1954-19

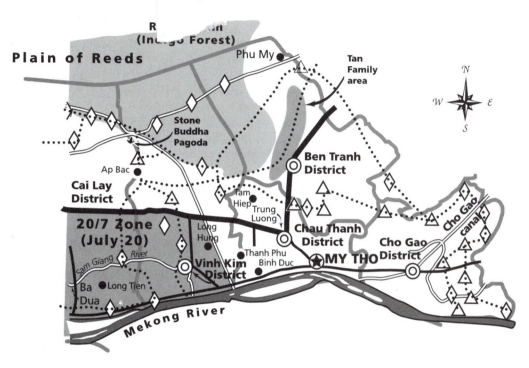

Plain of Reeds

R___ ___n
(Ind___o Forest)

Phu My

Tan
Family
area

N
W   E
S

Stone
Buddha
Pagoda

Ap Bac

**Ben Tranh
District**

**Cai Lay
District**

Tam
Hiep
Trung
Luong

**20/7 Zone
(July:20)**

Long
Hung

**Chau Thanh
District**

**Cho Gao
District**

Sam Giang River

Thanh Phu
Binh Duc

**Vinh Kim
District**

★ **MY THO**

Cho Gao
canal

Ba
Dua

Long Tien

Mekong River

KIEN TUONG PROVINCE

LONG AN
PROVINCE

KIEN PHONG
PROVINCE

Ben
Tranh
District

Cai Be
District

Cai Lay
District

Long Dinh
(Vinh Kim)
District

Chau
Thanh
District

Giao Duc
District

Cho Gao
District

GO CONG
PROVINCE

SA DEC
PROVINCE

VINH LONG PROVINCE

KIEN HOA PROVINCE

A Pacific Basin Institute Book

THE PACIFIC BASIN INSTITUTE AT POMONA COLLEGE

Now entering its third decade of service, the Pacific Basin Institute at Pomona College remains dedicated to its original goal of furthering intelligent communication between the nations of the Pacific Basin and increasing knowledge among Americans of the cultures, politics, and economics of the Asia/Pacific countries.

Since moving to Pomona College in 1997, PBI has greatly extended the scope of its activities. Our Pacific Basin Archive of film, video, and documentary material, based on the footage used for *The Pacific Century* TV series, has expanded to include more documentary and feature films. PBI's on-going Library of Japan, the first in a planned program of translations from Asian languages, has just published its ninth volume.

Pacific Basin Institute Books published by M. E. Sharpe

SENSŌ: The Japanese Remember the Pacific War
Letters to the Editor of Asahi Shimbun
Frank B. Gibney, editor
Beth Cary, translator

The Nanjing Massacre
A Japanese Journalist Confronts Japan's National Shame
by Honda Katsuichi
Frank B. Gibney, editor
Karen Sandness, translator

Silk and Insight: A Novel
by Mishima Yukio
Frank B. Gibney, editor
Hiroaki Sato, translator

The Kwangju Uprising
Eyewitness Press Accounts of Korea's Tiananmen
Henry Scott-Stokes and Lee Jai Eui, editors

How Asia Got Rich
Japan, China, and the Asian Miracle
Edith Terry

The Vietnamese War
Revolution and Social Change in the Mekong Delta, 1930–1975
David W.P. Elliott

T

THE VIETNAMESE WAR

Revolution and Social Change in the Mekong Delta 1930–1975

CONCISE EDITION

DAVID W.P. ELLIOTT

An East Gate Book

M.E.Sharpe
Armonk, New York
London, England

An East Gate Book

Copyright © 2003, 2007 by M.E. Sharpe, Inc.

Library of Congress Cataloging-in-Publication Data

Elliott, David W. P.
 The Vietnamese War : revolution and social change in the Mekong delta 1930–1975 /
David W.P. Elliott. — Concise ed.
  p. cm. — (Pacific Basin Institute book)
 "An East Gate Book."
 Includes bibliographical references and index.
 ISBN-10: 0-7656-0603-8 (pbk. : alk. paper); ISBN-13: 978-0-7656-0603-7 (pbk. : alk. paper)
 1. Dinh Tuong (Vietnam : Province)—History. 2. Dinh Tuong (Vietnam : Province)—Social
conditions. 3. Vietnamese Conflict, 1961–1975—Vietnam—Dinh Tuong (Province)
4. Mekong River Delta (Vietnam and Cambodia)—History. 5. Mekong River Delta (Vietnam
and Cambodia)—Social conditions. 6. Vietnamese Conflict, 1961–1975—
Mekong River Delta (Vietnam and Cambodia) I. Title. II. Series.

DS559.92.D56E44 2006
959.704′3—dc22   2006008303

Printed in the United States of America

The paper used in this publication meets the minimum requirements of
American National Standard for Information Sciences
Permanence of Paper for Printed Library Materials,
ANSI Z 39.48-1984.

BM (p)   10   9   8   7   6   5   4   3   2   1

Contents

Acknowledgments

This book was long in the making, and made possible only by the contributions and sacrifices of a large number of people. Hence, any acknowledgment of the immense debt owed to others is bound to be inadequate and incomplete. The core of the book is built around the narratives of those who served the revolution, who had left it by force of circumstances or genuine disillusionment. Some of these did not survive the war, and many faced severe retribution for their action after the revolution came to power in 1975. Several of the Vietnamese interviewers who elicited and shaped these narratives with consummate skill and insight also met with tragedy after April 30, 1975. Whatever value this book may have was gained at a very high cost for those directly involved.

It is my hope that in telling their story and recording their accomplishments this debt may be acknowledged, though it could never be repaid. The interviewers who worked with me in My Tho for the Rand Corporation were my companions, colleagues, and teachers. Three of them did nearly two-thirds of the interviews carried out between 1965 and 1974. Each brought unique skills to the task. One was a journalist, another a writer, and the third a high ranking military officer caught in temporary limbo by the convoluted politics of the Saigon government. Two had been imprisoned during the Diem period, and the third had been a close aide and fervent supporter of President Diem. Two were northerners, the third was a southerner. Two were urban intellectuals, the third deeply conversant with rural society in the South. But though they were different in many ways, they were united in their firm anticommunism. Paradoxically, it was this factor that resulted in what many have felt were the most consistently interesting and insightful of the interviews with "Viet Cong" prisoners and defectors done under the aegis of the Rand Corporation during the Vietnam War. It was precisely because these interviewers were strongly committed to an anticommunist brand of Vietnamese nationalism that they were intensely curious about the reasons the revolutionaries were such formidable opponents. Unlike many anticommunist Vietnamese who reflexively avoided any inquiry into their opponents and simply recycled the crude stereotypes typical of the times, these three approached the task of understanding the strengths and weaknesses of the revolutionaries with rigorous objectivity because they knew that complacency and self-deception were the surest paths to defeat. The extraordinary insights the interviews afford and the invaluable historical documentation they provide are a testament to these three remarkable individuals.

Nguyen Huu Phuoc was a prominent officer in the Saigon military brought down by his refusal to renounce his loyalty to Ngo Dinh Diem while other contemporaries of similar rank were quick to jump onto a new bandwagon. Many of his contemporaries attained positions at the very top of the Saigon power structure in the wake of the anti-Diem coup.

It was my good fortune to work with Phuoc during his years in the political wilderness. He taught me about life in rural South Vietnam and many other things. His interviews documented the complex and changing panorama of rural life in the Mekong Delta in a depth and scope made possible by his intimate knowledge of the countryside. After the Tet Offensive of 1968, Phuoc was remobilized into the Saigon army. He paid for his service to the Saigon cause with five years of harsh incarceration in various "reeducation" camps after the war before being reunited with his family in the United States. Dinh Xuan Cau was a writer with a rare ability to capture the inner dramas of the often tragic stories he encountered in the interviews, and convey them to the reader in ways that told a compelling story while at the same time being faithful to the words and thoughts of the people he interviewed. (All interviews were either taped and transcribed or recorded in near-verbatim handwritten notes). Cau was the most politically involved of the three, and for his bold activism was arrested after April 30, 1975. He died in jail. Vuong Bach was a journalist with a flair for seeking out the most unique and interesting facets of the lives of his interlocutors. This well-honed journalistic sense for the "story" of each individual respondent greatly extended the range of our understanding beyond the broad commonalities of the archetypal narratives of revolutionary prisoners and defectors, and also led to a better understanding of when and how significant change was occurring in a complex and evolving situation. He was my principal colleague in the 1971–73 period of the interviews. Bach remained in Vietnam after 1975 and died in 1998. Bach's assistant, Tran Van Thi, was very helpful in the latter phase of the research. Although we sometimes drew different conclusions from the interviews, they are the real co-authors of this book.

Two of my fellow graduate students at University of Virginia in 1961–62 introduced me to a country I had scarcely heard of. Dr. Nguyen Manh Hung, now a professor at George Mason University, and Dr. Ta Van Tai provided the entree into a world of fascinating complexity. Hung, in particular, unwittingly launched me on a trajectory where Vietnam came to be a consuming preoccupation in my life. After his return to Vietnam following his studies, Hung gave me valuable advice on the problem of translating American social science concepts and methods into a very different environment, and Tai helped out as well in the initial stages of the Rand project. While neither can be held responsible for the direction that this inquiry took and its ultimate conclusions, Professor Hung and Dr. Tai were in many ways "present at the creation."

My graduate studies at Virginia were interrupted by military service and the first phase of the Rand project from 1965 to 1968. The Rand "Motivation and Morale Project," which launched the interviews with prisoners and defectors, was controversial at the time and remains so today. The Dinh Tuong interviews were a separate undertaking that evolved in a different direction. I am thankful that I was afforded exceptional latitude by Rand to pursue the study of the revolutionary movement. Rand also allowed the use of a map that provides the basis for the schematic map of Dinh Tuong province at the beginning of this book. Dr. Robert Sansom, the author of an important book on land and revolution based on field work in Dinh Tuong, was instrumental in arranging for a second phase of interviewing in 1971 while he was working for the National Security Council staff. His timely support made it possible to extend the research into one of the most complex and important phases of the conflict.

I had little academic training on any aspect of Asian politics, culture, or society prior to my first stint in Vietnam (1963–68) with the U.S. Army and the Rand Corporation. Most of what I knew, I learned "on the job" from my colleagues mentioned above, my work with captured "Viet Cong" documents in the military, and from the rural people of My Tho whom I interviewed. Interviewing these "simple peasants" was a transforming experience. I was astounded by the political sophistication and analytic skills (that would put most American graduate students to shame), as well as the truly remarkable ability to relate their experiences with concision and introspection. I agonized over the hard hand dealt to them by fate and force of circumstances and admired what for many had been genuine idealism and real accomplishment, whether or not one agreed with the ends toward which it was directed. In the case of the defectors, this was tragically negated by the lingering suspicion from the Saigon side, and the implacable and unforgiving search for vengeance against them by the revolution. I learned vicariously from this world class "school of hard knocks."

The time came, however, to put this experience into a broader perspective, and to equip myself with the appropriate academic training I had sorely missed. It was my great fortune to be admitted to Cornell University for a second try at graduate school. It was there I encountered a remarkable cohort of graduate students, passionately interested in Southeast Asia and the Vietnam War, and two inspirational mentors. George McT. Kahin and David Mozingo provided not only intellectual guidance, but were also moral exemplars. They were teachers in the most profound sense. I cannot surpass the encomiums offered at the May, 2000 memorial to George Kahin at Cornell, or the testimonials given by several generations of scholars to the personal and intellectual example he offered. His thoughtfulness and support of his students were legendary. David Mozingo was an equally powerful inspiration. His integrity, intellectual rigor, uncompromising standards and moral force were a beacon in a time when passion often trumped reason, and advocacy sometimes deflected objective analysis. These two remarkable and generous people made possible my academic career, and therefore this book. Ben Anderson was and is a formidable intellectual presence at Cornell who left an indelible imprint on every student of Southeast Asia, even those with modest abilities and interests ostensibly quite remote from his. David Marr introduced me to the study of modern Vietnamese history while at Cornell and I, like so many others, have attempted to stand on the shoulders of his magisterial corpus of work on modern Vietnamese nationalism. He was kind enough to read chapters 3 and 4 of this book, providing his usual copious and meticulous commentary, and throwing out many intellectual challenges, which I am afraid I have not fully met. I hope that this book reflects their influence to some small degree.

Pomona College, where I have taught since 1977, has been a stimulating and supportive environment. I have been blessed with outstanding and congenial colleagues who have contributed to this book in many indirect ways that even they may not realize. Peter Stanley, past president of Pomona College and a distinguished authority on Asia himself, was strongly supportive of this book project and I am deeply grateful for his assistance. Thanks to his efforts, a portion of the publication expense of this lengthy book was met by a grant from the Rose Hills Foundation through the Independent Colleges of Southern California. Frank Gibney, founder of the Pacific Basin Institute at Pomona College, also played a key role in facilitating the publication of this work. His outstanding books and films have pioneered in explaining the turbulent "Pacific Century" to Americans and providing the larger historical context for smaller pieces of this dramatic story such as this study. Lynn Thomas, my colleague at Pomona, was exceptionally generous with his time and computer skills and helped introduce me to ways of accomplishing the research and analysis of a vast sea of data. His skill and creativity were also crucial to most of the computer-generated charts and maps in this book. Lynn Thomas also put many of the photographs in this book into publishable shape. Indeed, this would have been a very different and much more limited work in the pre-computer era. Kim Peasley performed computer miracles in restoring some crucial and historic photos from an unpromising original state to the point that they now convey a general impression of some key episodes in the rarely photographed early years of the conflict. Mimi Chang did meticulous work in digitizing a number of the maps used in this book.

Perhaps the most direct and indispensable role in allowing this long manuscript to see the light of day has been that of the former executive editor for Asian Studies at M.E. Sharpe. Douglas Merwin is surely the person "without whom" publication of this book would not have been possible, and for that, my profound thanks. The world of Asian studies is the beneficiary of his unique talent for identifying interesting projects and finding ways to bring them to fruition. M.E. Sharpe's rich and unique list of Asian books is testimony to this. Angela Piliouras, managing editor at M.E. Sharpe, performed the miracle of putting together the many elements of this long and complex work with patience, insight, and professionalism. To this set of "without whom/which" contingencies, I must add the heroic labor of William Turley, whose own studies of the conflict have set a very high standard, in reading the entire manuscript and passing a favorable judgement on it.

The extended process of research was supported by grants from the Social Science Research Council and the Haynes Foundation as well as a stipend from the Lyndon Baines Johnson Library to cover travel and research expenses. In addition to the helpful cooperation of the Johnson Library, I received valuable assistance from the Library of Congress, and obtained computer tapes of the Hamlet Evaluation Surveys from the Electronic Records Division of the Library of Congress. Many key documents from the American military side were found at the Center for Military History, and I thank their helpful and very knowledgeable historians for assistance in locating documents. In this regard, I especially want to thank Dale Andrade and John Carland. The Douglas Pike collection of documents, consulted when it was housed in Berkeley and now mainly located at the Vietnam Center at Texas Tech University in Lubbock is a unique resource. Douglas Pike was unfailingly helpful and generous with his vast knowledge of the documentary record of the war.

The most personal debts are the most difficult to express. My father, William Y. Elliott was known to the outside world in his later years as a vigorous "Cold Warrior" and as the mentor of Henry Kissinger. Refracted through the abbreviated caricatures in the various Kissinger biographies, his life has been reduced to a misleading footnote that leaves out his contributions as a poet, philosopher, New Dealer, anti-Fascist activist, wartime "czar" of the American civilian economy, adviser to presidents and teacher to generations of students who went on to important careers. To me, he was not only a person of brilliant and penetrating intellect along with passionate attachment to deeply held ideals but also a loving and supportive parent who made a genuine effort to understand why his son, on the other side of the Vietnam era generational divide, had moved away from Cold War orthodoxy and how the Vietnam experience had led to this. At a deep level my personal and intellectual journey was the consequence of the values and profound insights on the human condition that he communicated to his children, as well as many of his students, applied to a situation that I saw from the very different perspective of direct immersion in the tragedy of Vietnam. I wish he had been able to read this book. My mother, Louise Ward Elliott, had a very different but equally profound impact. She left a lasting impression even on those who have known her casually for her extraordinary empathy, love, and understanding of those around her. For her children, the influence has been immeasurable.

Most of all, it is my wife Mai that I must thank. She lived this book in circumstances that were often difficult. She contributed to it with her interviews and translations. Naturally I have been deeply influenced by her wisdom and insights not just about Vietnam, but about the human condition—as readers of her remarkable family history *The Sacred Willow* will readily understand. But to her I owe much more, for her love, the joy of her company—for the happiness and fulfillment of our years together.

A Readers Guide to
"The Vietnamese War"

This is a study of the revolutionary movement in South Vietnam's Mekong Delta covering the period 1930–75. The primary focus is on a single province, which was called My Tho during the French and Viet Minh periods (up to 1954) and Dinh Tuong during the 1954–75 period by the Saigon government. After 1975 the province was renamed Tien Giang. It is largely based on interviews with prisoners and defectors conducted mostly under the auspices of the Rand Corporation and the U.S. Department of Defense during the 1965–71 period. A small number of interviews were conducted in the 1972–74 period. In addition some important historical accounts of the revolution in My Tho and several surrounding provinces have become available in the last twenty years, along with a number of invaluable autobiographical accounts by leaders of the revolutionary movement in My Tho. Finally, there is a large quantity of documents captured from the "Viet Cong" during the war and now available on microfilm.

The main purpose of this study is presented in the introduction. In general, each chapter describes and analyzes a chronological period, but at the same time tries to focus on an important aspect of the revolution that is best exemplified by that period. Thus, there is no systematic discussion of the role of the Communist Party until after the chapter which describes the reemergence of the revolutionary movement in 1959–60. First, during the earlier periods the Party was less visible and dominant in the nationalist movement than it became after 1960. Second, in the following period there were important changes in the composition of the Party, and the Party as an organization was at the center of the strategy and mobilization for the next phase of the revolution. Though it is often referred to in earlier chapters, it is not systematically discussed until this point.

There are a number a terminological pitfalls in the study of this revolutionary movement. The most obvious is what to call the movement and the people in it. This is especially perplexing after 1960. Calling the movement and its members the "Viet Cong" is more comprehensible to a general audience, but is also a pejorative term which was devised for psychological warfare purposes by the enemies of the revolution. It is sometimes used in a sarcastic way in postwar revolutionary accounts, but given the origins and purpose of this term, it seems inappropriate for a scholarly study. An even more important drawback of this term is that it blurs the distinction between the more and less committed members of the revolutionary movement, and thus confuses the key issue of nature of the movement and the extent of its base of support. Nonetheless, there are some occasions dictated by the context when the term the "Viet Cong" is used in parenthesis to indicate the post-1954 revolutionary movement in South Vietnam. In the Rand project, interviewers were requested to use the term "National Liberation Front" (NLF) or, simply, "the Front." This had its drawbacks as well. Sometimes when it was important to make a distinction between the NLF and the Communist Party, for example, the respondent would take the cue from the interviewer and say "Front" while meaning "Party." I have tried to be clear about this whenever using the exact term is an issue, but in general have retained whatever term was used in the interview in the quoted citation, with an explanation when necessary.

The revolution itself would have preferred the term "the Liberation" movement, but I rarely use this term for two reasons. First, it applies only the post-1954 phase of the revolution and does not capture the continuity with the Viet Minh period, or indeed the pre-Viet Minh period (prior to 1941), and often leads to confusion about the connections of the northern movement with the southern movement. Second, since not all Vietnamese regarded the goals of the revolution as a "liberation" I have tried to use a more neutral term or place it between quotation marks to indicate the problematic aspects of this term. Therefore, the term "revolutionary" or "revolutionaries" is employed throughout the manuscript. It is often repetitive and cumbersome, but it is the best solution I can think of. Similarly I frequently use the terms "insurrection" or "insurgency" to describe the uprising in 1960, not to imply that one side was legitimate and the other was not, but in the same spirit a new leadership group trying to oust the incumbent leadership in an American trade union are called "insurgents."

Since the study by its very title is a commentary on the fact that the term "Vietnam War" has come to mean what happened to Americans in Vietnam—or even in the United States, when "the Vietnam War" is used for convenience to refer to the 1960–75 period, it is also usually placed in parentheses. The geographical object of the study also poses difficulties. The province studied, as noted above, changed names three times during the period covered by the research. During the 1930–75 period, the revolutionaries continued to refer to it by the colonial name "My Tho" while the Saigon based Government of Vietnam (1954–75) renamed it "Dinh Tuong." Both terms are used in this study to refer to the province in the post 1954, but My Tho is most frequently employed. This too, creates some confusion. The town which is the province capital was also called My Tho (at all times and by all sides). Sometimes there is a possibility of confusing the town with the province, and I have tried to clarify in these instances.

Yet another issue is the fact that for every one of the parties involved in the long conflict, the territorial boundaries of this province changed at least once. Most often, the change was either splitting off the easternmost districts into a separate province of Go Cong (which included the former My Tho districts of Go Cong and Hoa Dong), or re-attaching these two eastern districts to My Tho province. During the Resistance and briefly after 1954, My Tho province was itself combined by the revolutionary side with several other Delta provinces including Long An (then called Tan An). For the most part, this study focuses on the districts that were always part of My Tho. For the revolutionaries these were Cho Gao, Chau Thanh, Cai Lay, and Cai Be. After 1954, the Saigon government split off parts of these to form three other districts and called them Ben Tranh (northern Cho Gao and eastern Chau Thanh), Long Dinh (southern Chau Thanh) and Giao Duc (western Cai Be). Unless there is a specific reason to use these names, the revolutionary boundaries and terminology are used here because they are the terms most often used in the interviews and written historical sources.

From time to time neighboring provinces are brought into the analysis either for comparative purposes, or because they confirm or document something important happening in My Tho. The most frequently mentioned province is Kien Tuong to the north of My Tho. This province covered much of the swampy Plain of Reeds, which was a crucial base area for the entire region, and especially My Tho. Although it was administered by the revolution as a separate province, it is so closely tied to My Tho that it merits considerable reference in this study. The territorial parameters of the study can be confusing. During the colonial period, Vietnam was divided into three parts; Tonkin was North Vietnam, Annam was Central Vietnam, and Cochin China was South Vietnam. What is most often called "South Vietnam" as we know it after 1954 consisted of part of colonial Annam and all of Cochin China. Especially during the Resistance period, the revolutionaries called the three areas "bo" as in Bac Bo (North Vietnam), Trung Bo (Central Vietnam), and Nam Bo (South Vietnam). Sometimes the term "Ky" was used instead of "Bo." For example, until the "Viet Nam War" the highest Party headquarters in the southern part of Vietnam was called the Xu Uy Nam Bo or sometime the Xu Uy Nam Ky. The Cochin China insurrection of 1940 is termed the Nam Ky Khoi Nghia in most sources.

Nam Bo (Cochin China) consisted of the Mekong Delta and the areas immediately north and west of Saigon. It did not include the areas from, say Dalat up to the Demilitarized Zone which were considered part of central Vietnam. There is often confusion between South Vietnam meaning everything south of the 17th parallel under the jurisdiction of the post-1954 Government of the Republic of Vietnam and "south Vietnam" meaning Nam Bo or Cochin China. This book normally capitalizes South Vietnam or "the South" when the territory of the "Republic of Vietnam" from the DMZ south is meant, to help maintain the distinction. When the more limited territory of Cochin China is meant, the old Viet Minh term "Nam Bo" will be used or, occasionally, "southern Vietnam."

A related confusion arises over what to call the territorial echelons of revolutionary leadership. During the Resistance War, Vietnam was divided into nine zones by the Viet Minh. The Nam Bo area contained three of these; Region 7 (Eastern Nam Bo), Region 8 (Central Nam Bo) and Region 9 (Western Nam Bo). Only the latter two of these were in the Mekong Delta, so "Nam Bo" and the Mekong Delta are not synonymous. Central Nam Bo (Mien Trung Nam Bo) was the upper Delta, and included My Tho in both the Resistance and the "Vietnam War" periods. Western Nam Bo was actually south of My Tho, and included most of the provinces of the lower Delta down to the Ca Mau peninsula. During both the French and the post-1954 period the top leadership of the Party was in the North. The next level in the South below the Central Committee—which was located in the North for most of the period covered in this study—was first called the Xu Uy and, towards the end of the Resistance, the "Central Office for South Vietnam" (of the Central Committee), most often referred to as COSVN or by its code name "R". In both cases it covered the old Nam Bo area. During the French period, the Xu Uy was variously translated as the "Committee of the South" and the Southern Region (Xu) Committee or simply the Region Committee. Since the term "Region" is also used to translate the next lower echelon, the nine zones (khu or sometimes mien) into which Vietnam was divided during the Resistance, and the three zones of the old Nam Bo area after 1954, it would be needlessly confusing to call to top leadership in the South the "Region." Therefore, I have retained the Vietnamese term Xu Uy when discussing the top revolutionary headquarters in the South during pre-

1954 period, or occasionally referred to the area they commanded as Nam Bo, while using the term Region or Military Region to refer to the next lower echelon.

In the post 1954 period I use "COSVN," the English language abbreviation for the updated Xu Uy, now known as the Truong Uong Cuc or Central Office (of the Party Central Committee) or COSVN. My Tho belonged to Region 8 during the Resistance which was redesignated Region 2 after 1954 when the Regions were re-numbered to conform with the new situation. Regions 5 and 6 in central Vietnam from the DMZ down to the jungles north of Saigon retained their old designations. Regions 7, 8, and 9 in Eastern, Central and Western Nam Bo were renumbered Regions 1, 2 and 3 because Nam Bo became in effect a separate jurisdiction whose three Regions all reported to COSVN, while Regions 5 and 6 had a different chain of command. Confusingly, many post 1975 revolutionary histories continue to refer to Central Nam Bo by its Resistance period designation of Region 8, instead of the correct (for the 1954–75 period) designation of Region 2. Probably this is intended to underline the postwar position that the "Vietnam War" was a nationwide struggle, hence the pre-1954 unified numbering of regions from north to south is generally used in post-1975 revolutionary histories. Alternatively, many older revolutionaries had simply gotten used to the older term. When citing these sources I note the correct term in parenthesis. To summarize, after 1954, Region 2 or Central Nam Bo reported to the Xu Uy/COSVN. Thus the chain of command for the revolution during this period ran from the Politburo through the Central Committee in the North, to the Xu Uy/COSVN in the South, to Region 2, to My Tho province, to the various districts in My Tho, then to the villages, and finally to the lowest level of territorial administration, the hamlets. There were roughly 90–125 villages in My Tho and about 350–450 hamlets—the numbers fluctuated considerably over time as boundaries of villages and hamlets were split or consolidated.

The Communist Party itself changed its name several times. From 1931 to 1951, it was the Indochinese Communist Party (though it went underground from 1946 to 1951 and stopped publicly identifying itself as a Communist Party). In 1951 the name was changed the Lao Dong (Worker's) Party (VWP). In 1962 an ostensibly separate Southern communist Party was set up and called the Dang Nhan Dan Cach Mang or People's Revolutionary Party (PRP). This was recognized by all members of the Southern Party as a tactical ploy, and they considered themselves members of the VWP. For the most part, it is referred to here as "the Party," whatever the period. Recognizing that the revolutionary movement was much broader than the Party, though led by it, I have tried not to reduce the whole movement to the Party itself except when constant repetition of the term "revolutionaries" makes it more convenient to refer to the "Party" as the embodiment of the leadership of the revolution.

The selection of My Tho as the focus of this study is due to its intrinsic importance, which led the Rand Corporation to conduct a special study of this province during the period 1965–68 and again in 1971. This effort produced the materials described in the introduction to which this study is heavily indebted. A leading revolutionary military commander said of this region that "It could be said that in war, whichever side can control Highway 4 and the Cho Gao canal [which runs through the province of Dinh Tuong] can control the entire Mekong Delta and directly threaten Saigon."[1] Dinh Tuong thus was the vital link between the vast population and food resources of the Mekong Delta and the national capital. My Tho was designated the primary target of the Tet Offensive in the upper Mekong Delta by the revolutionary command in the South. It was considered by the Saigon government to be the most threatening staging base for military coups, and great care was taken to place loyal commanders in charge of Dinh Tuong province and the ARVN Seventh Division which was headquartered there. In the last desperate moments of the conflict the Saigon government thought that if all else failed it might be able to retreat to the Mekong Delta and make its last stand there. The American side also recognized the strategic importance of this province and periodically made it the focal point of "pacification efforts" in the South, although as the book shows, this fluctuated with changes in the political and military situation in the entire country.

In his perceptive and generous review of the hard cover edition of *The Vietnamese War,* Jonathan Mirsky took the book to task for not providing essential historical background on the long tradition of anti-foreign struggle in Vietnam and the deeply entrenched nationalism that was so evident during this conflict. I acknowledge that this was a defect in the longer original text, and that it has not been remedied in this abridged edition. But a brief discussion of this important issue should alert the reader to one of the critical historiographical issues which the evidence presented in this book implicitly addresses, concerning the nature of Vietnamese nationalism and national identity. These issues are so complex that it would take another lengthy book to merely lay out the broad contours of the subject, let alone provide a comprehensive historical context for the discussion. So I hope I may be excused for not dealing more explicitly and at greater length with this subject which is, as Mirsky states, at the very core of understanding the Vietnamese conflict.

Broadly speaking, there are two schools of thought on the elusive subject of Vietnamese nationalism which we could call "Vietnam conflict era conventional wisdom" and "postwar-postmodern." Keith Taylor, the author of a path breaking study of the formation of Vietnamese identity, has written about a longstanding scholarly consensus on depicting a "unified Vietnam, a Confucian Vietnam, and a revolutionary Vietnam." This is especially problematic, some scholars feel, because the "Vietnam War" unfolded in the southern part of Vietnam, a region with a quite distinctive history. Victor Lieberman notes that "in recent years scholarly research has focused ever more insistently on the polyphonic, localizing, fragmenting implications of post-1550 southern settlement in what Pierre Gourou as early as 1936 termed 'the least coherent territory in the world.'"[2]

Gourou's comment, of course, refers mainly to the Mekong Delta, the object of this study. If there is any validity to the dominant consensus among foreign scholars during the Vietnam War ("Vietnam conflict era conventional wisdom") of Vietnamese nationalism as a fusion of commitment to the ideal of national unity and resistance to foreign intervention as espoused by the revolutionaries whose leaders were, in Alexander Woodside's memorable term Confucian-influenced "proletarian mandarins,"[3] the most challenging test would be to apply this model of Vietnamese nationalism to "the least coherent territory in the world."

The Vietnamese revolutionaries themselves promulgated this view of Vietnamese nationalism as a combination of a seamlessly unified Vietnamese population and territory with a visceral and historically derived impulse to resist foreign interference in Vietnam. There is some ambiguity about the role that China's influence on Vietnam has had in forging this sense of unity both by giving Vietnam the tools of statecraft to build effective institutions and an ideology that provided cohesion for the ruling elite in the pre-colonial era (see the writings of John Whitmore on this subject[4]), but also by providing a unifying threat that would consolidate a distinct Vietnamese identity. North Vietnam's leading intellectual publicist during the conflict, Nguyen Khac Vien, frankly acknowledged the Confucian legacy[5] even while Vietnamese revolutionary leaders were trying to construct a more indigenous model[6] It should be noted, that the Confucian legacy was much more pronounced in northern Vietnam, and tended to recede as one moved further south, and would thus support the "postwar-postmodern" view of a more fragmented Vietnamese identity. The central issue of understanding what politically motivated large numbers of Vietnamese in the Mekong Delta to engage in a struggle for national unification under the guidance of a distant leadership based in North Vietnam requires that we explore the extent to which their vision of national identity—whatever its actual historical accuracy—was internalized by the revolutionaries in the South.

David Marr's extensive writings on Vietnamese modern history have amply documented the deep nationalist roots of the Vietnamese revolution, but he was also one of the first of the "wartime" scholars to challenge the view that the Vietnamese Communist Party had a monopoly on Vietnamese nationalism or that there was a single Vietnamese nationalism which had been passed down unchanged across generations. While the war still raged in 1971, he wrote "to date, in the West, the focus has been almost entirely on the Indochinese Communist party, the Viet-Minh, and the National liberation Front . . . In part this is because the study of Vietnamese anticolonial movements has been largely the preserve of the political scientist, the practicing journalist, and the intelligence specialist."[7] Nevertheless, Marr's conclusion was that "By 1945 salvation from the foreigner was taken by the peasantry to include salvation from hunger, tenantry, and taxes—a merging of activist and reformist ambitions that continues to motivate many in the conflict now under way," clearly implying that the diverse strands of early modern nationalism had been fused by the revolutionary movement.[8]

Whether or not the revolutionaries were viewed as the authentic exemplars of Vietnamese nationalism by a majority of Vietnamese, it was clear that there were important differences between the political activists in the North and in the South of Vietnam, even within the Party in the South, as this book will amply document. It is significant that the social and cultural heterogeneity in the Mekong Delta made it very difficult for the orthodox Viet Minh movement to gain control of and unify the anti-French Resistance until it was well underway in the late 1940s. But it is also clear from the interviews on which this book is based that through indoctrination or through mere exposure to a persuasive political analysis, those who joined the revolution accepted and even internalized the Party's view of its historical role and its definition of what nationalism entailed.

This was not a preordained outcome. A revealing indication of the fragility of the revolutionaries' position in the Mekong Delta at the beginning of the anti-French Resistance is the encounter in early 1946 of Le Duan, later to become the leading architect of the war in the South, and the head of propaganda for the central Mekong Delta (the newly established Region 8) Nguyen Thanh Danh, a native of the town of Cai Be in My Tho province who later became a famous literary figure under the pseudonym Bao Dinh Giang (the name of the river that circles the province town of My Tho). Le Duan urged Bao Dinh Giang to use Ho Chi Minh as a great patriotic inspirational figure of the Vietnamese people to induce youth to join the revolution's armed forces. Giang recollected that "In the early years of the

Resistance, the majority of the peasants here were not very clear about Uncle Ho and how he had undergone hardships to find the path to national salvation and how he was revered and made President (Chu Tich) of the country to lead the people in opposing foreign aggression," and so he had to embark on an extensive propaganda campaign to underline Ho's leadership and, therefore, the leading role of the revolutionary movement he headed. But in order to do this he had to link Ho to the leading anticolonial figures of the 19th century in the Mekong Delta, such as Nguyen Dinh Chieu and Nguyen Huu Huan.[9]

Hanoi's own historians have, in recent years, acknowledged the great differences between the society in the Mekong Delta and other parts of Vietnam stemming from the frontier character of this area, the last major territory brought under unified Vietnamese control, and the related factors of prolonged civil war and ethnic as well as cultural diversity. To some Vietnamese scholars, the pluralism of Mekong Delta society is a distinctive and enriching feature of Vietnamese identity, but nevertheless encompassed by it.[10] For other Vietnamese scholars the distinctive feature of a "Nam Bo" or indigenous South Vietnamese culture is its impermanence and constant transformation—a sharp contrast with the more traditional Vietnamese insistence on immutable cultural legacies from the past. "Huynh Ngoc Trang described the cultural distinctiveness of *Nam Bo* as an enduring property —his was not a snapshot of contemporary cultural developments but an abstraction, synthesizing more than 300 years of Vietnamese settlement of the region. Yet it would be inappropriate to describe this durable quality as a 'cultural tradition,' for one of the properties he claimed for this regional culture was its constant propensity to change."[11] It should not come as a surprise that the more tradition bound North Vietnamese soldiers coming to the Mekong Delta during the latter stages of the conflict sometimes said that "these Southerners are totally uncultivated." (khong co hoc thuc gi ca).

Developments inside Vietnam since the end of the "Vietnam War" and shifting academic fashions in the world outside Vietnam have combined to challenge the view of a cohesive Vietnamese nationalism or even a well defined Vietnamese national identity. The failure to impose the revolution's model of Northern socialism on the South and the ultimate disillusionment with that model was one factor. Another was the way southern revolutionaries were shunted aside from positions of leadership after the conflict. The vogue of deconstructionism and postmodernism in Western academic circles is yet another factor. This book documents the great diversity of the modern Vietnamese experience, in large part because of its deliberate focus on the microsocietal level of individuals and localities. But despite the stress on these distinctive perspectives, and the focus on the "least coherent territory in the world," I think the reader should pay close attention to the implicit acknowledgment of the now "problematized" picture of national unity that is contained in the interviews.

Much of this is implicit—what is not said, rather than what is articulated, since the interviews did not anticipate the subsequent emergence of the deconstruction of Vietnamese nationalism and did not emphasize the nearly universal appeal on the part of those interviewed (the majority of whom had left the revolutionary movement out of disillusionment or force of circumstances) of the ideal of a strong, unified Vietnam, and acceptance by the interviewees of the way that Vietnamese nationalism was defined by the revolutionary leadership. Another set of Rand interviews dealt more directly with the role of nationalism in the revolutionary movement, and the interviews on which this book is based did not attempt to retrace this ground.[12] It should also be kept in mind that most of the interviews were conducted by Vietnamese who held a sharply opposed view of nationalism, and who were keen to detect any doubts about the revolutionary message on the part of its adherents, yet a quite consistent and uniform account of this message emerged. For those who, during the war, were engaged in investigation of the motivations which drove the revolutionaries in the Mekong Delta, far from the Northern leadership (who in fact had initially impeded the revolution in the South in the late 1950s, and sacrificed its interests in the 1954 division of the country), it was very clear that the ideal of resistance to foreign intervention and a strongly held view that Vietnam was a single country were powerful and deeply held beliefs among even the rank and file of the revolutionary movement and a large segment of the society from which they came.

The fact that this now contested view of national cohesion resonated so deeply in the farthest reaches of Vietnamese villages and hamlets in the Mekong Delta during the conflict is, in part, a reflection of the importance of situational context. It was foreign intervention in Vietnam and the division of the country imposed from the outside that created a receptive audience for the simple nationalist message. When this situation no longer obtained, the potency of the message evaporated as Vietnamese turned inward and their own internal differences were accentuated. It is the old pattern of division following unified struggle against foreign dominance that so many historians have noted in Vietnam's turbulent history.

For another evidence of the power of this straightforward wartime message, consider Jonathan Mirsky's own eyewitness account of a village entertainment, witnessed in the company of John Paul Vann, whose career was closely linked to the fortunes of war in the Mekong Delta. "We were watching a puppet show," Mirsky recalls, "in which the Vietnamese puppets were bashing the Chinese while the rural audience was loudly applauding. 'That's us they're really smashing,' Vann remarked."[13]

The tension between oversimplifying stereotypes and deconstructed fragmentation or, to put it in more generic terms, between "lumpers" with a penchant for generalization and "splitters" for whom the essence of analysis is making ever finer distinctions, is inherent in analyzing social movements. In presenting a picture of a coherent revolutionary organization which survived and ultimately triumphed by finding a common vision that would elicit the support of its adherents, even under the most adverse conditions, this book is not denying the complexity of motivations and behavior of the individuals studied here, or the ambiguity in many of their actions. Indeed the very purpose of this study is to document these complexities. The fact remains, that this was an extraordinary feat of social and political mobilization, which could not have been accomplished by a rabble of unconnected people and groups. Without some community of purpose on the part of the actors who shaped its modern history, today's Vietnam would be, for better or for worse, a very different place.

Perhaps the necessary counterpart to the postmodern urge to deconstruct, is the attempt to understand why communities and political movements cohere, and how they construct an identity through common experience. Anthropologist Charles Keyes writes, "In reflecting on 'national integration' it is still useful, I believe, to begin with the seminal work in the effort to understand the nature of the problems attendant on national integration— Clifford Geertz's 1963 essay, "The Integrative Revolution: Primordial Sentiments and Civil

Politics in the New States," Geertz stressed that if a new state was to succeed as a nation-state, means must be found to establish a 'civil' order that transcended the existing 'primordial' differences between the peoples living within the boundaries of the state. Finding such a means was neither obvious nor the same from case to case. There is a direct line, I believe, between Geertz's ideas and those of Benedict Anderson (1991), Ernest Gellner (1983), Eric Hobsbawm (1990), Hobsbawm and Terry Ranger (1983), and others who have shaped the contemporary approach to problems of 'nation-building' and 'national integration.' Today we speak of the 'imagining,' 'invention' and 'construction' of national communities out of the diversity that is found within the politically recognized boundaries of states."[14]

Keith Taylor has asserted that "A 'common history' lies in the realm of mythology and indoctrination."[15] The revolutionaries would not necessarily disagree, and it is perhaps a tribute the energy of propagandists such as Bao Dinh Giang that they were so successful in purveying their Party sanctioned mythology through extensive indoctrination. Indeed, all nations are built in one way or another on constructed visions. Civil societies were built largely by forging a consensus on a shared vision of community. The same could be said about revolutionary movements. The outcome and ultimate form of successful revolutions are not preordained by the elements that form a revolutionary movement, but painfully forged in a common experience of struggle. In Vietnam's case, this also resulted in post-revolutionary complacency along with arbitrary and oppressive rule based on a sense of victor's entitlement, that undermined much of the initial promise of the revolution, and which has led some to question not only its original purposes, but also its very historical substance. But, as this work will attempt to illustrate, the historical record of the revolutionary movement in Vietnam is concrete and clearly visible—thanks to the voluminous record of contemporary sources from which its actions can be reconstructed.

Still, because of the great diversity of the revolutionary movement, it cannot be said that My Tho/Dinh Tuong is "representative" of the larger situation in Vietnam during the 1930–1975, nor is any other region or province. Yet the history of the Vietnam War will remain incomplete be until the important pieces of the larger picture at the province level are better understood. And by closely analyzing the role that Dinh Tuong played during this thirty year conflict, many of the continuing questions about "big picture" issues may be clarified. It was, after all, in the countryside and at the local level that the outcome of the thirty year conflict was decided. Although Dinh Tuong cannot tell us the whole story of this complex period, it is a significant step closer to the underlying fundamental realities of the Vietnam conflict than even the most revealing record of strategy, politics and diplomacy in the corridors of power in Saigon, Hanoi, Paris and Washington.

Notes

1. Le Quoc San, *Cuoc Do Suc Than Ky* [The Incredible Trial of Strength] (Hanoi: NXB Quan Doi Nhan Dan, 1991), p. 201.

2. Taylor quote and following comment are in Victor Lieberman, *Strange Parallels: Southeast Asia in Global Context, c.800–1830,* Volume I: Integration on the Mainland (Cambridge: Cambridge University Press, 2003), pp. 343–43.

3. Woodside, Alexander B., 1976, *Community and Revolution in Modern Vietnam* (Boston: Houghton Mifflin Company, 1976).

xxiv   A READERS GUIDE TO "THE VIETNAMESE WAR"

4. A listing of Whitmore's works can be found in Lieberman, *Strange Parallels*, p. 340, fn. 4.

5. See his classic essay "Confucianism and Marxism," in David Marr and Jayne Werner eds., *Tradition and Revolution in Vietnam* (Washington D.C.: Indochina Resource Center, 1974).

6. "While recognizing that the Vietnamese nation is made up of distinct ethnic groups, the government of the Socialist Republic of Vietnam (like its predecessor, the government of the Democratic Republic of Vietnam) have promoted the premise that all constituent dan toc in Vietnam shared a common heritage in that they are all descendants of the legendary Hung kings who lived circa 2000 BCE. By tracing the descent of the nation to the Hung kings, the assumption is that all the dan toc in Vietnam shared common pre-Chinese cultural traditions. The national narrative—which is promoted through compulsory education, public holidays, commemorative events and holiday, and documentary programs on radio and TV—also posits that the diverse dan toc of Vietnam also share a common heritage in resisting foreign domination. The leaders in resistance against the Chinese in the period from second century BCE to the fifteenth century CE, the French in the nineteenth and twentieth century, and finally the Americans in the twentieth century are recognized as national heroes. Ho Chi Minh is only the latest such hero to become apotheosized in the pantheon of deity-like national heroes. But even local leaders of resistance, including members of ethnic minorities, have been accorded recognition for their role, thereby serving as foci for local cults of the nation." Charles F. Keyes, paper on "Ethnicity and the Nation-State: Asian Perspective," presented Friday January 17, 2003. Center for International Ethnicity Studies at North Carolina State University's College of Humanities and Social Sciences. www2.chass.ncsu.edu/CIES/KeyesPaper.htm.

7. David G. Marr, *Vietnamese Anticolonialism* 1885–1925 (Berkeley: University of California Press, 1971), p. xv.).

8. Ibid, p. 277.

9. Biographical note on Bao Dinh Giang dated June 1999, published in Nhan Dan December 31, 2002. It is noteworthy that Giang focused on the literary figure Nguyen Dinh Chieu, and did not even mention the two gentry figures who were most effective in fighting the French in the upper Mekong Delta, Truong Cong Dinh and Thien Ho Duong.

10. "It would be impossible to recount all the cultural interchanges between Vietnamese and other peoples in the region in all spheres, such as: making a living, life style, clothing, houses, transportation, education, play and entertainment, and maintaining health. In these interchanges, Vietnamese culture in the region was enlarged, extended, distilled, and developed." Nguyen Cong Binh et.al., *Van Hoa Va Cu Dan Dong Bang Song Cuu Long* [Culture and People of the Mekong Delta] (Ha Noi: Nha Xuat Ban Xa Hoi Hoc, 1990), p. 41.

11. Philip Taylor, *Fragments of the Present: Searching for Modernity in Vietnam's South* (Honolulu: University of Hawai'i Press, 2001), p.102. Taylor has a valuable discussion of the distinctiveness of Southern culture in his chapter "Indigenising Modernity in Nam Bo," pp. 89–118.

12. John C. Donnell, Guy J. Pauker, and Joseph J. Zasloff, *Viet Cong Motivation and Morale in 1964: A Preliminary Report.* Santa Monica: Rand, 1965. RM-4507/3-ISA. xiii, 74 pp. The text has been placed on-line in the Virtual Vietnam Archive of the Vietnam Project at Texas Tech University, in two parts: Front matter and pp. 1–31 and pp. 32–74. See also Joseph] J. Zasloff, *Political Motivation of the Viet Cong: The Vietminh Regroupees.* RM-4703/2-ISA/ARPA. Santa Monica: Rand, May 1968. (Original edition: August 1966). xiv, 183 pp. The text has been placed on-line in the Virtual Vietnam Archive of the Vietnam Project at Texas Tech University: Front matter and Introduction (pp. i–xiv, 1–22); Part One, "The Regroupees in the North" (pp. 23–65); Part Two, "The Regroupees in the Front" (pp. 67–102, pp. 103–146); Part Three, "The Defectors" (pp. 147–183).

13. Jonathan Mirsky, "Wartime Lies," *The New York Review of Books,* October 9, 2003, p. 42.

14. Charles F. Keyes, "Ethnicity and the Nation-State: Asian Perspective."

15. Keith Taylor, "Surface Orientations in Vietnam: Beyond Histories of Nation and Region," *The Journal of Asian Studies* 57, no. 4 (November 1998), p. 972.

MY THO
(area of study)

THE VIETNAMESE WAR

1

The Vietnamese War

Introduction

This is a study of the origins and development of the war in Vietnam in a single province of the Mekong Delta during the period from 1930 to 1975. More precisely, it is a study of the Vietnamese dimension of the war, focusing on the revolutionary movement that became popularly known as the "Viet Cong." Historian Robert McMahon has observed that the writing on the war is "overwhelmingly produced by Americans, asking American-oriented questions and seeking answers in documents produced by other Americans." George Herring, who has written one of the standard histories of the Vietnam War, chided a colleague for writing yet another American-centric history of the war in which "the more deeply America becomes involved, the more the Vietnamese recede into the background, becoming shadowy figures whose actions remain obscure." Commenting on a newly published history of the war, he adds that this book, "[like] most American writing on Vietnam, . . . does not fully bridge the chasm of ignorance that separated us from our Vietnamese allies and enemies at the time. Our inability as a nation to make this cultural leap is of more than academic importance. There is little indication in recent political debates on possible American intervention in the world that we have learned an essential lesson of Vietnam: the need to understand and respect the history, cultural, and local dynamics of places where we contemplate involvement."[1] Historian Ronald Spector takes yet another work on the Vietnam War to task for its "ethnocentrism, the same assumption of American omnipotence, for which McMaster pillories the leaders of that era. It largely leaves out of the account the ideas, plans and actions of the Vietnamese."[2] In short, Americans will never learn the elusive "lessons of Vietnam" by looking only in the mirror.

Perhaps it is not coincidental that the end-of-century wave of postrevisionist books on the Vietnam War, each claiming that either the war could (or should) have been "won" by America and its South Vietnamese ally "if only . . . ," or that it was a necessary and justified intervention by the United States even if in historical retrospect it was bound to fail, are all overwhelmingly based on American sources and perspectives.[3] To the extent that the Vietnamese realities of the period are taken into consideration, they are typically filtered through the views of Americans with their own agendas and limited understanding of the environment in which those realities operated. Even postwar memoirs written by American participants present a picture of the country that is all too often distorted by remembered personal trauma. A recent book by an American officer who served in the Mekong Delta portrays this region in stark and negative terms as a Southeast Asian "Heart of Darkness": "The reader can almost smell the dank Mekong River, the fear, the rotting flesh. Mud, blood and vegetation swirl on the page, and author Nathaniel Tripp pounds home the sights and sounds."[4] While these images are part of the reality of Vietnam, the full picture is much larger and much more complex. It is, however, the dominance of these personal and therefore limited impressions in American writings that explain why Vietnam has come to represent a national American trauma rather than a real place with real people. As former Secretary of State Madeleine Albright said on her June 1997 trip to Vietnam, "The time has come to think of Vietnam as a country, not as a war."[5] For that reason, this book is titled *The Vietnamese War,* an effort to provide a more complete understanding of one of the defining events of the twentieth century.

The present work, though written by an American, is an attempt to elicit Vietnamese voices to explain what happened during the Vietnam War and why. The object of study is the revolutionary movement in My Tho province (as it was called by the French colonial government as well as the revolutionaries), known during the 1954–75 period as Dinh Tuong province (as the Saigon government called it) and now as Tien Giang province, in Vietnam's Mekong Delta. Its population during most of the period under consideration was over 500,000. The province is located 45 miles south of Saigon and is bordered by the Mekong River to the south, the vast swamp to the north called the Plain of Reeds (which served as a major revolutionary base area), and the South China Sea to the east. Because the principal land and water routes from the Mekong Delta to Saigon run through My Tho, it is considered the key province in the delta and the gateway to Saigon.

Analytic Themes

There are four distinctive features of this study. First, it presents a thesis that explains a paradox: why was the revolutionary movement so successful during the war, but far less effective in overcoming the challenges of postwar development? This thesis is supported by a detailed analysis of the effect of the revolution on Vietnam's rural social structure. The evidence suggests that the revolution was a victim of its own success. Its land reforms set in motion a fundamental transformation of South Vietnam's rural society, but at the same time the revolutionary agenda led to a prolonged and disruptive war, which itself became the main engine of social change and took it in a different direction than the Communist Party had originally planned. Subsidized American consumer goods and equipment flooded the countryside. Peasant communities were dislocated, and the depopulation of the countryside led to even more sweeping change in rural class structure than anything the Party could have engineered. The unintended result was the emergence of a rural middle class that included nearly 70 percent of the rural population in the Mekong Delta and, after the war, proved stubbornly resistant to collectivization. Eventually, this brought socialist transformation in South Vietnam to a halt and created a crisis that spread to North Vietnam. It ultimately forced the entire country to abandon collective agriculture and many other features of state socialism and adopt a sweeping program of market reforms.

In some ways it could be said that in winning the war, the Communist Party lost its revolution, and this book tries to explain the roots of this dilemma. This study also attempts to analyze why even this fundamental transformation of the socioeconomic base of rural society in South Vietnam did not change the outcome of the war. If the United States could take any satisfaction from the postwar travails of the communist revolution in Vietnam, the delayed impact of this war-induced change came far too late to salvage American political and strategic interests in Vietnam. Moreover, this transformation was not the result of deliberate U.S. or South Vietnamese policies, but of the war itself; thus, Vietnam's postwar difficulties cannot be taken as a vindication of the political and social policies of the opponents of revolution during the war.

A second feature of this study is its conclusions about political behavior, based on a study of the motivations and actions of both the committed revolutionaries and the peripheral supporters of the movement. It challenges the dominant school of contemporary political analysis—which, not coincidentally, is itself dominated largely by the study of American politics by Americans—and which assumes that people are "rational actors" responding to fluctuating incentives with careful calculations of self-interest and of costs and benefits. Although this rational-choice approach has considerable explanatory power, its individual-centered theory of politics often makes it difficult to account for the way in which a larger framework—a social movement or a community—shapes individual behavior. In addition to analyzing the complex and often contradictory pulls of ideals and self-interest, the present study examines the much misunderstood role of compulsion in revolutionary mobilization. Compulsion is not well integrated into the dominant paradigms of political behavior. This study graphically illustrates the terror and intimidation that were prominent features of the revolutionary movement, but the documentation also clearly shows that although these were effective tactics at critical junctures of the conflict, they were not the main factors in mobilizing widespread popular support. The text discusses how force was a supplement to but not a substitute for incentives and moral suasion. When the revolutionary movement encountered problems, compulsion alone did not provide a solution. The role of coercion in politics cannot therefore be ignored, but should be viewed as one factor among many that affect political behavior.

The study also clearly shows the centrality of values and ideals to most revolutionaries, and the responsiveness of even ordinary people to moral appeals. At the same time, it shows the validity of some aspects of the "rational actor" approach which are helpful in explaining the behavior of the emerging rural middle class. At times, political behavior of the revolutionaries and peasants in My Tho is best analyzed in collective terms, but at other times analysis at the level of the individual is more productive. James Scott's *The Moral Basis of Political Economy* and Samuel Popkin's *The Rational Peasant* are the most influential formulations of the contending schools of thought on the relative utility of taking community and values (Scott) as the starting point, as opposed to considering rationally calculating individuals (Popkin).[6] The My Tho case suggests that Scott is somewhat more helpful in understanding the early stages of the revolution, and Popkin more pertinent toward the end.[7]

A third feature of this study is the close examination of province-level documentation that casts light on a number of important historical controversies about the Vietnam war or offers a new perspective on the turning points of this conflict. In many cases, the province-level documentation provides crucial pieces of the puzzle that general Party histories of the war gloss over. Memoirs and interviews give an unusually detailed view of the struggle within the leadership of the southern branch of Vietnam's Communist Party in the 1940s and especially during the pivotal revolution of August 1945. This evidence shows that the Party's control of the Resistance movement in the South during the war against the French was less complete than most general accounts imply, but that the Viet Minh's governance style was quite dictatorial despite its great political popularity and broad nationalist appeal. Little mention has been made in most histories of the temporary success of French pacification in the Mekong Delta in the early 1950s, because most French and Vietnamese studies focus on what was happening in North Vietnam at the time. The reasons for the collapse of French pacification in the South in 1953–54 and the hope this precedent gave the revolutionaries during a similar low point in 1970–71 are important to our understanding of the struggle. Memoirs of My Tho province cadres and province Party histories shed important new light on the dispute over resuming armed struggle in 1956–59. The reasons why, within the space of a year, the Diem regime lost its near-total grip on the countryside in 1960 are brought out in more detail than in previous studies and are vividly illustrated by eyewitness and participant accounts. The role of terror, which has been downplayed in some sympathetic accounts of the revolution, was indispensable to the uprising during one relatively brief stage, and this study carefully documents this role while at the same time placing it in a larger perspective of highly successful, longer-term mass political mobilization. The complex impact of the Party's land reform in the South has been almost totally ignored or misunderstood, as has the topic of the popular associations that were the instruments of revolutionary governance at the grass-roots level. Most writings on the actual mechanics of guerrilla warfare in Vietnam are superficial and often erroneous, and the detailed reconstruction in this study of the military dimension of the revolution by its own cadres is a useful corrective. A number of turning points in revolutionary strategy, especially some still mysterious aspects of the Tet Offensive, and the debates between Hanoi and the southern guerrilla leaders over strategy in the late stages of the war, can be more fully understood by examining documents and memoirs relating to the way general strategies were perceived and implemented in the Mekong Delta and Dinh Tuong province in particular.

The fourth feature of the book is the sheer volume of unique and comprehensive documentation on which it is based. No other study of the Vietnam war has drawn on such extensive documentation, especially firsthand accounts in which the Vietnamese participants in the events described speak directly to us. Much of the analysis is based on interviews with prisoners and defectors from the revolutionary movement. These were conducted largely during two periods, 1965–68 and 1971–74. There were 288 interviews in the first set, averaging around 35 typewritten pages of verbatim transcript after translation. The second set, from 1971 to 1973, includes 103 interviews totaling about 2,200 pages, or an average of about 20 pages per interview. (Statistics for the second set are harder to calculate, since not all interviews were typewritten). The interview data thus amounts to nearly 12,000 pages of transcribed material. In addition, the study utilized documents from provincial revolutionary units captured during military operations. These comprised several thousand pages, of varying degrees of analytic usefulness. The study drew upon tens of thousands of documents captured by U.S. and South Vietnamese military forces and summarized by U.S. military intelligence translators. Many of these pertain to Dinh Tuong or the Mekong Delta. Finally, this book utilizes a large number of revolutionary accounts and memoirs that have rarely been employed in studies of the Vietnam war, especially local Party and military histories and memoirs of revolutionary leaders at the region and province level.

Availability and Use of Data

Two major deficiencies of the available data on the revolution in Dinh Tuong province from 1945 to 1975 underline the caution with which analytic conclusions must be drawn. The first deficiency is the lack of systematic contemporaneous input from participants in the revolutionary movement who were not either prisoners or defectors. The constraints of the environment in which the interviews were conducted are obvious. Fortunately, toward the end of the writing of this work, a wealth of official histories and biographies of leading members of the My Tho revolutionary movement became available. These reflect the higher-level perspective missing from the interviews, as well as the unconstrained presentation of the revolutionary point of view, albeit in retrospect. Second, both the terms under which much of the interviews were conducted (for the Rand Corporation under the auspices of the U.S. Department of Defense) and the political obstacles involved in doing research on the most sensitive areas of Vietnamese political life rendered systematic inquiry into the policies and actions of the Saigon government (the Government of the Republic of Vietnam or GVN), impossible, though the interviews include numerous evaluations of the personnel and actions of the GVN by those who had served in the revolution. I hope the reader will be persuaded that these limitations do not invalidate the findings derived from the extraordinarily rich data that were available, and that there are ways of compensating for these problems.

The post-1968 interview data are unique. At a time when most studies of the revolutionary movement which accompanied the early period of U.S. direct combat involvement in Vietnam had been terminated, the Dinh Tuong study was continued in the 1971–73 period and provides valuable documentation of an area and a situational context that was considered largely irrelevant by many U.S. officials. For one thing, the true test of the strength and cohesion of an organization or social movement is its response to adversity, and the post-Tet period certainly provided that for the revolutionary side. Even more important is what an examination of the war in the post-Tet period can tell us about the relationship of the Mekong Delta to other areas of Vietnam, especially North Vietnam, which combined to produce a revolutionary victory. In addition, much of the local postwar Vietnamese autobiographical material and research on the war at the village and provincial level has not been available or consulted in prior studies written outside Vietnam.

For the reader, the strengths of this book may prove a mixed blessing. The book is very long, even in its abridged paperback version, and requires close attention to a level of detail that may at times seem excessive. But the payoff is truly in the details. First, they provide a rich mix of voices that illustrates the complexity and individuality of the Vietnamese participants in the conflict. Second, they show the great diversity in the way revolutionary policies were perceived and carried out at the village level, which should demonstrate conclusively that the revolutionary movement was not monolithic. The ultimate aim of this book is to show the human face of a movement that is pictured by Americans largely in abstract and stereotyped terms, and to illustrate its diversity. These details will also help us understand the evolution from one stage of the conflict to another—how the situation changed and the reasons for the changes.

Implications for "Postrevisionist" Studies of the War

The meaning of the Vietnam War still remains highly contested despite the decades that have elapsed since the end of that conflict. President George H.W. Bush mistakenly concluded that America's apparently decisive victory in the first Gulf War had "kicked the Vietnam Syndrome" once and for all.[8] But the Clinton-era debates over America's global purpose by the late 1990s had revived attempts to reconsider and even rewrite the history of the Vietnam War, to erase the cautionary sting of defeat and clear the way for a more expansive use of military force. Some argued that if the Vietnam War was not a victory, it could have been and should have been—or actually was a success (though we did not recognize it at the time). When "Iraqification" surfaced as a means of achieving victory in the Second Gulf War in President George W. Bush's second term, some of the postrevisionist accounts were cited as evidence that the earlier historical parallel, Vietnamization, was not a failure and that the US had belatedly found the right commander (General Abrams) and the right strategy ("clear and hold" rather than "search and destroy") but, unfortunately, only after political support for the war had evaporated. The evidence cited in this book does not support this analysis. Only the "clear" element of "clear and hold was a success, and this lead to a significant depopulation and devastation of the countryside—not a model of "pacification" that would win "hearts and minds."[9] The two most serious challenges to the revolution were the loss of population and the erosion of the class base of the movement as the war transformed Vietnamese society. Neither of these factors was the result of carefully crafted counterinsurgency tactics. Both were products of the disruptive impact of the war itself.

Many of the postrevisionist studies which claim that the revolutionaries could have been defeated "if only . . . ," might do well to consider several points that emerge from this study. The first is that while the opponents of revolution often were able to find answers to revolutionary tactics later on in the conflict, the inescapable historical fact is that the war unfolded in real time, and these innovations were never timely enough to be decisive. If the United States had been in Vietnam with 500,000 troops in 1945 or if the anticommunist Saigon forces existed as they had in the later period of the "Vietnam War"—with more than one million men armed with modern weapons against ragtag Viet Minh guerrilla units of that period—the outcome would have been different. Of course this anachronistic scenario is absurd, but it reflects a logic often employed by those who claim that the revolution could have been suppressed if these later resources and tactics had been available earlier.

Two other examples of the "if only . . ." school are the belated Saigon land reform, which might have been politically effective if it had occurred much earlier but was essentially irrelevant by the time it was implemented, and the post-Tet 1968 change in U.S. military tactics from "search and destroy" to "clear and hold," which was far more devastating to the revolutionaries (as well as the rural civilian population) but was still not able to achieve a decisive result. The record also shows that though the revolutionaries were often knocked down, they were never knocked out. They seemed to find ways of recovering from every setback by devising new approaches when old tactics faltered, from the French period right through to the end. A related point is that the opponents of revolution could never "lock in" their temporary advantages when they gained the upper hand (as in 1970–71), despite overwhelming material superiority; explaining this failure is a major task for the postrevisionist historians. Third, as Henry Kissinger once observed, "the guerrilla wins if he does not lose." The implications of this observation pose another challenge for those who believe that "victory" over the revolutionaries was in sight at any point in the conflict.

Conclusion

I am not arguing, of course, that the revolutionary side emerged unscathed from thirty years of war, or suggesting that their victory was necessarily the best long-term outcome for the Vietnamese people. This book documents several periods of extreme crisis and devastating setbacks for the revolutionary movement. Whatever one's view of the outcome, however, in the end it was fundamentally decided by the Vietnamese themselves, bringing to a close 100 years of foreign intervention. As noted above, the protracted conflict eroded the political base of the revolution, and the staggering losses of cadres and soldiers also seriously weakened the revolutionary movement and constrained its ability to achieve economic growth and prosperity in the postwar period. In "real time," however, the revolutionaries sustained enough of an advantage—even in places like My Tho, where the movement had been badly damaged—to defeat their opponents—though at heavy cost for all concerned and only by mortgaging some aspects of Vietnam's future development. This study aims to examine these ups and downs in detail, because grasping the underlying dynamics of these cycles in the conflict is the key to understanding why it ended as it did. Too often, the Vietnam war is portrayed as a long but essentially unchanging struggle that ended because one exhausted side ground down an even more frustrated and weary opponent. As a capsule version of the Vietnam war, this may pass muster, but we will never get beyond recycling inadequately substantiated generalizations about this conflict until we make the effort to dig deeper. That is the purpose and aspiration of this study.

2

Postlude

June 1975. One month after the end of Vietnam's thirty years of warfare, Nguyen Thi Thap's automobile sped down Highway 4 from Saigon to the Mekong Delta, carrying her back to her native village after a three-decade absence. Dragonflies skittered away from the onrushing windshield and with startling evasiveness and agility ended up in their original places after the car passed by, as though nothing had happened. Thap remembered her many fruitless attempts to catch dragonflies as a child and thought that she herself was like these elusive creatures. Her return to the village where her long revolutionary career had started was like the dragonfly returning to its starting point, she thought.[1]

"Muoi Thap" [Sister Ten] was born in My Tho province in 1908 into a poor peasant family. Now she was one of the top leaders of the Democratic Republic of Vietnam and the chair of the Vietnamese Confederation of Women. Her revolutionary road had been long and arduous. As a dedicated revolutionary she knew that she should stay in Saigon to socialize with the surviving members of South Vietnam's female activists, but she couldn't resist indulging her personal feelings with a quick trip back to her native village of Long Hung accompanied by her brother Tam.

Everything had changed. Even from the airplane arriving from Hanoi, the once-familiar city of Saigon looked strange, with its tall buildings densely packed together. The railroad tracks that had connected My Tho to Saigon had been pulled up, leaving no traces. The formerly placid two-lane road that passed through the rice fields on the way to the Mekong Delta was now a modern wide, smooth highway, built by American engineers. In the old days, after leaving the Saigon suburb of Phu Lam there had been nothing but vast expanses of open rice fields or clusters of orchards. Now there were continuous strings of houses and small shops along the road. The old thatched-roof peasant houses with attached buffalo sheds were gone, replaced by concrete box houses with tin roofs. A jumble of big advertising signboards was interspersed with gas stations, government administrative offices, and militia posts of the former government.

Thap felt disoriented and did not recognize any landmarks. She looked for a familiar face but saw only strangers. Everything, from their market baskets to their conical hats, looked strange, and the style of dress of even rural women and the petty traders with their baskets of goods suspended from carrying poles was nothing like the old days. Suddenly, in the midst of all the enthusiasm of the recent victory, Thap felt a sense of sadness. Her old comrades were almost all gone, killed during the protracted struggle. This return trip after the victory of the revolution had been made possible at a very high price.

Near the village, the car was of no further use. Suddenly, like stepping through the looking glass, the transforming "modernization" of the main route gave way to scenes of decline and decay. Where was the old road into the village, she wondered. Unlike the modern highway that had replaced a modest colonial road, the route into the village had deteriorated from a well-maintained, all-weather laterite road that allowed cars to proceed all the way into the village to a narrow dirt path passable only on foot. Alongside the route the trees had been cut down, and brambles from the overgrown tangle of bushes on both sides of the path snagged the clothes of passers-by. The neat and well-maintained houses of former times were gone, replaced by a thin scattering of run-down shacks. The only familiar sensation was the pungent odor of tiny crabs, emanating from their burrows in the rice field banks—a special smell that was the sole reminder of the countryside of her childhood in an otherwise radically transformed landscape.

Revolutionary Rectitude Versus Material Prosperity

On the flight from Hanoi, Thap had noted the contrast between the flourishing trees and plants surrounding prosperous red-tiled roofs in areas formerly controlled by Saigon and the barren and war-ravaged zones controlled by the revolution, which had been bombed and sprayed with chemical defoliants. She consoled herself with the lines of poet and Politburo member To Huu: "In the South, where the foliage is flourishing, the people are withered, and where the foliage is withered the people are flourishing." Despite the outward prosperity and the beauty of their surroundings, she reasoned, the people in the Saigon zones must be morally and spiritually impoverished and burdened with a guilty conscience for having enjoyed the seductive but short-lived "sweet and fragrant morsels" set before them by the Americans, while those who had suffered in the revolutionary zones were bolstered by "revolutionary optimism" and had emerged from their ordeal still upbeat and positive.

As events would soon demonstrate, the population in the South did not as readily accept the trade-off of political rectitude for material prosperity as veteran revolutionaries like Nguyen Thi Thap. One of the ironies of history was that the "modernized" villages along the main roads were the ones that had initially been the most fertile ground for the revolution, but this very "modernization" eventually led the people in these areas in a very different direction. By the end of the war in 1975, the revolutionary base of support was strongest in the more remote and isolated villages, where the tidal wave of war-induced social change had not overflowed the channels in which the Party had attempted to contain it.

Thap sought out the wife and daughter of her older brother, Tam, her last close relatives still living in the village. Her brother was also a long-time revolutionary and had also just returned to the South after years of struggle. He was the one who had persuaded her to make the trip. Thap and Tam asked directions. Suddenly, one face was familiar. Sau Danh was one of the few remaining local revolutionaries who had survived both the anti-French Resistance and the later war against the Saigon government and the United States. It was Sau Danh who in 1959 had dug up the cache of weapons hidden after the 1954 Geneva Accords sent the province military forces to the North. With these weapons a new insurgency had been launched. Sau Danh had been the leading military figure in the province throughout the "Vietnam War" (1960–75).

With Sau Danh's guidance, Thap and Tam arrived at Tam's wife's house. Tam did not recognize his wife, whom he had not seen since he left for North Vietnam in 1954. Once a beautiful woman, she now looked wizened and bent. Tam's daughter rushed to embrace him. "Father, you've come back!" she exclaimed. Breaking into tears, the daughter sobbed,

"They're all dead now. There's nothing left." A crowd gathered, including a few old revolutionaries who tried to brighten the atmosphere by focusing on the survivors rather than the casualties of revolution.

In late afternoon, sounds of gunfire were heard. Sau Danh urged Muoi Thap to leave the village: "The gang of disbanded soldiers [of the former Saigon forces] who have not come out to report are hiding and sneaking out to get food. We are still hunting them down. Better to be careful." The sun gradually disappeared behind a clump of bamboo trees as Thap prepared to leave. The bamboo trees growing up from the foundation were all that was left of the family home, and even the bamboo had lost all its leaves. A few rotted cornerposts were overgrown with a tangle of vines. The family's armoire, made from a rare and precious wood, which had been hidden in a clump of bamboo throughout the conflict, was back in its old place, but its mirror was shattered. The symbolism of the broken images reflecting back from this relic of the past did not escape her. An expanse of what had once been well-tended orchard was now an overgrown empty plot of land with a few scattered huts belonging to recent arrivals who had been displaced from other villages by the war. Leaving the village, Thap walked along the banks of ditches built to impede American armored vehicles.

As Thap ended her nostalgic trip, memories flooded her consciousness. Images of the anticolonial demonstrations of the 1930s were followed by remembrances of the brief but bloody 1940 uprising against the French. The August 1945 revolution, when the revolutionaries first seized power, came back to her. A generation of fallen revolutionaries had been replaced by a new generation. Writing of her impressions of this 1975 trip a decade later, Thap asked her readers to forgive her "moment of weakness" as she was gripped by melancholy. Every trace of memory from childhood was gone—even softly reverberating sounds and sensations such as the plop of a ripe mangosteen hitting the ground or the smell of a durian wafting through the moonlit night. She tried to shake this unsettling sense of loss by remembering the heroism of past revolutionaries and focusing on the promise of the future now that the revolution had triumphed.

Nguyen Thi Thap's vivid account of her life as a revolutionary illustrates one of the main themes of this book. Vietnam's revolutionary movement fundamentally transformed its society, but at a heavy cost and not always with the results intended by its leadership. Because the struggle lasted for decades, most of those who initiated it were not around to see the end, and the character of the revolution itself evolved during this protracted conflict. As Thap's memoir reveals, there was another, even more powerful transformative force at work—the war itself, set in motion by the revolutionary struggle. This study examines in detail a small piece of the extraordinary attempt of the Vietnamese revolutionaries to remake a society that they felt had been deformed and stultified by feudalism, colonialism, and capitalism. This ambitious project of social transformation did achieve many of its goals. In the end, however, the social engineering of the revolutionary leaders was constrained by the vast spontaneous social change that resulted from decades of destructive war.

Legacies of War

The scattered remnants of the Saigon army that still lurked around Thap's village were eventually dispersed. Either they were detained and incarcerated for often lengthy periods in "re-education camps" or they melted back into society. The legacy of an alternative to the Party's vision of the good life was not as easily eradicated, however. During the war the revolutionaries had tried to insulate the areas under their control from both the market forces emanating from the Saigon zones and the cornucopia of goods avidly sought by the rural farmers—fertilizer, pesticides, and the humble but revolutionary small motorized water pumps that changed the face of rural agriculture. The Party cadres warned their people against becoming "addicted to the Americans" by becoming dependent on these goods, which the revolutionary zone could not supply; however, they could not stem the tide.

Thirty years of rigid revolutionary discipline created a reservoir of animosity that even peace could not dispel. Many one-time revolutionaries had faltered in the face of prolonged sacrifice and left the movement. So many ordinary people had worked for the Saigon regime that after the war it was hard to find a solid base of revolutionary supporters. Even those former Saigon soldiers and functionaries who were prepared to collaborate with the Party after 1975 were discouraged by the ineradicable blot of their past connections and the suspicion and hostility they faced. The overwhelming support the revolution enjoyed in My Tho during most of the war of Resistance against the French and the early years of the post-1960 insurgency had dissipated as a result of political fatigue, war weariness, and the heavy demands often harshly imposed on the peasants by the revolutionaries. By the end of the war, committed activist followers of the revolution in My Tho were almost certainly a minority of the population.

Though the war undermined many of the revolutionaries' accomplishments, these achievements were still quite remarkable. Considering the revolution in historical retrospect, we should not look at the entire period only through postwar lenses. The vast popularity and fervent support enjoyed by the revolution at critical junctures in its history is now easily overlooked, but it is important to record and to evaluate in order to understand the revolution as a social movement. The tenacity and effectiveness of the many admirable, idealistic, and dedicated revolutionaries contribute to our understanding of their political behavior, especially in assessing the relative weight of values and self-interest in motivating individuals to act. And the significant number of revolutionaries who were ruthless in pursuit of their objectives, who believed that their Party positions gave them complete authority over the people in whose name they struggled, and who were convinced that the ends justify almost any means, are equally worthy of study.

Like Thap's destroyed family home, little was left of the rural society that had existed before the revolution. Wholesale change had altered not only the clothing styles and the architecture of the countryside, but also its class structure. The Communist Party's Marxist analysis of rural society, which had provided the foundation for the revolutionary program and strategy of the Vietnamese Communist Party, fell behind the pace of social change as the war finished off the old landlord class and created a new strata of small independent "middle peasant" farmers in place of the oppressed tenants of Thap's youth. Despite these developments, Party perceptions and policies remained rooted in the old realities. In part, the rise of this new socioeconomic stratum was due to the impact of the early revolutionary land reform, but the lasting consequences of this restructuring of rural society were quite different from what the Party leaders had initially envisaged.

Revolution and Social Change

In fact, the whole texture of rural society was dramatically transformed between 1930 and 1975. The often stultifying but tightly cohesive traditional rural society was irreparably fragmented by decades of war and dislocation. Large numbers of refugees, forced off their land by the war, flooded into the cities or into anomic temporary refugee settlements. When they did occasionally return to their villages, they brought with them influences from the outside and helped to obliterate the formerly sharp distinction between village life and the outside world. The result was the erosion of the collective sense of moral community that, even though less powerful than in other areas of Vietnam, had traditionally provided the context for social and political action in the villages of the Mekong Delta. Peasants increasingly became farmers, and members of the collective village enterprise were transformed into individuals responding to their own interests more than community pressure. By 1975, the "moral economy" had largely given way to the "rational peasant."

Tran Van Giau, who had once been the political nemesis of Muoi Thap in My Tho and the Mekong Delta, had similar impressions of the great changes that occurred there during the war. Giau had once been in charge of the entire Southern revolutionary movement and was a key figure in Vietnam's 1945 revolution. Thap had resisted Giau's leadership in the period leading up to this pivotal event. But Giau's impressions on returning to the South after 1975 were comparable to those of Muoi Thap. After several years of unsuccessful attempts at realizing a "socialist transformation" in the South, Giau noted that powerful changes had taken place in the countryside, especially between 1954 and 1975. These were the consequence of the "development of commercialized relations between the countryside and the city, and the city and the countryside, which was the result of the American 'commercial assistance program.'"[2]

The result was the "creation of opportunities for a number of upper middle peasants and rich peasants to become a rural bourgeoisie," which, in turn, "changed the rural lifestyle in a number of ways and thus altered the traditional way of thinking of the peasants in some ways. The people here [in the southern countryside] actually lost some of their traditional qualities. According to Giau, "Commercialization also created a mentality of running after self-interest on the part of the small peasant proprietors and tenants who never—or hardly ever—used to think this way. When you speak of commercial relations you are talking about the pursuit of self-interest. Whenever the mentality of 'for profit' advances, the mentality of 'for righteousness' retreats. How can it be avoided? People from the Nam Bo countryside who return after being away for two or three decades can't help but feel pained when they notice this phenomenon of psychological degeneration!"

Giau observed that "Because the struggle to win over the countryside was fierce, prolonged, and incredibly tense, our revolutionary organizations were not in the villages at every moment, the liberated zone wasn't always extensive, and we didn't win every battle in the war. We chiseled incisions and the enemy effaced them; the enemy sullied things and we washed them clean—the struggle went back and forth like that for thirty long years." He concluded: "If you look at the most recent generation it is like a grove of bamboo in which some have been twisted and bent, we also know that the nature of bamboo is to grow upright, and that if pains are taken to remold and straighten out them out, the bamboo will stand tall as before."

Perhaps Muoi Thap should not have been so surprised by the extent to which the rural society of her childhood had changed. She herself was both an agent and a product of that change. Her revolutionary career had taken her into the cities and factories to organize workers and to the privations of jail in close and enforced intimacy with a cross section of people from all walks of life. Three times she traveled the length of Vietnam under conditions of extreme hardship and danger to get support from the central Party leadership. Her ability had taken her to the very top of the revolutionary leadership. Not many peasants reached this high or traveled this far, but significant numbers were pulled far enough away from their village moorings that they became very different people. The one shaping value that remained unchanged for Muoi Thap and many others of her revolutionary generation was an unshakable faith in the collectivity and the necessity to subordinate individual interests to the greater good.

The altruism and idealism of this position are inarguable, and it provided an extraordinary level of social cohesion for a society dislocated by colonial rule and wartime stress. This conviction, however, did not provide strong support for democratization based on recognition of individual rights, or for an economic system motivated by individual profit seeking. In this sense, Muoi Thap and most other revolutionary leaders remained attached to the "moral economy" framework, shaped by their rural origins. Even a "Westernized" urban intellectual like Tran Van Giau had a similar view, not only because of his Marxist training, but also because of his Confucian background, which emphasized the absolute priority of "righteousness" (*nghia*) over self-interested profit seeking (*chay theo loi ich ich ky*).

Despite the heavy losses of decades of struggle, the revolution survived. One generation was supplanted by the next, illustrated by the meeting between Thap and Sau Danh, who represented the next generation of revolutionaries in My Tho province that carried the brunt of the struggle in the post-1954 period. During the succession of generations, however, the original character of the revolutionary movement also underwent significant transformation. The revolutionaries launched their struggle because there was no other way to bring about the sweeping changes they desired in the face of determined opposition from a stubborn French colonial regime, and the still more powerful antirevolutionary forces of the Americans and their Saigon allies after the French departure from Vietnam in 1954. In the end, the war engulfed the revolution itself and deflected the course of societal change in ways that were beyond the capacity of the victorious Party leaders to fully control. How and why this happened is the focus of this study.

Railroad connecting My Tho and Saigon. A French guidebook published in 1887 reproduced this picture and said that My Tho, like most places in the Mekong Delta, had no real towns and was "nothing but an agglomeration of villages." The railroad was abandoned in 1962. Today, a modern (American-built) highway links Saigon and My Tho.

The All-Women's Theater Troupe of Vinh Kim (Dong Nu Ban) was an early nationalist group from the area around Vinh Kim whose patriotic plays had an impact in My Tho province.

As a young man from an elite family in My Tho, Bay Phong stole a sum of money from his mother equivalent to nearly 2,000 bushels (*gia*) of rice in 1926 to finance a trip to Canton, where he joined Ho Chi Minh's revolutionary organization. He returned the following year to organize the revolutionary movement in My Tho.

Nguyen Thieu was the first Communist Party leader in My Tho (1930–31).

Nguyen Van Con (Chin Con) was another early Party leader who played a key role in the 1930s and 1940s and helped bridge the gap between different revolutionary groups.

Dan Ton Tu (Sau Vi) was a founding organizer of the revolutionary movement in My Tho, and played a prominent role in the August 1945 revolution.

After the war's end in 1975, Nguyen Thi Thap meets a former constable of the colonial period who had shielded her from the French authorities.

Nguyen Thi Thap, known as "Sister Ten," was a revolutionary leader in My Tho in the 1930s and 1940s, and later became the head of the Women's Association in the Democratic Republic of Vietnam (North Vietnam).

The communal house of Long Hung, the native village of Nguyen Thi Thap and other prominent early revolutionaries in My Tho. This building served as a command post of the 1940 Nam Ky uprising.

A postwar reconstruction of the Long Hung communal house (1998). The current structure is a memorial to fallen revolutionaries and is referred to as the "House of Tradition" (Nha Truyen Thong), which implies a convergence between Vietnam's historical tradition and the tradition of the revolutionary movement.

Author in Vinh Kim with parents of revolutionary heroine Le Thi Hong Gam in 1982. The two people on the right were veterans of the 1940 Nam Ky uprising.

Author with Tran Van Giau in Hanoi, 1999. Giau was the revolutionary leader for all of South Vietnam during much of the period from the mid-1930s through the August 1945 revolution. At one critical juncture his leadership was challenged by the Liberation group of Nguyen Thi Thap.

Phan Dinh Lan was a youth and sports leader of the Japanese occupation period who later became the key Vanguard Youth organizer in My Tho.

Vanguard Youth in Nam Bo 1945, marching with sharpened bamboo stakes for weapons.

Duong Khuy, the leader of the Vanguard group of the Indochinese Communist Party aligned with Tran Van Giau and opposed by the Liberation group, which included "Sister 10" (Nguyen Thi Thap) in the period leading up to and including the pivotal August 1945 revolution. Shortly after this event, Khuy was removed as province Party leader, and was subsequently killed by the French reoccupation force in 1946.

Nguyen Tan Thanh (Bay Kinh), the first "military affairs commissioner" in My Tho province. He was killed during the anti-French Resistance.

Nguyen Van Chim (Ba Chim, the "Birdman") became the top Party leader in My Tho during the later years of the anti-French Resistance and played a key role throughout the next three decades.

Ambush of a French convoy at Giong Dua along the national highway in My Tho. This was the first major military success of the Resistance period in South Vietnam. Tran Van Tra was the commander of this action.

Another view of the 1947 ambush of the French convoy, which was taking ministers of the separatist French-created "Autonomous Government of South Vietnam" on an inspection tour.

Tran Van Tra at a Resistance base. He led the attack on the French convoy and was commander of Viet Minh forces in the central Mekong Delta.

Tran Van Tra headed a Viet Minh delegation from South Vietnam which met with Ho Chi Minh in the Viet Bac (North Vietnam) in late 1948. (Tra is standing immediately to the right of Ho.)

Peasants in the Plain of Reeds dig a trench to impede French mechanized vehicles during the Resistance.

Tran Van Tra, commander of revolutionary military forces in the central Mekong Delta was "angry and distracted" at being ordered to regroup to North Vietnam, but promised those who stayed behind that "one bright and happy day we will return."

Le Van Nhung (Viet Thang or "Victorious Viet") was Party leader in My Tho from 1957 to 1962.

Dao Dua, known as the "coconut monk," an eccentric religious figure in My Tho and Ben Tre who started to gather a following in the tense and unsettled time of the late 1950s.

3

Prelude

Spring 1945. They were an odd couple. The urbane Tran Van Giau looked a little out of place sitting on a pile of straw in the middle of a deserted rice field, talking politics with Nguyen Thi Thap and trying to persuade her to accept his leadership of the revolutionary movement in the South. It was the third lunar month of the year and the dry rice fields had just been harvested. In the distance, they could see American planes bombing the town of My Tho. World War II was coming to a close, and the impending defeat of the Japanese occupying forces who had just taken over from the discredited Vichy French colonial administration offered an unprecedented opportunity for Vietnamese independence.[1]

This brief encounter of two revolutionaries in the Mekong Delta is only a footnote in the grand sweep of Vietnamese twentieth-century revolution, but to understand its significance is to understand a great deal about how that movement unfolded in an important part of southern Vietnam. The background to this meeting in My Tho illustrates the nature and origins of that movement. It also situates the revolution in My Tho within the larger national context and introduces some key aspects of the relationship between the top leadership of the Communist Party, located in the northern part of Vietnam and the regional and local Party organizations in the south. My Tho's distance from the central leadership of the Party had very significant consequences for the way in which the subsequent history of the province developed.

Revolutions are shaped by the forces that produce them, and it is therefore essential to grasp the conditions that led to the drastic step of armed struggle, and the interplay between global, national, and local factors that influenced the course of events in My Tho and in Vietnam as a whole. Social movements are also decisively influenced by the aspirations and values of the leaders who organize them. Introducing the cast of characters who were central figures in the early stages of this drama will help us to understand their motivations, and their connections with the society that produced them. Finally, it will help us to see both continuity and change. At the end of the long conflict, in 1975, the revolutionary movement was very different than it had been at the beginning, in 1930, and that is the main story of this book. It is impossible to understand the later phases of this struggle without knowing how it started and where it came from.

Two different perspectives can be used to illuminate the significance of the Thap–Giau meeting in the rice field. One is to look at the events that immediately preceded it, and the other is to examine the origins in the 1920s and 1930s of Vietnam's revolution. On the surface the meeting may be part of a power struggle or a dispute over strategy and tactics, but underlying the rift between these two southern leaders was a deeper divide between social classes. As we will see, Thap's constituency tended to be more rural and lower on the socioeconomic scale, while Giau appealed to a broad coalition of urban intellectuals and rural elites.

One of the main arguments of this book is that social change in the Mekong Delta reflected a reality and followed a dynamic that did not always reflect Party dictates or expectations, and that ultimately undermined the revolution. In the early stages of the revolution, the Party tried to lead a social revolution while pursuing a patriotic struggle for independence, but these aims were not always compatible. In the crucial period leading up to the revolutionary assumption of power in August 1945 in the wake of the French and Japanese collapse, Party unity in My Tho and other places in the South was strained by its own internal diversity. The bedrock of the rural revolution was the mobilization of poor peasants, which began in 1930. Yet the poorest peasants were not always the first or most enthusiastic supporters of revolution, and many of the urban and rural elites who were drawn to the revolution out of idealism and patriotism were not always responsive to poor peasant interests. In addition, there were problems of coordinating revolutionary policy, especially after the Party headquarters moved to North Vietnam after the Japanese occupied Indochina, and the local strains in the My Tho revolutionary movement were exacerbated by their distance from an authoritative power center that could definitively resolve questions of policy and personnel.

To understand the complex elements that were combined into the revolutionary movement, we must start with the early history of the Party in My Tho. Although many of the people and issues that were prominent in the 1930–45 period do not figure in the later story of the revolution in My Tho, which is the main focus of this study, the significance and meaning of what happened in the thirty years from 1945 to 1975 cannot be fully grasped if the preceding period is ignored. Moreover, this study contends that the nature of the revolutionary movement was fundamentally transformed between 1930 and 1975, and that this helps explain the difficulties its leaders encountered after its decisive military victory in 1975. Thus the roots of many postwar problems lie in the now nearly forgotten past. In this chapter we first introduce some of the leading figures in the early revolutionary movement in My Tho, with a special focus on their socioeconomic and family backgrounds. These biographical profiles will give us some insight into the types of people attracted to the revolution and the reasons they joined it.

The origins of the rift within the revolutionary movement in the South in the mid-1940s may be faintly discerned in the class and status differences among the early activists, even before the events of the Japanese occupation led to a split based on strategy and policy differences. Then we place these early revolutionaries in the context of the broader socioeconomic crisis that followed the worldwide depression and resulting impoverishment of even relatively prosperous areas like the Mekong Delta. The course of events leading up to the 1945 watershed of Vietnamese history is traced. The peasant uprisings of the early 1930s, the Popular Front interlude of open political agitation in the mid-1930s, and the Nam Ky uprising of 1940, which was followed by brutal repression of the revolutionary movement, are the key benchmarks of this period. Finally, we examine in detail the origins and significance of the split between two elements of the revolutionary movement in the 1943–45 period: the Liberation group of which Nguyen Thi Thap was a member, and the Vanguard group of Tran Van Giau. This, in turn, will set the stage for the next chapter's discussion of the complex events of the August 1945 revolution and the legacy of this historic turn in the revolutionary road.

Early Revolutionaries in My Tho

One of the first Party activists in My Tho and an important leader in My Tho in 1945 was Dan Ton Tu (Sau Vi), who became a member of the Liberation group along with Muoi Thap, and who ran the Liberation cadre training school in 1945. The Liberation Group emerged during the Japanese Occupation. It adhered to the anti-Japanese party line laid down by the central leadership in North Vietnam, while Tran Van Giau led a rival Vanguard group which resisted cooperating with nonrevolutionary elements and, when the opportunity arose, advocated exploiting Japanese support for the liberation of Vietnam. The Liberation group was sometimes called "the old Viet Minh" and the Vanguard Group "the new Viet Minh." Although none of the revolutionary histories mention it, Dan Ton Tu's name strongly indicates that he was a descendent of the *minh huong*—Chinese refugees (Ming dynasty loyalists) who fled the Manchus and settled in the Mekong Delta in the seventeenth century. Although he was certainly fully assimilated, the strong tradition of Chinese-style secret societies that gave revolutionary activities in the delta a distinctive character must have affected him. He came from the village of Vinh Kim, right next to Thap's own village of Long Hung. Vinh Kim had been at the center of the provincial revolutionary movement since its inception in the late 1920s, and its revolutionary leadership was initially comprised of local teachers and rural gentry. Whereas Tran Van Giau's revolutionary lineage stemmed from both his Western education, his study in Moscow's "Stalin School" (the Oriental Workers' Institute), and his high-profile political agitation in Saigon during the Popular Front movement of the 1930s, Sau Vi, like Muoi Thap, came from more traditional roots.

Sau Vi's mother was widowed early and, unusual for a woman at the time, supported herself as a rural teacher of Chinese classics (*ba giao nho*). His father had been connected with the traditional secret societies of the early twentieth century such as the Thien Dia Hoi (Heaven and Earth Association), as well as nationalist groups such as the Duy Tan association. Sau Vi, recognizing that the older nationalists had been unable to formulate a solution for Vietnam's problems, turned to the inspiration of transitional "modernizing" leaders such as Phan Chu Trinh. Sau Vi was galvanized into political action by the highly charged atmosphere in Vietnam of the mid-1920s, which was catalyzed by the funeral observances for Phan Chu Trinh in 1926. He joined with rural schoolteachers in Vinh Kim to organize a memorial service for Phan, and headed a fund drive in Vinh Kim to send a like-minded patriot overseas to find an answer to Vietnam's problems. Even this local group, without the Western education and sophistication of Tran Van Giau, was already thinking about politics on a global scale.[2]

What directly motivated them, however, were the injustices of colonial society close at hand. Their anger was directed at the "ruling class" in My Tho, especially big landowners such as the Frenchmen Duquesnay and Brondeau, *Huyen* [District Chief] Tru, Le Phat An, Le Phat Thanh, and—the big landlord most frequently mentioned in the interviews of the 1960s—Nguyen Thanh Long; Francophile Vietnamese such as the wealthy entrepreneur Truong Van Ben; and high-ranking Vietnamese administrators such as Doc Phu Kia and Doc Phu Mau, Doc Phu Luong, Doc Phu Thuong, Doc Phu Kinh, Doc Phu Hai (Doc Phu was an official grade in the colonial bureaucracy equivalent to chief of a small province). During the mid-1920s, there was an unprecedented concentration of land the hands of big landlords. Sau Vi's own family, which had owned two hectares of rice fields, became impoverished tenants. "From the time I picked up my books and went to school until the day I joined the revolution," said Sau Vi, "there was not a moment that I didn't see my family in a situation of material deprivation."[3]

Muoi Thap also came from an impoverished background, somewhere slightly above the poorest peasants and at the fringe of the small rural gentry. As a young child she had ascribed her family's poverty to fate. As an old saying went, "the son of the emperor becomes an emperor, while the monk's assistant in the pagoda will go on sweeping the courtyard." Not until she was ten did it occur to her to ask why some people are happy in life and some are sad or miserable. Her oldest brother had been sent as a servant to a wealthy notable in Vinh Kim, and when he returned to Long Hung with his annual hair-cut and once-a-year Tet gift of a new white shirt, the whole hamlet was impressed by his good fortune.[4]

Thap's father was also a member of the Thien Dia Hoi, which saw itself as a continuation of the traditional anticolonial movement in the Mekong Delta. Its members practiced martial arts, swore blood oaths, and repeated the oath of the great nineteenth-century patriot and writer Nguyen Dinh Chieu: "While we live we will fight the enemy, when we die we will continue to fight and our soul will follow and aid our troops; we will take revenge for eternity." Thap's brother had fled home from his servant's job in 1917 because the French had begun to forcibly recruit coolies to send to the Western Front. Then, in 1918, the usually prosperous village of Long Hung was devastated by crop failure. A few landlords continued to live well, but the tenants and sharecroppers suffered. The local village constables (*huong quan*) took advantage of the desperation of the poor peasants to loan out money and then set up gambling dens to take it back, as the impoverished peasants frantically tried to raise more money by risking everything. When all was lost they left their native villages for the "wild west" frontier of Bac Lieu, further south in the Mekong Delta.

In 1920, Muoi Thap's mother died. Her strict father became reclusive. His health failed, and he could no longer earn even a modest living as village carpenter. Using his slight knowledge of Chinese characters, he was able to eke out an existence writing auspicious couplets on rice paper for buyers to hang in their homes, and by weaving baskets. Sitting at work, he regaled his daughter with stories of feudal virtues and proprieties. As a woman and an independent person, these models of subservient behavior did not appeal to Muoi Thap. She had to take over her mother's role in managing the household at age twelve, at the expense of her education. Some more educated revolutionaries had the impression that she could not write and was called Muoi Thap because she signed her name with the equivalent of an "X," the Chinese character for ten "+" (*thap*) [DT136]. Thap describes herself as a voracious reader, however, and it is unlikely that she could not write. The impression rather than the reality is significant, since it indicates the view of some revolutionaries in My Tho that she was illiterate until she remedied her educational deficiency after the regroupment to North Vietnam in 1954.

At the age of seventeen, Thap's father forced her to marry a man she did not love. The bridegroom came from a more prosperous background and from a family that had been close to Thap's own. After a vigorous argument and an attempted suicide, Thap acceded to her father's wish. Her philandering husband later became a Party member; nevertheless, she finally walked out the door and into a revolutionary career. She later married Le Van

Giac ("King Giac"), who subsequently led the 1940 Nam Ky uprising in Long Hung and was killed in its aftermath. One son was killed during the Resistance and another son was killed during the "Vietnam War."

In 1927, she met Sau Vi (Dan Ton Tu), who was a member of the local branch of the proto-communist Thanh Nien Cach Mang Dong Chi Hoi (Association of Revolutionary Youth Comrades), which had been organized by the man then known as Nguyen Ai Quoc and later known as Ho Chi Minh. From Vinh Kim the movement spread quickly to neighboring villages. Thap's brothers joined first, and then allowed her to participate. At first Thap supported herself as a seamstress, sewing for the peasants in the village. When harvest time came, she would go out to work in the few hectares of land her father rented from a landlord. She became active in the revolutionary-sponsored peasant associations, which adapted the traditional practice of labor exchange at harvest time to a larger scale, organizing groups of forty to fifty people. Within each group were secret revolutionaries.

Another early leader of this movement, Thai Van Dau, was based in the village of Tam Hiep, which was another revolutionary center in My Tho province not far from Long Hung. He was a friend of Thap's family, and though she did not know it at the time, a member of the My Tho Province Party Committee. Thai Van Dau was a poor peasant with dark sunburned skin who wore his hair in the traditional topknot, but Thap noted that he nevertheless also wore a "proper" black *ba ba* outfit (which later became famous as the "black pajama" uniform of the "Viet Cong" and a symbol of peasant poverty, not of being well dressed and respectable) and carried an umbrella, the mark of the rural gentry.

When Thap learned that Dau was a revolutionary, she asked him if she could join the Peasants Association. "The Peasants Association is an organization of the Communist Party," he said. "If you join the Peasants Association you will have to struggle with the gang of landlords and the gang of imperialists and make demands for the interests of the peasants. If you engage in struggle, you will be arrested, tortured and exiled. Are you scared?"[5] So eager was Thap to be part of the organization, she always paid her monthly dues in advance.

Eventually, Thap joined the Party itself. "Why do you want to join?" she was asked. "I want to join the Party to fight the imperialists, to fight the feudalists, and to kick the French out of the country," she replied.[6] Although this was not a sophisticated answer, it neatly sums up the motivations of the revolutionaries through their struggle. Other Party members, such as Sau Vi, studied a tract called the *ABCs of Communism,* which focused on the lessons of the 1905 Russian Revolution for Party leadership, and was prepared by the Thanh Nien group in Canton in 1924–25, as well as Ho Chi Minh's article on the "Peasant Situation in Vietnam" and, to get a sense of the broader revolutionary movement, the report of the 1924 Fifth Congress of the Communist International in Moscow.[7]

In December 1929, Ngo Gia Tu, one of the most famous early communists in Vietnam, came to organize a Communist Party chapter in Vinh Kim. In the name of the *Xu Uy,* he admitted Sau Vi and Thap's future second husband Le Van Giac to the chapter, along with several others. "Now we are comrades," said Tu, "and are brothers headed in the same direction with the same ideals. We must protect the Party and protect ourselves."[8] This illustrates both the positive and negative legacies of a revolution forced to operate clandestinely and in conditions of extreme danger. Idealism is an important part of the revolutionary story in Vietnam, but so is the secrecy, which gave rise to intense suspicion of those outside (and even inside) the Party, reinforced an authoritarian style of leadership, fueled the "paranoid style of politics" (a term political scientist Richard Hofstader once used to describe American politics), and gave rise to terrorism and arbitrary punishment as revolutionaries responded in kind to the suppression directed against them. In the face of French colonial repression, this style of politics was necessary for their survival.

During the Japanese occupation, Sau Vi was aligned politically with Muoi Thap and the Liberation group and became the head of the (Liberation) Provisional Province Party Committee after his return from imprisonment in Ba Ra (discussed below). He had been a member of perhaps the strongest Thanh Nien organization in My Tho, based in Vinh Kim since at least 1927, along with Thap's second husband Le Van Giac. Ton Duc Thang, a senior figure in the revolutionary movement, also met occasionally with this group.[9] Sau Vi could trace his political lineage back to this early recruitment as a Communist Party member by Ngo Gia Tu, one of the founding members of the Indochinese Communist Party (ICP) and an associate of Ho Chi Minh, as well as the head of the South Vietnam predecessor of the *Xu Uy* in 1929–30.[10]

After the March 1945 Japanese coup, Sau Vi escaped from Ba Ra prison, returned to My Tho, and helped set up a provisional My Tho Province Party Committee, which included Ba Chim (Nguyen Van Nhan) and Muoi Thap's brother. Thap was not on the province committee, according to Ba Chim, because she was a member of the (Liberation) *Xu Uy* that was in overall charge of the movement in this area.[11] Ba Chim later became the leader of the My Tho Province Party Committee during the crucial years following the 1954 Geneva Accords. Called the "bird" (*chim*; a term reminiscent of the "birdman of Alcatraz") because of his uncanny ability to escape from impossible situations, he was a poor tenant farmer from Kim Son village, which was adjacent to Vinh Kim and one village away from Long Hung.

One of the anomalies of the Vanguard–Liberation split was Chin Con, another key leader of the 1945 revolution in My Tho, who was a member of the 1943 Vanguard *Xu Uy* but also had close ties with the Liberation movement. When a nominally unified My Tho province committee was formed after the March 1945 Japanese coup, Chin Con was part of it.[12] Chin Con came from a rural gentry background. He was a direct descendent of Truong Dinh, a famous leader of the anti-French resistance in My Tho in the nineteenth century. Con was older than most of the other members of the group, with different formative experiences as well as social and political connections. Born in 1894, he became politically active at age sixteen and, together with other young men in Go Cong (at times a district of My Tho and sometimes a separate province) set up the Republican Association of Go Cong. As a political activist, he became acquainted with Ho Chi Minh's father (who spent his last years in the Mekong Delta and is buried in neighboring Kien Phong province) and with Nguyen An Ninh, a radical but noncommunist figure who was probably the most prominent anticolonial figure in the Mekong Delta during the 1930s, as well as other delta notables such as Tran Van Giau's relative, village chief, Hoai, who hosted the crucial 1943 *Xu Uy* meeting in Cho Gao, which reestablished a Party leadership in the South under the control of Tran Van Giau.

Chin Con clearly came from the upper gentry, though a prison term in Poulo Condore had somewhat lowered his status. When he resurfaced as the leader of the revolutionary movement in Go Cong in 1945, people remembered him as "a person who lived by selling *nuoc mam* [fish sauce] or occasionally teaching Chinese characters." A few people knew that he had been imprisoned, but very few knew about the extent of his revolutionary background, going back to the 1920s.[13] He and his friends often sat around discussing classical Chinese literature. One day shortly after the funeral of Phan Chu Trinh in 1926, Bay Phong, a younger member of his circle, rushed into Chin Con's house and pleaded with him to repair the family damage that was sure to follow from a rash act. He had just stolen 700 piasters from his mother to finance a trip abroad to find out how to make revolution. At the time, the average annual income of tenant farmers was 151 piasters, two-thirds of which was spent on rent and living expenses and much of the rest on debt repayment.[14] The sum of 700 piasters would buy nearly 2,000 bushels (*gia*) of rice, so this story clearly indicates the wealth and status of Bay Phong's family and, by implication, Chin Con's own social circle.[15] Bay Phong used the money to finance a trip to Canton, where he joined Nguyen Ai Quoc (Ho Chi Minh) and studied revolutionary tactics and theory. He returned in September 1927 and passed on his excitement about discovering Leninism to Chin Con (perhaps significantly, he did not refer to Marxism, which was more theoretical and of less practical use to an aspiring revolutionary).[16]

Nevertheless, Bay Phong did learn the Leninist position on the relationship between the Communist Party and society. Ho Chi Minh's teaching on this subject to the Thanh Nien group in Canton presented the "conflict in colonized Vietnam as one between the French colonialists and the 'most oppressed elements' (the peasants and workers); the other social groups were considered 'intermediary elements' who could at best be 'friends,' 'allies,' or 'fellow travellers' [*ban cung duong*] of the revolutionary peasants and workers. . . . The students, small merchants and small landowners are also oppressed, but not as miserable as the workers or peasants. Those three groups are only the friends of the workers and peasants."[17] Those three groups, however, were precisely the ones to which Bay Phong and Chin Con belonged. The Thanh Nien itself was certainly not a proletarian-dominated organization. Forty percent of its membership were petty bourgeois intellectuals or students, and another 15 percent were craftsmen and small traders. Another 40 percent were lumped into the category of "peasants" (which certainly included people from the upper reaches of rural society and probably consisted largely of this element), while only 5 percent were workers. One study of the revolution and the peasants in Vietnam concludes: "The fact that 40 percent of the members had a peasant background was an advantage for the Thanh Nien. The return of this group of rural elites, after having been trained in organizing peasants and in agitprop techniques, allowed the Thanh Nien to develop its contacts with peasants."[18] The "peasants" of the Thanh Nien were, then, clearly from the rural gentry or were self-sufficient farmers; they were not landless tenants or sharecroppers.

Formation of Revolutionary Organizations

The first Thanh Nien group was formed in My Tho in late 1927. Over the next several years it spread mainly to the districts surrounding the province town, especially Chau Thanh district, which contained the strong revolutionary villages of Long Hung and Vinh Kim, as well as Go Cong district. Radical political activism seems to have developed in those villages that were closer to the main routes of communication and more deeply engaged in the cash economy. The western districts of Cai Lay and Cai Be, the more remote villages in Chau Thanh, and the eastern districts do not figure as prominently in the early history of the revolutionary movement. Subsequently, in the later phases of the "Vietnam War," it was precisely these remote villages that became the revolutionary strongholds, for reasons discussed in later chapters. The "modernized" villages, which were more closely integrated into the commercial nexus of the colonial economy, also underwent greater social and cultural change.

Vinh Kim village, for example, organized a remarkable group called the United Women's Troupe (*Dong Nu Ban*), which was a theatrical troupe consisting entirely of young women, who put on patriotic plays and plays with an antifeudal message, all aimed at building a spirit of solidarity in the countryside. This group was organized by the My Tho province branch of the Thanh Nien Cach Menh Dong Chi Hoi. The troupe was personally supervised by one of the leading figures of the early Vietnamese revolution, Ton Duc Thang, whose wife came from the area. It consisted of about thirty of the "youngest and most beautiful" girls from the Vinh Kim area, all between about seventeen and twenty years old. These girls came from the upper strata of village society, and only the patriotic cachet of their work overcame parental disdain and prejudice against the traditional low status of actors.[19] This group traveled all over the Mekong Delta during 1927 but disbanded the following year. One source says that it was the "repression and sabotage of the imperialists and their lackeys" that forced an end to the Dong Nu Ban's activities.[20] Another source says simply that the group "decided on its own" to cease activities after two years.[21] Many of its members subsequently joined the Communist Party or its youth group. This group illustrates the three most salient characteristics of the early revolutionary movement: its members were young, generally from higher-status rural families, and concentrated in the "modernizing" villages of My Tho.

Like Sau Vi, Chin Con joined the Thanh Nien Cach Menh Dong Chi Hoi, possibly recruited by the younger Bay Phong, who had a direct line to the outside world and Ho Chi Minh. Huynh Kim Khanh noted the importance of this proto-communist group: "Thanh Nien was a new type of anti-colonial organization in that it attempted to unite political with social issues. Earlier patriotic movements had been exclusively political: their sole object had been freedom from foreign domination. . . . Thanh Nien . . . postulated a new Vietnamese society on the basis of a double revolution, both political ("national independence") and social ("land to the tiller"). . . . Thanh Nien was the beginning of Vietnamese communism."[22] Like earlier patriotic groups, the Thanh Nien emphasized secrecy and solidarity among a small group of like-minded individuals and stressed violence as a political method.

The Thanh Nien was supplanted by competing communist groups organizing in My Tho in 1929 and 1930, which were integrated only after the national unification of the communist movement under the leadership of Ho Chi Minh on February 3, 1930. Both the southern Party (*An Nam Cong San Dang*), which was organized in Go Cong under Chin Con, and the northern Party (*Dong Duong Cong San Dang*), which was strong in Chau Thanh district, had representation in My Tho. From February to April 1930, a delegation of cadres from the newly unified southern Party headquarters under the leadership of Ngo Gia Tu was in My Tho trying to unify the two groups, and the representative of the predecessor of the *Xu Uy*, Nguyen Thieu, was designated the first My Tho province party secretary in late April 1930.[23]

Jailed on the prison island of Poulo Condore (Con Son)—the "revolutionary university" in the early 1930s—Chin Con was released and returned to Go Cong, but he lost contact with the higher levels of the Party even though he continued to recruit for the revolution. When Tran Van Giau came to Cho Gao in 1943 to reestablish the Party organization in the South, Chin Con was selected as a member of the *Xu Uy*. Chin Con became identified with Tran Van Giau and the Vanguard group but was evidently acceptable to the Liberation group as well. Because Go Cong was somewhat separate from My Tho and had many noncommunist political forces in the underdeveloped revolutionary movement of this rural backwater Chin Con was probably the only game in town and was thus courted by both groups within the Party. Ba Chim (the "bird") recalls that Chin Con was a member of the Liberation province Party committee formed in April 1945, which included Liberation stalwarts such as Muoi Thap's brother and was headed by Sau Vi.[24] Chin Con's main political ties were to the Vanguard group of Tran Van Giau, but clearly the line between the two groups was much less distinct in Go Cong than in My Tho. Go Cong's weakness and isolation gave it an advantage in some ways, because it had not been an active area in the Nam Ky insurrection and was thus less affected by the post-1940 repression than other districts.[25]

Early Revolutionary Agitation

All of these early activists were drawn to the revolution by patriotism. It was not just the legacy of traditional nationalism that strengthened the political appeal of the revolutionaries, however, but also their social program. If they were angered by "the loss of country" that became a prominent nationalist rallying cry in the mid-1920s, the worldwide Depression of the 1930s set in motion an economic crisis that led to great misery and social dislocation, which aroused their concern for the poor peasantry and workers, even though most of these revolutionaries were not as directly affected. The Great Depression magnified the rural poverty of Vietnam and gave rise to a new wave of political activism.

Even before this economic crisis, the commercialization of agriculture had led to an increasing divorce between peasants and the land. Awash in a sea of debt or simply unable to produce proof of ownership, the small peasant proprietors now increasingly sank into tenancy. The spread of plantation-scale agriculture is described by Alexander Woodside, who notes that, by 1943: "The number of Cochin China [South Vietnam or Nam Bo] landowners who owned more than fifty hectares of land were less than 3 percent of all landowners in the region, yet they occupied more than 45 percent of all the cultivated land. The rate of land concentration in the South was more rapid than elsewhere in Vietnam. Acreage owned by small peasant landholders (five hectares of land or less) was small and continued to shrink, being less than 13 percent of all cultivated land in Cochin China at the time of the world depression. The potential political force represented by landless peasants also seems to have been greatest in Cochin China: it has been estimated that in 1930 more than one-half the farm families in Tonkin [North Vietnam] owned land, as opposed to about one-third of all the farm families in Cochin China."[26]

Although tenancy and concentration of landholdings was higher in the western Mekong Delta than in central delta provinces such as My Tho, the problem of landlessness was already serious before the Depression, and was made worse by that cataclysm. Pham Cao

Duong notes that, by 1930, "in the province of My Tho, where small properties were more widespread than in the west of Cochin China, 96,000 men over eighteen years of age and 34,600 proprietors were counted; thus, 61,000 persons—approximately two out of three— were classed as proletarians."[27] Of these landowners, 18,000 had less than 1 hectare and another 6,000 less than 2 hectares. Thus, as Duong notes, "at least 18,000 persons were virtually proletarian, or a total of 80,000 peasants out of 96,000."[28]

Despite the high level of political tension over land questions in the Mekong Delta, the most significant political action resulting from the initial shock of the Depression came in central Vietnam. The "Nghe Tinh Soviets" were mass demonstrations of workers and peasants in those two provinces that were eventually ruthlessly suppressed, touching off a wave of arrests that crippled the revolutionary leadership throughout Vietnam until a general amnesty during the Popular Front period released many of these leaders. These were also the only large-scale mass movements of the period that included extensive involvement by the newly formed Indochinese Communist Party.[29] There was, however, rural unrest and agitation in My Tho at this time. In some areas of the province, apparently spontaneous village demonstrations got out of hand and the Party role was to attempt to impose restraint. In a number of villages around Long Hung, "the struggles had some extreme leftist manifestations, including burning rice crops, pulling up rice, destroying seedlings, etc.," according to the Party history. "This situation was remedied by the Party in timely fashion."[30]

In 1930–31 there were Party organizations in possibly a quarter of My Tho's villages, and the province Party history claims that there were peasant organizations even in villages without a Party presence. The average size of each village peasant association was between twenty and thirty members, clearly a small but active minority of the village population.[31] One of the early Party leaders was arrested in 1931 for destroying the village communal hall, which housed the village tutelary deity.[32] Perhaps such iconoclastic acts were also regarded as "leftist manifestations." They do indicate the rejection of village tradition and solidarity by some early revolutionary activists. As noted earlier, it was the "modern" villages that were hotbeds of revolutionary unrest. The more prosperous market towns, on major province roads or close to the province capital, such as Vinh Kim, Thuoc Nhieu (the market section of Duong Diem village on the main national highway through the province), Nhi Binh (also on this road), and other prominent market areas such as Cho Bung (Tam Hiep village), Cho Rau Ram (Kim Son village, near Vinh Kim), Cho Xoai Hot (also in this area and closer to My Tho town), that were the centers of agitation.

With a memory perhaps influenced by a touch of local chauvinism, a native of the Vinh Kim area claimed: "We had a revolutionary Youth Association in Vinh Kim by the 1920s, and then when the Vietnamese Communist Party organized, a representative traveled from the mountains way up north on the Chinese border to choose three bases in the south. Vinh Kim was one." Reacting to the surprise of his foreign guest (Lady Borton) that the revolution would focus on this modest center of petty commerce, the old revolutionary said, "Never underestimate a market."[33] Markets like Vinh Kim were centers of a concerted demonstration against market taxes on May 1, 1930.[34]

Toward the end of the long revolutionary struggle, the center of gravity in the revolution shifted from these market towns to the more remote and less developed villages in the province. Ironically, the reaffirmation of rural values and communal solidarity would become an important aspect of the revolutionary movement in My Tho toward the end of the

"Vietnam War," and was particularly strong among the poorest peasants for reasons that will be discussed in later chapters.

Rural Agitation in the 1930s

Although demonstrations in My Tho province were not on the scale of the "Nghe Tinh Soviets" in central Vietnam, My Tho was certainly not quiet. Muoi Thap described the years 1930–31 in the area around Vinh Kim and her village of Long Hung as "boiling": "Almost everywhere you went you could hear the poor people and the peasant folk openly talking about patriotic things, opposing the French."[35] There were no mass peasant demonstrations on the scale of those in central Vietnam, but on May 1, 1931, a bold demonstration to bring the overbearing local policeman Constable Trau to justice was organized by Pham Hung, who was the province Party secretary of My Tho at the time (later the leader of the revolution in the South and, in the 1980s, the Premier of Vietnam's government), and Muoi Thap's brother. In Muoi Thap's account a large group of peasant demonstrators carrying the hammer-and-sickle flag marched to the Indochina Highway (later Highway 4), stopping buses and propagandizing the passengers about the meaning of International Labor Day. Proceeding on to Constable Trau's house, they saw him attempting to escape on horseback. Trau was run down and surrounded by 3,000 angry peasants. He was forced to kneel while the leaders of the demonstration read their list of his political crimes. Muoi Thap, among others, was strongly impressed by the transformation of this ferocious and arrogant power holder into a quivering supplicant asking forgiveness for his crimes. The mob shouted for the death penalty, and Constable Trau was dispatched with three pistol shots.[36]

In the repression that followed, nearly all of the Party members in the Vinh Kim area were arrested, and Party activities in My Tho subsided. Millenarian religious sects such as the Hoa Hao and the Cao Dai moved into the vacuum. The Hoa Hao had been strong in other provinces of the Mekong Delta, but their influence in My Tho was not great and was largely restricted to the western districts of the province. The Cao Dai, whose mother temple in Tay Ninh province was memorably described by British novelist Graham Greene as a kind of Oriental Disneyland, were strong in Ben Tre province to the south, but now began to gain ground in My Tho itself, even in Muoi Thap's own village of Long Hung.

After the repression of the early 1930s, the countryside of My Tho was relatively quiet until 1940, with the exception of some intermittent agitations during the Popular Front period (1936–1939). Muoi Thap left her village to go to Saigon and organize workers in 1933.[37] In 1935, Thap was elected to the *Xu Uy* (headed by Tran Van Giau) as a candidate member because of her effective work in organizing workers in Saigon. Her long membership in the *Xu Uy* was no doubt one reason why she felt able to challenge Tran Van Giau's leadership in 1943–45, even though she was clearly on the outer margins of the leadership.

Not long after her elevation to the *Xu Uy*, Thap was betrayed and arrested. The French *Sûreté* quickly picked up on the class and status differences in the revolutionary movement and tried to use it to their advantage: "You are just a peasant, how can you compare with the intellectuals like Tran Van Giau, Nguyen Van Duc, and Nguyen Van Kinh [who was a French citizen as well as a revolutionary]? They all have lawyers to defend them. As for you, who will argue for you? Think it over."[38] In the end the *Sûreté* could not find enough evidence to build a strong case and were forced to settle for a sentence of one year. Thap returned to My Tho as a former political prisoner in 1936, just in time to participate in a brief burst of open political agitation made possible by the new policies of the French metropolitan government.

The Popular Front Period in My Tho

The Popular Front was formed as a French attempt to unite groups of the left and center as the fascist menace grew increasingly threatening. In the colonies there was a general amnesty for political prisoners, and open political debate was sanctioned. For the first time there was a direct link between international and local politics, as a French leftist delegation traveled around Vietnam meeting with peasants and recording the abuses of colonial life. A poor peasant remembers a Than Cuu Nghia village meeting attended by 1,000 people from this and neighboring villages in 1937 to greet the delegation of Justin Godard, a representative of the Popular Front government sent to investigate conditions in Indochina. Their hope was that well-intentioned allies from the metropole might make their life better.[39] Although these expectations were soon dashed by the end of the Popular Front and the advent of world war, this period opened a significant window on the world for many ordinary peasants in My Tho.

During the Popular Front period in My Tho a diverse array of groups headed for the villages to win converts to their cause. Trotskyites of the Fourth International vied not only with the Moscow-affiliated local communists but also with rival nationalist groups including the Cao Dai, who were quite active in rural My Tho. Saigon newspapers were widely available in the villages and were read avidly by rural schoolteachers and literate villagers. In Thanh Phu village near My Tho during the Popular Front period, the following newspapers were available: *La Lutte* (of Nguyen An Ninh, a very popular noncommunist opponent of colonialism who was quite prominent in the Mekong Delta), *Tin Dien, Duoc Nha Nam, Cong Luan, Dan Quyen, Saigon, Viet Nam*, and *Phu Nu* (*Phu Nu Tan Van,* or Women's News).[40] Even though this list includes some anachronisms (*Phu Nu Tan Van* was shut down permanently in 1934), it suggests how much the political and social horizons in the villages expanded during the period. Ba Con, who was politically active in the 1930s and survived to serve at the district level in the post-1960 period, recalls being especially impressed by the political writings of several women journalists at the time.[41] In this more relaxed political environment the Party went about restoring its strength. Most of the political agitation centered around reformist aims such as tax and rent reduction rather than sweeping revolutionary goals or demands for national independence, but the confrontations with landlords still had the sharp edge of class struggle.

A landless peasant from Binh Trung village, next to Long Hung, vividly recalled more than three decades after the miseries of his life during the late 1930s: "The brothers were extremely poor, and if they couldn't pay the yearly tax in full they would be fined or imprisoned. You would be held in the village for a week to give you time to get the money. If you couldn't you would be given until the following month, but if you still couldn't come up with the money the village chief would send you to the district jail. This happened quite a lot—the poor peasants constituted 70 percent of the village." For most, the only recourse was to borrow money from wealthier villagers to pay the tax, and then to work off the debt. "You would work for one sou [*cac*] a day in order to borrow one piaster or six or seven sou, but the interest was equal to half the money you made in a day. In this way people got poorer every day, and many had to steal to survive. Even if you got caught, your wife and children couldn't be worse off" [DT310].

During these struggles against rent and taxation, the revolutionaries began to develop techniques of mass organization that became familiar during the Resistance and post-1954 struggles. One of these was to organize the night watchmen in the villages of the area so that the cadres would be informed when an arrest was made. A communications chain linked all the villages in the area. Then all the villages would launch a barrage of noise, using percussive implements ranging from traditional decoratively carved hollow wooden tocsins used by Buddhist monks (the "wooden fish" that became a hallmark of the 1960 Concerted Uprising), to pots and pans. In one such protest of the arrests of two Party members, an urgent appeal was made by the local militia to the French province authorities for help. Because the Long Hung village constable was a secret Party member, Thap and the other cadres found out about this immediately. When the French arrived, they were confronted by a group of 2,000 peasants. For her leadership of this demonstration, Muoi Thap was arrested and sentenced to six months in jail, indicating the clear limits of mass agitation even during the Popular Front period.[42] One important development during this period was that the Communist Party was able to organize in the western districts of Cai Be and Cai Lay in a number of large villages that later became important revolutionary strongholds. Go Cong also expanded its Party chapters in the villages.[43] By 1940, the Party claimed to have chapters in 60 of My Tho province's 125 villages.[44]

When Thap was released from jail she returned to her native village to find that the local revolutionary leader had "begun to pay attention" to her. Le Van Giac was a former carpenter and martial arts specialist who had been imprisoned in Poulo Condore for his political activities in an antitax demonstration in 1930. He was released in 1936 with the Popular Front amnesty and returned to his village. Thai Van Dau, the province Party secretary of My Tho during the difficult years of the early and mid-1930s, and a *Xu Uy* member who had recruited Thap into the revolutionary movement, said that if they wanted to get married they would have to do it "in the new style," to set an example for the people. It was a revolutionary wedding, with a large number of newly released revolutionary activists attending, and even a representative of the non-Party Saigon newspaper Dien Tin. The comrades made sure that no backward, extravagant feudal practices were followed at this "new style" wedding.[45]

The Nam Ky Uprising of November 1940

A startling turnabout in international politics put an end to the Popular Front and its leniency toward open political agitation. The collapse of the Popular Front in 1938 meant an end to the center–left alliance, and the colonial government resumed its repression of the ICP and other revolutionary groups. Now the international communist movement and the ICP changed their focus to "opposing imperialist war," and in Indochina directed their efforts to opposing the efforts of the colonial government to recruit Vietnamese soldiers. In August 1939 the Soviet Union and Hitler's Germany signed a nonaggression pact, and the international communist movement shifted sharply away from its opposition to fascism. In

June 1940 the French capitulated to Germany, maintaining a tenuous claim to sovereignty in the form of the Vichy regime. Taking advantage of French weakness, Japan forced the French to accept the stationing of Japanese troops in North Vietnam in September 1940. Encouraged by this development, the Thais began in December 1940 to threaten to take back territory lost in the nineteenth century to French Indochina. Cut off from reinforcements from the metropole, the colonial regime attempted to recruit more Vietnamese into the army. The Vietnamese heard that the target was 1.5 million recruits.[46] In addition to the conscription, the colonial regime escalated its efforts to arrest revolutionaries, including Muoi Thap's brother Tam Canh. This new imposition, on top of existing grievances concerning colonial taxation and landlordism, created conditions for an intense outburst of peasant rebellion, in which Muoi Thap's husband Le Van Giac was immortalized by the peasants as "King Giac" for his prominence in the most significant movement in My Tho's early revolutionary history, the Nam Ky Uprising of October 1940.

Around May 1940, the My Tho province committee sent out a directive to organize for armed self-defense. Muoi Thap described the international tensions of that period: "In France, the Germans were pouring across the border, in Lang Son [a province in North Vietnam along the Chinese border] the Japanese had already stepped in with their hobnailed boots. In Cambodia the Thai army had opened fire and attacked the border—a plot urged on them by Japan—to demand the return of the provinces that they asserted used to belong to Thailand."[47] In addition to the demands for more Vietnamese manpower, the French government stepped up its requisitions of basic commodities, making life even more difficult for the peasants. To pay for all this activity, the government increased taxes. The cost of living escalated and scarcities increased. Even matches were hard to find. Poor peasants improvised clothes out of burlap, and some could not afford even this.

The countryside fell into darkness, both figuratively and literally. There was no oil for the lamps of peasant households, and there were no more meetings or demonstrations. A nervous rural population jumped at sounds in the night and whispered their important affairs to each other for fear that someone was listening. Even the foundations of the colonial government were shaken, according to Muoi Thap. Vietnamese soldiers in the colonial army feared they would be sent to France or Cambodia to fight. Muoi Thap wrote: "The situation was very tense. The village authorities [te] only worried about two things: hunting down the communists and hunting down new recruits. The middle peasants, the rich peasants and landlords with a bit of national spirit in this situation, supported the revolution. They were very afraid of the Japanese fascists coming [and said] 'The Japanese are a hundred times crueler than the French; even a worm or a cricket could not live under their brutal violence.'"[48]

In part, Thap's comments were a retrospective and "politically correct" judgment of Japan (and another dig at the later Vanguard ties with the Japanese), but it is clear that many Vietnamese were aware of Japan's behavior during its occupation of China and did not relish the prospect of their arrival in Vietnam. Thap's later opposition to the Vanguard tactical collaboration with the Japanese certainly stemmed not only from this perception, but from the realities of the Japanese occupation of Vietnam, which were abundantly clear by 1945. Even before the main brunt of the Japanese occupation was felt in the Mekong Delta, their reputation had preceded them. A witness from this period recalled that the people in his area "considered the Japanese just like the French. However, there were some

people who were even more afraid of them, since they heard that when the Japanese dominated Manchuria they were very cruel. For instance, every seven families in Manchuria
could only share one kitchen knife" [DT226].

This view was not universal, however, and the same source, a middle peasant from Cai
Lay who was a teenager at the time, also recalled: "In 1940, the Japanese army was victorious all over Southeast Asia. Their prestige was very high, and they forced the French
colonialists to let their Imperial Army occupy Vietnam, Laos, and Cambodia. There were
many Japanese troops in Saigon, then and it was easy to earn money. Most of the youths
joined pro-Japanese movements or, if not, they at least liked the Japanese because they
considered them a victorious and glorious army" [DT226]. This young man went to Saigon
and obtained work with a Japanese engineering company. His experience from 1940 to
1945 illustrates the rise and decline of pro-Japanese sentiment. He joined the Viet Minh
after the August 1945 revolution, in part to hide his pro-Japanese past. The extent of such
initial enthusiasm for Japan in Vietnam can probably never be accurately ascertained because it is now buried in a "winner's history," which disparages those who took a pro-
Japan line, and because of the subsequent disillusionment with the Japanese occupiers.
There is no reason to doubt, however, that Japan exerted considerable appeal even for rural
youth at the outset of the occupation, which provided a challenge to Muoi Thap in her
political organizing.

Although Muoi Thap was pregnant in the period leading up to the Nam Ky insurrection, she continued her travels and political agitation around the district. In June she was in
the Tan Hiep market area when she heard people buzzing about the French surrender to
Germany. This made the French colonial regime even more desperate, although it also
saved them by putting them on the side of Japan's European allies, Italy and Germany.
Muoi Thap continually moved around, staying in different houses to avoid detection and
arrest. She and other local revolutionaries were sustained by financial contributions—sometimes 3 to 5 piasters. Wealthy sympathizers gave 50 or 100 piasters.

Thap's luck ran out, however, and the provincial Sûreté arrested Thap in her village
along with several other revolutionaries. The Vietnamese official in charge of the operation
said, "You people are mobilizing the people to become communists and oppose the French
State! Look at me; my father was also pained at the loss of country and went with Prince
Cuong De to Japan to find a way to save the country, but even he wasn't able to do it. I
myself have to cooperate with the French and assure the security and prosperity of the
people. You people don't have the strength, don't have the power. How can a grasshopper
kick an automobile? Those people have airplanes and artillery as well as combat tanks,
while you people only have bamboo stakes and swords—how can you fight them?" Muoi
Thap seethed inwardly but sat silently, because she had secret papers listing all the local
Party members and sympathizers hidden on her, and because every movement caused the
sawteeth of her handcuffs to cut deeper.[49]

Thap was rescued from this perilous predicament by a band of villagers who surrounded
the house and forced the Sûreté man and the militia to flee and barricade themselves behind the high masonry walls of the village chief's home. Thap again went into hiding,
placing her young daughter with a relative and changing the girl's name. During the rainy
season Thap, pregnant with a second child, was forced to sleep in rice fields or graveyards,
sometimes climbing into a tree to avoid the flooded ground, and with only a conical straw

hat to fend off the downpour. She spent so much time in the open at night that she memorized the positions of many stars. Despite the hardships, Muoi Thap continued her political organizing. From May to November 1940, tensions continued to rise, as more young rural men were conscripted. The methods used by the recruiters were none too gentle, and created a backlash among the new recruits in the regular army (*linh tap*) who went around in groups to beat up the gendarmerie (*ma ta,* or Civil Guard as they would be known under a later Saigon administration), who had cursed and beaten them as civilians being dragged off into the army.

Thap had returned to the vicinity of her village in July 1940. She was called to a meeting by the local Party leaders, who passed on a directive from the *Xu Uy*. (Despite being a candidate member of the *Xu Uy*, Thap had apparently not been consulted by it. The head of the *Xu Uy* at this time was not Tran Van Giau, but rather Ta Uyen who gave the order for the uprising.[50]) The time for action had come, the directive said. The French were bogged down in problems, with their defeat in Europe and the impending Japanese occupation of Vietnam, which began in September 1940 and was completed in July 1941. An opportunity was presented by the combination of increasing French weakness and its simultaneously increasing repressiveness. "We must rise up in revolution and change the government, and gain mastery over the country," said the *Xu Uy*.[51]

Unable to communicate with the Party center in North Vietnam the *Xu Uy* itself hesitated to give the final uprising order but was forced by the accelerating pace of events to give grudging assent to a rash and ill-coordinated uprising in the early morning hours of November 23, 1940. My Tho was the most active center of insurgency. As in the Tet Offensive of 1968, the revolutionaries briefly gained control of the situation in the rural areas of the province. In a report to the governor of Cochin China, the My Tho colonial province chief stated that, as of November 23, 1940, "the situation is as follows: the provincial militia on patrol only controls the ground they are standing on. . . . The rebels have gained absolute control of Colonial Route 4 and the province routes 20 and 25, as well as the villages of Binh Duc, Thanh Phu, Long Hung, Dong Hoa, Vinh Kim, Ban Long, Kim Son, Phu Phong, Tam Binh, etc., along Local Route 4."[52] But the planned uprisings in Saigon and elsewhere did not succeed, and My Tho's isolated action was doomed to failure.

French Repression Following the Nam Ky Uprising

When the full French response came, it devastated the revolutionary organization and their rural supporters. The movement did not recover until the collapse of French authority in 1945. As the first planes arrived, the peasants ran out to look. Seeing the letters "S-V" on the tails of the planes, they cheered: "Soviet planes! Soviet planes!" They were sadly mistaken. It never occurred to them at that time, recalled Muoi Thap bitterly, thinking of the experience of the later "Vietnam War," that the rifles they had could shoot down an airplane. For that you needed antiaircraft guns, they thought. The technological superiority of the French threw the peasants into confusion. Only two or three people were killed in the first bombing and a dozen were wounded, but it was an ominous portent of things to come. The "Tiger of Cai Lay," the notoriously ruthless district chief Nguyen Van Tam, came in five days after the insurrection with reconnaissance biplanes and conducted a four-day military operation. In Long Trung village alone there were 200 arrests.

Many were killed, and only fifteen members of this group made it alive to Poulo Condore prison island.[53]

Constables and Communists in the Villages

Though they were defeated, the revolutionaries' boldness had left a strong impression. One positive result of this was that it established their patriotic credentials and their position as the cutting edge of the anticolonial struggle. The negative side was that this rash attempt and the harsh repression it provoked branded them as people with whom it might be dangerous to associate.

The moral and political edge gained by the Party's effective domination of the nationalist movement in the struggle against the French even before the August 1945 revolution is well illustrated in its early form in Muoi Thap's dealings with village authorities. Many village constables (*huong quan*), who represented the colonial authority at the local level, knew her identity but either looked the other way or actively offered to assist her after she became a political criminal and fugitive as a result of her prominent leadership role in the 1940 Nam Ky insurrection.[54] And, as noted above, the constable of Thap's own village of Long Hung was a secret Party member.

A number of sources refer to the negative connotations of the term "communist" during this period. Among officials, the term conjured up an image of fiends whose main aim in life was to disembowel them. A formerly landless peasant who was an adult at the time of the Nam Ky uprising said that even in the late 1950s the people were still frightened by the term "communist," though less than in the 1940 period: "They were afraid because they heard that communism meant pooling all the property of the people in common. This meant that the individual would lose all his personal property and the right to trade. This was why the people didn't like communism. They thought that under the communists, those who worked well wouldn't be better off than those who did sloppy work" [DT148]. It was, he said, the landlords and the intellectuals who spread this view among the people, although later the very poor peasants lost their fear of "communists." Nevertheless, in 1945, during the August revolution, rumors circulated that the communists had arrested people and stuffed their disemboweled corpses with straw, and as the next chapter shows, there was considerable substance to these allegations of revolutionary brutality. "This was why at that time all the villagers were extremely afraid of the communists, and whenever they heard that there were communists in the area, they shook with fear, even though they didn't know who was a communist and who was not" [DT148].

Although this attitude later changed among the poor peasants, in the pre-1945 period the term "communist" was associated with recklessly dangerous political outlaws who were stirring things up with no real chance of success. Any connection to them could bring down the wrath of the authorities. A revolutionary writer reconstructing the history of Long Trung village in the early 1960s found that after the 1940 Nam Ky insurrection, "The movement was submerged as in 1930. The masses were scared and confused and their subconscious hatred of the revolution was elevated because their family members had been killed."[55] A poor peasant, who in the 1960s became the zealous head of the Nhi Binh village Peasants Association, had been so scared by the 1940 insurrection that he fled to Saigon until it was over. When he returned he found that the telegraph lines had all been pulled down and that four persons had been arrested, including two who had taken advantage of the insurrection to loot [DT207]. Some of the wealthier peasants may have feared the communists for their political program, but many poor peasants who might stand to benefit from this program were terrified of being implicated as "subversives" by connections with the revolutionaries. This psychology changed significantly in 1945.

Although they feared being linked to the messengers, the message left a powerful impression on the peasants. Prior to their exposure to the concept of the relationship between social class and exploitation, the peasants had ascribed their poverty to fate. "When poor people regarded rich people at that time, they didn't talk at all in terms of class categories, and they didn't understand anything about this," said a landless peasant. "They only said that it was fate (tai troi) and it was our lot to be poor because it had been decreed in heaven." He described how this began to change: "At the time of the Nam Ky insurrection, the leaders spoke to the peasants and pointed things out for them: 'Why do we have to be poor?' 'The brothers here are miserable, and what is the reason for this misery?' The peasants had never known the answer to this question. The rural people just listened attentively, but didn't say anything. Then the leaders explained; 'You can see that before you didn't have even a piece of land to support your wife and children because the landlords had grabbed it all. And if they rent it to you, you have to send your child to be a servant for them. Or if it is a middle peasant, you have to lease it from them for 50 or 70 piasters. It is because of this class that you are miserable, and if you want land to till you have to oppose them" [DT310]. From the revolutionary point of view, therefore, the chief result of the Nam Ky insurrection was that it got the poor peasants' attention, though not yet their commitment.

Impact of Repression on Revolutionary Organization

In the wake of the Nam Ky insurrection the Communist Party in My Tho and the South was devastated. The Party ordered its members to split up and try to escape the repression as best they could. While Muoi Thap was in hiding, her husband "King Giac" was cornered and died, still defiant, in captivity. The official province Party history of the period states: "The Party headquarters was heavily damaged; the Province Party Committee of My Tho, the district committees, and a great many of the ground level organizations were smashed. The majority of the cadres and Party members were shot or imprisoned and exiled. A number of Party members who escaped the repression of the French colonialists had to escape temporarily to other places. Only a very few Party members who hadn't yet been exposed were able to cling to the [grass-roots] infrastructure."[56]

An authoritative history of the Vietnamese Communist Party asserts: "The course of Vietnamese communism changed as the result of the Nam Ky Insurrection. The repression of November–December 1940, the ICP's most severe setback since 1931, left an indelible mark on the Communist organization in Nam Ky. Until November the Nam Ky section had been the strongest wing of the Party. . . . The 1940 repression delayed the ICP's recovery, especially in the South, despite the increasingly favorable political conditions occasioned by the war."[57] The Party's own statistics, based largely on French colonial reports, indicate that in the repression following the insurrection, 3,000 people were captured in My Tho province—about 50 percent of all those arrested throughout South Vietnam—and "hundreds" killed within a single month.[58] In a single village, Cam Son in Cai Lay district, 120 people were arrested [DT309].

After this savage repression, the revolutionary movement was at a low ebb. Its leaders in the South were dispersed and in hiding, or in jail. The occupation of Indochina and the transformation of Saigon into a center for Japanese military operations in Southeast Asia was an additional complication for the independence movement. To compound matters still further, the revolutionaries in the South were cut off from the central Communist Party leadership in the North.

Attempts to Reestablish Party Leadership in the South

Ho Chi Minh had returned from a long exile to take over direct leadership of Vietnam's revolutionary movement in 1941 and to set up the Viet Minh alliance. Although the ICP provided the leadership of the Viet Minh, the immediate goal was national independence, not social revolution, and the alliance reached out to a broad cross-section of patriotic groups. In the South, however, the revolutionaries were unable to restore direct contact with the Party leadership in the North. Their regional organization had been shattered by arrests and repression, and it was not entirely clear who was guiding the revolution in the South.

Tran Van Giau managed to escape, along with some other prisoners, from Ta Lai prison north of Saigon in 1941, and in this communications vacuum set about rebuilding the revolutionary organization in the South. As far as the Mekong Delta was concerned, however, Giau did not play the lead role until late 1943. Duong Quang Dong, one of Giau's fellow escapees, began rebuilding the shattered Party organization in the Mekong Delta in 1941, when he appointed Duong Khuy as Party secretary of My Tho province and Nguyen Van Con as Party secretary of Go Cong. By early 1943 he had extended his activities into the lower delta and designated a number of Party secretaries in this region. Returning to the central delta in May 1943, he set up the Interprovince (Region) Party Committee for central Nam Bo, which included Duong Khuy and the other province Party secretaries in the region.[59]

From October 13 through 15, 1943, Duong Quang Dong met with Khuy and others in the home of village chief Hoai (a relative of Tran Van Giau) in Cho Gao district of My Tho to officially reestablish the (Vanguard) *Xu Uy*. Dong recalled that "Because it was very difficult to move around at the time, there were only 11 representatives from 11 of the 21 provinces [of South Vietnam] in attendance. The agenda was a discussion of the national and international situation, the possibilities provided by the situation, setting forth the mission for the Southern Party headquarters, and electing a provisional *Xu Uy* to lead the movement. . . . In the election for the Standing Committee, I received the most votes and had to assume the post of Party Secretary. I asked the Congress to agree that this be temporary until we could contact comrade Tran Van Giau, the person who, more than I, had the requisite qualities and talent to assume this position. This proposal of mine was accepted."[60] Tran Van Tra also noted the establishment of this group, with Tran Van Giau as the Party secretary: "It was called the Vanguard group [Nhom Tien Phong] because of the newspaper which this *Xu Uy* published, called *Tien Phong* [Vanguard]."[61]

Xu Uy Nam Bo was the name of the top Party organization for the entire area of French

Cochin China, which included Saigon and areas north of that city as well as the entire Mekong Delta. Later during the "Vietnam War," the *Xu Uy* would become the Party Central Committee Office for South Vietnam (more widely known as COSVN), which was the main target of U.S. President Richard Nixon's "incursion" into Cambodia in the latter stages of the war. Although the *Xu Uy* is commonly referred to in the English language literature as the Regional Committee (and sometimes as the Committee of the South), to avoid confusion with the standard terminology of the later period, in which "Region" referred to the next lower level (known as the Lien-Tinh or Interprovince Committee until 1945), we will use the original Vietnamese term *Xu Uy* to refer to the Party leadership of all of South Vietnam (Cochin China) during the French colonial period.

Clearly Muoi Thap was not involved in the Vanguard *Xu Uy* reconstitution, since she erroneously asserts that Tran Van Giau was present at the Cho Gao meeting. Moreover, in her view this was an unauthorized act because a representative of the Party center, Nguyen Huu Ngoan, had already given official sanction to another group led by Sau Vi and including Tran Van Tra.[62] Tra's own account of this confirms the blessing of Nguyen Huu Ngoan and the designation of this group as the provisional *Xu Uy* in August 1943, several months prior to the formation of the Vanguard *Xu Uy* in Cho Gao. Sau Vi's group became known as the Liberation group because of the newspaper of that name that it published. At the end of 1944, Nguyen Huu Ngoan and Tran Van Tra, who says that he "was responsible for" (*phu trach,* i.e., in charge of) the Liberation *Xu Uy* at the time, were arrested, and, according to Tran Van Tra, "Nam Bo again lost contact with the Center."[63]

When Giau contacted Muoi Thap after the October 1943 establishment of the Vanguard *Xu Uy* and asked her to join, she refused. "It's a little difficult," she told him. "Difficult in what way?" asked Giau. "Difficult because although the old *Xu Uy* is almost all in jail, even though there are only a few members, it has never been dissolved. Now we will meet and get together with a few of the remaining comrades and assign them to strengthen and restore the organization, and after that we will unify with your *Xu Uy*."[64] The second meeting between Thap and Giau in the rice field in the spring of 1945 came to the same result. Not until after the August 1945 revolution did the two groups merge into a single Party organization.

My Tho and the "Big Picture" of Revolutionary Struggle

For the purposes of understanding the revolutionary movement in My Tho, two aspects of the Vanguard–Liberation conflict are of interest. First is the question of the relationship of the revolution in My Tho to the "big picture"—the regional leadership of the entire South and the national leadership based in the North. As the historian David Marr observed "it may be that some ICP leaders in the south, still disgruntled at the 1940 transfer of the Standing Bureau/Central Committee operations to Tonkin [North Vietnam] after many years in Cochinchina preferred not to receive instructions from General Secretary Truong Chinh and his associates. In an interview much later, Tran Van Giau intimated that he would not have followed Central Committee orders based on the 1941 Eighth Plenum resolution [which set up the Viet Minh front and shifted away from class struggle to resisting the Japanese] even if he had received them. Giau particularly insisted that workers and peasants ought to be able to develop their own class-based organizations rather than subordinate them to front control."[65] By contrast, the Liberation group asserted that it was following the official Eighth Plenum policy of the northern-based leadership.

This was not the only time that North–South issues were central to the revolutionary movement in My Tho. In the late 1950s, a growing number of southern revolutionaries in My Tho and elsewhere chafed under the restrictions imposed by the Party leadership in the North on armed struggle as they were hunted down by the Saigon government. Eventually, pressure from the South forced a reconsideration of this policy. In 1968, the Tet Offensive followed a vigorous North–South debate on strategy and resulted in heavy casualties on the part of the southern guerrillas, from which they never fully recovered. Increasingly, the burden of the heavy fighting shifted to northern troops infiltrated into the South. After the Paris Accords ended the U.S. combat role in Vietnam in January 1973, there was another period reminiscent of the 1950s, when the northern leadership ordered restraint in the South. Again the policy was reversed, largely because of southern pressure and defiance.

In the final analysis, however, the revolution in My Tho cannot be divorced from the larger revolutionary movement throughout the country. There are many distinctive aspects of the My Tho situation, and these help underline the complexity of Vietnam's revolution. A participant in the turbulent politics of 1945 called the Vanguard policy in the province "very My Tho" (*rat* My Tho).[66] These local characteristics, however, were always decisively shaped and constrained by the larger context of the revolution. The impact of the Great Depression, World War II, and the Cold War on My Tho and the Mekong Delta are cases in point. This study concentrates on the interplay among local, regional, and national forces and events. A broad national study cannot capture the full complexity of a large social movement, and a narrowly confined local study would seriously distort reality by attributing all local developments to purely local sources. The extensive discussion of revolutionary strategy in this book may seem peripheral to the study of a social movement, but this is precisely the point at which the inner and outer dimensions of the revolutionary movement in My Tho province are connected.

Implications of the Vanguard–Liberation Split in My Tho

A second point raised by the Vanguard–Liberation struggle is the social composition of the revolution itself. To a large extent, Tran Van Giau's Vanguard group represented urban intellectuals and the upper strata of the rural society, while Thap's Liberation group was dominated by people from more modest rural backgrounds—though not the very bottom of the socioeconomic ladder. Giau was an educated person, Thap observed, and very logical and persuasive. He had the support of the intellectuals and notables in Saigon and My Tho. His Vanguard-controlled *Xu Uy* included intellectuals such as Bui Cong Trung, trained in Moscow like Giau, and, from My Tho province, *Tu Tai* (baccalaureate degree winners) Hien (Tran Van Hien, a son of village chief Hoai and relative of Giau) and Duong Khuy.[67] A member of the Liberation group who later became the Party leader of My Tho province recalled: "In the countryside the Viet Minh front was built up by organizing the national salvation youth (liberation youth). Out in the urban areas the Vanguard Youth was built up—in outward appearance this was a legal organization. The Vanguard Youth was developing in a fast and widespread manner, including the rural villages of Cai Lay, Chau Thanh, [and] Cai Be."[68]

Even though the Vanguard Youth was both an urban and a rural organization, the perception of Muoi Thap's followers was that the Liberation group had a more rural, less urban character than its rival. The My Tho province Party history describes the Vanguard Youth as "a mass revolutionary organization operating openly under the leadership of the Party headquarters." It acknowledges that "There were two Party headquarters at the time in My Tho." The Party history states: "The movement developed tumultuously and spread all over from the cities to the countryside, especially in the province town of My Tho, the district towns, and the rural areas of Go Cong, Cho Gao, and Cai Be [districts]. This movement was not only comprised of workers and peasants and all strata of the working class, but was also able to draw in a large portion of the intellectuals, students, and other patriotic forces. The movement operated under many creative forms, such as practicing martial arts, training cadres, organizing neighborhood watch groups, maintaining security, and setting up teams [that combined being] medics with propaganda."[69]

A peasant witness of the period who lived in a Liberation group stronghold in the province observed that the Vanguard Youth, "were those who had schooling. Whenever there was a festival in My Tho the Vanguard Youth would assemble or go camping. They would go from Binh Trung to Vinh Kim and join up with the Vinh Kim group, and then go to Thanh Phu to link up with that group. They were a minority of youth who had education" [DT310]. At least some of the Vanguard Youth came from the lower rural strata, as in the case of a poor peasant who later became a Viet Minh hamlet chief in Xuan Son village (Cai Lay district) [DT265], but the leadership was clearly drawn from the village elite.

When she met with Tran Van Giau in the spring of 1945, Thap represented a rival group within the ICP which claimed continuity with the old leadership and fidelity to the Viet Minh United Front policy of Ho Chi Minh, implemented in 1941. Once again nothing was settled. The rice field meeting between Thap and Giau failed to resolve their differences. Muoi Thap saw that Giau's group had a distinct advantage, because it could openly recruit and organize under the sponsorship of the Japanese or, at least, with the tolerance of the occupiers. Japan had cynically held out the prospect of independence, which excited many patriotic and impetuous youth. This was certainly an easier sell than the Liberation policy of opposing the Japanese as well as the French, which deflected attention away from Vietnam's colonial masters who were the main target of the boiling nationalism of the period. Only by building up the "old Viet Minh" organization to some sort of parity with the rapidly expanding Vanguard group could the Liberation forces hope to negotiate Party unification from a position of power. Thap and others set out to try to revive the province Party organizations in key areas of the Mekong Delta and the Saigon suburbs, including My Tho, Cholon, Tan An, Gia Dinh, and Sadec.

By the time of the second Giau–Thap meeting (probably in April 1945) Japan was losing the war, though some Vietnamese groups continued to try to play the "Japanese card." Nevertheless, Japan continued to hold the reins of power. By March 1945, Japan had incarcerated the French soldiers and administrators and had seized direct control, governing through a weak dependent Vietnamese administration operating under a facade of independence. A secret ICP member named Pham Ngoc Thach had been appointed the official organizer of Vietnam's youth by this government. By June 1945, Thach had transformed the youth group organized by the isolated French regime during the war as a proactive defense measure. It had been established to channel their energies away from politics into sports and outings, and into the *Thanh Nien Tien Phong* (Vanguard Youth).[70]

The Vanguard Youth were an outgrowth of the youth and sports movement initiated by the French after the Japanese arrival in Indochina. Although the name was similar, the Vanguard Youth were separate from Tran Van Giau's Vanguard group within the Communist Party and were not directly controlled by it. Since the Japanese did not want to disperse their energy in taking on the burdens of colonial administration, during the occupation the Vichy colonial regime clung to a semblance of authority at Japanese sufferance and tried to insulate the Vietnamese youth from the ideas of a Japanese-led, pan-Asian, anti-European colonialism movement by taking the calculated risk of unleashing the forces of Vietnamese nationalism. Boy Scout groups were organized and a cult of physical culture and character building in the mold of Outward Bound was officially encouraged. Careful injections of Vietnamese history and tradition were incorporated into these activities to remind the Vietnamese of their national distinctiveness.

The French colonial authorities did this as a desperation measure of co-optation, and some wondered if the risks involved had been sufficiently appreciated. This unleashed patriotism might easily spin out of control and endanger the colonial regime itself.[71] These fears were soon borne out when the sports instructors and other youth leaders became the cadres of the Vanguard Youth, headed in the South by Doctor Pham Ngoc Thach, who soon became a major Viet Minh leader. The Vanguard Youth was the main revolutionary force in the Mekong Delta and much of South Vietnam during the August 1945 revolution.

The conflict between the Vanguard and Liberation groups within the ICP is one of the most vexing historical questions about these seminal events leading up to Vietnam's August 1945 revolution, which more than any other event set the course of the future revolutionary struggle. This is the point at which a scattered band of clandestine revolutionaries became the leaders of a mass movement, which swept them into power as the first government of an independent Vietnam and invested them with nationalist credentials that no other political group could match—which is all the more remarkable considering how severely the Communist Party was split in South Vietnam, and how much opposition they had from other groups during 1945.

Apparently the split in My Tho left no lasting impact. When yet another attempt was made at Party unification after the August Revolution, Vanguard leader Duong Khuy was put in charge of the revolutionary movement in Cho Gao district until he was killed by the French in 1946. In postwar Party histories he is considered "a picture of a My Tho province Party Secretary in the years which led up to the uprising of August 1945 who will still live forever in the revolutionary history of the people of Tien Giang [My Tho]."[72] Muoi Que, a member of the Vanguard province committee was put in charge of Cai Lay district after the August revolution. But Tran Van Giau had been eased out of his leadership position in the southern revolutionary movement by representatives of the northern-based Central Committee, along with members of the old Party leadership who had returned from imprisonment in Poulo Condore. The influence of many former members of the Vanguard group was greatly diminished by their arrival in My Tho.[73]

Conclusion

The story of the Vanguard–Liberation split raises many issues important to understanding the origins of the revolutionary movement in My Tho. It suggests that there were discernibly different socioeconomic groups within the Party itself. The "front" tactic of the Viet Minh and later the National Liberation Front was meant to unify the upper strata of Vietnam's society with the nominally proletarian or worker-peasant leadership of the Communist Party by placing them in the framework of mass organizations outside the Party that had no autonomous leadership and were led directly by Party representatives. But the Party had influences from these other groups within its own ranks, as the composition of the Vanguard group suggests.

Over the course of the three decades following the August 1945 revolution, the upper strata among the revolutionary followers and sympathizers in My Tho was largely stripped away, and even the Party itself within this province was increasingly comprised of poor peasants, as hardships and conflicting interests drove many of those who had joined on mainly patriotic grounds out of the revolutionary movement. However, as suggested earlier, by 1975 the Party was to some extent a victim of its own success. Large numbers of former poor and landless peasants had joined the ranks of the middle peasantry, thanks in part to the Party's land reforms. In short, as the class structure of the rural society of My Tho shifted toward the middle, the poor peasant class base of the Party contracted. This was not a linear or inevitable evolution, however. These profiles of the early leaders of My Tho's revolutionary movement come mostly from their own words, often as dictated to transcribers or redacters. They are not intended to be fully researched critical biographies, but they are meant to illustrate the self-described motivations of the revolutionaries as well as their perceptions of the conditions that prompted them to join the revolutionary movement. Their self-analysis also provides material for our understanding of the complexities of the motivations for political action. Moreover, this first generation of revolutionaries, who became active in the 1920s and 1930s, provides a good basis of comparison with the generations that followed, especially the 1945 generation, which joined at the time of the August Revolution, the 1960 generation, which joined when the insurrection against the American-supported Diem regime began, and those who joined during or after the 1968 Tet Offensive. Are these "rational peasants"? Were they responding to the ethos of a communitarian "moral economy"? Or were they mere pawns playing out a role dictated by large impersonal social forces, cogs in the wheels of a faceless social movement?

How did the early period of August 1945 revolution shape what came after? As noted above, the clandestine nature of the revolutionary movement deeply affected the way its members behaved and influenced their conception of politics. The nature of the post-1975 political system in Vietnam and the reluctance of its leaders to open up politically is made more understandable by considering how their own experiences contributed to their deep skepticism of political pluralism and their penchant for secrecy. They had learned from their early revolutionary experience that splits and disunity can seriously weaken a political movement. The very complexity of the social composition of the early revolutionary movement made it susceptible to fragmentation into rival interest groups, and this tendency was held in check only by strong organization and authoritarian leadership, which left a deep imprint on Vietnam's authorities. The strong antagonism to capitalism and the free market stemming from the identification of those structures with the French colonial regime, as well as landlordism and other structures of oppression, makes it all the more remarkable that Vietnam's current leaders—many of them former southern revolutionaries —have embraced opening up their economy and supported the post-1986 program of economic reforms.

Not least important are the many roads not taken and the dead ends encountered by the revolutionaries along the way. In particular, the lost opportunity for a more open style of political mobilization following the August 1945 revolution was largely the result of the French attempt to reimpose colonialism. The broad patriotic appeal of the early National Liberation Front's opposition to the Ngo Dinh Diem government and its American supporters attracted many idealistic and patriotic youth into the revolutionary movement after 1959. The very intensity of the nationalist commitment to ridding Vietnam of foreign influence, however, led to an authoritarian and often ruthless style of revolutionary politics that eventually dimmed the glow of idealism, and the prolonged and destructive nature of the war took a heavy toll on the idealism of this generation of revolutionary youth.

Although many crucial events occurred in My Tho before the August 1945 revolution, notably the Nam Ky uprising of 1940, and the movement changed dramatically in the years after 1945, it is with this great event that the main story must begin. This was the point at which the clandestine organizational efforts of a handful of revolutionaries finally encountered the favorable conditions of a large mass movement. The synthesis of these two elements had momentous consequences.

4

Revolution

The origins in My Tho of the movement later to be known as the "Viet Cong" were modest. In the 1940 Nam Ky insurrection the revolutionaries were armed mostly with bamboo spears and machetes. By 1972 they had Chinese- or Soviet-supplied SA-7 guided missiles. During their struggle to gain power in 1945, they were not the only armed group, or even the strongest, yet they were the ones who prevailed. The 1945 revolution in My Tho was led largely by urban and rural elites. When the first Indochina war came to a close in 1954, many of these elites had left the revolutionary movement, which by then rested on a broad base of support by poor peasants. As a result of revolutionary and patriotic political mobilization, the political and conceptual horizons of the peasantry had been vastly enlarged. By the end of three decades of conflict, the result of this education and awakening was a rural population whose interests and aspirations had changed in ways that the revolutionaries had not anticipated when they set this vast transformation in motion.

A year before the August 1945 revolution, the Viet Minh were isolated and divided, and during that watershed period they were militarily weaker than rival nationalist groups in many areas. French reoccupation of South Vietnam and My Tho a few months after the revolution disrupted the fragile new Viet Minh administration, which did not recover for over a year, and it took still more time to develop an organized mass base of support. After several years of Viet Minh dominance in the countryside of My Tho (1947–50), the French devised new alliances with local enemies of the Viet Minh; by 1952 My Tho was nearly completely "pacified," and the local Viet Minh cadres and guerrillas were in exile in the Plain of Reeds. By the end of 1953, however, the situation had again changed, and when the July 1954 Geneva Accords ended the first Indochina war, the Viet Minh revolutionaries were again the dominant force in My Tho. How the revolution prevailed in the face of these obstacles is the subject of the next two chapters.

Revolutions are by definition aimed at replacing the existing power structure of society. This is why mass mobilization is an essential requirement for revolutions to succeed. It is also why revolutions so infrequently produce democratic outcomes, since the mass forces are rarely motivated and organized by gentle persuasion and patient reasoning. Once mobilized, their continued participation in difficult times of repression and reaction must be sustained by whatever means possible. After the appeal of patriotic sacrifice to begin French colonialism began to lose its luster, the Viet Minh turned from the upper rural strata that had provided the initial leadership in the independence struggle to land-hungry peasants.

In My Tho, the August Revolution was the first step toward achieving the aims of the revolution, but the fact that the first Viet Minh government included many holdovers from the privileged sectors of colonial society reflected both its inability to dominate the political scene in 1945–46 and the fragility of the political alliances it was forced to make. Many of the urban intellectuals and rural gentry who had been attracted to Tran Van Giau's Vanguard movement, and then the Viet Minh coalition, fell by the wayside over the course of the nine-year Resistance against the French, and both the leadership and the mass base of the revolution rested increasingly on the poor peasantry. The simultaneous narrowing and deepening of the revolution's class base is a primary theme of this study, and the process began in the aftermath of the August Revolution, which mobilized a large majority of the population in support of the revolution. Given the aims of the movement, and the tortuous history of the next three decades, shrinkage of this vast reservoir of support was inevitable. In My Tho, unlike many areas of Vietnam where the Communist Party was the dominant political force from the beginning, the revolutionary movement started from an initially fragile position and had to overcome significant obstacles before it eventually gained ascendency in the anti-French struggle. As the Party unified its own ranks and consolidated its position in My Tho, it was gradually able to cast aside the temporary allies with which it had aligned in the initial phase of the revolution.

Changing Class Base of the Revolution During the Resistance

The main story of the revolution during the 1945–54 period in My Tho was the shifting class composition of both the leadership and the base of the movement. Intellectuals, landlords, and rich peasants, who had led the Viet Minh in its formative years or were key allies of the revolution, were cast aside in favor of leaders whose class interest bound them so tightly to the revolution that they did not vacillate when the going got tough. This changing class composition was accompanied by a related shift in the geographic center of the revolution, from the prosperous "modernizing" villages along the main roads and near the major towns in the center of the province to the more remote villages at the fringe of French control, as the colonial reoccupation spread to control the roads and towns.

In some ways the quick French reoccupation of My Tho was advantageous to reasserting central Party control over the Viet Minh, because the less committed members of the movement, usually from the higher social strata of society, dropped out rather than face the hardships of guerrilla struggle. It also provided the top Party leadership who were returning from prison the opportunity to purge the ranks of the revolutionaries and reassert their own authority. Tran Van Giau was quickly replaced as the leader of the Southern movement. By accident of geography, many of the highest-ranking leaders of the Indochinese Communist Party (ICP) found themselves based in My Tho on their return to the mainland from the island prison of Poulo Condore. During the first phase of the nine-year Resistance against the French, My Tho was under the direct supervision of leaders such as Ton Duc Thang, Le Duan, and Pham Hung—all of whom were national leaders in the revolutionary power structure and overshadowed the local Party activists during the crucial period following the August 1945 revolution. They were not on the spot to assist the local revolutionaries during the actual takeover of power in August 1945, however, and the Party organization in southern Vietnam was not completely unified and brought under control of the northern leadership until mid-1947.

It was not armed strength, or even overwhelming political superiority that launched the local revolutionaries into power in My Tho during the August 1945 revolution. At this time, as at so many other critical junctures over the next decades, revolutionary strength was not overpowering either in numbers or in weapons, but was sufficient to maintain an edge over the opposition. The revolutionaries had a comparative, not an absolute, advantage. In fact, in My Tho the Communist Party was even smaller and more vulnerable than in most other areas of the country. At the time of the August Revolution there were about 5,000 Party members in the entire country; in the twenty-one provinces of Nam Bo, including My Tho, there were only about 200.[1] In a province with a land area of 3,000 square kilometers, whose population numbered 341,000 at the time, the revolutionary forces were stretched painfully thin.[2] In the final analysis, it was the national strength of the revolutionary movement that was the key factor in helping the local activists overcome their initial disadvantages, and that carried them through many subsequent periods of crisis and hardship.

A future province Party secretary of My Tho who was imprisoned in Poulo Condore during the Japanese occupation saw prison records indicating that only about one-third of the ICP revolutionaries on that prison island survived until 1945.[3] Those who did survive were not liberated and returned to the mainland until the August Revolution was over. Small wonder that in most provinces of southern Vietnam " . . . it was the leaders of the Vanguard Youth, not the ICP, who took the insurrectionary initiative."[4] My Tho was no exception: Party control over the province during and immediately after the August Revolution was tenuous, and it took more than a year to consolidate a mass base under direct Party control.

During the period between the failed 1940 Nam Ky uprising and the August 1945 Viet Minh seizure of power, the ranks of the revolutionaries in My Tho had been decimated by arrests and repression. The conflict between two factions of the Party, the Liberation and Vanguard groups, also diminished the impact of revolutionary agitation. Even before the March 1945 Japanese coup against the French authorities in Indochina, however, the independence movement was beginning to stir. Both the Vanguard and the Liberation factions had regained enough breathing space to reorganize starting in mid-1943.

In the summer of 1944, Muoi Thap traveled around the province contacting the scattered revolutionaries, including her brother and his group hiding out on Truong Van Ben's Plain of Reeds plantation. Among this group was Ba Chim (the "Birdman"), who became the province Party secretary in 1954 and was a major link between the 1945 leadership of My Tho and the 1960 group. Thap also met Bay Kinh, a fellow villager from Long Hung, and ordered him to build up an armed force for Chau Thanh district. The province supply of forty weapons, buried after the failure of the 1940 uprising, had rusted, and new weapons were urgently needed. Bay Kinh (Nguyen Tan Thanh) went to Saigon at the moment of the March 1945 Japanese coup against the French and returned with a pistol and two ancient rifles picked up from the fleeing French and Vietnamese troops. That this pitiful cache of arms should be remembered as a major event in My Tho's revolutionary history is a mark of their nearly complete lack of military supplies, as well as their small numbers and rudimentary organization at the time of the August Revolution.

Bay Kinh gave the pistol to Chin Con, and the rifles were hidden in a pile of straw. "At the time," says one history, "a single musket was a rare commodity, because the informers would tip off the Japanese Kenpetai [military police]."[5] By this time, however, the French regime had collapsed and the Japanese grip was weakening. A new village chief had replaced the

French-installed militia corporal in Long Hung. He was "controlled" by the revolutionary forces and so only "went through the motions" of looking for the rifles. Bay Kinh's young neighbor was assigned the task of searching the haystack for the weapons by the lackadaisical militia and deftly kept them from being uncovered. The young man later became a general in the People's Army. During the August Revolution, Bay Kinh parlayed these modest weapons along with a few still serviceable from 1940 into a takeover of the Long Hung post and capture of all their weapons.[6] This set a pattern of finding ways to overcome a militarily stronger opponent that was to continue throughout the next three decades.

It is clear from the accounts of the August 1945 revolution in My Tho that neither Viet Minh armed force—whether by the Vanguards or the Liberation groups—nor revolutionary mass mobilization was the key to the actual seizure of power in My Tho after the Japanese surrender. As described below, the temporary end of foreign rule was accomplished by negotiation resulting in a peaceful transfer of power. The first group of province leaders in the August Revolution included many from the old regime and the privileged classes. Thus the revolutionaries in My Tho entered into one of the most critical phases of the revolution in a weaker position than their comrades in most other areas of Vietnam.

As the main group opposing the Japanese during the war, the Viet Minh was positioned politically to use the opportunity afforded by Japan's defeat. It was not the only nationalist group, and in My Tho as elsewhere other forces vigorously contested the Viet Minh claim to lead the country to independence. Nevertheless, it was Ho Chi Minh who proclaimed the first independent government of modern Vietnam, and the prestige of his leadership strengthened the Viet Minh position in the faraway South. The Viet Minh seized power in Hanoi on August 19, 1945, and Ho Chi Minh declared Vietnam's independence on September 2. Viet Minh political dominance could not be sustained by appeals to patriotism alone, however. In March 1946 the Viet Minh found it difficult to defend their reluctant compromise with the French, which allowed the hated colonial regime to consolidate its position. And later, after several years of Resistance, the power of patriotism did not prevent an erosion of the Viet Minh movement, and many could not withstand the extreme rigors of guerrilla war.

Political Competitors of the Viet Minh

There was plenty of political competition for the Viet Minh, as a bewildering array of groups jockeyed for position during the period after March 1945 when the Japanese overthrew the French colonial administration following the collapse of the pro-Axis Vichy regime in France, and installed a nominally independent Vietnamese government headed by Tran Trong Kim, which tried with limited success to establish its authority. Following the Japanese surrender of August 15, 1945, a power vacuum existed in My Tho, as in most of the rest of the country. From this time until the Viet Minh succeeded in gaining tenuous control of My Tho city on August 25, the fierce contention between the Communist-led Viet Minh and their rivals was complicated by the split within the Viet Minh's own ranks between the Vanguard and Liberation groups. A tense and often violent struggle between the Viet Minh and its Vietnamese rivals continued well into 1946. Despite the eventual dominance gained by the revolutionaries, the outcome was not settled conclusively until 1975—and even then the victory was less than total. Throughout this period, however, the

Viet Minh's opponents were never able to achieve the level of political cohesiveness necessary to overcome the revolutionaries decisively, or to exploit fully the opportunities afforded them in times of revolutionary weakness and decline.

In the accounts of the actual takeover of My Tho city, Duong Khuy and the Vanguards were the most visible.[7] The Vanguard Youth became active in the villages shortly after the March Japanese coup against the colonial administration. The Japanese did not occupy much of the countryside, but confined their troop presence to My Tho city and the villages along the Mekong River, as well as major market towns such as Vinh Kim. For the most part, in other villages—such as Nhi Binh along Highway 4—the same local authorities continued in their posts, but according to one account: "the village officials were then very weak. They were not enthusiastic in their duties" [DT226]. In Tan Ly Dong village, the officials were "totally demoralized" and left their posts at the beginning of August.[8]

A combustible combination of elements was set in place in My Tho's villages after the March 9 coup. The first element was the weakening of the village authorities. The second element was the rural poverty that had intensified during the Japanese occupation. A third element was the rising patriotic fervor of the rural youth, especially the educated youth in the countryside who were the core of the Vanguard Youth movement there. This nationalist sentiment had been building up even while the French were still in power; in fact, the French had sponsored nationalist youth groups out of a sense that they had to make some concessions to their colonial subjects to create a counterweight against the Japanese. The March coup installed a weak and dependent government in power, but the fact that it was Vietnamese made the youth thirst even more for real independence.

"At the time," recalled a villager from Nhi Binh, "the inhabitants of my village lived in poverty. Almost 70 percent of the women had to wear shorts made of local cloth. Several people had to wear clothes made of burlap. A meter of poor-quality local cloth then cost a bushel [gia] of rice, and even then was hard to get. A bushel of rice cost over 10 piasters. At that time people did not have enough rice for their meals, so how could they buy clothes? . . . There were families in which husband and wife only owned one pair of trousers between them and they had to take turns wearing it when they went out or attended ceremonies. Otherwise they had only shorts" [DT226].

In the light of this immiseration, it is remarkable that a political movement with primarily patriotic aims could develop. Presumably the Vanguard Youth did not have to worry about where their next meal was coming from, since they were primarily from the upper strata of rural society. In Nhi Binh village where the Vanguard Youth had been active since April, more than 300 members were organized into squads, platoons, and companies, and were led by the local elementary schoolteacher. According to one source: "They were equipped with sharp pointed bamboo stakes. They had no rifles. The activities of this group lasted for three months," until it was disbanded (presumably after the August takeover) and replaced by a Viet Minh-organized self-defense militia. Their schoolteacher leader was transferred to Go Cong [DT226].

Initial Revolutionary Actions

In the vacuum of power that existed in My Tho's countryside following the March coup, several major rice depots were commandeered by revolutionaries. Since most of the sources on these actions are official Party histories, they are presented as being led by Party cadres. An official history of the period based largely on the recollections of Sau Vi relates the seizures of two main rice supplies: the granary of Brondeau, who was one of the biggest French landlords in the province, which provided 800 bushels of rice; and *Doc Phu* [a title given to province-grade officials from the colonial period] Mau's granary.[9] The purpose was to provide food supplies for the growing guerrilla militias. One granary was able to supply the immediate guerrilla needs of the entire district of Cai Lay, and the other supplied the district forces in Cai Be.

The situation in the South was considerably different from that in the North, which had suffered a catastrophic famine in which 1 to 2 million people died. In the North, the storming of the rice depots by peasants was a matter of life and death, and many (if not most) of these actions were driven by hunger.[10] The relatively small number of Viet Minh cadres in the North were able to take advantage of these movements, and in some cases assume the leadership of them, but they did not play a big role in launching these peasant movements. In short, in the North the peasants were spontaneously mobilized by hunger and desperation, and the Viet Minh cadres gradually took over a mass movement already in motion.

Both the Vanguard and the Liberation groups had set up their own training schools. The Liberation school, first set up in Thanh Phu village in April, graduated over 100 students, trained in guerrilla tactics and indoctrinated in the orthodox Viet Minh political line. In Long An village, the rival Vanguard school also had both military and political training and graduated about the same number of trainees.[11] In addition to these training camps, a number of Vietnamese soldiers trained by the French joined the Viet Minh and acted as military instructors.

Power Seizure

Not surprisingly, the revolutionary takeover of My Tho's rural areas began in Muoi Thap's village of Long Hung which gave up without a shot fired, surrendering all its weapons. The local Civil Guard [*ma ta*] forces in Chau Thanh district were thinly scattered among seventeen posts, each with only five or six militia, most of whom were demoralized and ready to surrender. The disarmament of this force aided the seizure of the remaining posts in Cai Lay and Cai Be districts. Despite the loss of posts, some troops in Cai Lay refused to surrender. The revolutionaries were concerned that if Cai Lay held out, Chau Thanh district would be isolated. Crowds of demonstrators and psychological warfare tricks (such as smashing coconuts to produce a sound like gunfire) finally forced the surrender of the holdouts in the district town.[12]

The My Tho province Party history lists the dates of power transfer in the districts as follows: Cho Gao, August 21; Chau Thanh, August 22; Cai Lay, August 23; Cai Be, August 24; Go Cong, August 24.[13] "Thus, before the seizure of power in Saigon and before taking over the government in My Tho province capital, [in] the majority of districts in My Tho [the revolutionaries] had already assumed power, and the government administration of the enemy had completely fallen apart," concludes the Hanoi history of the August Revolution.[14] Although the exact sequence of events cannot be reconstructed from the available information, it is clear that the seizure of power in the districts of My Tho was not the result of a prior collapse of authority in Saigon or the province capital.

Most of the revolutionary histories of this period naturally stress the role played by the Viet Minh, but it is clear that the Viet Minh was not in full control of events. For instance, a group from the Vanguard training center in Long An village set out for My Tho on August 18. According to the My Tho province Party history, the three platoons of this group succeeded in taking over key installations in My Tho city, such as the *Sûreté* headquarters, the gendarmerie command, and various civil administrative and judicial offices. According to the history, this was accomplished with the aid of "internal planted supporters" [*noi ung*]. By August 24, the Viet Minh leadership was able to establish the My Tho Province People's Committee in a meeting held in the My Tho court building.[15]

The actual transfer of power in the province capital was a prearranged affair, with none of the drama of violent revolution. The Vanguard group's close connections with the Japanese and the province elite smoothed the transfer of power. Unlike events in Hue and Hanoi, which are vividly described in many revolutionary histories, the details of the Viet Minh takeover in My Tho must be pieced together from scattered available sources. The probable reason is that it was not a very dramatic revolutionary event. This is implicitly acknowledged even by the Party history, in noting the role of "internal planted supporters." Although the transfer of authority involved members of the Communist Party, the event was dominated by a group still professing a political line that was at odds with the main Viet Minh policies. As a result, subsequent Party histories are somewhat vague about who did what at this time. Finally, the Viet Minh administration set up in My Tho city did not last long, unlike its counterparts in the North, which remained in power for over a year. A month after the revolution in My Tho, the French launched their reconquest of South Vietnam and the My Tho administration had to flee the city. This also proved to be the end of the brief moment of glory for the doctors, lawyers, and administrators who had been the titular leaders of the new government.

A rural schoolteacher with close ties to this group of local elites said that "on August 18, 1945, the Viet Minh took over the government [this actually happened on August 24]. It wasn't a sudden takeover. In fact everything had been arranged beforehand. Diep Ba, a Viet Minh cadre, knew Mr. Kono, the Japanese official in My Tho province, very well. Also, another Viet Minh cadre who worked at the Tribunal was very close to Mr. Kono. They both arranged with Kono in advance for the takeover" [DT136]. Diep Ba was a lawyer in Saigon with roots in My Tho, who subsequently became the head of the Nam Bo security police and the nominal supervisor of Pham Hung, who in turn later headed the Party in the South during the Resistance.[16]

The Vanguard Group Remains Strong

The leading figures of the new government in My Tho province were mainly notables aligned with the Vanguard movement, or holdovers from the old regime. *Tu Tai* (baccalaureate degree holder) Tran Van Hien was the chairman of the new government, and Diep Ba, the Saigon lawyer, also played a prominent role along with several medical doctors and a *doc phu*. Tran Van Hien was the son of a village official who was linked to the Vanguard group.[17] He recruited additional members of the province elite to the My Tho Province Viet Minh Front, with the evident approval of the (Vanguard) Viet Minh province Party Secretary Duong Khuy.[18] Moreover, there is evidence that village elites, including landlords and village officials, remained in power after the August Revolution. This raises the question of how much the Vanguard policy of co-opting the incumbent power structure was a tactical expedient during a period of revolutionary weakness, as opposed to a reflection of its social base.

When Muoi Thap returned to the South in late August after her trip to the North to meet with the Ho Chi Minh leadership, she found that the Vanguard group was in control of many provinces. Thap described the situation in her memoir: "Since the seizure of power, the brothers on the Vanguard side had assigned various doctors, engineers and teachers as the heads of administrative departments. And the brothers called the 'old Viet Minh' [the Liberation group], who had come from peasant backgrounds with a poor level of education, for the most part were training guerrillas and setting up mass bases of support. In our missions we frequently encountered many problems because we couldn't decide anything on our own."[19]

Class and Power in the Villages of My Tho

There were wide variations in the outcome of the August Revolution in My Tho's districts and villages. In many cases the new government was formed from the old power structure. The first chairman of the Cho Gao District Administrative Committee was *Tu Tai* Giong. His deputy was *Tong* (canton chief) Kinh [DT116]. A poor peasant from Hoa Dinh village in Cho Gao district observed: "When the Viet Minh first arose in 1945–46, the landlords and the rich peasants were still the leaders and the poor and very poor peasants were still very miserable—did not have enough to eat or wear. The Viet Minh didn't pay any attention to them and [the peasants] didn't support [the Viet Minh]. Only the middle peasants and the higher classes supported the Viet Minh. At the time the Resistance Administrative Committee was composed entirely of middle and rich peasants and landlords. I think that these people joined the Viet Minh in order to protect their wealth" [DT148].

Another poor peasant from the nearby village of My Tinh An said, "in 1945 the village Administrative Committee was led by former supporters of the French, since at the beginning nobody from the Viet Minh league cared to come out and lead the people" [DT142]. Needless to say, these leaders all belonged to the village elite of the time. The head of the village administration after the August Revolution was the son of a landlord who "confiscated the rice and money of the smaller-scale rich people [*nguoi giau nho*] in the village and brought in some rich peasants" to the government. Asked to estimate the percentages of each social class in the village who supported the revolution in 1945, the poor peasant respondent answered: "About 80 percent of the landlords and 100 percent of the rich peasants. These two elements supported the Viet Minh a lot because they were able to hold on to power. At the time the Viet Minh had just emerged and these two elements stepped up to lead. At the time the people were not clear what communism was and only talked of the Viet Minh Front for opposing the French—they didn't know anything about social classes. . . . About 50 percent of middle peasants supported the Viet Minh, because they weren't allowed in leadership positions. . . . As for the poor and very poor peasants, they didn't give any support because they couldn't participate in the leadership and they didn't know if they would get any benefits from it. Moreover, they saw that the people in the movement in 1945 were the same as [i.e., had also been local leaders] during the French colonial period" [DT142].

Despite these assertions that the revolutionary movement was dominated by local elites, there is considerable counter evidence of violent assaults on the existing power structure. In Cam Son village in southern Cai Lay district, the revolutionaries appear to have gone after the *te* (village officials) with a vengeance. "That bunch was all tracked down—no one escaped," a poor, landless peasant recollected with satisfaction decades later. "They were tracked down because they had tyrannized the people too much, exploited the people, and ferociously beaten them. Of these a few were punished [i.e., killed], one or two to set an example for the others, and a number were granted clemency" [DT309]. As in many villages of the province, the big landlords saw the handwriting on the wall and fled for the towns, abandoning their land. In Binh Trung village, one of the biggest landlords in the province, Nguyen Thanh Long, fled for the city, leaving his vast lands under the care of a relative. Some of his lands were handed out to tenants. It was the beginning of one of the most sweeping socioeconomic transformations in modern Vietnamese history [DT310].

My Thanh village of Cai Be district had been an active center of Vanguard Youth activities. People who had worked for the French were arrested and the granary of a French landlord was seized. The next targets were the religious sects who had been aligned with the Japanese. According to a Cao Dai follower from the village (who later joined the "Viet Cong"), the Viet Minh launched a "movement to exterminate religious groups" (*phong trao diet dao*), closing the local Cao Dai temples and forcing believers to dispose of altars and religious statues from their homes. Some families refused to carry out this order, and in Chinese Cultural Revolution fashion, zealous Viet Minh youth came into their houses and smashed their Cao Dai altars. His step-brother, who was a high-ranking local Cao Dai official was buried alive. The brother pleaded with his persecutors, "Please spare a bullet to give me a sweet death so that it won't be painful." To which his executors responded, "Bullets are reserved for killing the pirates [French], not to waste on you" [DT146].

Although a significant number of Catholics sympathized with the Viet Minh, the revolutionaries were generally hostile to Catholics because of their past association with foreign rule; however, these feelings were not as intense as the mutual enmity between the Viet Minh and the Cao Dai and Hoa Hao. "The Viet Minh didn't do anything to the Catholics," said a villager from An Thanh Thuy. "There was a Catholic and a Buddhist representative in the Resistance Committee. I heard that the Cao Dai and Hoa Hao would slit the stomach of any Viet Minh they captured, so the Viet Minh hated these religions. But the Buddhists and Catholics didn't have such savage behavior toward the Viet Minh so they were left alone" [DT373]. In My Duc Tay village, however, with a population one-third Catholic and the remainder Hoa Hao or Cao Dai, the Viet Minh burned the village Catholic church and forbade the practice of religion in the village. Three Catholics were taken away, never to return. This act caused many of the Catholics in the village to leave and join the French army, so that they could come back and take revenge, but by the time they were able to return, the Viet Minh had fled [DT379]. Later, the revolutionaries disavowed acts like these as violations of the Viet Minh Front policy. Given the general chaos in the countryside, lack of communications between various Viet Minh groups, and splits within the province leadership between Liberation and Vanguard forces, this is a plausible excuse. Nonetheless, these excesses were committed in the name of the Viet Minh, were not isolated incidents, and were not confined to the turbulent period of mid-1945.

Engaging the Poor Peasants in Political Action

Alongside power struggles between contending groups in My Tho's countryside, a more profound social transformation was taking place. Peasants who had ascribed their poverty to fate were now increasingly convinced that they could change their lives through political action. This process is described by a formerly landless peasant from Binh Trung:

> During the August Revolution in Binh Trung village a number of people from other places came in—I estimate that there were about twenty of them. They agitated among the people. Though they were from other villages there were also a number of hard-core supporters [*nong cot*] in the village, who knew the situation in the village and who the poor people were so they could go and propagandize them. I don't know exactly how this was organized. At the time I was just a hard-working peasant trying to make a living and didn't know anything at all. I just saw a number of people involved in these activities. . . . The people from Vinh Kim and Long Hung came to Binh Trung to organize and detain the people who had been the government, and then they assembled the people. "The revolution has now stood up, and you brothers can see that we are working for you and defending your interests, so that you should join us in securing a better life for yourselves. You have led a hard life and have suffered for a long time. If you don't stand up with us now, you—and your descendants after you—will have to resign yourselves to servitude forever." They propagandized like this and mobilized the people and, at the same time forced them to act along with them.
>
> As a result of this motivation these people who had suffered misery for so long began to believe that they could do something about their lives, and if they didn't [act] they would have to accept the consequences. The majority of them felt like this, while some others didn't agree. [When they returned from the meeting] the majority worked on the minority and said, "Heavens! Those people really spoke the truth. If you don't act, then you and your descendants will have to be as miserable as you and your forebears have been. . . . If you act you can have a little land to work, enough to feed your children." They persuaded each other. Those who were persuaded first then persuaded others. Thanks to this motivation of people in misery . . . they supported each other in responding and acting [DT310].

This account of peasant mobilization starts with the classic pattern of "outside agitators"—who in this case were from neighboring villages, though they were probably not landless peasants (as the previous chapter's discussion of Muoi Thap's group makes clear). It is evident that there was a receptive audience in this village—once they had broken the psychological barrier of ascribing their misery to fate and had accepted the proposition that collective political action could change their lives.

Vietnam's August Revolution in My Tho and elsewhere was a watershed event because it marked the beginning of a fundamental shift in mass attitudes about politics. In past actions the goal had always been immediate and limited: to take revenge on exploiters and relieve a direct source of oppression. Now the peasants' horizons had expanded. Especially important was their new confidence in their political efficacy. Political action could overcome what had once been thought the immutable dictates of fate. The peasants also now saw the necessity for collective action. The Nam Ky uprising had failed because it occurred in isolation, and the greater success of the August Revolution was due largely to coordinated and simultaneous action. Finally, the Japanese occupation and the world war had introduced the peasants to the relevance of the larger world of international politics to their own lives. But in order to know the world outside the village, they first had to develop tools to tap into the flow of available information.

Popular Education Programs

Despite the pressure of coping with a French reoccupation, the Viet Minh did carry out social programs during the months following the August Revolution. In villages like Thanh Phu (in Cai Lay district), a popular education program was carried out from October to December 1945. About sixty people in the village were selected for a training course that lasted a month. This course trained popular education teachers and emphasized pedagogical methods such as "learning through play" (*vua choi vua hoc*) for children and "enjoying yourself while studying" (*vua vui vua hoc*) for older people. "The new educational method was very appealing," said a middle peasant, "because folk songs were invented to help the students learn the alphabet and so on. Community pressure helped encourage the illiterate to study hard. The day before the classes were officially started, the Administrative Committee sent people around the village with megaphones around the clock. Slogans and banners hung all over the village, and every night plays which satirized the illiterate people were staged. At the beginning of January 1946, the entire village launched a campaign against illiteracy. All the Popular Education classes started on the same day in all the hamlets. There were so many pupils that many of them had to sit outside the classrooms, since each one could hold only forty people. Many women brought their babies along so that they could breast feed during classes and not have to go home" [DT229]. Each of these courses lasted three months and had the sole aim of teaching peasants to read and write. They also taught lessons about citizenship and political participation to a population for whom the word "citizen" (*dan*) had traditionally meant "subject."

By the end of the anti-illiteracy campaign in Thanh Phu village, 70 percent of its inhabitants could read and write, and this in turn had a significant impact on the political education of the population: "The Popular Education program changed the face of Thanh Phu village completely. Every family read newspapers and leaflets distributed by the Viet Minh Front, or they went to the village information office to read books about the Revolution. The Viet Minh set up an information booth displaying newspapers sent from Hanoi" [DT229]. Now reading became useful not because of any direct material benefit, but because it opened up a world of information that peasants increasingly saw as vital to their survival. This was the beginning of a long process of political education that, in the end, did produce "rational peasants" at every socioeconomic level, who were able to acquire and process the information necessary to make decisions about their own interests. It did not happen overnight, and there were always competing pressures from the community and from the revolutionary authority, who increasingly wanted to restrict the flow of information to what was advantageous to the revolution.

Revolutionary Repression Following the August Revolution

What was in the interest of the poorer peasants in the villages was not necessarily in the interest of those who had benefited from the previous status quo. Thus village mobilization did not always promote village solidarity. In the retrospective accounts of the period it is often difficult to distinguish among class warfare, elimination of French collaborators or sympathizers, sectarian violence, infighting between rival political groups, and settling of personal scores. In some cases all of these factors were involved. Because of the rapid return of the French into My Tho province, the Viet Minh found it easy to label their opponents as "Vietnamese traitors" (*Viet gian*) and get rid of them, often without even the pretense of a "people's trial." "Antitraitor sections" (*Ban Tru Gian*) were among the first organizations set up after the August Revolution. Some of the rural violence may have been due to the lack of centralized control by any political group in My Tho. This may be indicated by the fact that the reported incidents of antireligious group persecution come from the remote northwestern villages of the province along the Plain of Reeds, which had a more heterogeneous population and less cohesive corporate identity, whereas the accounts of traditional village elites taking over come mainly from villages such as those in Cho Gao district close to My Tho.

Invoking the call of patriotism, the Viet Minh would brook no defiance of their demands for support. From the beginning of the Resistance, the revolutionaries were implacable toward citizens who did not do their duty as the Viet Minh defined it. Even the return of the French and the resulting reduced Viet Minh control over populated areas did not change this. A poor peasant (who became a Viet Minh soldier during the Resistance and later a Party member), describes the situation in Hoi Cu village after the French reoccupation:

> [The people] didn't support the Viet Minh as much as before because they were afraid of the French troops and the Civil Guards that were stationed close by. But they were afraid of the Viet Minh also and continued to contribute money to the Resistance. If they didn't contribute enough to the Viet Minh they would be taken away to the Plain of Reeds to be indoctrinated. Those who refused to contribute money to the Viet Minh and argued with them were kidnapped at night, blindfolded and buried alive in the fields. At that time the Viet Minh's motto was: "it is better to kill even those who might be innocent than to let a guilty person go." This was why the Viet Minh killed a lot of people. Their favorite method was to bury people alive or behead them or slit their bellies open with knives. [There were no People's Courts]. [When] the Viet Minh suspected anyone, they just arrested him and sentenced him to death. . . . From my house I sometimes heard a single shot during the night and I knew someone had just been killed by the Viet Minh. The villagers, therefore, were frightened to death and had to make contributions to the Resistance [DT173].

The frequency with which the harshness and brutality of the Viet Minh was mentioned in later interviews, and the fact that those who experienced the Resistance felt that the "Viet Cong" were, comparatively speaking, "kinder and gentler," and more politically patient and sophisticated, is a measure of the iron-fisted rule of the Viet Minh. Since the stock phrase about "better to kill by mistake than let a guilty person go" [*giet lam hon tha lam*] appears so often, and is even referred to in Party-sanctioned biographies, it is unlikely that this was a canard or an anticommunist fabrication. It also indicates that political mobilization was not accomplished only by political persuasion and positive inducements.

Local Revolutionary Leadership After the August Revolution

Inexperience and lack of cohesion made it difficult for the fledgling Viet Minh government in My Tho to respond to a rapidly changing situation. Ba Chim recalled that after the seizure of power in My Tho the province government worked at the province headquarters, while the permanent staff of the province Party committee was located some blocks away. Not long after, and before the French attacked in late October 1945, for the first time, the Vanguard and Liberation groups within the Party worked together, or at least at the same physical location. Duong Khuy, former head of the Vanguards, now worked alongside Chin Con, the Vanguard leader from Go Cong with some Liberation ties, and with others from the Liberation group. Sau Vi, the former head of the province Party committee of the Liberation group, was evidently not active during the brief period of Viet Minh rule in My Tho town, though he was a visible presence after the revolutionaries were forced into the countryside. Still, the Liberation and Vanguards continued to communicate with their supporters in the countryside through their own channels. The energies of both the Party leadership and the province government were devoted to establishing a system of local administration, building up the self-defense militia, dealing with social and health services, and maintaining order.[20]

By late September 1945, the ICP leadership had begun to assert firmer control over the My Tho administration. Le Duan, who later became the top Party leader in the South and then of the entire Party, had settled in My Tho after his release from the prison island of Poulo Condore along with Ton Duc Thang and Nguyen Van Tiep, a prominent local revolutionary from My Tho. Hoang Quoc Viet, another top Party leader had already arrived in the South with Muoi Thap's delegation returning from Hanoi and thus represented Ho Chi Minh and the Party leadership in the North. This group now represented a *de facto Xu Uy* as far as My Tho was concerned, and is referred to as the *Xu Uy* in postwar Party histories. The province Party history identifies Ton Duc Thang as the secretary of the *Xu Uy* as of November 1, 1945.[21] He may have served as head of the *Xu Uy* since late September. What little authority Tran Van Giau had been able to exert on the revolutionary movement there now came to an end. Giau himself was formally replaced shortly thereafter.

Meeting at My Phong village on the outskirts of My Tho town in late September, the new southern leadership reorganized the Party and government in My Tho.[22] Duong Khuy was replaced as province Party secretary, and Nguyen Van Tiep replaced Tran Van Hien as chairman of the province government. This was the end of Vanguard leadership in My Tho, but it was not an unqualified victory for the Liberation. Muoi Thap was summoned by telegram to return to My Tho from Saigon to attend this meeting. She was subjected to harsh and hostile questioning (by Le Duan and Ha Huy Giap among others) about why and how the split had taken place—why, for example, two separate military training camps had been organized without permission from the Nam Bo Resistance Committee. Thap maintained that she had permission, but she was contradicted by the former Vanguard leader Duong Khuy. Only when the signed authorizing permit was produced did the matter end.[23]

Coping with the French Reconquest

In addition to the Party and government changes, the September meeting decided on a number of measures to cope with the impending return of the French. First, they decided to set up a system of Resistance Committees (later called Resistance Administration Committees), which replaced the People's Committees at each level. Second, they determined that the revolution had to prepare for a protracted war, and it was necessary to preserve forces for the long haul. Their immediate strategic objective was to frustrate the French plan of quickly reestablishing its control of South Vietnam—a strategy they characterized as "attack fast, win fast" (*danh nhanh, thang nhanh*). In a strategic conception that prefigured the guerrilla aim of "winning by not losing" in the "Vietnam War," the *Xu Uy* leaders based in My Tho aimed to deny the French an easy reconquest. By raising the price of restoring colonial rule, they hoped to do their part in contributing to a negotiated solution. At the time, this was the only feasible strategy, since the Viet Minh forces were too weak to confront the French head-on.

Nevertheless, the *Xu Uy* did believe that they could confine the French to the towns and cities and at least delay their penetration into the countryside. Thus, the My Phong meeting ordered Viet Minh forces in My Tho to evacuate the cities and apply a "scorched-earth" resistance policy (*tieu tho khang chien*) of "barren orchards and empty houses" (*vuon khong nha trong*), which would leave the French with no people and no resources when they reoccupied the towns. The Resistance would set up a base in the Plain of Reeds, and its forces would establish lines of resistance to block the French advance into the countryside. One decision that had a lasting impact on the minds of the Party leaders was to set up an economic blockade of the towns. The revolutionaries believed that the wealth of the province lay in agricultural production in the villages, and that denying supplies to the towns would cripple the French economically. This was the rationale for the first of many attempts to create "economic blockades" of the towns, which were revived again during the "Vietnam War" even though by that time the villages were more dependent on towns than the urban areas were on them.[24] This view of the economics of the region, and the policies that stemmed from it, was later to create difficulties for the revolutionaries as politics and market forces pulled the peasantry in opposite directions.

Instead of attacking My Tho by land down the highway from Saigon, the French conducted a stealth operation and came by ship at night in late October 1945. Two French craft brought troops to seize Go Cong town, and fighting began. The Viet Minh's sabotage of roads in Go Cong and Cho Gao went for naught, as the maritime force continued on to My Tho by water and quickly reoccupied the town. A Vietnamese doctor in My Tho town recalled that "at eleven o'clock at night suddenly there were sounds of gunfire from the direction of the Mekong River, and sounds of running footsteps and shouts in the streets that the French bandits had arrived and were landing. The French repeated the story of Admiral Page 85 years earlier by assaulting My Tho town by surprise, not by land but by using ships coming in from the sea."[25] Ton Duc Thang, who had just had minor surgery, was bandaged up to play the role of a postoperative hospital patient returning home, and was thus smuggled out of the town. Tran Van Hien, the first Viet Minh chairman of My Tho province, drowned trying to get out of the town, and Duong Khuy, the former province Party secretary, was killed by the returning French force.[26] Ba Chim, in one of his many escapes, succeeded in eluding the French. Together with Bay Kinh (Nguyen Tan Thanh), Chin was ordered to set up the first line of resistance to the west along the Kinh Xang Canal (also known as the Canal Commercial)—later renamed the Nguyen Tan Thanh Canal to commemorate this initial stand against the French.[27]

The French assault caught the newly formed province leadership off guard. Although it had been anticipated, the timing and direction of the attack were a surprise. The My Tho Viet Minh police chief said that "ten days before the landing the Province Administrative Committee had met to discuss the plan for withdrawal. We were told that each of us should have a set of Chinese clothing ready, and a small Chinese flag which we should pin on the upper pocket of our shirts. When the French came, we didn't put up any resistance and simply withdrew" [DT136]. Among the Party leadership, the confusion was greater. "When the French opened fire to seize My Tho," wrote Ba Chim, "the comrades in the Province Party Committee couldn't assemble together but had to organize common sense measures to cope with it wherever they happened to be."[28] The Party leaders eventually ended up in Long Hung village, where they tried to delay the French reoccupation of the countryside long enough to carry out Vietnam's first national election. The Kinh Xang Canal front held out until the completion of the national election on January 6, 1946, and was then abandoned.

Following the French assault on My Tho, Muoi Thap, who had been operating in Saigon and throughout the Mekong Delta, was once again summoned to the province, where she found the defense crumbling under the French assault. The main line of defense between My Tho town and Vinh Kim–Long Hung was a unit of the Republican Guard grandiosely called the First Division and consisting of formerly pro-Japan elements. The First Division consisted of three fully armed companies and was led by a non-Viet Minh commander, Do Van Khanh, whom Thap blames for the retreat. Do Van Khanh was a former officer in the French army. A burly, light-complected man with a "chinstrap" beard that was always neatly trimmed, he always dressed in a khaki military uniform with boots, a steel helmet, and sunglasses, and he always had a pistol at his side. Thap admits that this dashing military rival of the Viet Minh did win the admiration of some, but she also notes his impositions on the people. Not only did he force them to dig trenches and build fortifications (the Viet Minh did too, but they always joined in the work), he demanded to be quartered in lavish style, with the finest delicacies, the best bed, and an embroidered pillow.

His staff headquarters was filled with beautiful young girls from the towns, and the houses surrounding his headquarters were requisitioned for these "Red Cross units" of "medics." "These girls," said Thap disapprovingly, "wore fancy shoes and wooden sandals, dressed provocatively, and did their hair in waved permanents. They wandered carefree through the villages singing. Every night there were sounds of mandolins strumming and the melancholy strains of songs like 'Happily we set out, although without being able to promise our sweethearts when we will return,' or 'Who can forget the pledges etched in our hearts?' The people really hated it, especially the older women, who didn't want their daughters to associate with this group of females."[29] This was a different reception than that given the patriotic United Women's Troupe (*Dong Nu Ban*) of the 1920s, in this area, and it foreshadows the peasant conservatism that surfaced as a reaction in the countryside to the "forced draft urbanization" in the late 1960s.

The My Tho Viet Minh police chief had somehow linked up with Khanh and the First Division during their retreat, though his staff had largely melted away. (Presumably, the majority were holdovers from the colonial government) "Only ten of my staff members were determined to follow the Resistance. We stayed in Ben Tranh [Tan Hiep] for a week and then we withdrew to Cai Lay. Khanh and 100 of his Republican Guard went to

Cai Lay with us. We had been in Cai Lay for a month when the French troops arrived. We didn't suffer any casualties in our withdrawal, because Khanh had given the order to withdraw before the French took over Cai Lay" [DT136]. The complexity of the political situation in the anti-French ranks is illustrated by this collaboration between the top province Viet Minh security official and the generally anti-Viet Minh First Division of the Republican Guard.

In Cai Be, there was more Viet Minh influence in the Republican Guard. Chin Om, who later succeeded Ba Chim as province Party secretary, was active in Cai Be after his return from Poulo Condore, and a Party member was the commander of the local Republican Guard. This unit was stationed in the former district headquarters. Inside was a melange of uniforms ranging from black pajamas to starched pants, as well as regular military khaki uniforms with Viet Minh insignia sewn on. Some Japanese equipment, including leather belts, boots, swords, and leggings, was also in evidence. Someone found a horse and rode wildly around with a trail of children in his wake. But no matter what they wore, says Chin Om, or what their rank, "they were all comrades."[30]

Muoi Thap encountered problems not only in her dealings with non-Party rivals, but with comrades as well. She had returned to Saigon to continue organizing in the suburbs after the My Phong meeting. She worked closely with one of the main military commanders in the area surrounding Saigon, Tran Van Tra, who subsequently played a major role in My Tho, in the Mekong Delta, and in the Nam Bo area as a whole. Thap again found that the living conditions of a revolutionary were not always ideal, as another guest in the house where she stayed—who was also a Party member—started to pursue her, making suggestive remarks and even groping inside her mosquito net. She moved out, but Tra asked her why she had left this revolutionary household. "Brother Tran Van Tra was very young," she wrote, "but his thinking and way of settling things was very mature and creative. He told me to go back to the house of brother Hai Tieu as though nothing had happened. Then he said, 'a single spark can start a forest fire.' At an appropriate time, the Party Chapter will advise comrade X. If we blow this out of proportion—and the matter isn't really important—we will embarrass him in front of the people and comrades, and he will flee to the city, and what then? Communist virtue in matters of relations between the sexes must be strict and proper. We don't excuse him at all, but let's not lose a Party comrade over this matter."[31] Whatever the Party Chapter said to "comrade X" seems to have done the job, and the harassment ceased. Later, when comrades were more plentiful, stricter measures against sexual harassment and illicit sex by cadres were employed.

During the first phase of the French reoccupation, Viet Minh weakness provided the opening for these rival groups of Republican Guard to seize the initiative. In November and December 1945, Vinh Kim was retaken by the French, and then Cai Lay fell, then Cai Be. The guerrillas could only fire ineffective "pot shots" from behind the rice-field banks. Toward the end of 1945, the French forces in the Saigon area had reached 5,000, including 2,000 who, according to Muoi Thap, were equipped by the United States with American weapons and brought to Vietnam in eight American ships. Opposing them in Region 8 (central Nam Bo) were a mix of guerrillas, local Viet Minh-oriented Republican Guard units like those in Cai Be and Cho Gao districts, and Republican Guard troops dominated by the Third Division of Nguyen Hoa Hiep. "In Region 8 at that time," says Thap, "the majority were Third Division troops, and our guerrillas were in the minority."[32]

The Party Attempts to Regroup and Reorganize

In a postmortem of these early military efforts decades later, Party military historians concluded that organizing the Republican Guard was a misguided effort because such a "complicated organization" was bound to fragment and fall apart—that is, the class composition of the unit was too diverse and the leadership was not completely under the control of the Party.[33] This was probably an easy judgment to make, considering the fact that the Party was not the dominant force in setting up the Republican Guard. After a tour through the delta provinces in October 1945, Le Duan (the chief architect of Party strategy in the South for nearly three decades, and the main instrument of reasserting Party control from the northern-based Central Committee) was said to have analyzed the organizational complications of the Republican Guard. He predicted its dissolution, and urged that asserting central Party control over the units be given the highest priority.[34]

Unlike the situation in North Vietnam, where the Viet Minh had gained an early edge over their nationalist opponents and had a year's respite to consolidate their power before the French challenged them, the Viet Minh in the South were caught in a crossfire between French forces and internal opponents before they had a chance to consolidate their power, develop a strategy, and recruit a mass base. The headlong retreat from the French assault disrupted the command and liaison structure for months, making it difficult for the Viet Minh leadership to respond to the situation. When the French retook My Tho city in late October 1945, the Viet Minh command had withdrawn to Hau My, at the edge of the Plain of Reeds. Muoi Thap, who had returned to the province from Saigon, along with the new province Party secretary, Ba Trong (Nguyen Van Trong) and a group of over fifty cadres, evacuated to the new Hau My base. Communication among the various Party groups in My Tho was interrupted for an extended period. Muoi Thap spent considerable time trying unsuccessfully to locate Nguyen Van Tiep, the Viet Minh province chief of My Tho. Ba Chim stayed behind in the Vinh Kim area, but he was not able to contact key province Party members such as Chin Con until March 1946.[35]

As part of the effort to reorganize military forces under a unified Viet Minh command, Muoi Thap was assigned to set up liaison routes to link the central delta with the other regions, especially the Plain of Reeds base and Sadec to the south, and with Tran Van Tra's base in Duc Hoa (in Long An province) to the north. This was a major challenge considering the fact that for the most part liaison between the province and district committees was cut off until March 1946. A further complication that must have affected communications within the far-flung Viet Minh movement was the decision of the northern Party leadership to publicly disband the Indochinese Communist Party in order to allay the suspicions of noncommunist members of the Resistance that their patriotism was being exploited for a covert agenda they did not support. Dissolution of the Party was, of course, a political charade. It was also the result of a necessity imposed on them by their own weakness and the need to unite a broad cross-section of Vietnamese society against the French reconquest. The ICP continued to operate clandestinely and provide the leadership of the Viet Minh movement, until it finally resurfaced in 1951 at the Second Party Congress as the Lao Dong (Workers' Party). My Tho's official province Party history states: "To continue to lead the protracted resistance struggle in an exceptionally tense situation, on November 11, 1945 the Party proclaimed its 'self-dissolution.' This proclamation reached My Tho at the end of November 1945. The reality was that [as the 1951 Party Congress stated] "when the Party proclaimed its self-dissolution, the truth was that the Party had withdrawn into clandestinity . . . and although it was clandestine, the Party still led the government and the people."[36]

Like the other Party organizations in Vietnam, the My Tho Party renamed itself the Association for the Study of Marxism and continued as before. The deception involved in the Party's tactical decision to hide its true revolutionary colors was not forgotten by non-communist opponents and was often cited in later years as evidence of communist duplicity. In the shorter term, it did constrain the Party from carrying out a radical social agenda until it launched a land distribution campaign in 1948. For the most part, the revolutionaries operated under the banner of the Viet Minh during the Resistance period, although semipublic Party ceremonies in villages and military units were not uncommon during the "clandestine" period and, at least in My Tho, the Party did not take any great pains to conceal itself.

Along with the rest of the country, My Tho participated in elections for a National Assembly on January 6, 1946. Three representatives from My Tho were chosen: Nguyen Thi Thap and two non-Party members, Diep Ba (the Saigon lawyer) and Nguyen Phi Oanh. Although an election apparatus was organized and participation appears to have been fairly widespread, the election was not entirely a model of democratic practice. The Viet Minh police chief of My Tho said that "before the elections [Nguyen Van] Tiep gathered all the cadres and told them how to get Diep Ba and Mrs. Muoi Thap elected to the National Assembly" [DT136]. Since the National Assembly was nominally a non-Party body—indeed the Party had been publicly disbanded—it is notable that Muoi Thap traveled to the North in a predominantly Party delegation which did not include her fellow delegates from My Tho (Diep Ba somehow managed to get there on his own). She was given a sendoff in February 1946 by Nguyen Binh, the military leader of the Viet Minh. On the return trip, according to Thap, "the "Party prepared the trip back for all the southern National Assembly delegates. Almost all were Party cadres, with a few who were notables."[37] Muoi Thap brought back with her two trunkloads of Viet Minh documents. The main function of the trip seems to have been reasserting the primacy of the northern based Viet Minh leadership. Muoi Thap's main activities during her brief say in Hanoi seem to have revolved around a meeting with Ho Chi Minh and a crash fifteen-day political training course held by Truong Chinh, the Party's top theoretician. Because the attendees were not allowed to take notes, they had to strain to grasp and memorize every detail of the Party line.[38]

In Hanoi, Muoi Thap was appointed by Truong Chinh as a member of a "Committee to Consolidate the Southern Party Headquarters" led by Le Duan whose mission was indicated by its name. With her two trunks of documents, Thap completed a dangerous return trip to My Tho, arriving in August 1946. Not knowing how to link up with the local revolutionaries, she took a horse cart from My Tho town to her aunt's house near Ben Tranh (Tan Hiep), where she had stayed while hiding out from the repressive aftermath of the 1940 uprising. Since her departure from My Tho province at the beginning of the year, much had changed. Thap's aunt described the changes: "The old village neighborhood was still there, but was different from before. Since the French reoccupied it, a number of old people have fled as refugees. Among the youth, some have joined the Republican Guard and some have joined the guerrillas, the *te* [village officials] gang has fled out to the Ben

Tranh market. The people don't drink and gamble as they used to."[39] The aunt was amazed that Thap had been able to navigate through the web of newly established French posts. The initial Viet Minh withdrawal from the populated villages made it easier for the French to "pacify" the delta, and by February 1946 the French had reestablished colonial administration down to the hamlet level.

Despite the reservations of some Party members, the Viet Minh continued efforts to attract the upper strata of provincial society to support the revolution. After the controversial March 1946 modus vivendi compromise between the Viet Minh and the French, which permitted the return of some French forces to Vietnam, the local Viet Minh leadership, including Province Chairman Nguyen Van Tiep and Ba Trong, the leader of the now-disguised My Tho province Party organization, convened a meeting in Long Hung village which was attended by "old civil servants and intellectuals" from the towns (i.e, those who had served the colonial regime). The purpose of the meeting was to explain the compromise and the necessity of being flexible in dealing with the French and, at the same time, to appeal to those elites to join the Resistance. Ba Chim, who was present at these meetings along with Sau Vi and others, said that "as a result of inviting a rather large number of people from the towns to motivate them in this way, a brother Duc from the old Land Service office left the town to join the Resistance. Following that, a number of people came to the 'boonies' [bung] to join the Resistance, such as Lawyer Dieu, Dr. Nghiep, Teacher Nguyen, Teacher Thuan, [police] Commissioner Trang, etc."[40]

In mid-1946, not only was the political and administrative situation in My Tho province in confusion, the military forces were still a hodgepodge. In addition to the infamous Third Division of Nguyen Hoa Hiep and, presumably, the remnants of the First Division of Do Van Khanh, other Republican Guard units, such as the Cho Gao Republican Guard unit that operated with the Duong Van Duong battalion, reflected the continuing impact of individual command personalities, much like the personally recruited units in the American Civil War. To replace the Republican Guard, a number of provincial units called *chi doi* (subunits) were organized; the first such unit was Chi Doi 17 in Cai Lay, organized in July 1946 and consisting of three companies.[41] One source indicates that Chi Doi 17 also had a "political officer," though the formal imposition of Party political control did not come until much later.[42]

My Tho and the National Revolutionary Leadership

Just before the French attack in North Vietnam on December 19, 1946, which spread the conflict to the entire country and marked the official beginning of the Resistance, the *Xu Uy* somehow received a warning cable (*buc dien*) from the Hanoi leadership.[43] This was the start of a new period of improved communications between North and South that continued even after the Viet Minh evacuation of the cities. In the past, prolonged interruptions in communication had marked the relations between the northern and southern branches of the Party. The long delay in communicating the North's decision to cancel the 1940 insurrection was one illustration of the problems this caused. Another example was the Liberation–Vanguard struggle, which had occurred largely as a result of the lack of timely and authoritative directives from the northern-based Party leadership. Radio communications soon replaced the laborious trips which Nguyen Thi Thap and others had previously made to get directives and support from the top echelons of the Party. It was another full year, however, before the Party center finally achieved full control of the southern revolutionary movement.

The magnitude of the problem of integrating the various elements in the southern Party is indicated by the fact that despite this and numerous previous "unification" efforts, the problem of bringing the Party together under firm control of the leadership in the North persisted into 1947. The introduction to a series of memoirs by protagonists from both sides of the Vanguard–Liberation issue in these early years says that "after many preparatory meetings, a Provisional *Xu Uy* was set up in mid-1947," which allowed a Party Congress of delegates from the Nam Bo Party headquarters to take place. This account notes that the meeting took place in the headquarters of the Region 8 (central Mekong Delta) Military Command, headed by Tran Van Tra, the former Liberation stalwart who, along with Nguyen Thi Thap and others, had opposed the leadership of Tran Van Giau and the Vanguard movement.[44] Tra's version of the final imposition of top-level control over the southern Party organization (in the same volume) states that while Le Duan again returned to the South in mid-1947 (this time from the Party's central headquarters in the Viet Bac base area of North Vietnam), it was not until the end of the year that Le Duan convened a meeting of province Party leaders (again at Tra's Region 8 military headquarters in the Plain of Reeds) and took direct control of the southern revolutionary movement as the Secretary of the *Xu Uy*.[45]

Resistance to the French reconquest of Vietnam had already begun in My Tho and South Vietnam in September 1945. In the North, the Viet Minh had over a year to consolidate their authority. When the French attacked the North in December 1946, the national Resistance began. In later years, people in My Tho would refer to the nine-year-long Resistance simply as "the nine years." What started out in 1945 as an exhilarating adventure dragged out to become a painfully protracted struggle. Because of the length of this Resistance struggle, the revolutionary movement changed over the course of time, especially in the social origins of those who led it and those who sustained it.

The removal of Tran Van Giau as the dominant leader of the southern revolutionary movement, and his eventual replacement by Le Duan, has often been viewed as a northern "takeover" of southern revolutionary politics. As this chapter shows, the matter is considerably more complex. The southern revolutionary movement itself was quite heterogeneous and required some time and effort to organize into a coherent organization. Le Duan's assumption of leadership in the South certainly did provide tighter central control (and this meant control by the northern-based Party leadership), but it also served to unify a fragmented Party organization in the South. From the perspective of My Tho and the local revolutionary leadership, this local unification, rather than greater northern control of the movement, was the main result of Le Duan's leadership during this period.

On the national scale, the Communist Party's leadership of the independence movement in 1945 created a deep reservoir of political legitimacy that sustained the revolution through hard times for the next three decades, even though that legitimacy was considerably depleted over time as the revolutionaries drew down their original political capital without adequately replenishing it. Toward the end of the "Vietnam War" (1959–75) the most important function of the legacy of Vietnam's August Revolution was not so much to mobilize support for the Party-led revolutionaries as to immobilize its opposition, who often suffered from a political inferiority complex stemming from their failure at the decisive moment of Vietnamese history when the nationalist dream of independence had been briefly realized, and the subsequent dependence of the anticommunist groups on foreign support to gain and hold power.

The August 1945 revolution also launched a momentous process of social mobilization. The patriotic resistance against the French broadened the revolutionary movement, and the land reform deepened it. Despite this, the patriotic and class struggle aims of the revolutionary movement were not always mutually supportive, and much of the original leadership of the Resistance, which was drawn largely from the middle and upper strata of My Tho's society, was either removed or left on their own. The Party made the calculation that greater sacrifices would result from offering more rewards to more people, and instituted land distribution and rent reduction to solidify the support of poor peasants, while putting them in positions of political power in the villages to bind them closer to the revolutionary movement. As the movement regained its equilibrium from the shock of the French reconquest, the Viet Minh turned their attention to organizing a military force to oppose French forces, and political mobilization to provide the manpower and resources for this formidable task.

5

Resistance

In the early stages of the 1946–54 Resistance the Viet Minh improvised a military response to the French invasion of the Mekong Delta. The revolutionary leaders had little military training and had to learn on the job. Some of their instruction came from Vietnamese soldiers who had served in the French army and from Japanese soldiers who stayed behind after the Japanese surrender. For the most part, however, the Viet Minh learned by trial and error. Surprising military successes were followed by crushing defeats, but each time the revolutionaries regrouped, analyzed their performance and set about devising a new response to overcome the difficulties. French military efforts combined with tactical alliances between the colonial regime and the religious sects in the Mekong Delta led to the near-complete "pacification" of My Tho during 1950–52. By the time the war ended with the Geneva Accords of 1954, however, the Viet Minh were in control of most of the province. The reasons for their success lay as much in the inherent political weakness of the French position as it did in the military prowess of the Viet Minh. This should have been a lesson for the U.S. military, which later claimed to have won every battle with the "Viet Cong," who nevertheless triumphed in the end.

What has come to be known outside Vietnam as the First Indochina War had an important international dimension. Since this study focuses on the internal aspects of the war, this realm of the conflict is mentioned only in passing. It should be noted, however, that there was a significant difference between the First (1946–54) and Second (1959–75) Indochina Wars (known to the Vietnamese revolutionaries as the anti-French Resistance and the anti-American Resistance) in this respect. The international dimension of the first conflict grew increasingly more prominent as the Korean War led to a major increase in U.S. support for the French military effort and transformed a colonial war into a Cold War battle. The conflict was terminated in 1954 by fiat of the great powers, though it was clear to most observers that without international intervention the Viet Minh would have triumphed in the South as well as the North. The Second Indochina War started out as a conflict heavily influenced by the dynamics of the Cold War, but the international dimension lost its salience over time, as new global realities such as the Sino–Soviet split and the U.S.–China rapprochement divested Vietnam of most of its significance to the superpowers. At the end of the Second Indochina War in 1975 the contending Vietnamese parties returned to where they had been in 1945, face to face in a struggle to determine Vietnam's future.

In order to mobilize support for the Resistance struggle (1946–54), the Viet Minh relied initially on patriotic appeals but, as seen in the previous chapter, the result was a military force that was not under firm revolutionary control and that in some cases turned on the

Viet Minh when their interests conflicted. Following the proclamation of "nationwide Resistance" in December 1946, the Viet Minh turned their attention to organizing military forces that would be more reliably under their control. In order to provide manpower and supplies for this force and to rally a larger segment of the population to sacrifice for the war effort, a land reform was introduced. To supplement this positive incentive, the Viet Minh employed strict sanctions and control measures in the zones they administered, and attempted to isolate and encircle the French areas. The heavy-handed methods they used during this period left a lasting impression, and tempered enthusiasm for Viet Minh rule among many people. In the end, however, the opponents of the revolution proved to be an even less attractive alternative. As in the second Indochina conflict (or the "Vietnam War" as we will call it), the race was not always won by the swift but rather by the side that had a marginal or comparative advantage over its rivals, whatever its own faults.

As the nationwide Resistance was launched at the end of 1946, Tran Van Tra, the "minister" of armed forces for Region 8, convened a meeting at Go Luy near Ap Bac and decided to transform the five *chi doi* of the provinces into five "main force regiments." This was a somewhat overblown designation for units that were, at most, battalion sized. The total strength of the five units was 3,307, indicating an average size of just over 600 per unit.[1] Chi Doi 17, which had operated in My Tho, became the 105th Regiment. Go Cong, a district in the eastern part of the province, formed the 305th Battalion.[2] Chi Doi 17 and its successor unit later designated the 309th Battalion, were the precursors of the 514th province unit of My Tho, formed in 1960, which became internationally famous in the 1963 battle of Ap Bac.

On January 27, 1947, along with the province unit of Sadec and a "regular unit" (*chinh quy*) of the military region, a My Tho province unit conducted one of the most sensational attacks of the early Resistance—an ambush in Cai Be district of a French convoy accompanying a high-level delegation that included some prominent members of the puppet "Autonomous Government of South Vietnam" on an inspection tour. This ambush along Highway 4 in My Tho province was aimed at a group of dignitaries from the separatist Le Van Hoach government traveling in convoy on an inspection tour of the delta. The education minister was killed, and a French engineer and a veterinarian were captured [DT136]. Fourteen vehicles were destroyed, and revolutionary sources claimed that eighty people were killed. Like the later battle of Ap Bac, the engagement was significant as much for its symbolic implications as for its actual results. It showed that after the retreats of 1946, Viet Minh units were now able to take bold military action. French policy had been to withdraw the smaller and more remote posts from the countryside, and consolidate them into larger posts to protect the key routes of communication.[3] This attack illustrated that the Viet Minh could challenge these strong points and French control of the major road in the Mekong Delta. The leader of this action was the region commander Tran Van Tra himself, who commanded the force led by Chi Doi 17 and Chi Doi 18, and who gained considerable local and national notoriety for the daring act. "Tra had a great talent for bolstering the morale of his subordinates," said a former Viet Minh. "I met him only once at a conference, but that was enough to make me admire him for his eloquence and persuasiveness. Tra became famous for his attack on National Highway 4 in 1947" [DT136].

Bay Kinh, who had been ordered by Muoi Thap to set up the Chau Thanh district guerrillas and had traveled to Saigon in early 1945 to pick up a few pistols, was also involved in contesting French control of Highway 4. From mid-1946 on, he directed sabotage activities along the road. During 1946–47, for example, he was in charge of mobilizing large numbers of villagers to dig up Highway 4. One source extravagantly claims that 100,000 villagers were involved in each one of these operations.[4] In March 1947, when another My Tho province military unit was set up, it was placed under the authority of Bay Kinh in his capacity as the "military affairs commissioner" of the My Tho province government.[5] In this position, Bay Kinh was in charge of organizing military training courses for province troops, including a group of 120 female militia members (nu dan quan) trained in mid-1947. Despite his background of consorting with rural riff-raff, Bay Kinh had contacts with people such as the three brothers from a "bourgeois intellectual" background that he recruited to help take over military posts by subversion from within. Bay Kinh was himself the victim of treachery and was killed by one of his own penetration agents in the course of what should have been his last attack on a post prior to going to Xu Uy headquarters for political training in early 1949.[6] Chin Om (Nguyen Chi Cong), the Party leader of the province in the mid-1960s, recalls that by 1947 "the movement had been restored rather well" and that popular associations of the Viet Minh were now organized throughout the province. In Cai Be district's fifteen villages, six or seven Party chapters had been set up, and Chin Om had been appointed the deputy secretary of the reconsolidated Cai Be District Party Committee. By this time, the Third Division of the Republican Guards had moved out of northern Cai Be and west of My Tho province to Cao Lanh. When the French attacked them there, Nguyen Hoa Hiep's forces fled to the Plain of Reeds, where they were attacked and scattered by the strengthened Viet Minh military forces in the area. This action gave the Viet Minh in western My Tho some breathing room, with only the French to deal with. (The Hoa Hao had already turned against the Viet Minh but do not seem to have been a major presence in My Tho at this time.) The French mainly controlled the villages along Highway 4, while the Cai Be district committee was based in Hau My and, occasionally, Hoi Cu village. The Nam Bo Viet Minh headquarters was based in northern Hau My at Thien Ho market, which had been retaken from the French and "completely liberated" in September 1947.[7]

The situation was similar in Chau Thanh district, to the north and west of My Tho town. According to Ba Chim (the "birdman"): "In late 1946 and early 1947 the enemy had only set up a number of posts in key positions like Vinh Kim, Kim Son, Duong Diem, Xoai Hot [Thanh Phu village], Nhi Binh, Cho Bung [Tam Hiep village], Tan Hiep, Ben Chua, Trung Luong, Tan Huong, . . . but most of these were manned by the partisans [Vietnamese militia serving the French] and they only stayed in their posts, occasionally venturing out along the major roads, but not daring to probe deep and create destruction among the people."[8] Ba Chim acknowledged that from the end of 1946 on the French had established village administrations everywhere, but they were staffed by only three to five officials who stayed either in the posts or in the towns and therefore exerted only limited control over the population. In addition, many were intimidated by the active "traitor extermination sections" of the Viet Minh and felt it wise not to be too energetic in their work. Under these circumstances, the Viet Minh found it relatively easy to organize in the villages. The French plan of attempting to control the major market towns along Highway 4 and along the western approach route to My Tho city was almost exactly duplicated by the American-inspired pacification plan during the "Vietnam War"; as in the later period, the French met with limited success.

"From mid-1946 to the beginning of 1947," says Ba Chim, "we were practically masters of the countryside. The movement of the National Salvation popular associations of the Viet Minh Front was boiling. Almost all villages and hamlets had organizations and activities of these popular associations. The people enthusiastically participated in all revolutionary activities in the hamlets and neighborhoods such as organizing self-defense forces to patrol and stand guard, motivating the youth to join the armed forces, creating solidarity and mutual assistance, setting up a 'guerrilla-support rice jar' collection [in which each household poured a measure of rice into a big jar]." By the beginning of 1947 the ostensibly dissolved Indochinese Communist Party (ICP) had Party chapters in nearly every village. As Ba Chim comments, "At this time in theory the Indochinese Communist Party had disbanded, but down at the district level and below it continued to operate normally, but without using the name."[9] The Party committees at each level controlled the corresponding Viet Minh Front government administration.

Erosion of Elite Support for the Resistance

Although there was a gradual erosion of support for the Viet Minh among the rural and urban upper strata, it was not immediate or total. One Party source claims that after a May 1947 appeal from the Nam Bo Resistance Committee to civil servants and teachers (most of whom were state employees) to break with the unpopular separatist Vietnamese administration of Le Van Hoach in Saigon, 6,000 civil servants and 100 "specialized workers" left Saigon for the Viet Minh base in the Plain of Reeds. This exodus proved to be a double-edged sword, however. The French found it easy to plant agents in this mixed group of urbanites to spy on the Viet Minh in their base area, along with "prostitutes and riff-raff" who "popularized a pleasure-seeking and decadent life-style."[10] The lessons from this episode were deeply engraved in the minds of the revolutionaries, and in My Tho they resulted in a profound aversion to influences from the enemy-controlled towns that continued into the "Vietnam War" period and became particularly acute in the later phases of that war.

In the countryside of My Tho, Ba Chim and others continued to recruit members into the Party with a combination of patriotism, internationalism, and socialism. One of the main sources of new Party members were activist poor peasants who had proved themselves in the National Salvation Peasants Association. A poor peasant from Phu Phong village recalled:

> I was one of the poor peasants in the Association who was admitted into the Party. At the time, I found communist doctrine very appealing, because Hai Lu and especially Ba Chim, a cadre from the district, were very eloquent and persuasive in explaining it. I don't know what job Ba Chim had at district level. [He was elected secretary of the Chau Thanh District Party Committee in mid-1947.] He gathered about thirty Party members from all the villages in the district and talked to them about communist doctrine. When I heard that socialism would grant rights and material benefits to everyone, and would bring material benefits to the people, I was bowled over, and thought that socialism was a correct doctrine. I found it very appealing because I wanted to see the world living

under universal communism. When universal communism was achieved, there would no longer be any national boundaries, and all the people in the world would live as brothers. I liked this very much. I was poor, and I liked the idea of bringing material well-being to all the people—all the poor liked this idea [DT153].

The idealism, universalism, and appeal to personal and class interest brought an enthusiastic response from many people like this poor peasant. At the same time, it was made clear that becoming a Party member to implement this "correct doctrine" would not provide a free ride. Ba Chim told the recruits that "a Party member always had to sacrifice for his own class and he always had to set that example for others—he had to be the first to do everything, and benefits would come to him only much later." While accepting this idealistic view of revolutionary duty, the poor peasant from Phu Phong also noted: "I joined the Party because I wanted to protect my interests and those of my family" [DT153]. Later, around 1950, as the Cold War came to Asia with the outbreak of the Korean War, Ba Chim returned to the village and painted a glowing picture of Russia as the future to which Vietnam could aspire. The establishment of the People's Republic of China in 1949 had evidently not yet been included in Party indoctrination, and nothing was said about it. Ba Chim also talked about Leninism, but he linked revolutionary heroism to revered names in Vietnam's precommunist anticolonial movement, such as Phan Dinh Phung and Phan Boi Chau. Curiously, he also seems to have noted favorably the contributions of two leaders of the staunchly anticommunist VNQDD [Viet Nam Quoc Dan Dang, or Nationalist Party], Nguyen Tuong Tam and Nguyen Hai Than [DT153]. Clearly, the appeals of communism were quite diverse, ranging from internationalism to traditional nationalism, and from the loftiest spirit of self-sacrifice and altruism to the nitty-gritty of personal and class interest.

Some personnel reshuffles in the leadership of the Party took place in 1948–50. After the death of Nguyen Van Tiep in 1948, he was replaced by Nguyen Thanh A, a member of the Region 8 Party Committee, who used the opportunity to "consolidate" the My Tho Province Party Committee, demoting Ba Trong and replacing him with a young and inexperienced northerner, who clearly did not inspire much confidence among his subordinates.[11] This was an example of tighter and more centralized Party discipline having negative effects, and initiating a period of instability and frequent turnover at the top levels of the My Tho Party organization that did not end until the appointment of Sau Duong (real name Nguyen Minh Duong and known at the time as Tu Mui), the predecessor of Ba Chim, as My Tho province Party secretary in 1951 or 1952.[12] In what was to become a worrisome trend for the Viet Minh, the deputy chairman of the Viet Minh Front in Chau Thanh defected, one of many from the upper strata of provincial society who found the protracted sacrifices of revolution too difficult to endure.

Separating Two Zones of Control in My Tho

By 1948 the revolution had reached a turning point. Its "fellow travelers" from the upper strata of society were vacillating in the face of hardships, and the French pacification efforts were shifting into a higher gear. French forces were able to gain control of the "Co Chi system" of villages between Tam Hiep and Phu My along Highway 4 north of My Tho (later known as the "Tan family" of villages), and to extend their control deep into what later became known as the July 20 or 20/7 zone of villages in the heartland of the province, in a quadrangle between Vinh Kim to the east, Ba Dua to the west, Highway 4 on the north, and the Mekong River to the south. At the end of 1947 and the beginning of 1948, says Ba Chim, "the enemy set up many new posts, and almost all the villages along the routes of communication and the towns had them. Every bridge along Highway 4 had a post. But [the enemy wasn't] able to break out of them [into the surrounding areas]."[13]

A sharp division between two zones of control emerged in 1947–48 as the French consolidated their grip on some areas of My Tho, and the revolutionaries continued to strengthen their hold in others. To a large extent this was the result of the Viet Minh policy to "draw a sharp line between the zones" (*phan vung chia tuyen*), forbidding civilian movement between French and Viet Minh zones and establishing a "no man's land" or "white belt," which was a zone cleared of people (*vanh dai trang*) that delineated the border. Civilians who violated this order would have their goods confiscated and be sent off for "education" (*giao hoa*) the first two times. If caught a third time they would be executed [DT331]. This "three strikes" policy was also applied to gamblers and other petty miscreants [DT136]. A debate about eliminating the "contested area" (no-man's land) and drawing a sharp line between two zones of control also resurfaced after the post-1973 cease-fire accords.

Land Reform During the Resistance

Within their own zones of control, the Viet Minh initiated policies such as the popular education program to reshape rural society, but it was their land reform program that had the most sweeping impact. Some aspects of this program had already been applied in scattered instances in 1945, such as rent reduction, distribution of property of landlords who had fled the villages, and even some distribution of village communal lands. Not until 1947, however, did the Viet Minh control enough territory and have sufficient administrative capacity to deal with the land question on a more systematic basis. In many villages, the main land reform came in 1948 and 1949, as the Viet Minh tried to expand their base of support into the ranks of the poor peasants.

Land reform in My Tho unfolded in stages during the Resistance, and the timing varied from village to village. In My Tho "land reform" generally meant the distribution of land taken from absentee landlords or from those who had collaborated with the French, rather than the more radical land reform later undertaken in the North, which aimed at egalitarian redistribution of all land and punishment of even small landowners unlucky enough to be labeled "landlords." Nearly 30 percent of the cultivable land in My Tho province was "redistributed" to poor peasants during the Resistance—mostly land expropriated from large landlords or smaller landlords who had fled the Viet Minh areas to resettle in the French zone. One of the largest landlords in the province was Nguyen Thanh Long. As we have seen, he had already fled for the safety of the town in 1945, and some of his land and that of other large absentee landowners who cast their lot with the returning French had been distributed at that time. The Party confiscated all the land of the biggest absentee "reactionary" landlords and pressured those who supported the Resistance to reduce tenant rent by 50 percent. The desired effect was to increase production, tie the poor peasants closer to the revolution, and give them an incentive to pay taxes and send their children off to fight.[14]

Land reform also was intended to show the poor peasants that the revolutionary government was the best guarantor of their personal dignity as well as their political and economic interests. During a low ebb of the revolution after 1954, Ba Chim was housed and fed by a villager named Hai Tri, a grateful beneficiary of the Viet Minh land reform, who explained why he did this at considerable personal risk. As a tenant of Huyen (District Chief) Tru, he along with the other tenants, had to tend hundreds of bonsai plants, carrying water every day from the distant creek. Tenants took turns rocking Huyen Tru's hammock during his midday siesta. One day, after a hard morning in the fields, Hai Tri was performing this duty when he nodded off and fell on top of the mandarin-like Tru. "Are you trying to kill me?" Tru screamed, and made Hai Tri kneel for three lashes of the whip. "I wasn't afraid of the blows," said Hai Tri, "but I was really angry and resentful." When bad weather caused a crop failure, Hai Tri begged the wife of Huyen Tru for a break on his rent. She offered him a pittance of relief and, when he persisted, said: "I'm talking to you like a Frenchman [i.e, with a power that brooks no argument]. Don't waste any more time begging [*Tao noi nhu Tay vay, may dung co xin xo nua mat cong*]." During the Resistance, Huyen Tru fled to Saigon with his entire family, and his land was confiscated and distributed to tenants, including Hai Tri. Some time later, shortly after the Geneva Accords, the landlord's nephew returned offering gifts of pastries and pleaded with the former tenant to pay a rent of ten *gia* of paddy a year, but he was turned down. The nephew then tried to appeal to the village authorities, but they now included officials from a different social background, and the police chief was a relative of a former tenant. The nephew then went back to Hai Tri and tried to wheedle a concession from him. Remembering his earlier humiliations, Hai Tri threw the words of Mrs. Huyen Tru back at the nephew: "I'm talking to you like a Frenchmen. Don't waste any more time begging!" Ba Chim noted, "he saw that as a way of taking revenge against the family of Huyen Tru. After he had told the story, he laughed uproariously and looked very pleased with himself."[15] Not only did the tenants feel exploited by exorbitant rents, they were also forced to act as unpaid servants, and this led to slights and indignities that made the lot of the poor peasant even more bitter. In addition to the economic benefits of land reform, the revolution brought the peasants the psychological satisfaction of being able to talk to their former masters "like a Frenchman."

Although the province history states that official policy was to unite the middle peasants with the poor and landless peasants, this does not seem to have been what actually happened in My Tho. In Ban Long and other villages, the middle peasants had dominated village government at the beginning of the Viet Minh period. "At that time," said a poor peasant, "they made a general appeal to all patriotic elements including any religion or political party. All could participate, most of all those who had some education. So the people in leadership positions were all educated middle peasants, and it was they who called on the people to throw out the French administration. But gradually after this the revolutionary administration purged this element. In my opinion, the middle peasants could not be counted on to stick it out, because their interests were adversely affected. For example, a middle peasant might have one or two *mau* of land but would have to share some with a poor peasant, so he would become dissatisfied. If the war dragged on, he would not be loyal to the revolution. The revolution gave its strongest support to the proletarian class" [DT372].

The transformation in the class base of village leadership took place gradually and coincided with the land reform. By 1949 and 1950, the initial rich and middle peasant leadership of the villages was largely gone. "They replaced the middle peasants gradually," said a Ban Long respondent. "It was very cleverly done, not clumsy. They would purge you and you wouldn't know it. For example, you might be working on the military staff, and they would transfer you to another place or another branch." Evidently, the middle peasants were not purged because they were soft on landlords. The middle peasant who was the first chairman of the Ban Long Resistance Administrative Committee was something of a petty tyrant toward all classes in the village. He would beat up anyone who refused to go on labor missions to dig up roads and the like. "At the time, it was not very democratic," said the Ban Long respondent. In addition, when these groups were directed to destroy a landlord's house, the middle peasant leader would appropriate whatever took his fancy, including furniture and books [DT372].

In Hoa Dinh village of Cho Gao district, by 1949 "there were no longer any landlords or rich peasants among the high-ranking cadres and in the village Resistance administrative committees. They resigned gradually and were replaced by middle, poor, and very poor peasants. This was the situation in the entire district at the time. The poor and very poor peasants were given land and they saw that the Viet Minh took care of their interests. They said that the Viet Minh had somewhat improved the life of the poor." The result was a shift in both the class structure of the village and the base of support for the Viet Minh. "The very poor peasants who had been given land by the Viet Minh had become poor peasants, and the poor peasants who had been given land became 'new' middle peasants [also called 'Resistance middle peasants' in My Tho]. So these two categories supported the Front in large numbers—about 70 percent. About 10 percent of the old middle peasants and 20 percent of the landlords still supported the Viet Minh, but none of the rich peasants did" [DT148]. Even if these estimates do not have social scientific precision, the general trend is clear.

The Resistance Economy and Military Mobilization in My Tho

Of course, the benefits conferred on peasants by the revolution were not entirely altruistic in intent. The peasants were expected to contribute to the revolution. In the early years, Resistance activities were financed largely by fund drives and contributions that were nominally voluntary. In 1947 the Party instituted an organized fund drive, tapping all sources from landlords and rich peasants to poor people, in both Viet Minh- and enemy-occupied zones. Cho Gao district was supplying the province with 30,000 to 40,000 piasters a month in 1949.[16] Initially, most of the revenues came from urban areas and merchants. The 1945 Viet Minh police chief said that "There were no taxes at the beginning of the Resistance, only collections, and the amount contributed was small compared to now [1966]. I remember that in My Tho city in 1945–46 we used to send the money we collected from the people once every three months to the province. Usually we collected from 80,000 to 100,000 piasters. This money was collected from the merchants by the city security police. From 1947 on, agricultural taxes were levied, but I don't know the rates" [DT136]. The province Party history says: "From the middle of 1951, the Party headquarters set forth the policy of collecting agricultural taxes," but it does not elaborate. When the Viet Minh were forced to evacuate the towns, the contributions continued but became more difficult to collect. The Viet Minh had to shift to a rural tax base, while at the same time giving the mass of peasants greater incentive to contribute to the revolution.

Building Viet Minh Military Forces

The dominant security issue in My Tho was the continuing French military effort to reimpose colonial rule. One of the rationales for land reform had been that it would help expand the base of support for the Resistance. It was not the material incentives of land reform that provided the main recruiting incentive, however. "Among the inhabitants of Nhi Binh village who enlisted in the Front army at that time, about half of the young peasants were volunteers. The main motives which encouraged them to join the army were their patriotism and their hatred against the colonialists and feudalists. It was not the land reform that stimulated them to enlist in the army. Since there were too many volunteers and not enough places to house them and weapons to equip them, a number of these youths were not accepted" [DT207].

By early 1948, the French had sixty-two infantry battalions in Indochina, including three paratroop battalions, six Legionnaire battalions, and thirteen North African battalions. The remainder was filled mostly with Vietnamese troops. The total number of colonial military forces in central Nam Bo at the beginning of 1948 was 26,258, of which 2,333 were French soldiers, 266 were Legionnaires, and 2,643 North Africans. There were 847 posts in the region, manned by forces ranging from a squad to a company.[17] Military initiative had largely passed to the French, though they had been stymied in their attempt to deliver a knockout blow to the Viet Minh command in the mountainous redoubts of North Vietnam. This failure was considered a major strategic success by the Viet Minh, because it once again dashed the French hopes of ending the war quickly.

A number of battalion-sized formations were already operating in the delta, but they had been split up into small units for several years. To cope with the French pressure on the delta, three units had been established to operate in central Nam Bo (Region 8), the 307th, 309th and 311th battalions. The class composition of these forces was quite different from that of the earlier Republican Guards. At the time, according to a Resistance veteran who had joined the 307th Battalion in the Plain of Reeds in early 1948, the Viet Minh "paid the most attention to virtuous character" in selecting military cadres. By one estimate, two-thirds of the soldiers in these units were poor peasants who, among other motivations, looked forward to getting enough to eat. Unlike the main force soldiers of the "Vietnam War," they lived in open fields and not in bunkers, trenches, and tunnels [DT116].

The 309th Battalion operated frequently in what was later known as the 20/7 zone, the populated heartland area between Highway 4 and the Mekong River. French spies reported its activities but, as in the later period, the response was always two or three days late. The first commander of the 309th was Le Quoc San (Tam Phuong), who by the time of the Tet Offensive in 1968 was the commander of Military Region 2 covering the entire central Mekong Delta. During this initial phase of operations, the people considered the arrival of the 309th a great occasion and crowded around the soldiers to celebrate their arrival. Knowing that retaliation would come soon, the villagers then hid their goods and prepared to flee the village. "At the time, being in the *bo doi* [main force troops] was great fun. The aunts and uncles would run up in large numbers and invite [the *bo doi*] to join them for food and lodging" [DT372]. Another survivor of the period had joined the 309th Battalion in 1949, when it moved in independent companies and did not fight big battles. Nevertheless, the 309th was constantly engaged in lower-level combat—which its members felt made life more difficult than in the larger, concentrated (i.e., not dispersed into small units) battalion units that fought only occasional, carefully prepared battles. The primary role of these independent companies was supporting guerrilla forces in the villages [DT338].

French Pacification in the Mekong Delta

To defend their expanding military post system, the French conducted sporadic large-scale sweep operations into the Viet Minh base areas. One of the largest of these was a 5,000-troop, seven-day operation in the Plain of Reeds conducted by the French in mid-1948. The Party's military historians consider this one of the most important attempts to eliminate the revolutionary military safe havens, and its failure a major defeat for the French.[18] However, despite being unable to crush the elusive guerrillas in the difficult terrain of the Plain of Reeds, the French did force the Viet Minh to go on the military defensive in My Tho province. A cadre in the Nam Bo Resistance headquarters, located in the Plain of Reeds just north of My Tho, said that "For a person traveling by sampan the Plain of Reeds was an immense area, and it would take a day and a night to traverse the Duong Van Duong and Nguyen Van Tiep Canals. But from the end of 1948 when the enemy used amphibious armored vehicles, the Plain of Reeds became far too small an area and was no longer safe for the [Resistance] agencies that had become far too numerous."[19] By 1950 the French had assembled 10,000 troops for continuous patrols and military operations in My Tho and Go Cong, and had enlisted the support of the Cao Dai and Hoa Hao to replace the Legionnaires who had been withdrawn from the province and to man military posts, especially along the fringe of the Plain of Reeds.[20]

By 1952, Go Cong had 400 French posts and was regarded as the most completely pacified area in My Tho.[21] The French and their local allies were able to control Cai Lay district with only 200 men, and in the zones "temporarily controlled" by the French, "they furiously collected taxes and recruited soldiers. "Counting only the villages of My Hanh Trung, Phu Hiep, Tam Qui, Thanh Hoa, Phu An, and Cam Son (Cai Lay district), over 400 youth were forced to go to Vinh Long [province] to be trained as soldiers for the Tay Ninh [province] faction of the Cao Dai." By May 1952, French posts, artillery, and frequent operations gave them complete control of Nga Sau—the "wagon-wheel" intersection of six canals (Nga Sau) that would later become a key "Viet Cong" base.[22]

The loss of control in the villages and threat to their base areas led the Viet Minh to soften their political approach even while they were simultaneously hardening their class line. Arbitrary executions and severe punishments had been justified during the early years of the Resistance on nationalist grounds: there was a war on, and treason would be dealt with summarily. With the growth of internal Vietnamese opposition to the revolution at the same time the Viet Minh were losing their military grip on the countryside, they increasingly resorted to "re-education," although summary punishment was still common in some areas. For re-education purposes the Viet Minh required a reasonably secure rear base area. They took people into the Plain of Reeds, often for months at a time, and subjected them to both the physical hardships of that environment and constant political indoctrination [DT372]. The French tried and failed to deliver a crippling blow to the Viet Minh with a massive operation in the Plain of Reeds in 1952. An interviewee whose brother was killed in this operation says that the French attempted to conduct an elaborate operation with eleven rings of encircling troops spread out across this broad expanse of swamp [DT147].

"Resistance bases in Nam Bo weren't like anywhere else," says the military history of the Resistance, "and each base had its own distinctive character."[23] The Plain of Reeds was a marshy sea of reeds interspersed with mangrove swamps stretching over an area of 700,000 hectares. A touch of seasonal color is provided by lotuses blooming in an otherwise bleak and forbidding terrain. The Plain of Reeds not only provided an escape route to Cambodia, it also linked up with the Duong Minh Chau base in Tay Ninh province, where the COSVN headquarters was located in 1952–53 and for much of the early part of the Second Indochina War.

At the eastern edge of the Plain of Reeds was the Hung Thanh My jungle, often called the "indigo jungle" (*rung cham*) for the indigo trees that proliferated there. This was an important base during the Resistance and was the location of the main province headquarters in the early years of the "Vietnam War." A veteran cadre described a village on the edge of this zone as a contested area during the Resistance but at the same time "an ideal location": "Behind it were the Hung Thanh My jungle, and an immense rice field almost 5 square kilometers in size. Dozens of Viet Minh administrative committees had their headquarters in this strategic area, such as the villages of Trung An, Dao Thanh, Long An, Long Dinh, Phuoc Thanh, and Binh Duc, to name a few. This rice field was nicknamed the 'Killing Field.' It was in this place that many French and Resistance soldiers were killed. Since the Killing Field had good terrain, all the members of the various village administrative committees poured in there to set up their offices. From there they went out to conduct their activities, and returned when they had fulfilled their mission. Later, when I worked for the NLF in Chau Thanh district, I often moved around to visit the families of dead Resistance fighters, and found that most of them had lost their lives in the Killing Field" [DT233]. The fact that all these Viet Minh village administrations had to take refuge in this remote base area illustrates the effectiveness of the French pacification effort of 1951–53.

In recognition of the pressures the cadres were under, the My Tho province leadership directed them to go into hiding and to "lay low" (*dieu lang*)—the same term that was used to describe the cadres who went underground in the 1954–59 period. Since they could not be supported by the Resistance, they were told to become self-sufficient and to take refuge in the Plain of Reeds [DT310]. As the cadres withdrew, the circularity of their problems intensified. "The movement went down in 1952–53," said one. Taxes could not be collected in some areas, and the troops had nowhere to stay. "A bunch of people left the unit to go to work as civilians. In the hungry year of 1952 the government provided [the troops] with one small can of rice a day, which was not enough. We had to go out and find vegetables to eat" [DT338]. The Viet Minh leadership in the base areas was nearly paralyzed not only by the French posts and operations but also by a devastating flood in northwestern My Tho and the Plain of Reeds in 1952 which forced them to focus on mere survival. Ba Chim confirmed that no taxes could be collected, and this along with the flood forced cadres to hire themselves out as harvest laborers to get enough money to live on.[24] The troops in the Plain of Reeds had to search for high ground or, when they could not find it, live on rafts constructed from the trunks of banana trees. These setbacks caused the mass movement to sink even lower and prevented the Viet Minh from responding to the expansion of French control.

Without the supporting presence of armed forces, the political cadres ran into problems. In Hoi Cu, a strategically located village which linked the Plain of Reeds and the populated area of My Tho, the cadres operated only at night. "During the day the women [sympathizers] contacted the young men to proseletize them and urge them to join the Viet Minh forces, or they talked to the villagers and asked them to contribute money to the Resistance. They never gathered in large groups so as not to draw suspicion. Usually a girl talked to a young man, or a woman talked to a farmer, or the two of them went into a hut and the female agent told them what the Viet Minh expected of them in a low tone of voice to avoid suspicion" [DT173].

Instability of French Alliances with Sect Forces

There was a political price for the French successes in pacification. The behavior of the French and their allies was just as brutal; indeed, the atrocities were far more widespread and arbitrary than the more precisely targeted Viet Minh reprisals. In order to find the manpower to expand the number of posts in the 1950–53 period, the French were forced to make political alliances with the religious sects, the Hoa Hao and the Cao Dai, whose irregular units became incorporated into the French control system and termed "partisans." Although this split the unity of the Resistance, the Hoa Hao and the Cao Dai remained minority groups in the province, and their interests did not always correspond with those of the French. Their sectarian solidarity made it easy for these groups to regard other Vietnamese as enemies, to be treated accordingly. Their parochial interests and outlook, however, made it impossible for them to pursue a long-term strategy, and their fickle shifts of allegiance eventually left them isolated and without allies.

Perhaps the most important eventual cause of the French decline was the inherently unstable nature of the political alliances they had devised in order to pacify the province. The history of French relations with the Hoa Hao sect is a telling illustration of the pitfalls of short-term political deals between forces whose long-term interests conflict. This story is colorfully told by French Major A.M. Savani, a military intelligence officer in South Vietnam who was largely responsible for dealing with the wildly disparate anticommunist political forces in the South. In a preface to his book, dated September 1953, Savani wrote, "Pacification will be completely realized not when we have occupied every inch of land, but when we have conquered all the hearts and 'occupied' all the minds."[25] This was to become a familiar mantra during the "Vietnam War" that followed.

Savani recounts the tenuous anti-French alliance between the Viet Minh and Huynh Phu So, the charismatic founder of the Hoa Hao sect, and its termination with the assassination of So by the Viet Minh in April 1947. Despite large-scale bloody clashes between Hoa Hao and Viet Minh forces in 1945 throughout the Mekong Delta, a National Front Alliance (Mat Tran Quoc Gia Lien Hiep) was established under Viet Minh leaders in May 1946, bringing together a number of nationalist anti-French groups including the Hoa Hao, and in June 1946 a Hoa Hao army was formed and sent into battle against the French. Huynh Phu So, however, split off from the military leadership to found his own political force, the Dan Xa (Social Democratic Party), with an anticommunist and anti-French program. He was nevertheless given the title of special delegate to the Xu Uy Nam Bo until the Viet Minh finally concluded that his political ambitions were going in a dangerous direction and—motivated also by the history of bad blood between the two groups—they assassinated the Hoa Hao leader. This led to a further fragmentation of an already badly split Hoa Hao movement and a continuous series of internecine struggles between rival factions.

Enraged by the death of Huynh Phu So, the Hoa Hao now aligned themselves with the French. Nam Lua, one of the major faction leaders, was given a French commission as a general in May 1947. The following year he negotiated an alliance with the Cao Dai, who had been anti-French but who also had grievances against the Viet Minh. The various Hoa Hao factions slid back and forth between alliance with the French and neutrality but generally maintained their vigorous opposition to the Viet Minh. As the preceding accounts of the pacification of My Tho indicate, the Hoa Hao military forces sent to the province were crucial in the campaign to contain the Viet Minh in their Plain of Reeds base. The marriage of convenience between the French and Hoa Hao (as well as with the Cao Dai) came to an end because French political weakness forced them to turn in another direction.

As early as 1951, General De Lattre de Tassigny ordered a policy of "Vietnamization" which would give the Vietnamese government operating under French direction more political latitude and also more responsibility in the fight against the Viet Minh. Conscription of Vietnamese into the fledgling National Army began. This was the origin of the Bataillons Vietnamiens or BV. In December 1952 the "old provinces" in the Mekong Delta—the first ones conquered by the French in the nineteenth century—were handed over to the "Vietnamese authorities," as Savani terms them. "In fact," he notes, "the Hoa Hao understood perfectly that the expansion of central power had as its corollary the limitation on their privileges and the gradual disappearance of their autonomy. . . . The transfer of the provinces of My Tho and Vinh Long to the FAVN [Armed Forces of Vietnam, the National Army] on June 1, 1953, marked the beginning of a tension characterized by regrettable incidents. This conflict was manifested in a brutal way by the massive desertion of Ba Cut's forces [Ba Cut was a Hoa Hao warlord], who pulled out on the night of June 25 with all their weapons, burning the posts that had been assigned to them to guard."[26]

To supplement and support the sect groups, the French assigned regular army troops from the colonies. In 1948 a battalion of Moroccans swept through Nhi Binh, burning all the houses and raping the women, prefiguring a similar performance by some GVN units in 1970–71. Nor were the occasional depredations of the colonial units the only threat to the villagers. The partisans were hardly models of decorum. "The majority of women in my village were raped during this period. Any girl who heard of Mot Chieu in Nhi Binh or Mot Hue in Cai Lay coming had to run away and hide" [DT226]. A peasant from Ban Long village next to Vinh Kim, a major center of French control in Chau Thanh district, said that the French regarded anyone they came across as Viet Minh. During the 1949–50 pacification, men and boys of all ages were arrested and often sent to jail in Cai Lay district for four to five months, while the women were raped [DT372].

In addition to burning houses and raping women, the French and their allies were also brutal in suppressing opposition. If a French soldier was killed while on operation, houses in the area were burned and civilians shot in retaliation. Even the Hoa Hao, who were considered "not as tyrannical as the French," were said to follow a practice of shooting five civilians for every one of their troops killed. "All these acts worked to the advantage of the Viet Minh," said a villager who became a cadre in the post-1959 period. The Viet Minh used these acts as propaganda to "foster the people's hatred toward the French. In other words, the Viet Minh won their political war due to these acts." Return of French control also meant the return to old patterns of exploitation by village officials—but with different people. "In 1950, the members of the village administration were all new faces. The former members had ceased working, thinking that they were all now 'out of date.' The new officials sided with the French army, felt arrogant, and thought only of plundering the people's land" [DT226].

Opposition to the Revolution

Major questions in evaluating the political aspects of the conflict include determining who the Vietnamese opposition to the revolutionary side was, why they opposed the revolution, and the reasons for their success or failure. Unfortunately, the interview data do not allow a thorough investigation of this important subject, since almost all respondents were or had been members of or sympathizers with the revolution. An exception is a poor peasant interviewee who joined the partisans in his village, introduced by his brother, who had joined previously. The commander was a Hoa Hao from another province, though the unit was not exclusively Hoa Hao. Disgruntled with the commander because he "oppressed the villagers," he tried to join the French commandos in My Tho city but was told there were "no vacancies"—indicating that the French had little difficulty recruiting. He remained with partisans who were manning a post in a neighboring village and were commanded by a French noncommissioned officer, and then he transferred to another post commanded by a Vietnamese. The salary was 800 piasters a month, "enough to live on." Finally he quit in 1952 and returned to farming [DT241]. The French readily found soldiers; for example, in two hamlets in the western part of the province, sixteen young men volunteered for the French Union Forces in 1950. The same two hamlets provided fourteen volunteers for the revolutionary forces in 1960–62 [DT229].

Another poor peasant enlisted in the Bao Quoc Doan (Protection of the Country Group), part of the Vietnamization program during the Bao Dai period (1949–54). In 1950 the French concluded that they did not have enough manpower to win the war militarily, and would have to make enough political concessions to attract anticommunist Vietnamese into the armed forces. In My Tho this policy resulted in the creation of forces such as the Bao Quoc Doan, which controlled the 20/7 heartland zone. The interviewee later re-enlisted in Bao Dai's Royal Guard and went to the mountain resort town of Dalat, where the emperor was ensconced in his Art Deco villa, to be a security guard. "It was a good chance to see the country and have a higher salary," he said [DT152]. In the estimation of a Viet Minh sympathizer, the people who joined the French forces during the Resistance were people who lived in zones controlled by the French: "Most were poor peasants, or the sons or brothers of those who disagreed with the revolution, those who had lost land or had their families punished. They became French soldiers to get a salary. At the time you could get killed on either side, and fighting for the other side [the Viet Minh] was very tough—you got bombed and were constantly deprived. It was more pleasant being a soldier for the French, and you got a salary to live on besides" [DT372].

Much of the support for the French came from sects such as the Hoa Hao and the Cao Dai, which was comprised largely of poor peasants, making any analysis of the conflict based purely on class difficult. In addition, there were the Catholic forces of Jean Leroy, who was half-French and had been empowered by the French commander in the South to form what Leroy termed "Mobile Units for the Defense of Christian Communities."[27] Leroy was based in Ben Tre province across the river from My Tho, but his forces also operated in My Tho. Some remnants of the Lien Minh ("Alliance" of Catholics, Cao Dai, and Hoa Hao) formed the nucleus of the post-1959 NLF guerrilla forces in at least one village in Dinh Tuong, as they forgot their previous enmity and united against the government of Ngo Dinh Diem [DT142].

Though much of the strongest animosity toward the revolution came from the religious sects, there was a class element to it. The hardening of the class line that accompanied land reform gradually resulted in elimination of rich and even middle peasants from the local leadership, and turned many middle peasants away from the revolution while alarming the rich peasants and landlords. In 1949–50 a country-wide hemorrhage of the urban middle class from the ranks of the Viet Minh happened at the same time as much of the rural middle class was being pushed out of the revolution. Thus Vietnam was engulfed in a complex conflict that was simultaneously a patriotic nationalist struggle, a conflict between sects and religious groups and the secular and nationalist revolutionary ideology of the Viet Minh, and a class struggle. Taken together, the forces lined up against the Viet Minh were quite significant, but badly divided internally. When the United States added its support to the French in 1950 for Cold War reasons, the challenge to the Viet Minh grew even stronger but still failed to find internal cohesion.

Although this opposition to the revolution ultimately failed, more for political than military reasons, it posed great difficulties for the Viet Minh in the 1949–53 period. The problem was again a vicious circle: to build up large units the revolutionaries first had to expand their guerrilla operations, both as a source of recruiting and as an intelligence and logistical support structure for the main forces. But it was difficult to build up the large units needed to attack the posts because of the posts. This chicken–egg dilemma was not fully resolved during the Resistance. The dramatic comeback of the Viet Minh in the delta in late 1953 was the result of a deterioration in the French position in other parts of Vietnam. As the attention of the French and the Viet Minh shifted to the North for the last years of the First Indochina War, the Mekong Delta was left largely to its own devices. No longer a military priority, both sides looked on it as a source of human and material resources for more important battlefields. The war in My Tho became largely a holding action until the very end of the Resistance.

Viet Minh Resurgence in 1953–54

Generally unnoticed in the shadows of the big-unit war in North Vietnam, the Viet Minh in My Tho quietly began regaining control of significant areas of the province. In many of the villages where posts had been built in 1949–52, resulting in the exodus of Viet Minh cadres and guerrillas, the posts were destroyed by resurgent Viet Minh military forces and the villages once again fell under the control of the Resistance. Part of the change was due to a more aggressive policy on the part of the Viet Minh, which was in turn made possible by a weakened French position as a result of military setbacks in other areas of Vietnam and growing opposition to the war in France itself. During 1951–

52, the Viet Minh had relied on political action more than military pressure out of necessity. The Joint Military Proselytizing–Political Affairs Section (*Binh Van Hop Chanh*)
was established in order to coordinate political agitation among supporters with political subversion of the Vietnamese troops who manned French posts. "Under this policy,
military activities were deemphasized and efforts were concentrated on political affairs
and military proselytizing. During these two years, whenever the GVN forces conducted
operations in the area, the Viet Minh troops usually fled" [DT226].

In early 1953 this policy was repudiated as too passive, and military operations were
once again stressed [DT226]. "Later, as higher authorities reviewed the problem, they
found that the Joint Military Proselytizing–Political Affairs policy was wrong, and took
corrective action. In early 1953 the military forces changed their tactics and began to take
the offensive. During 1953–54 they resolved to stay in the [Viet Minh] areas and not abandon them" [DT226]. Ironically, just as the general policy of military proselytizing was
being repudiated, the specific policy of subverting the Hoa Hao and weaning them away
from the French was decided on and implemented. In fact, the Viet Minh continued to try
to undermine their opposition through political means, even while they were stepping up
military operations.

A conference of the My Tho Province Party Committee, in March 1953 decided to
renew the effort to win over the Hoa Hao and split them off from the French; however, the
continual large French military operations still "created passivity and confusion" and drove
the Viet Minh forces even deeper into the Plain of Reeds. The majority of the village
guerrilla units, the Party history says, were so dispirited that they turned their weapons
over to the district forces, which, in turn, gave them to the province unit. The 309th Battalion stayed deep in its base in the Plain of Reeds, split up into smaller units, and focused on
producing enough food to avoid starvation. "In general," says the history, "in 1952–53 the
operations of the local force troops dropped off a great deal, both in terms of morale and in
terms of forces." Despite this pessimism in early 1953, rapid recovery of the Viet Minh
movement was about to begin.[28]

Responding to political currents emanating from North Vietnam and more aggressive
leadership from Tran Van Tra, the region military commander and the province Party
secretary, the My Tho province committee held another meeting in June 1953, criticized
the passivity and "rightist ideology," and ordered more pressure on the contested and
French-controlled areas. This pressure was not only military, but also included a revival
of class conflict. Without elaboration, the history notes that a "land policy was carried
out in the Independent Zones [Viet Minh controlled areas] in accordance with the policy
of the Party."[29] Refocusing on land issues was an apparently delayed response to the
January 1953 decision of the northern-based Party Central Committee that the "time had
come for a real class struggle to weaken feudalism economically and smash it politically."[30] This decision set in motion a political campaign that led ultimately to the ill-
fated land reform in North Vietnam, which reached frenetic heights in 1956. This reference
to land issues in the province history reflects only a faint echo of a policy designed
largely for north and central Vietnam; it was never fully implemented because the Viet
Minh in the south and in central Nam Bo did not have sufficient control to do so until
shortly before the Resistance War ended.

Thus, mass political mobilization was not the factor that triggered the Viet Minh revival in My Tho in 1953–54. The major causes of this rebound were French demoralization, which spread to their local allies; political conflicts between the religious sects and the Vietnamese administration under the French; developments in other areas of the country (including land reform in the North), which may have energized the core supporters of the revolution; and a renewed determination on the part of the local Viet Minh leaders to take advantage of this opening. Fittingly, Tran Van Tra, who showed up at so many crucial junctures of the three-decade struggle in My Tho, initiated the new, more aggressive policy. Ba Chim describes Tra's leadership after a Region 8 conference which decided on this line in early 1953: "Brother Tra came down to pass this decision on directly and to lead the My Tho Province Party Committee.[31] Tra pointed out that increasing French military difficulties in North Vietnam had forced the French to transfer soldiers from their posts in the Mekong Delta to the newly formed "Vietnamese battalions." "The enemy is now extremely weak," Tra argued, "and he is presenting us his back to be whipped but we are afraid it will sting our hand and don't dare." He chastised the cadres in My Tho for being too "rightist in dispersing units and thus reducing their ability to attack the enemy." How could they expand the Viet Minh zone under these conditions, he asked.[32] The new policy was to go on the offensive into the French zones. First, however, the troops had to prepare themselves by being more aggressive in repelling French attacks into their zones. Tran Van Tra's critique of Hanoi's post-1973 cease-fire policy in the South suggests how deeply this experience affected him in his strong rejection of Hanoi's "politics first" approach.

It was right after Tra's visit that the My Tho Province Party Committee met in June 1953 to repudiate "rightist ideology" and order more pressure on the French, as mentioned above. At this meeting, Ba Chim was elected deputy province Party secretary, and shortly after, the Viet Minh forces won a major military victory that is viewed retrospectively as the turning point in the Viet Minh military comeback in My Tho.[33] Starting in late 1952, the French had "pulled almost all of their expeditionary force to the northern battlefield, central Vietnam, and Laos, and replaced them by a massive infusion of puppet troops." They still maintained the military initiative, however, and in January 1953 the My Tho Party committee acknowledged that there was no longer an expansive base area and that most of the province was contested or enemy controlled.[34] This situation encouraged the French to press their advantage further.

As part of their Vietnamization program, the French decided to try out one of the Vietnamese battalions in a large-scale attack on the Kinh Bui Canal base of the Viet Minh on June 24, 1953, and sent in a 1,000 man-force with 40 amphibious vehicles and supporting artillery. In response, the 309th Battalion, using a tactic that became famous in the later "Vietnam War," hid in well-fortified concealed trenches and took advantage of the tactical mistakes of a Vietnamese captain (who was captured during the battle) mechanically following his French military training. The result was a heavy defeat for the Vietnamese battalions which, in the view of the My Tho Viet Minh military leaders, "created an important transformation in the face of the war in the My Tho battlefield" by showing that the Viet Minh could now defend their base areas.[35] The parallel in the "Vietnam War" was the Easter Offensive of 1972, which tested Richard Nixon's Vietnamization program and the ability of GVN troops to manage on their own, and led to the signing of the Paris peace agreements the following year.

One of the most important consequences of this battle was that Ba Cut's Hoa Hao soldiers who had been manning the string of posts along the border of the Plain of Reeds pulled out and went back to the Hoa Hao stronghold of Chau Doc province. There is no doubt this was triggered by the Viet Minh victory at Kinh Bui, but it was also a culmination of the "Hoa Hao proselytizing" program of the Viet Minh. Savani wrote in late 1953 that "The first months of 1953 were marked by a complete turnabout of Viet Minh political policy toward the Hoa Hao. The ferocious hatred of the [Viet Minh] rebels gave way to the policy of an 'outstretched hand.' Taking advantage of the unrest and defiance of the sects, the Viet Minh first tried to neutralize their military action with the hope of leading to the next step of getting them to turn their weapons on the Franco-Vietnamese authorities. This tactic was all the more skillful in that it took into account their mutual economic interests. Either a tacit or a formal truce would be particularly advantageous for them. A great propaganda effort was made in Nam Bo, with results that were not negligible, based on the fact that Hoa Hao had shown themselves to be extremely sensitive to anything that touched on their sovereignty. They had no sympathy for the Viet Minh [and] they also had a deep sense that their immediate interests were being jeopardized in the current situation."[36] Five companies of troops belonging to the Ba Cut and Nam Lua factions of the Hoa Hao left My Tho and abandoned the Nguyen Van Tiep Canal defense line that had sealed up the Plain of Reeds.[37] Even the Hoa Hao forces in the center of the province withdrew. Ho Van Nam's group in Binh Trung village next to Long Hung asked the local Viet Minh to let him "borrow the road" back to his own home province. Two companies of Hoa Hao pulled out of eight posts in Binh Trung. A local Viet Minh leader said, "After they withdrew we gained control of all those places."[38]

The Hoa Hao departure in effect opened the door to the populated areas of My Tho, and Viet Minh military units were sent into the heartland of the province in the villages around Vinh Kim to exploit this opportunity. Encouraged by the initial results of this move, the province committee met in October 1953 and decided to push into the most difficult and pacified areas of the province, the districts of Cho Gao and Go Cong east of Highway 4.[39] Posts in the villages of Binh Ninh, An Thanh Thuy, and Hoa Dinh in Cho Gao were evacuated in late November 1953. Hau My and Hoi Cu villages linking the Thien Ho base with the core province area now came under increasing Viet Minh control, as did the 20/7 heartland area. Interviews corroborate the crumbling French security situation in My Tho. One describes how An Thanh Thuy, where the Viet Minh hamlet chief had become the French *te* hamlet chief in order to "protect the people," was retaken [DT373]. Other interviews describe the Viet Minh revival in Binh Trung [DT310], Ban Long [DT239], Hau My [DT254], and part of Hoi Cu [DT173]. The Viet Minh claimed a total of sixteen villages liberated by mid-1953. By the end of the year, Cai Be and Cai Lay districts had each built up a local Viet Minh force of around 100 troops. The deteriorating position of the French caused problems for the Vietnamization program, and one revolutionary history claims that "in the 39 villages temporarily controlled by the enemy, 1,136 young men dodged the [French] draft, and there were 1,476 refusals to go to basic training between September 1953 and May 1954."[40] The figures may be inflated, but there is little doubt that Vietnamization in My Tho encountered serious problems because of French decline and the Viet Minh recovery.

Viet Minh military activity continued to accelerate in 1954, as the Dien Bien Phu siege demoralized the sect groups and the Vietnamese working with the French administration.

An interviewee noticed that the village authorities were scared into treating the villagers with respect: "They were no longer arrogant for fear of punishment by the Viet Minh if the situation changed, and they became rather kind to the people" [DT226]. A recruit who joined the resurgent Cai Be district local forces in 1954 saw a high level of military activity and constant clashes with French forces. He had been arrested by the Viet Minh eleven months before, just as he was about to join his brother-in-law in a French commando unit, and was held for indoctrination in the Plain of Reeds. He was asked to join "because the Viet Minh wanted to carry out their plan of expanding their area from the Plain of Reeds all the way down to the Indochina Road [Highway 4]. At that time the Hoa Hao had withdrawn from the area and became neutral" [DT173].

In one case, the Cai Be forces encountered a multibattalion French operation and lost thirty to forty men. In all, the unit fought four big battles in the last months of the Resistance War. The most painful incident for the unit was a triumph turned to tragedy: After the Cai Be local forces successfully ambushed a large wooden sampan carrying clothes and money to pay salaries of the colonial troops, the bales of clothes and money floated down the canal toward a remaining (but inactive) Hoa Hao post, where the treasure was fished out while the Viet Minh watched in impotent rage. The recruit explained their disappointment: "We were very mad, and said we had slaved for nothing. At the time we badly needed these clothes and the money—we lacked money and wore shabby white clothes dyed gray" [DT173]. The Cai Be local force unit was unable to carry out its plan to regain control all the way down the national highway in the heart of the province, but while the remaining Hoa Hao sulked in their posts, it did succeed in regaining control of the Nguyen Van Tiep Canal area and the big market areas, which had been lost earlier, and which provided a springboard for operations in the populated villages of the district. In Nhi Binh village, where the six posts set up in 1950 had crippled the local Viet Minh movement, the Viet Minh forces arrived in the final months before the July 1954 cease-fire and hit these posts hard. As a result, the overall situation "became favorable once again" [DT372].

According to the proud, and possibly inflated, claims of the My Tho province history (the account of DT173, for example, makes it clear that the Viet Minh did not have complete control over Hoi Cu village close to the Plain of Reeds even during the last months of the Resistance), by the beginning of 1954, 78 posts had been destroyed by military action (a figure also mentioned in the 309th Battalion's history); 139 had been forced to withdraw; 681 enemy soldiers were killed; and 508 were captured.[41] One of those captured when he had returned to his village to join the militia was the unfortunate partisan who had been rejected by the French commandos. When the Diem Hy post was taken in November 1953, he was interrogated for two weeks and then sent to a Viet Minh prisoner-of-war labor camp in central Vietnam, where he spent the rest of the Resistance War [DT241].

Viet Minh Gains in 1954

One indication of the Viet Minh control in My Tho was their ability to collect taxes again and use the money to supply their troops. By the end of 1953, the main force units were provided a twenty-five-liter ration of rice and a 9-piaster allowance. The previous year they had been starving and had to work in the fields for their food. At the beginning of 1954, by contrast, a number of key posts had been taken—217 according to a revolutionary history, which also claims that 1,006 of 1,182 Civil Guard soldiers had left their units, most of them returning to their villages.[42] This is another of the many striking parallels between the ends of the First and Second Indochina Wars. In 1974–75 there were also large-scale desertions of the government's province militia, reminiscent of 1954.

The unit history of the 309th Battalion claims that by March 1954 a "leopard spot" pattern of guerrilla control had been established in the strongest French areas of Cho Gao and Go Cong.[43] As in the final offensive of the "Vietnam War" in 1975, the eastern districts of Cho Gao and Go Cong were the last holdouts against the Viet Minh military resurgence. At the beginning of 1954 the French had been forced to send one battalion from My Tho to Ben Tre province and another to central Vietnam. These were replaced by two newly formed battalions and a Hoa Hao battalion commanded by Ba Ga Mo ("Pecking Chicken"), which had suffered heavy casualties in the lower Mekong Delta and was sent to My Tho to regroup. The Hoa Hao force was an inadequate replacement for the departed troops of Ba Cut, whose forces according to Savani numbered 1,000 men, while Ba Ga Mo had a modest force of 400. Nam Lua, another Hoa Hao leader whose forces had withdrawn, had a total of 7,000 troops, though it appears that only a small part of these had been stationed in My Tho.[44] By spring 1954 this time the French were able to conduct sweep operations only in contested areas like Cho Gao, and to restore posts in the most critical locations, usually those near towns and major roads. The Hoa Hao were still a formidable presence in Cai Be district north of Highway 4, even though the Ba Cut faction had abandoned the posts along the Plain of Reeds. Under pressure from Viet Minh guerrillas and certainly influenced by the impending collapse of the French at Dien Bien Phu, the remaining Hoa Hao contented themselves with staying in their posts and awaiting the outcome of events.[45]

My Tho's province history contends that by the signing of the Geneva Accords in July 1954, almost the entire rural area of the province was under Viet Minh control, as well as many of the secondary roads in the province.[46] The French military's assessment of the situation in the Mekong Delta at the time the Resistance War ended was that pacification remained "fragile": "Its eventual success requires a perseverance which we sometimes lacked. A characteristic example of this is the deterioration of the situation in Cochinchina during the last months of the war. At that time there occurred a renewal of Viet Minh military activity that would have required the initiation of a new pacification campaign. 'Only the zones held by the sect forces remained relatively healthy; all other zones supposedly under our control became gangrenous.'"[47] As Savani pointed out, however, in the end even the sects abandoned the colonial cause.

As in the 1973–75 period, this political and military resurgence followed the lead of events in other parts of the country, and people in My Tho were certainly deeply affected by the declining French military fortunes in north and central Vietnam, and above all the battle of Dien Bien Phu. Yet the fact that it happened in both cases demonstrates the French conclusion that "pacification" can be quite transitory if the larger issues of the conflict remain unresolved, and that the 1950–52 period was only a temporary setback for the revolution. Enough of the cadres and troops held on through the years of adversity to provide a nucleus for a resurgence of the revolutionary movement, based partly on existing assets and partly on recruiting new ones. The decline in morale of their opposition was the key factor that enabled the Viet Minh to exploit these assets. In any event, had the war not been terminated by a negotiated settlement, the Mekong Delta as a crucial source of food and manpower would have again become a central focus of the conflict, and in both the First and Second Indochina Wars, in the end the momentum in My Tho had swung back to the revolutionaries.

The Geneva Accords of July 20, 1954, brought this momentum to a halt. In accordance with the provisions of this agreement, all Viet Minh troops in organized military units were regrouped and sent to North Vietnam. Civilian cadres at the lower levels generally stayed behind in order to prepare for the anticipated election and in the belief that they would be protected from reprisals by the provisions of the agreement. This departure of military forces and cadres marked the dissolution of the My Tho province Resistance-era military units, which faded into history. It was a bittersweet ending for many of the revolutionaries. Immediately after the agreements were signed, Muoi Thap returned in triumph from the North, carried part of the way in a French staff car. When she reached the South, however, she discovered that one of her sons, the guerrilla chief of Long Hung village, had been killed in June. With mixed emotions, she reluctantly joined the Viet Minh soldiers and high-ranking cadres regrouping to the North in accordance with the Geneva Accords, consoling herself with the thought that it would only be for two years and never imagining that it would be nearly twenty years before she returned to the South.[48]

Conclusion

It is important to understand the Viet Minh failures in the 1950–54 period as well as their earlier and later successes, because the lessons they learned are the key to understanding the remarkable military expansion of the revolutionary forces in 1959–65. In essence, the revolutionaries concluded that no single approach would be sufficient to break the vicious circle of problems and difficulties. Their attempts to build up large units and move to mobile warfare responded to the theories and directives of the highest Party leadership, but were not suitable for local realities. An approach which stressed only political struggle failed to budge the sects and the partisans, but the military recovery in My Tho would not have been possible without a concurrent political policy that neutralized much of their opposition. The contributions of Viet Minh victories in other parts of Vietnam as well as the international forces which affected the outcome of the Resistance War point to the importance of understanding the links between the local situation and the larger national and global context. What was needed was a balanced approach, in which all components of the revolutionary forces were gradually and proportionately strengthened so that they became mutually supporting. Concentrating on one element at the expense of others did not work, because the strength of the strategy lay in making the whole system stronger than the sum of its parts. With the brief exception of late 1964 and early 1965, when a massive military draft and buildup of main force units unbalanced the local system, this lesson was the central guidepost to post 1959 military strategy.

Just as important is the legacy of the comeback staged by the revolutionary movement after My Tho province was nearly totally pacified in 1951 and 1952. When the same situation recurred years later, many older peasants harkened back to this reversal of fortunes during the Resistance. In 1971 the core areas of My Tho province were more or less pacified, but the recollection of Viet Minh experience bolstered the morale of the revolutionaries. It also may have diminished the political impact of the "Land to the Tiller" program and other initiatives of the Saigon government during this period, because the recipients of the land knew that the titles were only as good as the future of the regime that issued them. Another similarity between the resurgence of the revolutionary forces at the ends of the two conflicts is that neither movement was self-generated; both followed dramatic changes in other areas of the country and in the international situation. The end result in both cases, however, was an extraordinary reversal of fortunes, as the Viet Minh grew stronger and their opponents weaker—all the more remarkable considering how near the French had come to total pacification in My Tho.

For a brief period during the early 1950s, the social and political mobilization that followed the August 1945 revolution faltered, as the French and their local allies regained control over most of the province, separating the cadres from their mass base. Even so, much of the socioeconomic change brought about by the August Revolution was irreversible. The old power structure had been irretrievably overthrown, and most of the pre-August Revolution village elites were no longer willing to serve as local officials, either because of fear or shame, or because of a feeling that they were "out of date" (*lo thoi*)—yesterday's men. During the height of the pacification many of the landlords did return to the countryside and claimed rent from their former tenants; however, the events of 1945–50 made them aware that the situation might change in the future. As a result, they were somewhat tentative in their demands. Though the interviews do not discuss it, the returning landlords once again fled the countryside during the Viet Minh resurgence at the end of the Resistance War. After 1954 some landlords tried to restore the old ways, but, as we shall see, they ultimately failed. In this sense, the 1945 shattering of the traditional power structure had a lasting impact.

An even more fundamental change brought by the revolution was the transformation of the mental world of the peasants. They no longer resigned themselves to fate or felt that their lot in life had been predetermined. Peasants were now keenly aware of the political world around them, the larger national situation, and even the global forces that shaped their lives. Constant indoctrination may have been onerous and the framework of Marxist class analysis limited, but they did provide rural people with powerful tools with which to make sense out of the society and economy they lived in.

My Tho's rural society was in fact transformed by revolutionary policies. In addition to driving the big landlords out of the countryside, the land distribution set in motion a pattern of upward mobility that moved poor and landless peasants into the ranks of "middle peasants" as independent cultivators. This move, which was intended to win stronger support for the revolution and to bring about a more egalitarian society, however, also led to the unintended consequence of an increasingly large segment of rural society becoming attached to their new-found independence and prosperity. This would later pose an insurmountable obstacle to completing the Party's social revolution after the wars against foreign intervention were won, as this newly enfranchised class stubbornly resisted collectivization and forced the Party to drastically change its own thinking about society and economics.

Despite the progressive alienation of the upper strata of My Tho's society during the Resistance, the euphoria as a result of the Viet Minh victory over of the French gave the movement a powerful boost in the eyes of My Tho's population. Although the Viet Minh were harsh and vindictive, they also inspired exceptional dedication to a cause that was admired even by many of their bitterest opponents. This legacy of nationalism was a major asset in facilitating the recovery of the revolutionary movement after its near total suppression during the period following the Geneva Accords of 1954. As we shall see in the next chapters, however, the Viet Minh legacy to the next incarnation of the revolutionary movement was quite complex both in the minds of the people, who saw both similarities and differences between the Viet Minh and the "Viet Cong," and in the minds of the Party leadership, which decided to bring in an infusion of youthful zeal and obedience to the revolutionary movement at the expense of some of the old Viet Minh members.

Finally, the Resistance provided the revolutionary leadership a wealth of lessons for the future. Most of the debates about military organization and strategy during the "Vietnam War" had already been rehearsed during the Resistance. The same was true for many key policies, such as land distribution and taxation. Techniques of political mobilization employed in the later conflict stemmed mostly from the experiences of the Viet Minh, and Party organizational forms and leadership practices also had their origins in this period. Yet the conflict that followed was in many respects quite different from the Resistance, especially in terms of the nature of the opposition to the revolution and the extent to which My Tho's countryside was devastated and its society uprooted by the ferocity of the war. The government of the Republic of Vietnam for all its deficiencies, posed a more formidable challenge to the revolution than the succession of collaborator regimes and the melange of parochial religious sects that had lined up against the Viet Minh. The United States was richer and more powerful than the French; its military operations immensely more destructive; and it was the proponent of a somewhat more plausible political message than the French. In the end, however, the result was the same. The remainder of this book attempts to explain why.

6

Six Years of Peace
1954–59

Among the Viet Minh followers in My Tho, rejoicing over the end of the conflict signaled by the Geneva Agreements on July 20, 1954, was intense but transitory. The Democratic Republic of Vietnam (DRV), representing the revolutionary side, signed a cease-fire agreement with the French. A more general Final Declaration was signed by the DRV, France, Britain, China, and the Soviet Union. Bao Dai's representative refused to sign the Final Declaration as did the United States, which, however, pledged to "refrain from using the threat of force to disturb" the agreements. A temporary line of demarcation at the seventeenth parallel would divide Vietnam into two zones of control to separate the military forces. Viet Minh military forces would be regrouped north of this line, and French and Vietnamese military forces aligned with the French would move south of the line. The agreement stipulated that this demarcation line at the seventeenth parallel would be "provisional and should not in any way be interpreted as constituting a political or territorial boundary" pending a general election that would bring about the unification of Vietnam. This military regroupment was to be accomplished within 300 days. During this period civilians were free to relocate to either side of the line.

One authoritative study of this period notes that neither "the adherents of the Vietminh nor any other party or group were called upon to leave their home areas; all were to be protected against reprisals or discrimination, with the International Control Commission charged with ensuring that this and other features of the Geneva Agreements were respected. There was no provision limiting Vietminh political activity in either of the two zones; and it would, of course, have been impossible to prepare for elections if such a provision had existed. Geneva did not leave two separate states, but rather two contesting parties within a single state. These two rivals—the Vietminh (the Democratic Republic of Vietnam) in the north and the Bao Dai regime (the State of Vietnam) in the South—each continued after Geneva, just as each had done before, to lay claim to the whole country."[1]

Military units which had led the revival of the Resistance in My Tho were regrouped to North Vietnam after send-offs that were both festive and emotional. Lower-level political cadres and guerrillas stayed behind, with only a paper agreement fashioned in distant Geneva to protect them from retribution. The promise of national elections and reunification in two years was equally tenuous. Many of the Viet Minh who stayed behind were bitterly disappointed that they had not been able to exploit the political and military momentum of 1953–54 and bring the revolutionary movement to power in the South as well as in the North.

Looking back on the period that followed the Geneva Accords, people in My Tho called it "the six years of peace" or simply "the six years" (1954–60). (Similarly, the nine years of Resistance from 1946 to 1954 became "the nine years.") The people of My Tho were relieved to see an end to the fighting, even if the Viet Minh were frustrated by being compelled to forego the advantage they had gained in the final year of the conflict. In interviews conducted later, during the "Vietnam War," the "six years" were often described as a "golden era" of peace by people plunged into a second war even more devastating than the first. But these interviews also show that this period was not as idyllic as some remembered it. Landlords returned to the villages to reclaim their rights and demand back rent from tenants. The government of Ngo Dinh Diem launched a sweeping Communist Denunciation campaign (*To Cong*—pronounced Toe Cong) in 1955 which arrested, imprisoned, or killed even marginal supporters of the Viet Minh. New impositions by local government officials fueled peasant discontent as they were forced to labor without compensation on projects like the Agrovilles, which were designed to control them even more. By 1959, the escalating arrests of former Viet Minh and innocent civilians had increased the political tension in My Tho to unprecedented heights, and in 1960 the Destruction of the Oppression campaign began, marking the beginning of the insurgency which evolved into the "Vietnam War."

In the first two years after Geneva, life was tolerable for the revolutionaries who stayed behind. The Diem government was preoccupied with its own survival and engaged in a bitter struggle with the sects—the Hoa Hao, the Cao Dai, and the Binh Xuyen mafia—and the political influence of the Viet Minh was still very strong in My Tho. Gareth Porter writes: "The Chief of My Tho province told American officials in 1955 that the people were refusing *corvée* labor, which had traditionally been demanded of them by the government. 'The influence of the Viet Minh is very great,' he said, 'and we are not really opposing them in the village. . . . '"[2] By 1956, however, the situation for the revolution and its sympathizers took a turn for the worse. The Diem government refused to participate in elections for national reunification. The intended two-year delay of revolutionary victory now looked as though it would stretch out indefinitely. After defeating the sects, the Diem government turned on the revolutionaries and intensified the Communist Denunciation campaign, which created turmoil within the ranks of the cadres.

After the 1954 cease-fire, 1,500 cadres and soldiers from My Tho had regrouped to the North, leaving behind around 3,000 Party members and cadres in My Tho province.[3] At the time of the cease-fire, there was a total of 30,000 Party members in the entire central Mekong Delta (Region 8). By 1959, there were 3,000.[4] In My Tho, on average every village had twenty Party members in 1954, and some, like Hau My, had over 100.[5] When the insurgency started up again in 1959 there were less than 1,000 Party members in My Tho province, and nearly half of these were inactive. Only ninety-two cadres operated in direct contact with the civilian population. In many villages there were only one or two Party members left, and many more had none at all.[6] Tran Van Tra's figures for My Tho are slightly different but tell the same story: in 1954 there were 4,000 Party members, but only 100 were left by the time the 1960 uprising started.[7]

This chapter will focus on the aftermath of the Geneva Accords in My Tho, including the regroupment of the Viet Minh armed forces to North Vietnam, the initial takeover of the countryside by the new Government of the Republic of Vietnam (GVN) headed by Ngo

Dinh Diem; the response of the Viet Minh cadres to the GVN; and Diem's repression of the revolutionary forces via the Communist Denunciation campaign as well as the even more draconian Decree 10/59 (National Security Law). During this period, the revolutionary movement in My Tho lost control of the countryside as its cadres were imprisoned or forced into hiding and its supporters were intimidated into passivity. The Viet Minh suffered a similar setback toward the end of the First Indochina War, and these cycles of decline and revival raise important questions regarding the nature of the movement. Of course, the revolutionary movement also changed as a result of both the repression of the six years and the social and economic transformations in South Vietnam that occurred during this period. The "Viet Cong" movement that emerged in 1960 was somewhat different from the Viet Minh movement that preceded it, a shift which can only be understood by examining what happened during the six years of peace.

On the other side of the political divide of this period, the Saigon government gradually seized the initiative, and its actions shaped the course of events in My Tho and South Vietnam, especially in the period from 1956 to 1959. The GVN was also the beneficiary of a "peace bonus"—a period of prosperity that stood in sharp contrast to the misery of the wartime period and the Viet Minh-imposed economic restrictions. The GVN also had American aid to further bolster the economic appeal of its rule to the people of My Tho. However, the material benefits of GVN rule did not translate ultimately into a victory over the revolutionaries, even though these benefits were accompanied by a massive effort to regain control over the countryside by administrative, military, and political means. What seemed at the time to have been a nearly complete pacification of My Tho province by 1958 looks in retrospect to have been the point at which the essential groundwork for a revolutionary revival was laid.

Thus, one of the key analytic issues in this chapter is the extent of the Diem government's role in bringing about the revival of the revolution through its very attempts to suppress it. A major part of the story of this period is the increasing isolation of local officials from the villagers, as they became more arbitrary and oppressive. The blame does not fall on these officials alone, however, since they were caught between the escalating demands of their superiors to mobilize unpaid *corvée* labor and the inevitable backlash from below. And as the demands increased, the Anti-Communist laws gave these officials almost total and unchecked power in their jurisdictions. This mix of more demands and less accountability was ultimately fatal for the GVN.

It is somewhat misleading to view the six years of peace and the post-1959 insurgency as a political race between competitors who were starting from the same line in 1954. The contest for the "hearts and minds" of My Tho's peasants did not start in 1954, or in 1960, or in 1965, as many Americans thought when they first appeared on the scene, assuming that the end of colonialism had neutralized the nationalist edge the Viet Minh had held over the Vietnamese who opposed them. As the previous chapters have shown, each side carried heavy baggage into the post-1954 era. Although the Viet Minh had been as harsh and autocratic during the Resistance as the Diem government became in the late 1950s, they had been able to justify their actions as a patriotic necessity, whereas the repression of the Diem government appeared to be more self-serving and its local officials seemed to be an extension of the old colonial regime.

In addition, programs like the Viet Minh land distribution made it clear to many poor peasants that a return to the old regime would not be in their interests. The Diem land reform during the six years of peace did benefit many rich and middle peasants, and the "middle peasantization" of My Tho and South Vietnam would later become one of the most important developments of the post-1954 period. One respondent asserted that the middle peasants were the first to abandon the legacy of the Resistance: "During the six years of peace they could easily go to the cities to sell their produce and thus they became richer. They could also afford to send their children to the towns for an education. They thought that with the money they had they would get even richer and let their children stay in the towns to go to school and enjoy an easier life" [DT156]. This connection between leaving the villages and abandoning the revolution is a theme that will be discussed extensively in later chapters. The immediate impact of the land reform, however, was to create fear and uncertainty among many poor peasants about the security of their tenure on the land they were tilling.

Despite the return of landlords in some areas and the various costly impositions by local GVN officials, including bribery and *corvée* labor, the six years of peace were almost universally remembered by the interviewees as a time of prosperity. A typical statement is the remark by a poor peasant that in his village of My Long "even the poorest could make ends meet" [DT266]. A poor peasant from Cai Be district said, "During the six years of peace from 1954 to 1960 the villagers enjoyed relative prosperity. They had good crops and trade flourished. As for myself, I regarded this period as something from a fairy tale; I was carefree and enjoyed my youth" [DT277]. A villager from My Loi (a strong Resistance base near the Plain of Reeds) agreed: "During the 1954 to 1959 period the life of the poor and miserable class in My Loi village had really improved. They represented about 20 percent of the villagers. They had money for food and savings—not like during the Viet Minh times or now [1971]." He described the Resistance as a period when the villagers in My Loi had been "virtually bankrupted." In 1955–56, production was restored and with it people's incomes. "At that time the people's life was really comfortable. There was rice in the fields, fruit in the orchards, produce in the gardens, poultry and pigs around the house, and fish in the pond. All these sources of income helped the people of My Loi to rapidly restore agricultural production. In only a few years, the dilapidated huts were replaced by wooden houses. People bought tables and chairs, armoires and other things—at the time there was a competition in buying furniture and a rush to keep up with the neighbors. They had surplus income so they could do this. People at that time were really living the good life [*phong thai*], healthy and happy. You could say that up to 90 percent of the people in the village fixed up their homes during the six years of peace. Ninety percent had bicycles and motorized sampans" [DT331].

A poor peasant from Vinh Kim recalled that during this period his children were "well fed and well clothed, and I had 1,000 piasters in my trunk for an emergency fund" [DT197]. Another had a surplus of 6,000 to 8,000 piasters a year at a time when rice cost 70 to 80 piasters a bushel (*gia*) [DT264]. Others also mentioned possession of consumer items such as radios and luxury goods that had been forbidden during the Viet Minh rule, sending children to school, and in some areas even acquiring motorized water pumps, which eventually entered the province in large numbers in the mid-1960s and thereby revolutionized agricultural production in My Tho. Freedom of movement and freedom of consumer choice were highly valued aspects of this period to many, but not all, of My Tho's rural people.

"During the six years," said one poor peasant disapprovingly, "the youth liked to compete with each other to buy clothes and liked to have a lot of money." The women were "interested in material things and luxury" and "gambled and engaged in frivolous activities." After the revolution regained control in his village in 1960, he said, "they . . . stopped thinking that they [could] only marry nice girls or boys if they [had] money. Instead they [paid] more attention to the political stand" [DT257].

The remembrances of an idyllic six years were, of course, partly a product of later devastations and privations, which made the period of peace seem like a golden era despite all the difficulties and frustrations they also recounted, and which make it clear that this period was not viewed at the time as a "fairy tale." Not all villages were well off, and grinding poverty and indebtedness were still widespread. Nevertheless, the interview accounts of the six years indicate that it was not primarily economic deprivation that fueled the renewed insurgency in 1960, but anger and frustration at the way the people were ruled by the GVN local officials, mixed with a spirit of nationalism that the revolutionaries were still well positioned to benefit from. This again can be inferred from the overwhelming number of interview accounts of resentment and grievances against the impositions of local officials which pushed the respondents into revolutionary action. In the village of My Loi, described above, an estimated 200 people were arrested during the six years of peace, and by one account, 50 of these people were innocent civilians [DT371].

The two turning points in the political alienation of the population of My Tho were the Communist Denunciation campaign that began in 1955 and Decree 10/59 of 1959, which pushed tensions in the countryside to the breaking point. In addition, the reintroduction of military conscription, which was related to the internal suppression policies, hit My Tho's villages with an impact that jolted them out of their peacetime reverie. One implication of this is that the political policies of the GVN, more than the underlying socioeconomic grievances, were the immediate cause of the insurgency. A logical corollary is that, had the GVN taken a different direction, the later course of events might have been different.

It is, however, hard to imagine the Diem government of that period acting differently. The one-man rule and the political rigidity of President Diem himself was an immutable element of the situation, as was the American support which underwrote his government. Political isolation of the regime forced it to take measures which a more confident administration might have avoided. And, in the final analysis, there was a rough correlation between the contending political sides and the underlying socioeconomic factors. The GVN certainly did not represent the lower social strata in South Vietnam and it had a very tenuous link to the countryside, largely through ties with the rural elites who had opposed the Resistance. Though economic factors were not the primary or proximate causes of the insurgency, they were still extremely important elements of the revolutionary revival. And unlike the situation in 1945, when the poor peasants stood on the sidelines while the middle and upper strata took the lead, in 1960 the poor peasants overwhelmingly responded to the cadres' appeal, while the middle and rich peasants were hesitant.

Was the 1960 insurgency therefore a reflexive response to political oppression? Was it to some extent simply a revival of a suppressed and temporarily dormant social movement which resurfaced when it encountered more favorable conditions? Were the forces mobilized during the "concerted uprising" of 1960 different from the revolution's base of support in the Resistance? The answers to these questions are complicated by two factors. First, in any long-term process of social transformation, nothing ever stays the same, so the question is whether a difference in degree (the increasing reliance of the revolutionary movement on poor peasant support) became a difference in kind (did the movement become so narrowly class based that socioeconomic issues crowded out the broad appeal of the revolution's patriotic agenda)? Second, there is the question of the extent to which social mobilization was based on incentives and persuasion as opposed to compulsion and fear. Assessing the relative contributions of voluntarism and coercion in this mobilization has important implications for understanding the revolutionary movement in My Tho.

Still another question to be examined is the extent of change in the composition of the revolutionary leadership at the village level, the reasons for it, and the consequences of these changes. To put these questions another way, was the "Viet Cong" movement the same as the Viet Minh which preceded it? Much of the background necessary to answer this question is included in this chapter, though the question itself is addressed more systematically in a later chapter.

Depart in Victory, Stay Behind in Glory

Many of the original leaders of the August 1945 revolution in My Tho were dead or inactive by the time of the Geneva Accords, and most of the rest regrouped to North Vietnam. Of the major August Revolution figures, only Chin Con stayed behind and was eventually put back in charge of Go Cong district, where he had begun. Muoi Thap, who was in the North when the Accords were signed, was escorted by French soldiers from the military truce negotiation site of Trung Gia to Hanoi's Gia Lam airport to return to the South. Habituated to years of operating underground, she tried to avoid having her picture taken, but the sight of a woman with a military knapsack, carrying an enamel mug decorated with a painted Viet Minh flag and an inscription praising the Dien Bien Phu victory, attracted a swarm of photographers. It was Thap's first brush with international revolutionary celebrity.

Muoi Thap, Le Duan, and others in their group traveling south were to carry instructions covering the new situation to the Party Central Committee Office of South Vietnam (COSVN) and then to Region 8.[8] The initial message was encouraging: only a few would have to leave their native areas for the distant North. "The question of who goes and who stays was emphasized," Muoi Thap recalled. "Cadres, members of popular associations, and members of the [Viet Minh] government would go, but only a few, and the remainder would stay behind and consolidate the infrastructure and lead the masses to struggle with the enemy and force them to abide by and implement the provisions the two sides have signed. Only a [small] number of troops and cadres would regroup."[9] In fact, it was mostly the troops that regrouped, while many of the political cadres and most low-level supporters stayed behind.

Thap was a hit as she traveled around the Mekong Delta with her Dien Bien Phu victory mug, but she did not know how to answer questions about what would happen if promises of the Geneva Accords were not implemented. The mothers of the departing soldiers were particularly worried. "The responsible cadres couldn't satisfactorily answer," Thap wrote, but "in the end the people accepted it and carried out the order of the Party, the government, and the local activists. Sending their children off for regroupment, the people were both excited and concerned, especially the mothers with their characteristic sentimentality, which caused them to be emotional as well as to worry about the future."[10] The "sentimental" mothers, it turned out, had a clearer view of the situation than did the Party leaders. Muoi Thap reluctantly complied with Central Committee orders to go North again. "See you in two years," she told the members of the Women's Association. "In my mind I wasn't thinking of two years, or twenty years as it turned out, but I thought that if there were difficulties and complications it would be five or six years at most."[11]

Tran Van Tra's mixed emotions about the regroupment were symbolized by the shifting weather in the Plain of Reeds. At the end of September 1954, the rainy season was drawing to a close and the entire area was an endless glassy sheet of water. In the afternoons there were heavy rains and gloomy skies, but in the morning everything was sunny. The vegetation was bright green, and the sight of remote settlements dotting the expanse was pleasing to the eye. "Was this scene happy or sad?" asked Tra. "Who could say for sure. Perhaps a mixture of both." The questions asked by the soldiers were obviously on his mind as well. "Why did we stop the attack when we were winning? We still had enough strength to press the advantage and completely liberate our beloved Fatherland. This opportunity was exceptionally favorable, so why didn't we seize it instead of stopping halfway?"[12]

Some of Tra's retrospective regret about leaving for the North was clearly influenced by the fate of those who stayed behind, such as Hoang Du Khuong, the deputy secretary of the consolidated Eastern-Central Nam Bo Region, who was arrested by the Saigon government during the six years and released only after the 1973 cease-fire, after being reduced to a vegetable from years of torture. Much as Tra wanted to stay behind, as commander of the region, it was his duty to organize and lead the troops going to the North. COSVN rejected his request to stay, saying that because he was the region commander of the combined Eastern and Central Nam Bo zones and deputy commander of all Nam Bo forces, he was too well known and too high ranking to stay behind. "I was angry and distracted for a week," Tra wrote later. "But at the time there was a concern that it would be a violation of the Geneva agreement."[13]

At the send-off ceremony for My Tho's 309th Battalion in early October 1954, the unit commander read a message issued in the name of Tra's command headquarters: "We promise our beloved compatriots that one bright and happy day we will return."[14] The constantly repeated Party slogan was "Depart in victory, stay behind in glory" (Di la thang loi, o lai la vinh quang). A week-long series of banquets and entertainments was organized in My Loi village, and relatives came from near and far to see the departing soldiers. There was no effort to save the sons of landlords and rich peasants from regroupment, said a member of the 309th Battalion, who suggested that poor peasants were the only ones allowed to stay behind [DT331]. One poor peasant, who had fought in the 309th Battalion but stayed behind, ultimately became the Party secretary in his village [DT275]. Another landless peasant, who had fought with the 309th since 1949 but was one of the few members of his unit allowed to stay behind, went with remnants of his unit, mostly squad-level cadres, to War Zone D jungle base in Eastern Nam Bo during the six years, which was "just like going for regroupment" [DT338].

The poignancy of the regroupees' departure is captured in the account of a member of another unit who, like the 309th Battalion, left from Cao Lanh.

That day there was a swarm of relatives of the regroupees going North, but my wife wasn't among them. I was depressed and angry. The thought that my wife had not been true to me made me miserable, and I couldn't think of anything else. The boat weighed anchor and departed from Cao Lanh. I moved off from my comrades and stood on the deck looking at the countryside. When the boat pulled abreast of a small island rising out of the Mekong River, I suddenly saw my wife in a small boat near the shore. She was alone on the boat and I knew that she had been waiting there to bid me farewell. I called out "Ut! . . . Ut! What are you doing here?" Hearing my voice, my wife turned toward me, but when she saw me she couldn't say a thing. I saw her lower her head and wipe the tears from her eyes. I felt so sorry for her that I almost went crazy. I wanted to jump over the rail, swim to the bank, and go back to my native village with my wife and give everything up, even my comrades-in-arms and the revolution that I had—and still was—engaged in. But the ship was a French boat. They were responsible for taking us as far as Vung Tau, where we would be transferred onto a ship from the Soviet Union. If I jumped overboard, what would happen? Probably there would be a big commotion on the boat, it would stop, and the French would find out about it. What would they think of a revolutionary soldier like that? I saw that I would be shamed, and would disgrace my entire unit. So I pulled myself together and silently watched the silhouette of my wife, with her head lowered, fade into the distance. When it had disappeared, I didn't have the strength to remain on deck any longer. I went below to the sleeping quarters and lay down, ignoring my friends who were joking and bantering. When we reached Vung Tau we were transferred to a Russian [actually Polish] ship as planned, and during the week we were on this ship we were shown movies, but I remained stretched out on my bunk, thinking of the wife I had just married, and asked myself when we would meet again [DT101].

When this soldier returned from the North in 1961, he asked to visit his wife but was refused on the grounds that it would compromise the secret that regroupees had begun to return to the South. Two years later, "I couldn't stand it any longer and went to seek out my wife . . . but she already had a husband. This made me furious at the Party. What was even worse was that I found out that her husband was part Cambodian with a brutish temperament, who frequently beat her" [DT101].

Although the frustrations of regroupment reinforced the "southerness" of many troops who went north, they were changed by their stay in the North. And their return to the South in the early and mid-1960s, many "regroupees" became equally resentful of their southern commanders because they had not endured the hardships of regroupment and did not recognize the seniority and experience of those returning from regroupment. Many of these regroupees came to pose a serious disciplinary problem for the Party in My Tho and the central Mekong Delta. Many had been changed by the experience of living in the North. "Nam Tam, from Quon Long, who had served in the 309th Battalion in the Resistance, returned to [the] South in 1963. He dressed neatly. His leadership was average. He stuck to prescribed principles. His reasoning was rather poor. He had lived in North Vietnam and learned to be thrifty from the North Vietnamese; for instance, he would pick up a button or the top of a lighter, etc., and store all this junk in a box and in his spare time sort it out. But he was stingy with his possessions—no one could touch his radio" [DT233]. All these quirks were traits that southerners often ascribed to northerners. Most of the cadres who had returned from regroupment (hoi ket) were easily recognizable because their southern accents had become inflected with a sharp northern edge [DT338]. These soldiers later became key military cadres in the My Tho buildup of large military units that began in 1962. Despite the northern influences, many of these cadres retained their southern individualism and defiance of authority and thus gave their superiors major headaches. Both the positive and negative experiences they brought back with them when they returned to the South later became an important source of information for people in My Tho about what the postliberation phase of the revolution held in store for them.

Post–Cease-Fire Party Policy

According to one witness, the 1954 ceremony to hand over Doc Binh Kieu, one of the main Viet Minh bases in the Plain of Reeds, to the GVN inspired a mix of fear, resentment, and cautious optimism among the people assembled. Each side had four representatives. The GVN of Ngo Dinh Diem was represented by the Cai Be district chief who came in by water on an LST. The witness did not know who the Viet Minh representatives were, but he saw that they were accompanied by an armed platoon. Though there were soldiers accompanying the GVN representative, they were not allowed to get off the boat, because the Viet Minh had been designated as the party responsible for maintaining security. While waiting for the ceremony, a crowd of curious people surrounded the GVN district chief. He said, "If anyone has any questions about past events, stand up and speak up." One person in the crowd raised his hand and asked, "Honorable Mr. District Chief, the Nationalists [GVN] often boast of being humanitarian and all, so why did they always raid and arrest the people, and kill them and burn down their houses?" "That was all done by the French," the district chief replied and pointed to a grove of coconut trees. "From now on, I can assure you that these coconut trees will bear fruit forever." Someone else in the crowd commented, "They must be the Nationalists and not the French, otherwise we would have been arrested already" [DT146]. The term rendered in the interviews as "nationalists" was a literal translation of *Quoc Gia*, which carried the meaning of "government authorities of the nation" more than "patriotic nationalists," which would be better rendered by the term *ai quoc*. *Quoc Gia* was a term used by the Diem authorities to describe itself. Even anti-Diem peasants prudently employed this term when GVN authorities were within earshot. Still the GVN's position that it represented a force different from the French was cause for some optimism. The Diem government's initial position that the Resistance was good, (though most of his officials and soldiers had opposed it) but the communists were bad, soon gave way to an indiscriminate campaign against anyone who had been connected with the Resistance.

Post–Cease-Fire Leadership in My Tho

After the troops were sent to the North, there was a wholesale change in the My Tho province leadership. The central Mekong Delta provinces of My Tho, Tan An (Long An), and Go Cong, which had been combined in 1951, were divided into separate provinces by the revolution shortly after the Geneva Agreements, and in late August or early September 1954 Ba Chim became the My Tho province Party secretary in 1954 and served for the next three years. His eventual successor, Viet Thang ("Victorious Viet"), worked closely with him during this period. (Viet Thang was from Muoi Thap's village of Long Hung.) Other key leaders who stayed in the South during the six years of peace were Chin Om, who became the Party secretary following Viet Thang, and his successor, Le Van Pham (Chin Hai). Nguyen Chi Cong (Chin Cong) is referred to in the interviews as either Chin Du, Chin Gia ("Old Brother Nine") or Chin Om ("gaunt Brother Nine"). "Om" means "skinny" in the South and "sickly" in the North. Here both meanings are implied, and he will be referred to as Chin Om (ohm). The two most important military leaders in the province for most of this period were Muoi Ha and Sau Danh, both of whom are prominently mentioned often in the interviews.

Right after the Geneva Agreements were signed, the Party Central Committee in the North relayed the contents of the accords to the My Tho province headquarters. Ba Chim and the other members of the committee were jubilant, believing that the accords represented a major step toward victory. During the meetings and discussions about the agreements, Ba Chim "did not even consider the possibility that the enemy would not carry out the accord, and didn't think of the difficulties in the struggle to implement it, even though the Province Committee did take note of the possibility that the enemy might sabotage the accord and not carry it out."[15] "Some of the military cadres in the province (Sau Danh and Muoi Ha among them, no doubt) urged continuation of attacks during the interval between the signing of the cease-fire accord and its coming into effect. (The cease-fire was signed on June 20, 1954, and was to take effect in Southern Vietnam on August 11, 1954.) The political leaders agreed, and the Viet Minh forces that remained in My Tho resumed their attacks until My Tho was told by the Region authorities that the attacks were contrary to the Party's policy, and any land seized would have to be turned over to the enemy when the Agreements went into effect.

As part of a new strategy, My Tho was ordered to divide its Party organization into two branches, one overt and one secret. Ba Chim became the secretary of the secret province Party committee in 1954, and Viet Thang was promoted from his previous job as head of the Chau Thanh District Party Committee to be the number three leader in the secret province committee. He was replaced in Chau Thanh district by Muoi Ha, who was assigned to go with Sau Danh to find three secret places to bury three large boxes of weapons. As in the case of the weapons buried in 1940 and dug up in 1945, these weapons became the nucleus of the subsequent revival of armed struggle in My Tho. The top political cadres were given the highly prestigious Colt 45 pistols for self-protection. Thinking his Colt was unloaded, Viet Thang pulled the trigger and nearly ended his revolutionary career. He was probably happy to give up this pistol to Sau Danh, who used it in the assassination of District Chief Nguyen Trung Long in 1957, an event which jarred the apparent calm of My Tho during the "six years" and was criticized by higher Party authorities as rash and premature.[16]

Following the transfer of control of the Plain of Reeds base area to the GVN, Ba Chim and Viet Thang discussed where they should relocate the clandestine province Party headquarters. It could not stay in the Plain of Reeds, because the GVN would be looking for it there and it had no protecting military forces to keep the Saigon forces at bay. In the end, they chose the established revolutionary center of Long Hung. The province Party committee stayed there for several years, until the growing efficiency of the GVN military and police operations forced them to move. "During that period," said a poor peasant from the

Vinh Kim area, "only Long Hung village was still strong and had retained its 'backbone.' Long Hung had high-ranking cadres, it had its activists [*nong cot*], so they kept the village strong. Places without the activists couldn't organize. Besides, Long Hung had a revolutionary tradition, so you see that right up to now [1971] there have been very few ralliers from Long Hung" [DT372]. "At the time the situation was still pleasant," recalled Viet Thang about the relocation to Long Hung. "The people were still enthusiastic and the enemy's repressive machinery was not yet completed and they didn't attack us, so that liaison and finding a place to stay was easy. The brothers had only to ask and the people would agree right away."

Political Struggles in the Villages: 1955–56

In 1955–56, according to the province Party history, 40 to 50 percent of the GVN local officials at the grass-roots level were controlled by the Party, including village and hamlet chiefs.[17] "The policy of the Party headquarters was to block, slow down, and neutralize the implementation of policies by the enemy administration, and prepare to transform their government into our government when the general election came, and use this government to protect our cadres." Ten of the twelve militia members in Phu Qui were Party members, and the other two were sympathizers. In Xuan Son and Hoi Son (Cai Lay), the Self-defense Corps militia protected the meetings of the Party chapter.[18] As late as 1958, the GVN discovered that 151 of the 500 Civil Guard soldiers in Cai Be were penetration agents.[19] In late 1959, just before the full-scale outbreak of the insurgency, the entire "GVN" village council of Binh Ninh village was arrested on charges of having served as a front for the revolution during the post-1954 period, and were sent to the prison island of Puolo Condore [DT399].

The province committee rarely met as a group in this period, to avoid drawing attention to their presence in Long Hung village. In March 1955, however, the entire province committee assembled in Ap Bac for a review of the post-Geneva situation. The Xu Uy (as the overall southern leadership was briefly renamed before going back to the late-Resistance organizational title of COSVN) provided My Tho with 1 million piasters for incidental expenses. The monthly allowance for a single cadre was 60 piasters, which at the time was equivalent to 4 *gia* of rice. In this meeting, the Xu Uy stressed the importance of leading the people in political struggle against the Saigon government. Among other things, this involved protesting the growing trend of landlords reclaiming their land and demanding back rent.[20] According to the Party history, in the villages of Dao Thanh, Long An, Phu Phong (Chau Thanh), Phu Qui, and My Hanh Dong (Cai Lay), peasants killed landlords as well as the police and militia who were hired to collect rent for them. Such measures, the Party claimed, kept 80 percent of the land tenure intact during these first two post-ceasefire years.[21]

A number of interrelated developments occurring in 1956 changed the land tenure situation in My Tho's countryside, and began to undermine the indirect Party influence on the village administrations. The first was the failure to hold nationwide elections as required by the Geneva Accords and the realization, even before the election deadline passed, that reunification would not come soon. This meant that the people of My Tho would have to accept GVN rule for a prolonged period. Second, by 1956 the Diem government had eliminated its most serious opposition: the pro-French elements within the GVN army and the religious sects in the Mekong Delta. As a result, the political power of the Diem administration began to take hold in the countryside, challenging and supplanting the Viet Minh influence in the villages. Finally, the Diem land reform was inaugurated in that year.

Ngo Dinh Diem's political dilemma in the Mekong Delta was that he needed to attract the natural base of anti-Communist political support to his side in order to control the countryside and the rich resources of that area, but as a Catholic from central Vietnam he was mistrusted by much of the southern urban and rural elite. His solution to the dilemma was to break the power of the big southern landlords and create a peasant yeomanry of small landlords and rich peasants. This was done by implementing an American-conceived land reform plan which called for breaking up the landholdings of large southern proprietors by placing a limitation of 100 hectares on allowable holdings. The beneficiaries were the rich and middle peasants who already had some land, for only they had enough ready cash on hand to purchase what the big landlords were forced to sell off.

This reform not only limited the amount of land that landlords could retain and placed a ceiling on the rent they could charge for the remainder, it also required that contracts be signed between landlords and tenants to provide secure access to the land for those who tilled it. As landlords became more confident that an anticommunist regime would stay in power, they once again tried to assert their claims to land distributed by the Viet Minh and to demand back rent. Often, local village officials or militia were hired to collect it. Diem's land reform actually resulted in throwing some peasants off the land, as the big landlords sold to rich or middle peasants the hectares beyond what they were allowed to keep. Poor peasant tenants who could not afford to purchase the land were evicted, and the new small owners either tilled the land themselves or hired laborers to do it. There is some uncertainty about how far this process of undoing the Viet Minh land reforms had gone by 1960 and how many people were actually affected, but there is no doubt that the fear of losing land granted by the Viet Minh was an important factor in enlisting peasant support for a renewed insurgency.

The Denunciation of Communists Campaign

Another policy of the Diem government, however, had a more direct impact on the political situation in My Tho. This was the Denunciation of Communists or *To Cong* campaign. If the Diem land reform disrupted the social and economic patterns of the countryside and provided conditions which could be exploited by an insurgent political movement, the government's other policies unwittingly assisted reconstitution of the depleted ranks of the former Resistance cadres who had provided the local leadership for the Viet Minh. The Denunciation of Communists campaign begun in 1956 encouraged the rural population to identify and turn in former members of the Resistance to the Saigon authorities. This had been preceded by duplicitous offers of amnesty, which did not instill much confidence among the former Resistants in the good will of the GVN. In Hoa Dinh village, "In 1955 the government set a trap by urging those who had participated in the Resistance to come out, and promising to give them tools and rice." Four Viet Minh cadres took the bait and presented themselves. "A few months later the government arrested them and pumped them for information. One showed [the GVN] where a cache of over thirty weapons was located. All four were imprisoned for about a year and then released" [DT268]. The Denunciation of Communists campaign followed on the heels of this deceptive offer of clemency.

Many problems for both the GVN and its opposition emerged in the course of the *To Cong* campaign. First was the problem of distinguishing between anticolonial patriotism and actual membership in the Communist Party. A potential flaw in this "Resistance is good but communism is bad" strategy was the conspicuous abstention of most of the central and local leadership of the Diem administration from the armed struggle against the French, which made it imperative to provide some explanation which would rationalize their nonparticipation and legitimate their authority after 1954. The Saigon authorities claimed that they had in fact opposed the French but that the communists had hijacked the Resistance. It was not resistance to the French colonial regime (and its largely Vietnamese administration, which most of the post-1954 Saigon leaders had served) that was targeted, therefore, but rather the communist leadership of this movement.

Continuity between the old colonial village administration and the Diem local governments undercut the GVN's attempt to claim solidarity with the independence struggle of the Resistance while persecuting those who had led it. At the hamlet level, the situation was a bit less clear. The pool of potential leaders was more limited, and the longstanding interlocking social networks of the hamlet communities provided a challenge for both sides in finding people who were more loyal to their superiors than to their neighborhood. There are many mentions in the interviews of people who had been village and hamlet officials for both sides at various times. This may also help explain the ease with which the revolution was able to "plant" sympathetic people in the GVN local administrations in the early Diem period.

Political Activists and "Simple Citizens"

To some extent, the largest distinction in the villages was between those who were the "political class," no matter which side they served, and those who were less actively involved. This contrast is implicit in common parlance: members of the nonpolitical class are commonly referred to as "ordinary citizens" (*thuong dan*). A frequent response of villagers angered by political demands of any kind is "Do whatever you like, I'll still be a [simple] citizen" (*lam gi lam toi van la dan*), in which "citizen" (*dan*) is used in the traditional sense of "subject" rather than in its modern sense of the political or civic dimension of an ordinary person's life. Being a subject meant accepting the rule of the incumbent authority and the impositions inflicted on the ordinary villagers, but being a *dan* in this sense meant the opposite of being a political person. "I'll still be a simple citizen" meant accepting a nonpolitical role in society and not incurring the high risks of demanding a citizen's rights to be politically engaged. A similar distinction was made on the revolutionary side, and cadres often used the term "the masses" (*quan chung*) to refer to people outside the revolutionary organization who had not made a full-time commitment to political action. In sharp contrast to the traditional view of the peasant as a passive subject, however, the "masses" were required to participate politically in some way. As will be discussed later, the peasants' predilection for styling themselves "simple citizens" does not mean that they were apolitical, as Vietnamese peasants have often been portrayed, as in the French view that the peasants wanted only to be left alone to till their "little plot of land" (*petit lopin de terre*).

The primary distinction between the political class in the villages and ordinary people is in the level of risk taking in pursuit of political interests and objectives. Members of the "political class" were risk takers, and those in the nonpolitical class were not. A bold young cadre operating in the late 1950s found it "very difficult to recruit 'backbone elements' [sympathetic activists] because they were very afraid of jail" [DT109]. Another illustration of this is the case of a poor peasant from Nhi Binh who was deeply imbued with class hatreds and strongly sympathetic to the revolution, yet had been throughout his life only marginally active in the revolution. He described the people's reactions to the arrests of cadres in his village: "They said that these people were assigned to stay behind and wait for the general election but unfortunately the higher powers somehow decided that it wouldn't happen so they had to accept it. They had the responsibility of acting, to attack and throw out the French so that Vietnam could be free. Now their fate is that they have not succeeded so they are in jail." He differentiated between the determined political participants and their occasional followers: "A number of people only followed along with the tide of the movement. When it rose, they would participate, and when it fell they would drop out. These people who only followed the movement were innocent [*khong co toi*] and stayed behind to work, and got legal papers. They just lived and worked and no longer were active" [DT316]. Whether there are any larger explanations for the propensity to accept risk, and whether there are patterns in the decisions of marginal adherents of the movement to engage and disengage will be also be discussed elsewhere.

GVN Measures to Control the Villagers

Unfortunately for the GVN, recourse to authoritarian rule to control the countryside also distanced the village officials still further from the rural population and built up powerful political pressures which were released with great force in 1960. As one interviewee put it, "When the water pressure is too great it will burst the dike" (*tuc nuoc vo de*) [DT313]. Unchecked by laws or higher authority, local officials were able to settle political scores from the Resistance. The village chief of Tan Binh Thanh in Cho Gao had two sons who were killed by the revolutionaries during the Resistance, and he took vengeance during the six years by arresting around fifty former Viet Minh [DT264]. The repression also led to the counterterror applied by the insurgents in 1960, who felt that the only way to shake the peasants' fear of the Saigon government and get them to side with the insurgency was to make them even more afraid of the revolutionaries. This was the most important reason for the assassinations of village officials in 1960–61, which was viewed by many villagers as fitting retribution for their own abuses during the previous period.

At first, the distance between the GVN and the rural population was bridged by the natural relief of enjoying a relatively peaceful environment and greater prosperity, some of which was due to government policies. The void left by the Viet Minh cadres who had been driven out or underground was temporarily filled by the introduction of Civic Action teams (*Cong Dan Vu*) comprised largely of educated North Vietnamese refugees who came to the villages ostensibly to promote rural development, but primarily to assist the GVN in consolidating is grip over the countryside. Over 500 of these GVN cadres were sent to My Tho in mid-1955.[22]

Civic Action teams, like the Revolutionary Development cadres of a later period (1966–75), were in the final analysis outsiders who could not have a lasting impact on the village or compensate for the deficiencies of the local administration, which was the real face of the GVN in My Tho's villages. While their stated objective in the villages was to promote development and "civic action," their most visible function was to identify villagers according to a political classification that identified regime supporters, by an auspicious gold or white sign attached to the front of the house on which the interfamily group number was painted. Ominous black signs were used for suspected opponents. "People with no ties to the Viet Minh were regarded as good citizens and those who had relatives in the Viet Minh were regarded as 'incomplete citizens' [*cong dan khong hoan toan*], who were kept under watch and given indoctrination. These families were isolated in every sphere. Even in going to the rice fields they had to report . . . and 'good citizen' families were not allowed to assist them" [DT331].

These Civic Action teams were not able to compensate for the absence of close ties between the local province officials and the villages. In My Long, "no high-ranking officials of the district or province ever came to the village. The people didn't pay attention to them and didn't even know their names. Once in a while the district sent a Civic Action team to [the] village to teach animal husbandry. They also explained the general political situation to villagers, but as they hadn't studied the local conditions carefully before starting to talk about what should be done, their work turned out to be a failure. For example, a Civic Action team came to [the] village to teach [the] villagers to transplant trees, use fertilizer, burn the grass before planting rice, etc. But My Long is situated near a river and for seven months of the year all its arable land is covered with water, so how could we put their advice into practice?" [DT266]

By late 1956 the Diem government felt that it had sufficient control of the situation in the Mekong Delta to take the vital next step in traditional Confucian statecraft, which was to provide its own designations for the provinces and districts to replace the old French designations. The province had been named Dinh Tuong in precolonial times, but became My Tho as the French imposed colonial rule. After the GVN assumed control of South Vietnam, My Tho province again became Dinh Tuong. The districts were renamed with unfamiliar, stiff, and didactic terms that were intended to "civilize" this former frontier area and draw it into President Diem's own Confucian frame of reference. The unpretentious traditional district appellations, drawn some say, from earlier Cambodian place names, were replaced in official use by high-sounding new designations. Cai Be was split into two districts, Giao Duc (Teaching Virtue) and Sung Hieu (Venerating Filial Piety). Cai Lay became Khiem Ich (Modest Usefulness), and part of Chau Thanh, the traditional generic designation for the capital district surrounding the province seat, was split off to become Long Dinh (Settled Dragon).[23] Only Cho Gao (Rice Market) district remained unchanged. In President Diem's Confucian world, the renaming of the administrative units not only solidified his claim to rule and showed his power, the names also carried an intrinsic moral force that would rub off on the inhabitants of the area. Not surprisingly, the people continued to use the old familiar names, and this attempt to turn the individualistic South Vietnamese into proper Confucians only underlined the distance between the world of Ngo Dinh Diem and the realities of My Tho.

GVN Officials in Dinh Tuong During the Late 1950s

Not everyone in My Tho felt this gap between themselves and the GVN district and province officials. In 1956–1958, the My Tho province chief was the dynamic Nguyen Tran, a fervent Diem supporter who had shown a flair for provincial administration in central Vietnam. Tran supplemented his relentless pursuit of communists with an effort to convert them politically and to prove that the GVN could respond to the needs of the people better than they. One of his most famous initiatives was challenging a group of revolutionary sympathizers incarcerated in My Tho to a public debate about the relative merits of communism and the Diem regime, described in the official Party history as a "debate between Nguyen Tran and fourteen reporters and progressive intellectuals imprisoned in My Tho" in June 1958.[24] The accounts of who got the best of this debate naturally vary according to the political inclinations of the source. The owner of a bookstore in My Tho town in the mid 1960s, who had been one of the "progressives," presented the debate in a casual conversation during the "Vietnam War" period as a clear polemical triumph for the prisoners. Nguyen Tran's own account of this describes a debate about Marxism at a high level of abstraction and sophistication, after which a representative of the "progressive intellectuals" promised to cut off all ties with the communists.[25] Whatever the case, in GVN circles Nguyen Tran became famous for his boldness in challenging the communists on their own ground and attempting to defeat them by political means. This effort did not further his political career, however, and in the end he was removed by an increasingly paranoid Diem, who saw any successes or even initiatives from his subordinates as unacceptable challenges to his position.

Another interviewee had favorable words for some of the village officials, as well as a Cai Lay district chief of the period. Reading between the lines, however, the village officials were damned with faint praise (it was their subordinates who did the actual dirty work) and sly innuendo (it was their power more than their character or behavior that villagers respected): "I was on friendly terms with village officials. The people respected them, first of all for their power and position, and then for their prestige and behavior. They satisfied the needs of people without posing conditions. Each time [there was] a funeral or wedding, people respectfully invited these officials. When they were too busy, they hired assistants. It was these assistants who abused power and oppressed people in public works like digging canals and ditches, etc. They shouted at people and cursed them for not observing the measurements prescribed by the government, in order to extort money" [DT229]. This respondent's assessment of the district chief was more positive: "The Cai Lay district chief Nguyen Dinh Xuong was highly respected by the people. Later he became chief of Tra Vinh Province and now [1967] is Secretary General of the Ministry of the Interior. He visited the village often to check on the aid programs of the GVN and to find out what people's aspirations were. He was [a] good leader who carried out government policies faithfully. Unfortunately he left Cai Lay district in 1960 to become province chief in Tra Vinh, exactly at the time the Front emerged. His departure plunged Thanh Phu village into a chaotic situation" [DT229]. Another poor peasant said, "Mr. Nguyen Dinh Xuong often came to oversee the digging of canals, etc., and conversed amiably with everyone regardless of social class. He joined the workers in digging. When distributing buffalo, he himself led buffalo to each one. He was quick to settle all the affairs submitted to him. Everyone in the village in fact liked him very much" [DT237].

The district chief of Chau Thanh was also a presence in the villages, though he appears to have concentrated more on tracking down former Viet Minh than winning the hearts and minds of villagers. A native of Dong Hoa reported that in his village all the Party chapter committee members were arrested: "When Mr. [Nguyen Trung] Long was district chief, he used to disguise himself as a farmer or a trader to go into the hamlets to capture the ["Viet Cong"] cadres. He and his family were shot by Sau Danh later on" [DT196]. This happened while Long was attending a ceremony in Long Hung village [DT207]. According to one eyewitness account, in 1955, Nguyen Trung Long organized a ceremony in which 200 members of the Resistance, including the witness's father, publicly tore up the Party flag. The ceremony was attended by over 5,000 people. During the ceremony, a canton chief (an official mediating between the district and the villages) singled out one cadre and denounced him for "eating Nationalist rice but worshiping the Communist ghost." A number of Party members refused to tear up the flag and were sent to the prison island of Con Son [DT196]. Chin Om, the province Party secretary in the early and mid-1960s, notes that in 1957, Nguyen Trung Long had captured two district committee members in an assault on the Chau Thanh district committee.[26] The reason Long was later singled out for elimination was the threat he posed to the revolutionary movement in his jurisdiction.

Impact of the *To Cong* Arrests on the Revolutionary Movement

Certainly the mass arrests of the *To Cong* campaign devastated the revolutionary organization in My Tho. The official province Party history states that "more than 2,000 cadres and Party members were arrested, exiled, or forced to go into hiding in other areas. Some Party members who had been arrested could not withstand the torture and become confused and demoralized. Some surrendered and gave information which caused losses to our Party. The basic-level infrastructure of the Party in the villages was broken up or paralyzed; some district committees were all arrested, like the Cho Gao district committee; many comrades in the province committee were arrested or killed."[27] Another postwar revolutionary source says that "between October 1957 and May 1958, [the GVN] killed, arrested, or exiled nearly 3,000 people who were backbone cadres and Party members, or civilians [*quan chung*] who had connections with the revolution."[28]

In his memoirs, My Tho Province Chief Nguyen Tran asserts that documents captured from the My Tho province Party committee stated that 5,000 out of a total of 5,800 Party members had been arrested and the remaining 800 had scattered.[29] He states that at the time he was removed from office in mid-1958 there were 2,000 "communist cadres" in jail in My Tho and Go Cong (which was now part of the GVN Dinh Tuong province).[30]

"Sow the Wind, Reap the Whirlwind": Decree 10/59 and Escalating GVN Repression

In achieving this apparent triumph over their revolutionary opponents, however, the Saigon government also created some serious problems for itself which were not apparent at the time. These mass arrests showed conclusively that the former Viet Minh could not coexist politically with the Diem regime. In addition, the early Saigon position that it was not ties to the Resistance but membership in the Communist Party that was objectionable was belied by the indiscriminate arrests of marginal sympathizers.

An even more convincing demonstration of the insincerity of the GVN claim to have supported the patriotic goals of the Resistance was the classification of the village population into "good" and "bad" or "incomplete" citizens based on affiliation with the Viet Minh. Nguyen Tran had promised My Tho's villagers that they would not be punished. "On behalf of the Government," he told a group of villagers in Cai Be, "I gladly accept your return to the Just Cause of the Nationalists. Anything you have done before now will not be considered a crime in any way, because your actions were for the Resistance and were patriotic actions. They are worth inscribing on a golden plaque."[31] This message evidently did not penetrate to the lower levels of GVN administrations, and the "bad" citizens with personal or family connections to the Viet Minh continued to be isolated and put under surveillance. The "golden plaque" went to those who had collaborated with the French, not those who had participated in the Resistance who, instead, had a black signboard affixed to their homes indicating their political pariah status. The partial return of the landlords also tied the Diem government to the old order of the French colonial regime in the eyes of many villagers and made it clear that the GVN would not protect their interests.

Another problem concealed within the apparent triumph of the Diem government was what to do with the people they had arrested. One of the reasons it is difficult to get a clear picture of the extent and severity of the *To Cong* arrests is that interviews often did not distinguish between brief periods of detention and indoctrination and actual jail sentences. There was a wide range of penalties imposed on people with Viet Minh connections, ranging from a few weeks of indoctrination or "boarding school study" (*hoc noi tru*) at designated government locations to prison terms of six months to three years, many of which expired, conveniently enough, just at the time the insurgency was launched. Although some of those arrested fled to other areas following their release, the majority returned to their villages, now smoldering with resentment.

Another problem stemming from the repression was that in seeking absolute control the GVN overreached, even from the perspective of the Diem government. While there was deep resentment against the *To Cong* campaign of 1955–58, it was the passage of the infamous Decree 10/59 in May 1959 which proved to be the straw that broke the camel's back. "Sow the wind, reap the whirlwind" (*gieo gio gat bao*), a familiar Vietnamese saying, perfectly describes the action–reaction cycle initiated by the 10/59 law.

Decree 10/59 was a sharp escalation of the political repressiveness of the Diem government. It widened the scope of political crimes from past affiliation with the Viet Minh to any political opposition, which was now labeled treason. The new sanctions attached to this decree were far more menacing. A non communist critic of the Diem administration summarized Decree 10/59 as providing "for a faster judicial procedure through special military tribunals to sentence to death or life imprisonment people involved in sabotage activities."[32] Now opposition had become treason, and the range of political actions that were potential threats to "national security" was almost unlimited. By definition, anyone labeled a "communist" was a threat to the state under this law.

Decree 10/59 dramatically raised the stakes of political opposition and increased the powers of local officials, who now could arbitrarily consign anyone they designated to life imprisonment or death. For most villagers the seriousness of arrests during the previous *To Cong* campaign usually ranged from the irritation and inconvenience of a few weeks of indoctrination camp to sentences of six months to three years in prison. One poor peasant from Xuan Son village, who was a former Viet Minh hamlet chief, went through a month-long indoctrination program and in 1958 was even appointed as hamlet chief by the GVN. It is clear that he was not a "plant" because this strategy had been abandoned since 1956 (although it clearly continued well after this in many places, as shown earlier in this chapter), and he was rebuked and warned for his collaboration when the revolution reemerged in the village in 1960 [DT265]. By 1959, the GVN was less forgiving.

The draconian 10/59 law coincided with the removal of the GVN province chief Nguyen Tran and marked the end of his political approach to pacification. At the same time, the Saigon government failed to strengthen its security machinery and lapsed into a fatal combination of complacency and harsh repression. Since the Party leadership in Hanoi had already given its qualified approval to the renewal of armed struggle in the South in January 1959, it cannot be said that the 10/59 law of May 1959 was the only factor that triggered the insurgency, but it greatly accelerated the tensions in the province and the pace of the insurgency.

The extreme consequences of the penalties for being branded a communist, along with the ease with which the village authorities could make this charge, were a dangerous combination. In Thanh Phu village (Chau Thanh), "villagers were threatened that anyone who reported corruption would be charged with cooperating with the VC [Viet Cong] or being [an] underground cadre and [would be] sentenced by the 10/59 law. That's why everyone was very scared of the Village Council members" [DT181]. The fear instilled in the villagers by the threat of execution or life imprisonment under the terms of Decree 10/59 proved to be a profitable lever with which village officials extracted bribes from a terrified population.

As a tactic of intimidation, the draconian measures to stamp out the revolution did have an impact, but they also negated whatever progress the GVN had made in legitimating its claim to rule and now made it clear that the regime would rest on naked power and coercion. In Ban Long village, the repression had severely curtailed cadre activities by 1959, and those few who remained could not operate effectively because they could trust only a few households and could not risk trying to recruit others. "But thanks to the 10/59 decree," said a poor peasant who was marginally connected to the revolution at that time, "new life was blown into the political movement, and a patriotic appeal was made to overthrow the government of Mr. Diem because this government was killing people like that, so it led to another war and renewed fighting" [DT372]. The extreme measures of the Diem government had increased the risks for the marginal adherents of the revolutionary movement to the degree that they now had little to lose and were fighting a serious threat to their survival. "At the time, the people outwardly were deferential to the government, but inwardly they didn't respect it. Their outward deference was based on fear of imprisonment and death. They were really scared, but they still protected the cadres" [DT372]. Moreover, this law signaled to many peripheral supporters of the revolution that there was no turning back and that only the overthrow of the Saigon government could assure their safety. One postwar history recounts the story of a peasant women who had harbored district cadres in her home. When her husband returned from detention for GVN "political education" and was afraid of resuming political activities, she told him that the GVN would never forgive them for giving refuge to cadres and that their only safety lay in the survival and success of the revolution.[33]

Decree 10/59 created an atmosphere of terror in the countryside of My Tho and exacerbated the corruption and authoritarianism of local officials. Ironically, the actual number of executions under Decree 10/59 in My Tho seems relatively small. Only a few interviews specifically mentioned actual executions. A young organizer in Chau Thanh district said: "[My] work became easier when Ngo Dinh Diem issued the Decree law 10/59. With this decree, the opposition to Diem became heavier. The courts set up by its provisions sentenced five or six people to death in My Tho. The people became more angry and, as a consequence, many volunteered to join us" [DT135]. A Party history of the 1960 Concerted Uprising says that in the nine provinces of Nam Bo, "within a short period at the end of 1959" there were twenty death sentences and twenty-seven life sentences decreed by the mobile special military court.[34] One Party history claims that in all of South Vietnam between January and the end of October 1959, the Diem government killed 469 people, and that the figures for the entire 1954–59 period were 68,000 killed, 466,000 arrested, and 400,000 imprisoned or exiled.[35] This large number of people killed does not seem to reflect what happened in My Tho, even if accurate for other places. Nonetheless, Decree 10/59 had an impact that went far beyond its actual application.

Whereas the actual executions in My Tho apparently involved a relatively small number of people, the terror and corruption affected most of the villagers in the province, as did the increased burdens placed by the GVN on the people via corvée projects such as the Agrovilles. One villager said, "I was only forced to take part in construction of Agrovilles three times. I had to bring [my] own rice and was only given one piaster a day to buy soy sauce at each meal. I had to work three days each time. . . . I didn't hear any [complaints], because the villagers were split up and assigned to various groups with workers from other places. All of the workers were very scared and they dared not complain to strangers. They only said that it was very dangerous to complain against the government because Ngo Dinh Diem had issued the 10/59 decree which aimed to put every malcontent into jail. Nevertheless, some villagers said that it was not right to force the workers to eat their own rice while working for the government. The Front later on accused the GVN of treating the people like slaves, and that made every villager pleased because this statement reflected their own feelings" [DT83].

Inevitably, the heaviest burden of corvée labor fell on the poorest members of the village. Corvée labor could involve repeated jobs ranging from several days to several weeks, often during peaks in the agricultural calendar. Not only did people have to pay for their own food, they also lost valuable time and money by not being able to do their own work. The means of avoiding the corvée all involved money or connections, and usually the two were related. In one village, the going rate for exemption from corvée on the Agrovilles ranged from 1,000 piasters (more than the monthly salary of a Civil Guard soldier) to 2,000 piasters [DT239]. One person decided that a single day of corvée was more than enough and was able to hire a substitute to complete his service for a bargain 90 piasters [DT195]. Those who were higher up on the socioeconomic scale tended to have connections that would exempt them, leaving only the poorest to do the work. In My Phuoc Tay, the site of one of the two Agrovilles in Dinh Tuong province, the hamlet chiefs selected people to do corvée for periods of four or five consecutive days. One poor peasant complained that he was mobilized by his hamlet chief, who was a middle peasant, as were the members of the village council: "The assignments were not fair. The clever ones did not have to go, only the simple and straightforward ones" [DT340].

When asked which of the revolution's aims, he liked better, one interviewee responded, "Social justice was the aim I liked most" [DT143]. "From the time I grew up and had a little understanding," said a poor peasant from Ban Long village, "I have always dreamed of living in a just and equitable society—a society in which class would not exploit class. That's all I want. The daily life in my village led me to have this aspiration. During the six years in the village the people with money hired people to stand guard for them as well as to substitute for them in working on the Agrovilles. The hamlet and village officials 'ate' all that money, but the poor people who didn't have money and had already done these tasks were forced by the hamlet and village officials to do more, replacing the rich villagers who had put out the money to 'hire' them. I saw that these things were very unjust and at the time people had no freedom to speak out about these injustices. Whoever did speak out would be arrested or punished. So people just silently held in their hatred and anger. And when the Front rose up this hatred and anger burst powerfully to the surface" [DT393].

Forced Labor and Relocation of Peasants: The Agrovilles

In 1959 the Diem government began a program of population relocation to consolidate control over key areas of the countryside, especially the areas bordering the Plain of Reeds. The Agrovilles (*khu tru mat*), and later the more famous "strategic hamlets," were presented as a way of bringing development and the amenities of urban life to the countryside, but the underlying motivation was rural security. The purpose of the Agroville program was to relocate the peasants in a concentrated settlement area covering approximately 2 square kilometers, for more effective population and resource control. As an incentive, the peasants were promised better services and marketing facilities. In Hau My, a former stronghold of the Resistance, some villagers had to dismantle their houses near their rice fields and move to the central area of the village. Their fruit trees were leveled and their rice fields dug into canals and creeks. As a result they lost their source of income. A village midwife describes the impact of this relocation: "During the time they lived in the Agroville their life was miserable, and this was why a number of them moved elsewhere and supported the Front. The VC recruited their men among the dissatisfied villagers and set up the Liberation Front in the village" [DT141].

The greatest negative impact of the big construction projects, such as the Hau My Agroville, was on the people brought in from other villages to build it. One construction worker describes the dismal conditions: "We were then in the rainy season and the fields were flooded so that it was impossible to dig the well. The thousands of workers were forced to dive into the water and scoop up the mud with their own hands until we finally had a well. All the workers were covered with mud from head to toe, and many of them died because they had to stay in the water too long and the weather was cold. . . . In all about twenty people were killed while building the Agroville" [DT141]. In Ban Long village, "Whenever the Republican Youth came to the village to talk to the people about the benefits of the Agrovilles, all they had to do was to stay at the village headquarters, sound the gongs, and all the able bodied men in the village had to go to the meeting. The village council jotted down the names of the absentees on a list of VC suspects. Therefore, no one dared to get a job outside the village—if you went away, you went away for good. The suspects had to sleep at night at the village headquarters and lie on the floor without a straw mat or mosquito net. In order to [get] the Agrovilles in My Phuoc Tay and Hau My built on time, the villagers in Ban Long village were forced to do corvée labor ten days in a row, twice a month. The able-bodied men between eighteen and forty received no compensation when they did corvée labor and also had to bring their own food. Their wives and children had to take food and supplies to them, which meant they couldn't do their own work. The people were very frustrated and frightened [DT239].

The intensified political repression also affected nominal supporters of the GVN. The peasant who had initially regarded the six years of peace as "paradise" said that this came to a definitive end when the 10/59 campaign struck: "In 1959 village officials suddenly changed their attitude toward the villagers who became quite angry. These officials, accompanied by militia and [Self-defense Corps] troops went through the hamlets arresting any man or youth. They arrested them all and beat them up so cruelly, accusing them all of working with the VC with no exceptions. I was no exception either, even though I was a Republican Youth member. I was given three slaps across the face by [a Self-defense Corps] member while I was walking about in the hamlet. I protested, saying I was a Republican Youth member. He shouted 'Republican Youth indeed! You are VC. I'll tie you up first and bring you back to the post and see if its true or not' " [DT277].

A demobilized Army of the Republic of Vietnam (ARVN) soldier (GVN army), who returned to his village so poor he could not buy civilian clothes, was asked by the village council in Kim Son to serve in the unremunerated Youth for the Defense of the Countryside. When the Hau My and My Phuoc Tay Agrovilles were inaugurated, he was charged by the village council to lead the village youth delegation at these ceremonies. On his way to carry out this mission, a militiaman ordered him to do a job for the hamlet chief. He declined because of his conflicting engagement with the village delegation, but the hamlet chief interpreted this as insulting behavior and threatened to throw this ex-serviceman in jail. Although the matter was eventually sorted out, the former serviceman felt he had been dishonored: "There I was, a reserve soldier who had just completed his service in the army. The village and hamlet officials should respect and honor me because I had done my duty to the country and for one whole year had suffered all sorts of hardships in the army. But instead they despised me and dishonored me. They thought that they could arrest me whenever they liked and for whatever reason. I got mad and left the village to look for the Front cadres. This is the only reason that pushed me to join the Front. At that time I didn't know anything about the revolution and didn't join the Front out of any revolutionary fervor. I was young and impulsive then" [DT205].

Throughout the six years of peace, the GVN militia had free rein in the rural villages. They were supported by a substantial "control" structure in Dinh Tuong and Go Cong. At the end of 1956 the GVN had four battalions and nine companies of Civil Guards and fourteen composite Self-defense Corps (*tong doan Dan Ve*) groups, as well as a Self-defense Corps unit in every one of Dinh Tuong's 123 villages. By 1957 the GVN had a total of 250 posts in the province.[36] The Civil Guards were the main armed force controlled by the province authorities, supplemented by the Self-defense Corps who manned the smaller village posts. They were supported by a control infrastructure that included unarmed Youth for the Defense of the Countryside *(Thanh Nien Bao Ve Huong Thon)* and the Republican Youth *(Thanh Nien Cong Hoa)*, which was part of President Diem's National Revolutionary Movement. Other interviews mentioned the Combat Youth *(Thanh Nien Chien Dau)*. The paramilitary youth groups in the villages had different names at different times and the interviewees probably employed anachronistic terms, but whatever the designation, there was probably the same membership in the various youth groups throughout this period. These youths were stationed in small thatched huts or flimsy watchtowers along village paths, which supplemented the fortified posts that housed the Self-defense Corps and were used as a base. Since each village normally had only one or two Self-defense Corps posts, many hamlets had no permanent Self-defense Corps unit. The village policeman was in charge of the Self-defense Corps. Only the most important villages had a permanent Civil Guard (province militia) presence. Thus, most of the hamlets were controlled by the unarmed youth organizations and the administrative network of hamlet chiefs and interfamily chiefs who were responsible for keeping track of a small cluster of adjacent households and reporting to the hamlet chief. Local Self-defense Corps militiamen were responsible for enforcing unpopular policies such as the corvée duty, and they went house to house to check for evidence of compliance with orders to work on the Agrovilles. Those who had no certificates to prove that they had done so were arrested and turned over to the village council, which then sent them off to the Agrovilles.

Local Security Forces

By 1958 Dinh Tuong province had a total of 4,000 Civil Guard soldiers and Self-defense Corps militiamen. On average, each district chief had at his disposal about 450 Civil Guard and Self-defense Corps militiamen. Nguyen Tran proposed to cut the number in half and double the salary of the remainder, on the grounds that unmotivated and underpaid soldiers could not be relied on, but this idea was not accepted.[37] At the time, a Civil Guard soldier earned 900 piasters a month and a self-defense militia soldier earned 800 piasters. The standard monthly allotment for all revolutionary cadres at province and district level was 60 piasters a month. President Diem's brother, Ngo Dinh Nhu, felt that it was dangerous to equip the Civil Guard and Self-defense Corps with automatic weapons, because they would just fall into the hands of the guerrillas; Nhu ordered that they be withdrawn from the province forces and replaced by World War I French army rifles (mousqueton Indochinois) and machetes. "In my view," said Nguyen Tran, "this was in effect abandoning them, because if they didn't have enough strength to protect themselves, how could they be expected to carry out the missions we entrusted them? [They] will become half-hearted shirkers and will be easy for the Communists to win over like the 151 Civil Guards and Self Defense Corps in Cai Lay."[38]

Despite the apparently near-total control of the GVN in Dinh Tuong's most populous villages, there were some vulnerabilities in its security position. Several of the big villages near the Plain of Reeds included so much territory that they could not be adequately controlled by the relatively few posts, and these were the areas in which the resurgent revolutionary armed forces first operated. The "wagon wheel" intersection of six canals in northern Cai Be was essential to the control of the northwestern part of the province.

During the latter stage of the Resistance, the French abandoned the key post that controlled the area, and it was not reestablished during the six years [DT382]. There was, however, a Civil Guard post near My An village, along the extension of the Nguyen Van Tiep Canal marking the border of the Plain of Reeds at the boundary between Kien Phong and Dinh Tuong provinces [DT25]. Thanh Phu village in Cai Lay had a Civil Guard post and a Self-defense Corps post, which were capable of dealing with the small guerrilla forces until the 1960 uprising [DT203]. Still, these were only two posts for one of the province's most sizable villages.

In more compact and heavily populated villages such as Nhi Binh, next to Highway 4, there was a "post reduction" program which reduced the six posts of the French period to only two. One was located in the marketplace and the other along Highway 4, each with one squad of militiamen [DT207]. This meant that there was no permanent military presence in most of the hamlets of Nhi Binh. Xuan Son village, which lay in the heart of the province, evidently had a single post manned by a platoon of Self-defense Corps. For the most part, the village was patrolled by unarmed Republican Youth [DT120]. My Long village, at the geographic center of the populated 20/7 zone south of Highway 4, had three posts. "The Self-defense Corps militia at My Yen post was assigned to protect the village council. The Civil Guard was stationed at Long Dien bridge and at the post at [the] former market. Before the Concerted Uprising the troops in these posts often patrolled the whole village. When off duty, they came to villagers' houses for a visit and once in a while ate and drank and had [a] good time together. They did no harm to villagers but nothing to help them. Everybody minded their own business" [DT266]. In nearby Cam Son, the members of the Self-defense Corps who were all natives of the village, constantly patrolled and knew everyone in the hamlets and were familiar with all the local paths [DT286]. During the six years, ten posts and watchtowers were set up along the Ba Rai River, which led from the upper Mekong River through Cai Lay into the Plain of Reeds, making it perhaps the most important internal waterway except for the Cho Gao Canal, which led eventually to Saigon itself.

On the eve of the uprising, the GVN appeared to have the security situation in Dinh Tuong well in hand. The two big Agrovilles along the Nguyen Van Tiep canal, along with strong military posts in Phu My to the east and My An to the west, seemed to present a solid line of defense along the border of the Plain of Reeds. Most villages in the heavily populated areas of the province had strong posts manned by Civil Guard and Self-defense Corps militiamen. Although there were not posts in every hamlet as during the French period, the routine patrols covered the outlying areas. As the next chapter illustrates, it was not a lack of military resources that led the seemingly impregnable GVN position in Dinh Tuong province to collapse almost overnight.

Signs of Unease in the Villages

As the next chapter also shows, there was considerable evidence that by 1959 the revolutionary forces were rebounding from the near-total suppression of the 1957–58 period. Although it would have been difficult to predict this at the time, there are, in retrospect, signs that reveal the extremely unsettled conditions in the countryside of Dinh Tuong underneath the placid exterior of an apparently "pacified province." Some of these indications are not directly political but illustrate the restlessness and anxiety in the rural population that provided the context for the revolutionary upsurge. A few interviews mention in passing such things as the revival of interest in offbeat Buddhist figures such as Dao Dua, the colorful "coconut monk" who, during the subsequent conflict, became an advocate of peace and reconciliation. Dao Dua at this time lived in Ben Tre province across the river from My Tho (he later founded a small community populated largely by youths trying to escape the war on a small island in the Mekong River opposite Dinh Tuong, in a garish Disneyland-style replica of a unified Vietnam on a platform). A villager from Dong Hoa reported that "those who followed Dao Dua often went to Ben Tre to listen to him. In 1959 I went to see him since I had heard rumors that he was really good [*nghe tin don Dao Dua hay*]. I met him personally. In 1959 and 1960 many people went to Ben Tre, and the prophet's house was constantly crowded" [DT193].

Some interviews also noted the appearance of traditional "sorcerers" (*thay phap*) or faith healers, who often proliferated in troubled times. In Tan Ly Dong village there were "plenty of sorcerers in [the] village during the six years. Once every few days noisy sounds of gongs and drums to chase away the evil spirits were heard. Most of the villagers were very superstitious at that time. . . . There were around five sorcerers and about ten witches and countless so-called psychic mediums and fortune tellers. My uncle was a sorcerer and still is. He sold talismans to people which were supposed to protect very young children from the evil spirit and save those possessed by the devil." He added that "when the NLF emerged, sorcerers became unemployed." The man who became the village Party secretary from Tan Ly Dong after the uprising came from a family of sorcerers and had been one himself prior to 1945 [DT233].

Perhaps we should not read to much into this revival of folk religion since it probably involved mainly the more prosperous rural inhabitants. In Xuan Son village, "Mr. Hai Quon built a pagoda in the village and recruited five members all from the village. About 100 members came from other areas. The faithful of this sect all belonged to the rich class. Their pagoda was in Xuan Sac hamlet. Mr. Hai Quon's religious leadership [was] very unusual. No worshiping was done. Every time a woman member came to the pagoda Mr. Quon took her into a private room and committed a sinful act with her. Sometimes Mr. Quon practiced sorcery and made his members babble as though they were in a trance; he shaved his head, but dressed like an ordinary person. He only put on a brown robe when he officiated. I noted that the prayers he recited were from Cao Daiism and Buddhism and that most of the members were wives of GVN officials. The remainder were citizens who belonged to the rich class. No poor people in this sect. The faithful contributed money to the pagoda and each time each of them gave 50,000 piasters or less. This religious sect appeared in 1958 but did not have any members until 1962 and the pagoda was built in that year" [DT257]. These types of behaviors suggest the restlessness and anxiety in My Tho before the uprising, however.

Conclusion

As the pressure built up in My Tho, the Party was preparing to take action to protect itself before the GVN completely destroyed or neutralized the revolutionary forces in the province and to respond to the opportunity presented by popular discontent in the countryside.

The evidence summarized in this chapter suggests that an explosive situation existed even before the armed struggle began, and that the main cause of this was the actions of the Diem government. Certainly, a significant residue of sympathy with the revolution existed throughout the province, which provided a strong base of support for the insurgents, but it was the actions of the Diem government during the six years of peace as much as or more than the legacy of the Viet Minh that fueled the opposition to the GVN. A choice had been made to pursue pacification by coercive and arbitrary means, but without any legal or political restraints on abuse by local officials. The repression continued to escalate in 1959, alienating the population and leaving the GVN dangerously isolated at the height of its apparent triumph.

Tran Huu Danh (Sau Danh) was one of the main leaders of the armed guerrilla unit in My Tho province during the 1959–60 uprising.

A 1961 conference on the "self-defense militia" movement in My Tho.

Le Van Khuyen (Sau Dan) was the commander of the Kien Phong province unit that initiated the first major fighting in the central Mekong Delta at Go Quang Cung, prior to official authorization for this kind of armed struggle. He was later promoted to the Military Region military staff, but called in to take charge of the My Tho province military unit for the 1968 Tet Offensive.

Nguyen Chi Cong (Chin Cong, Chin Om, Chin Du) in a base area. The leader of the Party organization in My Tho from 1962 to 1968, he often appeared as a shadowy figure in interviews with the Party rank and file in the province and few had direct contact with him.

A studio portrait of Nguyen Chi Cong.

Nguyen Van Thanh (Tam Tao), leader of the My Tho province unit in the later years of the "Vietnam War," sums up conference proceedings. Behind him are pictures of the historical pantheon of Marxist-Leninist luminaries.

Photo of the major mass demonstration in My Tho at Chim Chim intersection in Dong Hoa village, January 20, 1961. This was the first direct political confrontation by a large organized group against the GVN authorities in My Tho in the early insurgency and was made possible by the growing military strength of the revolution.

Soldiers of the 514th Battalion, whose First Company also played a key role in the battle of Ap Bac. To emphasize the importance of local guerrilla units, the Party focused the spotlight on this province battalion rather than the better equipped and trained Region 261st Battalion.

Three members of the 514th Battalion who received special commendations for their actions in shooting ARVN paratroopers in this battle.

Nguyen Van Vu (Ba Vu), a leading cadre of Chau Thanh district who played a key role in attacking the GVN enclave of Phu My. He was described by a former subordinate as "a severe looking and quiet man" whom subordinates considered aloof and threateningly powerful. A district cadre described him as "serious, arrogant, and remote," but a good leader and a "resourceful and eloquent speaker" who was "forceful and assertive in everything he said."

A GVN soldier in Phu My circa 1965.

People destroying a Strategic Hamlet in My Tho following the overthrow of President Ngo Dinh Diem in November 1963.

Entrance to the restored "Stone Buddha Pagoda," 1999.

Nguyen Van Tiep canal as it passes the Stone Buddha Pagoda.

Civilian porters carrying ammunition at night.

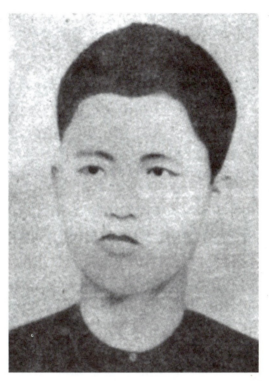

Muoi Quoc, Party leader in Go Cong in the early 1960s who transferred to the military as a political officer and led the 1965 class struggle sessions in the 514th Battalion during a "leftist" phase of the revolution. A soldier who served under him characterized him, "severe and a man of principle. . . . He is a good fighter." Another viewed him as "a competent military leader and cunning man with many ruses who reacted quickly in different situations." Yet another who served with Muoi Quoc said of this enforcer of the hard class line: "I sensed whenever I met him that he comes from the landowner class because he is very well mannered." Although he was not originally a military cadre, he became so skilled in combat that he was promoted to a regimental command position in the months following the 1968 Tet Offensive, but was killed in May 1968.

Muoi Ha, a key military cadre in My Tho province was also entrusted with the political education of the province military forces. He had been a major leader of the 1959–60 insurrection in the province. In "the year of the big change" Ha played an important role in orchestrating the class struggle and denunciation phases of the movement, especially in the May 1965 indoctrination for the 514th Battalion.

7

The Tiger Wakes

Within a year of the near-total suppression of the revolutionary movement in My Tho in 1959, a handful of cadres with rudimentary weapons and a few carefully selected recruits armed with stage-prop wooden guns managed to mobilize the rural population to intimidate and paralyze nearly the entire rural apparatus of the Saigon government in that province —in some villages in a space of a few months. Was this simply a case of providing the spark in an already incendiary situation? The often arbitrary behavior of local officials and militia and the onerous forced labor required of the peasants fueled the resentment of the populace. At the same time, however, there was fear and uncertainty among the peasants, and a reluctance to risk political involvement. How did a small contingent of revolutionaries manage to reverse the situation in such a short time, and what does it tell us about their movement?

Certainly, terror tactics played a key role, as many contemporaneous accounts of "Viet Cong" assassination and intimidation make clear. This does not by itself, however, explain how the several hundred political cadres who had managed to escape the massive arrests of the South Vietnamese Government of the Republic of Vietnam (GVN) or the even smaller number who actually carried weapons were able to turn the tables on their opponents so quickly. The terror was indeed central to the strategy of the revolutionaries, but for reasons quite different from the conventional belief of outside observers at the time, which held that raw coercion was the only way a minority with an unpopular political agenda could impose that agenda on a reluctant and fundamentally apolitical peasantry.

It is true that the peasants were initially reluctant to support the cadres, but the reasons were complex. A significant number of former Viet Minh supporters were still attached to the revolution but were too afraid of the consequences of GVN retribution to act on their sympathies. This situation is illustrated by an interview which describes the inhabitants of one village with a strong revolutionary tradition reluctantly complying when forced by local officials to sound the "wooden fish" alarm when cadres came into the area. The villagers did this "with tears in their eyes because the cadres were their own relatives"[DT145]. In addition to reactivating their traditional supporters from the Resistance, the revolutionaries tapped a rich vein of new support among young people and poor peasants who had been marginal adherents in the past. At the same time, although the brutality of the revolutionary methods used during the Destruction of the Oppression campaign (as the 1959–60 insurrection was called by the revolutionaries) did achieve the goal of matching and exceeding the GVN's intimidation and neutralizing Saigon's previous advantage in coercive power, it also appeared to many rural observers uncomfortably similar to the abuses that had aroused their indignation in the first place.

The uprising was a prolonged campaign that started in early 1960, took a major leap forward in July of that year, and lasted well into 1961. The process was similar in most villages but some villages went through the stages of revolutionary takeover earlier than others. There were also differences in the extent of revolutionary control even after the Destruction of the Oppression campaign was finished. Some villages were completely controlled by the revolution by the end of 1960, some were partially controlled, and some remained firmly in GVN hands. Naturally the situation differed in each case, and the accounts of people's behavior and attitudes reflected this. Many apparently incompatible recollections, reactions, and attitudes coexisted in particular people and communities. The mix of hope and fear, threat and opportunity, tragedy and triumph was different in each case. In the end, however, the year 1960 dramatically reversed the political situation in My Tho and set the stage for a deepening of support and commitment to the revolution that continued to grow for at least several more years.

An example of the contrasting impressions presented in the interview accounts is the evident growing excitement aroused by the spread of the revolution in My Tho, especially among the poor and the young, and the simultaneous backlash of revulsion against the killings that accompanied it. Another is the apparent disjuncture between the descriptions of boiling indignation among ordinary villagers against the Saigon government's local representatives during the six years of peace and the picture of initial great hesitancy of the same villagers to actively support the revolutionaries when they rose up to strike back at these officials.

At first glance, this may suggest a lack of support for the revolution and its objectives in My Tho's countryside or of an apolitical peasantry. Looking deeper into these interview accounts and tracing the subsequent emergence of a period of overwhelming and enthusiastic support for the revolution, it is clear that the initial caution of the peasants was a reflection of the situational logic of their predicament, rather than of their political beliefs or loyalties. In addition, as discussed in the previous chapter, some individuals were willing to accept a higher level of risk than others in acting on beliefs or defending personal interests. The bolder members of the village community were usually to be found among its youth, and it is therefore not surprising that enlisting their support as activists was a key ingredient in expanding the uprising to the point that the hesitant majority were willing to become fully engaged in the revolutionary movement. This chapter is about how the revolutionaries broke through the barriers to activating the rural population by a complex combination of appeals, incentives, psychological manipulation, group pressure, threats, and terror.

Resolution 15 and the "Destruction of Oppression"

During the six years of peace the cadres in My Tho had learned that only the most committed revolutionary sympathizers would risk revealing (let alone acting on) their political beliefs or harboring a cadre. Since, in the cadres' view, this attitude resulted entirely from the effectiveness of GVN repression, the obvious solution was to change the "balance of fear" in favor of the revolution—to make the rural population more frightened of defying the revolutionaries than it was of the Saigon authorities. The biggest impediment to this approach, however, was Hanoi's ban on armed struggle. After failing in their attempt to block the spread of GVN control to the countryside by political means during the first years following the Geneva Agreements of 1954, the local cadres came to realize that another approach was needed, but it took them several years to convince their superiors.

On the eve of the insurgency, the Party's ranks had been seriously depleted in My Tho. As of January 1960 there were only nine Party chapters in the entire province—seven in Chau Thanh district, one in Cai Be, and one in Cho Gao district. Among the villages of My Tho, thirty-one had no "backbone" or activist supporters (*nong cot*), and there were only ninety-two Party members at the "basic level" (*co so*). At the district and province levels there were just over 200 Party members, while about 500 cadres and Party members had returned from hiding outside the province. There were estimated to be around 500 activist supporters in the entire province.[1] While this may not be a complete inventory of the resources available to the revolution, it does show that this was hardly a powerful "organizational machine" at the outset of the uprising.

The Central Committee in North Vietnam finally authorized armed struggle on a major scale in January 1959 in the now-famous Resolution 15. Even then, it authorized armed struggle only for self-defense and with the proviso that it be clearly subordinated to political struggle. Resolution 15 was not communicated to places like My Tho until the middle of the year, and the details of the decision probably changed substantially before the end of 1959.[2] "In May 1959 the summary of the main content of the resolution was sent by radio to each battlefield, but it was not until November 1959 that the Xu Uy Fourth Plenum and the December 1959 Plenum of the Central Nam Bo Inter-Province Party Committee (Region 8), which met in Hong Ngu [Kien Phong province], that the resolution was presented in an organized [and] systematic way."[3] Apparent confusion over exactly how to strike a balance between armed and political struggle, and whether Resolution 15 constituted a "green light" for an all-out campaign to topple the Saigon government delayed formulation of a plan of attack until the end of 1959. In My Tho, the Concerted Uprising did not take place until mid-1960.

The insurrection was termed by the cadres the Destruction of the Oppression (*pha the kem kep*), of which the Concerted Uprising campaign (*chien dich dong khoi*) was one phase. The term was initially coined to describe the events of early 1960 in Ben Tre. "The term Concerted Uprising [dong khoi] appeared after three months of uprising of the masses in Ben Tre, and was the result of the contraction of two phrases '*dong loat khoi nghia*' [simultaneously rising up in insurrection]. After this, the Region started to use the term 'Concerted Uprising in Ben Tre' [Dong Khoi Ben Tre] in its correspondence."[3] The first broadly coordinated effort came September–October 1960, when the provinces of the entire central delta region were ordered by the Party Central Committee Office of South Vietnam (COSVN) to launch a simultaneous campaign of uprisings. This is referred to by the My Tho historians as the second phase of the Concerted Uprising.

The Origins of Armed Struggle

Some areas of Nam Bo apparently retained military units after 1954, both in the villages (under various pretexts such as antithievery "neighborhood watch" groups) and in some provinces of the lower Mekong Delta (which were said to have company- and even battalion-sized units).[4] At the beginning of the six years of peace, the Region leadership and the

My Tho and Go Cong Province Party Committees had planted some cadres in the Hoa Hao and Cao Dai armed units and had organized other units under the label of these dissident sects. Ba Chim (the "birdman") recalls that in mid-1955, Sau Duong, Party Secretary of the secret Party organization for the central Mekong Delta after the Geneva Agreements, had the idea of winning over the sect forces in the Plain of Reeds to help protect the area from the Diem army. Ba Chim explained: "We put a number of our cadres into the sect forces, and organized a number of armed cells operating in the name of the religious sects in order to eliminate a number of tyrants and reduce the oppression of the enemy. . . . In a way it was like both attacking the enemy and having a place to stay with rice to eat, and there would be a base of armed forces when the religious sects fell apart." Ba Chim himself disagreed with this policy and did not pursue it in My Tho, but the Region leadership went ahead with it.[5] My Tho seems to have organized its own revolutionary units disguised as religious sect units rather than trying to infiltrate exisiting military bands under sect command. In Go Cong, a forty-four-man unit was formed under the guise of a Binh Xuyen company (see below). Thanh Hai, the landlord's son, who was later instrumental in setting up the province military unit after the authorized launching of armed struggle, was a deputy commander of this unit. In My Tho, a forty-person unit disguised as a Hoa Hao formation was set up in Cai Be, operating in the Hoi Cu and Hau My areas. Sau Danh, the key military leader of the coming uprising in My Tho, organized a thirty-person unit operating as dissident Cao Dai in an area that became an important base for My Tho province in Hung Thanh near Phu My.[6]

Official Party policy was to stress strict compliance with the Geneva Accords and restrict revolutionary activities to political agitation. Sau Duong described this period to Tam Phuong, the new military commander of the Region, who returned from regroupment in the North in 1961: "Those of us in the leadership were in an extremely difficult position: if we carried out the orders from above forbidding armed activity, the people, cadres, and Party members would suffer, and if we allowed armed activity we would be disciplined by the Party."[7] Political assassination was a gray area between permissible "political struggle" and forbidden "military struggle." As the election deadline for North–South reunification approached it became clear that the Party's faith in the implementation of the political aspects of the Geneva Accords had been misplaced. In August 1956, Le Duan, the top Party leader in the South, spelled out the Party's aim of overthrowing the Diem government, but not yet by military means.

This was the grudging start of a process of gradual evolution toward the authorization of armed struggle in the South. Le Duan received this resolution by the Politburo in Hanoi while in Ca Mau, at the extreme southern tip of Vietnam. Although one Party history records him as "receiving the directive with pleasure," it appears from his subsequent actions that his enthusiasm for the restrictive Hanoi policy line on armed struggle was restrained. He traveled along secret liaison routes through the delta back to Saigon in order to "understand and grasp the situation better." When he arrived in Ben Tre province just south of My Tho, he met with the Ben Tre province Party secretary, and fended off an apparent demand to move directly to military action against the Diem government. Le Duan agreed that the Geneva Agreements would not be carried out and that the Diem government would have to be overthrown by force, yet he concluded that even Ben Tre, with its strong revolutionary tradition, was not yet ready to do this. In contrast to the hotheaded demand for immediate armed action in Ben Tre, Le Duan found that the approach in My Tho was more to his liking. My Tho had sent its cadres to report to the GVN authorities and "legalize" themselves by admitting their past revolutionary affiliation and registering as citizens of the GVN. After that they were to mingle unobtrusively with the people, operate clandestinely, and avoid suffering losses. Duan said approvingly, "This is the way to do it. Go ahead and do whatever is of benefit to the people and the revolution . . . only in this way can the people survive."[8] This policy was, however, soon repudiated by the Region Party authorities.

By December 1956 a more proactive approach was reflected in the following Xu Uy conclusion: "To a certain extent it is necessary to have self-defense and armed propaganda forces in order to support the political struggle and eventually use those armed forces to carry out a revolution to overthrow U.S.–Diem. . . . The path of advance in the revolution in the South is to use a violent general uprising to win political power."[9] Le Duan was evidently under pressure from below to be more aggressive but had still received no reaction from Hanoi concerning his call for a more active policy in the "Path of Revolution in the South." The Xu Uy "considered" a plan for "armed propaganda" drawn up by Sau Duong, who was the head of the Region 2 Party Committee (called Region 8 during the Resistance and briefly called the Interprovince Party Committee after 1954)—the echelon between My Tho and the Xu Uy.[10] This plan apparently attempted to define a more prominent role for armed struggle.[11] The Xu Uy still did not receive the go-ahead for an armed insurgency. The Xu Uy viewed armed struggle primarily as a means of self-defense, and still placed strict limitations on even this type of armed activity. Though the Xu Uy "had a policy" as of December 1956 of building up its armed forces, "as of 1957 the higher levels still prohibited armed struggle (to say nothing of some places where those who eliminated cruel and wicked tyrants were called up for criticism and sometimes were disciplined)." There were cases of cadres with weapons in hand being chased, but not daring to shoot at their pursuers. In some villages it took only a few GVN Self-defense Corps militiamen to control the area.[12]

In the remote Plain of Reeds environment, there was some sympathy among Region and province leadership toward the plight of these cadres and a tendency to turn a blind eye to violations of higher-level policy, as in the case of the Region Secretary Sau Duong, whose earlier efforts to persuade Le Duan to adopt a bolder policy on armed struggle had met with limited success. "Because of the urgent requirements of the local area, where you had to engage in combat to survive, even though the higher levels prohibited armed activities, the comrade Secretary of the Inter-Province [Sau Duong] didn't stop it even though he knew that the local areas were continuing to conduct military activities."[13]

But by 1957 the Xu Uy began to realize that their own caution on armed struggle was magnified at the lower levels. Some local cadres were so afraid of violating the Party's strictures on armed struggle that they "didn't dare use weapons in any circumstance whatever," though other lower-level cadres were hot headed and ignored Party restraints.[14] The central delta's Region command had started to organize self-defense militia in the villages, part of whose function was to obtain weapons for local armed forces "acting in the name of the religious sects." Le Duan referred specifically to this experience of the central delta Region, which had been designated Region 8 of the nine regions in the entire country of Vietnam during the Resistance and was now Region 2—the middle of the three Nam Bo military regions—as he moved toward his adjustment of the policy on armed struggle in 1956.

"In general," said Viet Thang, "from the [1954] Agreement until 1957 there were only scattered on the spot struggles."[15] At the beginning of 1957, in the face of a sharp decline in the revolutionary movement, My Tho and Go Cong were once again combined into a single province. Viet Thang became the province Party secretary, and Ba Chim went to the Region. Because of the expanding GVN security operations, it was no longer safe for the My Tho province Party committee to stay in Long Hung village despite the strong sympathy of the villagers. In April 1957, the committee moved to Hoi Cu village in Cai Be, which was closer to the Plain of Reeds, though some of its hamlets bordered Highway 4. After six months in Hoi Cu, the leader of the "armed squad of the province" defected to the GVN. Since he knew all the hideouts of the province cadres, this created a continuing problem. Viet Thang took refuge in the Plain of Reeds.[16] Viet Thang says that this experience in the Plain of Reeds and his observations of a "number of armed cells" in there made him "pay more attention to the matter of arms."[17]

My Tho Changes Direction

In its darkest hour, the province committee was finally able to arrange a meeting in May 1958 and called back some of its scattered cadres. This May 1958 province committee meeting must have been the signal that the time for renewed action had come. Cadres from the three western districts all traveled clandestinely along guerrilla-controlled routes, but those in the eastern districts had to take their chances going through GVN-controlled areas in disguise. This seminal meeting was presided over by Viet Thang. The next two future province secretaries, Chin Om and Chin Hai, were also there, as were the cadres who were to lead the guerrilla forces, Muoi Ha and Sau Danh. The meeting lasted for fifteen days. In addition to criticizing Ba Chim's 1956 decision to let some Party members "report" to the GVN, Sau Danh's assassination of district chief Nguyen Trung Long was repudiated as the Party tried to lay out a middle course between rashness and inaction. The meeting participants decided that "killing cruel and wicked tyrants is correct and necessary, but using armed force alone as in the killing of district chief Long and other such incidents should not be done and doesn't serve the movement." Killings should be combined with mass political struggles, they concluded, and should be resorted to only if it helped the people "throw off the yoke of oppression."[18]

According the memoirs of the My Tho leaders active at the time, in the aftermath of the May 1958 My Tho province Party committee meeting along the Kien Phong border to the west, the province committee began to expand the base at Tan Hoa Dong on the more exposed eastern fringe of the Plain of Reeds, which would be closer to the hard-to-reach eastern districts and the center of the province. The key members of the province committee, however, stayed along the Kinh Bui Canal in the western Plain of Reeds, the site of the great military victory of 1953. At the beginning of 1959 the province headquarters was again moved, this time to Kinh 3 (Canal 3), a secondary canal near the "wagon wheel" in northern Cai Be, and somewhat closer to the populated areas. Operations among the people would now be carried out by clandestine cadres, who were "illegal" in the eyes of the GVN and at risk of arrest at any moment.

Protecting the Province Base in 1959

The province committee had thus began to see that it could not simply flee to a distant base and hope to avoid detection but would have to move closer to the population if it wanted to operate politically among it, and being in this more exposed position would require an armed force to protect it. The decision to move to armed struggle did not come until the beginning of 1959, and even then there was confusion about how far it could be taken. As in 1945, the armed forces in My Tho were built up from a modest nucleus. A unit designated the "514th Unit" was established in 1958, fell apart, and was reformed and redesignated the "514th Battalion" in 1959. This and similar "battalions" formed in other provinces of the central Mekong Delta were actually composed of only one or two understrength companies. Their mission was to "defend their territory, conduct armed propaganda, build up political forces, set up secret armed forces, organize penetration agents in the enemy's ranks, intimidate the village officials, spies, and cruel tyrants, support the peasants in their struggle to hold on to their land, and help the people become masters of their hamlets and villages."[19]

In order to defend the new base, the Party organized the C211 Protection Company, composed of three squads, and started to recruit to strengthen this unit. In March 1959, one eighteen-year-old from a village close to the Tan Hoa Dong base decided to join. "In my hamlet lived a man to whom I paid particular respect," he said. "He was a former militant in the Resistance. I trusted him and liked to listen to him. I got excited whenever he told me about the youths' duty and about Vietnamese heroes. He told me that Ngo Dinh Diem had asked the Americans to come to Vietnam and help in their plot to put the country under their rule. He urged me to join the Front to perform the duty of a young patriot in fighting for the independence of the country to bring back happiness and prosperity to my compatriots. He led me to envision a brilliant future for myself if I followed his advice" [DT22].

This account touches on themes that arise frequently in interviews with these early recruits. Patriotic fervor was intensified by linking the unpopular Diem government to a foreign power. Idealism and hope for the future was mixed with personal interest in following a rewarding political career. This young recruit was among 100 who attended a three-month training session in Tan Hoa Dong village. Although he became homesick and depressed, and fifteen other recruits deserted the course, he stuck it out and was assigned to the C211 protection unit. "At that time I only saw the glory and didn't think of the hardships," he said. "I knew it would be dangerous but I was not afraid because the youth should sacrifice." This platoon had been set up "long before I joined it." There were three squads in the unit. Its job was to protect the base and arrest all strangers in the area [DT22].

Hanoi Gives Qualified Approval to Armed Struggle in South Vietnam

With the largely spontaneous move toward armed struggle gaining a momentum that threatened a crisis in relations between the impatient southern revolutionaries and the cautious leadership in North Vietnam, the Party finally confronted the issue in early 1959. At the Fifteenth Plenum of the Central Committee in January 1959, the decision was made to proceed with armed insurrection. Hopes of a political and diplomatic settlement were gone. For the first time, the Party spoke directly about the imminent prospect of the overthrow of the Diem regime by force, its replacement by a revolutionary regime, and unification outside the framework of the Geneva Agreements. The goal was "liberating the South from the oppressive yoke of the imperialists and feudalists to bring about independence and a national people's democracy." The means to be employed were "primarily . . . the strength of the masses, coordinated with the armed forces either a little or a lot, to overthrow the ruling power of the imperialists and feudalists and establish a revolutionary government of the people."[20] Some confusion still exists about the evolution of the decision on armed struggle in 1959. The foundation of the major policy shift was clearly the January 1959 Resolution 15 decision taken at an "expanded" plenary meeting of the Central Committee. A Resolution 15 of May 1959 is also frequently referred to, puzzling not only outside observers but some Party historians as well. Even after the May reformulation of Resolution 15, the exact role of armed struggle remained an object of controversy into 1960.

For the beleaguered revolutionaries in My Tho, however, Hanoi's Resolution 15 was eagerly interpreted as giving a "green light" to move from evasion and hiding from the Diem regime to armed struggle against it. According to Viet Thang, who was the Party leader in My Tho at the time, "On receiving the summary and new guidance I and the other brothers in the Standing Committee were very fired up, because for a long time we had wanted to use arms but it was not yet approved, and from the beginning of 1959 to this time [beginning of 1960] the Province Committee relied completely on our own armed force [i.e., the C211 company] on the spot at the province base, and the armed posture of Kien Phong and Kien Tuong which had solidified at that time. The main content of Resolution 15 was allowing armed activities." Viet Thang noted that the resolution referred to "armed propaganda activities," which was more restrictive than "allowing armed activities."[21] Viet Thang made it clear that in My Tho the more expansive interpretation was preferred.

Unauthorized Military Activities in 1959

By the summer and fall of 1959, province battalions in Kien Tuong (the Plain of Reeds) and the D502 Battalion of Kien Phong to the west of My Tho were "rather strong" and resisting ARVN sweep operations, harassing the Agrovilles, and conducting ambushes. Perhaps the first large-scale battle in the central Mekong Delta took place between the D502 province battalion of Kien Phong and an ARVN battalion stationed in the area in late September 1959, in which the revolutionary side claimed to have killed 100 ARVN and captured another 100.[22] This battle was for many years ignored by revolutionary historians because it was a major violation of Party policy at the time. An extensive account of this episode appeared only in 1991 in the memoir of Le Quoc San, who returned from regroupment to North Vietnam in 1961 to become the military commander in charge of the central Mekong Delta area for most of the "Vietnam War" period.[23] Even allowing for the customary inflated claims of revolutionary propaganda and historiography, this does appear to have been a military encounter on a large scale, and different from the small unit incursions into remote villages during the previous period. While the figures may be inflated, clearly the level of military conflict was escalating. The later claim that by 1959 there were 130 concentrated armed platoons operating in the base areas and "hundreds" of "secret action cells" (*to doi hanh dong*) operating in the Mekong Delta may also be a retroactive inflation of the reality, but the trend is clear.[24]

Insurrection Spreads and Fighting Escalates

Sketchy reports of fighting in the Plain of Reeds reached Hanoi by way of the BBC. Tran Van Tra was relaxing on a hot summer evening in 1959, seated outside to catch a breeze from the Red River in the sweltering heat of Hanoi and trying to tune in some light music on his small radio, when his dial came across a BBC announcement of a platoon-sized engagement on the fringe of the Plain of Reeds. The BBC reported that after two hours of fighting, both sides withdrew without casualties. Tra's military experience led him to ask how two sides could fight for two hours without inflicting any damage. He felt that this indicated a need for real military training of the insurgent forces if they were going to be involved in combat. The fact that even small-scale fighting was going on in the South gave him a pretext to request that a small military training group consisting of 100 regrouped Southerners return to the South. Tra presented his idea to Le Duan, now in Hanoi and holding the position of acting secretary general of the entire Party, who told him a group that large could not be approved without a Politburo decision. However, Duan was drawn to the idea. "Can you make do with fewer?" he asked Tra. "Maybe fifty," replied Tra. "I haven't yet reported this matter to the Politburo," said Le Duan, "and if I did they might not approve it. If it is only a small number, I could approve it and take personal responsibility, and then report it to the Politburo. O.K., let's settle for twenty-five."[25] This was the beginning of the return of the Southern forces that had gone North in 1954 and ultimately of the direct military assistance of the North to the South.

The date of the major battle in Kien Phong (known as the battle of Go Quan Cung) is significant because Kien Phong did not receive Resolution 15 from the Region until October 1959 at the earliest, and possibly not even at that time.[26] The battle started on September 25, 1959.[27] This means that Kien Phong province went ahead with this major military escalation without clearance from higher levels. Thus, Kien Phong, and not the more famous Ben Tre province, led the movement toward armed struggle in the Mekong Delta.

My Tho Takes the Offensive

Like Kien Phong, My Tho province seems to have jumped the gun on military activity. In December 1959, before receiving the Region decision on armed struggle, a handful of cadres orchestrated a daring attack against a post on the edge of the province base area in the Indigo Jungle (Rung Cham). Perhaps because action had not yet been authorized by the Party, the My Tho province Party history does not mention this attack. Three Chau Thanh district cadres were at the center of this operation: Ba Thanh (the district Party secretary), Tu Binh (who remained a key district cadre through most of the subsequent period), and Quoc Hong (who played a prominent role in the northeastern villages of Chau Thanh district throughout the conflict). They joined forces with the leading revolutionary military commander in the province, Sau Danh, whose platoon was the predecessor of the 514th Battalion. This attack on a post was one of the earliest military actions of this era in the province, and it pointed the way to the subsequent escalation of military activities in mid- and late 1960. The target was presumably chosen because it was accessible from the province base, which afforded a safe haven upon withdrawal. Putting the Saigon forces on the defensive in the area around the province base would both protect the base and lay the foundation for expanding action into the rest of the province.

In this December 1959 attack, Sau Danh's platoon, known as the Provincial Armed Unit, stopped a bus on the road leading from Highway 4 into the GVN stronghold of Phu My village at 0400 hours.

> They ordered all the passengers to get off the bus, and took their seats. Then they forced the driver to drive on and stop right in front of the Tan Ly Dong post. It was then dawn, and the gate of the post had been opened for the soldiers' dependents to go to market. When the bus stopped, the Viet Cong immediately got off and rushed into the post. The Self-defense Corps soldiers were caught by complete surprise. A number of them surrendered. Some of them were killed on the spot, including police officer Thong. The civilian laborers who had been gathered by the Viet Cong at a place nearby were also directed to enter the post to collect war booty. The post was then completely destroyed. A number of village councilmen were also captured, including the village chief, the chairman, and Mr. Ca Chat. After the attack, the aggressors retreated to the Tan Hoa Dong jungle. They then killed Mr. Ca Chat and released the other two. . . . After this attack the ARVN troops launched several operations to search for the Viet Cong, but without success [DT233].

In early 1960 the ARVN received intelligence about the location of the province unit and launched a regiment operation to encircle it in its Indigo Jungle base. The province unit had just returned from operations in Xuan Son and Cam Son villages in the center of what became the 20/7 zone and had not had a chance to regroup when they were forced to engage the ARVN operation. What followed was a harbinger of things to come: the inability or unwillingness of the GVN forces to close with their enemy, which drove generations of American advisors to distraction. According to one interviewee:

> The ARVN troops completely encircled the VC, and gradually tightened their cordon. But the tactical coordination of the ARVN troops was a complete failure. While an ARVN element was engaged in a fierce fight with the VCs, another element was directed to reinforce the first one. But when the soldiers of the second unit approached the area, they mistook the friendly troops for enemy troops, due to the dense bushes and trees that hampered visibility, and opened fire on them. One of the ARVN units was so beaten up by friendly firepower that it had to withdraw toward the river, where it was attacked by friendly gunboats. The fighting went on for three hours between the ARVN units and between the ARVN and the VCs. While the melee was going on, a squad of the VC platoon had been put out of action. The three VC automatic rifles ran out of ammunition and their rifle ammunition also ran low, down to five rounds for each weapon. The VC had to throw away their empty weapons and started wrestling with the ARVN soldiers to take their weapons. The VC were equipped with outdated MAS-36 rifles and they were only too glad to steal the ARVN's better weapons, such as carbines, Garands, and Thompsons. Unable to sustain the fight any longer, they had to "open a path of blood" to retreat, leaving the ARVN troops behind to fight each other in the ensuing confusion. When they realized their mistake, it was already too late, as they had suffered about 300 casualties [DT233].

Despite the initial success of the Ben Tre uprising in January 1960, the Xu Uy expressed concern that the revolution was being put on the defensive by large ARVN military operations into its base areas, and that the people were being forced to choose between surrender and death. At the same time, the Xu Uy may also have been impressed by the results of the military operations in Kien Phong and My Tho. On January 21, 1960, the Xu Uy upgraded the strategic priority to be given to military action: "Political struggle coordinated with armed propaganda is no longer enough to protect the revolutionary bases, and the masses have used armed struggle to resist the violent and barbarous actions of the enemy." The Xu Uy recommended to the center (e.g., Hanoi) that the strategic slogan in Nam Bo be changed to "Political struggle and armed struggle coordinated in tandem, both playing the key and decisive role in the movement."[28]

Now the military arm of the revolution had reached parity with the political arm, although it would take another year for Hanoi to formally acknowledge this. While this report was only a proposal to Hanoi, events were in the saddle, pushing both the southern leadership and Hanoi along. Because this proposal was made only a few days after the Ben Tre uprising, the southern leadership, who were located at some distance from Ben Tre and the delta, may not have realized the potential of lower-level guerrilla war to counter military pressure from Saigon. Or they may have felt that these initial successes could not be sustained unless supported by a higher level of military support. In either case, the immediate concern of the Xu Uy was the security of the rear base areas, not the villages on the front line of the uprising.

Ironically, the implications of the extraordinary success of the political action in the Concerted Uprising of early 1960 do not seem to have been immediately recognized by the southern Party leadership in the Xu Uy, soon to be renamed COSVN or the Central Office for South Vietnam. Their concern was with getting the insurrection going, and they evidently felt that this would require a higher level of military support than was actually needed at this early stage. Angered by Hanoi's stress on political action and flushed with victory, the Xu Uy may have been so preoccupied with getting Hanoi to authorize a major military buildup and offensive military action that it did not at first realize the military potential of the political forces that had been unleashed. Perhaps the lessons of the post-1950 period of the Resistance had fixated them on the absolute necessity of major military support for the political movement. It may be significant that what Sau Duong, the Party leader in the central Mekong Delta, singled out for study in 1961 was not the experience of political struggle combined with guerrilla war in Ben Tre, but the military tactics in the battle of Go Quan Cung.

Yet, as the many interview accounts of the Concerted Uprising show, the political aspects of the revolution far outweighed the impact of the still-understrength military units throughout the entire year of 1960, which culminated in the formation of the National Liberation Front (NLF) in December. The role of military units was limited to squads or platoons supporting mass political actions in the villages. Deception and psychological warfare compensated for the military weakness to give an impression of a greater military force than actually existed. Examining the way in which the Saigon control structure of military posts in the rural villages of the Mekong Delta was neutralized is a good way to understand the complex interplay between military and political action, and the process through which the military arm of the revolution evolved from small local groups of guerrillas to concentrated military units capable of taking on Saigon's regular army troops.

Preparing for the Uprising

When My Tho received the news of the decisions taken at the December 1959 meeting at Region 2, it first tried to strengthen the Party machinery at the province and district levels and called back the remainder of the dispersed *dieu lang* (in hiding) cadres. From January 21 to 23, 1960, the province Party committee met to determine how Resolution 15 as filtered through the Xu Uy and Region would be implemented. Chin Om recalls that "the January weather out in the desolate rice fields was cold, but sitting beside the flickering flames of a fire with our hearts burning with emotion, we did not feel the chill."[29] Ba Chim was now deputy Party secretary of Region 2, and he presided over this gathering. Sau Danh was not yet a province Party committee member, but he was called to the meeting because "he was the one in charge of the armed forces and had a lot of experience in the use of armed force, which was the main subject of the meeting."[30] Viet Thang explains the focus of the meeting: "The conference didn't much discuss the contents of the Resolution. [Resolution 15]. The comrades focused only on its general spirit, that is, giving permission for armed struggle. The only thing left to do was discuss a plan of action and ways of carrying it out."[31]

After an extended discussion the province leaders decided to concentrate on eliminating the GVN control structure at the hamlet level, and how to determine who would be "punished" (killed) and who would merely be publicly warned and ordered to resign or leave their village.[32] The specific actions called for by the province leadership were armed propaganda, intimidating shows of force, killing "tyrants," mobilizing the people to destroy watchtowers and break up the GVN hamlet control system of interfamily groups and hamlet chief, tearing down the black and white house signboards, tearing up GVN flags and pictures of Ngo Dinh Diem, and resolving "the land question wherever they went."[33] One nagging question which the meeting did not resolve was how to involve the people in political struggle against the local authorities without compromising their status and exposing them to retribution by the GVN. "Once they were involved in illegal activities," mused Viet Thang, "how could they stay legal? No one clarified this matter." Over the course of time, the revolutionaries tried to address the dilemma of the people caught between the two sides by formulating demands that "the enemy could not argue with," such as criticizing specific abuses but not openly contesting the authority and legitimacy of the GVN.[34]

The interviews suggest a somewhat different picture, however. Many witnesses of the Destruction of the Oppression conclude that there was a deliberate policy of implicating the villagers in illegal activities to force them to cast their lot with the revolution. Viet Thang was most concerned about protecting the identities of those already committed to the revolution so that they could operate under legal cover, while those not yet committed could be forced to embark on a revolutionary path by making them illegal with regard to the GVN. A poor peasant from Thanh Phu (Cai Lay) said that the village cadres "collected money from each family two or three times, deliberately making them illegal" [DT203]. A military cadre recalled that his revolutionary career started in 1960 when the village guerrillas tore up his ID card [DT70]. The aspect of this issue that apparently perplexed Viet Thang was the question underlying the matter of illegal activities—that is, how to gain the commitment of ordinary villagers to the revolution at a time when they lived under mixed control and were still subject to GVN retaliation.

Now that the revolution was expanding to a larger scale of activities, the question of finances arose. The uprising plan would cost around 200,000 piasters for its initial phase, with about half of that going to the armed force. Every district would require about 20,000 to 30,000 piasters. Chin Hai, who was province Party secretary in My Tho from 1968 until nearly the end of the war, promised to raise enough money for the province platoon. Cai Be and Cai Lay districts said they would raise their share of the money on their own. The total sum of money the revolutionaries expected to raise was a pittance compared to the resources of the GVN in Dinh Tuong. When Nguyen Tran arrived in the province in 1956, he had a budget of 124 million piasters.[35] About half of this was for the salaries of the province Civil Guard and Self-defense Corps.[36] During the entire year of 1958, the My Tho revolutionaries had collected 20,000 piasters, and only 10,000 in 1959. During the first six months of 1960 they would collect 800,000 piasters, but at the beginning of the year this fund drive was just getting under way.[37] Some agents had discovered that a Saigon payroll truck carrying around 40 million piasters would soon be coming through My Tho, so the leadership delayed the initial uprising to seize this tempting target of opportunity. An ambush was set up for the day before the scheduled province uprising, but the truck passed through the ambush site before the province forces could react. "Because we had this idea of attacking the payroll truck," wrote Viet Thang, "our uprising was later than [in Ben Tre], and we didn't consider the matter of surrounding posts and forcing them to surrender."[38]

The My Tho revolutionary forces available to accomplish these tasks were still minuscule in relation to the task that confronted them. As noted earlier, the province had a total of ninety-two "open" (illegal) cadres operating among the people. Chau Thanh district had only seven Party chapters, and Cai Lay and Cho Gao only one each. In eighteen villages without Party chapters, there were only one or two Party members. The remainder of My Tho's 125 villages apparently had no Party presence at all. In addition, however, over 200 cadres were operating underground and 500 *dieu lang* cadres could be called back from hiding. The province armed forces consisted of a platoon, which was now grandly designated the 514th Battalion, with thirty-three cadres and soldiers. A platoon from Kien Tuong province was sent to My Tho to reinforce the 514th Battalion. Cai Be, Cai Lay, and Chau Thanh districts each had an armed propaganda squad. In Cho Gao, the provisional Party organization had to double as the armed propaganda unit.[39]

On February 24, 1960, a month after Ben Tre had initiated its uprising, My Tho launched its own movement. Long An village was the main target, with the villages along the Nguyen Van Tiep Canal receiving the next highest priority.[40] In this pre–National Liberation Front period no effort was made to hide the Party's leadership of this insurrection or its connections with North Vietnam, and the revolutionaries shouted, "Long live the Lao Dong Party of Vietnam!" For purposes of military secrecy the 514th Battalion did not openly use its unit designation but simply called itself the "Liberation Army," and it also used this term on the seals stamped on official warnings issued to the local authorities.[41] In preparation for the uprising, the province headquarters was transferred to a forward base in Tan Hoa Dong village. Viet Thang observes that this move to a more exposed location "meant that we had to fight and there would be no more relying on legality and secrecy and other people like before."[42]

Uprising in My Tho

The My Tho uprising proceeded in two stages. The first stage was the relatively small-scale series of operations launched in late February 1960, which prepared the way for a second, much larger movement initiated on the anniversary of the Geneva Accords, July 20, 1960. In retrospect, the province leadership was not satisfied with its activities in the first phase. "The province Committee really bungled the uprising of the people with respect to coordinating armed and political action to eliminate the tyrants and destroy the oppression to gain control of the countryside," was Viet Thang's assessment. The main problem, according to a subsequent critique from the Region, was that the province had not been ruthless enough in eliminating its enemies. The plan for the first phase of operations centered on the villages bordering the Nguyen Van Tiep Canal. There were a few armed penetrations and "eliminations of spies" in the villages along Highway 4, but mostly this was done by the province force, which returned to its base in Tan Hoa Dong without triggering an uprising among the people. Seven posts were taken by small armed forces in coordination with penetration agents inside the posts. Thanks to the much stronger armed activities in Kien Tuong and Kien Phong, the GVN militias stationed along the Nguyen Van Tiep Canal began to "shrink back" (*co lai*) into their posts, and cadres who had previously operated only at night could start operating in the neighboring villages by late afternoon.[43]

Not surprisingly, the insurgents struck first at the weakest link in this control system, the rural youth militia, and in the most remote areas. Since many villages had only one or two posts, most hamlets relied on the unarmed youth, who were easy targets for kidnapping and intimidation. Saigon's control structure began to erode in the hamlets, which were distant from the village centers and the SDC (*Dan Ve* or Self-defense Militia Corps militia) posts. The Rural Defense Youth were intimidated by the sporadic presence of a few armed cadres, and the interfamily chiefs were neutralized by the threat of arrest or assassination. This outer fringe of the GVN control system was rendered ineffective by lack of support from the village officials and the SDC.

Even in areas close to Highway 4 there was significant revolutionary agitation, much of it directed against these weak links—the unpaid and unarmed youth militia and officials in the distant hamlets. In Ap Thoi hamlet (Diem Hy village), a young man who had been a member of the Rural Defense Youth since 1957 recounted how he had been apprehended by a group of guerrillas in January 1960 while returning to his hamlet from the village office. He was blindfolded and led before a crowd of villagers. "When they took off my blindfold I saw everyone from my hamlet already seated in front of me. The guerrillas took me to the center of the crowd and forced me to kneel. Hai Xinh, who was the village Party secretary, read an indictment. I was accused of having worked for the village council against the revolution and sentenced to death by the Front. But Hai Xinh said I would be reprieved if someone would agree to guarantee that I would give up working for the GVN. My wife's relatives stood up to guarantee that I would follow the right path and promised that they would be responsible for my behavior." The following day, the penitent youth was made to visit every resident of the hamlet with offerings of rice wine to apologize for his "crimes." The people in the hamlet were sympathetic and consoled the distraught youth. He said, "I wanted to die rather than to live with the shame. Therefore, a few days later I escaped from the hamlet and went to the village council. I asked them to grant me a salary in order to help me live outside my hamlet. They refused to give me a salary because they didn't have a budget for it, so I had to return to my hamlet" [DT151].

This "reduction of prestige" (*ha uy the*) became one of the most potent social and psychological weapons against the lower levels of the GVN administration. It combined public humiliation with the chance to redeem the "crime" of supporting the GVN by quitting. The authority of any GVN representative who had undergone this public humiliation was fatally compromised, most of all in the mind of the unfortunate victim of this shaming. Perhaps the most subtle and effective aspect of this procedure was that it tied the hamlet community to the goals of the revolution by implicating them in the impromptu "trials." Faced with the choice of condemning a fellow villager to death or taking collective responsibility for leading him down the "right path," neighbors and relatives found themselves maneuvered into the position of guarantors responsible for ensuring that the accused individual did not return to working for the GVN. This put the guarantors on the side of the revolution in silent collusion against the GVN and was an important first step in making the villagers "illegal" with respect to the Saigon government: by "burning their bridges" with the authorities, they were forced into siding with the revolution. In the Ap Thoi case, the young man appears to have been willing to let his wife's relatives suffer the consequences of his continuing to work for the village office. But even if the village had been able to pay him, he would no longer have been able to live in his own hamlet, thus negating his usefulness to the GVN. Not surprisingly, a month later he joined an existing group of twelve guerrillas, armed with a single grenade that had been dropped by the local Self-defense Corps [DT151].

Even before My Tho officially launched its uprising, the tactics that later proved so successful were being employed not only close to the Plain of Reeds but also in villages along the main highway. Cadres were operating in Phu Nhuan Dong village, only 5 kilometers from the district town of Cai Lay and bordering on a crucial stretch of Highway 4 that later became one of the main crossing points for revolutionary units and cadres. "The Front began to operate in my village in 1959," said a native of that village who had a brother working as an interfamily chief of Phu Loi hamlet and another in the Republican Youth. "At that time a military outpost with SDC was controlling the area. The first concern of the Front was to overrun it, which it did—some SDC were killed and the remainder fled. I don't know much about this attack since it happened while I was asleep. When I woke up the battle was over and the attackers were waging propaganda. In 1959 the [National Liberation] Front had not yet come into being and the attackers claimed they were fighters in the Liberation Army. 'The Liberation Army of South Vietnam,' they stated in their propaganda, 'orders the village council, the Republican Youth Group, and the interfamily system in Phu Nhuan Dong village to cease their activities. Whoever does not abide by our instructions will be severely punished.' " After a search of the village, the attackers arrested the village youth on guard and tied them up. Then they vanished without harming anyone. The killings in this village did not start until the second phase of the Concerted Uprising in mid-1960 [DT288].

Fear and Trembling in the Countryside

The morning after this attack, the district forces rebuilt the post and reinforced it. The hamlet chief and the Republican Youth reestablished control and resumed their guard duty.

But an important change had taken place. "The main psychological impact left by the attack obviously was fear. Although the campaign to Destroy the Oppression hadn't yet begun, the villagers were already terrified of the VC. The attack on Phu Nhuan Dong post by itself couldn't create such a widespread reaction—it only confirmed what the people imagined. Of course everyone kept their true feelings to themselves to protect family and relatives, because it was then commonly accepted that praising the strength of the Communists would make you a target for GVN anger and speaking ill of the Communists would invite savage repression from them" [DT288].

In April 1960, the Phu Nhuan Dong post was again assaulted. The attackers got the policeman in charge of the post drunk and then killed him. The attack was carried out in broad daylight, but by the time the district forces arrived in the afternoon, the "Liberation Army" had left. The guerrillas returned that night, however, and made the villagers demolish the post. The attackers identified themselves again as the Liberation forces. One interviewee said, "At the time, we had heard of the 514th Battalion, but I don't think it had anything to do with this attack." According to this interviewee, "From that time, the Front controlled the village" [DT288]. Chin Om states that after this and other attacks in northern Cai Lay and Chau Thanh, "from April 1960 on, cadres were able to operate openly in the area along the Nguyen Van Tiep Canal and the villages along Highway 4."[44]

Armed propaganda was carried out on a significant scale even in the southern villages of the province. Dong Hoa village lies to the south of Highway 4, at its junction with the road to Vinh Kim. Between Dong Hoa and Vinh Kim was Muoi Thap's village of Long Hung. Sau Danh's band of revolutionary cadres had been in this area since June 1959, broadcasting with megaphones and tearing up GVN flags and signboards. In March 1960 Sau Danh returned with two squads of armed guerrillas and convened a meeting of about 100 from all of Dong Hoa's seven hamlets. There were more symbolic destructions of GVN flags and signs, and hamlet and village officials were given a warning [DT196]. A villager from Thanh Phu (Cai Lay) describes how these guerrilla groups operated in the first half of 1960:

> The Front started to operate secretly beginning in February 1960. At first the secret guerrillas carried out armed propaganda activities in the hamlet at night. They went to the houses of the interfamily group heads and took them away for one or two hours to propagandize and reform them. When they entered the houses of these officials to arrest them, only those with genuine rifles came in. Those with fake rifles stood outside to lend support. The people who were arrested and their families couldn't distinguish between the real and the fake rifles. They were frightened and told others that the Front was strong and armed with many kinds of weapons. It was the families of the people arrested . . . who made unwitting propaganda for the Front and made it appear more powerful than it actually was. Along with the armed propaganda activities the cadres collected money throughout the hamlet. They appeared suddenly in people's houses and forced them to turn off all the lamps, then introduced themselves as members of the National Liberation Front of South Vietnam [at this time in early 1960 they probably said the "Liberation Army"] and requested the people to contribute money to feed the troops. Before going to see a family, the cadres studied the financial situation of that family and determined how much they would have to contribute, even though when they went to see them they said it was voluntary. No family refused to contribute money to

the Front. Each night the cadres operated in one hamlet. They divided the hamlet into different sectors and each of them took a sector to operate in. Before leaving the hamlet they hung banners, posted slogans, and disseminated leaflets. The cadres collected money from each family two or three times, deliberately making the people commit illegal acts in the eyes of the GVN by contributing money to the Front. It built up its strength by making the people commit illegal acts, because it really was not strong when it first rose up. The people who were suspected by the GVN of having committed illegal acts naturally were forced to lean toward the Front. At the start the secret guerrillas were the most important factors in implementing Front policies. They were chosen from the ranks of the poor and very poor peasants. Only a few were selected because at that time the GVN was still in control of the village and it was feared if the Front recruited a large group of secret guerrillas they would be uncovered by the GVN. At that time the villagers were frightened out of their wits when they saw how active the Front was and how easy it was for them to operate. The Front members came in and out of the hamlet as though it were deserted. At night when they saw shadows passing by, people quickly bolted their doors and pretended to be asleep, and didn't dare talk out loud [DT203].

As in Phu Nhuan, there were no killings at this time, but already an air of fear and uncertainty had permeated the countryside. The fear was a complex mixture of many elements. There was, first of all, fear of the revolutionaries. People did not know whether their compliance with the GVN's local rule or their family and social connections with GVN local officials and militia would make them vulnerable to retribution. One interviewee said that "the villagers were very scared because most had relatives working for the GVN" [DT152]. This concern was acute among the unpaid youth village guards and the interfamily chiefs, and especially for village and hamlet officials, but even ordinary people were worried. Second, there was the fear that being visited by the guerrillas would make them suspected by the GVN, which often treated villagers as if they were already actively colluding with the revolution. Finally, there was the fear of uncertainty. A peasant from Duong Diem village said that after the cadres started to come into his village, "the people were propagandized and every one of them became frightened of the Front. They were all afraid, but they didn't know exactly of whom or what. It was very strange indeed" [DT194].

The winds of change were blowing in the countryside, and the peasants were concerned that they might make the wrong move at the wrong time. Although the villagers were afraid of both sides, they were not politically equidistant from both the GVN and the revolutionaries. As the previous chapter showed, a probable majority of the villagers were seething with indignation against the GVN and its local officials. This was, however, a period of transition, with potentially devastating consequences for misjudging the evolving situation. In these circumstances, political attitudes cannot be reliably inferred from political behavior, since the villagers were trying to keep from being caught in a vise between the contending sides at a time when it was very dangerous to be linked to either one.

During the early phase of the uprising a hush fell over the countryside. The story of the shifting balance of power in the villages is illustrated by the changing significance of noise patterns. Far from the highway traffic and the bustle of the marketplace, life in the interior rural hamlets unfolded against a backdrop of low-decibel sounds of nature. People became self-conscious about what they said and who heard them, and began to talk in hushed tones. "People in the hamlet whispered to each other and worried about their own safety lest the Front misunderstand them," said one interviewee [DT239]. Night time was especially terrifying, because the smallest sound in the deep quiet of rural My Tho could be heard over a wide area. Any sharp or unusual noise which penetrated this tranquillity immediately captured the attention of all hamlet inhabitants.

During normal times in the villages of My Tho, the daily routine of life was punctuated by the sounds of gongs, bells, and wooden percussion implements emanating from small local Buddhist temples. However, noisemakers can be used for political as well as religious purposes. When the Viet Minh first arose in the Mekong Delta during the Resistance, they appropriated the wooden clackers of the temple and instructed the villagers to use them to produce a noise barrage [DT149]. The purpose was to demonstrate the extent of popular support for the revolution and to intimidate their opponents psychologically. During the six years of peace, GVN village officials sent subordinates around the hamlets with wooden clackers ("*mo*"—usually translated in the interviews as "wooden fish" because of the decorative patterns carved on the wood) to call the people to assemble for corvée [DT199]. The proliferation of rapid-fire volleys of percussive sound reverberating through the stillness of the countryside had an effect that was dramatically different from the reassuring call of the sounds announcing the hour for Buddhist prayers.

The use of megaphones to shout out the revolutionary message was a sharp contrast to the furtive "whispering propaganda" of the six years of peace and issued a bold challenge to the GVN control apparatus, in effect daring them to do something about it. A variety of methods were used in addition to the wooden clackers, including blowing whistles, beating metal drums, and raking sticks across corrugated tin roofs. One interviewee said that his view of the relative strength of the two sides was influenced by the noise barrages organized by the cadres: "My confidence stemmed from the fact that every night sounds [came] from the knocking on everything that could produce a sound. This created a diabolical concert. It made me think the whole population had decided to stand behind the Front and that this huge manpower would give the Front the necessary punch to overcome anything" [DT288].

Perceptions of Insurgency in the Villages at Higher Levels

By mid-1960 the insurrection had accelerated and activities conducted by the lower levels now had taken on a life of their own. In some instances the higher levels of the Party do not seem to have been aware of how far and how fast the revolution was spreading, and they were therefore slow to react with policy guidance. If the province was falling behind the revolutionary curve, the Region was even more out of touch, calling the My Tho cadres up for a reprimand just at the time the popular movement in the province was moving into high gear. As for the Xu Uy, by midyear it was largely preoccupied with GVN military counterattacks in eastern and western Nam Bo. When Region 5 radioed a query from central Vietnam about how the Xu Uy was progressing on developing the Ho Chi Minh trail and where they could expect to link up, "[the] leading comrades in the agencies of the Nam Bo Xu Uy were busy with a lot of things. The whole region was preparing an uprising on an even larger scale. The enemy was strongly stepping up sweep operations. A big sweep in Ca Mau begun in mid-May 1960 had just ended when in July 1960 seven main force puppet battalions with hundreds of Civil Guard troops in support had moved in to attack the base in Dong Xoai. The Xu Uy had to worry simultaneously about opposing this sweep and expanding on the results already achieved, as well as organizing a number of special teams with the mission of looking for a route to the outside [i.e., the Ho Chi Minh Trail toward central Vietnam]."[45] With all these tasks pressing in on it, the Xu Uy does not seem to have been exercising tight control over the central delta at this time. For its part, Hanoi was even further removed from the picture. If the evidence from the central delta is any indication, following its endorsement of armed struggle in the first half of 1959, Hanoi does not seem to have played a significant policy role in the South until its Third Party Congress met in September 1960.

The 1960 Insurrection: Phase Two

As the province cadres were preparing to initiate the July 20 phase of the insurrection, the GVN launched a major military operation to provide security for the inauguration of the My Phuoc Tay Agroville, along with a large sweep into the province base area of Tan Hoa Dong. Fortuitously, the province had concentrated its meager force of two platoons for an attack on a military post. When the GVN forces came in, they vastly outnumbered the province unit but were in an exposed position in the open rice fields, while the province unit was hidden in protected positions. After a two-hour battle on June 17, 1960, the ARVN forces suffered heavy casualties (Party sources say 200 ARVN and twelve members of the province unit were killed). The unit commanders were dismayed by the proportionately heavy losses among their small force. Viet Thang came across Chin Hai sprawled disconsolately on the ground, depressed by the casualties and not in a triumphant frame of mind. "Don't think anything of it," said Viet Thang. "In fighting you win some and you lose some, you can't win every battle. And taking casualties like that doesn't necessarily mean you lost."[46] In time, the revolutionaries would arrive at the insight that the guerrilla wins if he doesn't lose. The postwar evaluation of the battle is more upbeat: The action is said to have forced President Diem to call off his planned visit to the Agroville inauguration and to have stimulated the local population to contribute 800,000 piasters to the revolution. It was followed by the assassination of a key GVN official in the Agroville and the burning of the Agroville's model homes, which had been built to show to Diem during his intended visit.[47]

The first major political action in the July 20 phase of the uprising was a mass demonstration in northern Cai Be district where the movement had been building since 1959. This marked a turning point in the uprising, because it signaled to the population that the revolution had now gained a critical mass and that the "balance of fear" was swinging in favor of the insurrection. The transition is explained by a cadre who was actively involved in the uprising in the villages of northern Cai Be around Hau My:

> At that time the policy was to bring back the former cadres who had participated in the revolution as the main priority. This was because the people at that time didn't dare do anything. The people were still affected by Decree 10/59, so they were really scared. You could say that the people felt for the Resistance brothers even more than during the [first phase of the] Concerted Uprising, but they didn't dare put us up. There was a time when I myself was living in the woods, dying of thirst and deprived in every way. When I would come out, the people would cry. You could say that 80 percent of the people

would cry on seeing us. They really felt sorry for us. But they would only prepare something for us and send us on our way. They wouldn't let us into the house for fear of being implicated. They gave us enough to eat, but wouldn't let us stay in their house. At the time they had the red and black placards, so they were afraid of being implicated. But this underground support enabled the revolution to organize the large uprising of July 20, 1960. I witnessed the assembling of 27,000 people in My Thien organized by the district. At the time I was a squad leader of the [Cai Be district] armed propaganda unit. 27,000 people—they were thick as ants. My Thien was in the center of the district. I remember that 500 people from the town of Cai Be crossed Highway 4 to attend, and the other villages all had 1,000 to 2,000 people in attendance. Every village gathered groups of people to assemble in My Thien. Between 3 and 5 in the afternoon I saw people assembled in an inner and outer circle. They went on forever! I couldn't imagine that the guerrillas could do such a job of organization, and that there would be such a fired-up atmosphere. Every strata was gathered there, from people who had worked for the revolution before to old people. That is to say, at that time they had really linked up all different strata. At the time the GVN village council of My Thien was located on Highway 4 about 4 or 5 kilometers away, and there was nothing [no GVN presence]. It was empty. After the [initial phase of the] Concerted Uprising of 1960—actually, Cai Be had risen up from the end of 1959, but had only gone public before the people in 1960— every locality was organized and had popular associations and so on, which had clearly emerged, so they were able to assemble such a large number of people. I feel that only by that period was it possible to really evaluate the power of the masses and their belief in the revolution. For instance, in Dong Hoa Hiep, right next to the district seat, 90 percent of the people "understood" [hieu] the GVN, while only 10 percent "understood" the revolution, but they still leaned toward the revolution and they urged each other to go to My Thien. Some groups had not been able to cross Highway 4 in time because the sun had come up, but they crossed anyway and went to My Thien. There were two considerations. One was that the people in the zone had already risen up and they understood the revolution. The people living in the zone under the influence of the GVN had not yet risen up, but they responded like that thanks to the activist sympathizers [nong cot] who stirred them up and led them [DT415].

The most obvious sign of a major shift in the civilian population as they calculated the risks involved in supporting either side, was the willingness of people from distant, solidly GVN-controlled areas to go in groups in broad daylight to attend this mass rally, which was organized on a scale that would have been inconceivable even a few months before.

Various estimates of the crowd size are given in Party sources, but it is clear that the assembly was very large and moved without hindrance through the villages of northern Cai Be district. The province history records that "On July 20, 1960, a meeting was organized at the six-canal ["wagon wheel"] intersection of My Trung village in Cai Be, with more than 15,000 people participating. The meeting turned into a parade stretching 15 kilometers along Canal 28, which along with the supporting armed forces made the enemy in the posts so afraid that they fled."[48] Viet Thang writes, "The demonstration of 17,000 people marching in broad daylight from Hau My (Nguyen Van Tiep B Canal) went to assemble at the six-canal intersection in My Trung. The demonstration was carefully organized and had an electric atmosphere; there were banderoles, flags, and slogans. The demonstrators had staves . . . and walked along shouting slogans. Wherever the crowd of demonstrators went, hamlet chiefs and interfamily chiefs fled. The soldiers and village officials in the posts didn't dare to do anything." When Chin Om, who was attending a Region cadres meeting, heard the news, he exclaimed, "The Tiger has awakened!"[49]

The July 20, 1960, campaign marked the formal "coming out" of the revolution in many villages, and interviewees frequently confirmed this. It marked a major turning point of the uprising and a distinct new phase in the revolution, since this kind of political mobilization would now be in the open. The revolutionary forces would publicly identify themselves, and from that point on there could be no retreat back into clandestinity. This was another reason for the political killings, since the resulting intimidation could provide some of the protection for the cadres that the secrecy of underground activities had once furnished. A witness from Thanh Phu village said:

> The Front officially began operating [openly] among the people on July 20, 1960. . . . Every night they gathered the people for meetings, made appeals through megaphones, and hung banners which said "let us eliminate spies and wipe out traitors." The cadres motivated the people to destroy bridges and roads and, at the same time, they went to each house in the hamlet to collect money. . . . They tracked down the interfamily group heads, the intersettlement sectors, and the hamlet chiefs, who they brought before the people during meetings to indoctrinate them and forbid them to continue working for the GVN. If they disobeyed, they would be killed. At the same time, during the first week, Bay Dau Phong ["the peanut"—a nickname for the leader of the insurrection in the village], and his men ordered the execution of four people in the hamlet. Two of them were beheaded with machetes. After the Front killed these four in the hamlet, the people were frightened out of their wits. They obeyed the cadres in everything. . . . After they succeeded in frightening the people the cadres organized meetings, going from My Thoi hamlet to My Thanh, Thanh Hung I, Thanh Hung II, My Hung, and My Hoa hamlets, and on to Phu Nhuan village before dispersing. These demonstrations were organized for two consecutive months, and at the same time the inhuman killings went on without interruption in the other hamlets until June 1961. It was only in that year that the campaign to eliminate spies and wipe out traitors came to an end. The villagers lived in an atmosphere of terror. They only worried about saving their own skin, and didn't dare open their mouths to say anything [DT229].

There was a sort of domino effect as the insurrection spread from hamlet to hamlet, expanding the revolutionary zone of control and driving the GVN local administrators out of the exposed hamlets and into posts or district towns. Taking the "advice" of the cadres, many lower-level village and hamlet officials quit.

The following description of one such trial of eight "criminals," as told by an interviewee, fits the pattern of the revolutionaries' modus operandi:

> After making some propaganda, the cadres brought the prisoners in front of the people, read their crimes aloud, and then asked the villagers whether they should be killed or acquitted. A number of cadres who were in the audience stood up and said that they should be executed to set a good example for the rest of the villagers. So the cadres ordered their immediate execution. The guerrillas dug a big hole right where the meeting was held and beheaded all eight prisoners with machetes. Then they pushed the bodies into the hole, filled it in with dirt, and then ordered the villagers to disperse. A few villagers who attended the meeting were so frightened that they fell unconscious on the ground. The guerrillas were also shaking with fear" [DT223].

Fear fueled a torrent of rumors. The most effective of these were spread by the local Saigon officials themselves. An interviewee describes how rumors and deception caused fear in Binh Trung village:

> People became bewildered and confused. Hamlet and village officials went into hiding. The VC started a wave of denunciations which they called eliminating GVN security agents in order to liberate the people and eliminate the reactionaries. The first to be killed was a guy named Luong in Binh Hoa B hamlet. Next came Tan from Binh Phu hamlet, and a lot of people were given warnings. Most of the victims were members of the GVN administrative organs. This wave of denunciations frightened the people. . . . The village officials and the villagers overestimated the strength of the VC at that time. False rumors spread by the people frightened both the GVN officials and the villagers, and the officials retreated to the posts to live with the troops. The administrative organs were practically paralyzed. Ba Me of Binh Trung A hamlet was then in charge of recruiting a number of farmers and young men, arming them with wooden rifles, sticks, and machetes, and leading them in various shows of force before the people at twilight. The people were fooled. They thought the liberation forces were terribly strong [DT284].

Impact of Assassinations on the Villagers

As the panicked village and hamlet officials fled, the GVN paramilitary support structure in the hamlets, whose initial paralysis had been caused largely by the inaction of these officials, disintegrated further, and its own marginal supporters began to make accommodations. A vicious circle had started with the failure of village officials to support the paramilitary youth guarding the hamlets, which in turn demoralized the armed village militia and isolated the village officials further. One former Republican Youth explained his situation after the July 20 campaign was initiated in Thanh Hung village: "Seeing that the Village Council was so timid and didn't dare take strong measures, I also got frightened—so much that I didn't dare go out of my house, fearing that they would know I was an ex-member of the Republican Youth. The villagers became anxious and they wavered between the GVN and the NLF. Having one neck bound by two nooses, they had to do whatever they were told by both sides." This youth had built "a very beautiful house with brick walls and tile roof, with an iron gate" in 1959 and was clearly satisfied with his life until he had been detained and unjustly beaten by a Self-defense Corps militiaman during the 1959 anticommunist campaign [DT277].

Although there had been underground agitation in many areas since 1959, the sudden outburst of large-scale mobilization caught many of the villagers off balance. In the beginning they had not yet had time to assess the implications of this and were swept along by the tide. A middle peasant said, "I think the immediate propaganda about the Diem regime was what got me and the people. Not what might happen in a couple of years—that we weren't too clear about. I think that people could not yet assess the idea of struggling for the Liberation on behalf of their real interests. They couldn't analyze this because they were busy with their hard work to earn a living" [DT386]. Even those who might be drawn to the message of the revolution hesitated: "At the time people didn't have confidence in the Front because it had just arisen. They were afraid to commit themselves because the GVN had not yet withdrawn. Only those with children in the Front had confidence in it" [DT182].

This was a period in which collective pressures and influences on individual decision making predominated, but the "rational peasant" element of "what's in it for me?" was clearly important. Because of the abrupt change in the village context, many people had simply not had enough time to consider how the changes would affect them. In Hoi Cu, "the villagers were caught by surprise by the events and were too scared to adopt any definite attitude. They were like a herd of cattle which runs in any direction [the] herdsman wants them to go" [DT290]. My Hanh Dong was one of the three target villages in Cai Lay for this second phase. "The villagers were perplexed to hear VC propaganda cadres speak out against the government. All this came so unexpectedly that they didn't know what attitude to adopt. However, they abided by the decisions of the cadres and did exactly what they were ordered, without daring to react. In the meantime, the village council and the militia kept absolutely quiet and had no reaction against the VC activities, making the villagers even more perplexed" [DT237]. The lack of reaction is understandable considering that during the first month of this second phase of the Concerted Uprising thirty people were killed in the village, ranging from the village police chief to several leaders of the Combat Youth to "a mere villager whose friends happened to be SDC militia" [DT237]. One villager from Hau My said, regarding this early period of struggle over his village, "We are really miserable being caught in between. Whoever takes power, let it be just one of them!" [*Ong nao co quyen thi mot ong thoi*] [DT192].

Focus of the Insurrection Shifts to My Tho's Heartland

Only a month after the July 20 uprising, the movement in the northern villages of My Tho was well underway, and the focus shifted to the villages south of Highway 4. Not all the northern villages had progressed to the satisfaction of the province leaders, but the move south was a logical next step. Viet Thang assessed the situation at this time: "By about mid-August 1960 we had been able to rise up in almost all the villages north of Highway 4 in Cai Be, Cai Lay, and Chau Thanh districts. However, after reviewing the July phase, only Cai Be was really strong, while [the uprisings in] Chau Thanh and Cai Lay were not yet strong or broad." He explained that "strong" meant that the revolutionary forces had been able to surround the military posts and "eliminate traitors," while "broad" [*rong*] meant that the "masses had continuously participated in large numbers." Cho Gao was even farther away from the Plain of Reeds base and was more exposed than Chanh Thanh and Cai Lay. As a result, Cho Gao had initially been quiet. In May, however, the 514th unit (a platoon at this point) went to "stir things up" in the area. At the beginning of June it successfully attacked a post in Thanh Binh village and inflicted heavy casualties on the reinforcements the next day.[50] By August 1960 Viet Thang was relatively satisfied with the movement in Cho Gao, which had succeeded in gaining a foothold in the northern part of the district.[51]

In September 1960 the higher levels turned their attention toward My Tho and the delta. The Third Party Congress of the Lao Dong Party had just met and signaled the increasing interest and attention of Hanoi toward the South. The Xu Uy was now redesignated the Central Office for South Vietnam of the Party Central Committee (COSVN), thus reviving the title used in the latter stages of the Resistance and bringing it organizationally closer to the central Party organization in Hanoi. According to Viet Thang, the My Tho province committee prepared for a meeting to "pass on the Region resolution and review the lessons learned as well as prepare a plan for a Concerted Uprising throughout the entire Region which would be led by COSVN." The uprising "would start on September 23 and go until October 10, 1960, and would be the largest uprising in South Vietnam."[52] The verdict on this phase of the uprising was negative. A journal entry dated September 24, 1960, written by a leading cadre of the province military staff who was captured around 1965 says tersely: "24/9—Concerted Uprising in the entire Region—a failure [*that bai*]." But while this phase of the uprising may not have met the high expectations of the leadership, it set in motion or continued the process of undermining GVN authority in several key areas of My Tho.

The province Party committee met in its forward base of Tan Hoa Dong to discuss the new phase of the Concerted Uprising to start on September 23. My Tho decided to concentrate its armed forces and cadres and send them south of Highway 4. The 514th unit would support the movement in the Long Hung–Vinh Kim area, while a platoon borrowed from Kien Tuong province would do the same in the eleven villages of Cai Lay south of the highway.[53] The revolutionary base of support in these villages south of Highway 4 was considered "extremely weak."[54]

By the time the campaign reached the villages south of Highway 4 and east of the province capital, the villagers were no longer being taken by surprise and had a chance to think through its implications for them. The movement had picked up momentum, and the risks which had been a barrier to participation were correspondingly reduced. The two major centers of GVN power in this rich and populous area south of Highway 4 were Ba Dua in the west and Vinh Kim in the east. Although the Concerted Uprising occurred here months later than in the northern villages, this heartland of My Tho province was later designated the "20/7" or "July 20" zone. It consisted of the villages in Cai Lay and [GVN] Vinh Kim districts south of Highway 4 down to the Mekong River. The strategy of the Party was to isolate the strongpoints of Ba Dua and Vinh Kim and ultimately eliminate all GVN presence in this area.

The Destruction of the Oppression campaign was basically completed in My Tho and other southern provinces by the end of 1960. The movement had been particularly strong in the northern villages of Cai Be, Cai Lay, and Chau Thanh districts and had reduced GVN control in the southern villages of the 20/7 zone south of Highway 4 to the two isolated strongpoints of Ba Dua and Vinh Kim as well as some hamlets along the secondary roads in the area of southern Chau Thanh and Cai Lay districts near the Mekong River.

My Tho Assesses Gains in 1960

At the end of 1960, the My Tho province committee held a conference of village Party leaders in Tan Hoa Dong. It assessed the results of the last half of the year and noted some shortcomings. Not many weapons had been captured. Despite some success, the movement in the eastern districts of Cho Gao, Hoa Dong, and Go Cong was still not strong.[55] Nevertheless, the overall expansion of the revolutionary movement in 1960 had been remarkable by any measure. As 1960 drew to a close, the revolution had gained control of vast portions of My Tho province. The province Party history asserts that, as of March 1961, 88 of the 123 (by the revolution's count) villages in My Tho did not have a resident GVN village administration, and 33 of these villages were "completely liberated." At the beginning of 1960, 3 of the 6 key districts in My Tho had a combined total of only 9 Party chapters, but by the beginning of 1961, 119 of the 123 villages in the province had a Party chapter. The number of Party members had risen from several hundred to 1,500, and according to the history, there were a total of 20,000 members of the popular associations, each one (Farmers' Association, Women's Association, Youth Association) averaging 5,000 to 7,000 members.[56]

Limited Impact of Local NLF in My Tho

The growth of the revolutionary movement was marked by the formation of the National Liberation Front (*Mat Tran Dan Toc Giai Phong Mien Nam Viet Nam*), which resulted from the decisions taken at the Third Party Congress of the Lao Dong Party in September 1960. At this meeting, the Party distinguished two strategic missions of the revolution: "The North must advance to socialism, and the South must overthrow the fascist dictatorial My-Diem regime, liberate the South, and bring about the reunification of the country." In order to do this, the South had to "unite all the people to resolutely struggle against aggressive and warmongering U.S. imperialism, and overthrow the lackey ruling clique of the U.S. imperialists."[57]

The National Liberation Front was formed in Tan Lap village, Tay Ninh province, on December 20, 1960. "When they returned, the comrades who had gone from the South to the North to attend the Party Congress didn't forget for a minute Uncle Ho's instruction: when you get back down there, remember to urgently prepare to set up a Front. The required conditions have been fulfilled. It might take the name the National Liberation Front. Only in that way will it have prestige among the southern intellectual circles, and will have a chairman to assemble the various branches and circles and encourage the people."[58]

Although the NLF was designed primarily to gain noncommunist allies in the urban areas and among religious groups, the directive to form a branch of the national organization was dutifully carried out in My Tho. In January 1961, the founding congress of the National Liberation Front in My Tho was held in Ban Long village. The province Party history asserts that the province NLF was introduced to the public at a meeting of 25,000 people in My Long village, just to the west of Ban Long. After that, district NLF committees were formed. It is difficult to reconstruct the establishment of the NLF in My Tho for several reasons. Foremost among these is the fact that the NLF never played a significant political role in My Tho, and remained a "front" which eventually simply disappeared from view. Second, the Rand interviewers were encouraged to refer to the revolutionary movement as "the Front" because this was the closest thing available to a neutral term, and to avoid the pejorative term "Viet Cong." Thus, "Front" was used regularly in the interviews when it was actually the Communist Party that was being referred to. Third, there seems to have been a great variation in the amount of attention devoted to the NLF in My Tho even in the very early period after its formation. Some examples from the interviews illustrate the point.

Several interviewees stressed that the role of the Front was to provide political cover for the Party and to obscure the connection of the southern revolution with Hanoi. A cadre from My An village, north of Cai Be, said, "After the signing of the Geneva Agreement in 1954, the Hanoi government no longer had the right to interfere in the South, and yet it went on interfering because the Communists were the leaders. This is why it was necessary to change the name. In the South it became the 'Committee of the National Liberation Front of South Vietnam.' At the village level in the South it was known as the 'village Front committee,' in order to avoid violation of the Geneva Agreement of 1954" [DT156]. This considerably oversimplifies the situation but does make the point that rural cadres were aware that an important function of the NLF was to serve the diplomatic needs of the revolution by concealing Hanoi's role in the uprising in order to keep the focus on the role of the actions of the Diem government in sparking the insurgency and to maintain the appearance of Hanoi's compliance with the Geneva Accords. The irony, of course, was that Hanoi had endorsed the insurgency with considerable reluctance, and the main impetus for the Concerted Uprisings was local. A village cadre from Thanh Phu (Cai Lay) said, "During the period of clandestine operations from 1959 to December 20, 1960, all activities were carried out in the name of the South Vietnam Liberation Army. After December 1960, all activities were said to be carried out in the name of the South Vietnam National Liberation Front" [DT203].

Conclusion

Now that the die was cast, and the revolution was organizing for the overthrow of the Diem government, it would be the Communist Party organization and leadership that would provide the guidance and structure for the movement. The "fellow travelers" that the early revolutionaries had studied about were welcome, but not in leadership positions. The revolutionary movement was much larger than the Party which led it, and the mass organizations composed of non-Party members were crucial to the revolution's success. These organizations were also not under the political or administrative control of the NLF. The following chapter examines the people who led the 1960 uprisings in My Tho (including seasoned revolutionaries from the Resistance and those who were recruited in the course of the uprisings), the organization of the Party and the training of its members, and finally, the differences between the "Viet Cong" and the Viet Minh.

8

Forged by the Hammer of the Party

The revolutionary leadership in the villages of My Tho that emerged during and after the Concerted Uprising was very different from the leadership of the Resistance period. Many former Resistance cadres stayed on the sidelines after being released from jail, while others had left the province for good. A year following the 1960 Concerted Uprising, the Party purged many of those who had continued to serve the revolution and brought in young village cadres to replace them. Further, the Party itself changed with the times. Following the 1959 decision to authorize armed struggle in the South, the northern and southern branches of the Party were assigned different roles. At the Third Party Congress in September 1960, the northern Party was given the mission of building socialism, while the southern branch of the Party was to focus on "liberating the South."

During the Resistance, the Party organization had stayed in the background, letting the Viet Minh Front run local administration in the villages and in some cases allowing non-Party villagers to play important roles. There was no government separate from the Party for most of the "Vietnam War" period, and the Party itself led the villages. For a movement that had become accustomed to operating in secrecy, this required organizational and psychological adjustments. Because of the greater prominence of the Party organization, and the relative youth and inexperience of many of its members, political training and indoctrination were given unprecedented emphasis.

To understand the revolution it is necessary to understand the nature of the Party which led it. This does not mean, however, that the Party was the revolution. A number of analyses of the Vietnamese revolution have rightly pointed to the crucial leading role of the Party but wrongly concluded that the success of the revolutionary movement was due mainly to its organizational skills, its ruthless single-mindedness, or both. This "organization theory" explanation of the Vietnamese revolution is flawed in several respects. First, it does not account for the origins of the organization, which is often assumed to have sprung up full blown from some external source rather than arising from a social movement in a specific social context. Second, the Party had a number of ups and downs, reaching a point of near extinction in the South during the six years between the Geneva Accords of 1954 and the launching of the insurgency in 1960, and later suffering heavy losses after the 1968 Tet Offensive. Still, these blows to the Party organization did not cripple the revolution. Finally, there was great diversity of motivations and behavior on the part of individual Party members in My Tho and significant variations among Party organizations in its villages and districts.

The Party in fact included in its ranks a significant segment of the society in which it operated; it was not an external force imposing its will on Vietnamese society. In My Tho, the Party of post-1960 was different from the Party of the Resistance, and as its composition changed so also did its relationship to the society around it. Toward the end of the "Vietnam War" the Party became less representative of the social forces in the Mekong Delta, which had been radically transformed by the war, and this created difficulties for the revolution in the post-1975 period—but that is a story for later chapters. The first two points—the origins of the revolution and the early development of the Party, and the ebbs and flows of the Party over the nearly half-century of its independence struggle—are addressed in other sections of this study. This chapter deals with the third point: the Party as a reflection of the larger society. In order to do this, the distinctive nature of the Party as an organization must be closely examined, since the Party viewed itself as the "locomotive" of social change in its society and in some ways transcended the society from which it emerged. The purge of older members from the Resistance in the early years of the Concerted Uprising was an explicit attempt to create a revolutionary "fighting machine" that would act with one will and one accord. As this and following chapters show, the actual results fell short of that aim, but the more diverse and less regimented organization that evolved was in many ways more effective than the desired "machine" would have been.

In the first years of the insurgency the Party was especially secretive and cultivated a mystique about its operations in order to invest itself with an aura of wisdom and power as well as to protect its members from arrest and liquidation. As the Party gradually took an overt leadership role in the areas it controlled, and as its own ranks expanded, this image began to change. By 1971 in places like My Tho, the Party as an organization was not leading, but struggling for its survival, and had for the most part retreated back into hiding. After 1972 there were signs of regeneration of Party organization, but the military side of revolution on the larger battlefields outside the Mekong Delta was primarily responsible for bringing about the end of the conflict. This leaves open the question of whether, had the war continued, the indigenous southern revolutionary forces could have been rebuilt in places like My Tho to the point that they could have controlled the outcome without the assistance of the North. Of course, the North was an integral part of the larger society in which the revolution was occurring, and it was only an accident of history that diplomatic complications prevented Vietnam from becoming a single society in 1954. Nevertheless, the focus here is on the local social context within which the Party operated in the Mekong Delta and not on the broader and much more complex national scale.

In our examination of the Party organization, we will frequently refer to the Party's recruiting auxiliary, the Youth Group. Although the official designation of this organization following the establishment of a nominally separate southern Communist Party in 1962 was the Youth Group of the People's Revolutionary Party, most of the interviewees used the term "Labor Youth" (*Thanh Lao*), referring to the name of the northern Communist Party, the Labor Party or, as it is often translated, the Worker's Party (*Dang Lao Dong*), which they understood to be the actual leader of the revolution. One interviewee claimed that Party membership acquired in the North (that is, regroupees who went north, became Party members, and then returned south) was more "valuable" than Party membership achieved in the South. This could either be a tacit admission that the People's Revolutionary Party (PRP) in the South was a junior-varsity organization, or simply that the closer the admitting branch was to the center of the Party, the more prestige attached to Party membership [DT107]. There was a sense—especially among the regroupees—that the closer a person had been to the great Meccas of socialism, the more prestige and authority that person should enjoy. "Regroupees were haughty," said one interviewee, "and thought of themselves as older brothers. They had a superiority complex because they had studied socialism in the North or had been to Russia or China" [DT203]. Most interviewees did not feel that there was any fundamental difference between Party membership North and South, however, and we will use the northern term "Labor Youth" for the sake of consistency.

The Party as an "Organization Machine"

What emerges from a close study of the Party in My Tho and South Vietnam as a whole is the conclusion that it was both more and less than an organization machine. It was more in that the success of the revolution did not depend solely on the Party's unerring leadership and wisdom—this was an image which the Party liked to project for both internal and external consumption. The Party both locally and nationally committed many strategic and tactical blunders, but it succeeded in spite of this. Although the Party routinely used harsh methods, including terror tactics, and enforced rigid discipline on those it controlled, in the end it depended more on its ability to attract support from those outside its ranks than to coerce compliance and, even more important, its ability to prevent its powerful opposition from consolidating their own support. Neither of these fundamental successes was due entirely to the Party's wisdom or organizational skill, or even its intimidating coercive powers. The Party lay at the center of a formidable social coalition mobilized for revolution.

Party Training

Nevertheless, the Party did play a decisive role in shaping the human resources at hand through frequent, thorough, and extensive indoctrination, both as part of its normal organizational routine and in periodic indoctrination courses conducted at the province or higher levels. These courses ranged in duration from a week to a year. In the interview sample, seventy-three respondents specifically mentioned attending either Party or specialized training courses with an extensive political indoctrination component. The actual number was certainly much higher, but the question was not asked systematically. Of those asked, two had attended four such courses during their post-1960 careers, six had attended three courses, and eight had attended two, mostly within a span of five or six years. The average duration of training courses (in the cases where this was specified in the interviews) was forty-six days. Sending key village and district cadres off for this length of time when a war was going on represents, of course, a major commitment to training and indoctrination. Even during the most intense phase of the war, following the Tet Offensive of 1968, the training and indoctrination continued. A list of village-level Party trainees in My Tho between 1968 and 1971 shows a total of 378 who attended the province indoctrination course. This is an average of nearly 100 key village cadres a year sent for ideological retooling at the height of the war. Although this number represented a relatively small percentage of the total Party membership in the province (6,000 at the time of the 1968 Tet Offensive and 4,000 in 1972), it does represent a significant investment during a very difficult time (and does not include many members sent off to other types of training courses).

As the war progressed, demands on Party members increased. A village guerrilla leader compared the three Party guerrilla war-training courses he had attended in 1960, 1962, and 1964: "The third training course was carried out in February 1964 in Ap Bac and lasted twenty days. All the chiefs of the village Military Affairs Sections [of the village Party committees] had to attend this course. . . . There was much dissatisfaction among the trainees toward the instructor, who had also given the first course in 1960. This time he had become haughty and was not as good humored as the first time. He would scold the trainees and often used ugly words with them" [DT86]. The instructor was confronted by the trainees and reproached for his behavior during the mandatory self-criticism sessions (*kiem thao*). He promised to correct his behavior but was criticized a second time. The interviewee explained the instructor's response: "He didn't have to bother about our opinions. Being Party members, we had to be educated by other Party members the way the Party wanted. He also compared the pressure of the Party to the jaws of a vice, and said that the trainees were just like iron that had to be forged by the hammer of the Party" [DT86].

Although some Party members found this pressure oppressive, most felt that it was a help to them and a source of strength for the revolution. Another village guerrilla unit leader who seems to have attended the same training course described above as riven with dissension, said, "In early 1964 the village Party secretary proposed that I be given permission to attend a military training course for village guerrilla unit leaders organized by the province Party committee. I was very happy that the Front looked after my welfare" [DT224]. The deputy commander of the Cai Be local forces, who joined the Party in late 1962, said, "Thanks to the Party leadership and all the indoctrination classes organized by the Party, the soldiers have become excellent fighters, fully aware of the duties of Party members and ready to accept any sacrifice and brave any dangers. Because they are Party members they have to fight for their ideals—the ideals of a communist." After he had become disenchanted with the revolution, he reflected that "When I was with the Front I was like a man in a small dark room . . . I saw nothing outside. . . . Indoctrinated with propaganda, the cadres were exactly like me. They believed everything the Front told them" [DT176]. It was not usually the abstract or theoretical side of Party doctrine which made the strongest impression, but its demonstrated power as a method of achieving unity of purpose and action.

Party Policy Toward Holdovers from the Resistance

In the case of military cadres involved in the revival of the revolution in the South, the Party was willing to be flexible and settle for less than perfection in political training and personal behavior as long as they fought well; however, with the civilian cadres who were reactivated during and after the Concerted Uprising the Party was much less lenient. The Party wanted younger leaders who were more daring and energetic but also less independent than the veterans. From the perspective of 1967, a district security cadre said, "The majority of Party members are now between 22 and 25 years old. The older people are not eager to join the Party. Even the old Party members gradually quit. The Party paid more attention to the young people because they could be indoctrinated easily and were more enthusiastic than the old people" [DT233]. In My Tho and elsewhere, the Party took the opportunity provided by the hiatus in Party activity of many veteran revolutionaries during the six years of peace to refuse recertification of some older members from the Viet Minh period when the insurgency arose, and to reduce its ranks by attrition. One cadre, himself a revolutionary since 1945, said, "The upper echelon had the slogan, 'to each period its own cadres,' because people who were too old would be too weak" for the challenges of life in the revolution [DT153].

A more serious problem with the members from the Viet Minh period in the eyes of the Party was that many of them had been arrested during the 1954–59 period, and some had even renounced the Party under heavy pressure from their Government of the Republic of Vietnam (GVN) jailers. Even those who had managed to avoid the ritual denunciations of the Party were suspect because the revolutionary leadership feared they might have been secretly recruited by the GVN. During the Concerted Uprising, therefore, cadres in the villages were often new to the revolution, and many older Viet Minh cadres were ignored or gradually frozen out of the village leadership. Many of the revolutionary veterans who had been instrumental in mobilizing the uprising of 1960 were purged the following year. Most military cadres were more fortunate than their civilian counterparts. Many had regrouped to the North in 1954 and did not have to face the repression endured by the civilian cadres who stayed behind. The relatively few cadres with military experience who did stay in the South after 1954 generally had left their villages, either for secure base areas or for places where their past was not known. Because there were fewer of them, because their fighting experience was valuable, and because they were not playing highly visible and sensitive political roles, the standards imposed on the military cadres were less rigorous.

A former Resistance cadre recounted his experience in rejoining the Party in a way that illustrates the uncertainty of some Resistance members about what the new revolutionary organization was, as well as the Party's reluctance to readmit members who had been purged during the Resistance period:

> I went back to my village in 1957, and quietly worked to make a living. Life was comfortable and I avoided contacting the old Resistance cadres because I felt guilty for giving myself up in 1952. On July 20, 1960, the Front stood up to destroy the unbearable situation and the movement became stronger and stronger. I thought to myself, if I didn't join it, my family and I might be in trouble, i.e., arrested. My father had been jailed for 18 months by the Viet Minh because of his reluctant attitude. I waited for the cadres to contact me and ask me to join them, but none did. Realizing the weak position I was in, at the end of 1961 I looked up Bay Dien, who was from the same hamlet. He was a former Resistance cadre and was then enjoying some prestige with the village Front. I didn't know what his functions were, but knew that he had great prestige. I begged Bay Dien to let me join him and was willing to do anything he wanted me to. Bay Dien replied, "At the present time just be a member of the hardcore ["backbone element" or activist sympathizers], later I will see." From then on I acted as a member of that organization. Every time the cadres called the people on loudspeakers to take part in some demonstration, I went to individual families and urged them to come out. "We are citizens, we should obey their appeals and show up in great numbers and electrify the atmosphere with our enthusiasm." A few months later Bay Dien introduced me to Nam Lan, head of the village information section. It was then that I realized that Bay Dien was a Party chapter committee member and that the Party still played the leadership role. Before I had thought that the Front was an organization in the South and had no connection with the Lao Dong Party. Therefore I felt in greater danger because I had been purged from the Party. I begged Bay Dien to accept me as a Party member. Though

a good friend of his and coming from the same hamlet, Bay Dien didn't dare acquiesce. He replied, "Chicken boiled twice doesn't taste good." I tried to work very hard and, thanks to my educational background, which was better than the other comrades, I was accepted as a Party member three years later [DT239].

To this interviewee, it gradually became apparent that the new organization was in fact the old Party, but for former Resistance members, especially those who had wavered in their loyalty, this discovery was far from reassuring, and even personal contacts were no guarantee of readmission.

In view of the severe losses suffered by the Party in the South and in the Mekong Delta in particular, it is puzzling that such a hard line was taken, resulting in the exclusion of many capable and willing cadres. There was certainly not an oversupply of available cadres in 1960, since many were either still in jail or had been killed during the Diem repression of communists. Much of the decline in Party numbers during the six years of peace was due to arrests and defections, or simple inactivity of Party members, but some resulted from deliberate Party policy as some village Party organizations sharply reduced their numbers to preserve secrecy. From 3,000 Party members and cadres remaining in My Tho after the regroupment of 1954–55, the number of Party members was reduced to several hundred by the beginning of 1960. It rebounded to 1,500 members at the beginning of 1961, at which time, several factors induced the Party leadership to order a purge of older cadres and concentrate on recruiting young people from the villages to replace them. The first factor was that the revolution had already gathered momentum and the province Party organization could afford to be more selective. A second factor was that some of the new young Party recruits did not have as much experience or prestige in dealing with the villagers as the older Viet Minh-era cadres and had even more difficulty being accepted as equals by the older Party members in the village. Shunting the older members aside was seen as a way to expand the influence of the younger Party members.

After the Party reviewed the cases of Resistants who had already rejoined the movement, it turned its attention to those who had not rejoined. "As for the former Resistants who had not yet rejoined the movement," said one interviewee, "there was a Congress of Former Combatants. The goal was to again use the people who had some level of understanding [*trinh do*] to help the Front, because it was afraid that if it didn't use these people they would be dissatisfied and might create difficulties for the new cadres who did not have enough experience to deal with them in public, thus provoking turmoil among the people. But the majority of Resistance veterans were in fact entrusted with minor missions, in most cases pertaining to social tasks. That was why these Resistance veterans bitterly expressed their dissatisfaction, saying that they were the 'shunted aside' elements [*thanh phan bau eo bi suong—i.e.*, a fruit which is neither good enough to be eaten nor bad enough to be thrown away]. As far as I know, very few of them were entrusted with leading missions" [DT69].

Higher-level Party leaders were concerned that foot-dragging and lack of support from the older cadres for their eager but inexperienced young counterparts would undermine the unity of the Party at the village level.

In order to impress the new members—and the villagers—with the stern requirements of Party purity and to shore up the authority of the new recruits, the revolutionary leadership felt it necessary to purge those who had wavered in the face of hardships, at the same time eliminating alternative centers of authority in the village and ensuring a local leadership totally beholden to their superiors. Sometimes the disgraced Resistance cadres were simply ignored. In An Thai Dong village, "The cadres who renounced their Party membership and tore up the Party flag stopped working for the Viet Cong when they returned to their hamlets. When the Front emerged to destroy GVN control, it didn't contact these former cadres, and recruited new ones instead" [DT227].

Party Focus on Youth

The Party focused on recruiting youth because of their energy, fueled by a genuine idealism in most cases and often reinforced by ambition. Some interviewees claimed to have joined the Party purely for opportunistic reasons or to protect and further their interests, but in most cases, ideals and self-interest seem to have been mutually reinforcing. A Party member who had been jailed during the six years of peace for playing the peripheral role of a liaison agent first decided not to resume working for the revolution after his release in 1958. "But later I told myself that as a young man, I had always wanted to do something honorable to prepare for my future, and that I should do something for my country. Therefore I was predisposed toward Viet Cong propaganda. When they told me that if I joined the Front I would be given land, would have freedom, and could work for an era when there would be no exploitation of man by man and when there would be freedom and democracy and society would no longer harbor depravity, I joined them immediately. I thought that I was still young and had my whole life ahead of me, and if I joined the Front when I was only a teenager I would be bestowed with honors and would be considered deserving by my country when the revolution succeeded. . . . In my future work with the Front, I wanted to play a leading role. I wanted to become a high-ranking leader. Furthermore, I hoped that in the future I would be allowed to go abroad to study—my wish was to go to the North, to China, or to the Soviet Union to study about socialism. That is why I was eager to join the Front" [DT140]. This was quite an ambitious agenda for a young man who had only a few years of primary education.

Another typically idealistic recruit was a young woman who said, "When I attended the ten-day training course, I was told that it was an honor for me to attend the indoctrination session, that I was struggling for the Just Cause and for my own family, and that I was contributing to the liberation of the nation and so on. When I heard this, I was extremely enthusiastic. These things appealed to a youth like myself" [DT164]. A few respondents asserted that they joined for less idealistic reasons. One recruit who joined in late 1961 later became the deputy Party Secretary of his village. "When I joined," he said, "I had a lot of confidence in the Front. I thought that a cadre who was also a Party member would have his future assured." When the revolution took control of his village, "I told myself that being under the Front's control, it was better for me to be a Front cadre in order to keep my position in the village intact—that of a man with a little property and a certain reputation among his peers" [DT1]. For the most part, however, those who joined the Party had strong idealistic motivations along with ambitions and self-interest, and did not see any contradiction between the two. The possibility that being "a man with a little property," a traditional measure of prestige, might not be a career asset later on in the march toward socialism did not seem to cross his mind.

Party Purges and Rectification

As the Concerted Uprising drew in new recruits and reactivated old ones, the question of defining the qualifications for Party admission or recertification arose. At first, the leading province cadres in My Tho did not want to go into this politically sticky issue for fear it would slow the momentum of the uprising. Chin Om (Nguyen Chi Cong) recalled:

> There were a lot of new Party members. The Province Party Committee continued to organize training classes organized by brother Ba Niem. Many Party Chapters were set up entirely with probationary Party members not yet formally admitted into the Party— sometimes even the Party chapter secretary was a probationary Party member. From 300 Party members before the uprising, the number grew into the thousands following the uprising. In April 1960 the province committee assigned brother Tu Tranh to organize a short training course for backbone cadres in the popular associations in the villages and hamlets. This course trained over 1,000 people. At the July 1960 meeting of the province Party committee's Current Affairs Section, brother Bay Hiep, the deputy province Party secretary, raised the question of firming up the quality of Party members in the new situation. Within the ranks of the Party there were complicated questions. In each village nearly half of the Party members had surrendered to the enemy, broken with the Party, or denounced communism. Muoi Ha and I agreed in thinking that with regard to [the Concerted Uprising], "the Party is riding a high tide of attack, and we can consolidate through the challenges that come up in this attack. Struggle with the enemy is the best way to filter out and eliminate the opportunistic elements. In the process, we will re-educate the brothers on the Party regulations and get them to reevaluate themselves." Thus we decided not to halt the attack, but attack and consolidate at the same time. These two ideas were submitted to the Military Region Party Committee, and its Party Secretary, comrade Sau Duong, accepted the second idea. He directed, "Don't stop the attack. Through the attack we will consolidate and build the Party and recruit more members while eliminating the vacillating elements."[1]

Some time later, says Chin Om, the Party Central Committee "had some ideas for guidance" (*y kien chi dao*) on the matter of adjudicating the cases of Party members who "had problems" both before and after the uprising. These ideas were set forth in Directive 137, which legitimized the purge. "The way of resolving this matter was appropriate," Chin Om concluded.[2]

Purge or Fight?

Whether the Party should slow the momentum of the uprising in order to guarantee its purity was clearly a contentious issue in My Tho. The primary advocate of slowing the uprising in order to purify the ranks was the deputy province Party secretary, Bay Hiep. Possibly this stand cost him the job of province secretary the following year. Despite the fact that the Region Party secretary supported Chin Om on the policy question, Bay Hiep had recently served as the head of the Region 2 office, and therefore had powerful political connections at the Region level. In 1961, when the incumbent My Tho province Party secretary, Viet Thang, was promoted to the Region, Region 2 proposed that Bay Hiep replace him, "but, this decision was not clearly announced. At the same time, the comrades in the My Tho province Party committee proposed that Chin Cong [Chin Om] become the Party secretary. As a result, there was some disarray in sorting this out. . . . In June 1961 Bay Hiep came back, and in the end there was a proposal to hold an election to 'satisfy the upper level and placate the lower level' [thuan tren vua duoi]." However, the election was not held until the end of 1961. Ba Chim presided over the selection process, and Chin Om was voted the new Party secretary in a landslide. "Even Bay Hiep voted for Chin Cong [Chin Om]. Only at that time did I leave My Tho completely," writes Viet Thang.[3]

Consequences of the Purges in My Tho

The Party rectification, or purge of Resistance members whose actions during the six years of peace had been found wanting, was set in motion by an order known as Directive 137, also known as Directive 37. This policy certainly had local origins from 1960 although the specific order came the following year from the Central Committee itself. One factor which may have either precipitated or accompanied the proposal to purge Party ranks was a higher-level decision to recombine the secret and overt Party chapters. Many Party members who had operated clandestinely under "legal" cover in GVN areas were now regarded with suspicion. One interviewee explained, "In July 1961 as the NLF [National Liberation Front] movement grew, the higher NLF authorities decided that the "B" ["legal" and secret] village Party chapter was no longer needed. The two village Party Chapters were merged into one in order to simplify and facilitate the leadership." Shortly after this, Directive 137 was received in the village "decided on by the Central Committee of the Lao Dong Party, and aimed at screening and strengthening [the Party's] internal ranks" [DT233]. In Thanh Phu (Cai Lay), according to another interviewee, the village Party chapter actually started its investigation of jailed cadres at the end of 1960, "as part of the preparations to have the cadres start operating openly." Not long after, "In the middle of 1961 or thereabouts—that is, a few months after the cadres started operating openly—either COSVN or the Party Central Committee in the North sent to the province an important directive usually called Directive 137 for short"[DT203].

Directive 137 had a wide impact in My Tho. In many villages the majority of cadres had been arrested and jailed, and thus were subject to the scrutiny of Directive 137. An interviewee explained the effect of Directive 137 on the local Party structures and the purged cadres:

> Directive 137 was applied to the utmost in Thanh Phu village, but its application didn't affect the Front's activities and their leadership of the village because there were many former Viet Minh cadres and Party members in the village who hadn't been uncovered by the GVN. But in other villages the application of the directive affected the Front deeply because it lacked cadres with leadership capacity to organize the people when it emerged. The Party members who were purged were very dissatisfied, but they didn't react against the Front or oppose it openly. The gap between this class of cadres and that of the new cadres widened every day because of personal pride and because of the smoldering conflict between them. In the middle of 1963, the province wanted to end this harmful conflict and to mollify the former cadres and Party members, and so it organized a seven-day course to cultivate loyalty to the district for these former Party members during which their readmission to the Party would be considered and they

would be allowed to resume their work for the Front. About 100 [former] Party members in the village attended this course. Only a few didn't go, either because they were old or because they were too discouraged. To date [1967], none of those who attended the course have been readmitted and allowed to resume their work for the Front [DT203].

In some areas, the mid-1961 purge focused initially on those who had actually served the GVN and only later was expanded to those who had "lost their revolutionary virtue." A cadre who had served briefly in the Resistance said that, in 1962, the Party, through Directive 137, compelled all those who had joined the Resistance and were serving the Front at that time to attend a course to study this directive: "The course aimed [at] remolding [*uon nan lai*] the attitude and ideology of those cadres. After this course a number of cadres were completely abandoned by the Party, and others were able to join the Party. I was accepted into the Party after completing the course" [DT69]. At least one cadre who had torn up the Party flag rebounded to become the political officer and later the commander of the 514th Battalion. According to one account, he was readmitted "because of his contacts," but was "despised by the regroupees, who would never have done such a thing" [DT107]. In Nhi Binh village, twenty party members and twenty sympathizers were arrested by the GVN during the six years of peace. All were later released, and those who had "kept their integrity" were reassigned to Party membership. One who did not meet these exacting standards was told by the village Party leader upon his release in 1964 that he was being purged in accordance with Directive 137, though he was later readmitted, thanks to the efforts of another cadre who "helped me build my life again" [DT207].

Long Trung Village: Case Study of Social Changes in Local Party Leadership

When Directive 137 was first implemented in mid-1961, the immediate consequence was the rejuvenation of the Party and the purge of Resistance members who had committed "political mistakes." In a longer-term perspective, this was a critical stage in the process of narrowing the class base of the Party, which had roots in the Liberation–Vanguard conflict of the mid-1940s, and even in the 1930s. Many of the Resistance cadres purged were also people who came from the upper strata of rural society. In the period following the Concerted Uprising, these Resistance cadres were replaced by new Party members, many of whom came from the "basic classes."

A unique informal Party history of Long Trung village by the revolutionary writer-reporter Nguyen Thi (who traveled widely in My Tho until he was killed in the Tet Offensive of 1968) gives a good picture of the shifts in class composition of the Party leadership in Long Trung village over several decades.[4] In the early 1930s, the Party sent two outsiders to the village. Both were women. One, named Co Ho Lao ("Miss Tuberculosis"), was evidently in ill health but survived to play a key role in village Party history through 1944–45, when she again took the lead at age 73. They recruited a martial arts teacher named Nam Tranh, who became the nucleus of the village Party organization. In 1932 the two women returned to the district level, leaving behind three Party members and 100 backbone elements. Because of Nam Tranh, whose village status linked him to both the gentry and the peasants, the Golden House Society (*Hoi Nha Vang*) was transformed from a burial association reserved for the wealthy and the powerful to one that also served poor peasants. Nguyen Thi wrote, "[Nam Tranh] had prestige among the village officials and the governing association of the village communal house. A person with prestige was able to speak to the landlords and the cruel and wicked bullies."[5]

Following the countrywide repression after the Nghe Tinh uprisings of the early 1930s in central Vietnam, the three Party members in Long Trung became inactive. In 1935, when the colonial administration began to relax its tight political control, the two district women cadres returned to Long Trung and recruited fifteen Party members and a guerrilla squad of twenty people armed with sickles and knives. The social base of this group included poor and very poor peasants and "youth" (which Party writers often used as a euphemism for young people from the upper rural strata—as though poor peasants had no stage of "youth" in their life cycle—or as if the category transcended class). In 1938, Long Trung was the revolutionary center of a cluster of villages in the Ba Rai River area, and Nam Tranh was operating legally (*hop phap*) at a time when the Popular Front was collapsing and the Party (including several other cadres in Long Trung) was withdrawing into clandestinity. It was clearly the protection of his social position in the village that allowed him to do this. Some revolutionaries with the right connections had the protection of the village elite, but this also raised the question of how militant they could be when the revolution turned against this elite. This was an acute problem during the Resistance and was also at the root of Directive 137.

During the 1940 Nam Ky uprising, while the granaries of big landlords were being seized, the insurrectionists did not pillage the granary of the big local landlord Ho Khai Khoa because his son (who later became an engineer in the Diem government) followed the revolution. The son later gave 350 hectares of land in Long Trung to the revolution along with the sum of 50,000 piasters in taxes (presumably during the Resistance). Nam Tranh managed to escape the repression following the failed 1940 uprising "and found the money to get a legal status," while the two Party members who had gone underground in 1938 had to flee to a different province, presumably because they came from a less wealthy background and did not have the money or the status to bribe the local authorities. Another upper-stratum village Party leader who was also a martial arts expert (he was said to have fought twenty people by himself) had been arrested in the 1940 uprising. The "Tiger of Cai Lay" himself (Nguyen Van Tam, who was at the time the district chief of Cai Lay), tried to persuade this man to collaborate with the French, but after vehement refusals had him executed by firing squad.

During the Japanese occupation, the revolutionary movement in Long Trung sank out of sight, and there were only three activist sympathizers left. In 1944, Co Ho Lao, at 73 years old, returned and built the movement up to 100 sympathizers consisting of "good youth." They formed a Vanguard Youth group, and the majority were "from the upper strata" of the village. After an initially successful seizure of power by the revolutionaries, the French reconquered My Tho. During the Resistance, the village Party leaders were notoriously authoritarian and also aloof from the masses. The villagers often addressed them with a mix of deference and sarcasm, using the distant "mister" (*ong*), rather than the fictive kinship terminology normally used by villagers (Brother 5, Uncle 6, Aunt 7 etc.). "The guerrillas were very afraid of the Party chapter gentlemen [*may ong chi bo*]. They ate, and then went out to fight the enemy and guard the roads. There were no meetings or indoctrination. Spotting a Party chapter member from afar, they murmured to each other, 'There goes Mr. Party member, there goes Mr. Party Chapter member.' When the Party chapter secretary came to the people's houses, they were very scared."

The account of the Party history of Long Trung village, recorded by an outsider shortly after Directive 137 had purged the ranks of Resistance members, certainly reflects the Party's desire to justify this action, but it also explains why it felt compelled to do it. Nationalism had mobilized broad support for the Viet Minh, but it had also brought many of the old elite into its ranks. The Long Trung village history contrasts the blocked career of a poor peasant who had been a Party member from 1945 to 1951 without advancing in the ranks of the village organization with the faction-ridden and elitist behavior of the local Party leaders: "Those who advanced in the Party were rich peasants up to landlords, and middle peasants didn't advance. Every morning the Party chapter secretary and the deputy secretary and the leaders would each drink a cup of *café au lait* and smoke expensive cigarettes." These same leaders rigorously enforced the policy against luxury goods for other villagers. By 1951 there were eighty-three Party members in Long Trung village, "the majority from the upper strata of the high and mighty." When the French made a comeback, however, and requisitioned the two-story house of landlord Ho Khai Khoa to serve as a military post in 1951, the situation became difficult, and seventeen Party members surrendered while others fled the village. By 1953 there were only four Party members left in the village. Even Party members who had been promoted to the relative safety of the district level (in more remote and secure areas with fewer risks of exposure) returned to the village and turned themselves in. The Viet Minh guerrilla unit leader, who came from a landlord family, surrendered (although his unit members did not), and after 1954 he pointed out many of the former revolutionaries and their hideouts and used the Diem Anticommunist Denunciation campaign to extort money from his former revolutionary cohorts.

By 1960 the majority of Party members had surrendered or dropped out. Hai Luu, who was the last Resistance-period village Party secretary, was the only one left with any standing in revolutionary circles. Even though he, too, had been arrested in 1958, he had refused to name names. When the Destruction of the Oppression began, there was no Party presence in the village; aspiring revolutionaries were completely cut off from the district Party committee and did not know how to locate the district leadership. The first locals who tried to make contact were conscious that they were taking a great risk, because the security paranoia of the revolution was at a fever pitch ("at that time suspicions were very high"—*hoi do nghi van rat ky*). "If we weren't able to prove our good faith [to the district cadres], we would have already become illegal with the enemy [GVN] because of our running off, and people [the revolution] would pin the label of CA [cong an—i.e., security agent] on us and we would have to be constantly on the run, and that would be still more miserable (illegal with respect to both sides)."

Finally, the district sent in another woman, Ba Nhu, to organize a guerrilla unit and "destroy the oppression." This was not universally popular, both because of continuing resistance to women as political leaders and because Ha Thi Chinh, the female village Party secretary in the neighboring village of Long Tien, had defected in 1958 and turned in all the revolutionaries in the village. The fallout was also felt in Long Trung, where 100 persons were arrested as a result of her denunciations. "Women can't even stand above the grass to pee [*phu nu dai khong khoi ngon co*]," said some disdainful villagers. "Ha Thi Chinh surrendered, and now they didn't trust women." They said this to her face, not behind her back," wrote Nguyen Thi, no doubt heavily influenced by the "authorized" Party view of the period just after Directive 137, which was highly critical of what the Party considered the negative and obstructionist behavior of the old Viet Minh who had, in its view, failed the political integrity test during the six years of peace.

Leading the opposition to the inexperienced leadership of cadres like Ba Nhu were the old Resistance cadres. In addition to her inexperience, Ba Nhu was looked down on by many villagers because she used her political power to play a twisted game of sexual politics to humiliate her initially patient but lower-ranking husband. She used her Party authority to send him away from home during the six years, and then falsely denounced him for encouraging her to defect when he tried to persuade her to resume a normal married life. Nguyen Thi describes Ba Nhu as someone who plucked her eyebrows and had her teeth capped with gold—characteristic behavior of the rural upper crust who tried to ape urban fashions—and she recoiled at the touch of the calloused hands of her simple peasant husband. Ba Nhu was not a completely new recruit to the revolution, as she had been active during the six years of peace, but she was not tied to the old Viet Minh crowd and she had little leadership experience.

"The [old Viet Minh] comrades who had gone out to surrender [to the GVN] were now trying to gain merit, and because they were familiar with the working methods, knew how to conduct meetings, could use political argumentation, were educated, knew how to organize and lead, they therefore seemed to be in charge of even the new backbone elements." The result was that the "new and loyal brothers only stood guard, issued invitations to meetings, shouted through the megaphones, and ran around for those gentlemen." Knowing that those gentlemen had lost their conviction, the masses had no confidence in them, but didn't know where to turn, because they couldn't articulate it. Those gentlemen submerged the new brothers and didn't let them study or get any indoctrination." The irony was that these very "gentlemen" of the old revolutionary guard had been recruited to do revolutionary work by the new elements—"certainly the district Party committee didn't contact them."

The problem of village disdain toward and resentment of Ba Nhu in particular and women in politics in general was particularly acute in Long Trung, since at that time the Party did not have a formal organization in the village and the only Party member was a woman. Thus, disdain for her amounted to a rejection of the Party's leadership, the district committee reasoned.

Ba Nhu added insult to injury after Directive 137 was sent to the village in July 1961. As the Party soon discovered, she was neither a model of diplomacy nor an advocate of internal Party democracy. Later, she was criticized for excessive killings of suspected GVN sympathizers without any discussion among the village Party organization. The situation was later referred to as a case of *tien tram hau tau* ("a prerogative conceded by the king to an official to behead first and to report afterwards").[6] The Party eventually had to make an embarrassing apology to the families of a number of villagers who had been killed as a result of Ba Nhu's excess of zeal.

The directive ascribed the slowing down of revolutionary momentum after the upsurge of 1960 to the opportunistic "jumping in" of the surrendered cadres. In a meeting to explain and implement Directive 137, Ba Nhu said, "The cadres who surrendered to the enemy are worthless and can no longer be used [*can bo dau hang dau thu het xai*]." Enraged, these cadres grabbed their chairs and threatened to beat Ba Nhu, who fled the meeting. "After studying [Directive 137], these gentlemen were very upset and showed fierce opposition. If there was any weakness or opening they would jump right in. Our [e.g. the Party's] standpoint was to implement the directive and speak frankly. These gentlemen were angry and hit back at us. After that the Province Party Committee had to come in to overcome this. They forced these gentlemen to undergo indoctrination about their responsibility and how they should help the revolution and the young cadres." The Party also pointed out that during the risky days of the Destruction of the Oppression, "those gentlemen" had not participated, but later "muscled in" and "pushed aside" the young cadres after the movement was going strong.

The Long Trung story is not only a tale of a generational changing of the guard, it is also an illustration of one of the main themes of this study—the progressive narrowing of the class base of the revolution. From the martial arts leader Nam Tranh through the café au lait-drinking Party leaders of the Resistance, the village revolutionary leadership of Long Trung had come from the upper socioeconomic strata. Even after Directive 137, class conflict continued within Party ranks. In December 1961 the Long Trung Party had grown to fifteen members, and Son was elected as the deputy Party secretary of the newly formed village Party chapter. This was resented by Bien, who was only a lowly self-defense militia member, though he had joined the insurrection before Son. The problem was that Son was a petty bourgeois. Nguyen Thi's informal account is nevertheless politically orthodox in that he describes this group as vacillating and self-interested—which is why they should not be entrusted with leadership positions. Son was newly married and was constantly pressured by his wife's family to spend more time taking care of his family and less time on revolutionary work. Ba Nhu, now the Party chapter secretary, criticized him in her blunt and challenging manner. "What can a young man with a wife accomplish?" (Given her contemptuous disregard for her own husband this had a sardonic irony). Son was angered by the remark and asked to be allowed to work in his hamlet to be close to his family. The district committee criticized him for this. Finally, Son quit altogether and left for Saigon.

This did not put an end to class politics within the village revolutionary movement. Bien, who had been disgruntled by having the petty bourgeois Son surpass him in revolutionary rank, was now appointed squad leader of the village guerrillas because he struck his superiors as brighter and quicker to grasp plans and policies than Mau, who was evidently from even more humble origins and seemed slower on the uptake. After a province wide conference of guerrillas the province leadership tapped Bien rather than Mau. Mau was upset by this but was easily pacified: "The vexation of the brothers from the basic [class] was easy to resolve. When they were told about the interests of the revolution they immediately understood." By contrast, when a middle peasant was asked to take over as clerk of the village Farmers' Association, he refused. "He was a hard core middle peasant—what did he have to worry about [*trung nong cung, lo lang gi*]?" the Party members grumbled. He wanted a leadership position that would give him some prestige, and his attitude was "better the head of a rat than the tail of an elephant."

Continuity and Changes in Local Party Leadership in the Early 1960s

The purge of Resistance members marked the end of the village elite's dominance of the revolutionary movement. The son of landlord Ho Khai Khoa was no longer a progressive revolutionary donating land and contributing taxes to the revolution, but an engineer in the Diem government. The constables who had mediated between the gentry and the revolutionaries and who had protected Nguyen Thi Thap (see Chapter 3) were long gone. In fact, the Long Trung constable of the late 1930s had been a fawning subordinate of the ferocious "Tiger of Cai Lay" (Nguyen Van Tam) but had an epiphany in 1945, after which he gave away all his land and possessions to the revolution on the grounds that "the Great Harmony" ideal called for this now that both he and Vietnam were independent. His relatives, of course, thought he was crazy. After this impulsive act, he seems to have played no further role in the village. Gone too were the martial arts experts who could "speak to the landlords and bullies" but now had faded out the picture. The Vanguard Youth with its social base in the urban intellectuals allied to the upper strata of the rural villages had been eclipsed by the peasant-based Liberation force of Nguyen Thi Thap and others. The *café au lait* Party leaders of the Resistance, who had been mostly from the upper strata of the villages and feared by the ordinary peasants, had dropped out or been purged by Directive 137. Even the new generation of activists had been cleansed of elements like the petty-bourgeois Son, who, in the Party's view, showed his true class colors by abandoning the revolution and moving to Saigon.

While Directive 137 did mark a changing of the guard from veterans to youth and a shift in the class base of the revolution, a very complicated reality underlay these changes. In Long Trung village, despite the harsh and authoritarian record of the Viet Minh there, considerable residual sympathy remained for some of the Resistance veterans, and petitions to the province committee forced the Party to recall a dozen or so of them back to work in minor capacities.[7] And while the Party was purging old members, some with impeccable class credentials and a distinguished record of service to the revolution, it was also taking in new recruits who did not always come from the preferred classes or background. In 1960, when the revolution was expanding rapidly despite the deputy province party secretary's admonition to purify the Party's ranks before proceeding further, the few cadres who had continued operating in the difficult period from 1959 to mid-1960 found it hard to refuse eager new recruits. At first they concentrated on people with a "revolutionary tradition"—that is, those with personal or family connections to the Resistance. One interviewee described the rush to join the revolution in the "deep" villages near the Plain of Reeds base area: "People would run after [the revolutionaries] clinging to their clothes, crying their hearts out to be allowed to join. Two guys ran after me pleading to join, but two days later they were sent away. They cried like rain because they weren't accepted. In the [other] villages it was different. They didn't make distinctions on the basis of class, but accepted anyone who would dare stand up and act. . . . At the time there were even some people who belonged to the landlord class who surrendered their class to come over to the revolution to gain merit. The policy then was to use every element that responded. They were to be gradually filtered out later" [DT415].

Unfortunately, there is little empirical evidence on which to assess this claim. In the interview sample, the class breakdown of those who joined the revolution in 1960–61 was: 11 very poor peasants, 55 poor peasants, 22 middle peasants, 2 rich peasants, and 3 petty bourgeois. This does not suggest that class background was ignored during this period, but of course, it is impossible to say if the interview sample is in any way representative of the larger population of revolutionaries in My Tho. The general question of which classes supported the revolution during the Concerted Uprising and how this changed later will be considered in following chapters. Apparently, the Party became more strict about the class background of recruits after the first wave of recruitment. According to one respondent, at first the village was empowered to accept members into the Party, but starting in 1961, only the district had this authority: "Only the district had the means of verifying the class and thoughts of prospective members, and sufficient prestige to represent the Party" [DT285].

There is also no way of definitively answering the question of how many Resistance members continued to be active in the revolution after the 1960 uprising and the 1961 purge, but two sets of figures offer some insight into this question. In the interview sample of 154 Party members, 17 (around 11 percent) had joined prior to 1954. All but one of these was interviewed prior to the Tet Offensive. A roster of trainee classes at Party indoctrination courses for village-level members between 1968 and 1971 lists a total of 378 Party members, of whom 30 (nearly 8 percent) had joined the revolution before 1954. Although the 1971 roster covers the post-Tet 1968 period, by which time attrition had certainly diminished the ranks of Resistance cadres, the proportions in the two samples are quite similar. Probably a minimum of 10 percent of former Viet Minh remained active at the village level after 1960, but the maximum was probably still a clear minority of cadres at the village level. In contrast, 118 (31 percent) of 378 post-Tet Party trainees had joined the revolution between 1959 and 1962, despite the extremely heavy losses suffered by this generation of cadres. Therefore, in most villages only a handful of older Resistance-era Party members were still leading a revolutionary organization that now consisted mostly of new, young recruits.

By the end of 1961 there were 34,800 Party members in all of South Vietnam. As of December 1962 the number had increased to 69,580, of whom 19,600 Party members were in the armed forces and 33,465 were in the villages and hamlets. There were 5,073 female Party members as of December 1962 and 8,130 from ethnic minorities. These members were organized into 4,400 Party chapters [*chi bo*], half civilian and half military.[8] The expansion of 1961–62 was a significant increase above the 15,000 in 1957 and produced a total that was higher than the 1954 level of 60,000 Party members in the South. The scattered data on village Party membership reported by the interviewees seems to indicate that in My Tho the most significant expansion took place in 1963. In 1960–62 most villages had fewer than ten Party members, while in 1963 it was not unusual to have more than twenty. The Labor Youth was the key auxiliary of the Party and the major pool from which it recruited. According to a postwar history, the number of Labor Youth Group chapters in My Tho rose from twenty-three in 1960 to sixty by the end of 1962. During the Concerted Uprising there were 330 Labor Youth Group members. By the end of 1962 there were 2,100.[9] As noted earlier, the number of Party members in My Tho rose from several hundred at the beginning of 1960 to 1,500 by the beginning of 1961.

Becoming a Party Member

Initiation ceremonies for full Party members were important and solemn occasions. The room in which the ceremony took place would be decorated with banners. A Fatherland altar and a picture of Chairman Ho Chi Minh would be prominently placed, and the room would be decorated with flowers [DT393]. For civilian Party members, a leading district committee member would preside. A new recruit would need to have two Party members from his village to act as his sponsors. The inductee had to explain why he wanted to join the Party and take an oath that he would sacrifice "to the last drop of blood" for it [DT331].

Selectivity in choosing its members, extensive and ongoing political training, and tight organizational control of its members were the ways the Party set itself apart from society in order to lead and transform that society. The Party was "the organized vanguard" as well as the "highest organization" of the working class. Its members were the "most enlightened and bravest in sacrifice among the laboring people."[10] The organizational checks and balances like alternate monitoring and implementing levels and the vertical and lateral chains of command were supposed to keep the organization from becoming co-opted by local forces and ensure that the goals and interests of the Party always came first. Procedures such as the vaunted *kiem thao* (criticism and self-criticism) sessions were meant to bring up problems and resolve them so that Party solidarity would not be threatened. In addition, the careful selection of the most "advanced" and "enlightened" elements, combined with a systematic ideological formation, would ensure that individual members put the interests of the Party above everything else.

"Impartial assignment of tasks" (*chi cong vo tu*) was a cardinal precept and meant to counter any tendency toward favoritism or factionalism. To be sure Party members did not become arrogant the Party stressed that even as members of the Party they were individually insignificant, and that they had stature and value only as part of the group. When some Party members began to ask embarrassing questions about the Party position on the Sino–Soviet dispute in the early 1960s, they were reprimanded. Who were they to question Party policies? They were only "lowly Party members who were like grains of sand on the beach or pieces of garbage in a dump" [DT205]. A similar comment was that "Your presence in the Party is but a grain of sand in the desert" [DT233].

A soldier who chafed at self-criticism sessions said that he was constantly reminded by his superior that "the collectivity was Paradise, and the individual was Hell" (*tap the la thien duong, ca nhan la dia nguc*). "By this he meant that the collectivity was always clear sighted, while the individual was dull-witted" [DT22]. The soldier was not persuaded by this explanation, however: "As for myself, I noticed that in the collectivity there were factions who used the force of numbers to oppress individuals. Whenever I wished to argue against the collectivity's statements, the squad leader always referred to Ho Chi Minh's statement that everyone commits errors, thus compelling me to accept the collectivity's criticism" [DT22].

Part of the individual pride and excitement of becoming a Party member was precisely in becoming part of something larger and more powerful than oneself. Searching for an analogy to describe the high status and influence associated with Party membership, a rich peasant who was not anxious to join said, "People told me being admitted to the Party was just like having French citizenship during the French period" [DT189]. The first barrier to using the Party merely as a vehicle for advancement or promotion of self-interest was that the individual could not request admission directly but had to be invited. "I didn't apply to join," said one. "It simply wasn't done" [DT137].

On the other hand, Party membership had its rewards. A military cadre said he was asked to join the Party because "[The Party leader] observed that I had done rather well in my assignments. Thinking that if such a good cadre as myself was not admitted into either the Youth Group or the Party there would surely be bad political repercussions, and because I was too old for Youth Group membership, he helped me to get a Party membership." This somewhat immodest self-appraisal illustrates that the concepts that recruits were "grains of sand" and that no one was indispensable did not apply when the Party needed to enlist key cadres and good leaders. This military cadre explained how his life changed after joining the Party: "From the time I first entered the unit right up to the time I was admitted into the Party, I was only an ordinary guy from the masses, under the control of everyone. So when I entered the Party, I felt somewhat enthusiastic because I knew that from that day on I would no longer be bossed around by a number of persons. On the contrary, I also knew I was going to boss some people around myself" [DT157].

Political Indoctrination

Some of the 1960–61 recruits later were sent to higher-level Party training courses, where they marveled at the brilliance and erudition of their political instructors. A security cadre at a COSVN training course in 1964 described one of his instructors: "Hai Binh had been a member of the Hung Hoa provincial Party committee in North Vietnam before he came to South Vietnam. He was about forty-two years old, short, small, slim, and completely bald. Hai Binh was a lecturer in the history of ideology, the world of the prehistoric era, the origins of communism, and dialectical materialism. His lectures were profound and highly sophisticated. In the beginning, the students were unable to understand a word he said. Only a few chiefs of security sections who had previously attended a Tran Phu training course of the Party [for basic-level cadres] were able to understand about one-third of his lectures. Men like me, with only a sketchy knowledge of Party ideology were lost in his lectures" [DT233]. A military cadre said that "Sau Linh, the [Military Region 2] political officer, was very persuasive. He could teach a shrimp to swim [an idiom roughly comparable to "He could sell refrigerators to eskimos"]. He came down to the 261st Battalion a few times to explain the world situation and the situation in the South and the weakening of the Americans. His speech was very interesting and everyone, including the regiment cadres, listened to him with their mouths hanging open. He was an excellent political cadre. He was over fifty years old and a real hard-core communist. I heard he studied Party dialectics for six years in China. Everyone who had contact with him liked him very much" [DT149].

Not all the military cadres were interested in theory and dialectics, of course. One interviewee described a Party training class for platoon-level cadres:

> About twenty-five of the thirty-six liked to have freedom—they didn't like the restrictions on drinking and eating, for example. If only they had this freedom, they would be willing to die in combat. This is why during the fifteen days of political reorientation the majority of students were dissatisfied because they were forced to adapt themselves to the mold and discipline of the Party. The majority of platoon cadres were young and loved to have freedom. They liked to wear good clothes, have a fancy hair styling, and to play and joke, so they protested vehemently when they were forced to observe the Party's strict discipline during the political reorientation course, which forced them to live like

worn-out old men. Those who protested belonged to the drinking group. During the discussions they demanded to be left alone and allowed to enjoy the good things in life. They said that if they were allowed these things, they would be willing to fight to the death" [DT108].

Even at the province level, some cadres made a particular impression with their grasp of ideology. Chin Om, the province Party secretary, appears to have been more interested in practical matters than abstract doctrine, but others were accomplished theoreticians. Muoi Ha, in charge of province military affairs, was one such. An interviewee who attended a province Party training class conducted by Muoi Ha said, "He spoke with a northern or a central accent—he certainly wasn't a southerner. He had an extremely high level of understanding. He conducted the training on the political line of the revolution in the South. We just studied the theory, not any concrete plans. Communism meant that a communist must be brave, must set the example, and live gloriously and die with honor. After liberating the South we would build a really democratic regime, and then advance to socialism. After building socialism we would advance to the 'great harmony' [*dai dong*], which is the highest stage of communism. I really believed in this, and was very enthusiastic" [DT386].

The My Tho province cadre who did most of the political training for village-level Party members in the early 1960s was Ba Ky, who seems to have fit the stereotype of the humorless dialectician. He had been a major figure in the uprising in Cai Be district and he was relentless in arresting and indoctrinating or "punishing" GVN officials. Ba Ky appears to have been a rural Robespierre, ordering brutal executions and spreading terror wherever he went [DT215]. "He was lanky and tall," said a cadre who had attended his training classes. "He was a very fastidious person who abided by set principles. He neither drank alcohol and tea, nor smoked" [DT233]. A respondent who had been in the same work unit as Ba Ky said, "He was about forty years old, strong and severe. He was quiet and had a very high level of political understanding. The workers at the print shop did not like him because he was too severe and never joked." Ba Ky's behavior toward this respondent in a self-criticism session was "hateful." On the other hand, Ba Ky's deputy, Tu Thong, was friendly and liked to joke with the workers. Everybody liked him" [DT194].

Ideological indoctrination also had a practical side. It produced unity and strength, as well as an infallible diagnosis of whatever problem was at hand. Dialectical materialism, the same method that produced the diagnosis, also helped determine the appropriate course of action. "The Party cadres and members have always taken dialectical materialism as a guideline for the settlement of their problems. They think that everything in this world never stands still, but is always changing. A human being or thing experiences the same change of conditions. If a Party cadre or member does not believe this, he is a backward person. Thus a Party cadre or member must always try to improve himself" [DT233].

Reasons for Joining the Party

Given the dangers and hardships of being a Party member, and the difficult and distasteful nature of some of the duties of a cadre, why did people want to join? There are, of course, fundamental problems in using the interviews to assess personal motivations, and nowhere is this truer than in evaluating reasons for joining the Party. Even if a consistent and coherent pattern of motivations emerged from the interviews, the question remains whether these views are still representative. There is no way to answer this question, in view of the basic uncertainty about how representative the interview sample is, the conditions under which the interviews were done, and the fact that there was no fixed questionnaire and not every respondent discussed the same issues, so that even within the sample it is hard to make generalizations. The best that can be done is to indicate different types of responses, to suggest the diversity of motivations. How representative each of these categories of response is of all Party members in the province cannot be determined, and, of course, the mix of motivations changed over time.

The interviews reflect a mix of self interest and idealism in motives for joining the Party. For some, there was no tension between self-interest and the public good. An idealist who spoke of the Party's "lofty ideals" and of losing concern for self-interest after becoming a Party member said in another context, "I left my family to fight and bring rights and material benefits to the people, to my family and also to myself. If we achieved success, my family and other families in the village would share in the prosperity and happiness. There wouldn't be any more differences between classes—there wouldn't be anyone too rich or anyone too poor—and all injustices would be corrected" [DT159]. In theory, helping the community was also helping yourself.

For many young people in the villages, joining the revolution combined excitement with the prospect of being "on the inside." Party membership offered the prospect of learning the inner secrets of politics and becoming a person of authority with a voice in the affairs of the village. In short, it offered a road to maturity and full membership in the village community. A village guerrilla said, "After getting my official Party membership, I had the right to attend meetings of the village Party committee and I was able to present my ideas to the committee. Once in a while I was able to express my own ideas on certain questions. At that time my impression was that the Party sincerely looked after me. I had known nothing about the village committee's leadership before, and though I did not understand the exact purpose of my missions, I carried out all the orders of my superiors"[DT224]. One member explained how he felt about joining the Party: "My prestige rose, my assignments were more important, and I had more authority to speak on a wide range of issues [*duoc quyen an noi lon rong*]. I felt it a great honor of course—I didn't know all of the Party's policies but only what came up in each campaign." Of course, duties came with the privileges. "I was most put off by the discipline," he said, "and felt there was no freedom. I was most turned off by the pledge, 'Whatever the Party says has to be obeyed. I must be faithful to the Party for life, follow the Party to the end, serve the interests of the Party and put it above family interest. Wherever the Party needs me I must go. If sent off to die, I also must go'" [DT386].

In addition to giving its members a voice in politics, Party membership made them political insiders who might know what ordinary people did not. There are two dimensions to the appeal of being privy to the "secrets" of the Party. The first was simply being "in the know"—a political insider, as in the cases described above. The second was the more abstract appeal of access to the "secrets" of life embodied in a doctrine and a framework of analysis which others might not understand. To some, this had a quasi-religious dimension —the doctrine laid out a revealed truth that was the path to salvation. For others it was a comfort to know that they belonged to a large and powerful congregation of believers. The images of power, universality, and infallibility of scientific insight into history and politics were strongly appealing to most Party recruits.

For women, greater gender equality and leadership opportunities were offered by Party membership. "The Party paid special attention to women," said one interviewee, "because there were so few in the Front. Also, it was easier for them to operate under cover" [DT133]. There were practical reasons like this to expand the numbers of women in the Party, not least of which was that the Party had to have female Party members to deal effectively with other women in the socially conservative villages. The Party was genuinely progressive, however, in seeking to emancipate women from feudal constraints, and many women responded to the new horizons and opportunities opened to them by the Party. Still, as noted above, women constituted only 15 percent of the total Party membership in South Vietnam as of 1962. A captured document from Cho Gao district set a goal for 1965 Party recruitment in the district that would increase the number of women members to 20 percent of the total membership.[11] In the interview sample of 154 Party members, only 5 were women, all of whom joined between 1961 and 1967, and 4 of the 5 were poor peasants. Of the roughly 300 village Party secretaries mentioned in the interviews, 9 were women, all of whom had served in the 1960–65 period, before the major escalation of the war.

The travails of the woman village Party secretary who was chased from a meeting by angry older men brandishing chairs have already been mentioned, as has the traditional chauvinist contempt for women with political ambitions. There were no province-level My Tho equivalents of Nguyen Thi Dinh, who had a symbolic but highly visible guerrilla leadership role in Ben Tre. The most prominent woman revolutionary in My Tho was Nguyen Thi Thap, who had left for North Vietnam in 1954 to become the head of the Women's Association. There was, however, a move in 1965 to underline the importance of women in the guerrilla war movement. One postwar history of My Tho province mentions a woman cadre (Doan Thi Nghiep) who served as deputy leader of the province military unit in 1966.[12] She is not mentioned in the interviews, however. The interviews do mention two instances in which cadres in the District Women's Association were appointed to leading military positions. Bay Nga became deputy in the Chau Thanh district local forces in order to show that "in guerrilla warfare, males and females are of equal importance" [DT99]. Another woman, Viet Huong, had been a liaison agent for the security forces in Cho Gao [DT142]. During the Resistance, she was appointed deputy head of the Cho Gao Military Affairs Section [DT148]. In the interviews, the most prominent female cadre in My Tho was Chin Hoang, the daughter of a Vinh Kim landlord who had been bankrupted by his opium addiction. Her sister was a prosperous businesswoman in Saigon. Chin Hoang had worked her way up from head of the Women's Association in Chau Thanh district to head of the My Tho province Women's Association. She was married to a regroupee who had returned South and had been assigned to My Tho so he could be near his wife [DT135]. This kind of special consideration was usually frowned on in Party circles, however.

Party Organization

In some villages, there were not enough members to establish a formal Party organization until the end of 1961 or even 1962. Cam Son village, in the heart of the 20/7 zone, did not have a formal Party administration until the end of 1962 [DT69]. Dang Hung Phuoc village in Cho Gao did not have an official Party chapter until the end of 1963, when it included three Party cells, fifteen Party members, and eleven members of the Party chapter committee [DT49]. In Long Hung village, only four or five new Party members were recruited each year in 1961–62 [DT134]. A Party chapter was set up in Long Hung village only in 1962, "when the movement began to be strong" [DT182]. This village had fifteen Party members in 1962 [DT206]. This is more than most of the other villages for which figures are available for that year (five seems to be the median). An exception to this pattern of modest Party expansion is Hoi Cu, which, according to one source, mushroomed from six members in 1961 to sixty in 1962—but fell back to thirty members in the following years when that village encountered problems [DT109]. By 1963 it was not unusual for a village to have twenty to thirty Party members.

Party organization started with the cell (*tieu* to), but the crucial base of the Party was the *chi bo* or Party chapter. *Chi* indicates a "branch" off a main trunk, and "*bo*" means headquarters, which is why chi bo is sometimes translated as "Party branch." Party rules designated the Party chapter as the "foundation of the Party, which links the leading organs of the Party with the masses." A Party chapter would be formed with a minimum of three official Party members. The leading revolutionary organization at the village level was usually the Party chapter, which was led by a Party chapter committee (*chi uy*), consisting of the key Party members in the village, and the Party secretary (*bi thu*), a deputy secretary (*pho bi thu*), and a "member in charge of current affairs" (*uy vien thuong vu*), who was entrusted with the routine bureaucratic affairs of the Party chapter.

The Party Chain of Command

The Party as an organizational mechanism served a double function. One was the task discussed above, of recruiting and indoctrinating the leadership of the revolution. The other was to organize and energize the revolution. This was especially important because, unlike the Resistance period, there was no governmental administrative apparatus to oversee the implementation of Party policies from 1954 to 1969, when the provisional revolutionary government (PRG) was formed, and even this "government" was largely synonymous with the Party. The command hierarchy was also a communications system as well as an administrative system. As experience with other communist systems has shown, the danger of the Party assuming all of these functions is that it may lose its revolutionary zeal and become mired in routine administration. The Party tried to address this problem in a number of ways. One was to separate the decision-making and oversight functions by assigning them to different levels of the hierarchy.

At the Third Party Congress in September 1960, the Lao Dong Party in Hanoi created a "central office" to lead the revolution in the South. On January 23, 1961, the Central Committee established COSVN, which would "be responsible for the guidance of Party missions in the South, and organizing the implementation of all directives and resolutions of the Central Committee and the Politburo. Nguyen Van Linh, (Muoi Cuc) was named secretary of the COSVN."[13] The line of Party control ran from the Politburo representing the Central Committee in Hanoi, to COSVN, to the Region Party committees (in this case the Region 2 Party committee), then to the provinces. At the province level, the province Party committees directed the district Party committees, which in turn directed the village Party chapters or committees. In this chain of command the key decision-making levels were COSVN and the province Party committee. Although the district Party committees were the most direct and visible source of higher authority in the villages, the district was less a policy-making level of authority and more a supervisory body, overseeing the implementation of policies decided above. A training manual for district committee cadres in South Vietnam explained: "[The] District committee plays an important role because it is the leadership level that is in direct daily contact with the basic-level organizations of the Party, and links them to the Party committees at higher levels. The object of the District Committee's work is the Party Chapter."[14] The district Party committee level was entrusted with "overseeing and motivating" (*kiem tra va don doc*) the Party chapters.

Party Leadership at the Province Level

While the district level was a monitoring echelon, the province was a decision-making level that tailored central directives to the local situation. Directly above it was the region, which was also a monitoring body. The region could transmit policies and priorities determined by COSVN, and it could parcel out quantitative targets such as numbers of young men to be recruited for the military among the provinces. Except during periods when communications with COSVN were difficult, the region rarely initiated major political policies. It did, however, enjoy considerable latitude in the military sphere, where the Military Region Command played a decisive role in planning military strategy in its territory. In Party political and administrative affairs, the province was the main center of decision making as far as the villages of My Tho were concerned, though any major initiative had to be closely checked with the region party committee member in charge of My Tho, who was usually a former My Tho province Party secretary such as Ba Chim, Viet Thang, and later Chin Om, all of whom knew the province situation intimately.

In the interviews, which largely reflect the village perspective, the district leaders were in constant interaction with the village Party organizations, but the province leadership seems to have been remote and inaccessible. The anonymous nature of the higher leadership did not appear to be an issue with the lower-level cadres, who viewed it as a necessary security precaution and were not, in any case, looking for charismatic leadership beyond the towering figure of Ho Chi Minh. A cadre who was asked whether he knew the identify of any top Party leaders responded that he did not: "I think because of security reasons no one was allowed to know the names of the big bosses" [DT157].

In My Tho, the province Party secretary was an elusive figure who surfaced now and again in the interviews but only in brief, passing encounters, even in the responses of the few interviewees who had worked at the province level. The presence of this figure in the interviews was a far cry from the romantic image of the populist politician suggested by some French observers. Max Clos, for example, an experienced correspondent who had covered Vietnam for Le Monde and Figaro, contrasted the province Party secretary with the Saigon province chief, who lived in a big house, drove a Mercedes, and whose wife was loaded with jewelry: "[The Saigon province chief is] a man of importance who is approached with deference, protected by police, soldiers, and assistants. His Vietcong opposite number can be seen every day. He is out among the people. He is dressed like a peasant, in black calico and with sandals cut from an old tire. He makes his rounds in his district on foot, walking along the public roads. You can be sure of one thing, he is not getting rich on the back of the people."[15]

Although the austerity portrayed in this idealized view of the prototypical revolutionary province leader is quite accurate, the interviewees would have been incredulous at the idea of the province Party secretary sauntering down the (GVN-controlled) public roads or the idea that he would circulate widely among the rural population or even have "name recognition" among them. As for "face recognition," the Saigon government was never even able to produce an authenticated photograph for a "wanted" poster, and its erroneous and widely disseminated boast that a top province leader (Muoi Ha) had been killed in 1966 only revealed to the cadres how little the GVN actually knew about the revolutionary leadership in the province. Even among the cadres, very few of the interviewees who had been active revolutionaries had actually seen the province Party leader Chin Om or his successor Chin Hai. Even more fantastic is the idea that the province Party secretary would travel without security and a protective retinue, which routinely accompanied him even in the friendly confines of a rear base area. At the village level, the Party leaders were not the "faceless Viet Cong" that CIA analyst and publicist George Carver portrayed during the war. This characterization is somewhat more appropriate as a description of village perceptions of the higher leadership. The top province leader in My Tho was not known by sight to most village cadres, though they were quite familiar with other province-level cadres such as Muoi Ha and Sau Danh, who were mentioned frequently in the interviews. At the village level, the Party secretaries were the most likely to have encountered the province Party chief, usually in an indoctrination class organized by the province.

It might also be added that while many of the high-ranking GVN officials in leading positions in the Mekong Delta did fit the Max Clos caricature of the GVN province chief, and while it is also true that it was impossible to be a Saigon province chief and not be in some way implicated in the systematized network of corruption that characterized the GVN after the overthrow of President Diem in 1963, the two GVN province chiefs in charge of My Tho during the main phases of this study (1965–72) were modest, energetic, and very capable military officers. One (Tran Van Phuc), a reserved and dignified but unostentatious man, had been a former schoolteacher and was an intelligent and competent administrator.[16] The other (Le Minh Dao) returned to the military after his stint as a province chief and fought courageously to the end in 1975, while his colleagues fled the country. He led the last major resistance against North Vietnamese troops before they entered Saigon—hardly the actions of someone who was in it only for the money. After 1975, like Tran Van Phuc, he paid for his dedication with years in a harsh "re-education camp." During the Diem period, the most notable province chief was the highly respected Nguyen Tran, an austere figure who was intensely dedicated to his idealistic political vision. Probably Dinh Tuong was atypical in this respect, and this might be partly explained by the importance of the province to the GVN, which (with the exception of the later Diem period) put a premium on competent leadership.

A Revitalized But Different Party: 1961–63

Although Party organizational structures and procedures were very similar to the Resistance period, the Party itself had changed substantially. It took several years for the new

Party that emerged after 1960 to take shape. The post-1960 Party had stripped most of the Resistance veterans from its ranks and had rejuvenated itself. There are no exact figures on the differences in class composition, but it seems likely that the new Party had a proportionately higher level of poor peasants in its ranks than during the Resistance. Even though class background had been deemphasized at the very beginning of the Concerted Uprising, it quickly reemerged as an important factor in selection of new members. As the revolution progressed, the importance assigned to class background waxed and waned, but the overall tendency was toward even greater stress on the poor peasants, while many middle peasants dropped out.

Despite the fact that Party members were supposed to transcend their class backgrounds once enrolled in the "vanguard of the proletariat," class distinctions were still made among Party members. A middle peasant felt that although he was a Party member, he was not trusted by the Party. He did not get along with the village Party secretary. "I was a middle peasant and he was a poor peasant. He criticized the way I dressed and said it was not appropriate for a member of the revolution." From this experience he concluded: "Not being a poor peasant is detrimental to a Party member. I keenly sensed that in the eyes of the Party I would never be a trustworthy member" [DT288]. In such vital matters as land distribution, the poor and very poor peasants were favored as "the two classes closest to the Party," and the middle peasant Party members could not ensure their interests because of Party ideology [DT203].

As the war dragged on, even the poor peasants began to question the benefits of Party membership as compensation for the sacrifices. The burdens increased and the rewards decreased. This meant that the Party had to intensify its organizational efforts at mobilization and control at the lower levels to sustain the momentum of the revolution. After 1964, some district cadres were sent back down to the villages to take a more direct leadership role. This was perceived in the villages as a form of downward mobility, reducing the upward movement of village cadres. In Party chapter meetings, said one poor peasant, the members complained that "however much they tried to rub off their horns, they would always remain water buffalos [*mai xung cho lam van la trau*]" [DT203]. But although the life of civilian cadres eventually became worse, the expansion of territorial control of the revolution in 1961–63 and the general enthusiasm for the revolution in this time of growth and strength made the Party's tasks much easier. It is to the growth of the revolutionary military forces and the spread of revolutionary control in My Tho province that we now turn.

9

Creating an Armed Strike Force

Military Expansion, 1961–63

By mid-1961 the Concerted Uprising and the Destruction of the Oppression campaigns had run their course. The Communist Party had broken the hold of the Government of the Republic of Vietnam (GVN) over much of the rural area of My Tho province, and was moving from clandestine insurgency to exerting overt control over many hamlets. The revolution was faced with the need to administer a significant amount of territory while defending both their cadres and the population who had collaborated with them from GVN retaliation. Its success in neutralizing Saigon's village officials and intimidating the local security forces was a significant accomplishment, but the revolution had enjoyed the advantage of surprise and profited from the ensuing confusion on the part of the Saigon regime.

However, the Saigon government had now regained its composure after the stunning setbacks of 1960, and its overwhelming superiority in military manpower and weapons posed a serious threat to the revolution. The Party thus set about building up military forces to defend the areas they already controlled, and expanding them where possible in order to keep the GVN from concentrating its forces on known revolutionary strongholds. The creation of the 514th Battalion was aimed at creating an "armed strike force" (*qua dam vu trang–qua dam* means to strike a blow with the fist and *vu trang* means armed) of My Tho province.[1] Despite this vivid image, the description and analysis of the military side of the revolution in this and later chapters underscores the most important point about the military dimension of the Vietnam war in the Mekong Delta: military control and influence were based as much (or more) on psychological factors as on actual military capabilities or achievements. Still, without a real capacity to fight a more numerous and better equipped adversary, it is doubtful that the revolution would have survived.

Popular support for the revolution reached its highest level in the 1961–63 period, during which the power of the revolutionary forces continued to grow despite an effective GVN counterattack in 1962, from which the revolution quickly rebounded. Even before the overthrow of President Ngo Dinh Diem in November 1963, the revolution in My Tho was reclaiming control of territory lost in 1962 and expanding into new areas—thanks largely to its increased military strength and the impetus this military "strike force" gave to extending its base of popular support. And even without the chaos and confusion that followed Diem's overthrow, the revolution in My Tho and the Mekong Delta had developed a powerful momentum that probably would have led to the brink of victory even without the political crisis in the GVN ranks, and therefore confronted the United States with the same choice of either intervention or defeat by 1965. The fear and uncertainty that characterized the villagers' reaction to the Destruction of the Oppression of 1960 was transformed into a surge of enthusiasm for the revolutionaries once it became clear that the uprising was not just a reckless attempt to stir up the peasantry, which might leave them holding the bag if it failed.

The history of the conflict is replete with abrupt reversals of fortune, a pattern well illustrated by this early period of the "Vietnam War." By 1961 the revolution had gained apparently unstoppable momentum, and the peasants became much more receptive to what it had to offer. In this period the costs of supporting the revolution were relatively low, while the benefits were high. Saigon's military forces were reluctant to go into many parts of My Tho's countryside in small units, and big operations were initially sporadic and ineffective. There was no heavy bombing or shelling in the countryside—this started in 1963–64 and dramatically escalated in 1965. Taxes to the revolution were relatively light, and were assessed in the form of "voluntary contributions" in "fund drives" (*lac quyen*) rather than the higher and more rigidly enforced compulsory tax that was phased in during 1963–64. Although heavy social pressure was exerted on young men in revolutionary zones to join armed units, there was no mandatory draft until 1963–64, and most of the early recruits were eager volunteers. Most important, the Party quickly began to implement a land distribution, which gave an immediate reward to its closest followers and held out the promise of real benefits from the revolution to large numbers of poor peasants. In order to make the offer of land credible, however, the revolution first had to demonstrate that it had real control over the territory, both to intimidate those who possessed land to give some of it up and to protect the recipients from reprisals.

As in the Resistance, the Party established various types of military forces. In the first years after the Concerted Uprising, guerrillas operated in the villages, usually as a squad of a dozen or so, with the aid of part-time self-defense militia in each hamlet. At the district level there might be a local force platoon or company to support the guerrillas when needed. The province would have its own unit, also called a "local force" (*dia phuong quan*) unit. In My Tho this was the 514th unit, which grew from a handful of "armed propaganda" cadres to a platoon, then a company, and finally to battalion size. It was the successor to the 309th Battalion of the Resistance period. At the region level there were main force units, which also grew to battalion size in the early years. These were more heavily armed, and they operated throughout the provinces of Military Region 2 (the central Mekong Delta). A combination of units from the region's 261st Battalion and the province's 514th Battalion fought one of the most celebrated battles of the war, the battle of Ap Bac, in January 1963. It was several years, however, for these units to reach the point at which they could stand up to Saigon's regular army forces.

1961–62: The Armed Struggle Intensifies

In January 1961, the Politburo concluded that "the revolution in the South is progressing along the road toward a general insurrection with new characteristics, and the possibility of a peaceful development of the revolution is now nearly nonexistent." The uprising had the My-Diem (Americans and Ngo Dinh Diem) enemy on the ropes. "The temporary stabilization of My-Diem is over and a period of continuous crises and serious collapse has begun. Various forms of limited guerrilla war and partial uprisings have appeared, opening the way for the ever-increasing high tide of revolution." The policy prescription flowing from this analysis was to upgrade military struggle to a position of full equality with political struggle. To some extent this had already become a reality in the South, and the central Party leadership was ratifying a fait accompli. "Because the balance of forces has changed," said the Politburo resolution, "we must push political struggle even more, while at the same time pushing armed struggle to be on a par with political struggle, and attack the enemy on both the political and military fronts."[2] The Party leadership worried that although the struggle had eroded the GVN position in most of the rural areas of Nam Bo and the highland areas of central Vietnam, the revolutionary forces in big cities and in the central Vietnam delta were still weak, and the "armed forces had not yet become big and strong and the base areas were not yet secure."[3]

The buildup of military forces in My Tho accelerated in 1961 after the small paramilitary groups of armed cadres had fulfilled their supporting role in the uprising. During 1962 the Saigon government launched a military counteroffensive coupled with a population regroupment plan known as the Strategic Hamlet program, which threw the revolution off balance in My Tho and throughout South Vietnam. Tam Phuong (Le Quoc San), the Region 2 military commander who had returned recently to the South along the Ho Chi Minh Trail in mid-1961, later wrote that "At the end of 1961 and throughout the year 1962, right up until the victory of Ap Bac at the beginning of 1963, it could be said that the enemy was the 'master of all they surveyed' [*bau troi la cua dich*]. The delta was open terrain, so the American armed helicopters could operate freely. The appearance of helicopters on the scene completely changed the tactical situation from what it had been during the anti-French Resistance."[4]

The U.S. Responds: Pacification and Counterinsurgency

American aid and military advice had produced the new tactic of helicopter assaults, which gave the GVN forces vastly improved mobility and often the advantage of tactical surprise. This was the beginning of what the revolution termed the "Special War" (*Chien Tranh Dac Biet*) period—its translation of the Kennedy administration's obsession with "counterinsurgency war," by which the United States would try to suppress the revolutionary movement in a Third World country by arming and advising a proxy local client to do the actual fighting. American aid and military assistance, along with advisors, would back up the Saigon government, thus achieving the U.S. aim of defeating the spread of communism in Asia without the direct intervention of U.S. combat troops. From the American perspective, this required counterinsurgency tactics aimed at suppressing a peasant-based guerrilla movement in its earliest stages, which it hoped to accomplish by the Strategic Hamlet program along with the new military advice and assistance—the first of many "pacification programs."

"From mid-1961," says the province Party history, "the enemy carried out a pacification program in the guise of the 'Rural Construction Program.' On April 17, 1962, the 'Rural Construction Program' was elevated to the 'national policy of Strategic Hamlets,' and in August 1962 Diem officially approved its expansion to all of South Vietnam. My-Diem viewed the strategic hamlets as the backbone of the Staley-Taylor plan, which aimed at resolving the contradiction between concentrating military forces to search-and-destroy and the stationing of static occupying positions, especially in the large expanses of the rural areas."[5] This was an expression of the classic "pacification" dilemma of balancing defense with offence, "clear and hold" with "search and destroy."

In October 1961 the first of a planned 250 Strategic Hamlets for Dinh Tuong province was established in Tan Ly Tay village, along Highway 4 on the stretch leading from My Tho city to Saigon. The first of three waves of Strategic Hamlet construction was to be completed by mid-1962. During this phase the main targets would be populous villages along the main arteries of communication which were still controlled by the Saigon government. Because these semiurbanized villages were densely populated—and also tended to have more residents connected with the GVN by family ties—the Strategic Hamlet would not require population regroupment, and the main new feature was to fence in existing residential areas. The second phase would run until the end of 1962, would move deeper into the rural areas, and would require extensive population regroupment and often the forced dismantling of homes, which would be moved inside a government-designated area. The third phase would take people out of areas in or near the strong revolutionary zones in northern Chau Thanh and Cai Lay districts, including the Ap Bac area, and a nearby area that soon became the central focus of both sides' attempts to control movement between the Plain of Reeds and the populated villages in central My Tho, which was known by the designation of its most visible landmark as the Stone Buddha Pagoda (Chua Phat Da).[6]

Rising Mass Support for the Revolution in 1961–62

Despite the increasing U.S. involvement, at the end of 1961 the situation looked favorable to the Party leaders, both at the top levels and in My Tho. A district cadre summarized the political line laid out for 1962 as communicated to the cadres in My Tho: "Political struggle is to be coordinated with armed fighting. Armed fighting is to push the struggle forward." In general, he said, the Party leadership in My Tho was pleased with the results achieved in 1961. "The struggle in 1961 achieved several goals and good results. As the movement was reviewed throughout the Region, the masses' political struggle reached a very high peak. Moving from the scattered struggles in the beginning, huge mass rallies were held in Dinh Tuong province, such as the multivillage assembly of nearly 50,000 people held at the Chim Chim junction in My Hanh Trung village on July 20, 1961, in which the people demanded that the Agrovilles and Strategic Hamlets be disbanded, and American advisors go home" [DT233]. Official Party sources mention that this large demonstration took place at the busy intersection of Highway 4 and the Vinh Kim road, at Dong Hoa village in January or February 1961 (the reference to My Hanh Trung probably confuses this demonstration against the GVN with another large crowd in the Ap Bac area near My Hanh Trung, which was assembled shortly thereafter to witness the "coming out" of the 514th Battalion). One source calls the Chim Chim demonstration the first organized direct mass confrontation with the GVN, with the demonstrators organized into groups bearing slogans and petitions. Another source puts the number of demonstrators at 15,000.[7] The difference between the massive spontaneous demonstration in northern Cai Be in mid-1960 and this action in early 1961 was that the Party was now able not only to attract large numbers of supporters, it could organize them in risky direct confrontations with the GVN authorities and in areas close to GVN strongholds.

The Party leadership in My Tho concluded at the beginning of 1962 that "although not all the rice fields and orchards were liberated and some enemy posts still exist, the NLF [National Liberation Front] had won the people's hearts and minds" [DT233]. A thoughtful and politically sophisticated former district cadre who read the reports cited in the previous chapter, which stated that most people followed the revolution out of fear in 1960, elaborated that "from the beginning of 1962 to early in 1963 the people appeared to be more eager to support it. This success stemmed from the Front's ability to seize control over a lot of villages and also from the Front's skillful propaganda, which repeatedly acknowledged that its victories were due to the people's support. At that time the liberated villages enjoyed real security and real democracy, and the ARVN [Army of the Republic of Vietnam] didn't dare conduct frequent sweep operations in them. In my opinion the people thought they were then enjoying 'real democracy' because the cadres behaved nicely toward them. Before, the villagers bent their heads and were scared when they met GVN officials. Since their villages were liberated, the cadres' behavior and way of addressing them was different from that of the GVN officials and the peasants were so pleased with the change that they thought it was 'real democracy.' As a consequence they felt more at ease when they dealt with the Front's cadres" [DT135].

A cadre from Vinh Kim said that it was not until the end of 1962 that the villagers' fear disappeared, and "90 percent of the people enthusiastically supported the Front." The people liked the land reform and felt the Front was "more lenient than the Diem administration," which they considered "very cruel" [DT143]. The evidence of strong popular support was a widespread willingness to contribute to the revolution's fund drives, and an enthusiasm for the political meetings held by the cadres. [DT143] This positive face of the revolution, solicitous of the people's welfare, modest in demeanor, and moderate in the demands it imposed on the people, was most evident in 1962–63, between the harrowing "Destruction of the Oppression" and the 1964–65 push to end the war, which imposed heavy burdens on the peasants.

Strategy of the Revolution in the Early 1960s

Because the Party had decided on a balanced approach to building up military forces, it had to apportion its scarce military resources among all the different levels from hamlet to region; it could not afford to sacrifice the lower levels even while building up larger forces at the higher levels. Years after the end of the "Vietnam War," Sau Duong, the Region 2 Party secretary, addressed the question frequently asked of him: "Why didn't you set up big and strong main forces of regiment and division size?" His answer was that the weapons available to the revolutionary forces, mostly captured from the Saigon forces, were all small-caliber weapons, "which were dispersed to the provinces, districts, and villages, to build up armed forces on a broad scale to hold and expand our control and attack the enemy."[8] Building up larger units would have required heavy weapons for combat support units, and these were not available in the early years of the war. Interviews and Party histories suggest that these weapons did not start arriving in quantity in the Mekong Delta from North Vietnam until 1963.[9]

By the end of 1960, according to a cadre notebook captured in 1965, province forces had captured a modest 197 rifles, and half the village guerrilla units in My Tho province still had no weapons.[10] The Party concluded that at this stage, battalion-sized units were the largest feasible formations in the Mekong Delta, with its challenging combination of open terrain (where large units would be subjected to air and artillery attacks) and interlaced networks of streams, canals, and roads (which made movement of large units difficult).[11] In his February 1961 letter to Nguyen Van Linh (head of COSVN), Le Duan wrote that Hanoi had authorized the establishment of twelve battalions south of the Demilitarized Zone (DMZ), the North would send enough cadres to set up six battalions in Nam Bo, and both cadres and enough soldiers to equip an entire additional battalion.[12] This accelerated the return to the South of the military cadres who had regrouped North after the Geneva Accords. Those who returned were called "autumn cadres" (can bo mua thu), because their departure to the North had started in the autumn of 1954.

This balance of military and political struggle was also a logical corollary of the strategic role that the Politburo had assigned to the Mekong Delta in its January 1961 resolution. The mountains and forests of South Vietnam would be suitable for large-scale military operations, while only political struggle was possible in the cities and towns. In the delta areas, however, military and political struggle would have to be integrated and closely coordinated.[13] The need for a stronger armed presence in the delta was underlined by the military setbacks in 1962, which hampered the revolution's ability to respond to the Strategic Hamlet program and resulted in the loss of control in some areas of My Tho during this year. After the battle of Ap Bac in January 1963, the revolution regained its momentum. Despite some setbacks in 1963, the strength and influence of the revolution continued to expand up to the November 1963 overthrow of Ngo Dinh Diem, after which the revolutionary forces gained control of nearly the entire province.

As part of the Diem government's response to the 1960 setbacks in the Mekong Delta, the ARVN Seventh Division was transferred from the DMZ to My Tho in the late spring of 1961. Immediately after the deployment of the Seventh Division, a week-long operation was launched against the province and region base areas along the Nguyen Van Tiep Canal.[14] At the same time, the Seventh Division conducted sweep operations in the villages north and south of the crucial Highway 4. Emboldened by this new military support, the GVN province Civil Guard (later known as the Regional Force or RF) began to operate in areas on the fringe of those the revolution considered its "liberated zone."

Formation of the 514th Battalion in My Tho

As the military side of the revolution rose to a position of equality with political struggle in Party strategy, the role and capabilities of its armed forces rose accordingly. The arrival of the ARVN Seventh Division in My Tho gave additional urgency to the task of strengthening revolutionary military forces. The most noticeable evidence of this was the expansion of the My Tho province unit, which had been officially presented to the public in "liberated areas" as the 514th province unit on February 20, 1961.[15] In the same month the 514th province unit was presented to the public, another unit which gained fame in the battle of Ap Bac was officially established. Military Region 2 inaugurated a military unit known by the date of its formation—February 1961—as the 261 unit.[16]

The precursor of the 514th began to operate regularly as an organized military unit about the time of the main phase of the Concerted Uprising in July 1960. At that time, some of the older cadres who had been involved in the armed propaganda operations of the province unit were sent back to their villages to serve as political cadres, and were replaced by young recruits. The province unit expanded to five squads.[17] On July 17 it fought the battle of "Mighty Tiger Mountain" near My Phuoc Tay in Cai Lay. This indicates that the 514th was able to move around the province with relative ease. As the uprising gained momentum in the July 20, 1960, "second phase," the activities of the 514th intensified. There were several military successes over the next several months. By August 1960 Sau Danh, who had led the armed guerrilla activities in My Tho during the preceding period, was playing a more direct military role in the Concerted Uprising. From the perspective of one witness of the Concerted Uprising, the major turning point of the expansion of revolutionary influence in My Tho took place after the surge of activity in July 1960. It is evident from his account that it was this political tidal wave that made the extension of military action possible, rather than the reverse [DT415].

Initial Success of Insurgency Based More on Political Than Military Factors

Two key points emerge from examining the role of the province unit in the Concerted Uprising. First is that the entire political process was initially conducted in the name of a military organization, the "Liberation Army." This was the name the revolution most often used to identify itself until December 1960, when the National Liberation Front was established [DT203]. Second is that despite the military front being presented to the people, the vast majority of accounts of the Concerted Uprising in 1960 do not mention the support of the province unit, and it appears that its role was secondary until the military side of the guerrilla conflict intensified in 1961–62. In some cases combined squads of guerrillas from adjacent villages cooperated with a rudimentary district force. It was political action supported by small and poorly armed local guerrilla forces that led the Concerted Uprising.

During the six years of peace, from 1954 to 1959, the GVN controlled the roads, towns, and the villages of My Tho (numbering between 93 and 125 during the "Vietnam War" period), with 250 posts manned by province (Civil Guard) or district (Self-defense Corps) militia. In 1960 the GVN had a total of 4,450 soldiers and militia in My Tho. By the end of 1962 the number of posts had risen to 400. According to the province military history, the number of posts in 1966 was 324.[18] During the Resistance the number of French posts had reached 847. Later in the war, in 1971, the number of posts was 948. Clearly, the fluctuations in the number of posts reflected shifts in the security situation. When threatened by larger revolutionary units, the posts were consolidated into fewer but stronger and more defensible installations. When security improved, increased numbers of smaller posts and watchtowers could cover the "pacified areas."

By comparison with My Tho, Long An province to the north had a total of 200 "posts and watchtowers" in 1961.[19] Long An covered 4,338 square kilometers, compared to My Tho's 2,339 square kilometers.[20] Long An's population in the early 1960s was 350,000 in its towns and 127 rural villages,[21] while Dinh Tuong's population was nearly 518,000 in its towns and 93 villages.[22] Assuming for the sake of comparison that Dinh Tuong had about 300 posts by 1961, in both cases the ratio of posts to people is about 1:1,700. Ben Tre, with a population of 600,000 and 115 villages, had 300 posts at the time of the 1960 uprising, and a territory of 2,247 square kilometers.

The Concerted Uprising succeeded without having to defeat this control structure militarily, and the posts were neutralized primarily by political and psychological pressure in 1960. Only nine attacks on posts in 1960 are mentioned in the interviews (two interviews mentioned the same attack), and three of these occurred at the end of the year. The military history of the province mentions only eight posts attacked by organized armed units in 1960.[23] In contrast, twenty-one attacks on posts in 1961 were mentioned in the interviews, and the province Party history claims that sixteen posts were taken that year.[24] The interviews mention eleven post takeovers in 1962, when the military tide turned against the revolution. The province history claims that fifteen posts were forced to withdraw in Go Cong alone at the beginning of 1962, but it also concedes that, after the arrival of the Seventh GVN Division, many posts in critical areas such as the 20/7 zone, which had been withdrawn earlier were reestablished starting in February 1962.[25]

Neutralization of GVN Militia Posts and Expansion of Revolutionary Control

By the end of 1960 the revolution had a sufficient foothold in the heartland of the province to expand its military operations there, and it began to take direct action against the village militia posts which were the central feature of the GVN control system. Expansion of revolutionary control in My Tho was carried out in two ways. First, GVN presence in the villages was neutralized by intimidation or by direct military domination. Second, the security of areas controlled by the revolution was strengthened. Neutralizing GVN presence did not always require actually eliminating the posts and military forces in a hamlet or village. Many interviews describe the growing passivity of local GVN militia forces, who often simply holed up in their posts and ceded control of the village or hamlet to the revolutionary forces. In some cases the posts were forced to withdraw altogether. A native of Thanh Phu village (Cai Lay) recalled: "At the beginning of 1961, the Front succeeded in forcing the GVN troops to withdraw from the post. Actually, the Front's armed forces were still very weak at the time. There were only nine secret guerrillas armed with three rifles in the village, but they were very clever and pretended that they were numerous and strong. I was the one who led the attack on the post and forced the troops to withdraw. Throughout the eight or nine months after the Front had risen to destroy GVN control, the secret guerrillas fired at the post every night to harass the soldiers. During the day they fired at the post to prevent the soldiers and their dependents from going in and out of the post in order to put psychological pressure on them" [DT203]. In 1961 the village Party organization decided to destroy the post and started a political campaign to build up resentment against the post soldiers among the people, by pointing out that the soldiers were the enforcers of the unpopular policies of the Saigon government. At 6 A.M. on "D-Day," the cadres assembled the villagers at twelve separate meeting points and then led the 5,000 people to surround the post. Megaphone appeals to surrender alternated with the detonation of homemade explosives, which "made an awful noise" [DT203]. With only three rifles, the guerrillas orchestrated their shots to create the impression of great strength. The megaphone appeals went on until 10 P.M. By this time only 200 to 300 people remained around the post. Knowing that the soldiers would not come out at night, the cadres sent the people home, but they assembled the same crowd the following morning. This time an escape route was deliberately and obviously left for the soldiers to withdraw by. A home-made mine was exploded and a megaphone order to "assault" the post and destroy it was shouted out. "The soldiers were frightened out of their wits, and believing that the post was really going to be assaulted, left the post in a hurry and withdrew by the route left open by the Front. After all the soldiers were gone, the cadres and guerrillas entered the post and seized a large quantity of ammunition and grenades" [DT203].

The primary method of protecting revolutionary forces was also more psychological than overtly military. An imaginary umbrella of protection covered much of the revolution-controlled area, because the Saigon militia forces were increasingly reluctant to patrol in areas where they might encounter guerrilla ambushes. Even if they were stronger than the local guerrilla forces in a given area, they might be caught by surprise. As the strength of the revolutionary local and main forces grew, the GVN forces were deterred by the even more intimidating possibility that one of these larger units might be in the area. The obsession with secrecy of the revolutionaries had a very practical side, since it was uncertainty about the location of "Viet Cong" forces at any given time that was the most essential ingredient of the psychological restraints imposed on GVN forces.

Build-up of Local Guerrilla Forces

Even with some setbacks, there was sufficient expansion of liberated zones in the populated areas of the province to make it possible to expand the military resources of the revolution in My Tho and organize district local force units. This was part of a move to unify all levels of military force under a single Party command system. In May 1961 the My Tho Party leadership carried out a region directive to create guerrilla military units at all levels from the province down to the hamlet and to link these with a unified command structure. As part of this effort, some district local forces were sent to the province level to build the 514th, now at company strength, into an "armed strike force" of the province (*thanh qua dam vu trang cho tinh*)." The local forces were replaced with enough recruits to ensure that each district had at least a concentrated platoon at the core of district armed forces. At the village level, a variety of different types of guerrillas were to be enlisted: guerrillas operating as a concentrated full-time unit, hamlet guerrillas, secret guerrillas (*du kich mat*), underground guerrillas (*du kich ngam*), and sapper guerrillas who would perform sabotage missions (*du kich cong binh dac cong*).[26]

By mid-1961 every village in My Tho had a village guerrilla unit, and the total number of village guerrillas in the province was 1,350.[27] The experience of the resistance had shown that a variety of different sizes and types of military forces were essential in coordinating military and political action. The district and province local force units provided the indispensable link between big concentrated units and village guerrillas. As the 514th unit expanded, it gave the province more military muscle and the "strike force" called for by the Party, but it also made it more difficult to operate in certain situations where something larger than a village guerrilla unit but smaller than a company or battalion was needed. The district local forces were designed to fill the gap between the village guerrillas and the big units.

Local Force Units Help Draw an "Imaginary Line" Around Revolutionary Controlled Areas

District local force units were organized starting in 1960 and 1961. In Cai Lay, for example, the local force was organized in 1961 at a strength of two squads [DT160]. Its first commander was Tam Tien, a capable leader who won the respect of his subordinates and was "a man of few words," despite his origins as a political cadre and the fact that he ultimately returned to a political job [DT160]. He had been one of the most active cadres during the Destruction of the Oppression, going from village to village to get the process started. In some ways his assignment to the Cai Lay district local forces was an extension of this role, as the revolutionary movement grew and was protected by military pressure, although at a level not much beyond that of the village guerrillas. "While fighting he demanded respect from his troops, but off duty considered them his friends," said one of his soldiers [DT159]. "He was about forty, and his handwriting was beautiful," said the impressed poor peasant. "Tam Tien was very good at leading and deploying troops so it was easy for us to take advantage of GVN weaknesses" [DT159]. Even so, the three platoons of the 1962 Cai Lay local force were "still very weak" and could only "harass posts, reinforce combat hamlets and destroy strategic hamlets—it was unable to do anything significant" [DT159].

Although the Cai Lay local forces did not register any major military victories in this period, they did achieve a security objective of major importance. Their attacks and harassment of the GVN local militia, the Self-defense Corps, and even the better-organized Civil Guard "fixed an imaginary demarcation line between Front-controlled hamlets and GVN-controlled hamlets and allowed the civilian cadres to operate openly" [DT152]. Without the visible effect of a victorious military engagement, this development was of even greater importance to the revolution than a military victory—perhaps even greater in terms of local impact than a spectacular triumph like the 1963 battle of Ap Bac. "Fixing an imaginary demarcation line" between two zones of control had two crucial consequences. First, like the Viet Minh policy of "dividing the zones and establishing a boundary" between the Viet Minh and French zones of control (*phan vung chia tuyen*), the "imaginary demarcation line" established a border which made the control of people within the revolutionary zone and the surveillance of traffic between the two zones easier. Even more important, this demarcation line had the effect of discouraging smaller unit GVN incursions into "liberated" territory. It underlines the most important point about the military dimension of the Vietnam war in the Mekong Delta: that military control and influence was based as much (or more) on psychological factors as on actual military capabilities or achievements.

By creating the belief in the minds of GVN soldiers and commanders that certain areas could not be entered except by large units, the revolutionaries had put in place the essential foundation of their military system. If the liberated areas could only be entered by larger units of the ARVN, this provided two immediate advantages to the revolutionary cadres and soldiers. First, large operations were costly and difficult to mount, and by concentrating large forces in one area, operations could be carried out in fewer places and with less frequency. Second, the element of surprise was lost with larger-scale operations. Revolutionary agents quickly discovered when operations were being mounted and provided adequate warning for the cadres and troops to move elsewhere. The operations themselves were ponderous and slow moving, so even if advance warning was not given, the result was the same.

This major turn in the strategic equation in My Tho province was not primarily accomplished by direct attacks of larger units such as the 514th and 261st battalions, though the these attacks had a significant impact. The larger units' function was mainly to neutralize or eliminate military posts by harassment or large-scale attack, thus pushing back the GVN militia presence. The division of labor was that the 514th would surround and harass the posts and ambush any GVN reinforcements, while the better-armed 261st Battalion carried out the actual attacks. Counteracting the posts was a necessary but not sufficient condition of drawing the crucial "imaginary line of demarcation." The vital complement to neutralizing the posts was simply the frequent physical presence of the district local force or the larger units in an area which—whether they engaged in military attacks or not—dissuaded smaller GVN units from operating there. The result was the mutual reinforcement of function that was envisaged in the "three types of force" strategy of coordinating village guerrillas with district and province local forces, and both of these with the main force units.

Military Recruiting

From 1960 to 1963, recruits were volunteers. According to a Military Region recruiting cadre in 1963–64, when the draft was being phased in, "those who volunteered were very enthusiastic and those with wives and children who had been pressured to go far away were very sad but didn't dare complain, but the deserters reached 30 percent" [DT338]. The districts sent two to three groups of recruits to the province center each year in 1961 and 1962, in groups of more than 100 each time. Probably several thousand recruits a year passed through the center. For those two years a cadre at the center estimated the desertion rate at about 10 percent, rising to 30 percent in 1963–64 when the fighting became more intense and draftees entered the mix of recruits [DT215].

Although almost all of the recruits in the 1960–63 period were volunteers, they went with different levels of enthusiasm. Many went fired up with zeal for the revolutionary mission. Others went because of the intense social pressure put on young men to join by the popular associations and, in particular, the women [DT387]. One young man arrived in the new recruit camp in 1961 after a trip of six days. He saw two types of recruits, those with field packs and those without, and guessed that those who had nothing were reluctant inductees like himself. "Every evening I went to the edge of the jungle and wept," he said. "I climbed a tree and looked toward my village hoping to feel better in doing so" [DT243]. A cadre at the new recruit base observed that morale was quite high among recruits in 1961–62, because they were all true volunteers. "Starting in 1963 morale decreased a great deal because they had joined either to imitate others in their village or because they were induced by cadre propaganda. Once they came face to face with reality they became frightened and lost their ideological conviction and zealousness and only thought of deserting" [DT215].

Early Leaders of the 514th Battalion

As the recruitment of volunteers built up the 514th unit and the district local forces in My Tho, Sau Danh was promoted to the province Military Affairs Section to preside over the expanding province command structure, being replaced by Thanh Hai, in late 1960 as commander of the province unit. Thanh Hai, a fun loving free spirit from a privileged rural family, had been the leader of the guerrilla unit in My Tho that was the precursor of the 514th in 1959, apparently alternating in this role with Sau Danh. The military command structure was formalized in 1961 and in 1962 a new set of leaders were assigned to direct command of the 514th unit, but it appears from the interviews that Thanh Hai still frequently functioned as commander of at least some elements of this unit whatever his official rank and title, and was the most visible military commander associated with it. Several sources indicate that he played a key role in the early years of the 514th and a number of interviews identified Thanh Hai as the battalion commander in 1965 and 1966. A member of the 514th who joined in 1962 recalled the history of the unit as it had been told to him. At the time Thanh Hai became commander there were three understrength platoons. "Platoon B1 was led by Cho. He's still [1965] only a platoon commander and could not be upgraded because of his drinking. . . . I only knew Cho because later on I used to go out and get drunk with him. At the time Thanh Hai's company became famous thanks to the battle staged against Lt. Thinh, the Go Cong district chief. That's why the people nicknamed the unit "the Thanh Hai Battalion" [DT157].

Sau Danh, by contrast, was a more disciplined leader. A member of the 514th described him as a forty-year-old cadre who had been in the Resistance but had stayed behind after 1954 to lie low (dieu lang). "He did not seem to be a status seeker," said the interviewee. He wore black pajamas and not new clothes. Nor did he like women, because he was old" [DT106]. This last point must have seemed self-evident to a nineteen-year-old, and certainly distinguished Sau Danh from Thanh Hai, who in fact was about the same age. Sau Danh evidently had more success in indoctrinating strangers than he did one of his own sons, who was a squad leader in the 514th and a "maverick." "When Sau Danh tried to indoctrinate him, he would shout back at him. Sometimes Sau Danh got mad and hit him with a stick" [DT147]. All of Sau Danh's three sons were members of the 514th and died on the battlefield" [DT157]. In the estimate of one long-time military cadre, "Sau Danh has only a province level of competence. If he was promoted to a higher level, he wouldn't be able to handle it and it would be harmful to the revolution" [DT338]. Apparently the Party was well aware of the pitfalls of promoting people above their level of competence, because Sau Danh remained in My Tho throughout the conflict. He proved to be a dedicated and effective leader at this level, and was rewarded by elevation to the position of deputy province Party secretary, serving in 1973 under Chin Hai, the province Party secretary. "The fame and prestige of these two is now very great," said one respondent at the time [DT404].

A key Party overseer of the province military forces was Muoi Ha, who also provided a sharp contrast to Thanh Hai. "No one mentioned his wife or children." said one respondent. "He spoke well and was careful in words and action, so no one could say whether he had real faults or not. He was rather nasty when he saw his comrades getting drunk, and this made him rather unpopular with the lower-ranking cadres" [DT157]. While personality factors may have entered into this ("cadres didn't much like Chin Hai either, but didn't hate him as much as Muoi Ha"), part of Muoi Ha's unpopularity stemmed from his assigned role of conducting the dreaded self-criticism sessions during the annual "reorientation indoctrination" (*chinh huan*) sessions [DT157].

The Tide Turns Against the Revolution in 1962

Throughout the conflict there was a pattern of action and response that created a kind of ebb and flow in the fortunes of the two sides. A high tide of revolution like the Concerted Uprising created formidable political momentum, but also stimulated a countercurrent of GVN response. An interviewee from Kim Son village related the following illustration of this point. "Gradually we bought ammunition from the higher echelon and sniped at the GVN post, as the Viet Minh used to do during the Resistance. After firing a few shots at the post we would return to rest. Our sniping was only intended to make the presence of the Front felt. We were neither strong enough or well equipped enough to maintain complete control over the village. Sometimes the GVN soldiers sneaked into the hamlet at night to wait for us and capture us. They carried sacks along to put us in should they be able to capture us. One time they shot a guerrilla in the stomach, seized his machete, and captured him. At first, when we started sniping at the post, the GVN village council members were very afraid, and fled in their motorized sampans. But after they captured that guerrilla, they found out from him that we were very weak and didn't have any weapons. So they were no longer afraid of us and the GVN soldiers started laying ambushes in the village and carrying sacks along to throw us in if they could capture us" [DT205].

The "guerrilla theater" of posturing and deception had apparently reached the end of its usefulness. By this time, however, the guerrillas had begun to acquire real weapons and powerful military backup, and they continued to devise effective psychological techniques of intimidation. "Later on the main force units succeeded in capturing weapons from the GVN soldiers—even submachine guns—and began producing 'sky-horse' [*ngua troi,* a bazooka-like tube] weapons to fight the GVN. (The term used by Southerners to describe a praying mantis was evidently applied to this weapon because the gun's tripod configuration bore some resemblance.) Then the village council became frightened of us again because of the tremendous explosion of the 'sky-horse' [DT205]. Another cadre found this miracle weapon less impressive: "The Front forces' resistance was weak because their weapons were rudimentary. In order to fire a 'sky horse' gun, three men had to hold it while another pulled the trigger. When the gun fired, its blast hurled all four of them to the ground and they either got wounded or sick from the fall. Because they weren't well equipped, the guerrillas' morale began to slip" [DT109]. Although the "sky-horse" was essentially a glorified noisemaker whose main function was to produce a big bang, better-armed revolutionary units were becoming a reality and were increasingly able to provide the muscle that the poorly armed village guerrillas lacked. Further, the guerrillas themselves began to receive more and better weapons just at the time that the GVN was starting to understand how militarily weak they had been during the uprising. Not for the first time, the GVN would perceive and act on a reality that had already changed. For a while, however, the new GVN activism was quite effective.

Beginning in 1962, the fortunes of the revolution in My Tho began to shift. The Saigon government launched a pacification program and accelerated its military pressure against the revolution. The United States stepped up its military and civilian assistance. The Strategic Hamlet program regrouped scattered rural communities into concentrated agglomerations defended by fences and bamboo spikes, all more closely integrated into the system of posts and watchtowers than before. GVN forces were now more formidable than when the insurgency had begun.

The initial reaction of the local revolutionaries to Tan Ly Tay village, the first strategic hamlet in Dinh Tuong province, was a combination of bravado and complacency. Sau Duong, the region Party leader recalls that "The local cadres laughed, and said "let them go ahead and do it! After they have finished it, we will show our hand and their strategic hamlet will simply become our combat hamlet."" However, Sau Duong added, "The reality turned out otherwise. It was not just a question of rising up one time and destroying a strategic hamlet. There were times when the masses had to rise up dozens of time and had very strong forces within the hamlet, as in Ben Tre, but the strategic hamlet continued to exist."

The conclusion of Sau Duong was that the destruction of the strategic hamlets could not be done by political agitation alone, but would require military forces with enough strength to "oppose sweep operations and counterattack to annihilate, break up, and neutralize the enemy's military spearhead which they have used to create a sense of pressure in the areas where the masses once were in control but now had been herded [into the strategic hamlets] and did not dare return."[28] The key to opposing strategic hamlets was thus to strengthen the military forces, and find ways for them to operate in areas close to GVN controlled areas areas. In 1962 this was not an easy task.

Although Hanoi's February 1962 assessment of the situation in the South said that "the balance of forces had still not yet changed," the raw numbers of each side's forces indicates that, in strictly quantitative terms, the balance was unfavorable to the revolutionary side. After the war, Sau Duong, the Region 2 Party secretary, acknowledged the obvious fact that in 1961, "comparing our forces with those of the enemy, clearly those of the enemy were ten times as strong."[29] In the upper Mekong Delta there were 38,000 Saigon troops and, the GVN estimated, a guerrilla force of 15,000. COSVN listed 25,000 concentrated troops and 22,000 guerrillas for all of South Vietnam as of late 1961. The five-province area of operation for which the ARVN Seventh Division was responsible had 8,500 regulars in the division itself and 1,500 in independent ranger companies along with 28,000 territorial troops (the Self-defense Corps in the villages and the Civil Guard at the province and district levels). In the same area there were estimated to be about 2,000 main force soldiers in revolutionary units, and 3,000 in the province and district local forces along with some 10,000 village guerrillas.[30] In My Tho, in addition to the arrival of the Seventh Division in mid-1961 and a River Assault Group, the province had a battalion of Civil Guards and eight Civil Guard companies were stationed in the districts, along with two other independent companies, 3,606 Self-defense Corps (SDC) militia, and 242 police. As part of the American advisory buildup, a contingent of U.S. advisors moved into a former Catholic seminary on the outskirts of the province capital.[31]

Armored personnel carriers appeared for the first time in the delta in Long An province in the north during "Operation Delta" in June 1962.[32] New weapons such as armored personnel carriers (APCs) and new tactics such as helicopter assaults caused considerable difficulty for the revolution. The main ARVN force, the Seventh Division, became much more aggressive. After its operations in the Plain of Reeds, Long An, and My Tho, it moved for the first time in regiment strength to Ben Tre in July 1962.[33] In Ben Tre the result of this counteroffensive was that by the end of 1962, according to the count of the province Party committee, the GVN had retaken four liberated villages, set up seventy additional posts, and built 194 strategic hamlets.[34] COSVN later acknowledged that "[in] Central Nambo [MR2] the number of villages under our control decreased from 74 to 63 and we controlled only a million people. Our base area in the Dong Thap Muoi [Plain of Reeds] has been attacked severely between mid-1962 and early 1963 and the enemy has set up a series of outposts and a system of canals through the area."[35]

In My Tho, 184 strategic hamlets were set up in 1962, and the major military bases and Agrovilles controlling the border of the Plain of Reeds in Hau My and My Phuoc Tay were strengthened. The GVN built 400 posts during that year. The province Party history admits that the GVN "had basically finished pacifying the heavily populated areas and areas along the axes of communication [roads, rivers, and canals]. Only north of Highway 4 had they not yet commenced building strategic hamlets.[36]

From the perspective of the United States and the Saigon government, however, the situation in My Tho in 1962 was not entirely encouraging. Neil Sheehan's evocative account of this period describes the tenuous security situation in My Tho and the delta when John Paul Vann arrived in May 1962 to take charge of the American advisory group to the ARVN Seventh Division. ARVN operations merely "pushed the guerrillas into hiding or flight, in the way a ship displaced water. The moment they departed, the guerrillas flowed back."[37] This was true enough. However, focused as it is on the American side of the war and refracted through the prism of Vann's perceptions and the recent increase in U.S. attention to the war, this account does not fully reflect the trajectory of the situation from the Vietnamese perspective, in which the revolutionary side had been doing extremely well but was now encountering some new problems which had to be overcome. Much of the evasiveness of the revolutionary units during this period can be ascribed to an order from Military Region 2 to avoid GVN operations, which was a temporary expedient to stabilize the situation in a time of difficulties.

Even the region's 261st unit could not initially cope with the new ARVN aggressiveness. After the setback in May in Bang Lang it suffered another major defeat in July 1962 at Trai Lon in Kien Tuong province. Viet Thang, the former My Tho province Party secretary who had just been promoted to region level, wrote that "In mid-1962 the enemy had begun to carry out a new set of tactics: helicopter and armored personnel carrier assaults. At that time we really began to encounter difficulties, and were in disarray. At the beginning, the enemy used a helicopter assault to attack over in Kien Tuong, but it had a big impact on many places. When they attacked Trai Lon we lost a company, and this created consternation and demoralization among a number of our cadres and fighters. After that, the Region Party committee and Military Region committee put forth the policy of not allowing military units to resist sweep operations in order to preserve forces." Following the defeat at Trai Lon, a base for training new recruits near My Phuoc Tay was attacked in late August 1962 and 150 cadres and recruits were killed, "which created an extremely tense and stifling atmosphere. But we could not yet find a way to deal with it."[38] A cadre at the camp said that he later learned that a defecting deputy commander of a company of the

514th Battalion guided the ARVN forces in this attack. "There were only 24 men left in the company following the attack, including the command staff. It took us two days to bury the 82 dead. The remaining new recruits deserted" [DT215].

For much of 1961 and part of 1962 the 514th Battalion stayed in its home base near the province committee along the Nguyen Van Tiep Canal, often for weeks at a time before going out on an operation. Despite poor sanitary conditions, it was generally quiet and secure in the province base area. One reason for the quiet in the province Hung Thanh My base area was that the resident population of reed gatherers in the village had moved to the nearby GVN stronghold of Phu My and the village was "nearly empty," as was the area around the Stone Buddha Pagoda, which was another key province base [DT76]. The region base was even deeper in the Plain of Reeds, and even more quiet and desolate. A cadre who worked there at the time said that he was "located in a section of the Indigo Jungle right in the middle of the Plain of Reeds. The offices were scattered over many kilometers. In the villages [outside the Plain of Reeds] there was feverish activity, while at the Region there was total silence. There was no noise, and nobody spoke in a loud voice. Looking out, apart from the office, I could see nothing but trees and high-ranking cadres" [DT313].

In late August 1962, a high-level delegation from COSVN led by its third-ranking official, Vo Chi Cong, passed through My Tho on an inspection tour of the central delta. Viet Thang was assigned to accompany Cong on his way to Ben Tre and back. "At the time," recalled Viet Thang, "the situation was rather stable, so that we could go from My Hanh Dong [where the top province Party leaders were quartered, near the main province military base at Hung Thanh My] to Long Dinh [village] during the day."[39] Viet Thang continued his escort duty across the Mekong River to Ben Tre province and back again to My Tho. They even found time for a tourist visit to the island of the "Coconut Monk" on the Mekong River and were shown an ecumenical display of the monk's objects of worship, with Buddhist, Cao Dai, and Catholic icons and portraits of both Ho Chi Minh and Ngo Dinh Diem.

When they arrived safely back in the Hung Thanh My base area, "I must say that the entire region committee along with me and the comrades from the My Tho and Ben Tre Party committees felt that a burden had been lifted off our shoulders. This was a very historic trip, and we had organized it so that 'going was smooth and the return passed through safely.' In this happy frame of mind, we had been back in My Tho only a few days and had not yet had a chance to meet with the My Tho province Party committee when we encountered the sweep operation of September 2, 1962. You could say that this was a ferocious sweep, where they attacked right at the headquarters of the various province agencies, and many cadres lost their lives. But the COSVN group was safely protected."[40] The deputy commander of the Military Region 2 armed forces, who had been assigned to take direct charge of combat in My Tho in mid-1961, was killed in this encounter, however.[41]

The ARVN operation was so big that even some members of Madame Nhu's paramilitary Republican Women's Group went along, and came so close to the COSVN group that their boisterous banter could be clearly heard.[42] "We never suspected that enemy troops would make their landing from helicopters. Moreover, they landed in our rear and were able to advance directly to the target," said a cadre who was caught in the assault [DT233]. "For the COSVN comrades this was their first experience with such an enemy sweep, and they were no doubt quite concerned," observed Viet Thang.[43] This was not the first time the province base had been hit by bombing and artillery fire, but unlike the usual ARVN tactic, this was part of the actual assault and not a preliminary "softening up" of the target that gave advance warning of an assault to come later.

This defeat had an immediate negative impact on the revolutionary movement in My Tho. "In general," said one cadre, "because of the enemy's offensive, a number of our cadres and fighters became demoralized when they faced the enemy's new tactics and schemes. In fact, they were frightened by the enemy's weapons and heliborne tactics. Consequently, when the enemy launched the search and destroy operations on September 2, 1962, in My Hanh Dong, My Thanh, Thanh Phu, and some places in Cho Gao district, not only did the guerrillas and local force units [not] dare to resist the enemy's operation, but the province mobile battalion also split up and fled. As a result, the enemy freely conducted his activities and inflicted heavy casualties and damage to our forces" [DT233].

The pessimism of 1962 about the adverse turn in the military situation reached to the highest levels of the Party in the South. Sometime during this year (it is not clear whether it was before or after Vo Chi Cong's firsthand encounter with the military difficulties in the central delta), Tam Phuong, the military commander of the region, returned from a COSVN conference on guerrilla warfare. He reported to Sau Duong, the Party section of Region 2, the concerns of the top level revolutionary leadership in the South about the situation in the central Mekong Delta: "In the COSVN conference in Eastern [Nam Bo] the leading comrades were all very concerned about Region 8. In a situation where the enemy was carrying out special war, and with the material and manpower strength that they had, and the delta battlefield open and exposed as it was, would it be possible for [the region] to cope?" Tam Phuong also said that some COSVN leaders proposed transferring some of the region's rear base installations to the forests in Eastern Nam Bo.[44]

The Party later concluded that 1962 was a year when, because things seemed to be going well, the revolutionaries became too complacent and were not prepared for setbacks. Thus they overreacted when difficulties occurred. "They did not think of Uncle's [Ho Chi Minh] saying: 'if you have a river, remember its source; when it is day, you should remember the night' [*co song nho suoi, co ngay nho dem*]. When the movement is rising, you should think of the day it may become weak. When you enjoy advantages, you should think of the disadvantages. When you attack the enemy, you should think about protecting yourself." True, the GVN had recouped some of its losses, but the remedy was at hand, summarized in the saying "to attack the enemy is to protect yourself" [DT233].

The Revolution Strikes Back in Late 1962

COSVN leader Vo Chi Cong directed the My Tho province Party committee to meet and assess the battle of September 2. On September 7, he joined the province committee along with Viet Thang to formulate a response to this setback. The incumbent province Party secretary, Chin Om (Nguyen Chi Cong), had not yet returned from his lengthy ideological training, and the My Tho committee was represented by his defeated rival, the soon-to-depart Bay Hiep, along with Sau Danh and the wounded Muoi Ha. In addition to considering how to cope with the new ARVN tactics, the meeting's agenda also included devising measures to counter the Strategic Hamlet program. The attendees concluded: "With the enemy attacking in this way, if we want to survive, we have to attack them, and only by attacking them can we survive."[45]

This was easier said than done, however. Though it was only four months before its signal victory at Ap Bac, both the 514th and 261st battalions were reeling from major defeats. The province military and civilian units could not concentrate as called for in the resolution, but had to temporarily split up and disperse to regroup. But the lessons that the revolutionary leadership in the province learned from this period paved the way for the next and most successful phase of military operations from 1963 to 1965. Except for the recruit center they would no longer stay for long periods in a fixed base, vulnerable to the new firepower and mobility of the ARVN. The revolution profited from the lesson it had learned, and would eventually create a system of constant movement and deception, combined with unexpected attacks to keep the GVN off balance and reactive. This both provided better security and gave concentrated units like the 514th Battalion greater operational range. Until they perfected this system of operations, however, life in the 514th Battalion was difficult.

Yet even in the face of the heavy casualties inflicted on the 514th, the unit rebounded. In a move born of necessity, the units of the 514th began to move out greater distances from the Plain of Reeds and for longer periods of time. The expanded reach of the main military units, and their ability to fend off encircling attacks, increased their security. It allowed them to attack posts and strategic hamlets more successfully because they did not have to make long marches from their Plain of Reeds base or return immediately to the base. Even more important, the possibility that a big unit could be almost anywhere in the province at any given moment drew the "invisible line" around even more base areas in the more heavily populated parts of My Tho, and increased the security of these base areas.

The military region was so impressed by the 514th Battalion's performance in fighting off a heliborne operation in Cau Vong [My Hanh Dong village] in early October 1962 that in a conference the following month it adopted the policy laid down in the My Tho conference of September, and ordered all units to stand and fight when attacked, rather than fade away and preserve their forces as they had done before.[46] Chin Om, the My Tho province Party secretary who had been attending a year-long indoctrination course at COSVN, was preparing to return to My Tho when he heard the news of the Cau Vong victory over a GVN Ranger company. "The Cau Vong battle dissipated the worries that had been weighing down on me," he said. "I was even more confident in the correct policy of COSVN, which had now become a reality. We would definitely destroy their Special War on the Southern battlefield."[47] The American advisors also took note of the significance of Cau Vong. As Sheehan points out, this encounter was in some ways a preview of the Ap Bac battle soon to come. "The fighter-bombers struck with bombs, napalm and rockets. The guerrillas did not panic on this day. They stayed in the shelter of the foxholes until they could withdraw in good order. . . . Their performance seemed ominous to [U.S. advisor John Paul] Vann. Some of the Viet Cong leaders were teaching their troops not to let fear overcome judgment, to maneuver, and to take advantage of the terrain. The time of easy killing was coming to an end."[48]

The Battle of Ap Bac in January 1963

It is this context of military escalation and revolutionary reverses, and the new determination to stand and fight, that explains why the battle of Ap Bac was considered so significant by the Party. Ap Bac was a major turning point in the war because it marked a reversal of the military tide which had been running against the revolutionary side for much of 1962, and it allowed the revolutionaries to regain the momentum they had built in 1960–61. This battle also showed that the revolution could cope with the new weapons and more sophisticated equipment and tactics and bolstered the confidence of troops, cadres, and the civilian supporters of the revolution. It showed that "special war," the Kennedy counterinsurgency policy of relying primarily on local allies advised and equipped by the United States to defeat guerrilla war, could be defeated. Party General Secretary Le Duan said that "After the Ap Bac battle, the enemy saw it would be hard to defeat us."[49] The possibilities of a strategy based on winning by not losing were becoming apparent.

The battle of Ap Bac made the 514th Battalion so famous that the noted American political columnist Joe Alsop, a fervent supporter of the war, singled it out some years later as a symbol of how the early "Viet Cong" military prowess had faded, and pointed to several defeats of this unit as proof that the United States was winning.[50] It is safe to say that before its meteoric rise to international celebrity, members of the 514th would have found it difficult to predict that they would become global icons of guerrilla war. As we have seen, during its first two years of operation the 514th operated either in small units supporting village guerrillas and local force units or, rarely, as a company.

At the time of the confrontation between revolutionary and Saigon forces at the hamlet of Ap Bac in January 1963, the 514th Battalion had not fully recovered from its 1962 setbacks. Only one full company was combat ready. Second Company was seriously understrength and was refitting at some distance from Ap Bac when the battle occurred. According to a postwar Party history, the order to assemble a company from the 261st Battalion, a company from the 514th, a platoon from the Chau Thanh local forces, and guerrillas from Tan Phu village where Ap Bac was located, was given by the Military Region command, "based on an idea" of Nguyen Van Linh, then the Party secretary of COSVN and in the 1980s the Party secretary general in Hanoi. The purpose was to assemble this force to resist anticipated sweep operations against revolutionary bases.[51]

In one sense, the battle of Ap Bac was an accident or, as Tran Van Tra (then the deputy commander of COSVN military forces) sardonically put it, "they met without making a formal appointment."[52] The First Company of the 261st Battalion was in the area of Ap Bac because it had been on its way to coordinate in destroying a strategic hamlet in the next district, but for some reason it abandoned the plan and camped in the Ap Bac area of Tan Phu village (Cai Lay district). At the November 1962 Military Region 2 conference the First Company of the 261st Battalion and the First Company of the 514th had been designated to "move together and form a composite battalion which would both attack and destroy strategic hamlets and at the same time prepare to attack and defeat sweep operations."[53] Their movement, as Sheehan's account reveals, was discovered by U.S. radio intercepts.

According to Muoi Ha, "Ap Bac was a place chosen by the enemy because of its small area of treelines [*dia hinh mong,* e.g., there was little cover for concealment], its swampy terrain, and the fact that [they thought] the Viet Cong [sic] would not be able to retreat."[54] Though the revolutionary side did not choose this battle ground, some kind of similar encounter was inevitable, given the new "stand-and-fight" rules of engagement ordered by the region and the province. Region Party Secretary Sau Duong later commented, "Although from a leadership perspective there was no province plan for a battle at Ap Bac, once we had entered into the phase of activities [e.g., the more aggressive military campaign], if the battle hadn't taken place at Ap Bac, it would have happened somewhere else."[55]

The 261st Battalion bore the brunt of the attack, and the 514th played a secondary role as a blocking force [DT311]. This role fell to the 261st Battalion because it was the largest and best-equipped military unit in the area. It was the primary main force unit of the military region, and naturally had a feeling of superiority over province units like the 514th. A platoon leader of the 261st said proudly that the 261st was not only the best in the region, but the best in all of South Vietnam! "The women in there say if you are going to marry a soldier, choose a husband from the 261st Battalion. The 514th Battalion is held in less esteem. My battalion usually had to assist the 514th and if we won a battle it was announced that it was the 514th in order to create prestige for it" [DT101]. From its origins, the 261st Battalion was designed to do the heavy military jobs in the region. It was formed by the fusion of the early military units of Ben Tre and Kien Phong, which were the earliest and most successful in the military region.

The cadres of the 261st were experienced soldiers. Most were veterans of the First Indochina War who had returned from regroupment in the North. Sau Phu, a deputy commander of the 261st Battalion at the time and a regroupee himself, later made the point that "The quality of the southern armed forces changed as a result of the presence and concern of the comrade cadres who were sent back by the Center after six years of building up the armed forces in the North."[56] Sau Phu himself was well liked by his subordinates. One who accompanied him on a trip to his home village in Ben Tre province said that "he was tall and intelligent, and all his soldiers had great confidence in him. He behaved very nicely towards us and never failed to pay a visit to every squad after a battle" [DT77].

On the other hand, the fact that some of the attributes of Northerners, the smooth talk and the stern discipline, had rubbed off on these Southerners during "regroupment" led to some friction with many of the younger Southerners. One cadre of the 261st described the regroupee political officer of the unit: "He was quite status conscious and arrogant with the cadres who were his subordinates. He spent most of this time in his office, and didn't go to visit the company cadres often. He didn't think much of the company cadres, whose level of understanding he considered very low. He had attended political training courses organized by the Party in the North, and was very good at political argumentation, whereas the Southerners who had never been in the North were very bad at it because they had spent all their time in the jungle and had never attended any Party political training courses. He was articulate, clear, coherent, and eloquent. The Southerners didn't know how to embellish their speeches. Sometimes during meetings, the political officer oppressed the company cadres by, for example, ignoring them when they raised their hand requesting to express an opinion. Or, he interrupted a company cadre in the middle of his speech because he grew impatient with his inarticulate and incoherent style" [DT149].

Tu Khue was one of the two leading cadres of the unit at the time of Ap Bac. Unlike the Southerners who had returned from regroupment in the North, the interviews agree that he was a "Northerner" by origin. One said that he came from Thanh Hoa province [DT149]. It is unclear whether he had served in the South during the Resistance, as a number of Northerners did—including Muoi Ha, who was My Tho's top Party official in charge of military affairs (and who did not regroup to the North in 1954–55). Tu Khue was "bald, thin, and tall" [DT119]. In the approving view of a fellow regroupee in the unit, he was "very composed and meticulous" [DT101]. The military reporter, a Southerner who had not been North, was less enthusiastic, but not because Tu Khue was too "Prussian." He criticized him for being "too lenient and too slow for a military job" [DT313]. Another Southern cadre in the 261st Battalion from that period had the opposite complaint: Tu Khue was too strict and demanding. The cadre was criticized by Tu Khue for smoking Cambodian cigarettes, considered a luxury by the troops. "The people in the South are suffering," said Tu Khue, "and yet you are enjoying yourself at the expense of the people's sufferings." Fearful that this would go down as a black mark on his record, and angered by the criticism, the cadre snapped back at his commander. "I've been fighting for the revolution for many years now, and no one has ever spoken to me the way you do. I'm not afraid of death and I'm going to fight the enemy until I die. But as long as I have a few piasters to spare and as long as I'm still living, I'm going to buy cigarettes and enjoy myself a little. If you want to indoctrinate people, go back to the North and do it. We don't need you here. Without you we still can carry on the struggle." Tu Khue didn't reply to this outburst. "After that, every time he passed by my company I felt like jumping on him and throttling him to death. Tu Khue was the cadre I had arguments with the most often" [DT149].

Although Tu Khue seems to have acted on occasion as the commander of the 261st Battalion in these early years, it was actually another cadre who led the "composite" battalion during the battle of Ap Bac. Hai Hoang (Nguyen Van Dieu) was a Southerner and a regroupee. A fellow cadre described him in these terms:

> I've known Hai Hoang, the battalion commander, for two years and a half [as of 1966]. He was a regroupee and was very friendly with his subordinates. He was very fair, and never oppressed anyone. If a man had done something wrong, he criticized him for it, but he didn't do so in an arrogant manner. He never criticized someone for something they hadn't done. He was a very sympathetic man, and all the men in the 261st Battalion liked him very much, and it was because of this that he stayed with the battalion so long. The higher authorities didn't dare to transfer him to another unit because they were afraid that a new battalion commander might not command the same confidence and respect from the men in the battalion and this would seriously affect the unit's performance. Once every year, Hai Hoang used to go away for two or three months to meet with the cadres of other battalions and to confer with them about their own experiences and to learn new tactics. When he was away, Tu Khue took over as commander. The men were discouraged every time Tu Khue took over and anxiously awaited Hai Hoang's return. The other battalions also liked Hai Hoang for his nice behavior [DT149].

Later, Hai Hoang and Tu Khue apparently alternated as commanders of the 261st Battalion [DT149]. But Hai Hoang was clearly the right commander for this operation, which required command diplomacy to lead the "composite battalion" with its combination of Region and province forces. His performance at Ap Bac justified the selection. Tran Van Tra wrote, "It is clear that Hai Hoang fought a perfect battle, with a big victory that surpassed expectations."[57] The 261st Battalion operated effectively in the face of the challenge of the new ARVN mobility and firepower. At the time the ARVN uncovered the presence of a military unit in Ap Bac hamlet, they estimated a force of no more than 120.

It turned out that the combined force of the 261st and 514th was 320. During the course of the battle, First Company of the 514th downed two helicopters bringing reinforcements.[58] This feat became magnified by a curious combination of factors, and Ap Bac became one of the most memorable battles of the "Vietnam War."

The only extensive participant account of this battle in the interviews is the story told by a newly recruited member of First Company of the 514th Battalion—whose earlier military experience had been in the early 1950s as part of Bao Dai's Royal Guard in Dalat:

> At that time the 514th Battalion was still being built up. Apart from the First Company which was at full strength, the Second Company was only in embryonic form. It had only one squad when the 1963 Ap Bac battle took place and didn't participate. It stayed in Hung Thanh My village. The First Company was stationed at the Mieu Hoi [Pagoda] intersection in Ap Bac hamlet. The 261st Battalion was stationed about 1 kilometer to the southeast. Ba Thanh, the outgoing commanding officer of First Company, was about to hand over command to Muoi Diep, a regroupee. Therefore both of them took part in the battle. I had just been assigned to the battalion for three days. I didn't know much about what was going on when I was warned of the arrival of GVN troops. Later on I realized that a column of soldiers marched straight to our location at Mieu Hoi intersection. We opened fire when they came within range. While the GVN soldiers were busy fighting against us, the 261st Battalion, which was camped at the Cau Ong Boi bridge, moved toward the rear of the attackers. It succeeded in encircling the GVN, which had to call for help. The helicopters then came over, carrying heliborne troops, which jumped out in the open field, but their landing place was subjected to crossfire by the 261st Battalion and they suffered heavy casualties. Sometime later the paratroops came in and landed behind the 514th Battalion's trenches. However, the terrain there is spongy and the Ap Bac guerrillas helped our company shoot at the paratroopers. Many of them were killed while they were still in the air. Most of those who landed safely were pinned down by our fire. That's why the GVN suffered heavy casualties that day. The 514th Battalion withdrew to Hung Thanh My and camped on the bank of Canal 24, which flows into the Nguyen Van Tiep Canal. Then it celebrated the victory on the bank of the Kinh Xang Hau Canal on the other side of the Nguyen Van Tiep Canal [DT152].

His account is a useful supplement to Sheehan's extensive description of the battle in *A Bright and Shining Lie*.

The victory at Ap Bac apparently revived the spirits of the 514th Battalion. The newly arrived recruit found that "In 1963 when I joined this battalion every one of the cadres and soldiers were high-spirited. They looked happy and lively. They liked to sing and no one seemed to be homesick. They also felt very superior to the ARVN troops—especially after the Ap Bac victory—and felt that they could defeat them even at ten-to-one odds. Their faith in the final victory of the Front was unquestioned" [DT152]. A soldier from the 514th Battalion's Second Company also viewed 1963 as the high point of troop morale and civilian support. "In 1963 the soldiers seemed to be more happy and high-spirited. At that time the villages were still heavily populated and the soldiers were often welcomed by the Fighters' Mothers' Association or the Fighters' Sisters' Association." Looking back from the perspective of 1965, "the soldiers were nostalgic for the former celebrations of victories. Before, they could enjoy festivities which were enlivened by entertainment teams which flooded the village with songs and music" [DT60]. For the Vietnamese revolutionaries, the battle of Ap Bac proved that their forces could stand up to helicopters and armored personnel carriers, and gave confidence that the counterinsurgency strategy of the United States could be defeated.

The story of the coverup of a major military setback for Saigon became a symbol of the ill-founded optimism, self-delusion, and even mendacity of some U.S. officials and their GVN counterparts. At the national level, it was indeed a story of major proportions, and the repercussions from the extensive international coverage ensured that it would be a story of lasting local significance as well. In some ways this was the point at which the "Vietnamese War" became the "Vietnam War." The hitherto obscure struggles between the contending sides suddenly took on global significance just at the time that America's deepening involvement had raised the level of outside interest in Vietnam, and both the role of the United States and the impact of the Vietnamese war on the United States began to overshadow the local dimension of the conflict.

The shift in the momentum of the war signaled by Ap Bac put additional pressure on the Diem regime and certainly affected the upsurge of urban opposition to Diem in the spring and summer of 1963. This was a classic example of the interplay between the "three strategic zones" of the cities, delta, and mountain-jungle areas. The aura of invulnerability that President Diem had attempted to cultivate had been strengthened by the initial successes of the Strategic Hamlet program and intensified military operations of 1962, but was fatally undermined by the inability of Diem's government to cope with the resurgence of revolutionary forces in 1963, even before the final paralysis of his regime. This comeback was most noticeable in the Mekong Delta, and especially in My Tho.

GVN Pacification Efforts Following the Battle of Ap Bac

Despite the defeat at Ap Bac and the steady expansion of the revolutionary movement, in some respects the GVN actually improved its security position in My Tho during the first months of 1963 and was able to restore control in some of the villages and hamlets it had previously abandoned. On the eastern side of My Tho, the Hoa Dinh village post, which had withdrawn under heavy revolutionary pressure in late 1960, was reestablished in January 1963 [DT268]. In the Ap Bac area itself, the GVN managed a brief comeback with a flurry of pacification activity, and started resettling the population on the fringes of the Plain of Reeds north of Ap Bac to more easily controlled areas along the secondary roads, in hopes of redeeming its embarrassing loss and reasserting control in this area.[59] Thus one fateful consequence of the Ap Bac battle, which went unnoticed at the time, was the beginning of a GVN program of forced population resettlement which exceeded that of the Strategic Hamlet program both in the distances and extent of the uprooting involved and in the numbers of people affected. In the former Viet Minh stronghold along the fringe of the Plain of Reeds in Kien Tuong province the GVN "set up six posts in the My An area, mostly occupied by Hoa Hao. "The VC began having a hard time in the beginning of 1963 when the GVN began to set up posts in the village" [DT156].

However, it was one thing to establish conventional small military posts, and quite another to fortify an entire hamlet. One of the problems the GVN encountered in applying this Malaya-inspired counterinsurgency tactic of population regroupment in defended enclosed enclaves—to say nothing of controlling areas like this which were not strategic hamlets with scattered militia posts—is also indicated by the description of a strategic hamlet set up in My Luong village in southern Cai Be district. This was not a compact and defensible stockade, but like many hamlets in the Mekong Delta was strung out along a creek for 2 kilometers, and was defended only by a fifteen-man Self-defense Corps militia unit at each end [DT156].

In many areas the defeat at Ap Bac did not immediately reverse the 1962 gains of the GVN. For the first few months of 1963 the Saigon forces were carried by their own momentum. The beginning of the 1962 retrogression of the revolutionary movement started in Cai Be district when a large demonstration involving 2,000 people was suppressed. The GVN cracked down hard and arrested a number of the cadres leading the demonstration. This success was partly due to improved intelligence, as the GVN recovered from its original confusion and uncertainty about the real dimensions of the revolutionary challenge and began to organize a network which produced deadly accurate information on revolutionary cadres and units.

The retaking of Hoi Cu village is described by a cadre who witnessed this comeback by the Saigon forces. The "GVN had informers in the village who pointed out to them the Front cadres and the stationing points of the Front forces." Using these informers, "The GVN destroyed the Front forces; only five or six Front fighters were left and they had to withdraw to the fields in the back country. There were operations continuously and the people knew that they had all taken part in Front activities one way or another— taking part in demonstrations, beating drums, and so on—therefore, they were all afraid that if they just made the slightest move in support of the Front they would be arrested, beaten up, and jailed" [DT109]. "Once the GVN had the necessary information, it began to conduct operations inside the VC-controlled area. At first the GVN forces reoccupied the area about 1 kilometer from the post, and then little by little the GVN forces could go anywhere in the village. The GVN reaction was strong, and so the people became discouraged and demoralized because such a short time ago the Front appeared so strong, but now it seemed that the Front just couldn't oppose the GVN" [DT109]. This local reversal lasted from the beginning of 1962 until May 1963, perhaps not coincidently the month when the Buddhist struggles that led to the political unraveling of the Diem government began.

By the spring of 1963 the momentum of the previous year could no longer sustain the GVN in Cai Be. In Hoi Cu, "The Front reconsolidated its ranks and sent the Party members back to the village to reorganize and strengthen their organizations in the village. They assassinated GVN informers and once more destroyed the GVN grip. The GVN intelligence network was destroyed, and the Front revamped its organizations. From [May] 1963 on, the Front became strong" [DT109]. Even during the "reverse tide" of 1962 and early 1963 in favor of the GVN, "this post was encircled and soldiers couldn't get out to harm the people as they had done before, and its soldiers couldn't go out to buy things or contact the people. The [Cai Be] district supplied them with difficulty, because the road had been destroyed. The Front force encircling them consisted of only one guerrilla squad, who took turns sniping at the post. There were over forty Self-defense militia in the post and they could have easily defeated the guerrilla squad, but they were demoralized and did not dare put up any resistance" [DT223].

The Party Orders a More Aggressive Policy After Ap Bac

Province Party leaders were divided about how to deal with the loss of momentum during 1962. Bay Hiep, the outgoing deputy secretary of the province Party committee, who had antagonized the majority of the province committee by rigidly insisting on putting top priority on purging and purifying Party ranks just as the uprising was reaching its peak in 1960, now wanted to weed out the district leadership ranks in the face of the 1962 set-backs. At the province Party conference of January 1963 in the Hung Thanh My base area, the Party leadership acknowledged that "because of the establishment of Strategic Hamlets and enemy destruction, there is a lot of ideological tension among [cadres at] the district Party committees, and a lot of bad developments that have to be overcome, especially in the three lower districts [Cho Gao, Hoa Dong, and Go Cong]."[60]

A post-Ap Bac province Party committee meeting in January 1963 led to an upsurge in revolutionary activism in My Tho, and a renewed drive against the strategic hamlets. Although the GVN continued to register gains in early 1963, it also suffered some painful losses. The province Party committee gave orders to all the district committees to set up several "committees to destroy strategic hamlets," and the districts ordered the villages to do the same [DT233].

In the late spring of 1963 the My Tho province Party committee ordered the destruction of the Xuan Son strategic hamlet and sent in the First Company of the 514th Battalion, also under Thanh Hai's direct command, and the Cai Lay local forces and village guerrillas from the area to attack. At night these units lined up along a single front and "drove all the soldiers into the post—like chasing chickens into a coop." Although the revolutionary forces penetrated the post and achieved a temporary military success, they did not destroy the strategic hamlet until after the overthrow of the Diem government in November of that year [DT265]. Yet this military pressure had been sufficient to put the GVN on the defensive in Xuan Son.

Possibly encouraged by My Tho's initiative, and sensing that the time had come to build on the momentum of Ap Bac, Region 2 sent the deputy chief of staff of region forces to oversee military operations in My Tho in the area south of Highway 4. Tam Phuong, the military commander of Region 2, also went to the area surrounding Ap Bac to confer with the My Tho province leadership about how best to exploit the victory. While they were conferring, the GVN authorities launched their effort to erase the defeat by intensifying pacification in the area around Ap Bac, and started a major population regroupment effort. Tam Phuong concluded: "If we go on like this sending out the region and province companies one at a time to attack different strategic hamlets [as had been done before], and had no other approach, we would find it very hard to attack the enemy's system of strategic hamlets because they had concentrated all their resources and forces on a large scale." With this in mind, the region ordered a switch to a concentration of forces strategy and sent both companies of the 514th Battalion to the area south of Highway 4.[61] Not only did the revolutionary forces start to operate in larger formations, they also upgraded their firepower. A postwar military history finds that at this time even the modest addition of two bazookas, infiltrated from North Vietnam by sea, made a significant difference. My Tho province formed four combat support companies to use these and other heavy weapons, so that military attacks would pack a stronger punch. Earlier, the recoilless weapons available to revolutionary forces in My Tho had been unable to damage a fortified post. Now both companies of the 514th Battalion were sent to the area south of Highway 4, supported by these newly acquired heavy weapons.[62] They were also supported by the region's 261st Battalion.

The counter-pacification operations conducted by the 514th Battalion in other villages around Ba Dua had not eliminated the GVN presence in the area but, in Chin Om's view, they had "reduced the morale of the gang that governed the enemy's infrastructure so that they did not dare push the people around and control them as before." This initial success around Ba Dua encouraged the My Tho leadership to step up their efforts in the area. The province committee met and affirmed their support for Chin Om's "forward policy." "It was unanimous," he said, pointedly noting that Bay Hiep who had opposed this policy had returned from overseeing the reshuffle of Party organizations in the eastern districts also attended this meeting. Tam Phuong, the top military commander of Region 2, where Bay Hiep had close personal and political connections also supported the more aggressive policy. Tam Phuong "was very much in agreement" with the new offensive plan, wrote Chin Om with evident satisfaction.[63] At the province level, Muoi Ha was ordered to draw up a detailed plan of attack. While he was engaged in this task, COSVN convened a conference on destroying strategic hamlets, and My Tho sent a representative to participate. The My Tho Party leaders did not wait for further directives from COSVN, however, and decided that the time was ripe to try to destroy the strategic hamlets altogether. (COSVN evidently did not produce a detailed directive on destroying strategic hamlets until late August 1963.)[64] Cam Son and Xuan Son villages in the Ba Dua area were selected as the test case for this new effort.

On May 26, 1963, the province forces surrounded the Cam Son post and clashed with three companies of Civil Guard reinforcements. Chin Om's account says that the Civil Guards were repulsed with heavy casualties and that "the Cam Son post fled and Cam Son village was liberated." Muoi Ha pithily summarized the lessons learned from retaking Cam Son: "surround them, force them to surrender or pull out, stand up to sweep operations, liberate the countryside."[65] Tam Phuong, commander of Region 2, was also impressed by this lesson. "If you finish off the posts, that will be the end of the strategic hamlets."[66]

Chin Om recalled: "In the first phase the First Company of the 514th . . . led the assault and destruction of the network of strategic hamlets around Ba Dua, consisting of four interconnected hamlets in Long Trung, Long Khanh, and Long Tien villages. The result was that these strategic hamlets were destroyed. The troops carried out their armed propaganda mission well, and the local enemy government's morale sank and they didn't dare lord it over the people and control them as before."[67] The increased size and greater firepower of the 514th Battalion had an immediate impact. Using one of the new bazookas, it heavily damaged the main Cam Son post. Chin Om was less impressed by the contribution of the new weapons and points out that there was very little ammunition for them, implying that the military "strike force" at this time was an important but not yet dominant factor in the expansion of revolutionary control.[68] Whatever the role of the new weapons, a combined force of the 514th Battalion and local guerrillas inflicted heavy damage on the post in Cam Son and on the GVN reinforcements sent in after the initial attack. The Cam Son post along with posts in several surrounding villages, were forced to withdraw.[69] By May 27, 1963, the GVN forces evacuated Cam Son and the village was "liberated."[70]

After Ap Bac, these concentrated units found ways of staying for extended periods in exposed areas far from their secure bases in the Plain of Reeds. The key was establishing forward bases and logistical support in places like the 20/7 zone, so that big units could remain in the area and pressure the GVN forces continuously. The number of bases were increased so that there was always another base available within a short march. The surprise of a sudden appearance of a large concentrated unit could create a temporary numerical military edge for the revolutionaries in a given location, even though their overall troop strength in the province was much less than that of the GVN. By May 1963, the 514th Battalion was able to do this, and the result was a major shift in the military situation. In Sau Duong's words: "After the battle of Ap Bac, if we dared to deploy our big concentrated units in a given area, as I have described, the balance of forces in that area would swing completely over to our side, and that allowed us to destroy whole areas [*mang*], and knock off [*pha dut diem*] strategic hamlets more effectively and on a broader scale. It was precisely these ideas that, after the battle of Ap Bac, gave rise to the region's decision to open up the area south of Highway 4 in the days of July 1963."[71]

The "July 20" Campaign of 1963 Accelerates Revolutionary Gains Prior to the Overthrow of Diem

Because the available sources do not always agree on the exact dates on which the GVN lost control of posts in some villages of My Tho during 1963, it is not always possible to answer with complete certainty the important question of how much of the revolutionary recovery was due to the confusion and demoralization following the coup against Ngo Dinh Diem in November, and how much had occurred before this, thus contributing to his downfall. An additional difficulty in evaluating these accounts is that there was often more than one post in a village, and even if it is reported that "the" village post was withdrawn, sometimes it is clear from other interviews that some GVN militia presence remained in the village, usually in another hamlet. Often "the village X" post refers to the largest and best-fortified post at the village headquarters, sometimes guarded by a stronger provincial Civil Guard detachment rather than the district Self-defense Corps militia. Xuan Son village is a case in point. Clearly, however, the GVN position in key areas like Ba Dua and Hau My was in a state of near collapse by the end of May 1963, even though a military garrison still hung on in both places.

It was the Ba Dua campaign which led to the designation of the core area of My Tho province as the "20/7 zone," to mark the anniversary of the July 20, 1954, signing of the Geneva Accords. Tam Phuong writes that the July 1963 campaign resulted in the "complete liberation of a entire group of twelve adjacent villages in southern Cai Lay and Chau Thanh district, which linked [this area] to the [area] north of Highway 4 and the vast Plain of Reeds. From then on, this area was given a new and very meaningful designation: 'the July 20 zone.'"[72] Region 2 was impressed by My Tho's accomplishments and initiated a regionwide campaign to exploit this success, with My Tho designated as the top-priority area.[73]

The "July 20" campaign was actually launched on July 16. On the revolutionary side, the command staff selected for this operation was a composite region–province group. The region deputy commander (Chau Kim Son) was in charge, and Muoi Ha of My Tho province was the political officer for the campaign. Hai Hoang, the 261st Battalion commander at Ap Bac, and Sau Danh were designated as joint deputy commanders of this "unified command section."[74] The composite 261st–514th unit continued the attacks from the western part of the 20/7 zone toward the even more critical eastern GVN strongpoint of Vinh Kim. The province history claims that eight posts were forced to evacuate and seven posts were overwhelmed and compelled to surrender.[75] A recently infiltrated regroupee was the deputy commander of a recoilless weapon platoon, part of an entire heavy-weapons company of the 261st Battalion. With only a single heavy-weapons squad from its newly formed heavy-weapons company participating in the assault, the 261st Battalion overran the main Vinh Kim post (province sources say it was the 514th Battalion). "We captured some members of the Self-defense Force, seized a few weapons, and held a meeting of the local people for about two hours, and then withdrew, leaving over thirty of the GVN forces dead and injured, while we suffered three dead," said the platoon cadre [DT186]. According to Chin Om, the GVN tried to make the people rebuild the hamlets, but had to give up in the face of their protests.[76]

The GVN defeat in Vinh Kim left a powerful impression. "During that period, the morale of the troops and cadres was high," both because of the adequate supplies and because of the effusive civilian support at the time: "the soldiers were warmly greeted by the people everywhere they went." In addition, "there was not a lot of shelling at that time" [DT186]. A youth from a neighboring village was so impressed that he immediately joined. "When I arrived at the Vinh Kim market, I saw the whole post burned down, and the VC troops had taken over the place. . . . Frankly, I had just seen the VC troops take over the Vinh Kim post. I thought they were very strong. I believed that the country would be reunified very soon and it would be a glory to be part of a victorious force" [G35]. The GVN retook the town after the withdrawal of the 261st, only to lose it again for a time in the even more devastating assaults following the overthrow of Ngo Dinh Diem four months later.

It is clear that the position of the GVN in the upper Mekong Delta had been seriously eroded by the summer of 1963, and that even in the absence of the Buddhist crisis the Diem regime would have been badly weakened. However dimly the realities of the Vietnamese countryside were perceived in Washington, and even Saigon, a few young reporters like David Halberstam and Neil Sheehan reported the setbacks in the struggle against the revolutionaries. Halberstam made a particular splash with an August 15, 1963 article titled "Vietnamese Reds Gain in Key Area."[77] In a stunning example of the sophistry and self-deception that suffused official US thinking at the time, General Victor "Brute" Krulak, the Pentagon officer overseeing counterinsurgency efforts attempted to debunk the Halberstam article in which he asserted that "Halberstam, in his comments on the temperature of the battle in the Delta, exhibits a lack of understanding of our entire Vietnam strategy. From the start, that strategy involved a purification process, north to south; driving the Viet Cong southward—away from their sources of strength and compressing them in the southernmost area of the peninsula. This has proceeded. I Corps is fairly clean; II Corps, not much less so; III Corps, warmer; and IV Corps, still tough. . . . This was expected. The gradual redisposition of Vietnamese power, from the less to the more critical areas, portrays this. As General Cao, CG, IV Corps, said in June, 'We want to see all the Viet Cong squeezed into the Ca Mau Peninsula, and then rot there. . . . If Halberstam understood clearly this strategy, he might not have undertaken to write his disingenuous article. Perhaps this strategy should be more fully explained to the press.'"[78] In short, in Krulak's view, the growing numbers and aggressiveness of revolutionary forces in the Mekong Delta proved that the counterinsurgency strategy was working.

Party Assessment of Military Activities in 1963

During the last months of the Diem government, the GVN security situation in the rural areas continued to deteriorate. The nationwide target for strategic hamlets set in early 1962 had been revised downward to 11,000 by the end of that year. By mid-1963, 7,000 strategic hamlets had been built in South Vietnam, and many of these existed in name only. The revolutionary command at COSVN concluded that their major success in this period was in continuing to build up their own forces while the Saigon government was not able to expand its areas of control.[79] Another captured COSVN document covering the same period states that by July 1963 the revolution was "able to reoccupy the liberated areas and even enlarge them. . . . In central Nam Bo [Military Region 2] we controlled 1,900 hamlets," and 100 villages were "completely liberated."[80]

Revolutionary directives put considerable stress on attacking strategic hamlets in the 1962–63 period, but the available evidence suggests that they inflicted less damage on the GVN than might be inferred from the high profile given to this mission in the retrospective Party historical accounts of the period. In fact, the actual priority assigned to attacking strategic hamlets in South Vietnam as a whole during 1962–63 appears to be lower than it was in My Tho. A COSVN assessment of the 1961–64 period revealed that, countrywide, "Up to November 1963, there were 3,500 small and large-scale attacks against strategic hamlets, accounting for over 10 percent of our armed activities. The number of enemy soldiers captured and killed in strategic hamlets was 12 percent of the total enemy casualties. The number of weapons captured in strategic hamlets was 25 percent of the total number of captured weapons."[81]

Although this is an overall figure for all of South Vietnam and attacks against strategic hamlets in the Mekong Delta, where most of the strategic hamlets were concentrated, must have comprised a higher percentage of overall military activity than 10 percent, this proportion of military action devoted to such a high-profile task seems small. It is also curious that the primary COSVN directive on destroying strategic hamlets was issued only in August 1963. Perhaps this indicates that a lot of the military action in this period was either defensive (resisting sweep operations of ARVN—*chong can*) or aimed at militia posts as a preliminary to attacking the strategic hamlets themselves. The COSVN assessment says: "Especially in 1963, attacks against main objectives were conducted successfully in Regions 8 [Military Region 2] and 9. Our troops used raid tactics or combined these tactics with [attacks in] superior force to destroy enemy strongholds held by . . . one platoon up to one or two companies."[82] It was after the overthrow of President Ngo Dinh Diem on November 1, 1963, that the greatest collapse of the strategic hamlets took place, although My Tho province seems to have been more successful than other places in Vietnam in eliminating them prior to that time and clearly had the military initiative months before the coup that ended the Diem regime.

However, the Party's end-of-the year assessment of 1963 gave a mixed review to the military achievements of its forces. A January 1964 report to Bay Ba, a former soldier in the French army who had been promoted from deputy commander of the 514th Battalion to a key position on the province Military Affairs Section, provides a detailed account of the evolution of the military situation in 1963. There had been successes in mid-1963, especially in Cho Gao district and the Phu My area, showing that the morale of main force soldiers and guerrillas "was very high," and so "our forces were twice as strong as the enemy. . . . The concrete proof was that they continuously attacked posts at night and countered large-scale operations during the day. They endured and overcame hunger, fatigue, ferocious air and artillery, and were determined to achieve victory." With this conventional opening, which accentuated the positive, the report went into more qualifying detail, gradually shading the optimistic picture somewhat.[83]

There were four main phases in the evolution of the military situation in 1963, according to this analysis. "After the victory of Ap Bac," said the report, "designed to overcome the ideology [*tu tuong,* which, in this case might be translated "mind set," or "state of mind"] of fearing large-scale sweep operations, aircraft and artillery," the focus was on strengthening the spirit of self-confidence in revolutionary units, getting them to stand up to the ARVN sweep operations, while avoiding overconfidence. In the second phase of July–August 1963, "the enemy troops reduced their activities and operations. They stayed in posts; our troops could seldom engage them. We conducted only large-scale attacks (counter sweeps). . . . Then came the Doc Lap [Independence] phase (September 1963). Most of the units did not score good achievements. District units were hesitant and did not dare fight continuously (except units in Go Cong). Province units still lacked determination in the attacks on posts. Attacks on posts were continuously defeated. Cadres and soldiers were afraid of sweep operations and became pessimistic." Even the successes of the post November coup did not satisfy the demanding author of this report, who complained that while the surge of postcoup attacks "gained some results," subsequently, "due to long-range activity, they were tired and were forced to cope with enemy aircraft and artillery, therefore cadres and soldiers developed a fear of aircraft and artillery. They dared not stay to counter sweep operations and lost the courage to promote achievements."[84]

The Effect of the November 1963 Coup in My Tho

If the province leadership of the revolutionary side was not completely satisfied with its military achievements of 1963, their opponents had much more cause for concern. The urban political crisis stirred up by the Buddhist movement and other opposition groups had a paralyzing effect in the countryside, and the resurgence of the revolutionary position in the countryside also further weakened the position of the Diem government in Saigon. It was the type of vicious circle which revolutionary strategy hoped to create and exploit. The overthrow of the Diem government in a coup on November 1, 1963, accelerated the collapse of Saigon's position in My Tho and the Mekong Delta.

"At that time a GVN Civil Guard company and a Self-defense Corps platoon manned a post in the Phu My marketplace," said a cadre from the area. "I don't know when the staff of the 514th Battalion reconnoitered this place, but in November 1963 it took advantage of the revolution which toppled Ngo Dinh Diem in Saigon to attack and overrun the post. All the GVN posts in the area were affected by the revolution and the downfall of the Phu My post. They were also encircled by the liberation forces day and night. Finally the ARVN forces had to abandon the post and ran back to [Ben Tranh] district, where they assumed a defensive position" [DT233].

As the Saigon government was thrown into confusion by the overthrow of Ngo Dinh Diem, its position in My Tho rapidly disintegrated. Areas which had been pressured in previous months now fell under revolutionary control as the demoralized GVN soldiers withdrew from their posts. Xuan Son was one of the last islands of GVN presence in the Ba Dua area following the withdrawal of the Cam Son post in May. "In November 1963, when Ngo Dinh Diem was overthrown, the guerrillas began to besiege the guard post [of Xuan Son village]. On the fifth day of the siege, November 5, 1963, the 514th Battalion brought all its force and violent firepower against the post. The resistance from the post was very strong, and it held out for a day and a night. The following day the post received the order from the province to evacuate. As a result there was one killed and one wounded in the post. The VC had one killed and five wounded. From that day on the VC had full control of Xuan Son village. Half of the people in the strategic hamlet left the hamlet to join the GVN. The rest stayed and collaborated with the Front. No one was denounced or punished at that time" [DT265]. A slightly different version of the collapse of the last vestige of GVN control in Xuan Son asserts that, after the fall of President Diem, "the intervillage guerrillas from Long Trung, Hoi Son, Hiep Duc, Tan Hoa, and Phu An came in groups of six to twelve and encircled the Xuan Kien outpost continuously for half a month. Then the 261st Battalion came to attack the post and finally it was forced to withdraw" [DT293]. It seems that Xuan Son was not completely "liberated" until after the fall of Ngo Dinh Diem, but it was largely under to the control of the revolution by the spring of 1963, and GVN influence in the villages around the key point of Ba Dua had been essentially neutralized.

The crumbling Strategic Hamlet program collapsed altogether in the wake of the November 1963 coup. COSVN asserted that by December 1963, "3,800 strategic hamlets had been destroyed, of which 1,000 became liberated hamlets. The movement against the building of strategic hamlets is strongest in Regions 8 [Region 2] and 9."[85] In My Tho thirty-three posts were destroyed in the surge of revolutionary activity that followed the coup, while seventy-two strategic hamlets were destroyed and thirty strategic hamlets damaged [DT117]. Another estimate was that over 100 strategic hamlets had been destroyed [DT233]. In most cases these were never reconstituted, as in the case of a large strategic hamlet in Cho Ong Van, which had gathered 200 families from surrounding areas and moved them into cramped quarters much against their will. After the coup this was demolished, and the people returned to their homes [DT49]. Where the population had not been relocated to a strategic hamlet, the impact was less dramatic. Ap Trung A was a strategic hamlet in Nhi Binh village which had been built in 1963, before the coup. "People had lived there for a long time before it was set up," said one cadre, "and continued to live there after it was destroyed" [DT226].

Even allowing for the likelihood of exaggeration in these claims, the revolutionary gains were still dramatic. "At no other time," said one interviewee, "were members of the Front so enthusiastic." The larger GVN units stopped conducting "sweep operations" into revolutionary-controlled areas, while the guerrillas of Hoi Cu village who had been pushed out the village in 1962 moved the "invisible line" dividing the zones of control to within 200 meters of the paralyzed post, which ultimately had to be evacuated [DT117]. As the guerrillas became emboldened, the psychological pressures on the GVN forces caused a shrinkage in the area which they could influence or control, even in the areas where posts and bases remained intact.

The GVN collapse after the November coup was a case of "falling dominos," and revolutionary successes in one area led to victories in other places. This was not always a case of geographic spillover from one village to the next, but of a general demoralization of GVN soldiers and officials in My Tho that intensified with each new defeat. In the Phu My area, near the revolutionary province base, the local district Party committee did not wait for orders from above, but decided on their own to attack the posts in the area and liberate it. The Chau Thanh local force commander personally took the surrender of the Self-defense Corps of the Tan Hoa Thanh village post right after the coup, and Second Company of the 514th Battalion besieged the Phu My post. The following day the ARVN Seventh Division relieved the siege and evacuated all GVN military forces and civilian officials from the area, thus eliminating the last vestige of GVN presence in the immediate vicinity of the My Tho province base of the revolution. District cadres organized villagers to destroy the Phu My strategic hamlet to which they had been involuntarily moved and to return to their own hamlets, aided by the armed forces, who helped them move [DT179].

In the 20/7 zone, the two key control points of Vinh Kim and Ba Dua, which had been isolated and briefly occupied during the "20/7" campaign, were also evacuated by the GVN. "The people also came to the roads to uproot telephone poles. A number of strategic hamlets were destroyed right in the daytime. On those days the GVN soldiers didn't dare go out of their posts; they were all demoralized. They became powerless, while the NLF forces acted at will" [DT226]. After the fall of Ba Dua the deterioration of the GVN position in the Ba Rai area was felt even in villages like Thanh Hoa, at the intersection of Highway 4 and the Ba Dua road, and adjacent to Cai Lay district town. The interior of this village several kilometers from the district town had been contested for several years, but now "the withdrawal of the Ba Dua post permitted the VC to extend control over my own hamlet," said a resident of Hoa Hung hamlet in Thanh Hoa village—a little over a kilometer from the district headquarters [DT54].

As the balance of forces shifted rapidly in the wake of the November 1963 coup, the Party had to decide how best to exploit this political and military momentum. Should they move with the existing pace of events, further consolidating their control in the countryside with their current guerrilla war tactics, using this leverage to exploit the political and diplomatic possibilities that the coup had opened up? Or should they "go for broke" and try to defeat the Saigon army militarily, before the United States could react and come to their rescue?

Their decision to "go for broke" had momentous consequences not only for the revolutionary movement, but for the history of the twentieth century. In the short term, it led to gaining near-total control of My Tho as the growing revolutionary military forces swept the last remnants of GVN control out of the countryside. But this success also contained the seeds of two developments which had a profound impact on the future of the revolution. The first was the escalating demands the Party imposed on the peasantry to support the military offensive in 1964–65. The other was the U.S. intervention that this offensive triggered.

10

Going for Broke

After the overthrow of the Ngo Dinh Diem regime in 1963, the anticommunist position in South Vietnam precipitously declined. The Saigon army was confused and demoralized by the disunity and disarray in its ranks, and the local officials and militia in the countryside were uncertain about how the new Saigon government would develop. Taking advantage of this paralysis, the Communist Party devised and implemented a new, more aggressive strategy designed to exploit the opportunity created by the confusion. A major escalation of military pressure was ordered, in the hope that it would fatally weaken the Saigon forces and preempt large-scale U.S. military intervention. It nearly succeeded in its objective of shattering the Saigon army, but in the process triggered the very intervention of U.S. forces that the strategy had hoped to avoid.

In the Mekong Delta, this new strategy had several important effects. On a national level it marked the beginning of a decline in the strategic primacy of the Mekong Delta, which gradually lost the leading role that it had played in the revolution from 1959 to 1963. In the local and regional context, the level of military activity escalated in both the delta and in other areas of Vietnam. This increased military activity required a major increase in both troops and supplies, and the Mekong Delta was the best source of both these. As a result, two new policies were introduced in 1963–64 which produced some of the desired resources, but at a very heavy political cost for the revolution—especially in areas like My Tho. Voluntary financial contributions were replaced by a compulsory "agricultural troop support tax," which cut significantly into the budget of every rural family. Before 1964 the revolution depended largely on moral suasion and social pressure as well as genuine voluntarism to fill its military ranks, but now it turned to forced conscription.

These two policies of taxation and conscription fundamentally changed the nature of the relationship between the revolution and its supporters. More subtle and patient political measures were replaced by policies which reflected the urgent demands of the situation, and the mix of persuasion and compulsion shifted heavily toward the latter. The Party had offered the peasants land, and was now demanding its side of the bargain in the form of taxes. The Party had "Destroyed the Oppression" of the Government of the Republic of Vietnam (GVN) in the villages, but it was now asserting its own prerogatives as a governing power in conscripting young men into military service. And, as the scale and intensity of military operations escalated, increased burdens were placed on all the villagers to perform exhausting and dangerous service as civilian laborers, carrying supplies for the military units, digging up roads, and building combat fences and spike traps to impede the entry of GVN forces into revolutionary-controlled territory.

At the beginning of the Destruction of the Oppression, the balance of fear had to be tilted in favor of the revolution to overcome the aversion of the villagers to engaging in risky behavior. During the next several years the actual and potential costs of supporting the revolution declined sharply. Now, just as the revolution appeared to be gaining the upper hand, these costs began to rise once again. Perhaps for this reason, as well as the sudden demoralization of GVN officials and soldiers, some of the tactics current during the Destruction of the Oppression, such as "reduction of prestige" and the noise barrage beating of tocsins to psychologically intimidate GVN militia in the posts resurfaced immediately following the November 1963 coup in order to bolster the morale of revolutionary supporters and take advantage of Saigon's confusion.

Hanoi Decides to Intensify Military Struggle

Following the overthrow of Ngo Dinh Diem, the revolution had two choices. It could continue its patient political mobilization supported by a gradually escalating level of guerrilla warfare, or it could dramatically expand its military effort in order to force an early and favorable resolution of the conflict. After an apparently heated debate in Hanoi, the Ninth Plenum of the Party Central Committee decided on the more ambitious and risky strategy, which was laid down in considerable detail in Resolution Nine of the Lao Dong Party Central Committee, December 1963 (not to be confused with a 1969 strategic policy change also called Resolution Nine but issued by the Party Central Committee Office of South Vietnam COSVN).[1] As was the case with all sensitive Party decisions, the details of Resolution Nine were kept secret, though a full text of this decision was later obtained by U.S. sources.

In the Party's view, the overthrow of Diem offered new opportunities but also posed new risks. From Hanoi's perspective, the Diem government had been the vehicle for a disguised U.S. takeover of Vietnam. The armed conflict resulting from this effort could take any of three forms. It might be a low-level conflict, a "special war" *(chien tranh dac biet)* in which the United States would supply and support GVN troops but would not participate directly in the fighting. This had been the situation during the Diem government's attempt to repress the revolution until its demise in 1963. If the proxy war strategy did not work, the United States would be forced to intervene directly using its own troops, raising the costs of the conflict, but still restricting it to the territory of South Vietnam in a "limited war" *(chien tranh cuc bo)* like the Korean conflict. If the United States was unable to achieve a decisive military outcome in South Vietnam itself, it might expand the war to the rest of Indochina, even risking the possibility of Chinese intervention.

The Party outlined several possibilities. First, the United States might keep its commitment at the November 1963 level, or increase it slightly. Second, also within the framework of "special war," the United States might send in several times the current level of troops and even combine them with some allied forces from the Southeast Asia Treaty Organization (SEATO). Even if this major escalation occurred, it would remain a "special war" if the United States still relied primarily on Saigon forces.

Only if the United States took on the main burden of the fighting, or brought in SEATO troops on a large scale, would the nature of the conflict shift to "limited war." Hanoi estimated that the United States would intervene only if (1) they were convinced they could win, despite their current difficulties in Vietnam, (2) they were convinced that there would not be a strong reaction from North Vietnam if they intervened, or (3) they felt that there would not be a strong international reaction against the intervention. All three possibilities were largely discounted. "In the immediate future, these possibilities are not likely," the Party concluded, because "they clearly see that if they get bogged down in a protracted war on a large scale, they will be in a passive position throughout the world. On the contrary, that possibility [U.S. intervention] will increase if the revolution in the South is not strong."[2]

Thus the Party decided that the best way to avoid American military escalation in Vietnam was quickly to build up its own military forces for either eventuality. It hoped that a stronger military position would dissuade the United States from intervening, but if they did, the buildup would leave the revolution better prepared to cope. Because during twenty years of revolutionary struggle a high level of "enlightenment" among the people had been attained, "the revolutionary movement of the people has created the ever-increasing capability of strengthening and building up our military forces. If we lead the political and military struggle well, and lead the buildup of forces well, then we may be able to create a large military strength very quickly. Creating a basic change in the balance of forces between ourselves and the enemy is something that is entirely within the bounds of possibility."[3]

Ever since the battle of Ap Bac in early 1963 and especially since the overthrow of Ngo Dinh Diem, said the Party resolution, the internal ranks of the Saigon government had been disintegrating. This, in turn, increased the possibility of the Saigon army and government falling apart, leading to a general offensive and uprising, and total victory. In such a circumstance, if the United States was faced with imminent defeat of the Saigon government, they might send in forces to save the situation. If that happened, the war would be longer and more difficult but would be won in the end, just as the war against the French had been. So, the possibility that the impending collapse of the Saigon government might bring U.S. combat troops into Vietnam was considered, but the tone of Resolution Nine suggests that the overall assessment was that it was more likely that the United States would not intervene. Even if they did, it would not change the ultimate outcome, though escalation would raise the costs to the revolutionaries.

A final consideration was that the revolution in the South might pass through a "transitional phase," with "new and complex forms and methods of struggle," before complete victory was achieved. This was a reference to a negotiated solution and possibly a coalition government. Even in this case, as in all the other eventualities, "we must be resolved to mobilize the entire Party and army to *bring about the maximum victory,* and shouldn't have a half-hearted attitude of wanting to stop at the transitional stage."[4] The highest possible level of military pressure was called for to bring about the best outcome (no U.S. intervention), cope with the worst possibility (U.S. intervention), and even to complement a negotiated solution, which was viewed as only a stage along the way to a military resolution of the conflict.

Resolution Nine Shifts the Focus Away From the Mekong Delta

Starting from this strategic decision, the Mekong Delta began to lose its primacy in the revolutionary struggle. By Tet 1968 the fighting in the Mekong Delta was fierce, but compared to Central Vietnam and eastern Nam Bo, it was a sideshow. In 1964–65 the major strategic role of the Mekong Delta was to provide manpower and resources to the big units, while denying these resources to the GVN. "If we gain control of the rural deltas, then the mountain-forest regions will not be isolated and we can mobilize manpower and materiel resources to develop our forces both in the delta and in the mountain-forest areas. Gaining control of the rural delta areas will create a favorable posture to, along with the mountain-forest areas, support the movement in the cities and, when there is an opportunity, move in to attack the enemy's key positions and nerve centers."[5]

This formulation emphasized "control" of the delta areas, which could be accomplished by a mix of political struggle and guerrilla war, but it also suggested that the manpower and material resources from the delta would be used to build up military forces both in the delta and in the mountain-forest regions. To some extent this was true, but the clear priority was the big units in eastern Nam Bo and the Central Highlands, and recruits from the delta were sent to these areas. The strategic slogan for 1964 communicated to the My Tho cadres also suggested that they were essentially involved in a holding action. They were told that the mission was "to occupy the mountainous area, to firmly hold on to the delta, and to attack the urban areas [*chiem linh rung nui, giu vung vung dong bang, tan cong vung do thi*]" [DT233]. "Holding on to" the delta, the task assigned to My Tho, was a less expansive directive than Resolution Nine's admonition to gain "control of the rural delta areas," although it also implied that such control had already been fundamentally achieved and needed to be preserved.

Clearly, the strategic logic of Resolution Nine was to take the resources of the Mekong Delta and deploy them to other battlefields for other uses. Nevertheless, the delta was also to intensify its military efforts and build up its forces even while supplying manpower to the bigger units to the north. To keep up the military pressure in My Tho, the province was assigned the target of reaching a strength of seven companies for the 514th Battalion; but because of the requirement to send province troops to higher levels, this could not be done. By the end of 1964 the province unit had managed to form five companies, in spite of the drain of "upgrading of troops" (sending troops from concentrated units in the province to higher level units and replacing them with manpower drawn from local guerrilla forces) and a substantial number of casualties during the year [DT233].

Resolution Nine was a costly strategy in several respects. It succeeded in its immediate objective of demoralizing the ARVN forces and pushing them to the brink of defeat. However, this success not only failed to convince the United States that it had no foundation for a military intervention, it actually precipitated it by confronting the United States with the imminent prospect of a humiliating defeat and provoking a crisis which triggered the decision making that produced the American escalation. Whether a continuation of lower-level guerrilla warfare would have led to a more gradual decline of the Saigon government without a specific crisis to prompt U.S. intervention, or even to a negotiated solution, lies in the realm of historical speculation. At the least, Resolution Nine created the necessary if not the sufficient conditions for U.S. intervention.

Overthrow of Diem and the Assassination of President Kennedy Leads To U.S. Re-emphasis on the Mekong Delta Just as Revolution Changes Focus

Although the Mekong Delta was now accorded a lower strategic priority in revolutionary strategy, both the military and the political movement intensified in My Tho, as the Saigon forces began to lose their grip on key areas of the province. Ironically, just as the revolutionary side was shifting its strategic focus away from the area, the United States decided to concentrate its attention on the Mekong Delta. National Security Memorandum 273 (NSAM 273), issued on November 26, 1963 (and made famous by the movie *JFK*, in which it was alleged to show that Kennedy's efforts to disengage from Vietnam were thwarted by a warmongering clique led by Lyndon Johnson), was the first major policy review following the deaths of Diem and Kennedy. As the authors of the *Pentagon Papers* correctly conclude, "NSAM 273 was an interim, don't rock-the-boat document. Its central significance was that although two assassinations had changed many things, U.S. policy proposed to remain substantially the same. In retrospect, it is unmistakably clear, but it was certainly not unmistakably clear at the time, that this was a period of crucial and accelerated change in South Vietnam."[6]

At the time, the U.S. presumption was that it would not have to intervene militarily in Vietnam and, in fact (based on the assumption of an improved political and military situation), would have largely withdrawn from Vietnam by the end of 1965. This meant that the emphasis was still on assisting the South Vietnamese to win the war and this, in turn, suggested a concentration on the major populated rural area in South Vietnam, the Mekong Delta, where the struggle for manpower and material resources was most intense. "We should concentrate our efforts," said NSAM 273, "and insofar as possible we should persuade the government of South Vietnam to concentrate its effort on the critical situation in the Mekong Delta."[7] This decision came a month before the major shift in Hanoi's policy in Resolution Nine, but even had it been based on knowledge of the new revolutionary strategy, the focus on the Mekong Delta still would have had some strategic logic from the U.S.-GVN perspective. It would have acknowledged that the mountain-forest buildup in the Central Highlands and eastern Nam Bo depended ultimately on resources from the Mekong Delta, and by putting more pressure on the delta it would have made that strategy more difficult.

Situation in My Tho Following the November 1963 Coup

A reconstruction of the period from the coup of November 1963 to the U.S. intervention in the spring of 1965 shows that the general trend was the establishment of overwhelming military dominance by the revolutionary forces. But this was not accomplished easily or without setbacks, and during the year of victories in 1964 there were also serious defeats for the revolutionary side. Moreover, the victories were purchased at a heavy price. The political costs to the revolution brought on by heavy taxation and forced conscription have already been mentioned. In addition, the intensification of the fighting set in motion another process that was to have a devastating impact on the revolution. When the Party turned up the heat militarily, it provoked a desperate response from the GVN side. Lost in the remembered impressions of an unbroken string of GVN military disasters in 1964 and early 1965 are the significant counterblows ARVN delivered to the revolution's forces in My Tho during 1964. On balance, the revolution came out far ahead in this contest to see who could inflict the most damage on the other side, but it was by no means cost free.

The heaviest cost was not the military defeats in specific engagements, but in prompting a new GVN military tactic. Starting in late 1963, the shelling of the countryside by heavy artillery was escalated dramatically. Even with a much lower level of air and artillery bombardment in mid-1963, the impact on the revolutionary troops was substantial. The year-end military review of 1963 commented that "since the time the enemy increased airstrikes and artillery fire against our troops (August 1963), the principle of troop bivouac became the principle of troop concealment and all forms of entertainment stopped. We were more inclined to the protection of troops and disregarded their joyful and youthful activities. Story telling in squads and platoons could only be conducted separately, and other forms of entertainment such as playing the flute or harmonica, or dancing and giving shows, could very possibly be realized but lacked leadership and encouragement. The units and organizations were enveloped in a melancholic and uneasy atmosphere; troops in bivouac often wandered alone, violating the internal regulations, partly because they could not bear the melancholic atmosphere."[8]

Intensified Bombing and Shelling Launches Refugee Exodus From the Countryside

Already evident in 1963, this problem became more acute as the intensity of the war escalated. And, as the United States grasped for some military alternative to the faltering ARVN ground troops, the intensification of the air war also began to have a major impact on the civilian population in the populated Mekong Delta. By their very nature, air and artillery were not discriminating weapons, and they inflicted heavy casualties on the rural peasantry. The inevitable result was an exodus of civilians from the villages most under the influence of the revolution, since these areas were the targets of the bombing and shelling. One of the first villages to be depopulated by bombing and shelling was Xuan Son, near Ba Dua in the 20/7 zone. A village cadre described how villagers began to leave for Cai Be or Cai Lay district town or the relatively tranquil island of Tan Phong as a result of heavy shelling that began in February 1964. The cadres tried to make their own relatives set an example by returning to face the escalating danger, but they met with limited success [DT132].

Beginning in July 1964, the neighboring village of Cam Son became a target of shelling from Cai Be and Cai Lay district towns. "Each shelling lasted from 1500 hours to the end of the afternoon. During the last months of 1964, Cam Son was shelled 25 days out of the month" [DT2]. Probably this was a response to the daring attack on Cai Be district town in July 1964, discussed below. Dong Hoa Hiep was another village near Cai Be district which "was often shelled, especially after the Cai Be battle" [DT68]. Unable to meet the threat of attack on the district towns with aggressive operations and patrolling, the GVN relied increasingly on shelling the surrounding villages to break up any real or imagined troop concentrations.

"Free fire zones" were areas created in the province, initially mostly in the Plain of Reeds and adjacent areas, where bombing and shelling could be done without prior authorization from the province or ARVN Seventh Division command. Naturally, most of the civilian population in these zones, including the supporters of the revolution, left for safer locations. Artillery shelling became increasingly indiscriminate, and this trend reached its peak with the implementation of the tactic of "harassment and interdiction fire," random shelling of the countryside based on the presumption that the possibility of unexpected shelling would hamper the movements of revolutionary troops. Of course, the very randomness of this tactic also put civilians at risk, and in fact resulted in extensive civilian casualties, especially in the initial phases before the civilians learned to cope with the intensified air and artillery assault.

"Coping" meant moving out of their homes into the shaded orchards and treelines. For many this meant moving to squalid refugee settlements along Highway 4, and living in shacks in the broiling sun far from their rice fields. For others, it meant moving into improvised shacks in the middle of the rice fields, away from the treelines that were the refuges of the cadres and troops and therefore the targets of air and artillery. To convince the omnipresent L-19 observation plane forward air control spotters (mostly American), who identified the targets for air strikes, that they were innocent civilians, the peasants in the rice fields began to wear white clothes, on the reasonable ground that "black pajamas" had become so identified in the minds of Americans with the "Viet Cong" that anyone who wore the opposite color would be by definition a non-Viet Cong. When the civilians began to leave their homes in the hamlets, this set in motion a process of gradual erosion of the indispensable support network for the revolution. Former supporters were pushed from the revolutionary side by resentment against forced conscription of the youth, compulsory and dangerous civilian labor details, and the heavy increase in taxation. They were also pulled away from the revolution by the heavy bombing and shelling.

Peasant Attitudes Toward the Revolution After the 1963 Coup

It is precisely at this juncture that some of the key questions about the nature and extent of popular support for the revolution become especially salient—and especially difficult to answer. Certainly the honeymoon of 1961–63 between the revolutionaries and the populace at large was far from over; but new tensions between them were beginning to emerge. There were many reasons for the overwhelming popular support enjoyed by the revolution during this period: the benefits of land distribution and rent reduction, the elimination of oppressive GVN local officials and the end of the hated *corvée* labor and threat of arbitrary arrest, and a deep-rooted feeling that the revolution was the authentic face of Vietnamese nationalism and that the My-Diem combine was merely an extension of foreign domination. "In Vinh Kim, it was not until the end of 1962 that about 90 percent of the villagers began to support the Front energetically," said the head of the village propaganda and indoctrination section. "Their former fear had disappeared because they realized that (1) the Front had really taken care of the poor by giving them land, and (2) the Front was more lenient toward the people than Ngo Dinh Diem's regime. Instead of punishment and oppression, the Front was inclined to use reeducation. The people then thought that Diem's regime was very cruel because there were many people who were arrested, tortured, and imprisoned by GVN officials" [DT143].

The evidence of popular support was that (1) all families were willing to let their sons join the liberation military units, (2) they were at that time willing to pay taxes "and did not even ask us to reduce them," (3) villagers regularly participated in fencing the hamlets and digging spike pits, and did so with enthusiasm, and (4) they were so enthusiastic about attending the village meetings that sometimes they regretted that meetings broke up so soon. They lingered around the meeting place, discussing the Front's policies, the cadres' behavior, and the cruelty of the Diem regime until late into the night. (5) They eagerly protected the cadres by hiding them during sweep operations, and quickly came to the defense of the revolution by soothing people with complaints against cadres with the assurance the Front would definitely punish any misbehaving cadre because it "would never let its cadres bother the people" [DT143].

In this propaganda cadre's view, the high-level enthusiasm for the revolution lasted until the end of 1963. Starting in 1964, all the things that had created a surge of support for the revolution turned in the other direction. They were no longer willing to let their sons be drafted, and they complained about taxes and were reluctant to pay. They only attended meetings after being summoned four or five times by the cadres, and then went only out of fear of being punished by the cadres. And they "no longer liked the cadres as before. When they came across us, they just continued on their way, ignoring us." This change was ascribed to high taxation, cadre arrogance, the discouragement of the people because of the increased level of destructiveness of the war, and the decline in Saigon's coercive behavior since the fall of Diem (as it lost control over these areas) and the simultaneous rise in revolutionary coercion (as they gained control) [DT143].

The Party Leadership in My Tho Reacts to the 1963 Coup

The Party's exploitation of the opportunity afforded by the overthrow of the Diem regime began auspiciously. First, the coup did not come as a complete surprise to the cadres in My Tho, since numerous coup rumors had been floating around in the supercharged political atmosphere of the last months of the Diem administration, and some cadres discussed this possibility in pre-coup indoctrination sessions [DT120]. For several months prior to the coup, the Party conducted indoctrination sessions to discuss the evolution of the GVN crisis and its possible outcome.

During those study sessions the participants were briefed that "All our cadres and fighters should get psychologically and ideologically prepared to grasp the opportunity. A coup d'état will take place within the GVN ranks. We should take advantage of the occasion while the GVN authorities are fighting each other to deploy our forces to encircle and harass the neighboring GVN posts in order to enlarge our liberated areas." Those study sessions were held by all organizations at the hamlet level, and as a result of these sessions everyone was confident of the coming victory. When the coup d'état took place, drums and tocsins were loudly beaten in all villages in the area in response [DT226].

Tam Phuong (Le Quoc San), the Region 2 military commander at the time, indicates in his postwar memoir that planning for the eventuality of a coup against Ngo Dinh Diem began in October 1963, a month before the coup. Acting on a COSVN directive, Region 2 began to plan for the contingency of a coup in Saigon. "According to the Region directive, if there was no internal coup in the enemy's ranks by November 5, 1963, a coordinated campaign would be launched throughout the entire region." Thus it appears that the Region directive was less a contingency plan to exploit the coup than a means of intensifying pressure on the Saigon government if the coup was delayed. The central focus of the impending military effort would be the districts of Cai Lay and Chau Thanh. The Region's 261st Battalion and the province's 514th Battalion (now up to three companies in strength) would attack Ba Dua and Vinh Kim in order to liberate all the villages between them and motivate the people to rise up and destroy strategic hamlets. After this, these units would move to Phu My, where "they must finally finish off the company led by the contemptible Hue" and liberate all the villages in this area.[9]

The coup against Ngo Dinh Diem actually disrupted the execution of this plan, and the My Tho province authorities hastily decided to split up the two units, sending the 261st to the main target area of Ba Dua and Vinh Kim, while the 514th was dispatched to Phu My. The 261st overran the Ba Dua post and "liberated" the villages between Ba Dua and Vinh Kim, but was not able to take Vinh Kim itself and so moved back to the Ba Dua area to expand the area of revolutionary control. The 514th arrived in Phu My on November 2, and by November 4 was in full control of this strongpoint as well as most of the surrounding villages. The second company of the 514th Battalion then went on to Cho Gao and Go Cong districts to the east and forced the surrender of thirty posts. According to this revolutionary account, 162 posts were "eliminated" and 52 villages "liberated" by the end of November 1963. This month-long period following the coup was called—perhaps in retrospect—the "seizing the opportunity campaign" *(dot thoi co)*, though the campaign would have been launched whether or not President Diem had been overthrown.[10]

Local Antagonists Confront Each Other in Phu My

Because the concept of taking advantage of any "sudden situational opportunity" *(thoi co)* during the course of any revolution—a legacy both of Leninism and the experience of Vietnam's own August Revolution of 1945—had been so deeply inculcated in Party members at every level, they knew that they had to do something to respond to this major change, and not just sit back and await orders from above. In the "Tan family" of villages (villages whose names include the word "Tan," located near the market center of Phu My), which protected the province headquarters as well as access to the eastern districts of My Tho province across Highway 4, the local revolutionary movement responded quickly. "Sometimes things like the November 1963 came up so fast that waiting for guidance from above was impossible," said a district cadre. "Each village Party chapter had to hold a meeting to respond to the new situation" [DT233].

The response to the overthrow of Diem in Phu My village is of interest for a number of reasons. First, it shows that the Party was already headed in the direction of trying to eliminate this important GVN outpost. The "sudden situational opportunity" accelerated this plan but was not an initiative out of the blue. This illustrates the short-term impact of the coup in My Tho. It did not immediately result in new plans and objectives, but it stepped up the timetable for implementing existing plans, which were revised as circumstances dictated (the original plan was to have both battalions attack Phu My after taking Ba Dua, but the coup prompted the province to try to attack Ba Dua and Phu My simultaneously). Second, it is an interesting study in leadership and command organization. The devolution of Party leadership from the districts to the villages had just gotten underway, and much of what happened in Phu My was decided by a single district cadre and not the collective district party committee, or even the province and the region. Finally, the battle for Phu My illustrates the personalized nature of the conflict, featuring a showdown between the Party leader in the area and his GVN nemesis.

Ba Vu was born in Tan Hoa Thanh village on the eastern edge of the Plain of Reeds, and adjacent to Phu My, so he was very familiar with this critical area. He had been a Viet Minh cadre in the Chau Thanh district headquarters during the Resistance, but was arrested by the French during the period of Viet Minh decline in 1952. He managed the extraordinary feat of escaping from the prison island of Con Son on a raft in 1957, and in 1960 he reappeared in the "Tan family" to lead the Destruction of the Oppression along with a small group of cadres who constituted the first district armed unit of Chau Thanh [DT233]. By 1963, Ba Vu, with his Colt 45 at his side (a symbol of high rank), had been placed in charge of propaganda and indoctrination of the Chau Thanh district committee, but was also assigned to take direct charge of a group of villages in the northeast sector of the district, which included the "Tan family" and Phu My.

A woman clerk-typist in the district committee office characterized Ba Vu as "a severe-looking and quiet man," and said that his subordinates did not like him because he appeared aloof, but they were afraid to show it "because he was a powerful man" [DT182]. Another district cadre agreed that Ba Vu was "serious, arrogant, and remote," but added that his leadership was good and that he was a "resourceful and eloquent speaker" and "forceful and assertive in everything he said" [DT233]. He did not drink alcohol—or even tea (a luxury in peasant society)—nor did he smoke. Furthermore, he "did everything according to set principles" and would try to indoctrinate local village cadres on his visits, and pass on directives and criticism rather than socializing. He would not let up until "everything had been done to expectation." But even this dedicated and disciplined leader had his faults. He had two wives, and in addition had that very year (1963) become involved with a woman from Vinh Kim village. To make things even more complicated, one of Ba Vu's associates in the Chau Thanh district committee was also involved with the same woman [DT233].

Another problem with Ba Vu was that he had a tendency to ignore the district leadership. To some extent, this was built into the situation. Ba Vu had been assigned to take over this sector of the district precisely to allow for quicker and more responsive decisions in a rapidly changing situation. Moreover, the dominant view among those familiar with the district committee regarded him as a better leader than the district secretary. Vua Tau ("The Chinese King"), Ba Vu "usually ignored the Chau Thanh district committee and rarely submitted reports to it" [DT233]. The head of the village military affairs section (MAS) in Phu My village at the time said that after Ba Vu assumed leadership of the area, "the village cadres no longer attended any meetings by Thanh Viet [the head of the district military affairs section]. We only met with Ba Vu" [DT179]. Thus both the line (district secretary to village secretary) and staff (district MAS to village MAS) Party channels were sometimes circumvented.

Nonetheless, Ba Vu had come into the Phu My area with a mandate. "Ba Vu first came to Phu My village in October 1963 to strengthen the local Party chapter. Then the coup d'état broke out in Saigon. After the coup d'état the NLF took over Phu My and the surrounding area." The head of the Phu My guerrilla unit said he believed that "the district headquarters closely watched the evolution of the conditions in Saigon at that time. Ba Vu convened a meeting on the very day that the coup started. He said that we should take advantage of the confusion caused by the coup to launch and attack to liberate the area." Soon after the coup, the "Chinese King," as district Party Secretary, and Thanh Viet, as head of the district military affairs section, came into Phu My to join Ba Vu [DT179]. This concentration of top district cadres indicates that Phu My was considered the main priority of the movement in this district and that Ba Vu, though taking the initiative, was not acting in isolation.

One of the chief obstacles to the revolution in Phu My was a Cao Dai commander named Tu Hue, who played the role of a local warlord in the area. In 1960, during the Destruction of the Oppression, the revolutionaries had gained control over the entire area except for the central market. But Tu Hue led a GVN resurgence in 1962. He had formerly been a captain in the dissident Cao Dai Lien Minh forces and had been arrested by the GVN. He was persuaded to join forces with Saigon, however, and was allowed to form a Civil Guard company of his Cao Dai troops and with them he regained complete control of the village [DT171]. During his ascendancy, Tu Hue cut an impressive figure, and villagers were fearful and deferential toward him. The view from the other side was correspondingly negative. "Tu Hue used to be considered a cruel person who sowed death and destruction in the Phu My area. Everyone in the village, young and old alike, had to greet him respectfully whenever they met him. Every time he came in the village, innocent villagers were killed as well as revolutionaries, and this is why the revolution and the people hated him" [DT159]. Tu Hue's methods were effective, however. In 1962 he established a Strategic Hamlet and a defense system of posts and a fort. He also launched an aggressive system of patrolling that, unlike most GVN operations, did not fall into predicable patterns and was backed up by effective tactics such as hiding a reserve unit to be deployed when least expected. Tu Hue's carefully devised tactics soon put him in complete control of the village. He routed the village guerrillas, who had only four weapons and twenty bullets among them, and the cadres along with the guerrillas [DT179].

Even before the Diem coup, the revolution had decided to try to regain this territory, which is why Ba Vu was in the area, along with elements of the 514th Battalion, which immediately occupied part of the village following the coup. Three days later the 514th launched an attack against Tu Hue's fort and defensive system, and the entire Cao Dai unit under his command had to be evacuated under the protective cover of the ARVN Seventh Division, leaving Phu My occupied by the revolutionary forces for two months before it could be retaken. Right after gaining control, the local cadres called on the villagers, many of whom had been moved into the Strategic Hamlet against their will, to return to their homes. About half of them did, assisted by the revolutionary army [DT171].

On the GVN side, however cruel Tu Hue may have been, he was politically shrewd and an exceptionally resourceful tactician, who, apart from the setback in late 1963, almost always got the better of his revolutionary opponents. An example of his political sense is his intercession for Coc, the younger brother of a revolutionary guerrilla leader in the area, who had been arrested by the GVN provincial police. Perhaps even more relevant here is the persistence of family ties cutting across the political divide. Coc's wife was the niece of Tu Hue's wife. Tu Hue got the brother of his arch-enemy released, and cleverly enrolled him as a soldier at one of the Phu My posts after the village was retaken [DT179]. He was also astute enough to try to clean up the messes his troops created, though apparently only in areas controlled by the GVN. "The local population appreciated Mr. Tu Hue's kindness. But some of his soldiers often plundered their property, cutting down trees and stealing poultry. If Mr. Tu Hue found out about any of these things, the soldiers would be severely punished. All of his subordinates were scared of him, since he used to beat them when they made a mistake. When trees were cut down they would be used as firewood or sold to people living around the post. The owners didn't dare lodge any complaints, for fear of being punished." In spite of the fears of the civilian population, Tu Hue was given credit for having "good political sense, and therefore the people esteemed him highly." He also was able to use the people in the tight-knit and anticommunist Cao Dai and Catholic communities to obtain crucial and timely intelligence [DT179].

Not everyone agreed that Tu Hue and his men had the popular touch with the villagers. "Tu Hue fights by using commando tactics. When they enter a village, the people are all terrified because the soldiers arrest and beat civilians indiscriminately and steal and loot their ducks and chickens. They are aggressive and brutal, and never use political tactics with the villagers, who complain about them a lot." Tu Hue's anticommunist ally was Huynh Hoa, the commander of the Catholic military unit in Phu My. Huynh Hoa was also feared by the cadres for his surprise raids, but was considered less of a threat to the villagers because he didn't bother to arrest village youth evading the GVN draft and, though his men also stole ducks and chickens, unlike Tu Hue's men they did not carry out more serious pillaging [DT233]. Probably the extent of Tu Hue's concern about the behavior of his men toward civilians depended on whether or not the people concerned were sympathizers of the revolution.

In the final analysis, it was Tu Hue's military prowess that bothered the local revolutionaries. After two months in exile, he was supported by the ARVN Seventh Division to retake Phu My, and thereafter managed to thwart both the 261st and 514th Battalions in their efforts to dislodge him. "Regarding combat tactics and strategy," said a former antagonist of Tu Hue's, the ex-guerrilla chief of Phu My village, "I must admit that Tu Hue, who is an old man, has more experience than Chin Han, the commander of the Chau Thanh local force company, and his deputy, Sau Bon" [DT179]. Frustrated by their inability to counter the crafty Tu Hue, the revolutionaries put a price on his head. Ba Vu concluded that the civil guard company would not be broken up as long as Tu Hue was alive, and set about devising a long-range plan for his elimination, which called for maximum military pressure by sniping and encirclement until the big units could finish the job. This plan, however, did not succeed.

In the short term, the fall of Phu My after the November coup had a major impact. It was the birthplace of the then-GVN Chief of State Duong Van "Big" Minh and other Saigon notables. One native of Phu My later became a member of the Constituent Assembly in Saigon. After the takeover of Phu My, he was forced to attend a week-long indoctrination course, and since he had been the head of all the local Diemist political organizations, "he was forced to kneel and beg the people's pardon." In an atmosphere reminiscent of the Concerted Uprising, a crowd of 7,000 was gathered in the main market area of Phu My for a rally at the end of November 1963. A "warrior's memorial" was built in the main marketplace to commemorate the revolutionary dead. However, the population (and even the guerrillas) suspected that because of the importance of the village, the GVN would ultimately retake it, which they did in early 1964—rededicating the "warrior's memorial" to their own military dead in the process [DT179]. In the ebb and flow of the conflict, this is yet another example of a revolutionary upsurge followed by a setback: 1960 followed by 1962, and later the Tet Offensive followed by the decline of 1970–71. In this case, however, the damage done to the GVN position in My Tho by the post-coup offensive was fundamental and potentially terminal (had the United States not intervened in 1965), de-spite a temporary Saigon recovery in places like Phu My. Even here, the trauma of the revolutionary takeover prompted many of the anticommunist Cao Dai supporters to flee to the greater safety of the Cao Dai Holy See in Tay Ninh province, significantly weakening Tu Hue's position in the area.

The immediate impact of the post-coup revolutionary upsurge was a heavy but not fatal blow to the GVN in the province. In other key areas, such as Vinh Kim village, which anchored the eastern end of the 20/7 zone, the Saigon forces were overrun only to return later, as was also the case with Ba Dua, the strongpoint on the western end of the 20/7 zone. Though Phu My, Vinh Kim, and Ba Dua were retaken, they remained isolated is-lands of GVN control in a province whose rural population was largely under the control of the revolution in 1964 and the villages surrounding them came under the domination of the revolutionary forces. Despite the drain of military manpower to other areas, these forces continued to expand and gain the upper hand over their GVN opponents—though, as noted, at a major political price.

Assault on the Heartland of My Tho: Vinh Kim and Ba Dua

To understand the extent to which even the temporary occupation of these keypoints un-dermined the GVN position, it is necessary to examine the impact of takeovers of Vinh Kim and Ba Dua to supplement the case of Phu My, for these were the three incidents that stood out to the population of My Tho as evidence of the powerful growth of the revolu-tionary movement. "Mr. Ngo Dinh Diem was toppled in November 1963," said a village cadre, and "in 1964, the Front three points of attack movement was well coordinated and vigorously pushed forward in my district. The NLF military forces took the initiative and launched several attacks on the ARVN units. As a matter of fact, the NLF conquered Ba Dua and Vinh Kim villages and occupied the entire village of Phu My. Several ARVN posts were successively abandoned. The desertion rate of the ARVN units increased day after day. At that time the populace was very confident in the NLF" [DT226].

Vinh Kim village had been a problem for the revolution during the Destruction of the Oppression because of the strong GVN military presence of this strategically located area. As in Phu My, there was a strong antirevolutionary social base in the village, which was a small market town serving the surrounding villages. "Vinh Kim was a special situation in that it has two religious groups who can never cooperate with the VC. These are the Catho-lics who have never been able to coexist with the VC, and the Cao Dai, who at one time fought the Viet Minh" [DT97]. Vinh Kim may have been a "special situation," but it was not unique, since this was also true of Phu My. Although officially launched on July 20, 1960, the Destruction of the Oppression campaign in Vinh Kim did not really get under-way until January 1961, when Thanh Viet and elements of the 514th Battalion came in to support the local cadres. Even with this assistance, the campaign took a long time and was only partially successful. Two hamlets bordering the core inner area of the 20/7 zone came under revolutionary control.

Along with Phu My and Vinh Kim, the strategic crossroads of Ba Dua controlling the access to the western 20/7 zone from Cai Lay district also fell. Pressure on this area had begun before the November 1963 coup. Sau Duong, the Region Party secretary, recalled that in the summer of 1963 Region 2 had decided to make expansion of revolutionary control in the 20/7 Zone of villages south of Highway 4, the central task for My Tho province. This was coordinated with intensified activities in other areas of My Tho and the central Mekong Delta to keep the GVN from discovering where the main effort would be directed.

Two factors led to success in this effort according to Sau Duong; the overthrow of Ngo Dinh Diem and the arrival of weapons from North Vietnam. Duong's account implies that the weapons arrived "for the first time" only after the November coup, though other accounts (cited in the previous chapter) claim that some weapons from the North had arrived in the Mekong Delta as early as 1962. Sau Duong observed, "The weapons aid from the Center [the Party leaders in Hanoi] really came at an opportune time, and added fuel to the fire, which would make the U.S.-puppet schemes to salvage the situation go up in flames. Thanks to the wealth of guns and ammunition, Region 8 [Region 2] was able to set up many main force infantry battalions for the region and its provinces, and improve the district local forces along with the village and hamlet guerrillas. The weapons and ammunition which the region, provinces, and districts had on hand [before the shipment from the North] were given out to the guerrillas. The amount of gunpowder given to the military side of the local infrastructure was also plentiful."[11]

In addition to the weapons supplied by the North, the ranks of the revolutionaries in the Mekong Delta had expanded since 1960. This growth was accelerated by the revolutionary upsurge following the November 1963 coup. Sau Duong states that the number of Party members in Military Region 2 had expanded from 1,800 in 1960, to 6,000 after the Concerted Uprising (presumably by sometime in 1961) and had tripled from that number by late 1964, while the members of the popular associations in Region 2 had risen from next to nothing in 1960, to a "few hundred thousand" in late 1961 and triple that number by late 1963, while the region had two infantry "army groups" (called *chien doan*, these were actually regiments, or *trung doan*) totaling six battalions. The region military forces totaled 5,000 by the end of 1963. For the entire central Mekong Delta, the total of province and district local forces was 15,000, and the "five kinds of guerrillas" listed by Sau Duong (village guerrillas, overt hamlet guerrillas, secret guerrillas, sapper guerrillas, and individual guerrillas) were said to be over 50,000 for the entire region.[12]

These expanded and better equipped forces were quickly put to work in the populated 20/7 Zone of My Tho province. A member of the province demolition unit spent a month and a half reconnoitering the key post in Ba Dua. Then two companies of the 514th battalion supported by demolition units and heavy weapons successfully assaulted the post [DT147]. As a result, nearly the entire area between Highway 4 and the Mekong River came under revolutionary control. This was clearly part of the Region 2 plan to gain control of the heartland of the province, as suggested by a province demolition cadre who was in charge of reconnoitering priority objectives [DT157]. The impact of this would be to put the revolution in the position of being able to cut off Highway 4, the only land route connecting the Mekong Delta with Saigon, a parallel to the larger aim ascribed by U.S. military analysts to General Giap of cutting South Vietnam in half by gaining control of the central highlands.

The revolutionary gains in My Tho after the overthrow of Ngo Dinh Diem were substantial. The Strategic Hamlet program crumbled in the wake of the November 1963 coup.

One respondent recalled that 33 posts in My Tho were destroyed in the surge of revolutionary activity that followed the coup, while 72 strategic hamlets were destroyed and 30
strategic hamlets were damaged [DT117]. Another estimate was that over 100 strategic
hamlets had been destroyed [DT233] The official Party history of My Tho claims that 174
of 184 strategic hamlets were destroyed, leaving only ten.[13] Another official Party history
claims that by the end of November 1963, only twenty strategic hamlets remained in My
Tho province.[14] (By the end of 1962, 184 of a planned 250 strategic hamlets had been built
in the province.) The province history asserts that from March through December 1963
over 300 posts, including the strongholds of Phu My and Ba Dua, were forced to evacuate,
and that 52 villages were liberated while 40 others retained posts only along the main
routes of communication. On the revolutionary side, says the Party history, 122 villages
were transformed into combat villages and 573 of 857 hamlets were turned into combat
hamlets (this figure is much larger than the number of GVN hamlets, because it includes
Go Cong, which for the GVN once again became a separate province in 1964, and it may
also reflect a splitting of some hamlets).[15]

The GVN forces were in retreat, and the revolutionary side was supremely confident.
Confident did not mean satisfied, however. The year-end military report of the province for
1963 stated: "During the first days of November 1963, province and district units rose up
and took advantage of the coup d'état to attack the enemy, and they gained some results.
But subsequently, due to long-range activity, they were tired and were forced to cope with
enemy aircraft and artillery. They dared not stay to counter sweep operations and lost the
courage to promote achievements."[16]

A few months after the November 1963 coup, a countercoup occurred in Saigon, restoring some of the former Diemist leadership to power and heading off a rumored move
toward a political settlement of the conflict. Bolstered by this reaffirmation of the anticommunist position, the GVN forces in My Tho counterattacked and won back some of the
territory lost. The Seventh Division moved back into Phu My and Ba Dua, and Vinh Kim
was also retaken. This amounted to little more than a military reoccupation of these strategic points; the population was under the nearly complete control of the revolution.

The U.S. Reaction to Setbacks in the Mekong Delta

The U.S. government, itself in a state of some confusion following the assassination of
President Kennedy, reacted with consternation to the revolutionary gains. A report from
Long An province to the north of My Tho in late November 1963 epitomized the collapse
of American pre-coup optimism. At the end of September, Long An province officials had
reported 219 strategic hamlets completed, but this number was reduced to 45 by an upsurge of sober realism following the coup.[17] A U.S. assessment of Dinh Tuong province
cited in a Party military history stated that only 10 of 184 strategic hamlets remained by
the end of 1963, even less than the 20 strategic hamlets that the revolution conceded were
still in existence as of the end of November.[18] This new pessimistic reporting so concerned
Secretary of Defense Robert McNamara that he wrote in late December 1963, "Viet Cong
progress has been great during the period since the coup, with my best guess being that the
situation has been deteriorating in the countryside since July to a far greater extent than we
realized because of undue dependence on distorted Vietnamese reporting. The Viet Cong

now control very high proportions of the people in certain key provinces, particularly those directly south and west of Saigon."[19] The idea that the distorted Vietnamese reporting may have been due partly to a desire to cater to his own passion for statistics does not seem to have occurred to McNamara.

Faced with the need to devise a more effective approach to the collapsing situation, Roger Hillsman, Assistant Secretary of State for East Asia and the Pacific, a veteran of Burma jungle fighting and one of the earliest and most active Kennedy administration enthusiasts for counterinsurgency, devised a plan to deal with the crisis. His ideas were based on the assumption that "villages in Southeast Asia are turned inward on themselves and have little or no sense of identification with either the national government or Communist ideology—that the villagers are isolated physically, politically, and psychologically. In such circumstances," concluded Hillsman, "it is not difficult to develop a guerrilla movement." His other assumption was that villagers would respond "with loyalty" to whoever offered them security and "some simple progress toward a better life."[20] The idea that peasants would respond to whoever could best provide security and prosperity was reasonable enough, but the picture of apolitical insular village communities was a fundamental misunderstanding of the Vietnamese realities. This view is correct in pointing out that most Vietnamese peasants made decisions on the basis of rational calculations of political risks and benefits, but it was precisely because the revolution had linked them to a larger universe than the village and hamlet that they were plugged into an informational network that stretched far beyond the edge of the village, and were increasingly equipped with the political experience and sophistication to analyze the complex choices they faced.

Hillsman's practical prescription was a pacification program called the "oil spot" concept —an image of a drop of oil spreading from its original location like ink on a blotter. In fact, this idea dated back to the nineteenth-century French campaigns of colonial conquest, when it was called the *tache d'huile*. The parallel between French colonizers and the "pacifiers" of the 1960s, which is evident both in the use of the term and in its imagery of an external occupying force methodically subduing an indigenous population, does not seem to have troubled the proponents of the "oil spot." It also prefigured the later "clear and hold" military strategy, which replaced General Westmoreland's "search and destroy" approach after the Tet Offensive although in Dinh Tuong the pre Tet pacification strategy was a lineal descendant of the "oil spot" idea. The idea was that pacification should focus on thoroughly securing a few strategically located spots and then gradually expanding the secured areas.

As Hillsman described it, "the strategic concept calls for primary emphasis on giving security to the villagers. The tactics are the so-called oil blot approach, starting with a secure area and extending it slowly, making sure no Viet Cong pockets are left behind, and using police units to winkle out [sic] the Viet Cong agents in each particular village. This calls for the use of military force in a different way from that of orthodox conventional war. Rather than chasing Viet Cong, the military must put primary emphasis on clear-and-hold operations and on rapid reenforcement of villages under attack. It is also important, of course, to keep the Viet Cong regular units off balance by conventional offensive operations, but these should be secondary to the major task of extending security."[21] Such an approach, said Hillsman, would rely on two basic principles: first, the scattering and over-extension of resources symbolized by the Strategic Hamlet program should be replaced by a more focused concentration of effort; and second, "the way to fight a guerrilla is to adopt the tactics of a guerrilla."[22]

This idea reflected a fundamental misunderstanding of the reasons for the revolutionary side's success in guerrilla war, which went far beyond tactical commando-style small unit operations and were ultimately based on the total mobilization of society. The United States had, however, traveled a considerable distance from the imperious overconfidence of General Paul Harkins, who once proposed to end the war by a concerted, one-time "spasm" of military operations by every Saigon unit in the country, an ironic prefiguration of what the United States thought the revolutionary side was trying to do in the Tet Offensive of 1968. As the authors of the Pentagon Papers comment, Hillsman's recommendations were only partly implemented, and the air war and big unit operations increasingly overshadowed these pacification programs.

Revolutionary Response to "Pacification" in 1964

"Pacification" did, however, become a major project in the Mekong Delta. There was an obvious need to focus on the provinces around Saigon, which by 1964 had become an isolated island in a sea of revolutionary-controlled territory. The "Hop Tac" (Cooperation) Program envisaged concentrating resources on the provinces immediately around Saigon and especially Long An and Dinh Tuong provinces to the south, which were two of seven provinces recommended as national pacification priorities by U.S. planners in April 1964. (Perhaps another reason for doing so was that this would keep the ARVN commanders in these critical provinces too occupied to participate in Saigon coups—though this new assignment did not, in fact, deter the Seventh Division forces based in My Tho from getting caught up in the military conspiracies of 1964–65.)

By the late spring of 1964 the key areas of Phu My, Vinh Kim, and Ba Dua were again under tenuous GVN control. These were the "oil spots," which would be expanded and finally merge as pacification succeeded. The geographic logic of this is clear from a glance at the map, especially in the case of Vinh Kim and Ba Dua, which were at the center of the eastern and western portions of the 20/7 zone respectively. After the reestablishment of the Vinh Kim post by the GVN, persistent efforts were made to retake the area. In March a province demolition unit member furtively entered a post on the outer defenses of Vinh Kim and brazenly polished off the rice left by the sleeping defenders. "We entered the post at midnight, and found the pot of cold rice. We ate it, and reconnoitered every defense fortification. When we left the post it was 3:30 a.m. Sometimes we stayed in a post for thirty minutes or one hour only. We could have assassinated the GVN post commander very easily, but we never did it because we thought if we killed him the GVN would be alerted and we could not attack the post" [DT147]. This probe finally resulted in a major attack by the 514th Battalion on Vinh Kim on July 20, 1964, which was repulsed with twenty-six dead from the 514th [DT157].

Despite the GVN presence in Vinh Kim, the town was an isolated outpost in a "liberated area." Only a single road connected Vinh Kim with Highway 4 and the outside world, and it was constantly under attack. During 1964 and 1965 villagers dug up nearly 10 kilometers of this road and another leading to Binh Duc [DT206]. The Chau Thanh local force unit was given the assignment of interdicting the roads connecting Vinh Kim and

Phu My with Highway 4 [DT209]. An economic embargo was imposed in Vinh Kim by the local cadres, echoing the Viet Minh attempts at economic strangulation, with limited results. A village propaganda cadre from Vinh Kim described the difficulties he had selling this policy to the villagers:

> To date the Front has forbidden the villagers to attend this market not once but twice. The first time was in 1964. Tu Binh, a district committee member, and myself were then assigned to indoctrinate the villagers about this embargo. Although we did our utmost to explain to them that it specifically aimed at isolating the Vinh Kim military post in order to help the Front move to liberate the entire village, we did not gain their sympathy. They protested and said that this would simply deprive them of the means to earn a living. They argued that this market was indispensable to them because it had always enabled them to sell their fruit for cash with which to buy their daily ration of rice, and that if they were forbidden to go there, they would have to go to the My Tho market instead. But going to the My Tho market to sell their produce would make them starve, because their daily sales of a few dozen items of fruit would be just enough to cover traveling expenses. Their arguments sounded reasonable and therefore I was very puzzled about how to reply to them. Therefore, despite the embargo, the guerrillas themselves did not have the heart to carry it out for long. Only twenty days later, the market was reopened [DT143].

Economic warfare seemed to the revolutionaries a reasonable weapon to employ in their effort to liberate Vinh Kim, but it raised difficult and uncomfortable questions about the revolution's claim to be serving the interests of the people. Sacrifices were expected in many areas, including the draft, taxes, and civilian labor. However, the embargo threatened the daily livelihood of the villagers and provoked a strong reaction. When the Chau Thanh district committee tried to reimpose the embargo in 1966, "by this time the villagers couldn't care less, and they no longer observed the instructions. They just stopped going to the market for a few days to probe the guerrillas' reaction, and then they resumed going to market as if nothing had happened" [DT143]. The beginning of this slippage of authority was already evident in 1964, at the very height of revolutionary control of the province, and was due partly to the high political price exacted from the province population in the Party's haste to push the war to a rapid conclusion.

The GVN Attempts to Regain the Initiative in My Tho

In Phu My, the Seventh Division reoccupied the area after two months under revolutionary control, but it then pulled out, leaving Tu Hue once again as its main defender. "After the Seventh Division had withdrawn and Tu Hue led a civil guard unit to reoccupy the local post, Ba Vu formulated a long-range plan, which the district committee was in charge of, to subvert the area and eliminate Tu Hue. This operation lasted for over one year, until the end of 1965. During that period, the VC continuously attacked Tu Hue's unit to harass his soldiers, who, consequently, became short on food and sleep. Roads were dug up and bridges were blown. Sniping fire was used, and the post was shelled. All the Chau Thanh district forces studied this operation to eliminate Tu Hue. When Tu Hue was wounded, it was reported that he was killed. Consequently an even fiercer attack was launched to end this operation" [DT179]. Reports of Tu Hue's death were premature, however, and he continued to hold out in the besieged outpost. The 514th Battalion was frequently in the area looking for a way to attack Tu Hue, but it met with no success. In March 1964 a plan for the 514th Battalion to attack the area was disrupted when they were themselves surprised by the Seventh Division and driven from their fortifications with flame throwers. In August 1964 an attack on Phu My by the 514th was repulsed, and the unit suffered 42 dead and 13 wounded, all in Company First. After this defeat, the cadres of C1 were warned that further failures would be noted in their personnel files, and the threats resulted in a general demoralization [DT191].

In the neighboring "Tan" villages, the situation for the local cadres and the guerrillas became increasingly difficult after the reoccupation of Phu My. The leader of the village guerrillas in Tan Ly Tay, newly appointed in February 1964, found that "the military situation in the area from Tan Ly Tay village to Phu My turned critical because of repeated sweep operations of GVN troops in all the villages in the vicinity of Highway 4 in Ben Tranh district. All the guerrillas had to withdraw from their villages and retreat to the Nguyen Van Tiep Canal. As the situation in the area began to turn unfavorable for the Front, some guerrillas for the Tan Ly Tay unit became discouraged and deserted to go back home" [DT224]. In February 1964 the Seventh Division and GVN district militia launched a series of operations which resulted in the recapture of the GVN village office in Tan Ly Dong village, and the establishment of a post along the road to Phu My [DT233].

The high priority given by the GVN to pacification in Dinh Tuong province was having an effect. One of the most secure revolutionary bases in the province began to come under attack. The Stone Buddha Pagoda area had in 1962 been a base for the military region as well as a number of province civilian and military installations, including the C320 demolition company:

> From 1962 to 1964, the company's main staging area was at the Nguyen Van Tiep Canal, about 5 kilometers from the Stone Buddha Pagoda in the direction of Phu My. The company was stationed around the My Dieu hamlet communal house. There were still many houses along the canal. North of the canal there were as many as 500 houses. C320 only stayed in this position, and was never stationed in the pagoda itself, because the place was not good from a military point of view. During the period from 1962 to May 1964 this was a secure and prosperous area. There were neither bombings or shellings, and no military operations either. Then, from June 1964, the area began to be attacked by artillery and airplanes. No one in the company was killed, however. The area attacked extended from a place 2 kilometers from the Stone Buddha Pagoda toward Phu My. During the attacks the company usually withdrew into the woods about a hundred meters from the canal. In quiet times, the company stayed right on the canal banks in the people's homes. In this period there were about six air and artillery attacks [DT157].

The undisturbed security in formerly secure base areas like this was disrupted by the intensification of air, ground, and artillery operations. Defoliation with chemical pesticides began to be used against revolutionary base areas in 1963 and 1964 [DT179]. Even in villages close to Highway 4, such as Nhi Qui, which was a stopover point for district local force troops, defoliants began to be used in 1964. The village was also shelled every time Highway 4 was mined [DT15]. These actions were not sufficient to allow the GVN to regain the military initiative, but they fundamentally altered the tempo and intensity of the war. This was the first major step in an escalation of violence which ultimately depopulated vast areas of the province. Nothing in the way of direct military assaults by GVN (and later U.S.) forces would equal the devastating impact on the revolution of the forced depopulation of the villages. The grim and increasing dangers posed by stepped-up bombing and shelling shattered the tranquillity of the rural atmosphere in revolutionary-controlled areas, raised the costs of staying with the revolution for supporters as well as cadres, and started to drain the sea in which the guerrillas swam. Still, the revolution held on to many of the basic gains made following the November 1963 coup, especially in the heartland of the 20/7 zone. A document captured in August 1964 listed the villages in the province which were considered "liberated." In Cai Lay, 12 of 20 villages were liberated. In Chau Thanh district, only 7 of 37 were listed as "liberated" (Vinh Kim was number eight, but a notation added the updated information, "Reoccupied by F," e.g., the ARVN Seventh Division), but of the seven villages, five were in the vicinity of Vinh Kim in the eastern 20/7 zone.[23] In accordance with the "oil spot" pacification plan, the GVN began to concentrate its efforts on building further momentum from the return to Vinh Kim by taking back the Ba Dua area, the other key to controlling the 20/7 zone. This GVN initiative was temporarily deflected by a major revolutionary assault against the district town of Cai Be, near Ba Dua.

Attack on the GVN district town of Cai Be

The most daring assault by the 514th and 261st Battalions in 1964 was on the district town of Cai Be on the now-familiar July 20 anniversary date of the Geneva Accords. It was an extension of the earlier attacks on Ba Dua and aimed at gaining control over the central part of the province. The direct assaults on Ba Dua had not succeeded, but now the province and region leadership were embarked on an even more aggressive move to hit a much more vital target. Cai Be district town borders the upper branch of the Mekong River and is about 4 kilometers from the juncture of a road connecting the district with Highway 4 as it turns west to the My Thuan ferry. The Military Region began reconnoitering this target in March 1964 and continued the investigation until June, in anticipation of a major attack [DT150].[24]

A victory in Cai Be, said the Military Region, would "create military and political repercussions in the local area and throughout the whole region. It would create the conditions for breaking up the long-range pacification plan of the enemy along the border of the Mekong River." In addition, it would "annihilate the enemy's strength and build up our strength, pushing our forces one step forward." Responding to the importance of their assigned mission, the 261st and its commander declared their resolve to "overcome all difficulties in annihilating Cai Be town and carrying out the mission assigned by higher levels."[25]

"Let me tell you about the attack on Cai Be district town as an example of the pattern of operation of the 261st Battalion," said a former company commander of that unit. "At that time a special unit of the Americans was stationed in Cai Be district town, and they were on the point of destroying all Front infrastructure organizations in the district. So the province unit and the province Party committee asked Region 2 to send a main force unit down to the district to attack the Cai Be subsector in order to improve the political situation with the people and to destroy the reactionary elements—meaning this team. The 261st Battalion was sent to Cai Be to carry out this attack." Elements of the 514th were used as a blocking force to stop GVN boats from reinforcing the town [DT149].

The attack started at 1:00 a.m., one hour later than scheduled, and lasted several hours. "Our main tactic was to launch an attack south of the Iron Bridge on the Police Center, the Post Office, and the Civil Guard barracks." By 5:00 a.m. the withdrawal had been completed, after three companies of the 261st Battalion had inflicted heavy damage on the GVN military installations and part of the town. By their own account, the 261st Battalion captured forty weapons, killed or wounded over 230 ARVN soldiers, and killed the district chief. Some problems of coordination and communication were noted. Since it was one of the first major assaults with a full battalion-sized unit, this was not unexpected. Civilian laborers responsible for guiding the troops, carrying the wounded, and burying the dead ran away under fire, and the troops had to bury their own dead on the spot during the withdrawal.[26]

Soldiers returning from the attack on Cai Be district said that "they had been welcomed by villagers standing alongside the path when the reached the liberated zone. As a matter of fact, they felt slightly encouraged and proud, but their satisfaction soon vanished." The interviewer asked, "Did the villagers cheer?" No, said the respondent, "I was told that they were just standing alongside the road looking at the soldiers passing by. Nobody cheered but some of them said, 'Ah! You just won the Cai Be battle, didn't you?' " Many military sociologists have argued that soldiers do not fight for glory or ideology, but for each other. There is plenty of material in the interviews to dispute this, but this particular respondent said, "Afterwards we gathered in cells for a *kiem thao* [self-criticism] review and when it was over said, 'It's very sad to think about our missing comrades. Yesterday they were still with us and today they no longer exist. You never know what will happen to you tomorrow. Only our superiors enjoyed the victory, because they will be commended. As for us, we have nothing to enjoy.' I thought that due to this frame of mind the fighters were tightly bound together and they felt compassion for one another" [DT77].

The strategic success of the Cai Be battle was that it dealt directly with the challenge of the new pacification strategy of the United States and the GVN. The "special unit of Americans stationed in Cai Be" probably indicated the newly expanded U.S. military advisory effort, which in 1964 had reached the district level, and the pacification effort referred to was the Hop Tac program and the local pacification centers of Ba Dua and Vinh Kim. Since the pacification strategy was based on a concentration of effort, the revolution's task was to force a dispersal of GVN pacification forces. This is confirmed by the Region's after-action report. "While the enemy concentrates to cope with Cai Be, they are scared of losing Cai Lay, Cai Mon, Hau My, Vinh Kim, Long Dinh, etc. So they are forced to split up to reinforce the posts, and the morale of their troops is more apathetic than before." The Region asserted that the Seventh Division troops heaved a sigh of relief that they had survived the "July 20 phase of operations," and that the wives and parents of the GVN soldiers in the Region went to the pagodas to pray to Buddha that their sons would survive "July 20."[27]

In his postwar memoir, the military commander of Region 2 recalled, "After Thien Ho [Hau My] and Cai Be subsectors had been demolished, the liberated area of My Tho provinces expanded a great deal. At the beginning of June 1964 I directly proposed to the Region

Party Committee and the Command Staff of the Military Region the plan of opening a corridor along the Vietnam–Cambodia border. This corridor would be 100 kilometers long, beginning in Long An, running through Kien Tuong and down to Kien Phong and finally An Giang province, connecting the Eastern and Western Nam Bo battlefields."[28] This was an expansion of his 1963 plan to link to the provinces of Central Nam Bo with a corridor in the western part of the region, noted earlier, and a reflection of the confidence that these mid-1964 victories engendered in the revolutionary leadership in the central Mekong Delta.

Perhaps the fact that the Cai Be battle was one of the first major attacks on an important town was even more significant than its impact on forcing the dispersal of GVN pacification forces. "This time we attacked the town of Cai Be, not just posts like before." The attack was also intended to discredit the new district-level advisory effort, by demonstrating that American advice on defense of major GVN strongpoints was ineffective, and that revolutionary troops had attacked the very places "the enemy felt were secure, and had boasted about the new American fortifications." The GVN had relied on a system of fast reinforcement by water, air, and land (APCs), but this had not worked in Cai Be. The Region reasoned that if the defense system did not work in Cai Be, it would shake the confidence of all the lesser GVN installations in the area.[29]

In a way, this was a first step toward the strategic reasoning which led to the attacks on all the major towns and cities in the Tet Offensive of 1968. It was clear from the planning of the operation that this was not meant to achieve a lasting military objective. Inflicting casualties on the GVN was mentioned by the Region as an additional benefit of the operation, and the 514th Battalion and various demolition forces lying in ambush for reinforcements clearly hoped to contribute to this end. The main point, however, was to shake the confidence of the GVN soldiers both in their own troops and in the advice and support of their American advisors.

This was an indirect way of attacking the pacification program. Direct assaults on places such as Phu My, Vinh Kim, and Ba Dua were not working because they were too predicable and the range of targets was too small. So the Region decided to expand the scope of operations, and felt that it could attack even more important targets if it multiplied its options and lowered its goals from total destruction of the GVN forces in a key pacification point and occupation by Front forces to a broader strategy of hitting major targets in an unpredictable way, and hoping that the combined effects of the actual military damage and the psychological effects on the GVN defenders in the province would ultimately wear down the Saigon forces, and paralyze them in the same way that the tactics of the Destruction of the Oppression had done.

Despite Revolutionary Victories, Doubts Persist at the Lower Levels

These limited aims were to some extent forced on the revolution by the draining of manpower and experienced troops to central Vietnam and eastern Nam Bo, which made it more difficult to achieve a decisive military result in delta provinces such as My Tho. These areas were where the GVN had concentrated *their* resources, and one of the main purposes of building up the big units in other areas was to draw these GVN forces away from the delta and lure them into setpiece battles with the big units of the revolutionary side. During the latter half of 1964 and in early 1965 the heaviest fighting increasingly was taking place outside the delta. The focus on the main force military activities had a negative impact on the consolidation of the liberated areas and the expansion of guerrilla war in the delta. The local cadres and guerrillas

> . . . thought of modern weapons and were not confident in the rudimentary ones. They did not trust the masses' fighting capabilities. They also thought in terms of conventional warfare and underestimated guerrilla warfare. Therefore they relied on support from higher levels and were not confident in their own strength. The majority of the village Party chapters fled when the enemy came in. When the enemy withdrew they would return but were inactive. When they held meetings, they criticized one another and made excuses that the enemy was too strong and that our armed forces from higher headquarters did not come to fight them. Worst of all, there were Party cadres and members who inadvertently agreed with the enemy's propaganda themes: "How can you fight and win this war? You need strong units from your higher headquarters to fight it." Or, "Combat villages and hamlets are useless" because the enemy conducts heliborne operations while we still use guerrilla warfare, and so on [DT233].

The Party's stress on the need for main force military action had made some of its members lose confidence in guerrilla warfare, which was the only approach possible in the Mekong Delta. As they began to question the efficacy of guerrilla warfare, the cadres also began to neglect the task of consolidating defensible areas near the main bases in the Plain of Reeds, and combat villages in the more exposed and heavily populated areas of the province. A district cadre who operated in the Phu My area concluded that, in 1964, "The consolidation and strengthening of the VC base areas seems to have failed. The VC were unable to keep the people in their areas of control as they gradually expanded. For instance, the VC gradually enlarged their areas of control in My Tho province to cover the following villages: Tan Ly Dong, Tam Hiep, Long Dinh, Nhi Binh, Nhi My, Tan Hoi, My Hanh Trung, Binh Phu, Phu Nhuan Dong, Hoi Cu, My Duc Dong, and My Duc Tay, which run along Highway 4. These villages have served as the boundaries of the provincial VC base areas which cover the Nguyen Van Tiep Canal zone bordering Kien Tuong and Kien Phong provinces" [DT233]. During 1964, the revolution made considerable gains in these vital areas, connecting the Plain of Reeds base with the 20/7 zone south of Highway 4. Without control of these villages in northern Cai Be, Cai Lay, and Chau Thanh districts, access to all areas south of the National Highway would be restricted, and the concentrated troop units would have fewer options of places to stay in the province

However, the local guerrillas were evidently unable to consolidate their hold on these key villages in 1964, and "no combat villages could be conducted in these areas. The people's movement could not be developed and thus there were no secure areas for the VC main force units" [DT233]. The province Party committee ordered the buildup of combat villages and strengthening the defenses of the base areas as a top priority, probably to compensate for the loss of military forces to other battlefields as well as to cope with the intensified pacification efforts of the GVN. The results did not please province Party Secretary Chin Om. Only a few scattered efforts were made to follow through on creating a denser cluster of trees and bushes as a defense against detection and raids. "Only a few palm trees were planted in Tan Ly Dong and Tan Hoa Thanh. They looked like toys, in the words of Chin Du [Chin Om], the province Party secretary" [DT233]. A military cadre suggested that the Party had much more ambitious aims for 1964 which were not realized. "As far as I know, the Front's main goal from 1964 through 1965 was to liberate the rural areas, that is to say, 'to gain every inch of land so as to win every citizen.' The special mission for 1964 was to do everything to occupy the three districts of Cai Be, Cai Lay, and Long Dinh [Vinh Kim], so as to liberate the triangle formed by these three districts. That was the Front's aim back in 1964, but it was a failure" [DT157].

Perhaps the greatest setback for the revolution in 1964 was the inevitable reaction of fatigue and disenchantment following the heady successes immediately after the overthrow of the Diem government. At the beginning of 1964 it seemed possible that the confusion and disarray of the GVN and the new aggressive strategy of the Party might bring the war to a quick end. The Saigon authorities suffered significant military and political reverses in 1964, but in My Tho they managed to rebound from the debacle of late 1963. The Chau Thanh district cadre observed that in 1964, "The VC cadres and members from the district cadres down to the village cadres were still confident in the Party, but they have become afraid of protracted war," as evidenced in remarks like 'In the past the Party said that reunification of our country is not far away,' or 'the time has come, we should struggle to gain decisive victory" [DT233]. Too many promises of "light at the end of the tunnel" were beginning to take their toll, precisely at the time when the Party was, in fact, on the brink of a major breakthrough.

"Going for Broke" Begins to Succeed—But at a Price

This turning point came not in My Tho, but in eastern Nam Bo, where the Party's strategy had counted on a major success, in the form of a heavy defeat inflicted on a 2,000-man ARVN force in Binh Gia, north of Saigon. This battle had as much historical significance as the one at Ap Bac. Whereas Ap Bac had showed that the revolution could stand up to regular Saigon units in military combat, Binh Gia showed that they could defeat the biggest units the GVN could field and signaled the beginning of the military "unraveling" of the ARVN. Without U.S. intervention, the descending spiral of military defeat and political paralysis had projected Saigon on a path of defeat.

This was not immediately evident in My Tho, however, and the revolution was having problems of its own. The inability of the revolutionaries to build and defend secure base areas, especially in the more exposed areas of the province farther from the Plain of Reeds, brought to light a weakness that needed to be remedied. Some way had to be found to provide more security to the liberated areas, better protect the cadres, and offer greater freedom of movement to the concentrated troops in the province. Part of the answer was to restore the imbalance created by draining troops out of the area, both to augment the main force units operating in the province and to restore the effectiveness of the district local forces, which were the essential link between the big units and the village guerrillas. But the more essential answer was to find a way to multiply the effectiveness of the existing level of forces, because the revolution could not hope to defend every inch of "liberated territory" or to match the GVN's military strength unit for unit.

Beginning around mid-1964 and the battle of Cai Be, the revolutionary side began to view military operations more as a holding action, to protect revolutionary bases in the delta and access to manpower and materiel resources to be used in other areas. To an extent this was an affirmation of the view that the delta areas should balance political and military action, while military action would predominate in the mountain-forest regions and political action in the cities. The tactical consequence of this was that the revolutionary forces in the delta perfected a nearly perfectly balanced system of coordinated military-political operations in My Tho, which allowed the revolution to hold onto its areas of control even though its military forces remained inferior in numbers and weapons to the GVN forces in the province.

The basic elements of this balanced system have already been indicated in the previous chapter. It was to establish an interlocking network of prepared fortified positions as way stations for movement of concentrated units around the province. The fact that these prepared positions were not occupied most of the time did not detract from the umbrella of psychological protection they cast over the surrounding area even when no unit was present. The mere possibility that a big unit could be almost anywhere in the province at any given moment drew the "invisible line" around even more base areas in the more heavily populated parts of My Tho, and increased the security of these base areas. This system depended on having company and battalion size local force units menacing enough to deter small Saigon forces from entering these base area. Large GVN forces could operate only sporadically in any given zone, and their cumbersome operations rarely caught the revolutionary forces by surprise. This system worked fairly well even when the "upgrading of forces" depleted the middle sized local force units whose constant presence throughout the revolutionary controlled areas was essential to the functioning of synergies of this strategic system. When the "go for broke" period ended in 1965, and the Mekong Delta was allowed to retain more of its own military recruits, this stratagem was even more effective in protecting revolutionary zones—until the arrival of US combat forces with new and aggressive tactics seriously undermined the deterrent value of the occasionally occupied fortified positions.

Still "Going for broke" prevented the Mekong Delta revolutionaries from consolidating and expanding their gains of the late 1963- early 1964 period and also imposed heavy costs on the civilian population and marked the beginning of a process which led many initial supporters to drift away from the revolution. The two most important were taxation and the compulsory military draft which were, as noted earlier, initiated in 1963 and greatly expanded in 1964, raising the costs of supporting the revolution dramatically. In addition, the growing ferocity of the war forced residents in revolutionary zones to take measures for self-preservation. Realizing that it could not stem the tide of civilians fleeing the revolutionary zone when military clashes occurred, the Party leadership tried to turn it to advantage. Perhaps it is significant that the Region 2 commanders, who took the lead in devising a response to civilians fleeing the revolutionary zones, were themselves totally isolated from the civilian population. This may have affected their grasp of the rapidly changing realities of the situation. Even though the military tide had turned in favor of the revolution, there were still serious problems to be dealt with, and the Region 2 leadership seems to have assumed a level of popular support that had certainly peaked and was already beginning to subside despite the wave of revolutionary victories.

The View from Above: Region 2 in 1964

During this period the Region 2 leadership was located on the border with Cambodia in an isolated area of three villages, each with a name including the word "Thuong" (the "Tam

219

Thuong"), located in Chau Doc province about 50 kilometers up the Mekong River from the western edge of My Tho province. Starting in October, the flooding Mekong inundated the area for four months. A solid sheet of water 2 meters deep was interspersed with an occasional clump of scraggly trees and bushes. The Region 2 leaders had to split up in scattered lean-to huts built on elevated platforms suspended from the trees. About 1,000 people lived in this base area, subsisting on snails, snakes, turtles, and fish. The Region's "conference hall" was a platform of plywood planks of about 60 square meters, which could accommodate up to 100 people gathered in a circle like sitting around a campfire. It was here that Region 2 convened a large meeting in the fall of 1964 to review the situation in the upper delta.

The key Region 2 cadres were Party Secretary Sau Duong and Tam Phuong the military commander of the region. Many of the leading Party cadres of the region came from My Tho. Two were former Party secretaries of My Tho: Ba Chim ("The Birdman") and Viet Thang ("Victorious Viet"). Tu Long had been the head of the propaganda and indoctrination section of the My Tho Party committee before his promotion to region level. Bay Hiep was the controversial former deputy Party secretary with a penchant for purges, whom the region command could not persuade his My Tho comrades to accept as their leader. Several former cadres who had led the uprising in Cai Be had been transferred to the region level. Tu Hien was the Party secretary of Cai Be district during the 1960 uprising and was now in charge of security and administration of the Region 2 base. Sau Binh had been the deputy head of Cai Be military forces and later returned to My Tho as chairman of the My Tho People's Committee after the Provisional Revolutionary Government was established in 1969 and became province Party secretary in 1973. There was also an impressive aggregation of women cadres. Nguyen Thi Dinh, from Ben Tre, had become nationally famous for her leading role in the uprising in Ben Tre. A less famous but no less active leader of the My Tho uprising was Bay Ngoc Viet, who had held out while her husband surrendered to the Diem forces, and who joined Ba Chim and Viet Thang during the miserable years of the late 1950s when she was briefly put in charge of the movement in Cai Be. Another prominent woman leader at the region level in the early 1960s was Hai Huong, who became the head of the My Tho city Party committee after the 1968 Tet Offensive.

Of the 23 cadres identified as participants in a key Region 2 meeting on strategy in late 1964, at least 8 had close ties to My Tho—by far the largest provincial contingent, suggesting the importance and influence of My Tho in the region.[30] The conferees noted that while the basic strategic outlines for the conflict had been set out at the time of the uprising, and although the Mekong Delta merited a "gold star" for leadership by 1964, a number of "new and hot issues had arisen." They recalled that since the Resistance, the rural people of the delta had used the phrase, "when the roosters fight, the bushes get trampled," which was "an indirect criticism of the heavy reliance on military measures, which resulted in losses to the people." The region cadres were concerned about the level of damage that the escalation of the fighting had inflicted on the civilian population. During the discussion, a cadre from Ben Tre recalled that just after the uprising, there had been a concerted military counterattack by the GVN, and the accompanying bombing and shelling forced the civilian population into a "reverse evacuation" into the GVN zones with as many possessions as they could carry, to escape the fighting. "It became a habit to evade the fighting and no one could stop it." Sau Duong, the region Party secretary, laughed dismissively. The revolution always tried to get the people to descend on the GVN posts and towns to demonstrate against the military operations, he said, and here was a perfect opportunity to turn the situation to the advantage of the revolution by getting the people who were on a "reverse evacuation" to the GVN areas to confront the GVN, and demand as legal "nationalist citizens" (*dan quoc gia*) to be protected and not retaliated against. In this way the "reverse evacuation would be turned in to a political offensive."[31]

Still fired up by the great shift in the balance of forces since the overthrow of Ngo Dinh Diem, and confident in the support of the majority of the rural population which had reached its height in 1963 and early 1964, the Party cadres were sure that they had only to devise a tactical plan, and the people would carry it out. But the situation in the Mekong Delta was, as they themselves perceived, changing rapidly, and the "new and hot issues" that had arisen proved to be quite difficult to resolve. In historical perspective, the decisions to "go for broke" ended the strategic primacy of the Mekong Delta in Party strategy, not only because in the short term it shifted its focus to the heavy fighting elsewhere, and not even because the military push in these other areas drained valuable manpower from the Mekong Delta, which limited their ability to exploit GVN weakness there. A more fundamental reason was that the "go for broke" strategy provoked a massive U.S. intervention, which eventually turned the delta into a sideshow of the war until the final withdrawal of American troops. But the most significant consequence of this decision was that the compulsory draft and heavy taxation that were essential components of this policy constituted what was perhaps the political watershed of the revolution. Before this time, the success of the revolution in My Tho and the Mekong Delta was extraordinary. After the imposition of the draft and taxation, a long but steady decline in popular support for the revolution was set in motion. That the revolution managed to hold on and triumph despite this is an indication of how far it had developed since the 1930s and how deep its core support base was. But the cumulative effects of the disillusionment of much of the civilian population and the emergence of a rural middle class created serious problems for the Party after the war was won.

11

Year of the Big Change: 1965

By early 1965 the Saigon Army of the Republic of Vietnam (ARVN) was reeling from major defeats such as the battle in Binh Gia north of Saigon, and to many revolutionaries victory seemed near at hand. The big military push of 1964 was apparently paying off, and the Communist Party was determined to press its advantage and cripple the Saigon Government of the Republic of Vietnam (GVN) and armed forces before the United States could intervene. This would require exceptional sacrifices from the peasants, and so the political strategy of the Party in My Tho and elsewhere was to compensate the poor peasants by promising greater political and material benefits. To do so, it hardened its policies to appeal to its core support base of poor peasants at the expense of the wealthier elements in the countryside, and downgraded the United Front elements of its strategy as exemplified in the National Liberation Front (NLF) coalition of diverse social and religious groups. This policy was implemented in a campaign titled "Motivating the Peasants" *(Phat Dong Nong Dan)*.

Another reason for appealing to the poor peasants was that in 1965 large numbers of people began to leave their villages for more secure areas as the war intensified. Most of those who could afford to leave were wealthier peasants with some cash reserves to support themselves away from their land. This made it all the more important to appeal to the peasants most likely to stay behind, and these were generally the poor peasants. In the military units, poor peasants seemed to be less prone to desertion, and thus more reliable.

Because of the major shifts in political strategy, the intensification of the war, and the direct U.S. intervention, 1965 was a critical turning point in the war. One interviewee called it the "year of the big change," and another said the Party considered it a "hinge year." Initially, this reflected the Party's hope that it might win the war that year or, at least, decisively tip the balance in its favor. The possibilities of a negotiated solution based on neutralization of Vietnam and a coalition government faded, and the Party tried hard to press its advantage by tightening its direct control over the rural population in My Tho. At the time, the dominating fact in My Tho and Vietnam was the deteriorating position of the Saigon government throughout the country, and the rapid escalation of U.S. intervention in the conflict. This is the "big change" referred to in the interviews, and the reason why 1965 was considered a "hinge year" by the Party.

A second "big change" was a sharp radical turn in Party policy toward the peasantry. The "Motivating the Peasants" campaign was short-lived. It was soon eclipsed by the escalating intensity of the war and the necessity of coping with the effects of the exodus of peasants trying to escape the fierce bombing and shelling of "liberated areas." The evidence that the Party attempted to accelerate class-based policies of the revolution to support its military escalation in order to create irreversible momentum and make revolutionary dominance *a fait accompli* before the U.S. intervention reached a critical point is fragmentary but persuasive. Even more intriguing but much less well documented is the evidence that Hanoi ordered a sweeping land reform modeled on the disastrous campaign in North Vietnam during the early 1950s. This was quietly buried by the local Party leadership in My Tho, but it offers a preview of the postwar problems that the Northern Party leadership encountered in trying to impose unworkable policies on the South.

In historical retrospect, the year 1965 was not only the year of the U.S. direct entry into the war but also (and partly because of the consequences of that escalation) the year the Party began to lose control over the shape and direction of the social revolution in Vietnam. The wrenching upheavals of Vietnam's rural society caused by the war and the depopulation of the countryside became the driving force of social change, and eventually swamped the Party's attempts at political social engineering. That was the third and perhaps most important change of 1965, but it unfolded gradually, and its ultimate significance was not recognized or anticipated at the time.

Hanoi's View of the Changing Situation in the South

Strategic considerations pushed revolutionary social policy to the left in 1965. As in the period following the overthrow of President Ngo Dinh Diem, Hanoi's leadership became anxious to press their military advantage and bring about the collapse of the Saigon armed forces in order to eliminate the key foundation for prospective U.S. intervention. This, in turn, led the Party to offer more incentives to the poor peasants in the form of land and political preferences so that they would be willing to make sacrifices, while the wealthier rural strata balked at the spiraling demands of the draft, taxation, civilian labor, and participation in risky political demonstrations and battlefield support tasks such as carrying ammunition and evacuating the wounded. The "Motivating the Peasants" campaign was aimed at winning political support for this great effort, and specifically for the draft. In the end it was quietly phased out, because the big military push had brought about the very result it was intended to prevent—the large-scale intervention of U.S. troops.

Dean Rusk, the U.S. Secretary of State at the time, later explained that the gradual escalation of U.S. troop deployments in South Vietnam during the spring and summer of 1965 was calculated to avoid forcing China and Russia into a dangerous reactive response. Gradualism would make every day look like every other day, he said, and this would not push the Soviets and the Chinese into an "orgasm of decision making."[1] Perhaps a more protracted approach by the guerrillas would have avoided pushing the Johnson administration into making the crisis decisions that plunged America irreversibly into the "Vietnam War" and, in this sense, the Party's big drive backfired. The irony is that both Johnson's hesitation about defining the stakes in Vietnam until the stark reality of an impending defeat forced him to act, and the Party's rush to finish off the GVN worked in tandem to make war inevitable. Under the new circumstances of a massive U.S. intervention, a nationalist appeal to all social strata would seem to make more sense than a narrow class-based policy.

Le Duan, the Party secretary general in Hanoi, began the year 1965 confident that major U.S. intervention could be prevented by building up unstoppable momentum. Even if the United States did intervene, he argued, it would not change the basic character of the war. In a letter to Nguyen Chi Thanh, the controversial military commander in the South whose death in 1967 left lingering doubts and suspicions because of his apparent opposition to some aspects of Hanoi's strategy, Le Duan explained that he was passing along his own gloss on a Politburo resolution at the beginning of 1965. The strategic slogan which reflected the thrust of that resolution was ambiguous and even contradictory, perhaps reflecting a split within Hanoi's leadership about whether to step up the war immediately, or settle down for the long haul. "Fight a protracted struggle and go all out to seize the opportunity to gain victory," said the resolution. Le Duan's private letter to the top military commander in the South left no doubt about which option he preferred: "we feel that this is the opportune moment to seize the opportunity and not waste it."[2]

The 1963 battle of Ap Bac, he argued, proved to the United States that it could not defeat the revolutionaries, while the battle of Binh Gia clearly showed them they were going to lose the "special war." After analyzing the situation in detail, Le Duan posed the question, "Has the opportune moment to fight and defeat the Americans in the 'special war' come yet? And can we force the Americans to accept defeat without being able to change their strategy in time? I think that opportune moment is arriving; and that restraining the enemy to defeat them in the 'special war' is still a possibility."[3] Of course, he acknowledged, this depended on what the United States would do and how well the revolution took advantage of the opportunity. And the key was not to give the Americans enough time to change their strategy, which meant doing as much as possible to prevent direct U.S. intervention with its own combat troops, which would change the conflict from a proxy "special war" fought by Saigon government troops with American advice and logistical support to a limited war of the Korean War type.

In Le Duan's opinion, the best way to do this was to bring about a collapse of the Saigon armed forces before the United States could get geared up for such extensive intervention. "We must strive to shatter the base of support of the Americans. . . . For this reason we must *systematically break up the puppet army* [emphasis in original]." If this was done so quickly and completely that the United States had no time to react, it would reduce the possibility of direct U.S. intervention to "a low level."[4] At the beginning of 1965, Hanoi estimated that the GVN had a three-to-one superiority over the revolutionary forces in the South, or two-to-one if only the regular army units were considered and not the Civil Guard. This was about the ratio between the forces of Chiang Kai-shek and Mao Zedong in China in mid-1947. The ratio of armed forces was less favorable to the revolution than in the final period of the Resistance, but Le Duan felt that the political movement was stronger, and the morale of the ARVN troops weaker. The strategic reserves of the GVN would have to be depleted and their regular army pulled out of the cities, including My Tho, which would take the pressure off the urban political movement. "These requirements concerning the annihilation of the enemy can be achieved within this year," Le Duan asserted.[5]

This air of confidence that victory was in sight was also evident in the central Mekong Delta in early 1965. Tam Phuong, the commander of Region 2 military forces claimed, that the Strategic Hamlet (pacification) program had been rendered "bankrupt" and that fifty-one of My Tho's villages, or nearly half the villages in the province, had been "liberated" along with fifty-seven villages in Long An and fifty-seven in Ben Tre. (He did not note the fact that the revolutionaries had claimed fifty-two villages liberated in My Tho by November 1963). This, he asserted "expanded [revolutionary] control to the cities and towns and important routes of communication."[6] "In the Region 8 [Region 2] battlefield at the beginning of 1965," Tam Phuong recalled, "both main force puppet divisions, the Seventh and Twenty-Fifth Divisions, had been heavily damaged, and no longer had the strength to cope with our armed forces."[7]

The sense of an imminent and decisive breakthrough is vividly reflected in the words of Sau Duong, the top Party leader of Region 2. In early 1965, on one of his many trips to COSVN headquarters in Tay Ninh (as Region 2 Party leader he was an ex-officio member of COSVN), he discussed the situation with Nguyen Chi Thanh, who he identifies as the leader "delegated by the Politburo to go South and develop the leadership of the Party Central Committee in comprehensive preparations for carrying out the plan for a general offensive and general uprising in the South in 1965." Sau Duong adds that the "battles of Gia Lai and Binh Gia in the central highlands and in eastern Nam Bo made it even clearer that the goal of that policy was close and inviting." COSVN was further encouraged by intelligence reports that the top leaders of the GVN were worried enough to be making plans to escape to foreign countries, and that there were strong neutralist tendencies within the Saigon government and armed forces that would lead to a coalition government. This government would demand reinstatement of the Geneva Agreements, the United States' departure from Vietnam, and negotiations with North Vietnam for reunification. Sau Duong writes that in a COSVN meeting, Nguyen Chi Thanh said, "The situation now is very favorable and we can't drag our feet. We must quickly make comprehensive preparations to seize the opportunity. We have to run and form into ranks while we are getting dressed—we certainly can't wait to get dressed and only then fall in." Duong adds, "These electrifying and exhilarating words of the comrade were quickly passed down to the cadres and the staff personnel at the lowest levels and to every main force soldier, local force soldier, and guerrilla."[8]

"When the circumstances are ripe," Le Duan told Nguyen Chi Thanh, "we will launch a wave of uprisings in Saigon and other big cities like Hue, Danang, My Tho . . ." In a preview of the Tet Offensive of 1968, Le Duan envisaged armed forces attacking the cities from the outside, and if the attack was strong enough, "it would paralyze the enemy army and then the masses will have a base of support for acting with a high degree of resolve." The key would be not to allow the ARVN to send reinforcements to Saigon. To prevent this there would be a diversionary attack in the Central Highlands, a preview of the Tet strategy. The Party would try to pull the "intermediate classes" to its side and create a big surprise for the United States by carrying out the uprising under the flag of a "neutral Front"—again a parallel to the formation of the Alliance of National, Democratic, and Peace Forces in 1968, ostensibly to replace the National Liberation Front (NLF) as the rallying point for non-Party opponents of the United States. Even the revolutionary troops would style themselves a "neutral army." Le Duan cautioned that this could be done only if the conditions were right, but he was confident that it could be done "if we actively create them." In a display of supreme confidence, and even bravado, he asserted that even if the uprising in the cities failed and the forces had to be withdrawn "it won't make any difference. The forces of Fidel Castro attacked the city three times before they succeeded. We could enter the city and then have to retreat, but we shouldn't be put off, because the entire rural area and the mountains and forests belong to us, and there our posture is strong."[9] This almost cavalier confidence seems to have sobered by the time of the Tet Offensive, but the reasoning was much the same.

By May 1965, Le Duan's tone had become somewhat more cautious. The United States had launched a sustained bombing campaign against North Vietnam, and was already beginning to introduce combat forces into the South. Still, it was not clear how far this buildup would go, and Hanoi seems to have concluded that it was just a desperation holding action that would not amount to a major U.S. commitment to fight and win a ground war in Vietnam. In another letter to Nguyen Chi Thanh, Le Duan assured him that "sending more troops into the South and bombing the North is only a more aggressive defense," and "on our side, militarily and politically in the South, basically nothing has yet changed." The best way to keep the U.S. from turning the conflict into a Korean-style limited war is to keep "attacking even harder."[10] Nevertheless, he continued to hold out the possibility of an urban insurrection. Noting that Lenin had cautioned "never to play around with insurrection," Le Duan asserted that Vietnam's situation was different from the one Lenin faced, and he was still confident that even if the first attempt failed, it would not harm the revolution.[11]

The escalating U.S. intervention at the time Le Duan wrote his second letter in May had resulted in one major change of political strategy, however. "In my last letter, I foresaw the possibility of using political struggle to demand the establishment of a different government in Saigon which would have the policy of ending the war and negotiating with the Front. Now this is not necessary because the Americans have sent and continue to introduce expeditionary forces into the South to carry on the war, and bomb and destroy the North in order to create a strong position for negotiations." Now it was the United States that wanted to negotiate, to buy time for the Saigon government and armed forces, and they had even offered to negotiate unconditionally, the letter said. "In this circumstance, *we have to fight hard, fight even more effectively, and certainly this is not yet the time for bargaining and negotiations* [emphasis in original]." Only after an urban insurrection had succeeded would the Party raise the issue of a neutral central government.[12] The heady optimism of early 1965 had somewhat dissipated, but Le Duan was still convinced that the U.S. intervention was only a stop-gap measure to strengthen their negotiating hand. Even in the worst-case scenario, argued Le Duan, "the fraternal socialist countries are ready to assist us. Even if the U.S. recklessly sends their army into North Vietnam, we up here will also defeat them. Although it may cost hundreds of thousands of casualties, although Hanoi could be reduced to rubble, the North will be alongside the South, and will resolutely fight and defeat the American bandits and complete the liberation of the people and the reunification of the country."[13]

By November the emphasis was on protracted war and settling in for the long term, and Le Duan had heavily qualified his projection about an insurrection with the proviso that, in the future, it would have to be accompanied by a large-scale military "general offensive."[14] "The strategic slogan of the revolutionary war in the South is that we must fight a protracted war, and rely mainly on our own strength." This was because the United States hoped that its intervention would lead to "a decisive victory in a relatively short period of time."[15] The obvious strategic response for the revolution, which knew that it could not throw the United States out of Vietnam in direct military conflict, was a denial strategy of inflicting unacceptable casualties and preventing a decisive U.S./GVN military victory. Now the strategic roles had been reversed, and it was the United States which hoped that a big push would bring a quick end to the war, while the revolution had to figure out how to weather the impending storm.

In the Mekong Delta, the best way to defeat the Saigon army was to "hold and expand our control in the countryside." This would require a more rational deployment of troops than the 1964 and early-1965 strategy of draining the delta of manpower to send to the big battlefields north of Saigon and in the Central Highlands to finish off the ARVN. Now the manpower would be kept in the delta and the balance among the guerrilla, local, and main force units restored. Le Duan instructed COSVN in November 1965 that "we must strengthen the numbers and combat capacity of the local forces and expand the guerrilla network really strongly and on a really broad scale." It is not clear whether this was accompanied by an order to retreat from the radical "Motivating the Peasants" campaign, or whether the abandonment of this campaign was the result of Southern revolutionaries proceeding on their own.

Le Duan's message to COSVN strongly suggests that the hard class line of early 1965 was eventually moderated by a necessity to revert to a broader nationalist appeal, and that the land question was to be put on the back burner and resolved "step by step." "It is necessary to carry out the policy of great unity of the entire people well, and resolve step by step the land question for the peasants; firmly grasp the Party policy for the country-side, aim the sharp spear point of struggle at the American imperialists and the landlord gang of cruel and wicked tyrants who are lackeys of the enemy. Along with stepping up production and combat, we also have to be concerned about the health, education, culture, and social tasks."[16]

The War Intensifies in My Tho

To a great extent the sharp move to the left in revolutionary strategy in early 1965 was dictated by the Party's assessment of the situation prior to the major U.S. intervention. Giving more benefits to the poor peasants would encourage them to support the greater demands that the total mobilization strategy imposed on the rural population in an attempt to take advantage of the momentum gained following the overthrow of President Diem in 1963. But the leftward turn was also the result of several growing problems that confronted the revolutionaries in My Tho even as they surged toward an anticipated victory. The burdens of supporting the revolution were becoming increasingly heavy, not only because of the draft and taxation, but also because of the increasing insecurity caused by intensified bombing and shelling of the countryside. In the Party's view, an early victory would halt the erosion of the popular base of the revolution, and thus also help preempt an American intervention. As it happened, the accelerated decline of the Saigon government and the military successes of the revolution brought about the very intervention that the Party had hoped to forestall. Even at the height of the military momentum of the revolution nation-wide, however, in My Tho a number of problems were developing. The political and military disarray in Saigon and many key rural areas was greater than in My Tho, where the government forces were on the defensive but still able to mount effective operations despite significant setbacks in the province.

Expanded military assistance from the United States enabled the GVN to dramatically escalate the level of bombing and shelling in the delta. A document captured in the summer of 1965 itemized the specific increases in GVN firepower in Dinh Tuong province. It mentioned that the GVN had increased the number of artillery pieces from eighteen in 1964 to twenty-six in 1965. The average of daily bombing sorties was three to eight a day. In one 1965 battle they fired 1,500 rounds of artillery and dropped 200 tons of bombs. In the first six months of 1965, the document claims, the ARVN fired 75,000 artillery rounds and dropped 7 tons of bombs on My Tho. There were 810 sweep operations in My Tho during the first six months of 1965. "The result is that the enemy caused us a number of difficulties. They set up twenty-eight additional towers and posts, expanded the province capital defense zone, and put some liberated zones under pressure (in Go Cong and Cho Gao), and attrited some of our guerrillas (Cho Gao and Cai Be)."[17]

Increased American military aid not only had a direct impact on military encounters between the two sides, it had a far more important and lasting effect: it set in motion an exodus from the rural areas that in the course of five years was to result in substantial depopulation of vast areas of the delta, which drastically weakened the revolutionary movement there and profoundly disrupted rural social organization and peasant life. In addition to the bombing and shelling, the Saigon military achieved some local victories in early 1965, which were overshadowed by the more important large-scale defeats it incurred in other areas of the country. Stripping My Tho and other delta provinces of military personnel had an inevitable impact on the combat effectiveness of the local revolutionary units. This was belatedly recognized in Le Duan's November letter, which acknowledged that the ARVN had not fallen apart as he had apparently anticipated at the beginning of the year.

Land Reform Benefits to Peasants Eroded by Burdens of Tax and Conscription, and Growing Rural Insecurity

Another significant change in tone in Le Duan's November 1965 letter was a new concern for the costs of the "go for broke" policy to the peasantry in South Vietnam. The key element in expanding the base of political support for the revolution in areas like the Mekong Delta was the land reform which accompanied the expansion of its control over population and territory. This provided clear benefits for landless peasants which, however, were diminished over time. The former poor peasants now became self sufficient "middle peasants." But, in addition to the problem this later posed for the revolution (the "new" middle peasants didn't want collectivization any more than the "old" middle peasants), the benefits of receiving land were soon negated by the heavy taxes and military conscription that followed.

Despite the Diem land reform, by 1960 as much as 75 percent of the land was owned by 15 percent of the population, because much of the land distributed by the revolution during the Resistance had been reclaimed by its former owners during the 1954–60 period (a postwar Hanoi study estimates 80–90 percent in the Mekong Delta). The Hanoi study asserts that in My Tho, of the 46,415 hectares distributed by the Viet Minh during the Resistance (slightly less than 30 percent of the total cultivable land in the province), only 16 hectares were still in the hands of the Resistance beneficiaries by 1960.[18] Certainly more than 16 hectares of land were still in the hands of Viet Minh beneficiaries by 1960, but it is clear that much of the Resistance era land reform had been undone during the Diem period. It is hard to argue with the Party's conclusion that "the landlord class and the system of tenantry was not only not eliminated but was actually restored."[19] According to another revolutionary account, landlord rent, which had been reduced to between 2 and 2.5 *gia* per *cong* during the Resistance, rose to 3.5 to 6 *gia*. As much as 25,000 hectares in My Tho was affected by this escalation of rent.[20] Nevertheless, this brief resurgence of land-lordism has to be seen against the longer-term terminal decline of this once-dominant rural class, which had begun with the Resistance land expropriations and the flight of landlords from the countryside.

According to the official province Party history, 11,000 hectares of land or about 7 percent of the total were distributed in My Tho in 1961.[21] By the end of 1965 the Party claimed that a total of 126,623 hectares had been distributed, or an average of slightly over 20,000 hectares a year for the 1960–65 period. Most of the distributions were made in the period 1961–64, but distributions continued at a lower level after that. Not only did the land distributions take place over a long period of time, there was considerable variation in the amount of land given out, the number of families affected, and the amount of rent paid to the landlord after cultivation rights were assigned to a family.

A postwar Hanoi study of this period stated that "The process of collapse of the landlord class in the Mekong River Delta is also the process of development of the middle peasant strata. The tendency of middle peasantization [*xu huong trung nong hoa*] becomes clearer every day, though with different levels in different localities, and it had to pass through a period of fierce struggle."[22] As of 1965, the middle peasants in the Mekong Delta constituted 54 percent of the rural population in the "liberated zones" and tilled 76 percent of the land, while according to a COSVN study, "the landlord class has been dealt a heavy blow and is embarking on the path of disintegration."[23] In 1970, COSVN reviewed the situation since 1960 in the countryside and concluded that "the majority of the landlord class has fled, and the cruel and wicked landlords and bullies have had their land confiscated. Here only a few small landlords remain, and they are economically dependent and not a significant factor. They still collect some rent, some-times a very small amount, or live on the labor of their family, especially in the Mekong Delta."[24] COSVN's 1965 figures had showed that middle peasants were already a major-ity in the revolutionary-controlled areas. By 1969 a number of Party-ordered studies suggested that the middle peasants now comprised from 51 to 87 percent of the popula-tion, or from two to six times the number of middle peasants in 1945 by this calculation, and controlled 60 to 91 percent of the land. The equalization of land holdings is evident in the fact that "the ratio of middle peasant land to the total cultivated land is similar to the ratio of middle peasants to the total population in each locality," which means that "a middle peasant family occupies an amount of land equal to the per-capita average land holding in each locality."[25]

The "middle peasantization" that was already evident in 1965 posed a dilemma for the revolution. On the one hand, it represented the obverse of the decline of the land-lords, and was a sign of greater equity in land distribution. On the other hand, the Party did not trust the middle peasants, because their class interests would not necessarily carry them all the way to the end of even the "national democratic" revolution, let alone the socialist revolution. In Long Hung village, the "cradle of the revolution" in My Tho, "after the land reform was carried out in the village, the poor and very poor peasants contributed to the Front even more zealously. The rich and middle peasants began to leave their fields and orchards to go to the GVN areas." When the land distribution was first launched, the "middle peasants didn't dare oppose it. When the Front gained complete control over the village, the middle peasants saw that the Front didn't harm their interests and began to get to like the cadres and supported the Front from 1961 to 1963. But in 1964, when the Front imposed the agricultural tax in the village, they began to be disgruntled and left their homes to take refuge in the GVN areas. So now [1967] the village Front has concluded that the middle peasants belong to the vacillating and passive element of the national democratic revolution" [DT185]. Since the middle peasants had already become the dominant class in the countryside in 1965, this was an ominous portent for the revolution.

When the compulsory taxation imposed after the land distribution began to equal and even exceed the landlord exactions during the six years of peace, the GVN alternative with its low taxation (made possible by the fact that its American allies were subsidizing most of its budget) looked somewhat better, certainly to the middle peasants who were becoming the dominant element in the countryside. A poor peasant from Long Hung village whose family had lost 5 *cong* of land purchased from someone who had left the village permanently (probably a landlord or rich peasant) said, "It is common knowledge that after land distribution taxes to the Front were higher than rent to the landlords. In my family we paid 30 *gia* rent for 12 *cong* and now have to pay 21 *gia* to the Front for 7 *cong* [after it had taken 5 *cong*]" [DT190]. The exaction per *cong* was roughly comparable, but the reduction of land made the total burden comparatively greater.

By 1965, certainly by 1966, escalating costs to the peasants in the form of the draft, taxes, and the increasing violence of the war outweighed the material benefits that the revolution could bestow on them. The shifting patterns of control also reopened the issue of who supported the revolution and put the peasants' loyalty to yet another test. A Cao Dai middle peasant from Quon Long village described the evolution of the situation in his village. At first, "only the poor class joined the revolution, because the Front promised to protect their children from the GVN draft and restore leadership and honor to these people if they joined right away. The middle peasants were forced to follow in order to protect their interests. Two years later, when the Front finished its organizations among the people and installations in the village, to support or not to support the Front was no longer a problem. Everyone was forced to join the Front, whether he wanted to or not. From 1966 on, the situation became disadvantageous for the Front because the people's attitude changed with the situation. They were still afraid of the Front, but if the Front put on too much pressure they would take refuge in GVN areas" [DT276].

As the war intensified, land became increasingly devalued as a currency of revolutionary payoffs to supporters. Although more and more land became available as the wealthier peasants fled to more secure areas, the very insecurity that had made this land available also made it dangerous and unprofitable to cultivate. And by 1967 large numbers of refugees of all social classes had been driven out of the countryside by the bombing and shelling. Thus the land question diminished in importance, and the daily struggle for survival replaced land as the most critical issue for the rural population.

Taxes and Military Conscription

Compulsory taxation had been instituted in areas like My Tho in 1963 to replace the less onerous "fund drives" of the post insurrection period. By 1964 the burdens of taxation had escalated to support the "go for broke" military escalation. In November 1965 Le Duan, from his vantage in distant Hanoi, expressed his concerns about the tax burden on the peasantry to the revolutionary leadership in the South and implied that with a shift of strategy toward a more protracted guerrilla war, the burden of taxation might have to be adjusted. "The level of the Resistance agricultural tax imposed on the people must be carefully weighed so that it is reasonable *[vua phai]*. I am not clear on whether the level of contributions of the people in Nam Bo is high or low, but it seems that in Region 5 [Central Vietnam] it is heavy. In a situation where the enemy is fiercely employing sweep operations and destructive firepower, and stealing and pillaging resources with all his strength, if we ask the people to contribute beyond their capabilities, then I'm afraid that they will not have enough strength to endure a protracted struggle. To reduce the contributions of the people over the next few years, the Center will make efforts to meet the needs of the resistance in the South. However, the financial capacity up here [in North Vietnam] is limited. I propose that in each area of operations you brothers carefully figure out how to economize on outlays."[26]

The institution of forced conscription proved even more unpopular than escalating taxes. Sometime in 1963, probably before the overthrow of President Diem, a decision was made to institute "military service" (*nghia vu quan su*). Like the post-World War II draft system in the United States, the policy did not mean that everyone *would* serve in the military; rather, it meant that the military would no longer rely completely on voluntary enlistment, and that the entire able-bodied male population would be eligible for the draft. The three separate elements of this policy were (1) the introduction of compulsory service, (2) the idea that military service would be universal—that all eligible draftees should, in principle, serve, and (3) the enforcement mechanisms of this policy, ranging from persuasion and indoctrination to arrest.

In the beginning, the major change marked by the new military service policy in 1963 was that the concentrated military forces and the guerrillas would no longer be only carefully selected volunteers. The need for a larger military force, not only in My Tho but in other areas of the country where there was heavy military activity but a sparse population, forced the Party to abandon its reliance on highly motivated volunteers. At the same time, the fact that the war had already gone on for several years and was escalating in ferocity gave pause to those who imagined that military glory could be had at a relatively low cost. Finally, those youth who were most inclined to volunteer had already done so, and the revolution now had to find ways of recruiting less motivated individuals.

After the first shift in policy from a volunteer army to a mixed volunteer–draft regime, the second shift was in the scale of recruitment. By 1964 it had become the objective of the revolution to press every able-bodied male into service. At first those who were already serving as political cadres were exempt, but by 1965 the Party had initiated a policy of "reduction of administrative personnel" *(gian chinh)* aimed at transferring even key political and administrative cadres to combat units. The next stage in the evolution of the draft, from 1963 to 1965, was in the methods used to conscript reluctant recruits. In the early stages, persuasion and social pressure were the primary techniques, but by 1965 brute force and subterfuge were the main methods of dragooning reluctant recruits into a service which the rural youth had come to dread as an almost certain death sentence. When this policy proved counterproductive, and eventually ineffective, it was abandoned. The rapid military buildup of 1964–65 failed to produce a quick and decisive victory over the Saigon forces and, far from persuading the United States not to intervene, triggered direct U.S. military involvement. The final stage in the draft policy, in 1966–67, included the formation of a Volunteer Youth group *(Thanh Nien Xung Phong)* which functioned as a "halfway house" between civilian and military life, and an implicit recognition that direct transfers of large numbers of rural youth to fighting units was no longer possible.

By 1965 the aura of voluntarism and selectivity had faded. Rural villagers' "most frequent complaint," said one respondent, was that "although the Front's term for military service sounds nicer than that used by Diem, it amounts to the same thing—grabbing our sons as soldiers *[bay gio noi nghia vu, cung chi di bat linh thoi]*" [DT64]. Although the term *nghia vu,* with its overtones of high-minded idealism, had been retained in some places, it had taken on the less lofty meaning of a forced draft. In an attempt to distinguish military service for the revolution from military service for the Saigon government, the Party took pains to use different terms. Instead of the Saigon term *linh* 'soldier,' a term with ancient and negative connotations dating from the traditional images of a riff-raff of Imperial soldiery who preyed on the population instead of protecting them, the Party adopted the term *chien si* ("warrior"), or used the term *bo doi* (troop or troops, or "our boys"), employed during both the Resistance and later. (In the Second Indochina War, 1959–75, *bo doi* was most commonly used to refer to North Vietnamese troops, to distinguish them from the Southern guerrillas). Having the *nghia vu* compared to the dragooning of Army of the Republic of Vietnam (ARVN) soldiers (the GVN used the literal term *quan dich*—military service) was not the image the revolution wanted to project.

Like taxation, the draft policy imposed heavy costs on the revolution and eroded much of its political support. In the early 1960s the revolution had often contrasted its ideal of voluntary service in a just cause with the forced conscription of the Government of the Republic of Vietnam. Since the GVN draft was universally unpopular, this struck a responsive chord in the rural population. Not only were rural youth conscripted against their will, but because of Ngo Dinh Diem's fears of building up local power bases which might be used against him, and the ARVN high command's concern that serving too close to home would encourage desertion, many of the Saigon government's conscripts from the Mekong Delta were sent to units in Central Vietnam, far from home and family.

If there were doubts about how many demands could be imposed on the civilian population by Party leaders in Hanoi, they were even more pervasive among cadres and Party leaders who were closest to the villages where these policies were implemented. A district cadre described the reaction to the forced draft and taxation policies:

> When the cadres, including myself, were first indoctrinated about the new finance and military policies, they were very upset. When we learned that we would have to use repressive measures, we reasoned that we studied the policies and were then sent out to execute them [e.g., just followed orders]. But our families were among the people and we ourselves were from the people, and this meant that the new policies ran directly counter to our interests. All the cadres, even in the district committee, were upset. Bay

The, who was in charge of current affairs in the Cho Gao district committee, opposed the finance policy as soon as it was set forth. He opposed it to the point that they removed him from his job and sent him back to the village. He opposed this policy because it involved excessive taxes from the people and he himself would have to pay an excessive tax. He told the district committee that this was sheer exploitation, that this was stealing from the people, and asked how they could be expected to pay. [Q: Did the other cadres in the province know about this incident?] They all knew. A deputy district secretary who had opposed this policy and was demoted by the province Party committee back to the village had an impact all the way over to the Party ranks in Cai Be. A number of Party members opposed the new policies, but did not dare to do so openly [DT109].

Villagers Predicament in the Escalating Violence

Increasingly, life in revolutionary-controlled and contested areas became untenable for most peasants. Whatever their political sympathies, they were caught between two sides whose objectives threatened their hamlets. The Saigon government bombed and shelled indiscriminately, and the behavior of its troops toward the villagers was often brutal and contemptuous. The revolutionaries imposed the heavy double burden of conscription and taxes on the villagers, and were implacable in punishing those whose loyalties were suspect. In addition, as the people defied cadre orders and left the hamlets, the cadres often retaliated by sniping at the posts from near the New Life Hamlets where the refugees had relocated, to provoke shelling around these hamlets. The object was to neutralize the safety advantage of living in these Saigon-controlled areas, and force the people back into the revolutionary-controlled hamlets [DT34]. This tactic was a variation on the 1960–61 assassination campaign, which had also attempted to shift the "balance of terror" in favor of the revolution.

New Life Hamlets (*Ap Tan Sinh*) were updated versions of the Strategic Hamlets, renamed to project a more hospitable image. The "new life" designation may have been a result of the influence of Taiwanese psychological warfare advisors, harking back to the authoritarian "New Life" movement of Chiang Kai-shek's Kuomintang (KMT) in 1930s China. They differed from the former Strategic Hamlets primarily in that they did not generally fence the hamlet population within an armed fortress. At this stage of the war the population was not actually coerced into these hamlets, but were induced to leave their own homes and move to GVN-controlled areas by the more impersonal technique of bombing and shelling, which, in theory, still left the choice up to the individual.

Face-to-Face Struggles

The situation created by this rural depopulation sharpened the dilemma facing rural inhabitants, now torn between the desire to cling to their homes and the urge to move to a less dangerous area. It also put their loyalty to the revolution and obedience to the cadres to the test. The village cadres, fearing loss of support and resources, ordered the people to stay. They also tried to turn the indiscriminate shelling to advantage by using it to mobilize the villagers for political action. In many villages, the cadres organized groups of peasants to go to the GVN village office to protest the shelling. A cadre from the contested village of

Hoa Dinh recalled watching one such demonstration of about thirty women, "who did not bring banners or shout slogans, but looked rather sad and marched silently" [DT47].

By contrast, Dang Hung Phuoc, also in Cho Gao district, organized four major "face-to-face struggles" at the district headquarters, with about 100 people participating each time, which demanded an end to shelling from the district and, perhaps to deflect attention from the revolutionary draft, protested GVN conscription [DT49]. By the end of 1965, however, many villagers had wearied of the task of demonstrating, which did not seem to produce noticeable results and could lead to arrest. The Party did not, of course, tell the people that it had an ulterior motive for urging them to demonstrate, whether or not the GVN listened to their complaints. A veteran cadre from the Resistance asserted that the main point of face-to-face struggles was to create a diversionary "uproar in the East while striking in the West [*duong dong kich tay*]," and that the main purpose of the struggles was to "give political support for military activities and to keep the GVN security services occupied" [DT153]. In Tam Hiep the village Party secretary mobilized the people for three "face-to-face struggles" in November and December 1965, resulting in the arrest and over-night detention of three villagers.

As the potential cost of participating in demonstrations rose, the villagers became more reluctant. In response, the cadres assured them that if they were jailed, other villagers would demonstrate for their release in a show of solidarity—an attempt to underline the power of mass action as well as defuse the peasants' fears. As an additional incentive to participate in the demonstrations, the village Party secretary "tried to explain to the villagers that face-to-face struggles would help them avoid being shelled and losing their pigs and chickens," but the villagers were not persuaded and remained reluctant to go [DT59].

To cope with this situation, the district committee sent security agents to Tam Hiep village to conduct a "thorough investigation." This resulted in the arrest of three villagers. "They led them away, forced them to attend a reeducation course, brought them back to the village, gathered the Tam Hiep people once again, and compelled these three men to wage a face-to-face struggle. From dissatisfied people, these three villagers now became back-bone elements. Finally, a big face-to-face struggle was launched on the 'day of struggle of the entire province' [*ngay dau tranh cua toan tinh*]. That day the people from Long An, Long Dinh, and Tam Hiep villages were also motivated to participate in a big face-to-face struggle and they came back to the district in greater numbers. But none of them were arrested and when they came back to their villages, the Front waged propaganda, claiming that the people had successfully struggled against the GVN. That was the last struggle of last year [1965], and the cadres said they would wage other struggles in the year to come, if necessary" [DT59]. In addition, Ba Vu, the district cadre who had led the Concerted Uprising in this area and engineered the withdrawal of the nearby Phu My post in 1963, came and appealed directly to the villagers to participate in the demonstrations.

As in the concerted uprising of 1960–61 in My Tho, a combination of fear, persuasion, and appeal to interest was employed to induce villagers to participate in demonstrations. "The villagers were very scared, but they could not avoid being forced to participate in these struggles. Those who refused to follow the Front's orders would be placed under house arrest. I think that the villagers also feared the GVN, but they feared it less than they feared the Front. In there [in the revolutionary-controlled areas] the people had to comply with the cadres' orders, otherwise they would be accused of plotting to sabotage the struggle waged by the Front. The villagers who were on friendly terms with me often complained to me that they were very unhappy because they could not stay home and, besides, participating in face-to-face struggle was hard and dangerous" [DT59]. Despite the occasional success of these pressures in motivating more people to participate in these demonstrations, as in Tam Hiep village, cadres in other areas encountered increasing difficulties in mobilizing villagers to struggle. The numbers of participants declined, and so did the frequency and boldness of the demonstrations.

One of the political dilemmas the cadres faced in organizing face-to-face demonstrations was that the risks and burdens were shared unequally. Not everyone agreed to go, and this raised both the problem of equity and the problem of making those who did participate all the more exposed and noticeable. After a small group of Kim Son villagers returned from a demonstration in which three old women who had presented petitions to the district chief requesting an end to the shelling had been arrested, they blamed the cadres for not making all the villagers go, thus placing the burden on these old women. A village cadre in the Women's Association, which was largely responsible for organizing these demonstrations, recalled, "We had to reply that 'Those who didn't participate don't thoroughly understand the revolution. We have to give them time to understand where their own interests lie,' and we hoped they would do their duty next time" [DT65].

Seizing the opportunity to make a political point, the cadres added that the shells came from the United States, in order to stir up resentment against the Americans. "The villagers believed that, because they actually saw the Americans participating in sweep operations and they have never seen any Russians or Chinese. In fact, it was difficult to wage face-to-face struggles. The people were afraid and they did not want to go on demonstrations. But in the last months before I was arrested [August 1965], the people sustained excessive damage and this stirred them up to such an extent that they could care less about being arrested. They wanted to meet with the district chief and ask him to stop shelling their village. Many villagers wept profusely when they saw their hamlets wiped out. . . . The people just want to earn their living in peace" [DT65].

The Role of Village Cadres in Organizing Demonstrations

Because many peasants left the strong revolutionary areas which were the targets of the bombing and shelling, however, there were fewer people to demonstrate, and those who remained were more exposed, both because of their smaller numbers and because they were assumed to be closely tied to the revolution. As a result, the activists could no longer lose themselves in a larger crowd. The distinctions between the activists and the peripheral participants in these demonstrations were fairly clear. There was an inner core of "backbone" elements, a surrounding group of Women's Association members, and an outer group of "the people" or ordinary citizens.

Hoi Cu village, a large and strategically located village in Cai Be bordering Highway 4 but extending north to villages which were on the fringe of the Plain of Reeds, was under the leadership of Hien Mai, a former seamstress in Saigon who had returned to her native village in 1962 and had rapidly ascended through the position of head of the village Women's Association (1963) to village Party chapter secretary (1964). Her quick rise through the ranks was due in part to her very good rapport with the popular association members and, according to one account, ordinary non-Party people in the village [DT130]. The general consensus of interviewees from Hoi Cu, however, was that she had risen in the Party not because of her popular touch, but because she was hard-nosed in imposing Party discipline. Another cadre said that some villagers disliked her because she had been "undemocratic," showing favoritism to her relatives in the land distribution. "Hien Mai was harsh," he said, "and she offended everyone with her sharp tongue. She liked to press the people hard, and the villagers didn't like her. But the Front trusted her because she was the right hand of the revolution" [DT165]. Her strong family links to the revolution certainly helped her Party career. In addition, her male predecessor had been judged incompetent to lead at the village level by higher Party authorities, and was demoted to a hamlet-level Party position [DT117].

Hien Mai was disliked by many of her fellow cadres; however, some of whom attributed her harshness and inflexible application of orders and regulations to an inferiority complex [DT130]. Her tough enforcement of Party policy led to an appointment as village security chief before she became the village Party secretary [DT117]. A cadre who had been promoted to district level from Hoi Cu said the problem lay mainly with the guerrillas in the village, who were "swashbucklers" and resented being led by a woman, and, no doubt, the discipline she imposed on them [DT109]. "Hien Mai was harsh," said the former head of the village guerrilla unit, "and didn't like military people to eat and drink. She never praised anyone, but criticized them for errors right away" [DT165]. A main force soldier from Hoi Cu village presented a less than flattering picture of Hien Mai: "All her brothers are fervent Front followers. She is forty years old, looks ugly, and has never gotten married. She comes from a middle peasant family. The villagers are afraid of her because she likes to dress down those who didn't perform the tasks she entrusted them with" [DT93]. A very different account was given by a village cadre who admired Hien Mai, though he implicitly agreed with the cadres who thought she had an "inferiority complex." In his telling, she was a twenty-nine-year-old former Resistance member who had been married to a cadre who regrouped to North Vietnam in 1954, and now lived with her mother along with her twelve-year-old daughter. She was, he agreed, from a middle peasant family, and she had a third-grade education. Her father had been a cadre in the Resistance [DT130].

While other village cadres were having increasing problems assembling a crowd for political demonstrations, Hien Mai had some success. On the occasion of the July 20 anniversary of the Geneva Accords in 1965, she succeeded in mobilizing 100 members of the Hoi Cu village Women's Association and 200 ordinary villagers for a large inter-village demonstration in Hau My village. The secret to her success on this occasion was probably that this was not a risky face-to-face demonstration in a GVN district town, but a political rally in a secure liberated area. On this occasion the ratio of Women's Association members to "people" or *nhan dan* (in this context the term is used in the same way as the more frequently employed "masses" or *quan chung,* that is, ordinary civilians who were not members of revolutionary organizations) was one association member for every two nonmembers.

Hien Mai also got some results even in the more risky face-to-face demonstrations. In late August she organized a demonstration of 100 women in Cai Be district town, with five "backbone elements" (probably Women's Association members) for every thirty ordinary demonstrators. The smaller number of demonstrators (100 as compared with the 300 at the Hau My rally), and the lower one-in-six ratio of "backbone elements" to "masses" (as opposed to the one-to-two ratio at Hau My) reflects the greater difficulty of organizing higher-risk "face to face struggles," since both the activists and the "masses" were harder to persuade. In the march on Cai Be district, the crowd carried petitions urging an end to shelling of the village and forced GVN conscription. They also called for higher salaries for the GVN soldiers (to provide political cover for their demonstration by appearing to be acting on behalf of GVN soldiers, while also trying to sow discontent in the GVN ranks), and demanded U.S. withdrawal from Vietnam. The demonstrators from Hoi Cu village, who had been afraid before the march, returned enthusiastic and triumphant because none had been arrested. But then Hien Mai, according to the "official story," was promoted to the "district level," and no one in the village was subsequently able to match her success in organizing political participation [DT130].

As the War Intensifies, Peasants Are Faced with Difficult Choices

As the war escalated, the peasants were increasingly squeezed between the greatly increased risks of participating in revolutionary activities and the increasingly heavy-handed pressures used by the cadres when persuasion failed. In terms of actual participation in revolutionary actions, villagers not only were expected to engage in the political demonstrations, but also an even higher-risk task: serving as porters for revolutionary military units, often under combat conditions. When village cadres found it difficult to mobilize "front-line porters" (*dan cong tien tuyen*) starting in early 1965, district cadres came down to the villages to suggest techniques of dealing with the problem. If the young men in the village were tapped to go but refused, they would be arrested on the grounds that they now possessed secret military information (where and when the battle would take place). "As a result of these strong measures," reported one village cadre, "the mobilization of civilian porters always got results." The incentives for the local cadres to get results were also evident, because "this time the cadres were much more zealous and operated more forcefully than in the case of the military draft, because if they didn't round up the allotted number of civilian porters, they themselves would have to go" [DT146]. However, as people left the villages in revolutionary areas, these strong measures became less effective, and ultimately contributed to the outflow.

Many of the village cadres themselves felt ambivalent about the policy of forcing the people to choose between safety and livelihood. "In fact the Front cadres themselves felt that the measure was not only ineffective but incorrect as well, because most of them had some relatives who had also taken refuge in the GVN-controlled areas. The villagers' security problem is, for the moment, an unresolved problem for the Front" [DT69].

Province Party leaders acknowledged that the growing insecurity in revolutionary areas had created a serious problem. Chin Om, the province Party secretary, recalled:

> Going into 1965 the enemy fiercely and destructively fired into the liberated area, driving the people out to live along the roadsides, while they zealously prepared for a limited war [the intervention of U.S. troops]. The situation became difficult. How could we hold the people in the liberated areas? Before, when they [the GVN] used infantry to

grind down and round up the people, we could use the "three spearheads" of political and military action along with military proselytizing to stop them, because they were flesh-and-blood human beings. Now the instrument used is iron and steel raining down from the skies. The gang that does this is not there on the spot, so how can you stop them? The Current Affairs Section [of the province Party committee] constantly met to discuss this. I concluded that we should resolve to mobilize everyone, cadres, soldiers, and people, to dare to cling to their turf. The leadership must set the example, and the fiercer and more difficult it is, the more they need to set an example. Brother Muoi Ha raised the point that the people in Ap Bac had spontaneously left for the open rice fields and set up straw huts at the edge of their fields. At the beginning they only set up some crude straw roofs as shelters for them during the day, and returned home at night. But later, as the [GVN] continued to shell into the treelines [where the settlements were], they built more substantial houses in the fields. The other brothers said that it was not only Ap Bac that did this. By day the people wore white clothes and moved back and forth. When enemy planes came to strafe, they just went about their business normally and it appears that the enemy got used to this, so that this became a way of becoming legal with them. From this phenomenon a solution to the problem of holding onto the people gradually emerged.[27]

Impact of Rural Devastation on Support for the Revolution

Letting the civilians find their own ways of protecting themselves like moving to huts in the open ricefields or wearing white clothing rather than the "black pajamas" (which the U.S. pilots identified with the "Viet Cong") and not panicking when planes approached apparently worked better than the solution urged on the people by the Party, which was embodied in the slogan, "a good bomb shelter is better than a good home" [*ham tot hon nha tot*], which could not have sounded very appealing to the people living in the heavily shelled treelines.[28] Over the next several years, the villagers who remained in the revolutionary zones were forced from the clusters of neighborhoods in the shady treelines—which were also the hiding place of the guerrillas—to living in the rice fields in the blazing sun, protected only by a rudimentary straw hut. This was the beginning of a physical distancing of the people from the cadres, which made life increasingly more difficult for the revolutionaries in My Tho.

A former district propaganda cadre analyzed the problems the shellings caused the revolution: "During the years 1961 through 1963 almost all the cadres enjoyed the people's sympathy. Signs of anger among the people were then rare. The villagers and the cadres got along with one another very well. This was only natural, because the revolutionary movement was then in full swing, hatred against the Diem regime was still strong, the war was less bloody, and the security in the countryside was comparatively good" [DT135]. In this cadre's view, "The year 1965 was the year of the big change." The hatred directed against Diem had dissipated somewhat, and had not found a sharp new focus in the revolving-door Saigon governments, whose very anonymity and ineffectiveness were their best political protection against rural hostility. The behavior of local officials improved somewhat, in large part because their monopoly on power in the rural areas had been broken and the revolution had demonstrated its power to punish and deter.

The biggest change, however, was the intensification of the war, which had turned "violent and bloodier, while the Front's conscription and tax policies became unbearable. All this has contributed to making the villagers detach themselves from the cadres. To meet the Party's requirements, the cadres had to use threats and violent measures to compel the people to comply with the Party's orders, since they had failed in persuading them to freely agree with the Front. Consequently, they made the people angry at them" [DT135]. The shelling drove the people out of key base areas, thus depriving the troops moving through of food and support. Tax contributions dropped, both because many taxpayers had left and because production fell. Moreover, "the Front always claims it helps the people improve their living standards, and therefore it couldn't afford to make them pay when they were suffering from damage caused by the war. The cadres were reluctant to make these people pay, too. This occurred everywhere damage had been caused. In these places the Front has to stand financial losses from contributions and payment of taxes" [DT135]. It became difficult or impossible to motivate villagers to participate in ammunition transportation, destroying roads, or waging "face-to-face struggles." Cadres became acutely concerned about the welfare of their own families. This brought revolutionary activity to a near standstill in some places and had a serious impact on cadre morale.

The district cadre, with the interviewer's prompting, agreed that "if humanitarian considerations are to be discarded, I will say, as a purely military statement, that shellings really serve the final victory of the GVN," and added that, "from experience, I have realized that the Front is strongest in villages which haven't been shelled and that, on the contrary, it weakens where the shellings happen frequently." He concluded with the paradoxical observation: "To wage Front propaganda and to sow hatred against the GVN, Front cadres need quiet. In Long Dinh village, where shellings have greatly affected the people's welfare, it is very difficult for the cadres to win the people's support" [DT135]. The implication of this apparently contradictory statement is that a little shelling allows the cadres to stir up hatred and resentment by the concrete acts of the enemy, but continuous shelling dislocates the local society to the point that people can think only of survival. Many or most villagers fled from the danger, and those who stayed were difficult to mobilize for political action.

This logical conclusion occurred to others as well. In a famously controversial article, Professor Samuel Huntington of Harvard advanced the view that the United States may have blindly stumbled on the counter to guerrilla war in what he termed "forced-draft urbanization." The basic concept was to turn what most people regarded as a moral and practical problem, the vast refugee displacements in the rural areas, to advantage. In the cynical phrase current among some Americans in Vietnam at the time, "we've got the onus, let's get the bonus." The idea was that the people would come under the Saigon government's control in moving into towns and cities, and in the long run the effect of urbanization would be like that of the industrial revolution, bringing progress and modernization, and immunizing the population from revolutionary mobilization. This proposition would be put to the test in the remaining decade of the war.

The Party Responds to "The Big Change" with a Turn to the Left

Faced with the loss of both population and control, the Party tried to respond to the situation with new policies. Direct commands and threats had not worked. Two different approaches were tried. First, the Party offered greater material incentives to those who stayed. Second, sanctions against those who left were increased. Since most of those who stayed were either relatives of cadres or peasants too poor to be able to move, an appeal to this core group of the revolution was inevitable. The punishments and rewards centered on land, which was taken from those who left and given to those who stayed. Confiscation of the land of refugees who had fled to GVN areas was both a punishment for defying Party orders and a warning to others who might want to leave. In addition, it proved to be a way of revitalizing the flagging land distribution, which had ground to a halt for lack of available land after the first wave of confiscations from landlords and rich peasants, as well as middle peasants who had dispossessed tenants in the Diem land reform.

Although the departure of many of the wealthier peasants from the revolutionary zones was costly in terms of lost manpower and tax revenues, it did provide a new source of available land to pay off the core supporters of the revolution. In Hoa Dinh village, for example, the cadres controlled six of nine hamlets in 1965 (two were GVN-controlled and one was contested). Thus there was a second land distribution in Hoa Dinh in 1965. "Since many villagers left for the towns," a former cadre said, "the Front took their land and gave it to those who remained." Underlining the need to appeal to a narrower but more committed hard core of supporters was the fact that "among those given land in 1961, some also left for the New Life Hamlets" DT[84].

The second wave of land distribution in 1965 was both an expedient to deal with the rural exodus and a political policy connected to the Party's turn toward its core supporters. In Thanh Phu village (Cai Lay) the revolution had been so strong it had not needed to implement a land distribution to strengthen the movement. But in 1965 the villagers began to tire of the burdens of supporting the revolution, especially the draft, and the Party leadership introduced land distribution as an incentive to support its policies. "The peasants had served and made many sacrifices to the Front for five long years, but they hadn't enjoyed any benefits in return, so the Front now had to cajole them and grant them concrete benefits by distributing land to them" [DT203]. Thus the "rational peasant" began to emerge, having wearied of unrequited sacrifices and appeals to communitarian solidarity.

In April 1965 a wave of political indoctrination introduced a new policy to My Tho. Earlier, in February 1965, the annual conference on Party building declared that a major objective for that year would be setting up "people's self-administration" organizations (co quan nhan dan tu quan) from the village to the province level. These organizations were to be "solely composed of basic elements" (e.g., poor and landless peasants), and members from other social categories, "such as category 'A' middle peasants, rich peasants, and landlords, would have to be pushed aside and employed in other organizations" (category 'A' was a political label for "old" middle peasants who had not benefited from land reform) [DT135]. Thus the new hard class line was first announced within the ranks of the Party, and would apply to Party members as well as those outside its ranks. The "self-administration" organizations were a form of proto-government. The revolution had not to this point attempted to proclaim a "government." The National Liberation Front was just that, a "front," and the Party did the direct governing and administration at the local level. This tentative move toward a government in early 1965 proved abortive. Not until 1969, when the Provisional Revolutionary Government (PRG) was created did the revolution actually formally establish a "government" (chinh quyen).

Sweeping Land Reform Proposed by Hanoi
and COSVN is Rejected in My Tho

A platoon leader in the Cho Gao district local forces was told that 1965 would be the "year of victory" and that almost all villages in My Tho province had been fully liberated or were half or two-thirds liberated, and thus it was time to set up a government so that the villages could be "self-administered." Those villages which had been completely liberated or two-thirds liberated should set up a government. Eight of the twenty villages in Cho Gao fell in this category in early 1965. "The main goal of the government," said this respondent, a former village Party secretary, "was to have a land reform so that the people could rely on the [village] government's support to have a class denunciation of landlords in connection with the land reform." [DT108]

In May 1965, Region 2 held a conference on launching the land reform campaign, after which Muoi Ha, who had attended the conference, returned to My Tho along with some Region 2 cadres.[29] The My Tho Party committee held a meeting in May in Nhi Binh village which was devoted largely to the larger strategic issues of the conflict and how to cope with the escalating American intervention. However, this meeting also "discussed the Central Committee directive on land reform. In the face of a situation where almost all the landlords had lost all their political influence and had fled to the cities, the land had been seized by the revolution and temporarily distributed to the peasants. Only a few small landlords had permission to continue receiving rent under our regulations. The province Party committee decided that in June 1965 we would organize indoctrination sessions on the Central Committee's directive within [Party] ranks and motivate the people in a few villages like Nhi Binh and Long Dinh in Chau Thanh district. In July and August 1965 we would spread the motivation to the masses throughout the province and transform it into a denunciation of miseries and recalling of hatred campaign against the Americans and the landlord class."[30]

The official Party history version thus specifically identifies a Central Committee directive from Hanoi ordering the South to launch a land reform campaign in 1965 along the lines of the one carried out earlier in the North. It glosses over what actually happened to this directive, however. After Muoi Ha and the region cadres returned from the region conference and investigated the prospects for such a campaign in My Tho, they concluded that it could not be done. Chin Om (Nguyen Van Cong) wrote in his memoir that "the reality showed that you couldn't mechanically do [land reform] like in the North." As a result, the abortive land reform campaign was "transformed into a denunciation of the crimes of My-Diem, who represented the imperialists and the feudalists."[31] Thus, shifting from a land reform campaign to a campaign of verbal denunciations of exploiters, which emphasized the patriotic issue of their links with foreign aggressors, represented not the culmination of the "motivation of the peasants" but the sidetracking of a far more radical movement that had been ordered by Hanoi.

It took longer for Hanoi to finally acknowledge the failure of this abortive attempt at land reform. General Nguyen Chi Thanh, a tough and hard-line military leader from Central Vietnam who had also presided over the agricultural cooperativization program in North Vietnam, had returned to the South to oversee the military effort in 1964. In 1966 he was persuaded by reports from COSVN cadres in charge of "the rural mission" to advocate carrying out a land reform (*cai cach ruong dat*) in the liberated areas of Nam Bo, "to increase manpower and resources for the anti-American resistance, which had reached a ferocious level." Tran Bach Dang, a leading political cadre from the South, later criticized the COSVN cadres whose reports had led to this policy as being "out of touch with the situation in Nam Bo." Dang wrote: "Many comrades, including myself, did not agree with the policy of land reform for the following reasons: in reality, Nam Bo had carried out a land reform during the anti-French Resistance . . . [and] the peasants who had been 'temporarily allotted' land . . . had almost all become middle peasants, which formed the core force during the Concerted Uprising of 1959–60." After a heated debate at COSVN, Thanh agreed to send to matter to Hanoi for decision and the Central Committee decided not to carry out a land reform.[32] It is a revealing indication of how "out of touch" COSVN and Hanoi were with the grass roots that this decision came down long after the issue had already faded away, in My Tho at least.

Hard Line Complicates Relations With Religious Sects

Still, the harder class line made its impact in My Tho in many other ways. For the rural religious sects there was a clear link between the new political hard line directed against the wealthier peasants and the abandonment of the united front with religious groups in the countryside. When the "motivating the peasants" campaign was initiated in Cai Be district, where the Hoa Hao sect was especially strong, "when the religious groups hear of this class struggle, they didn't like it, and when they heard that the Party was going to play a prominent role they also didn't like this because they knew that the Party was heading toward a people's democratic revolution and the realization of a socialist society in which there would be no religious groups, no landlords, no capitalists, no exploiters—what they considered to be exploiters—and that they would be enemies of the Party. When they heard about this campaign, they reacted strongly" [DT109]. By mid-1965, this district cadre estimated that "at least 30 to 40 percent of the religious groups and about 30 percent of the rich peasants and landlords" had left the revolutionary-controlled areas for the towns. A captured document from Dinh Tuong reviewing the My Tho province situation during the first half of 1965 noted an upsurge in Hoa Hao activity in the province and said that "712 Hoa Hao youths were recruited or drafted in the service or [as] replacements for [GVN] local forces. And the majority of Hoa Hao believers had moved from our base area to the Cai Be [district] perimeter." In addition, former officers of the Cao Dai sect forces were used to recruit co-religionists in the province to form three GVN Regional Force companies.[33] Other interviews indicate that by this time there were very few rich peasants, to say nothing of landlords, left in the revolutionary zones, so the percentage who had left the villages was probably much higher. In a district where religious groups were estimated to comprise about 40 percent of the total population, the Hoa Hao and Cao Dai constituted up to 60 percent of the religious population, the relationship between the revolution and these two groups was a crucial political issue [DT109].

In the view of a district Labor Youth cadre from Cai Be, this policy toward the religious sects was a "subjective error." He reasoned that "most of the religious people are peasants and the Party line is that the peasants are the 'main force' of the Party despite the fact that they also have religious affiliations. The Party considered that their basic character was that they were peasants. Besides, the religious representatives were not very active, and this gradually shifted the effort of motivating the peasants toward the Party. . . . As a result, they subjectively let the Front disintegrate" [DT109]. During the radical phase of "motivating the peasants" in 1965, the Party tried to reduce the rural population to their class essence, ignoring cross-cutting ties and identities such as religious affiliation, thus attempting to get, say, a Hoa Hao poor peasant to feel class solidarity with all other poor peasants, rather than identify with his co-religionists.

A province propaganda and indoctrination cadre pointed to the importance of a letter written in mid-1965 by the province Party committee as part of the "motivating the peasants" campaign. "Its special importance was that this time it was the Party itself that had written the letter to the peasants, without going through the Front. It was the first time the Party had directly addressed the people" [DT145]. Though this experienced and committed Party cadre asserted that the people showed a lively interest in the "coming out" of the Party in presenting its policies directly to the people at the indoctrination sessions at the village and hamlet level where this letter was presented, he and his fellow cadres concluded that the results had been uneven. There had been some improvement in the tax collections, but the draft policy was still fraught with problems [DT145].

Still, the new hard line did achieve some initial results, as even the Cai Be district cadre who was critical of the policy conceded. "In Cho Gao, I heard that they got very good results. The tax collections went well, and the draft campaign also went well. They succeeded in stirring up the peasants' resentment to the point that one night five or six peasants went together and beheaded four landlords. I was told in Cai Be that the purpose of this campaign was to service military requirements and, secondarily, to isolate the upper levels of society and pay particular attention to the middle, poor, and very poor peasants in order to ensure a supply of manpower. We were told that the middle, poor, and very poor peasants composed the vast majority of the population and that, this being the case, the military and political objectives could be served at the same time" [DT109].

Impact of the 1965 Hard Line in My Tho

The effects of the 1965 hard line were felt for a long time. For one thing, the depopulation of the countryside had left the revolutionaries with a base of support largely consisting of poor peasants, and they had to take care of the interests of this constituency. By 1971, the base population of the revolution had been reduced to small clusters of poor peasants. It was not revolutionary policy or incentives that kept them there, however, but a combination of strong attachments to the revolution and a lack of capital and skills to move into more secure areas. There is some evidence in the interviews that portions of the harder class line were applied in selected test areas before it was officially adopted as a policy, and to some extent it predated the major refugee outflow of spring 1965. The rationale was clearly to mobilize manpower and resources for the big military push described in the previous chapter, though its momentum carried it on into the period of the U.S. intervention, by which time the foreclosing of the possibility of quick victory, the increased support from North Vietnam and the socialist world, and the political awkwardness of a divisive class policy in a new stage more suited to the united-front approach rendered this policy obsolete and led to its abandonment by the end of the summer of 1965.

"Motivating the Peasants" was a campaign designed to "stir up resentment in people who had previously not had any resentment against the landlords, the Americans, or the GVN. They were going to use the denunciation technique (*to kho* or denouncing with recitation of grievances and miseries), telling the poor peasants that they had been exploited, assaulted, enslaved, and impoverished by the landlords and the Americans and their lackeys, and that this was the source of their misery" [DT109]. A district cadre recalled that in indoctrination sessions, "We were told to write denunciations against the imperialists and the feudalists. Each of the participants had to relate all the past sufferings caused to him and his family by the imperialists and the feudalists. We had to remember all our ancestors' sufferings and make them known to other participants. Each of us had to read our denunciations aloud and, after our reading, other participants had to contribute to our denunciations by making additional comments aimed at increasing the degree of our hatred against the imperialists and the feudalists. . . . I witnessed many of them crying. The atmosphere of hatred, in my opinion, was notably increased. Everyone swore he would die for the Party. In fact, this stage of the training was the main key of the indoctrination course" [DT69]. In the short term, this political agitation had a significant impact, especially among Party members. Over the longer term, however, the temporary intensification of class consciousness was supplanted among most cadres by the emotions of war, and the hatreds generated by combat and killing.

Economic restrictions on the civilian population that accompanied the new hard line were reminiscent of the enforced poverty policies of the Viet Minh during the Resistance.

> The Front put all sorts of economic restrictions on the people, who were forbidden to use nylon materials [in the interviews "nylon" referred to any synthetic fabric, that is, something that could not be indigenously produced in rural Vietnam and was regarded as a luxury good] in clothing or to wear colorful and thin clothes. The women were forbidden to have gold teeth made and to wear shoes that cost from 400 to 500 piasters a pair, and the young men were forbidden to wear clothes made with Dacron and to wear wristwatches that cost from 3,000 to 4,000 piasters each. It was said that these restrictions were aimed at destroying the GVN economy. The cadres said that even though the money belonged to the people, they should economize in order to save the money and contribute it to the Front. The cadres said that if the people saved the money they could use it to buy food for themselves so they could remain healthy to fight the GVN. During the indoctrination sessions the people agreed with the cadres on this point, but they exchanged glances and said sarcastically, "Let's go home and destroy our nylon clothes. The money is ours. We worked hard to save it in order to buy nice clothes to wear and we are criticized for this trifle. During the six years of peace we could buy whatever we pleased—even an airplane!" This showed that the people always want to be free to earn their living as they see fit, to eat good food and to wear good clothes. When they go someplace they want to go by car and be comfortable. If they can do so, when they return home and have to work hard they won't complain. But in the Front-controlled areas they have to work extremely hard but are not allowed to spend their money as they please as a compensation for the hard work, so they feel too restricted under the communists and don't like it [DT148].

People in My Tho's countryside had chafed under the even more stringent sumptuary restrictions of the Viet Minh period but, on balance, supported the cause despite their unhappiness with its economic policies. However, as the screws were tightened once again, many people looked back on the "six years of peace" nostalgically as a time of relative economic freedom, despite the *corvée* labor, the landlord impositions, and the other darker sides of that period. Naturally, the wealthier peasants had stronger feelings among these economic restrictions than the poorest peasants. "Most of the villagers were dissatisfied about these restrictions, especially the middle peasants and the higher classes. The poor peasants just listened and didn't say anything" [DT148]. The "buying a plane" jest was half-serious; clearly, the consumer horizons of the wealthier peasants were greater than those with little discretionary income. When many of these poor peasants later moved up into the middle peasant class, the restrictions on economic freedom would become a more pressing concern.

Class Struggles in Military Units

Class struggle was also intensified in the military units, though with some variations. A former high school student from a middle peasant background who became a company clerk in the 514th Battalion described the new hard line: "After the Reorientation campaign [of March 1965], the 514th Battalion was to become a unit of very poor peasants with strict discipline. Its soldiers and cadres had to dress in black and wear woven reed hats. They had to burn all their nylon clothes and nylon hat covers. They had to listen to the radio collectively—nobody was allowed to own a private radio. Later this rule was relaxed; you could own a private radio but had to operate it within designated times. The 261st Battalion, on the other hand, was composed mainly of students and urban people, and its discipline was more flexible—you could dress as you pleased. Its cadres were capable and well educated. Comparing the 514th Battalion with the 261st Battalion, many members of the 514th felt disappointed. Some quit the unit to go home, some asked to be sent to Eastern Nam Bo, and others volunteered to go to Central Vietnam to fight" [DT107]. Another soldier transferred briefly into the 514th Battalion was made to buy a new set of clothes, because "nylon shirts" were forbidden in this unit [DT105].

One of the main instruments of this new emphasis on class was Muoi Quoc, a civilian cadre transferred to the 514th Battalion in 1965 to take over as the unit's political officer. Muoi Quoc had become so well known for his success in mass mobilization against the Strategic Hamlets in his native area of Go Cong, where he was district Party secretary, that he was selected to give a lecture to a 1964 COSVN conference on guerrilla warfare.[34] Although there were some reservations about sending a civilian specialist in guerrilla war to head a military battalion, he was evidently a success at the job. A soldier from this unit said that Muoi Quoc "visited us from time to time to tell us heroic stories like the one about hero Tran Van Tho, who threw himself onto a French gun barrel to immobilize it during the Resistance. He was very serious" [DT58]. A company clerk in the 514th said that Muoi Quoc was "severe and a man of principle. . . . He is a good fighter" [DT107].

Curiously, this enforcer of the hard class line did not seem to come from the poor peasantry himself. "I sensed whenever I met him that he comes from the landowner class because he is very well mannered," said the company clerk, who had spoken at length about the class line in his unit [DT107]. Despite his lack of military experience, a platoon cadre described Muoi Quoc as "a competent military leader and a cunning man with many ruses who reacted quickly in different situations" [DT214]. He did not hesitate to enforce discipline even among key battalion leaders, such as a company commander who was demoted for going home without permission [DT246]. As battalion political officer, Muoi Quoc was in charge of the unit's political education. A biographical profile of Muoi Quoc states: "After becoming the battalion political officer for a period, he was able to consolidate the 514th Battalion into a strong unit with regard to political ideology, as well as being rather good at the tactics of surprise raids and annihilating ambushes."[35]

In the military units, there was a clearly stated rationale for appeals based on class: the poor peasants were perceived as more enthusiastic fighters, and less prone to desert. After a series of setbacks for the 514th Battalion in early and mid-1965, nearly thirty soldiers deserted from First Company in a five-month period. When the company commander reported this to his unit, "some of the soldiers accused the defectors of having 'imperialist thoughts.' Those who criticized the deserters were high-spirited because they belonged to the poor peasant class, and their families had been exploited by the imperialists and the feudalists, who they strongly hated" [DT72].

Outside the ranks of the Party, the "motivating the peasants" campaign was significant for another reason. It marked the last effective large-scale attempt at social mobilization engineered by the Party. Henceforth the Party tried many times to motivate and direct the course of social change in the countryside, but these efforts were swamped by massive dislocations caused by rural depopulation, which destroyed the community solidarities which the revolution had earlier successfully employed to achieve their own ends, as well as the level of political control which this directed political and social change required.

Wartime Dislocation and the Allure of "American Goods" Challenge Revolutionary Policies

The anomie and social fragmentation caused by the wrenching large-scale dislocations of village life, along with the new economic opportunities and mobility of the unsettled wartime conditions, had a more profound and longer lasting impact on the rural population than the carefully organized revolutionary projects of social transformation. For Vietnamese rural society in the Mekong Delta, 1965 was truly a "hinge year." It was the year the revolutionaries lost control of the social revolution, never to regain it. In the end, they won the battle for independence but lost the war of "socialist transformation." Professor Huntington was partly correct, but his confidence that "forced-draft urbanization" would lead to an American victory was misplaced. What the United States accomplished was to leave behind a sociological time bomb, which exploded long after it would be any help in rescuing the United States from its greatest foreign policy disaster.

During the 1965 indoctrination the Party put its finger on what was to become the greatest challenge to its leadership: the pull of material incentives and interests beyond what the revolution could provide. A platoon political officer received what may have been a higher-level briefing on this sensitive point, not mentioned in the accounts of lower-level reorientation sessions. He described the Party analysis of the ultimate challenge posed by the United States in detail:

> The Americans planned to bring electricity to the countryside within a few years in order to win the support of the people. The Americans were ready to spend large sums of

money to build up the hamlets and villages. When they had brought modern conveniences to the countryside such as electricity, the Americans would point to the North and compare the progress made there by the socialist regime with that of the South. They would tell the people that the Socialist regime had been reconstructing the North for many years, but the progress wasn't as good as that achieved by the South in two or three years of American aid. The instructor explained that under a Socialist regime, the people had to contribute money and efforts themselves to rebuild the country, that they didn't have any foreign aid, and that this was why progress was slow. In the South the Americans poured out large sums of money, so the progress was quicker. The Americans wanted to give the people a happy material life. Before, agriculture in our country was backward, but after the Americans brought in aid money, it was modernized. Before, whenever a peasant tore his clothes, he had to sew it by hand. Before, when he wanted to go to market, he had to walk on foot. Before, when he wanted to tie his water buffalo to the plow, he had to make the rope himself. Before, when he wanted to have a basket to take to the market, he had to go and gather reeds, dry them, and weave them into a basket. But now he could buy nylon bags to take to the market, he could ride in motorized sampans to the market, and he could sew his clothes on sewing machines. Bringing all these modern conveniences to the people was a very poisonous scheme of the Americans. This was done to show the people that since the Americans came to the South, their life had improved a great deal, and to win the political support of the people, so that if the North wanted to start an insurrection against the Americans it would have a lot of trouble doing so [DT205].

Lyndon Johnson had hoped to undercut the nationalism of Ho Chi Minh and his followers with alluring promises of future material prosperity and New Deal-inspired visions of a TVA on the Mekong River. As this cadre's remarks show, there was enough appeal in this approach to merit concern by the Party leadership. There is little evidence in the interviews that the United States got much direct mileage out of its material aid, which those peasants who benefited received with pleasure, but not political gratitude.

As "Special War" Becomes "Limited War," the Party Reassesses

As the "special war" became a "limited war," the Party felt it necessary to have "supplemental" reorientation indoctrination sessions, to pass on its assessment of the U.S. intervention. One was held in December 1965 and another in March 1966. The reasons for the supplements to what was supposed to be an annual affair were twofold. First, the Party did not gauge the scale and speed of the U.S. intervention accurately. Second, the policies put forth in the first reorientation of 1965 were overcome by events. The "motivating the peasants" campaign was quietly dropped, and replaced by the "three large-scale movements" *(ba cao trao)*. "They saw that the campaign of motivating the peasants hadn't brought any results, and that it was diverting the efforts of the cadres from the military offensive. . . . In this campaign, great emphasis was placed on economic problems. This campaign was a recognition of the importance of all strata of the people and of the religious groups, and it marked a return to something along the lines of the Front tactic. . . . By December 1965 and in early 1966 they are still studying the 'three large-scale movements' " [DT109].

Sau Duong, the Party leader of Region 2 writes that "It was not until December 17, 1965, that the Party Central Committee met at the 12th Plenum that our policy was officially determined: postpone the preparations for a general offensive and general uprising to overthrow the government in the South [GVN]; the immediate goal is to concentrate all efforts on fighting and defeating the new war of aggression pursued by the Americans." Sau Duong felt that even though circumstances had changed, the peasant mobilization of 1965 had not been wasted effort. "The widespread motivating of the peasants campaign had created a higher sense of responsibility toward the revolution among the peasants, and because they had asserted their control [*lam chu*], the peasant's level of [political] enlightenment [*giac ngo*] was raised a level. After that, in 1965 when the American forces jumped into the South in a big rush and the general offensive and general uprising had to be temporarily suspended, this motivation campaign still had a big impact in that it laid the groundwork for the mobilization of all the people to fight the Americans to become a big and extensive movement."[36]

The introduction of U.S. and allied troops had changed the military and political character of the war. "Our country is being invaded and enslaved, so it is the duty of every citizen to fight. In their indoctrination sessions, they had landlords, rich peasants, religious representatives, and ordinary civilians. But they did make a distinction and did not allow those who remained wicked and exploiting landlords to participate. This was to mobilize—they called it 'total political mobilization,' *[dong vien chinh tri toan dan]* aimed at providing adequate and timely support in manpower, finances, and materiel to the revolutionary effort" [DT109]. As part of this campaign, the Party now took on direct leadership of political struggles, bypassing the popular associations, and tried to build up village guerrillas and local forces so that some of their number could be sent to the main force units.

The "big changes" of 1965 had created some serious concerns for the Party leadership. The first and most obvious was the impact of a large number of well-armed American troops on the military situation. Sau Duong recalls that, "Sounding out the views of the comrade cadres from the Center [Central Committee level] (whom I had met many times previously) while the resolution [of the 12th Plenum of December 1965] was being disseminated, I was able to grasp a bit of the [Party] secretary general's concerns about coping with the American army in a Limited War. Le Duan's concern was precisely that concern of all of the comrades in the Party Politburo and Central Committee. And how could they not be concerned when the opponent in the war was now the most powerful military force in the world? I listened to some of the Central [Committee] cadres passing on a considerable amount of top secret information about the advice of friends from all over the world, including some friendly countries with formidable military forces of their own, who were very worried and urged our Party to weigh things carefully before accepting a direct confrontation with the American armed forces. Some even had the view that we should compromise to some extent [a reference to the Soviet Union], and some had the view that we should accept volunteer military forces [from other countries—presumably a reference to China]."[37] These concerns were also expressed closer to My Tho. "In the COSVN base, when Resolution 12 of the Central Committee was being passed on, the brothers were worried for Region 8 [Region 2] which was encountering difficulties that would be hard to overcome—and this was not without reason."

Sau Duong spent sleepless nights trying to figure out the next move in this new situation. His answer, after much reflection, was to continue to rely on the strengths of the revolution in the guerrilla war environment of the central Mekong Delta. There was no other way, he concluded, than to continue the strategy of *"maintaining the overt and legal status of the masses for the revolution, to have them pretend to be nationalist [GVN] citizens. . . ."* [emphasis in original]. The delta didn't offer the protective cover of forests and jungles, so the people would have to have to serve as a substitute for this natural protection. For this reason, concluded Sau Duong, the revolution could not *"allow the people to slip into an illegal posture with respect to the American army and the puppet army"*[38] [emphasis in original]. The idea of keeping revolutionary supporters "legal" with regard to the GVN authorities is a recurring theme in Sau Duong's memoir, but it receives special emphasis in his discussion of the 1965 period. The clear implication was that direct political actions against the Saigon government like "face-to-face" struggles would be sparingly used because they would identify the participants as revolutionary sympathizers and make it difficult for them to remain "legal." Almost certainly this is related to the problems that the civilian exodus from the countryside had already caused for the revolution in 1965. This was an acknowledgment that the revolution would not be able to exert dominant control over a significant portion of the rural population and could not expect those living under some degree of GVN control to overtly identify themselves as sympathizers with the revolution. With the coming of the American army and an even greater escalation of the war, the problem would only get worse. Thus the revolution had to find ways to maintain its support base even when they were not under its constant and direct control. This became a major problem in My Tho and other delta areas in subsequent years.

By March 1966, the new reorientation reflected the Politburo's conclusion of the previous fall that the war was becoming "step by step a limited war," but was still "half a special war, half a limited war." A district propaganda cadre said, "With this new concept in mind, the cadres should know that political struggles are no longer able to help the Front to win, and therefore, military means should have precedence over military activities." Despite this priority on military action, the main target would not be the U.S. forces, but the ARVN, "which, in the Front's eyes constitutes the base which the Americans are leaning on to fight." The deputy district Party secretary explaining this policy concluded, "So, in case the Front succeeds in destroying the ARVN, the Americans will have to negotiate" [DT135].

The reluctance to state unequivocally that the war was now a "limited war" was due to the fact that such a determination would lead logically to the conclusion that the main target should be the U.S. forces. Since the main military effort was still focused on the ARVN, the "half a special war" formula was devised. It also reflected the Politburo position that the ARVN would have to be crushed militarily before the Party could afford to engage in negotiations with the United States because, as Le Duan explained in his May 1965 letter to COSVN, a coalition government could be accepted only after a successful insurrection, which of course required the defeat or neutralization of the ARVN. This would eliminate the main base of support for the U.S. intervention and deprive any coalition government of a power base independent of the revolution. In the Mekong Delta, this focus on the GVN and the ARVN was, in fact, the only choice, since U.S. units would not arrive in force until in the delta until early 1967. After a year of experimentation with political mobilization, the revolution turned to the more immediate task at hand: coping with the escalating military conflict and countering the GVN pacification efforts in the Delta.

Rand interviewer Vuong Bach in My Tho town.

Rand interviewers Nguyen Huu Phuoc (left) and Dinh Xuan Cau (right) visit Revolutionary Development (pacification) cadres of the GVN.

Vinh Kim market, 1966.

Hoa Hao Regional Force soldiers in a militia post in Ban Long village.

Regional Force soldiers in Dinh Tuong province on operation.

The GVN River Assault Group arrives at the Gia Thuan jungle in Go Cong at dawn and prepares to launch an assault in 1966.

A militia post guarding Vinh Qui hamlet in Vinh Kim village, 1966. Vinh Qui was rated as a "V" or "Viet Cong-controlled" hamlet by the GVN Hamlet Evaluation Survey, and was the most heavily shelled hamlet in Vinh Kim.

Bunker of the Vinh Qui post.

GVN Popular Force militia from the Vinh Qui hamlet post in Vinh Kim village, 1966.

Left to right: Don Oberdorfer, journalist Phan Ky Ngoi who wrote for Saigon newspapers but lived in Vinh Kim village (and who was assassinated by the revolutionaries in 1969), Master Sergeant "Binh," and the author, 1966.

GVN village officials, 1966.

Large U.S. produced tractors began to appear in Dinh Tuong to remedy the war-induced labor shortage. This movement presaged the emergence of a new type of rich peasant whose wealth was based on equipment rather than land.

A GVN propaganda poster says "Don't listen to the propaganda of the communists and die uselessly."

An aerial view of the town of My Tho as it looked just prior to the Tet Offensive of 1968.

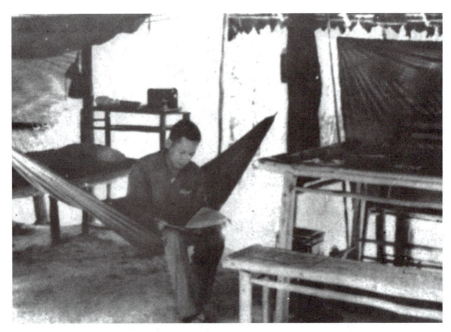

Tran Van Tra in a COSVN base.

Tran Van Tra and the author at a 1990 conference on the Vietnam War.

Nguyen Minh Duong (Sau Duong), the Party leader in the central Mekong Delta at the time of the Tet Offensive.

The opening assault of the Tet Offensive in My Tho town.

M-113 armored personnel carriers stand by as Vietnamese refugees evacuate the town of My Tho, Dinh Tuong Province during the Tet Offensive, 1968 (National Archives).

Dirt mounds marking graves of revolutionaries next to a traditional tomb.

The revolution's caption for this photo was "The United States bogged down in Dinh Tuong."

Revolutionary heroine Le Thi Hong Gam was designated "heroic killer of Americans." She was killed by an American unit in 1969.

U.S. planes defoliate revolutionary bases in Dinh Tuong (National Archives). During the war, many peasants moved their houses from the cooler and shady but heavily bombed and shelled orchards and treelines to the middle of the rice paddies, sacrificing comfort for safety. From 1962 to 1971 the U.S. Air Force sprayed more than 12 million gallons of Agent Orange over Vietnam in order to defoliate the jungle and areas like this in the Mekong Delta.

U.S. Ninth Division unit burns a "Viet Cong base camp" in Dinh Tuong (National Archives).

An expanded meeting of the Region 2 Party Committee in 1970. Nguyen Minh Duong (Sau Duong), the Party leader for the central Mekong Delta, is third from right in the front row. Next to him (fourth from right) is Nguyen Van Linh, the second ranking Party leader in the South. At this meeting Linh, seeing firsthand the military difficulties of the Region, advised Sau Duong to ignore a direct order that came from Pham Hung (Linh's superior at COSVN) while the meeting was in session to continue the disastrous head-on attacks against heavily defended GVN positions.

12
Winning Hearts and Minds

With the focus in 1965 on the escalating U.S. intervention, the fact that the international conflict was superimposed on an ongoing civil war often was put into the background. U.S. troops did not arrive in My Tho in force until 1967, and until then conflict there was fought largely on Vietnamese terms and in the villages. Despite the continuing clashes between revolutionary main force units and the Army of the Republic of Vietnam (ARVN), no decisive military outcome was achieved by either side, and the political and guerrilla struggle once again emerged as the key element of the struggle in the province. On the revolutionary side, continuing efforts to mobilize the village population required motivation, training, and protection of the cadres who mobilized the civilian population. The United States and the Government of the Republic of Vietnam (GVN) began to implement a new type of pacification program that stressed political and development goals more than the previous approaches, which had addressed only the military and security dimensions of combating the revolutionary movement.

Although the United States and the Saigon government devised an elaborate pacification program, the attempt to "win hearts and minds" in Dinh Tuong province was a failure. However, while both sides were focusing on these pacification efforts, a more formidable long-term challenge to the revolution was developing. The bombing and shelling of the countryside continued to intensify, and large numbers of refugees left their homes in revolutionary-controlled areas. The most effective challenge to the revolution was not Saigon's efforts to win over the rural population, but the devastation of the countryside, which "drained the pond to catch the fish." This chapter will discuss the U.S.–GVN efforts to win the "hearts and minds" of My Tho's rural population in 1966–67, the Communist Party's response to this challenge, and the revolution's own approach toward building a sympathetic and politically responsive constituency.

The Contest for Peasant Loyalties Becomes
More Complex as the War Intensifies

During this period, the jobs of village cadres became much more difficult, as the initial enthusiasm for the revolution among the population was dampened by the dangers of living in a "Viet Cong"-controlled zone and the heavy taxes the revolution imposed. The cadres found that they could not prevent people from leaving the villages either temporarily or permanently, and they began to lose control over the villagers. The political and security challenges to revolutionary control of the pacification program were met by a rigid, often arbitrary, and sometimes deadly system of village security which protected friends and ruthlessly suppressed enemies, whether real or imagined. Raw coercion, however, was never the primary tool of revolutionary mobilization, which also relied on moral suasion, interminable political indoctrination, and material incentives. Both coercion and persuasion, however, became increasingly difficult as the war drove large numbers of people out of the revolutionary-controlled zones. The failure of the "motivating the rural population" campaign of class struggle and appeals to the interests of poor peasants mandated an alternative approach to retaining the support of the rural population on which the revolution depended. As control of the revolution in some villages began to slip, the Party too had to pay more attention to the desires and interests of the rural people, and the cadres in some areas became more accommodating. Thus both sides had to consider how to win "hearts and minds."

"Winning hearts and minds" was not a one-shot affair, because the sympathies of the peasants depended to a large extent on what each side did for and to them, and this changed over time. The overwhelming and enthusiastic rural support enjoyed by the revolution in the 1961–63 period was badly shaken by the tax and draft policies, and by the escalation of the war. Even if "in their hearts they knew the revolution was right" (to paraphrase a classic slogan from Barry Goldwater's 1964 Presidential campaign), translating feelings into action, and sympathy to sacrifice is always problematic in political life.

The epic independence struggle of the revolution and the concrete benefits of ending the worst excesses of landlordism and the petty tyranny of local officials had attracted the peasants to the revolution and provided political capital for the long struggle. But political capital, like its monetary counterpart, has to be periodically replenished, and cannot be drawn down forever. The aims of the revolutionaries in this early period had been largely consistent with the interests of the peasants, and the land distribution and leveling of social and class differences in the villages were welcomed by the majority of peasants. The cadres, who, at great personal risk and sacrifice, had brought this about were admired for their dedication even when feared for their ruthlessness. Increasingly, however, the sacrifices demanded of those ordinary civilians who stayed in the revolutionary areas as the war became more deadly and violent equalized the moral edge that the cadres, as paragons of selfless devotion and service, had once enjoyed. By 1965 the cadres had largely lost their ability to intimidate and impress merely by invoking the mantra of revolution, so that the task of political leadership in the villages became increasingly difficult and new formulas of pressure and persuasion had to be devised for nearly every circumstance in the face of a rapidly changing rural situation.

On the Saigon side, a series of revolving-door governments in 1964–65 had been unable to formulate, let alone execute, a coherent rural strategy. By 1966 the new military-dominated government achieved some stability, despite the serious challenges to its authority in the cities by Buddhist and student demonstrators. Dependent as they were on U.S. support, the Saigon authorities had to take into account the American views about how the conflict should be waged. The greatest area of agreement between the United States and the Saigon government was on the subject of military pacification, but the two sides had quite different views about the "other war" and the political, economic, and social strategy based on the assumption of President Lyndon Johnson and some of his advisors that "winning hearts and minds" through a combination of TVA-style social policies and a program of populist democratization would steal the thunder of the revolutionaries and win the war.

Reemphasis on Pacification in 1966–1967

A reemphasis on pacification was reflected in a new 1966 strategy of territorial security, which identified a few key points in the province and placed top priority on securing them. This was also the year in which teams of "pacification cadres," later known in American circles as "revolutionary development cadres" and to the Vietnamese, more prosaically, as "rural development cadres" were trained and deployed. They were an updated version of the Diem era "civic action cadres" of the 1950s, though most of the American pacification planners seemed not to be aware of this, or of the limited success of that earlier program. The "oilspot" pacification program, which had been devised in 1964 and aimed at breaking the revolution's grip on the 20/7 zone, was abandoned in 1965 as both sides slugged it out with larger units. For the GVN, faced with a struggle for survival, there was not much long-range planning, and military operations largely followed the flow of revolutionary units around the province.

The 1966 and 1967 GVN pacification effort had more support, was designed around an underlying strategic concept, and was also more realistic. It concentrated largely on the area around the province airfield, which also blocked the easiest route of attack on the critical intersection where Highway 4, Saigon's lifeline to the Mekong Delta, turns west toward the lower delta. This airfield had been attacked several times in 1965 and was clearly a major military target for the revolution. A second zone designated for pacification by the GVN was a vital area between the 20/7 zone and the province capital. This new pacification program was not merely a local initiative, however, but reflected decisions made at much higher levels.

In early 1966, U.S. and GVN leaders met in Honolulu to discuss the next phase of the war. American intervention had stabilized the military situation and pulled the Saigon government back from the brink of disaster. The question was, what should be done now? Military strategy was the province of General William C. Westmoreland and his Saigon command. He had opted for a war of attrition. "Search and destroy" operations—aggressively pursuing the revolutionary forces and hammering them with massive firepower—were the essence of this approach. Since Westmoreland wanted to fight a big-unit war with minimal constraints, his geographic focus was on sparsely populated jungles and forests, and the Mekong Delta did not figure directly in the initial U.S. military operations.

The conferees in Honolulu were concerned more with political issues than military strategy. The broad themes, dictated by President Johnson's instincts and strong personality, were democracy and welfare—a New Deal for Vietnam. GVN Vice President Nguyen Cao Ky related that Johnson talked of economic development and social welfare. "Turning to the problem of winning over the peasants, he asked, 'How have you built democracy in the rural areas? How much of it have you built, when and where? Give us dates, times, numbers.' " Reflecting sensitivity about the displacement of the rural population, which was already generating concern in the United States, Johnson told the GVN leaders, "Next is refugees. That is just as hot as a pistol in my country. You don't want me to raise a white flag and surrender, so we have to do something about that."[1] In fact, the refugee problem was to become much worse as the war progressed, and the depopulation of the countryside proved to be the most effective, if brutal and indiscriminate, method of pacification.

Johnson's more realistic advisors talked not of democracy but of "pacification." As the

Pentagon Papers noted, "The resurgence of pacification was dramatically punctuated by three Presidential conferences on Pacific Islands with the leaders of the GVN—Honolulu in February 1966, Manila in October 1966, and Guam in March 1967. After each conference the relative importance of pacification took another leap upward within the U.S. Government—reflecting a successful effort within the U.S. Government by its American proponents—and the U.S. tied the GVN onto Declarations and Communiques which committed them to greater effort."[2] The American political strategy devised by Ambassador Henry Cabot Lodge was "based on the absolute necessity of controlling the villages. In day-to-day terms this meant that Lodge had to push pacification as hard as possible. Thus, he was quite pleased with the emphasis that came out of the Honolulu conference in February of 1966."[3]

Just as the Americans later spoke of "revolutionary development" while the GVN continued to use their own term, "rural construction," a similar gap in perception and terminology existed regarding "pacification." The American participants in Honolulu "decided to use the phrase 'social construction' in place of pacification. Then, according to the memorandum, everyone lapsed back into using the phrase 'pacification.' " The Vietnamese understood the term "pacification" *(binh dinh)* quite well, since the French had used it to describe their colonial conquest of the country. It had even earlier antecedents and sometimes a positive connotation in Vietnamese history. Le Loi, a national hero and the founder of the fifteenth-century Le dynasty, had styled himself the "Prince of Pacification" (Binh Dinh Vuong) as he set out to bring Vietnam under his rule. Still, the term "pacification" retained strong overtones of "suppression" and did not catch the spirit of undercutting the revolution with development and social reform advocated at Honolulu.

The reality that the hopeful declarations of Honolulu faced was reflected in a *New York Times* article reflecting official assessments (and quoted in the *Pentagon Papers).* It said that by early 1966 there were twice as many revolutionary troops in the country as there had been a year earlier, some 230,000 to 250,000 including eleven North Vietnamese Army (NVA) regiments, and that an estimated 20 to 25 percent of the country's area was "so firmly in control of the Vietcong guerrillas that no civic and political programs are possible there at all. Other large areas are so sharply contested that for the time being pacification and rural-improvement workers cannot operate. Thus rural-pacification work in 1966 is to be concentrated in one-third or fewer of the rural hamlets that the Government already claims to control. The limitation implies an admission that after five years of war the allies are starting from scratch in this field, and that progress must be slow."[4] The modest 1966 national goal was pacifying 192 hamlets (of the nearly 13,000 in the country) including 238,000 people (of a population of over 16 million).

An analysis of the available population control data by Thomas C. Thayer, a former Pentagon analyst who has provided the most comprehensive and detailed account of the available statistical data about the war, concluded that there had been "an increase of 4.2 million people in the 'secure' category between December 1964 and June 1967 and a reduction of about 900,000 in the number of people under VC ["Viet Cong"] control. In terms of percentages, the secure population increased from 42 percent to 64 percent of the total. The gains appear to be significant ones for the government, but Table 13.2 [in Thayer's book] suggests that much of the increase resulted from the movement of people coming into secure areas instead of the expansion of territory protected by allied military forces."[5]

Thayer observed that the 1.2 million officially registered refugees (there were, of course, many more "unofficial" refugees) accounted for 60 percent of the increase of population under GVN control during this period. He also believed that for a variety of accounting reasons, the "VC-controlled" population was understated, but ultimately concluded that the U.S./GVN assessments of population control were roughly accurate. By 1967, these estimates had 42 percent of the population living in "secure" areas, 25 percent "relatively secure," 16 percent "contested," and 17 percent under "communist control."[6]

Measuring Pacification: The Hamlet Evaluation Survey

The much-derided "Hamlet Evaluation Surveys" or HES ratings were monthly assessments of the security situation in each of Vietnam's hamlets, the component neighborhoods of the villages and the lowest administrative unit in Vietnam. Thayer has provided a balanced and thorough discussion of this issue. The HES, despite its remote and bureaucratic overtones, tried to confront one of the central issues of the conflict: how do you measure political control and political behavior? That the HES fell far short in this regard is not surprising. Even the most skilled and sensitive observer would have a difficult time answering these fundamental questions. And, as the present study demonstrates, the answers to such questions are highly conditional. Both political loyalty and political behavior in a high-risk, volatile, and constantly changing environment are very difficult to measure. As conditions and circumstance change, so do the calculations, perceptions, and even the values of the participants in the political process. Even coerced compliance is conditional: living in an area controlled by one or the other side does not mean that individuals or groups will act as the ruling authority desires in every circumstance, especially if they have the "exit" option of moving somewhere else. And, of course, the ruling authority in a given area may be changed or expelled.

The HES system became a symbol of both the technocratic-managerial mentality of Secretary of Defense Robert S. McNamara and some of his "whiz kids" and their failure to understand the underlying complexities of revolution and social transformation, as well as the inclination of successive administrations in Washington to manipulate information about the war for political advantage. In addition, demonstrating "progress" in the war was a political and bureaucratic imperative, and one function of the HES was to provide a mechanism for doing this. Stanley Karnow relates a revealing episode involving the first head of the U.S. "pacification" bureaucracy, Robert Komer. "Once, after producing an implausibly buoyant 'progress' report on Vietnam for the White House, he was discussing its contents with a group of correspondents. 'Come on Bob,' said one of the journalists, 'you know damned well the situation isn't that good.' Komer, undaunted, replied in his nasal twang, 'Listen, the President didn't ask for a 'situation' report, he asked for a 'progress' report. And that's what I've given him—not a report on the situation, but a report on the progress we've made.'"[7] Thus Komer followed in the footsteps of General Paul Harkins, head of the Ngo Dinh Diem-era U.S. military advisory team, who sent a regular "Headway Report" to Washington. As David Halberstam noted caustically, the format left "no doubt that things were going to get better."[8]

These larger issues cannot be addressed adequately in a study limited to a single province of Vietnam, but the information on Dinh Tuong province provided by the HES surveys is highly relevant to our concerns, despite the obvious flaws and shortcomings. The HES data, giving security and population information on every hamlet in the province from 1967 to 1974, offers the possibility of observing trends over time within the framework of the HES itself, and comparing the HES data with the less systematic but far more detailed and authoritative data provided in the interviews by people who themselves lived and operated in the hamlets. As for the problem of reducing complex political behavior to a single indicator, a "score" or rating for the hamlet, the Party itself determined that for its own purposes this was useful, and it had its own version of the HES, even eventually adopting a version of the ABC ratings used in the U.S./GVN HES.

What can the HES tell us? Essentially, it gave an indication of the "security situation" in a hamlet, based partly on whether there was a functioning GVN administrative presence in the hamlet, and provided a reasonable indication of the likelihood of a GVN force getting shot at if it operated in the hamlet. Second, there was population data for each hamlet in each monthly report, which in theory should be useful in dealing with the key issue of the extent to which "pacification" was accomplished by a transfer of population rather than an extension of territorial control. In terms of the present study, however, even the hamlet is often too large a unit to get an accurate picture of population displacements, and the vital HES category of "nonhamlet population" added to later versions to distinguish refugees from "permanent" hamlet population was not, apparently, taken seriously by the Dinh Tuong officials and they made no attempt to report data on this. Perhaps the most important limitation of the demographic data in the HES surveys is that hamlet boundaries changed over time as hamlets were consolidated, split apart, and even eliminated from the survey—as seems to have happened in some cases where revolutionary control was deeply entrenched. Despite these limitations, the population and security information at least provides a basis for discussing the question of whether pacification gains for the United States and GVN in My Tho during the post-U.S. intervention phase of the war were the result of extending Saigon's territorial control, or merely reflect the displacing of the rural population from areas of revolutionary influence into GVN zones, as Thayer's national-level data suggest.

What does HES not tell us? Political loyalties, as opposed to observable behavior are beyond the reach of HES, both in principle and by design. As the HES evolved, it was aimed increasingly at eliminating subjective judgments and concentrating only on verifiable facts. Did the hamlet chief sleep in the hamlet or not? Was a bridge being built or wasn't it? Both the binary logic of the computer and the desire to standardize local responses so some meaningful national data could be generated dictated this approach. One of the paradoxes of the HES is that as its designers sought less subjectivity, they also increasingly attempted to measure more subtle indicators of "progress" in the complex struggle. When the early versions of the HES merely attempted to reflect the security situation, its rough indicators were suitable to the task, but as it addressed the more abstract questions of socioeconomic development, the rating process seems to have bogged down in the task of measuring the unmeasurable.

By attempting to take the judgments out of the hands of the district advisors, who were closest to the scene, the HES managers in Saigon and Washington also created an ever-widening gap between the local reality and what came out of the computers at the other end, with dozens of "yes" or "no" answers massaged through complex models, statistically weighted, and translated into cumulative scores which were far less revealing than the rough-and-ready impressions of the district advisors about the relatively straightforward question of "security." Despite the fact that they themselves often did not know the exact situation in many of the areas in their jurisdiction, they certainly knew where they were most likely to be shot at. The basic problem of the later HES models was that they rested to at least some extent on unprovable assumptions about the relationship of economic and community development to political behavior in a revolutionary struggle. Would more fertilizer and pesticide immunize the peasants from the lure of revolution? Would GVN-managed village elections protect from intimidation the peasants who were not inclined to support the revolution? Would they elicit the active support of the peasants for the Saigon government? The implicit assumption of the HES seems to be "yes." The ambitious GVN land reform program attempted toward the end of the war is another example of the problem, and will be discussed in a later chapter.

Along with the increasing divergence between the local and higher-level perspectives in attempts to gauge the progress of the war was a parallel split between the military and civilian perspectives. As the HES managers fine-tuned their questionnaires with increasingly elaborate questions, and fed them into ever-more-complex mathematical models, the U.S. and GVN militaries began to abandon even lip service to the "other war" of "winning hearts and minds" with cement and bulgar wheat (which the Vietnamese found inedible and, despite its nutritional value, most often used it for pig feed) and, after the Tet Offensive, embarked on an "accelerated pacification" program whose hallmark was military operations of unprecedented violence and intensity. Perhaps it is not merely coincidence that this happened during the administration of Richard Nixon, whose close advisor Chuck Colson's view was "grab 'em by the balls, and the hearts and minds will follow."

Different American Conceptions of Pacification

From the start, there had been a fundamental disconnect between Washington and its war managers in the field. Intelligence professionals such as William Colby, then head of the Central Intelligence Agency (CIA) and later to become pacification "Czar" in Vietnam, believed fervently in a carefully calibrated program of pacification, which combined good police work with upright and efficient administration. He was scornful of some Johnson advisors who preferred the bludgeon to the scalpel and maintained a quasi-theological belief in the efficacy of bombing to break the will of the revolutionary leaders. "The fascination of higher levels of the Government with this subject, and their failure to perceive the nature of a people's war, was perhaps best expressed by Walt Rostow, President Johnson's National Security Advisor, when he said that bombing of North Vietnam would be our form of guerrilla war to match the attacks by the Communists against the Government in the South. At one point in these exercises, I exploded in total frustration to one of my colleagues, 'For God's sake, let them go bomb something, anything, so they can get it out of their systems! Then maybe we can get them to turn their attention to fighting the war where it has to be fought.' That place, as some U.S. leaders belatedly realized, was the war in the villages."[9] The CIA's top specialist on Vietnam, George Carver, argued that pacification required gaining the active support of the population. "If an attempt is made to impose pacification on an unengaged population by the GVN or U.S. military forces," he argued, "that attempt will fail."[10] While Carver in Washington talked of engaging the population, Colby, who had been the CIA station chief in Saigon and ultimately took charge of the pacification program, concentrated on "rooting out the infrastructure" of revolutionary cadres.

Colby's "counterinsurgency" approach, modeled largely on British police techniques in the Malayan "Emergency," rested on somewhat different assumptions. Much of what Colby advocated seemed to be predicated on the understanding that the population was either anticommunist or apolitical, and thus only had to be shielded from coercion. For those few who might be tempted to engage in revolution, keeping them separated from the revolutionary *apparat* and raising the costs of antigovernment acts would do the trick. In the end, both Komer and Colby's pacification achieved very modest results. To the extent that the revolution's political "infrastructure" was affected by pacification, it was not careful intelligence or even the infamous "Phoenix" operations that did the damage, but a combination of incessant bombing and shelling of the countryside, and the continuing outflow of civilian supporters from the villages and hamlets. The main blows in My Tho were struck by the U.S. Ninth Infantry Division, whose turbulent operations and massive and indiscriminate firepower seemed to vindicate Walt Rostow's view that bombing was the American answer to guerrilla warfare. The human and political costs of this approach were incalculable, however, and the end result a bitter failure.

It is ironic that not only the actual formulation of the objectives for pacification plan but also the underlying political and social philosophy was the work of Pentagon planners. A document known as PROVN ("The Program for the Pacification and Long Term Development of South Vietnam"), which was submitted in March 1966, noted that "The situation in South Vietnam has seriously deteriorated. 1966 may well be the last chance to ensure eventual success. 'Victory' can only be achieved through bringing the individual Vietnamese, typically a rural peasant, to support willingly the GVN. The critical actions are those that occur at the village, district, and province levels. This is where the war must be fought."[11] Thus the Pentagon's original pacification view of whether the peasants needed to be engaged or simply subdued was closer to Carver than Colby, and closer still to both of those than to Colson.

This commitment to the abstraction of winning peasant support did not long survive the realities of Vietnam, however. General Westmoreland's headquarters in Vietnam squelched the PROVN study and reduced it to a "concept paper." The authors of the *Pentagon Papers,* intimately familiar with the bureaucratic infighting of the period, concluded that the PROVN approach had two fatal flaws. "Proceeding from the unstated assumption that our commitment in Vietnam had no implicit time limits, it proposed a strategy which it admitted would take years—perhaps well into the 1970s—to carry out. It did not examine alternative strategies that might be derived from a shorter time limit on the war. In fact, the report made no mention of one of the most crucial variables in the Vietnam equation—U.S. public support for the Administration. Further, the report did little to prove that Vietnam was ready for pacification. This 'fact' was taken for granted, it seems—a fault common to most American-produced pacification plans. While PROVN did suggest geographical priorities, they were derived not even in part from the area's receptivity to pacification but exclusively from the location and strategic importance of the area. Thus the same sort of error made in Hop Tac [the 1964 "oilspot" pacification program] was being repeated in PROVN's suggestions."[12]

This critique itself rested on the assumption that there had to be at least some "receptivity" for pacification to work, and that this would vary among different areas. It did not suggest how a "receptivity" test could be administered, however. The *Pentagon Papers'* analysis of the time problem implicit in this strategy was more to the point and, as will be seen, the pressures to get quick results were incompatible with the approach advocated by Colby and Carver, though they appear to have been oblivious to this fundamental political reality. Without clear guidance on the conditions under which pacification might succeed (if indeed this was possible), but faced with the immediate requirement of designating pacification priorities, the military naturally chose target areas for their strategic location more than the political complexion of the village population with some exceptions.

The early 1966 Pentagon plan was that major combat efforts would be directed against military base areas in unpopulated areas, while top priority in "rural construction" would be given to the Mekong Delta, and specifically An Giang (already largely "pacified" because of its fiercely anticommunist Hoa Hao majority), Vinh Long, Dinh Tuong, and Go Cong.[13] In My Tho at the end of 1965, 105 hamlets in the province, less than a quarter of the total, were declared "secured." Even this number was dramatically reduced by a "central inspection team" that came from Saigon in February 1966 to refocus attention on pacification. This team said that only 33 of these hamlets met the strict "six-point criteria" of a pacified hamlet. The U.S. advisory team continued to use the 1965 figure, however, readjusting it only at the end of 1966 to a total of 59 hamlets "secured," 12 "undergoing securing," and 47 "undergoing clearing."[14]

It was not until mid-1966 that these high-level plans began to be implemented in My Tho, however. The first pacification teams arrived in Binh Duc and Thanh Phu villages, less than 10 kilometers from the province capital, in July 1966. Binh Duc subsequently became the Dong Tam base of the U.S. Ninth Infantry Division. This was clearly a less ambitious plan than the 1964 "oilspot" scheme of pacifying the two anchors to the 20/7 zone, since it did not target a large contiguous area of revolutionary control, but centered on a relatively isolated pair of villages that constituted a buffer between the 20/7 zone and the province capital. In early 1967, a second priority area was added. This was the village of Tam Hiep, near the province airfield, which had been a favorite target of revolutionary operations.

The Balance of Forces in My Tho in 1966 Indicates a Long Struggle

Although the revolutionary forces were still strong in My Tho province in 1966, there was a rough equilibrium of forces between both sides. American estimates of total revolutionary military strength in My Tho were 3,250 in 1964 (including 720 in district local forces and 1,500 village guerrillas), and 4,200 in 1965 (including 565 in district local forces and 1,800 village guerrillas).[15] On the GVN side, there was the Seventh ARVN Division, which had, among other assets, two regiments (each with two battalions and a reconissance company) assigned to protect Highway 4, along with two more battalions in defense of the province capital. In addition, the province had Regional Force companies in each district, and Popular Force platoons in the villages. There was an additional assortment of mobile Seventh Division units moving around the province, and a number of Ranger, Special Forces, artillery, and armored units, along with the airpower that was at the disposal of the province. Although the GVN had the decided numerical edge, neither side could easily overpower the other, and this further added to the impression that the conflict would not end soon.

A district cadre from Chau Thanh recalled the reorientation indoctrination for his Farmers' Association branch in late July 1966. "The second part was ideology. We should endure hardships and difficulties, and we had to prepare our ideological stand in order to fight longer. I noticed that everyone seemed to be bored and confused. They were all afraid of the duration of the war and of death." This attitude also affected his own morale. "The purpose of the indoctrination periods was to encourage the Party members so that they wouldn't be afraid of difficulties, of hardships, and so they would accept a long, hard, and difficult war. I myself felt more disturbed than before because of the probable duration of the revolution. If the revolution lasted a long time, I wouldn't benefit much from it. My desire was to fight until peace so that my children and I could live peacefully and enjoy life. But when we talked about the long-term war and the sacrifices, then naturally I was scared, because everyone wants to live and not to die. Everyone would be afraid of death, even though the Party called for sacrifices. Before, the Party had said that the war would end in the near future, thanks to the help of the different socialist countries. It was also trying to end the war by seizing power and creating turmoil in the ranks of the GVN. At that time, during the reorientation session, nothing was mentioned about quickly ending the war" [DT153].

For the soldiers the problem was even more acute, because the longer the war went on, the higher was the probability of their being killed. There were no 365-day tours of duty for them; they were in for the duration. Yet most seemed philosophical or fatalistic about what might happen. The interviewer asked a company commander of the 261st Battalion, "How did the fighters react when they were told the war would be a long-term one?" "They complained about it," was his reply. "But the majority of them said, 'Hell, what can we do about it? We don't have any choice but to fight on forever' *[Thoi ke me no! Bao nhieu thi bao; cu danh giac hoai vay thoi]*. They didn't understand anything. They only knew that they were doomed to die in the war. They only thought, whether they were communists or not they would be killed, so they might as well be communists and do something before they got killed. But sometimes when they got together to drink tea, they discussed the duration of the war and the intensification of the American bombing and shelling. Sometimes they worried that if the war lasted too long, the strength of the unit would be exhausted. Whenever the company political officer saw them gathered together, he broke up their meeting and forbade them to talk about these matters" [DT149]. For the soldiers, the "exit" from their situation was more difficult than for civilians. Their very function implied the risk of death, and they had—willingly or unwillingly—signed on for the duration. The only "exits" were death, capture, or desertion.

Under these circumstances it is remarkable that so many faced the prospects of protracted war with such equanimity. Naturally, the interviews generally reflect the views of those who had tired of the struggle. A platoon leader and veteran of the Resistance said, "The men of the Front said they'd prefer to have the Front carry out a General Offensive and Uprising. They wanted the Front to carry off a big offensive for a few days and win the war. They said that if this happened, they would be willing to fight and die" [DT147]. The impatience with protracted struggle among revolutionaries was reflected even among these adepts of guerrilla warfare. This attitude is also relevant to understanding both the decision to launch the Tet Offensive (though, as will be argued, the top leadership did not expect that it would bring an immediate end to the war) and even more to the great letdown among the Southern guerrilla veterans following the collapse of the Tet Offensive.

"Pacified" Without "Pacification": The Case of Vinh Kim Village

The length and intensity of the war, even as of 1965, had taken its toll on both the general population and the revolutionaries. An illustration of how these two factors interacted is the erosion of the revolutionary position in Vinh Kim village, where many of the top leaders defected in 1965–66 and revolutionary operations were severely hampered. In some ways this is a case of a village being "pacified without pacification," since this happened not because of any larger plan, but because of the unfolding of a local situation in the face of the intensified war.

In Vinh Kim, however, the near-paralysis of the local revolutionary organization did not really result in "pacification," even in the narrow sense of physical security for GVN activities, since after two years of difficulties, most of the hamlets of this village were still considered to be largely under the control of the revolution. In the HES ratings of January 1967, two of Vinh Kim's six hamlets were rated "V" and "E," or completely controlled by the revolution; the rest were rated "D," or nearly completely controlled by the revolution. If in this key location, a village where a district headquarters was located, the defection of most of the top cadre leadership did not cripple the revolution, the implications for a pacification strategy that hoped to bring about Saigon control by "uprooting the infrastructure" were ominous.

Vinh Kim was more than a village, with its large population and active market, but less than a major market town on the scale of Cai Lay and Cai Be. Its market served the surrounding area—seven or eight villages within a 10- to 15-kilometer radius. It had been taken over briefly by the revolutionary forces during 1964, when the defending GVN troops were forced to withdraw. It was one of the two major targets of the 1964 "oilspot" pacification program because it was critical to controlling the villages at the eastern end of the 20/7 zone. To some extent the attention given to Vinh Kim was responsible for the difficulties that the cadres and guerrillas encountered, and the ultimate decline in the revolutionary organizations there. The fact that Vinh Kim was made a separate district headquarters, on a par with the much larger and more important towns of Cai Be, Cai Lay, and Cho Gao, meant that it had a stronger GVN commitment to holding on to it, and thus it received far more security and administrative resources than ever before. Precisely because of its strategic centrality to control of the 20/7 zone, Vinh Kim had been a frequent target of attacks, especially in the annual campaigns to commemorate the July 20, 1954 anniversary of the signing of the Geneva Accords. The 261st Battalion had attacked the main post of Vinh Kim on that day in 1963 [DT186]. The following year, a combined attack of the 261st and the 514th battalions was successful and Vinh Kim was briefly controlled by the revolution [DT157]. By 1966 the GVN had caught on to the pattern, and conducted a lengthy military operation on that date that threw the revolutionary forces on the defensive [DT137].

During 1964, the villagers of Vinh Kim had been forced to cope with being on the front lines of the see-saw struggle between the contending forces. After forcing the Saigon administration out of the area for over a month, the revolutionary forces were themselves evicted when the GVN retook the area and made it a key element of the province pacification plan. The Chau Thanh district Party committee responded by sending two of its members to Vinh Kim to "carry out its plan of destroying 'McNamara's pacification plan' in this village" [DT99]. Vinh Kim's guerrilla unit was reinforced with a platoon from the district local force, and augmented by squads from each of two adjacent villages. This effort was momentarily stalled when the village guerrilla leader defected, throwing the guerrilla unit into disarray and creating tensions within the local Party organization. The village guerrilla unit was disbanded, and the village Party secretary, who had been the sponsor of the defecting guerrilla, came under suspicion [DT99].

The "oilspot" pacification technique called for concentrating resources on a few key points. In the case of Vinh Kim, this meant more regional force troops to defend the new district town, but the main addition was more firepower. With more troops in the area, larger units would be required to attack them, and these larger units would be more vulnerable to the air power and artillery now available to the district. An example of what additional resources could do for pacification is the bridge that was built across the river dividing the district seat in Vinh Kim from Vinh Qui hamlet. Until 1965 the guerrillas and cadres simply evaded the occasional GVN operations launched from across the river. "It was very easy for them to flee because, at that time, the bridge which connects the present District Headquarters to Vinh Qui hamlet hadn't yet been built. So whenever the GVN soldiers wanted to go into Vinh Qui, they had to cross the river by sampan, and there was always enough time for the village cadres to flee" [DT197].

The redoubtable journalist Marguerite Higgins found that the situation in August 1965 was considerably different from the previous year. "The last time I visited Vinh Kim in 1964, it presented a scene of desolation. All the bustle and commotion normal to a prosperous district headquarters in the Delta were absent. All but four families of Vinh Kim's normal population of 3,500 had fled because of the Viet Cong harassment, including the forcible kidnapping of some of Vinh Kim's best young men. Some fled to refugee camps, others to relatives, still others into Mytho, the province capital. In 1964, Vinh Kim had an eerie, ghost town, on the beach [the name of a then current movie about nuclear devastation] air. . . . today Vinh Kim is bursting at the seams. Virtually all of its old inhabitants are back. But it is also stretching to accommodate refugees from the countryside. Still, it has regained approximately the same degree of prosperity that prevailed in the summer of 1963." (Actually Vinh Kim had been briefly overrun in July 1963.) Higgins attributed this to a rededication of the ARVN Seventh Division to fighting the communists after a turbulent year of participating in coups, and a new district chief, whose American advisor regarded as "honest, fair, dynamic, and a man whose military competence is obvious. . . . Gradually he has given the peasants the feeling that Vinh Kim is reasonably safe from Viet Cong harassment."[16]

There was a reason, of course, why Vinh Kim was beginning to receive refugees. Surrounding villages and hamlets were constantly being bombarded by mortars in the GVN district compound, which made life in the outlying hamlets so precarious and unpredictable that large numbers of peasants moved into Vinh Kim to cluster around GVN military posts in the security belt around Vinh Kim. They felt "safe" in Vinh Kim because it was the source of the shellings rather than the target. Others moved into the rice fields to live in straw huts and escape the shelling directed at the orchards and groves of trees that had been the residential areas of the hamlet because of the shade they offered, and because they didn't take up valuable cultivatable land. The revolutionaries had a somewhat different assessment of the GVN district chief than did the American advisor on the spot. During the reign of the GVN district chief of 1965, "it was very easy to win the villagers' support," said the former head of the Vinh Kim Propaganda and Indoctrination Section.

> Everyone looked on Mr. D as a very cruel district chief who couldn't care less about the villagers' lives. He was the one who caused the most casualties among the villagers. Back then, when a shelling of his had killed someone, I gathered the villagers together in a meeting immediately afterward to denounce the cruelty of the GVN and to stir up the people's resentment. I only had to add new names to the long list of Mr. D's mortar victims. The villagers applauded me for everything I said. They even considered me a very kind cadre who cared a lot about their welfare because I advised them to dig shelters for their own safety. Many old people came over to see me and to tell me that they were grateful to me. Thanks to the shellings, the Front enjoyed more confidence from the people. This helped us perform many assignments. Mobilizing the Vinh Kim villagers to participate in planting spikes and fencing in the combat hamlets was an easy matter at that time. Even the collection of taxes was not a hardship for the cadres [DT143].

"Each day the Vinh Kim subsector shot about thirty rounds on the Front-controlled hamlets," said the former village Party secretary. "Sometimes there were apparent reasons for these shellings, but at other times the subsector shelled us at random. The Vinh Kim villagers often said, 'Each morning when we wake up, we don't know whether we are living until we open our eyes' " [DT99]. The former deputy chief of the village Farmers' Association said that there was great villager resentment against this GVN district chief, "because he used to shell at random, killing many innocent people and giving rise to strong resentment of the GVN," though he added the somewhat contradictory remark that "they only hated those persons who hurt them, and not the GVN as a whole" [DT111].

Another way in which the shelling assisted the revolution in its work was to provide an unwitting tool of coercive persuasion. The cadres "forced those who did not pay taxes to attend reeducational courses in the hamlets which were often shelled by GVN artillery. This method was designed to make the tax dodgers afraid. The village finance-economy cadres were then sent to reeducate them for two hours every day. Fearing that they might be killed by shellings, the tax dodgers had to write to their families to urge their relatives to pay taxes in order to have them set free" [DT99]. This two-pronged attack, combining the boredom of traffic school with the terror of a combat zone, rarely failed to produce results.

Although the shelling made the revolution's job easier in some ways, it created problems in other areas. As the people began to leave the hamlets that were the targets of GVN shelling for the relative safety of the areas around the posts that were doing the shelling, the revolution faced a problem. It initially tried to forbid the movement, but it was powerless to stop it. The cadres then tried to impose conditions on the refugees. "The Front agreed to let the people move into a 'pacified' area to settle, but the villagers must agree to work for the Front by informing it of what was happening in the area. They also had to be put into cells to facilitate their underground work" [DT99]. At least some villagers got the message that moving to the GVN New Life Hamlets in the village would not be a good idea. By 1967 there was still sensitivity on this score. A leading village cadre's relatives had moved to a New Life Hamlet, but like others, not in Vinh Kim. "The villagers' relatives who had left the village for good didn't dare settle in Vinh Qui New Life Hamlet because the Front forbade them to live there. So they moved to other places that are controlled by the GVN, such as along Highway 4 in Long Dinh, or along the banks of the Mekong River in Kim Son" [DT197].

One irony of this approach was that, in Vinh Kim at least, the cadres had tried to persuade some villagers to move to GVN areas to work as informants, but found few takers until the shellings intensified. "At the very beginning, when there were no shellings, the villagers did not want to move into the 'pacified area' to work for the Front. Later on, when their hamlets were shelled, the villagers moved into it without warning the Front of their departure. Therefore, at present, only a few of them agreed to work for the Front" [DT99]. The former village guerrilla unit leader said at the time of his defection in November 1965, "For a long time now, the people have been finding subtle ways to refuse the tasks assigned to them. They argue that because of the heavy bombing and artillery, their own rice fields are in sorry shape. Some say their child is sick, others that their health is failing or that they have a headache or a fever and can't possibly work. In addition, no one is able to guarantee their security while they are performing their mission. Before, every time they went to do a job—setting up a roadblock, for example—an entire platoon of guerrillas went to defend them, but now every time they go there are at most six or seven. Under these circumstances, how can they dare go on a mission?" [DT97].

As refugees began to move back and forth between their new residences in GVN areas and their former homes, it became more and more difficult to maintain a line of separation between revolutionary-controlled and Saigon-controlled areas. What had once been a hermetically sealed political and security environment, with civilian movement in and out of the area tightly controlled, now became porous. A guerrilla said, "Before, there were secret guerrillas in the village, but then the people uncovered them all. The secret guerrillas had been operating under legal cover, but after the villagers uncovered them they had to operate openly. There were secret guerrillas up until 1964–65, but after they were uncovered they had to become either part-time or full-time guerrillas. After they were uncovered by the people, the soldiers in the post found out about it, and the secret guerrillas no longer dared to go to the market or to other GVN areas to gather information for the Front" [DT188]. (In another context, the same interviewee mentioned that each hamlet retained a cell of secret guerrillas as of 1967.) But this leakage of information went both ways. The former guerrilla chief said that planting informers in the GVN areas was the job of the security section. "My guerrilla unit did not have any informers, because I did not find any trustworthy villagers living outside of the hamlet to take care of that. Nevertheless, I knew what was happening in the district town through the villagers who came back from the market. Even if I did not ask them, they were always eager to inform me about any concentrations of forces and about the number of military trucks and APCs which had been gathered in the district town" [DT97].

Another consequence of the erosion of a clear line between the two zones of control was that policies which had been possible to implement with varying degrees of success in earlier years, such as the brief 1964 economic embargo of Vinh Kim, now became impossible to enforce. When the Vinh Kim cadres tried to impose a second economic embargo on Vinh Kim in 1966, it was a complete failure. Living in two worlds, and sometimes between two worlds, opened up a range of political and social choice to many villagers that had been denied them in the more restrictive environment of the traditional village community. For better or for worse, the uprooting of rural society began to have a profound transforming effect on every aspect of the peasant's life.

Refugees and Displaced Peasants

No issue is more complex than the question of refugee movement. It was difficult to define "refugee" in the fluid conditions of the time and, therefore, to count the number of refugees. There were two ways that residential and population transfers would be noted in official statistics. One would be the list of people who were officially registered as "refugees," usually in designated refugee resettlement areas, and qualifying for some government assistance. As Thayer points out, "Refugees were people who were forced to move away from their homes and employment and registered for government benefits. If they didn't register, they didn't show up in the statistics."[17] Thayer adds that "Vietnamese Government records suggest that about seven million people at one time or another were official refugees or war victims during that period. More than a million were people whose homes were destroyed or damaged by the 1968 Tet Offensive."[18]

A U.S. government-sponsored study of refugees in Dinh Tuong province in the summer of 1966 cited a U.S. Agency for International Development (USAID) estimate that there were 5,177 refugee families in Dinh Tuong province as of that time, and interviews were conducted with 272 of these.[19] Since only 43 percent of these were receiving some form of official assistance, the interview sample appears to reflect both "official" and unofficial or quasi-official refugees. As Jerry M. Tinker, who supervised the study, wrote in his report, "it is frequently difficult on the surface to distinguish refugees from much of the general population of Dinh Tuong," because of the many informal mechanisms for absorbing people displaced from their homes. He distinguished between temporary refugees and long term "resettled" refugees. "In Dinh Tuong, government assistance has been directed almost exclusively to such 'resettled' refugees; the more 'temporary' refugees—those who move in and out of areas on their sampans for only a few weeks at a time—are difficult to count, much less to aid. Hence, the operational definition of a 'refugee' in Dinh Tuong is a rather simple one; first, a family must be more or less 'permanently' resettled long enough for officials to see and count them and recognize their request for assistance; and, second and most important, they must come from an area controlled or contested by the Viet Cong. Most officials interviewed did not feel that refugees should prove their need of assistance; it was generally assumed that if they ask for it and if they had abandoned their homes, they had also abandoned their source of livelihood and their need for government assistance was implicit."[20]

Despite this broad definition of a refugee, it seems clear that the relatively small number of officially counted refugees, amounting to about 1 percent of the province population, seriously understated the extent of war-induced population movement. Much of the government assistance appears to have been directed at officially sponsored refugee camps, such as those that were set up to take care of the population that left the villages around Hau My when the GVN pulled out its major base on the edge of the Plain of Reeds. "Although the original government announcement of assistance had been directed to 900 families from nearby hamlets, within three weeks after the closing of Hau My the movement of refugees grew from the expected 900 families to approximately 3,000 families from throughout the northern portion of [Cai Be] District. This unexpected flow seriously overburdened existing government facilities for resettlement and constituted a large part of the initial refugee problem in Dinh Tuong in the summer of 1965."[21] Thus much of the official province refugee total seems to come from these large concentrations of refugees. The more typical pattern was movement from one hamlet to the next or within hamlets. Even Tinker's study, which concentrated mainly on "resettled" refugees who had made a clear break with their former homes, and which reflects situations like villagers in the northern Cai Be area moving several villages south to camps (actually agglomerations of disheveled straw huts) near Highway 4, found that nearly 70 percent arrived at their new location within nine hours, and another 20 percent within a day, underlining the short distances traveled.[22] But the interview sample, drawn largely from officially designated refugee sites, found that nearly 75 percent of those interviewed did not return to their homes, even to harvest crops.[23] A detailed statement of the more prevalent pattern in My Tho was given by a former Vinh Kim village guerrilla in early 1967.

> Most of them still went back and forth between the hamlet and the GVN areas. Almost all the families in [Vinh Phu] hamlet were doing that—moving back and forth between the hamlet and GVN areas, such as My Tho and so on. They traded for a living, and once in a while they came back to their orchards to gather whatever they could find. When they came back to the hamlet and ran into the VC, the VC invited them to return to the hamlet. This was why the villagers just sneaked back in their orchards and hurriedly gathered some bunches of bananas or areca nuts or firewood, and then left. Only five or so families moved from the hamlet for good. These families didn't have to leave anyone behind because the VC didn't seize the land if they went back to the hamlet once in a while. All that the VC did was to send them oral messages asking them to move back to the hamlet. Grass invaded all the orchards, because no one took care of them. When the villagers came back, if they could find any fruit, they took the fruit with them, otherwise they just went away empty-handed. As for the rice fields, when the planting season came, the villagers came back to till their fields. The VC didn't do anything to them. ... But the villagers had to pay taxes to the Front. If they didn't have cash to pay the cadres, they had to pay in paddy. If anyone refused to pay, the VC wouldn't let them come back to the hamlet again [DT188].

Economic factors compelled the cadres to acquiesce to this form of commuting. First, it guaranteed the payment of taxes—indeed, facilitated it—because the villagers now had to pay on the spot as a form of entry fee to their land, whereas they had been able to procrastinate while they still resided permanently in the hamlet. Second, if there was a blanket prohibition against returning to the village, there would be no rice production, and no food for the cadres, as well as no income for the villagers to pay the tax.

Local Cadres More Reliant on Persuasion as Hamlets Become "Contested"

As the "liberated areas" shrank, the village cadres had to adjust their methods of dealing with the population in conditions of less than complete revolutionary control. A Chau

Thanh district Farmers' Association cadre said, "In the weak Front areas, the Front's policy has to be more flexible, and it should allow the cadres to alter it a little bit to meet each particular situation. In the case of taxation, for example, the cadres can't do it as forcefully as they would in the liberated areas. The cadres don't dare to operate too openly because not all the people in those areas can be trusted. They have to use persuasion instead, to make the people self-enlightened and willing to pay their taxes. In the towns and cities, the cadres also have to rely on persuasion and the people's self-enlightenment to collect taxes. I heard that in Vinh Kim this year [1966], the Front collected very little money from the people, but I don't know how much. About 30 percent of the families at the market place made financial contributions to the Front—they didn't pay taxes—and the money was collected by the guerrillas" [DT153]. As we shall see, in the view of some village cadres, it was actually easier to collect taxes in the weaker areas in some cases, but the essential point is that the village cadres now had to carefully calibrate the mix of coercion and persuasion used in each area and in each circumstance.

If the cadres relied on persuasion, it would have to be the time-consuming face-to-face variety. The popular associations were falling apart as the population left the hamlets, and no other mechanism for extending the Party's influence into the masses existed. "These associations," said the former village guerrilla chief, "needed to be reorganized because they had been disbanded before May 1965. The frequent bombings and shellings made the villagers and the association members leave the village for New Life Hamlets in great numbers. The Farmers' Association, which was the strongest association at that time, was disbanded. Before, it had seven members in the village Farmers' Association executive committee and about 500 members. By May 1965, only three committee members and about forty ordinary members were left. The village Party chapter was then incapable of motivating the association's cadres to go on working. A few of them refused to work and the others had settled in New Life Hamlets" [DT97].

By 1965, the Vinh Kim village Party secretary was under pressure to stem the tide of refugees and persuade them to return to their homes. "The Vinh Kim village Party commit-tee succeeded in calling back ten of the families which had settled in New Life Hamlets. It was not difficult because they often came back to their hamlets to watch their rice fields and orchards. I made them attend reeducation courses, but they refused to come back [for good]. I then had to forbid them to come back again, and they reacted by coming back in large groups, and said that if I were to kill them, I would have to kill the whole group. I should have left them alone, but I was strongly criticized by the other village Party com-mittee members, who said that my weak attitude would convert the whole area of Vinh Kim into a New Life Hamlet. We had a very long discussion about this problem and, in the end, I had to promise them that I would refer it to the District Committee for resolution. The situation was not the same in other villages. The village Party secretaries' behavior against those who did not comply with the Front's orders was harsher, and they eagerly confiscated the people's property. It was easy to do this, but I did not think it was a good solution. It only aroused hatred from the people" [DT99].

The villagers' response to the pressure was to come in large groups, thus reversing the community pressure that had been put on them when they were in a collective setting that was easily dominated by the cadre leadership and their "backbone" supporters. This turn-about in group pressure proved difficult to deal with, because it would have required harsh measures toward large numbers of people rather than a few selected scapegoats. In many cases, the village Party cadres had to take on the direct contacts with the people, without the aid of the popular associations and the "backbone cadres." The political buffer that these groups had provided was also largely gone. Pressure was now not exerted in the name of a civic association of the community, but in the name of the Party. With the reduction of non-Party collective structures, the revolution could not rely on community pressure as much, and had to resort to direct commands. This raised the profile of the village and district security apparatus, who had to step in from time to time to remind the remaining villagers that noncompliance had high costs.

Conflicts Among Cadres in Vinh Kim

The Party not only had to deal with those outside its ranks, in many areas it had serious internal conflicts. In Vinh Kim, the internal Party problems were of long standing. At the beginning, when the revolutionary movement was still strong, these problems had been contained. The population exodus of 1965–67 created new difficulties which brought the longstanding internal conflicts to a head. Defections crippled the village leadership, raised tensions among the cadres, and lowered the esteem for cadres in general among the villagers. The fact that a few key cadres had broken with the revolution diminished the general standing of the many other cadres who stayed and soldiered on for the revolution.

The first defection from the ranks of the revolution was the one with the longest-lasting influence. Hai Nam, the last Vinh Kim village Party secretary of the Resistance, had been promoted to district level during the "six years of peace." The local GVN authorities arrested his father and held him hostage, with threats of retribution if Hai Nam did not surrender. At the time, there was no Chieu Hoi ["Open Arms" program for defectors] policy to ease the sting of defecting from the revolution with flattering terminology like *hoi chanh vien* ("one who returns to the just cause"—which had been softened from the previous GVN term for defectors, *qui chanh,* which carried a stronger implication of submission). The revolutionary movement called cadres who abandoned its ranks "surrenderers" (*dau thu*). From the moment of his departure, Hai Nam became a mortal enemy of the revolution, though no friend of the GVN authorities. By the mid-1960s he had resurfaced as an important community leader, and by 1971 he had been elected village chief, in which capacity he led a struggle of the village leaders against an especially corrupt and arrogant GVN district chief.

Defections of at least five leading village cadres within a little over a year (late 1965 to early 1967) badly hurt the Vinh Kim village Party organization. After the defection in late 1965 of the Vinh Kim village Party secretary and the village guerrilla chief,

> There was a lot of turmoil inside the village Party chapter. First of all, none of the cadres and Party members trusted anyone. All of them feared that the village Party secretary would take GVN soldiers back to arrest and kill them, and everyone was suspected by the others on the grounds that he might be one of the Party secretary's henchmen. After that they split up and each one tried to secure a new hideout for himself alone. Before, they lived in groups, and had full confidence in one another. Second, the villagers lost confidence in the cadres. They feared that in the next sweep operation the ralliers would single them out to the GVN as VC helpers. As a consequence, they stopped giving

assistance to the cadres, arguing that they were no longer certain of the cadres' loyalty. Some of the villagers even declared, "Giving the cadres something to eat is like raising bees in one's shirtsleeves!" Whenever we called on them for a meal, they would say, "Let us make it clear that giving you something to eat is no different from giving GVN soldiers something to eat. We have to cook for anyone who tells us to. If I have more compassion for you, it is only because you are leading a very hard life. So if any of you rally, please spare me from being arrested by the GVN. In case you lead GVN soldiers back here, don't single me out as a VC sympathizer" [DT143].

This was not an isolated case. The defection of a key district cadre in Cai Be in early 1966, who had been falsely accused of being a GVN security agent, created a sensation in his home village. "The people were all confused, and didn't know who to trust. He used to work in the village and was a very zealous and effective cadre. When the people heard he had been arrested and charged with being a GVN security agent, they were frightened, because they said it had become impossible for them to tell which cadres were really revolutionaries and which were GVN security agents. They told us, 'We'll only know who among you are real revolutionaries when the revolution achieves success. Right now we don't know who to trust and we're afraid of all of you. Even some of the district cadres were GVN security agents, so can we trust you people down here in the village?' The people were terribly demoralized and said, 'If you ask us to come to meetings, we'll go. If you ask us to pay taxes, we'll pay. But we don't trust anyone anymore' " [DT165].

Following the defection of another key village Party cadre and the guerrilla chief, the Vinh Kim Party committee was reduced to four members. The district cadre who came down following the defections said, "They are now reactionaries, and since there is no leniency for such people you can shoot them if you come across them." Most of the land owned by the two defectors was confiscated, leaving their wives (who remained in their hamlets) just enough to subsist on. A village cadre who argued that it was unfair to punish the wives for their husbands' faults was sustained by the district committee, which relented and ordered the land given back. At the same time, however, this brought the cadre under suspicion. "Assuming the defense of reactionaries' relatives always raises suspicion in the Front, and therefore I acutely sensed I was being watched by the village chapter. My colleagues' attitude toward me changed suddenly, and they became more friendly and kind towards me than before, and I grasped the full meaning of the change." This sinister solicitude was the handwriting on the wall for this village propaganda chief, and he soon defected [DT143]. Other accounts indicate that there were other reasons, including allegations of womanizing. The cadres told the villagers only that he had been purged—to the rank of "deputy ordinary citizen" (pho thuong dan) they said sarcastically, to emphasize the depths to which he had fallen by losing his Party membership [DT188].

The district Party committee sent cadres down to dissolve the beleaguered Party chapter, but the new leadership did not fare much better. The new Vinh Kim Party secretary, Hai Hong, "couldn't maintain discipline either. He used to criticize us and talked until he was all red in the face, but we didn't pay any attention. This was why he got the nickname 'Hai Hong,' or 'Hai who gets red in the face'" [DT188]. Hai Hong had participated in the Destruction of the Oppression in Vinh Kim, and was promoted to the district level in 1963 to become a member of the district Farmers' Association. Despite the lack of respect from his fellow village cadres, Hai Hong apparently went over better with the villagers. "His personal conduct is good, his comprehension is fair, and he enjoys much confidence from the villagers," said the former propaganda chief [DT143].

In addition to his problems with the village cadres, Hai Hong apparently got little support from his superiors. "At present, he is very dissatisfied with the district committee, which seems to trust Nam Ri [the district committee member in charge of the Vinh Kim area] more than him. One day he became so depressed about the district committee's attitude, he wept in front of me, complaining that he was only a puppet village secretary."[DT143]. Hai Hong also found it increasingly difficult to control and motivate the village guerrillas, even though the guerrilla unit commander was personally courageous and effective.

"The guerrillas liked him a great deal. He had a virtuous behavior. He didn't drink, was over thirty years old, and was a capable and courageous leader. He wasn't afraid of death. For example, when he wanted to go on mission in a dangerous area and the guerrillas refused to go along, he went by himself. He had killed one GVN soldier and wounded a few others in clashes with GVN troops. He wasn't afraid of the Americans. He never fled with the guerrillas when the Americans conducted an operation in the village" [DT188]. Even this capable and brave cadre, however, had trouble getting the guerrillas to follow orders. "It was very difficult for the cadres to work with the guerrillas, because they refused to obey orders. For example, when the guerrilla unit leader told them to stay close to the Americans, they just said they didn't dare to, and he had to do it by himself. The guerrillas didn't listen to anyone, and the cadres' power existed only in theory" [DT188]. Just as discipline was breaking down, the Vinh Kim organization was faced with a new problem, the arrival of American troops. One result of this was that the red-faced village Party secretary was killed in an ambush in early 1967. "Now that Hai Hong has been killed," said a guerrilla, "things are going to pieces in there because he took charge of practically everything while he was alive" [DT188].

How Typical Were These Problems of Vinh Kim During the 1965–1967 Period?

The experience of Vinh Kim during the GVN pacification campaign of 1966–67 is instructive in several ways. First, it was atypical. The reason we have a fairly detailed grasp of the village politics and can chronicle the decline of the Party organization there is because of the unusual number of defections of leading village cadres over a fairly short period of time. There were only a handful of comparable cases in the interviews, which indicates that although Vinh Kim's case may illustrate particular problems and tensions that were widespread in My Tho province, Vinh Kim was unique in having to deal with all of these problems simultaneously. A major part of the story of the 1965–67 period is the number of problems contained in the interviews, which are typified by Vinh Kim. But another important part of the story is all the villages and cadres who were not heard from during that period, or whose occasional defectors revealed problems far less severe than those in Vinh Kim. Vinh Kim's experience does, however, indicate the difficulties encountered by the revolution in the villages closest to the center of GVN pacification activities, as well as the consequences of loss of village population for the revolutionary organizations. Evidently, Vinh Kim's special problems were forgotten after the conflict. A visiting anthropologist looking for a village to study in the early 1990s was told by the director of the province Party school that Vinh Kim was "the most typical village of Tien Giang province."[24]

The popular associations in Vinh Kim began to fall apart, depriving the Party of an essential instrument of revolutionary mobilization and recruitment. The decline in Vinh Kim was worse than in other villages, but the underlying reasons for it were widespread in My Tho. The main reason was the bombing and shelling forcing the people into secure areas, with the taxes and draft as supporting factors. Vinh Kim may have been an area where shelling was heavier than normal, in part because of a callous district chief, and in part because it had been a focus of pacification and its new status as a district seat called for more intense measures to secure it. Pacification involved a preliminary "clearing phase" in which artillery and mortar shelling was intense and continuous, and the same refugee exodus was seen in the next villages that became pacification priorities. Although this depopulation was not a formal part of the "pacification" strategy, the side effects of the shelling on the civilian population, and the consequent draining of the civilian ocean in which the cadres swam, could not have escaped the notice of the GVN.

As the population in the revolutionary areas shrank, so did the revolutionary organizations. Membership in the Vinh Kim Farmers' Association fell from 300 members [DT99 put the number at 500] and seven cadres in 1964 to 40 members and three cadres by May 1965. The Women's Association was reduced to a few faithful activists. By early 1967 the popular associations had been disbanded. "They have disintegrated because all the members have left" [DT188]. The Party organization itself had twenty-one members in mid-1965, before the wave of defections, and the district committee had targeted an increase to thirty, at which time the village Party organization would be considered fully developed, and would advance from a Party chapter to a full-blown Party committee [DT99]. Not only did the Party organization fail to meet this target, Party membership began to suffer a decline, though more in quality than in numbers. By 1967 there still appeared to be about twelve Party members in the village [DT188]. Even before the defections, the Youth Group had begun to drop off in membership because of the draft. There had been forty members of the village Youth Group in 1964, but by November 1965 there were only fifteen. Of the twenty-five who had left the group, twenty left the village and five were purged for insufficient zeal [DT97]. The village guerrillas, who had been reinforced in early 1964 by the district local force and guerrillas from surrounding villages, declined to fifteen by late 1966 [DT143]. By early 1967 their numbers had dropped to nine [DT188].

As might be expected, these organizational and situational problems sharply diminished the activities and the effectiveness of the Vinh Kim Party chapter and its cadres. Vinh Kim had the same problems recruiting for the armed forces as many other villages. Volunteers dried up in 1964, and through late 1965 only seventeen youths were drafted, of whom fifteen deserted [DT97]. Since the early years of revolutionary activity, the Party secretary estimated that about 10 percent of the youth had joined the Front, a total of about 100 in five years. Of these, seventy deserted or defected, and only about thirty continued to serve the revolution as of 1965 [DT99]. Vinh Kim village had only seventy unaffiliated young men as late 1965. "There have been about 200 natives of Vinh Kim who have left the village to work for the GVN in the Civil Guard [Regional Forces] and Popular Force units in Long Dinh district town, and about 150 others have volunteered to join the GVN divisions." About 200 men in the 18–45 age bracket had "fled to the cities to make their living" [DT97].

Family Ties of Cadres to the GVN

Because the interviews focused mainly on the revolutionary side of the conflict, they do not fully reflect the extent to which families were split along the fault lines of a civil war. But the cross-pulls between family and civic duty documented in these interviews reinforce the point that the revolution was not being carried out by an "organizational machine" and that the social context that conditioned its operations was all-important. Family tensions and the struggle between public and private interest was only one aspect of this social context. Families were split apart by the conflict, and ties of kinship suffused the village community and often spanned the gulf between the contending sides. This underlines the salience of the "hearts and minds" aspect of the civil war dimension of the conflict, in which personal and political matters were sometimes hard to disentangle.

Again, Vinh Kim is a good example. The former village Party secretary, for instance, had a nephew who was a GVN policeman in My Tho, a cousin in the intelligence service of the GVN district, and a brother who was a former soldier in the French Expeditionary Forces. The father of the former village propaganda chief had been a local Saigon official, and his brother-in-law was in the local Popular Force militia. A village guerrilla's father worked as a servant for an ARVN lieutenant colonel in My Tho, and his father-in-law had been executed by the Party for his role as a hamlet official. A province security cadre whose job required him to select security agents from those with "clean" backgrounds (i.e., with no family ties to the GVN) said, "I had served the communists from adolescence to adulthood. As I served them, I sinned against my family. When my uncle and my father-in-law refused to side with the Front, I denounced them. I deliberately displayed my ingratitude toward my uncle who had raised me. Later on, when I came to my senses, I felt my conscience gnawing at me" [DT233].

In the early years following the Concerted Uprising, the Party had been quite strict about not accepting people with family ties to the GVN into Party or cadre positions. But these ties were so widespread that the Party had to relax this stricture, especially as it expanded its ranks of cadres and soldiers. The Party members were told in indoctrination sessions, "The period of struggle of the Revolution is very arduous, and this was why the Front had to temporarily ally itself with all people who wanted to join the Front's struggle. But once the Revolution is successful, the Front will have to review the family ties of all cadres on both the paternal and maternal sides. If a cadre had a relative who had worked for the GVN, his advancement would be restricted, and then ways would be found to purge him from the Party. He would only be allowed to work in the popular associations" [DT203]. This prospect, no doubt, helps explain the defection of 145 of a total of 314 ralliers in the interview sample who at some time had close personal or family ties with the GVN. An additional 26 of the 79 interviewees who were prisoners had such ties. There is no way of telling whether the percentage of people with close ties serving the revolution was as high as in the interview sample, but in light of the nearly identical percentages of prisoners and defectors who had such ties (roughly one-third), it is certainly possible.

Since the interviews primarily reflect the views of those who had become disillusioned with the revolution, they naturally suggest more widespread disaffection than was actually the case, as some scattered but poignant evidence suggests. The former Vinh Kim Party secretary said that after his defection, "My wife was very sad, and my eldest son wanted to commit suicide. I met him on the day I went back to Vinh Kim. He complained that all his friends showed great contempt toward him because 'your father,' they said, 'has followed the American imperialists' " [DT99]. There clearly remained a strong and committed base of support for the revolution, even in weak areas like Vinh Kim. Some were shunned by family for the opposite reason. A village cadre from Long Binh Dien said that even her older sister, living in the province capital, refused to see her after her defection. "She said she didn't want to see me because I was a traitor, meaning I have been working for the VC. She sent me a message saying that when the GVN allows me to return home, she will support me through school, but right now she refuses to see me" [DT133].

Perhaps the best illustration of the complexity of local ties and connections is the case of Master Sergeant Binh, whose presence is strongly felt in the interviews. Technically a noncommissioned officer of the GVN Regional Force, Binh commanded an essentially autonomous force, much like that of Tu Hue in Phu My. Master Sergeant Binh and his forces had been the main Saigon military presence in Vinh Kim. It was his decision to evacuate the main post in the village in 1964, which led to the one-month revolutionary takeover of the village, and he was also in the thick of things as the GVN forces retook the village. Master Sergeant Binh seemed to be related to half the village, and intimately acquainted with the other half.

During this period of the war the US government launched a campaign to depict the revolutionary movement as "faceless" puppets of Hanoi, led by people with no indigenous roots in their society. The implication was that these were mere cogs in an externally directed organizational machine. The main focus of this campaign was to discredit the leadership of the National Liberation Front who were not, in fact, widely recognized figures in South Vietnam's villages and did not, for the most part, wield real political power. In addition, the real upper leadership of the Communist Party carefully preserved their anonymity for security reasons. But US officials went beyond these facts to imply that the "faceless" characterization applied to the entire revolutionary movement.[25] In Vinh Kim village here were no "faceless Viet Cong" here. He knew them all.

Master Sergeant Binh had, for example, taken the sister of the village guerrilla unit leader as a concubine, and was instrumental in smoothing the way for the guerilla's defection. He also arranged the defection of the village Party secretary (though an ARVN lieutenant who encountered the defecting cadre tried to take the credit). "When I was determined to rally to the GVN," said the Party secretary, "I got in touch with an intelligence agent of the Vinh Kim subsector, through my wife. As a matter of fact, he had advised my wife to urge me to rally long before, but for a very long time I didn't dare trust him. Meanwhile I came across an uncle of mine who came back to Vinh Kim to look after his property. His son is a policeman in My Tho, and I asked him to see Master Sergeant Binh on my behalf. Master Sergeant Binh was the agent's chief, and I wanted to be sure that he would agree to protect me when I rallied. My uncle called on Binh thereafter, and he gave his assent to help me" [DT99].

Unlike the revolutionary guerrillas and militia, the local GVN troops often were not only strangers to the village, they came from outside the province. In 1966 a Hoa Hao Regional Force unit from outside the district occupied the main post on the border of Vinh Kim and Ban Long villages. The deputy chief of the village Farmers' Association noted that the Popular Forces in Vinh Kim came mostly from Sadec province. "Although they are not natives of Vinh Kim," he added, "they behaved rather well toward the villagers. Those who camped in the Vinh Thoi military post got along with the villagers well. They looked as dissatisfied as we did that Vinh Thoi was shelled without apparent reason. One of them was also killed by these reckless shellings because their post once suffered a direct hit, so they were as resentful of the former district chief as the villagers were. Out of discontent, many of them deserted." The Regional Forces, controlled by the province, were a different story. "They have arrested and beaten up the people many times. Among the Regional Forces, only Master Sergeant Binh is a good man" [DT111].

The GVN Makes Some Progress in Winning Hearts and Minds—But Not for Long

To the revolutionaries, the GVN authorities were also anything but "faceless." They knew Master Sergeant Binh well, and they were also quite well informed about the Saigon-appointed district chiefs, who were the top authority in the area. Captain D had become infamous for his destructive shelling of the area, and the villagers were relieved to see him go. His replacement caused a great stir among both the villagers and the cadres. In the view of the village propaganda chief, among the GVN district chiefs, "Only Mr. Minh caused much trouble to the Front. This is also the opinion of the village Party chapter of Vinh Kim as well as those in the surrounding villages. Before he came into Vinh Kim, I never ran into difficulties in waging Front propaganda. Everything that I said met the villagers' approval. During the time that the previous district chief, Mr. D. ran Vinh Kim district, it was very easy to win the villagers' support. It was also the time that I was most active" [DT143]. Callous disregard for the peasants' lives and property created a propaganda bonanza for the local cadres.

"But the situation in Vinh Kim changed after Mr. Minh took office. He stopped shelling the hamlets indiscriminately, allowed the people to come back to live in their hamlets if they wanted to. He stayed close to the people by frequent contacts with them and, finally, he won the people's sympathy. Henceforward, my job of propagandizing for the Front ran into more and more difficulties, and the villagers no longer seemed willing to listen to my speeches. Before, when I talked, the audience kept very quiet. Now the people became fidgety and talked among themselves before I had completed even half my speech" [DT143]. Losing the audience was a fatal problem for a propagandist, and reflected the general problems the revolution was encountering in Vinh Kim. It also, as the propaganda cadre acknowledged, was due to the extraordinary personality of the new district chief.

Captain Minh was a dashing and energetic man, with an instinctive popular touch and a flair for dramatic personal and political gestures which had considerable impact on the people in his district. He was not unique among ARVN officers, though this kind of officer was rare. The tragedy of Captain Minh was that he was the exception that proved the rule. His common sense, his accessibility, and his effective but controlled military activities and good tactical sense were the model of what the Saigon government required to prevail in its struggle. His downfall illustrates why the Saigon regime ultimately failed. Not only did it not support its most capable and aggressive officials, it sometimes turned on them either because they were perceived as a threat to the less effective members of the GVN or because of corruption, or both.

After a few months in the district, Captain Minh had capitalized on the disarray of the local Party organization. He sought out Hai Nam, the former Resistance Party secretary of the village, now a community leader, and enlisted his support in winning the people over to the GVN side. Hai Nam was a close cousin of the Party propaganda chief, who began to notice that the Party leaders were growing more distant toward him. Finally, a Party member told him in confidence that his cousin Hai Nam was now working with Captain Minh and was now "very powerful in Vinh Kim." This news "reminded me of the last conversation I had with Hai Nam, who had spoken well of the GVN. He said, 'The GVN these days is no longer a bad government sponsored by the colonialists. It is really a government which cares about the people's interests.' Hai Nam also complained about the way the Party had treated him regardless of what he had done during the Resistance" [DT143].

The combination of the populist district chief, the affable but omnipresent Master Sergeant Binh, and the former Resistance village Party secretary posed a formidable challenge to the Party in the struggle for the "hearts and minds" of the villagers. "We all knew that Hai Nam was skillful in winning over the villagers' support. We also realized that he had succeeded in detaching some members of the Farmers' Association from the Front, and turning a certain number of villagers into GVN supporters. As a consequence of all this, the outlying portion of Vinh Kim village from Ong Ho Creek to the Kinh Xang Canal has become a dangerous area for the Front to operate in. Before the cadres of the Vinh Kim town Party chapter often came there, but not now." "Why was Hai Nam so successful with the Vinh Kim villagers?" the interviewer asked. "Hai Nam has always enjoyed the villagers' confidence since the Resistance," replied the propaganda chief. "Even during the time he was shunted aside by the Front, he still remained a good man in the villagers' eyes. He is a rather kind and gentle man, and people love him. The Vinh Kim Party chapter also trusted him, and the village Party members often called on him for a chat while he was living in Vinh Kim and before his cooperation with the GVN" [DT143].

After a few months of this effective political warfare, Captain Minh was suddenly arrested and jailed. The circumstances around his case remain murky, but the essence of the charges were that a unit under Minh's command operating in a swampy guerrilla base in distant Camau province had killed civilians during an operation in 1960. The legal points at issue were (1) whether these were really civilians, or were revolutionary cadres, and therefore fair game, and (2) whether then-Lieutenant Minh had personally ordered the shooting. He had already been tried once, in 1964, on these charges and acquitted. No one could explain why this case had suddenly been resurrected, or who was behind it—other than a vague impression that it was relatives of the deceased who had reactivated the case.

Why, in a war where such occurrences were commonplace, was Captain Minh singled out for an event that had occurred years before and despite his previous legal exoneration? Many close to the case felt that the Party had arranged for surrogates to revive this case to put this devastatingly effective officer out of commission. Dark hints of corruption and bribery in the Saigon legal system circulated widely as an explanation for why the GVN would arrest and try one of its own best officers, who had, in any case, been legally exonerated once. This is a probable explanation for a case of singular mystery and complexity and, if true, helps illustrate why the Saigon regime did not prevail in the political struggle. Minh was convicted and sentenced to jail, and cashiered from the ARVN. Captain Minh's well-liked American advisor had considerably more political sensitivity than his predecessor, who interpreted the prior district chief's reckless shelling of neighboring hamlets as a sign of aggressiveness. He was a U.S. military officer who enjoyed an exceptional rapport with the Vietnamese in his district and had effectively supported Captain Minh. But some months after Minh's arrest he too left the district. The province advisor's report for November 1966 noted, "In a remarkable tribute to the American advisory presence, leading citizens of Vinh Kim petitioned President Johnson to extend the tour of Long Dinh subsector advisor Major William R. Wilcox. He has, the petitioners said, "brought many advantages to the people of Long Dinh District from the military, political, economic, and social points of view."[26] Sentiment, or even a desire to do a more effective job, could not prevail over military bureaucracy, however, and Wilcox too departed.

Without any support from people in positions of authority, the former revolutionaries who had hoped to wage a populist struggle against the Party were relegated to the sidelines. The Saigon administration in Vinh Kim went through a turbulent period in 1966. Following the arrest of Captain Minh, the village chief of Vinh Kim, who had served since 1961, was also arrested, along with the deputy district chief (a civilian administrative functionary who did the paperwork for the military officers who were appointed as district chiefs), and two members of the village council. The charges were embezzlement and bribery. In the villagers' view, these charges were well founded. A hamlet Farmers' Association chief said, "They seemed to be very pleased to see them arrested and jailed. They said, 'They accepted so many bribes in the past, they deserve to be killed!'" [DT197].

A Limited Exercise in Democracy

Nearly a year after the Honolulu conference, Lyndon Johnson's democracy came to Vinh Kim in the form of village elections on April 9, 1967. A recently defected hamlet cadre said he had wanted to participate, but couldn't.

> Although I wanted to vote very much, I wasn't allowed to do so. The reason was that my name wasn't registered in the list of voters. Apart from me, there were a lot of other people who didn't have the right to vote—for the same reason, of course. According to the former Vinh Kim Party secretary, only the people living around the Vinh Kim market, that is, in Vinh Thanh [I] hamlet, will be allowed to vote. Many people in Vinh Qui, Vinh Hoa, and Vinh Thoi New Life Hamlets couldn't participate in this election. . . . [The former village Party secretary], who had many contacts with the local [GVN] authorities, told me, in private, that the Vinh Kim district officials hadn't conducted any election campaign. They just selected those who enjoyed their confidence and gave them the right to vote. They also pointed out the name of those they wanted the people to elect when they came into the booths. That's why the Vinh Kim villagers didn't put any stock in that election. They think it wasn't a fair election and that, consequently, the GVN isn't a democratic government either [DT197].

Honolulu had brought democracy to Vinh Kim, but it was democracy Texas style, reminiscent of LBJ's early political life. Later village elections expanded the electorate. In fact, possession of a clipped voter's card, indicating participation in the GVN election and therefore acknowledgment of its authority, became a form of ID, and was often checked by police and soldiers along with the official GVN identity card. By 1971, Hai Nam had succeeded in getting elected on a reformist ticket, but he proved such a thorn in the district chief's side that the village administration was disbanded and Hai Nam and his group publicly reviled by the district chief as a "pack of mangy dogs."[27]

The relationship between the GVN authorities in Vinh Kim and the Americans also took a turn for the worse following the departure of Captain Minh and Major Wilcox, partly due to a change in people, and partly because by 1967 the small American advisory presence had been submerged by the arrival of United States' combat troops in the area. Captain Minh was ultimately succeeded by another ARVN officer who had earlier earned the reputation of the "Tiger of Cho Gao" for his tough rule and aggressiveness as a regional force commander and then chief of that district. "He's a little tiger" was the somewhat condescending title that his American advisors regarded as the ultimate accolade for the kind of fearless warrior they constantly hoped would come their way and "Tiger of Cho Gao" seemed to be an answer to this wish. For the Vietnamese, this term was an intentional reminder of the "Tiger of Cai Lay," Nguyen Van Tam, who ferociously suppressed anti-French revolutionaries during the colonial period. His American advisors might have been less enthusiastic about their counterpart if the story about the "tiger's" views told by Sau Duong, the top Party leader in Region 2, has any basis in fact. After describing some apparently successful "face-to-face struggles" by women from the Vinh Kim area, he adds: "Another amusing story regarding these face-to-face struggles is [that] the District Chief Pho led hundreds of compatriots from the Vinh Kim district seat to Dong Tam [the newly constructed base of the U.S. Ninth Division]. As they passed the [GVN] posts along the way, the puppet soldiers in the posts, upon hearing that the district chief was going along with this group to struggle [protest] with the Americans, were all for it. They were antagonized by the behavior of the Americans toward the Vietnamese, which awakened the nationalist spirit of the puppet soldiers regardless of how hectically they propagandized within their own ranks about American-Vietnamese cooperation, how the Americans were saviors and bosom allies, etc. The reason the contemptible District Chief Pho agreed to lead the people to struggle with the Americans was that he felt his self-respect and prerogatives in the area under his control had been encroached upon." Pho was asked by the Americans in the Ninth Division if the demonstrators were affiliated with the GVN. "The contemptible District Chief Pho resolutely replied, 'correct, these are nationalist [GVN] citizens who are under my tight control.' " Sau Duong makes it clear that he considered this a demonstration instigated by the revolution.[28] Whatever the case, the escalation of war damage in Vinh Kim caused by the arrival of American forces had a disruptive impact on local Vietnamese of all political affiliations and persuasions.

Vinh Kim's struggle for hearts and minds ended in a draw. The revolution had been the clear victors up until 1965, but the social dislocation of the refugee exodus and the disintegration of the Party organization was a major setback. The GVN briefly exploited this opportunity, with the remarkable alliance of a populist district chief, a respected former Resistance leader, and an active and effective master sergeant in charge of the GVN local troops. The larger realities of the Vietnamese situation brought this brief period to an end. From this time on, the outcome of the struggle in places like Vinh Kim, and in My Tho generally, would not rely on "winning hearts and minds," but would be dictated by the larger political, military, and diplomatic currents of the Vietnam conflict.

13

Stalemate

In late 1966 the revolution was buffeted by a double challenge. The first was a natural catastrophe: the monsoon season brought a record amount of rain, resulting in flooding of most of the province north of Highway 4. This drastically reduced the dry and accessible base areas available to the revolutionaries, and sharply curtailed their military operations and movements. The second setback was the arrival of elements of the U.S. Ninth Infantry Division in Dinh Tuong. Both of these events prompted a reassessment of the revolution's military and counterpacification strategy in My Tho. Throughout 1967 both the civilian and military sides of the revolution encountered increasingly serious difficulties, yet the military successes of the U.S./Government of the Republic of Vietnam (GVN) side did not produce a decisive military or political breakthrough, and the year ended in stalemate.

The revolution's problems did force it to adopt a different military strategy, focusing increasingly on the towns and cities, whose logic led ultimately to the 1968 Tet Offensive. Much of this change in the military situation was the result of the introduction of U.S. combat units, whose massive firepower and aggressive tactics upset the carefully designed protective system that had been established in previous years. Many of the revolutionary units in My Tho took a terrible pounding during 1967. The 514th Battalion, the mainstay province unit, suffered continuous setbacks during the year, and the operational area of the region main force battalions shrank. At the end of 1967, however, the revolution was still the dominant presence in most of the countryside, at least as measured by the newly instituted U.S./GVN "Hamlet Evaluation Surveys" (HES), which attempted to assign a letter grade reflecting the security situation in every one of the hamlets in the province.

The hamlet ratings system was primarily a managerial tool designed to inform American and South Vietnamese officials about the month to month progress of the war. There were, however, other ways of assessing the key question of the conflict: who was winning the war? This was a hotly debated issue in 1967. President Lyndon Johnson called General Westmoreland back to the United States twice during that year to assure the American public that progress was being made and the U.S. policy was on a winning track. Yet, as Henry Kissinger and others were soon to acknowledge, "the guerrilla wins if he does not lose." The military setbacks suffered by the revolutionary forces were not sufficient to force them to abandon their objectives of overthrowing the South Vietnamese government and reunifying the country.

This chapter examines the impact of sending U.S. combat forces to the Mekong Delta, the losses they inflicted on their adversary and the Party's response to this challenge, the increasing pressures on revolutionary cadres in the villages and, finally, the evidence that despite all these problems for the revolution, the United States and GVN forces were unable to turn the tide of war decisively in their favor despite an extended period of heavy U.S. military involvement. We begin the analysis by examining the evidence concerning the gains and losses of the contending sides during 1967.

Measuring Territorial Control

The extent of revolutionary control measured by the first HES report in January 1967 showed predominant revolutionary control in Dinh Tuong province. The figures for January 1968 were nearly identical. This suggests that the U.S. military operations in the Mekong Delta and in Dinh Tuong during 1967 had a limited impact on pacification. Pacification itself was limited to a fairly small area of Dinh Tuong province. As of January 1968, only 28 of 603 hamlets were listed as "undergoing pacification," and in 1967 only three villages in the entire province were designated priority pacification areas, while there were some signs that progress had stalled in one of them. The American military province advisory report of December 1967 noted problems in a major pacification area near the U.S. Ninth Division base. There was "poor security in the Thanh Phu [village] area" and there were "few people living in Xom Vong, Giap Nuoc, and An Duc Lo [hamlets]." Only half of the hamlet area was controlled by the cadre in daytime. The second pacification priority was Binh Duc village next to Thanh Phu. Binh Duc had become secure largely as a result of the fact that it bordered the main base of the newly arrived U.S. Ninth Division. The third priority pacification area was Tam Hiep village, near the province airfield. The province advisor judged pacification there to be "on schedule," but due to the efforts of the ARVN Seventh Division rather than the GVN pacification team. The U.S. province advisor sensed that despite a significant defeat of the revolutionary forces in the western part of the province the security situation in the province remained tenuous and wrote in his December 1967 report that "VC efforts continue to be directed against the GVN population centers and RD [revolutionary development or pacification] areas, and the mood is still uneasy even if it is improved from last month."

Some of the numbers reported in the HES were based entirely on the military security situation in each hamlet—the likelihood of getting shot at in a particular hamlet. The more complex ABC "HES" rating, initially called "U.S. category," was based on a weighted score which took into account the development status of the hamlet, that is, the extent to which GVN personnel and programs were operating in a hamlet, as well as a variety of other measures. Since the HES province map printouts used this benchmark, they were presumably considered more revealing. The HES alphabetic ratings were A, B, C, D, E, and V. Only the V rating was purely a security assessment; it meant "VC controlled." The other measures were composite scores on a scale of 100 to 500, with factors other than security included in the assessment. It is clear, however, that the D and E category hamlets were under the predominant influence, if not nearly total control, of the revolution.

Clearly, despite the setbacks to revolutionary military units and cadres during 1967, and the securing of a few priority villages, the security situation at the end of the year remained more or less what it had been at the beginning of the year—with some important exceptions. The major difference was that the mobility and firepower of the U.S. Ninth Division created a fundamental change in the military equation, even though this had not been translated into dramatically improved security ratings by the end of 1967.

Second, the pacification program did dislodge the cadres and guerrillas from several villages that had been high-priority areas, notably Tam Hiep, Binh Duc, and Thanh Phu (Chau Thanh)—despite the continuing insecurity in Thanh Phu noted by the U.S. province advisor. Third, the concentrated units were less able than before to perform their deterrent function of inhibiting smaller GVN units for entering hamlets near a known base area even if it was not certain that there were revolutionary main force units physically present there at the time.

Revolutionary forces found it increasingly difficult to defend their zones. During 1967, the "psychological umbrella of security," which had cast an invisible protective cover over much of the liberated area, began to lose its effectiveness. Escalating revolutionary pressure on the towns and cities suggests that the Communist Party had concluded the best defense was a good offense, and began to stress a more aggressive strategic and tactical posture for every level of military force. For the most part, however, the guerrillas and concentrated units were unable to accomplish the demanding tasks assigned them, and in reality the "offense" was largely limited to sporadic mortar fire and small-unit sniping, not major assaults on military units or installations.

The rough sequence of events in the year and half preceding the Tet Offensive of 1968 was as follows. First, the pacification effort of mid-1966 concentrated on two villages (Binh Duc and Thanh Phu) adjacent to a U.S. military base being constructed at that time. In response, the regional Party military command ordered a change in mission and tactics for concentrated units and demolition forces. Movement along the key interprovincial supply routes from Kien Hoa and the sea began to experience difficulties, and more reliance was placed on bringing supplies from Cambodia. This, in turn, prompted the region command to shift some forces to the Cambodian border and to Long An province, where U.S. units had first entered the Mekong Delta. Shortly afterward, the first U.S. units began to arrive in My Tho, although their presence was not fully felt there until 1967.

In September 1966, a disastrous flood engulfed the northern part of My Tho and the Plain of Reeds base areas, creating serious problems for the revolution there. The flood lasted until late November. By late 1966 new strategic guidance came from higher headquarters, beginning the shift of emphasis to a strategy which emphasized creating insecurity in GVN areas by special unit attacks on the towns and cities. This strategy culminated ultimately in the 1968 Tet Offensive. At the beginning of 1967, the GVN shifted its pacification effort to Tam Hiep village near the province airfield, which had been a favorite revolutionary target in 1965. Strong Saigon control of this area would present major problems for the movement of big units and supplies from the eastern district of Cho Gao to the base areas in the Plain of Reeds and the western districts, and protect both the key Trung Luong intersection where Highway 4 turns west toward the lower delta and the most obvious route of attack on the province capital. By mid-1967 the operations of the U.S. Ninth Division had intensified, and the 514th Battalion and other concentrated units engaged in a series of very costly battles to maintain a toehold in the 20/7 zone. As a result of military setbacks to revolutionary units in 1967, and the devastating U.S. firepower which created still more refugees, the popular associations in many villages fell apart, communications between the villages and higher levels were disrupted, and many key cadres deserted or were killed.

In the face of all these difficulties, the revolution in My Tho was on the defensive, but far from incapacitated. The HES data shows that most of the territory in the province was still under predominant revolutionary control, even though much of the population had fled to GVN areas. The fact that territorial control did not reflect the extent of population control is underscored by the fact that, according to the August 1967 report of the U.S. province advisor, there were nearly 105,000 people (out of a total population of somewhat over 500,000) registered to vote in the upcoming GVN election in Dinh Province, although only 51 of 93 villages would have polling places. Even though being registered to vote did not signify allegiance to the GVN (in fact, an election card was considered a form of compulsory identification by GVN police and soldiers rather than a gateway to democracy) it does suggest that a large number of people lived within reach of the GVN's authority in mid-1967—more than a map based on the HES scores reflecting dominant influence in a given territorial area would suggest. However, even though a single secure hamlet in a village might have served as a polling place, nearly half of the villages of Dinh Tuong did not have one.

The badly battered concentrated units still managed to operate in the province, even though they suffered extremely heavy casualties, had great difficulties recruiting replacements, and had lost much of their supporting civilian infrastructure in the villages. Perhaps the most telling indicator of the extent to which the revolution retained a reserve capacity in the province was the extraordinary resurgence of both its military and civilian sides during the Tet Offensive of 1968, the subject of the next chapter. A reader of the litany of woes told in the 1967 interviews would not have anticipated this resilience, and it poses a central challenge to studies like this, which rely heavily on the available documentary record provided by these exceptionally detailed, but perhaps misleading sources. It also provides a major test for our understanding of the revolution itself, as the following chapters will discuss.

Pacification and Arrival of U.S. Troops in 1966–67

In early 1966, the Party was already apprehensive about the double challenge of intensified pacification and the arrival of U.S. troops in My Tho, even though the outlines of the new GVN pacification strategy had not yet been decided, and no decision had yet been made about sending U.S. troops into the Mekong Delta. A security cadre operating in the area of the province airfield, which later became a priority pacification target, recalled that Chau Thanh District Deputy Secretary Ba Vu had expressed these concerns during the indoctrination.

> In early 1966, I attended a course on the projects made for the first quarter of that year, otherwise known as the Spring–Summer campaign. The course was conducted by Ba Vu. The main theme of the course was the American plan to send 40,000 troops to My Tho province to pacify the Mekong Delta. As far as the general situation, on the enemy's side and ours, it was assessed as follows. The U.S. forces that were to be sent to My Tho appeared very large and strong. In actual fact, they would create difficulties for us. As far as the population was concerned, the majority had been confused and demoralized due to the enemy's intensive bombing and shelling. As a matter of fact, a large number of the population in the district had taken refuge in GVN controlled areas. Reports from top authorities talked of a high revolutionary stand among the people, but for the last few years, the people's morale has become seriously hurt by bombing and shelling. In fact, if we look right into the heart of the matter, the people's demoralization is due to their fear of a protracted war [DT233].

One of the controversial issues in analyzing the Vietnam war is the question of whether the Party at some point concluded that time might not be on their side, leading to an abandonment of a protracted warfare strategy and a go-for-broke effort to bring about a quicker end to the war via the 1968 Tet Offensive. This is the subject of the next chapter, but it should be said here that the revolutionaries were not, at this time, pursuing a strategy of "protracted war" as it is conventionally understood. Moreover, the evidence cited here suggests that the "top authorities" did not perceive any crisis of morale or slackening of popular support. Still, the obvious evidence of civilian demoralization greatly concerned the local cadres, since they were face to face with the realities on the ground. The evolution of the situation in 1966 and 1967 intensified these concerns, but the truly remarkable thing is how quickly the population was mobilized for the Tet Offensive of 1968 and how, for a brief but crucial period, their support for the revolution was reenergized.

In 1965 and 1966 the Party's attempts to counter Saigon's pacification efforts were complicated by the fact that the GVN's own plans and priorities changed during this period. During 1965 the "oilspot" approach was still the basic pacification strategy of the GVN, and it centered on the two geographic keys to the 20/7 zone: Vinh Kim in the east, and Ba Dua in the west.

By mid-1966 a new pacification plan was in operation, and the main targets were Binh Duc and Thanh Phu villages to the east of Vinh Kim, next to the future U.S. military base and on the opposite side of the 20/7 zone from Ba Dua and Long Tien. In early 1967, Tam Hiep village became "phase two" of this pacification effort, extending the pacification focus north of Highway 4, protecting the province airfield, as well as the approaches to My Tho city and the ARVN Seventh Division headquarters. Like Long Tien, Tam Hiep had still been able to mobilize its villagers throughout 1966, and had held a rally for 200 people in observance of the July 20 anniversary that year, with no reaction from the GVN [DT179]. By early 1967, however, intensified GVN pacification activities made this impossible. Together, these two pacification zones provided a screen between My Tho city and the revolutionary base areas. This buffer was generally effective in 1967, but it failed completely to detect or deter the attack on My Tho city in the Tet Offensive of 1968.

Changes in Revolutionary Military Operations: 1966–67

Although the primary main force units were still active in Dinh Tuong during mid-1966, their level of activity was sporadic. During 1966 some significant battles were fought, but the level of attacks was much reduced from the previous year. The 261st Battalion spent most of the time between May and July 1966 in training, reorganization, and "reorientation" or ideological training. After that, the encroaching flood waters restricted its activities. Although the flood waters also restricted the ARVN's movements, and in some ways facilitated the movement by sampan of big revolutionary units, it was more dangerous for the main force units because it slowed their withdrawal and left them open to air and artillery fire [DT149]. By mid-1966 the larger revolutionary military units were concentrating their efforts on the area around Ba Dua in the western 20/7 zone, where the 261st and 263rd Battalions frequently operated, and in the Tam Hiep area, where elements of the 514th Battalion attempted to protect the lifeline to the districts east of Highway 4 [DT179].

In a mid-1966 reorientation session, the cadres of the 261st Battalion were informed of the anticipated arrival of U.S. troops in the delta. They were told that U.S. troops were unfamiliar with guerrilla war and could not withstand hardships. Nevertheless, the dispatch of a U.S. unit to neighboring Long An problem caused some concern. "They said that the presence of the American unit caused the Front some strategic difficulties. The regiment command staff said that the Americans had come to Vietnam in order to take up the defense of the cities and to force the puppet army to conduct sweep operations. This made things difficult for the Front because the enemy divisions—such as the Seventh, the Ninth, the Twenty-First, and the Twenty-Fifth—would be more aggressive now that they were relieved of their defense duties. This meant that the Front forces would have less security because the enemy divisions would conduct sweep operations more continuously and also meant that the enemy divisions would be more aggressive in trying to wrest territory from the control of the Liberation Front and that the war would become fiercer. The cadres said that this was going to be the situation in 1966, 1967, and in the following years" [DT149]. Although, as pointed out in this revolutionary assessment of U.S. plans in the Mekong Delta, the initial idea was to have U.S. units relieve the ARVN of its static defense responsibilities so they could engage in more aggressive operations, the pattern over the next three years was the reverse. After a brief period of base construction and consolidating perimeter defense, it was the U.S. Ninth Division that went on the offensive.

In early 1967 the revolutionary main force units were ordered to hit the enemy in GVN controlled areas as part of a strategy to force it to stretch out and spread itself thin was an important element of the even more ambitious Tet Offensive strategy, which aimed to do on a national scale what this strategy proposed for the Mekong Delta. Another objective was to keep ARVN on the defensive so it could not assume a more offensive role as U.S. troops came into the area. Although some units were ordered out of the province because of this strategy and also because of difficulties in My Tho, the Party also decided to respond to the difficulties by adopting a more aggressive posture in both strategy and tactics.

Recruiting Problems in Military Units and the Arrival of Northern Reinforcements

Recruitment problems reduced the strength of most units, and forced them to begin relying more on military cadres of Northern origin. The military region finally deemphasized the practice of upgrading troops, which drained the village, district, and province units to reinforce the region main forces. Transfers out of the region had been reduced, but they had not stopped completely. A former village guerrilla was sent with a group of 100 recruits, the My Tho province total for June 1966, to eastern Nam Bo. If this was a representative monthly average, it would have meant a total of over 1,000 new recruits in My Tho for the entire year of 1966—in contrast to the estimated 1,000 for *each* district in 1964. Still, even this is more than most interviewees implied by their assertions that recruiting was impossible. Part of this manpower came from cadres in the civilian specialized branches who were transferred to military units [DT246]. Part came from village guerrillas who were still being upgraded, though since it was getting more and more difficult to replace them, this practice was decreasing, particularly because it promised diminishing returns for the revolution. It had become a zero sum game, and was seriously hurting the villages at a time when they needed to gear up to counter pacification. Increased infiltration of North Vietnamese troops supplied the manpower to eastern Nam Bo and the Central Highlands for the big-unit encounters with U.S. troops, and allowed the Mekong Delta to deploy its own resources locally, where they could be used more effectively in a guerrilla setting.

The 267th Battalion commander was a Northerner, a fact that underlines the emerging shortage of capable local cadres. This commander evoked a wide range of reactions from his subordinates. An assistant squad leader said, "He has been the commander of the battalion since the beginning. When I came into Long An to join my company [1965], he was already there. Hai Lieu is a man of over forty. His hair has turned gray. He is tall and slender and his teeth were dyed black. [The translator noted, "This shows that Hai Lieu comes from a Northern peasant background."] I don't know what social category Hai Lieu comes from, but I learned that his family is living in the North. The fighters' opinion of Hai Lieu were quite contradictory. Some of them thought he was a good leader, very kind toward the fighters and very able in military matters. But many others who didn't like to fight were very displeased with him. They often said, "These spinach-eaters are worthless for fighting. Even if we didn't have those sonsofbitches, we in the South could still handle things! *[Cai do rau muong thi chien dau khi gi! Khong co tui no thi tui tao o Mien Nam van lam duoc viec ma!]*" [DT198]. "Spinach eaters" was a derisive label for people from the poverty-stricken North, whose austere diet featured a type of spinach-like aquatic plant sometimes called "bind weed," which was skimmed off ponds and which symbolized to the Southerners the difference between the abundance of their region and the hard living in the North.

The 267th, which spent a lot of time along the Cambodian border, and some time recuperating in Cambodia, was comprised mostly of Southern ethnic Vietnamese. One former soldier, however, who was himself an ethnic Khmer, told a story of constant discrimination and scorn from his Vietnamese comrades. Because he was labeled a troublemaker for quarreling with his comrades, he was kicked out of a more desirable rear service unit that rarely engaged in combat and sent to the 267th, where he was assigned to cook and dig trenches for Hai Lieu, the battalion commander, whom he described as "tall and big, frank, cheerful, and who commanded great prestige among his men." The Southern-born deputy battalion commander was "small, hotheaded, belligerent, and shouted loudly every day." The Fourth Company's commander was also a Northerner who was "aggressive in his duties," while the Southern-born deputy company commander and political officer, on the other hand, was "hostile and hotheaded, his conduct and behavior were inferior and he often oppressed his soldiers. He was big, tall and fat, and walked slowly" [DT231]. Clearly the North–South question was a matter of individual qualities as well as regional stereotypes, and Southern rank and file could appreciate considerate and able Northern leaders and prefer them as individuals to those Southern cadres who had less attractive qualities.

Disruption of Supply Routes and Rear Base Areas

The move of units such as the 267th to Long An, the Cambodian border, and into Cambodia itself, was probably due partly to problems on the main region supply route from Kien Hoa and the sea, which came through My Tho to the base areas in the Plain of Reeds and on to the Iron Triangle region and the COSVN bases near the Cambodian border. This, in turn, was probably due to the effective U.S. river patrols along the upper branch of the

Mekong River, begun in 1966. The failure of the local civilian cadres to provide a reliable supply of civilian porters forced the region supply units to rely mainly on their own personnel, and sharply reduced the quantity of goods that could be sent along this route.

The supply problem itself was due to the increasing intensity of the war. First, the refugee outflow meant that fewer civilians were available for transport service, and the popular associations that had mobilized them were falling apart. Second, the dangers of the trip, because of massive bombing and shelling, made it hard to recruit even committed supporters of the revolution to do this dangerous work. The problem was not supplies but getting people to move them. "It became more difficult for us to get civilian laborers. Almost all the supply routes were more or less insecure because the GVN had uncovered them. When a liaison route that we used to take was uncovered, we transported the supplies by sampans—because this was easier—instead of transporting them by land, and we had the civilian laborers carry the supplies to the canal or river and load them on sampans, and then we rowed away. Sometimes we could obtain only about twenty civilian laborers, while there were up to 100 cases of ammunition, and bags containing weapons. In this case the civilian laborers had to make many trips from the place where the supplies were to the canal or river bank" [DT205]. The main supply bottleneck had, by the end of 1966, become people, not supplies, dramatically reversing the situation of the early 1960s, when there was a vast surplus of manpower, but a severe shortage of weapons and supplies.

The flood waters submerged most of My Tho province north of Highway 4 from September through November 1966. The already reduced level of revolutionary military operations ground to a near halt during this period, as the units concentrated on surviving, and on the challenges of daily living in their flooded base areas. An assistant squad leader in the 267th Battalion said that during the flood his unit "camped along the banks of the Nga Sau [which the U.S. military called the Wagon Wheel] intersection of six canals, or along Bang Lang canal, or in Hau My. We just moved around here and there by sampans. The banks of the canals were also flooded and we had to hang our hammocks on the trees to sleep in. Life was very dull. We used to sit in our hammocks all day long doing nothing but looking around" [DT198].

During the flood, the troops lived on sampans and rafts. They cooked, ate, and slept there. Although the flood deprived them of the protection of the familiar fortified trenches, "the floating rafts offered some protection for the troops, because when airplanes came to drop marble bombs [*bom bi,* cluster bombs with exploding pods of pellets], they could dive under water and stay beneath the rafts to hide from the bombs." In these miserable circumstances, the health of the troops deteriorated. Malaria was chronic, along with flu and rheumatism from the cold and damp. With sufficient medical supplies, the 261st managed to deal with these health problems, and the daily average of five to fifteen men in the company who reported sick still left the unit with enough healthy troops to function [DT149].

Living on the rafts and sampans had less serious but still demoralizing drawbacks. There were not many snakes in the Kien Phong and My Tho areas, [but] sometimes we found *ran luc* poisonous snakes, and centipedes in the sampans at night. The fighters had to watch out for snakes. Usually before going to bed they checked the sampans and rafts to make sure that there were no snakes. During the flood season living conditions became worse than before. Sometimes three men had to sleep under the same mosquito net because the sampans were small and they couldn't hang three mosquito nets in one sampan. They had to lie like sardines in a can. Then it rained very frequently at night, and we were caught in the wind and the rain. There were many things that made life very hard for the men" [DT149]. As is the case with many accounts of life with the revolution, this gripping account of the miseries of life in revolutionary units can be read at least two ways. It explains why so many did ultimately leave the revolutionary ranks, but it is also a testament to the extraordinary dedication and endurance of those who persevered, and it is this which is much more difficult to explain.

Attitudes Toward Americans and Responses to the Arrival of U.S. Troops

The hardships, the resentments against the revolution for being unable (or unwilling) to assist those who suffered in its service, and the comparative largess in GVN disaster relief and refugee resettlement (made possible by U.S. aid) all reflected unfavorably on the revolution. However, this slightly more positive image of the Saigon government did not extend to the Americans. A Diem Hy cadre told the interviewer, "To tell the truth, I must say that everyone in my hamlet thought of the Americans as invaders. On this point, they think the Front didn't lie when it said that the Americans wanted to take over the country. Front propaganda also accused the Americans of having instigated this war. Therefore the people of my hamlet are very resentful of the Americans" [DT151]. Though this view might be expected of a member of the village propaganda and indoctrination section, it was not a statement calculated to improve his status with the GVN, and must be considered sincere. A company commander of the 261st, who had made his own peace with the GVN, also did not extend it to the Americans. Asked by an ARVN sergeant right after his defection whether he still hated the Americans, he replied, "I have rallied to the GVN, and not to the Americans," he said. "You see, in the Front we were always told that we had to fight against the American invaders, and this stuck in my mind." It is clear from his account of the reorientation sessions that the anti-American theme struck a very responsive chord [DT149].

It was in this context that Americans started to arrive in My Tho province. Their mission was to support the pacification effort. The preceding comments, however, reveal the political difficulty of the task. Pacification was a GVN responsibility, and the political, administrative, and security tasks of pacification could only be done by Vietnamese. In a shift from the Party's initial conclusion that American troops would assume the static defense to release ARVN units for more aggressive offensive operations, it now appeared that the U.S. troop presence was intended to provide a shield behind which pacification could proceed, and to keep the larger revolutionary units from disrupting it. The political costs of a highly visible American presence had been hotly debated in the U.S. government, and it was only two years after the first major combat troops arrived in Vietnam that they were assigned to the heavily populated delta. The calculation was that the military benefits they could bring by keeping the main force units off balance would compensate for the indirect damage that would be caused by underlining Saigon's reliance on the United States, and the direct damage that the thunderous presence of the U.S. Ninth Division would inflict on the rural population.

Building "Combat Hamlets" to Counter Pacification

Along with the well-established "people's guerrilla war" tactics of holding onto territory in the rural areas by using spike pits, thorny bushes, and grenade traps to render the area impregnable, the leadership decided to take the offensive, and make a virtue of necessity. The necessity was to resist the loss of even more territory, while at the same time trying to roll back the pacification program. Just as the Military Region 2 main forces had tried to pursue a more aggressive strategy from mid-1966 to take the war to the GVN strongholds and force both the U.S. and GVN forces to spread themselves thin, the province and district forces in My Tho now were told to put more pressure on the GVN-controlled villages, district towns, and even the province capital.

To keep GVN operations at arms' length, or at least slow down the ARVN troops until people had the opportunity to evade oncoming "sweep operations," they were told to construct and reinforce "combat hamlets" *(ap chien dau)*. In places where the terrain permitted, thorny hedgerows were planted around hamlets or neighborhoods, closing in the hamlets. In the Mekong Delta, unlike North and Central Vietnam, hamlets consisted of small scattered clusters of homes strung out along canals more often than they were concentrated in a compact grouping, which somewhat complicated this task. Nevertheless, the dense foliage in many areas allowed the "fencing in" of fairly large residential groups with this combination of thorny hedge and bamboo fence. This channeled access along a few paths, which could be interdicted with spike pits over a meter deep with ten sharpened bamboo stakes embedded at the bottom, or with grenade traps and mines. In some cases these fences were as much as 2 kilometers long [DT161].

"Combat hamlets" were not a new innovation; they had been established in some areas after the Destruction of the Oppression in 1960. Where circumstances permitted, peasants were continuously urged to build them. In late 1965 and throughout 1966 and 1967, however, there was a reemphasis on building combat hamlets as the big-unit clashes of 1965 diminished and the battle for the villages intensified. Quon Long village cadres, for example, were ordered to complete the transformation of four hamlets into "combat hamlets" by December 1965 [DT95].

Combat hamlets played a central role in the 1965–66 response to pacification. As the U.S./GVN pacification program shifted direction somewhat in mid- and late 1966, this approach was supplemented by other measures, such as the "anti-American perimeters," but combat hamlets remained the foundation of the counter-pacification effort. The reason is simple: the greatest problems for the revolution were not being created by clever pacification tactics or "revolutionary development" cadres, but by the bombing, shelling, and military operations that made it nearly impossible to stay in the hamlets being fought over. Combat hamlets were a device to protect the village cadres and guerrillas, while at the same time—along with bunkers and bomb shelters—offering some measure of protection to the villagers who stayed.

Life in the combat hamlets was hard, and villagers chafed at the lack of freedom of movement under the new fenced in hamlets—not unlike the hated Strategic Hamlets of the Diem period in that regard, except that they did not require relocation of houses. Many peasants, however, began to move to temporary shelters in nearby open rice fields to avoid bombing and shelling. Combat hamlets also meant a reversal of the earlier revolutionary policies of community development in the village, and "public works" assumed a destructive and defensive character. In a hamlet of Vinh Kim, "the village Party committee did urge the villagers to repair roads and bridges during the early years of the revolution. They didn't provide any funds for this, but only forced the people to do public works. But in 1966 the village Party committee ordered the villagers to destroy every road and bridge and forced the people to use new paths. Spike boards have been planted in the old paths. The village Party committee also forced the villagers to make many fences. Whenever they got news that the GVN soldiers were approaching their hamlets, the guerrillas closed the fences and planted grenades. In April 1966 one GVN soldier was wounded and another killed when they tried to open the fence gate" [DT197].

Villagers often stepped in the spike pits themselves [DT84]. Occasionally they were injured by grenade traps. The trenches, ditches, and canals that criss-crossed the hamlets and impeded GVN operations also inconvenienced the residents and ruined many valuable fruit trees [DT10]. One of the first things the GVN forces did upon regaining control of a former combat hamlet was to rebuild the bridges and fill in the ditches to facilitate movement [DT12]. "I did not feel secure in my hamlet since it was converted into a combat hamlet," said one former resident. "People have to take great care when going out to the rice fields to work or going to fish. We feared being arrested, beaten, or shot at by GVN soldiers. We also feared being shelled by GVN mortars" [DT28].

In many cases the cadres and guerrillas did not themselves live in the "combat hamlets," and this created a number of complications [DT28]. First, it accentuated the separation between the cadres and the villagers. Second, it created a "law-and-order" problem in the fenced-in combat hamlets. A guerrilla chief from Dong Hoa said:

> The Front set up combat hamlets only to slow GVN soldiers down. The cadres and guerrillas did not live in them—they always lived in hamlets distant from the post, in order to have enough time to hide before the soldiers arrived. Therefore, in combat hamlets, nobody took care of collective security and, because the villagers were poorer, many things got stolen at night. There were many thieves at night, and the villagers complained a lot about stolen things. In 1963, when my hamlet was not yet fenced, the villagers often showed contempt for the Strategic Hamlets, which were carefully fenced. They felt that life in the Strategic Hamlet was not pleasant and often said that life in the Strategic Hamlet was like being in jail because you had to ask for permission to go out. But since the hamlet has been fenced in the villagers also had to ask for permission to go out. And, the Front never gave it to those who were undesirable elements [that is, with family ties to the GVN]. At present, they prefer to live in the New Life Hamlet because they receive assistance from the GVN and their children can go to school [DT86].

Whereas the Strategic Hamlets had once been targets of guerrilla war, the combat hamlets were now the more dangerous place to live, and in many ways they imposed more constraints on villagers than the old Strategic Hamlets. The shelling and insecurity had caused the few primary schools that continued to operate in revolutionary areas to close down. In addition, many peasants did not feel that the textbooks used by the revolution's teachers, with their heavy ideological content, were real education [DT86]. Moreover, a revolutionary education might be of limited value if the children had to move to a GVN-controlled area and this, along with the physical danger and actual destruction of schoolhouses, meant that the GVN could use the promise of education as a powerful magnet to draw people out of revolutionary-controlled areas.

Another problem with the combat hamlets was that the amenities of life were sadly lacking. The previously lively rural atmosphere had dissipated, and many of the combat hamlets became depressing to live in. In Long Binh Dien village, life in one of the combat hamlets was described as "dull," and the place looked "deserted and sad." "The villagers left it for the rice fields because they hated the Front, and feared shellings and sweeps. They hated the district cadres and the guerrillas who often called on them and asked them to put them up, and disturbed their way of living. Life in the [Saigon-controlled] New Life Hamlets was certainly better. They were not shelled, and the people could therefore afford to buy good furniture, whereas in the combat hamlet the houses are empty" [DT94].

Combat Hamlets were no answer to the rain of mortars and artillery that fell on the villages of southern Chau Thanh district during the clearing of the area around the U.S. base. A liaison agent from Song Thuan village said, "My hamlet has been regularly shelled from mid-1966 on, after the GVN Seventh Division soldiers came into Binh Duc to pacify it. Shellings happened almost every day and night. Therefore, there have been a lot of casualties among the villagers. I don't know the exact figure, but it is probably about four dozen. Most of the dead were children." Not surprisingly, the villagers were "very resentful of the GVN. They cursed Thieu and Ky and the Americans violently. They accused the Americans of bringing mortars into Vietnam to kill the people. They also went on demonstrations in Vinh Kim, but since the GVN authorities arrested some of them they were afraid and became reluctant to wage face to face struggles" [DT169].

As the local situation deteriorated, the village cadres tried to impress on the villagers that the "big picture" was more encouraging, but this was not effective. "The cadres kept telling the villagers many times that the big units would come to attack the GVN troops, but nothing happened. Then the cadres had to change their line and said that the Front forces were attacking the enemy fiercely in many areas, and that the GVN troops would have to withdraw to reinforce the other beleaguered units. But the people remained frightened. During the meetings they kept silent, but deep down they didn't think much of what the cadres said. Their aspiration was to move out of their hamlet [DT164]

Some village cadres were not disturbed by the arrival of U.S. troops. A village Party secretary was asked, "Did you ever think that since the Front couldn't defeat the GVN alone, it would be impossible to defeat both the ARVN and the Americans?" The cadre replied, "While I still worked for the Front, I never thought so, because we were heavily indoctrinated that the Front would have the ability to cope with any increase in strength by the Americans. Although the cadres never plainly stated that the Socialist countries would send troops to help the Front, the implication that Red China would send its troops to Vietnam when necessary was very clear. That's why we felt confident. We didn't worry much about the GVN's increase in strength brought about by the presence of the American troops in My Tho" [DT247].

Impact of U.S. Military Operations on Pacification and Revolutionary Military Operations

For the ordinary people, however, the impact of the American arrival was unsettling. The original U.S. military designation of "Base Whisky" was changed to Dong Tam ("With One Accord"), after an alert U.S. Information Service officer suggested that the original name did not convey the professed high ideals of the U.S.–Saigon relationship. Many Vietnamese in My Tho may have remembered that phrase *dong tam* had been used by the GVN to describe its aim of "annihilating the communists with one accord" *(dong tam diet cong)* during the terrifying year of 1959.[1] The base was completed in late 1966 and the U.S. forces arrived, worrying the villagers, who now had a new problem. "The people were afraid that when the Americans came to stay in the village, the VC would fire at them and the Americans would retaliate with mortar shellings. They said that if this happened, they would all get killed. They had never met any Americans before, so they were frightened of them. They said, 'We don't speak their language. If they come and arrest us, how can we plead with them?'" [DT164].

The concerns about the frightening potential of U.S. firepower were amply justified, though after the initial clearing phase, the villagers of Binh Duc began to enjoy the security of living outside a combat zone as the destruction moved to other villages. The revolutionary military units could not get near the base, and the village guerrillas and cadres had been forced to take refuge in neighboring villages. Eventually, the villagers learned to live with the U.S. presence. "They found things rather easy. The American troops let the people go and work in their rice fields as usual, as long as they wore white clothes. I've seen the Americans from the base dealing with the people—they treated the people very well, even though they couldn't communicate with the villagers. When a farmer wanted to ask for a cigarette from the Americans, he put two fingers close together on his lips, the Americans understood and gave him the cigarettes. As for the children who came to see them, the Americans gave them candy and cookies. I think the Americans were very nice. The GVN soldiers in the posts nearby were also very nice to the people and didn't cause them any troubles, and the people had nothing to complain about" [DT162].

This idyllic picture was clouded by the fact that many of the peasants, including this hamlet Farmers' Association cadre, lost their land to the military base. In his hamlet, only five of twenty tenants had land rental contracts; the others had worked for landlords without contracts, and thus could not prove that they had a claim to the land that was appropriated for the military base. The alternative was to get a construction job. The hamlet cadre said, "My aspiration is to work for some agency so that I can support my wife and children. I want to work at the American base doing things like scooping dirt or mixing cement, but the only thing is that the job might not last long. If I work for the GVN Rural Construction or Armed Propaganda teams, I'll get paid less, but the job will last longer. My specialty is farm work, but I no longer have any land to till" [DT162].

One advantage to the residents of newly pacified villages was that they were no longer automatically considered "Viet Cong citizens" and, therefore, fair game for abuses by ARVN troops on sporadic operations. As the ARVN presence became routinized, their behavior seems to have improved, at least in the areas now under Saigon control. "Before the village was pacified, the Front propaganda told the people that when the GVN or Allied troops entered the settlements in the hamlet, they would arrest, kill, and rob them. This was why the people were very afraid of GVN operations. Whenever there was an operation, the villagers with legal papers, the middle-aged farmers, and the young boys and girls, all fled from their hamlets and buried their possessions because they feared that the GVN soldiers would steal them. Since a number of GVN soldiers had, in fact, stolen poultry and a number of other possessions when they came in on operation, the VC propaganda was very effective. Since the village was pacified in the beginning of 1967, the GVN troops who conducted operations in the village have stopped looting, and this is why the people have lost their fear of the troops. They have become less hostile toward the GVN troops" [DT216].

But, having accommodated to the ARVN soldiers, villagers in the expanding path of the pacification program soon had to adjust to a new challenge. From the outset of the first sustained U.S. operations at the beginning of 1967, the American military presence made a considerable impact in Chau Thanh district. Small U.S. units had conducted intensive patrols in the villages around the Dong Tam base, and were gradually clearing the areas north and south of Vinh Kim, pushing cadres and guerrillas back into the heart of the 20/7 zone. The mobility and firepower of the U.S. Ninth Division troops were a major problem for the revolutionary forces. The tactic of "snaring prey with a conical hat" *(chup non)* was particularly effective. This involved small U.S. units being transported by helicopter from one point to another in a checkerboard fashion, making rapid probes and then moving on to the next area if there was no contact. If a guerrilla unit was encountered, massive air and artillery support came immediately, and other heliborne units would rapidly converge on the spot and pile on. In the villages closest to the base, from Vinh Kim and surrounding areas north to Highway 4, the Ninth Division conducted constant small-unit patrols during January 1967. In Song Thuan, "Americans were constantly in the village" in platoon strength, staying several days in each hamlet. The guerrillas were unable to detect any set operational patterns in these patrols, and thus were unable to devise countermeasures [DT183]. U.S. troops heavily patrolled the hamlets along the Vinh Kim road, disrupting liaison between the village cadres and higher levels [DT193]. In Nhi Binh village, U.S. troops first appeared in January [1967]. Prior to their entry into the former base area hamlets of this village, heavy artillery shelling destroyed the prepared fortifications which the big units had used while stationed there [DT207].

Under these circumstances, the carefully calibrated "security umbrella" provided by the fear that a large revolutionary unit might be in the area was ineffective. The "security umbrella" relied on raising the threshold of force for invading troops to battalion, regimental, or divisional size, thus reducing the frequency of operations and the area of coverage, as well as tipping off any units or cadres in the area with the ponderous preparations for an operation of that size. In addition, when the attacking unit did get there, it would find the main force units dug in and protected by prepared fortifications in favorable terrain. Speed, mobility, and withering firepower brought in by the U.S. Ninth Division changed this equation. However, this success came at a very high moral price because of the heavy civilian casualties resulting from indiscriminate use of firepower.

Another advantage of the American "checkerboard" system of operations was that it did not rely on timely and accurate intelligence, but simply kept troops moving until they ran into something. On routine patrols, the U.S. troops would destroy the prepared fortified positions they encountered, and in the depopulated countryside the main force units had neither time nor labor to restore them. The frequency of operations also kept both the concentrated units and the local guerrillas off balance. In Nhi Binh B village, U.S. troops came in on operations about ten times in the month of January in a strength of about forty each time, and destroyed all the fortifications in the area. As a result of the intensifying war, the Nhi Binh B cadres had been unable to gather civilian laborers for ammunition transport since August 1966, and after March 1967 could not even mobilize civilians to evacuate the wounded [DT203].

Apart from the military measures devised to cope with the new American presence, the cadres were given instructions to pass on to the villagers on how to confront the U.S. soldiers politically and psychologically.

> As far as educating and indoctrinating the people is concerned, we had to proselytize American troops. A number of leaflets and declarations in English had been printed and sent to us by top authorities at some level. The leaflets were distributed down to every hamlet and village. Since it was recognized that American soldiers would not willingly pick up any type of paper from the ground to read it, we were instructed to drop the leaflets in clean and attractively decorated places for their benefit. It would be even better if could be done through intermediaries, whose job would be to find ways to place the leaflets into the hands of the American soldiers. In fact, all the villagers living in the 20/7 zone were taught to speak forty-one English phrases. They were very simple phrases such as "I want peace," "Do you miss your wife and children?," "We are civilians," "This route is dangerous," etc. These sentences were intended to appeal to the American soldier's love for his home country, family, and so on, and by this to affect his morale [DT233].

It is unlikely that these language lessons made a deep impact on the villagers, though at first they were terrified of the possibility that they would be unable to communicate with the U.S. troops in circumstances that might be life threatening, or at least might lead to arrest and possible imprisonment. A postwar revolutionary account of crossing the language barrier shows how quickly the peasant apprehension about the Americans dissipated and also gives some indication of the depth of the underlying cultural divide." The people of My Tho province and the folks around the base, especially school children, were very bold with the American soldiers, and all learned a number of common American phrases to win the sympathy of the Americans, like 'Hello,' . . . 'No VC' [I'm not a Viet Cong], 'Vietnam number one,' . . ." According to this account, a U.S. company marching down the Vinh Kim road took down some NLF flags and marched for 2 kilometers with the flags on their heads, saying, "VC number one!" to the passers-by. The Party leadership interpreted this as an antiwar demonstration.[2] If such a thing did in fact take place, it was far more apt to be GI clowning to lighten the stress of the routine of boredom interspersed with moments of terror that was the general lot of U.S. soldiers in Vietnam, or a derisive taunt to the "VC."

Ultimately, the villagers found that the universal language of commerce transcended the language barrier. In Song Thuan village, next to Vinh Kim, "A lot of women are now selling fruit and food to the Americans. They crossed the Kinh Xang canal with their supplies and sold them to the Americans. They are making big profits. I came across some of these women and had a chat with them. They told me that the Americans were good buyers. 'If you are not pleased with the price they give you, you just shake your head. Then they raise the price. When you get the right price, you just nod. Then they pay you and take the things away.' Despite the language barrier, the Vietnamese women and the Americans could communicate with each other very well. They communicated with sign language" [DT169]. In Binh Duc, the villagers even found the lack of communication an advantage, since the U.S. troops "paid whatever price they were asked. They were good customers." Naturally, "The people who had business dealings with them were very pleased. They only complained that they couldn't communicate with the Americans. The all said, 'the Americans *si so* [indicating a sibilant rush of incomprehensible sounds] with us, and we don't understand a thing they say" [DT164]. To the extent that the My Tho villagers developed an English language vocabulary, it probably did not reflect the revolution's approved forty-one phrases.

Villagers' Attitudes Toward Cadres in 1967

The interviews portray a clear decline in popular support for the revolution that resulted from the loss of physical control, but the precise extent of this shift is difficult to document, and the reasons for it are even more difficult to determine. Was this a temporary drop-off in the active support of villagers still loyal to the revolution because of the increased risks of overt support? Had the villagers become fed up with the cadres and turned away from the revolution in order to take care of their personal concerns? Were the majority of peasants simply political opportunists who would accommodate to whichever side had the stronger force? Or were the villagers relieved to be liberated from the exactions of the cadres? And what were the reasons for the decline in confidence in the revolution? Was it only changes in the village situation, or did the peasants use a larger framework to assess the way the conflict was going? Was there a single major factor, or was it a combination of things? Or was this an area where the interviews were unreliable or, because they largely reflected defector accounts of the situation, skewed by the attitudes and circumstances of the sources?

Evidence of declining support for the revolution in late 1967 is an essential background to the next chapter on the Tet Offensive. To what extent was there a perception at high levels of the Party that the support base was eroding, and that a dramatic new approach to the conflict was needed? Equally important, how can the apparent decline in popular support between 1965 and 1967 be reconciled with the powerful evidence of an overwhelming, though brief, resurgence of popular support for the revolution only a few months after some of the most pessimistic evaluations of the revolution's in My Tho were recorded in the interviews?

An illustration of the changing villager attitudes toward local revolutionaries is the following description of the evolution in village attitudes toward the cadres in a My Hanh Trung, a village with a strong revolutionary tradition. At the beginning of the insurgency, "the cadres, who often got in touch with the villagers, were highly esteemed and respected. But little by little the villagers began to lose faith in them because of the increasing ferocity of the war, the inevitable payment of taxes, and the numerous assignments they had to carry out, such as meeting their military obligation, working as civilian laborers without pay, setting up fences around combat villages, digging foxholes, etc. As a matter of fact, the friendly atmosphere that existed in the early days between cadres and villagers began to wane, and finally the villagers' attitude toward the cadres became one of complete indifference" [DT238].

"It should be mentioned here," said the respondent from My Hanh Trung, "that the cadres did not do anything concrete and realistic to help the villagers. They were just trying to win the people over to their side by coming to their house to have a friendly chat with the people, to ask about the health of other members of their family, or to give some advice on certain matters. In short, they knew how to use the psychological factor to win the sympathy of the people" [DT238].However, the "psychological factor" unsupported by any concrete benefits for the peasants by was beginning to wear thin as the war dragged on and intensified. By the end of the 1967 the "rational peasants" were coming into evidence. It was no longer enough to talk persuasively; the question of where the peasants' interests lay was becoming an increasingly important factor.

Moreover, the awesome authority of the cadres had been diminished over time by familiarity born out the very proximity that had once worked in the revolution's favor. In a hamlet of My Hanh Trung, the hamlet unit leader "was a benign person. He was very fair in dealing with his subordinates. Unfortunately, he was not worthy of his job, as he did not have any military experience at all. He was a very determined follower of the Front and undoubtedly the only one in the hamlet unit whose interest and enthusiasm in carrying out his missions never seemed to flag. However, the fact that he was too kind diminished his value in the eyes of his subordinates. Nobody was afraid of him, and it was obvious that no mission could be carried out effectively under these conditions" [DT238].

A village guerrilla from Quon Long said, "From the first days of the Destruction of the Oppression up to 1965, the villagers did have respect and faith in the hamlet cadres. But since 1966 their respect and faith in the cadres has greatly diminished. Indeed, they no longer welcome them warmly in their homes, wining and dining them as they used to do before. The people are no longer so respectful toward the cadres in their hamlets in their speech and behavior. Besides, they no longer comply with the cadres in civilian labor or paying taxes as they did before. In other words, the people are indifferent or even cold toward the cadres. The reason for this change in the people's attitudes is the destructive character of the war, the weakening of the Front, the fear that the GVN will cause them difficulties, and the fear of having to pay heavier taxes while their crops have been heavily damaged by the bombing and the war" [DT279]. Another guerrilla from the same village concurred:

> The villagers' attitudes toward the cadres is very complicated. It changes with the situation. When the Front first took over, everyone was afraid of the cadres. The villagers obediently carried out all the orders given by the cadres. When the Front was really strong and had taken over control of various areas, the villagers still feared the cadres, but they also respected the cadres. They looked up to them as national heros who dared to sacrifice themselves for the people. In 1965, when the Front simultaneously promulgated three policies—the military duty, the tax duty, and the civilian labor duty—the villagers' attitude changed from respecting and fearing to secretly resenting. The villagers resented the cadres secretly because if this attitude were known to the cadres, they might be watched closely or sent for reeducation. When the war came to the area, the Front's secure base was attacked and the cadres' prestige decreased a great deal. Whenever there was a military operation or an air or artillery attack, the cadres always ran away quickly, ahead of the villagers. They were the last to return to the village. The villagers realized that the cadres were no better than themselves. . . . In short, the villagers' attitudes toward the cadres varied sharply from respecting, to despising and resenting, but always fearing [DT275].

Of course, these statements came from people who themselves had been deeply demoralized and no doubt projected their own feelings onto others. Nevertheless, the attribution of widespread disaffection to other villagers in these interviews is more prominent than in interviews from 1965 and 1966. Given the extraordinary turnaround in the level of popular support during the 1968 Tet Offensive, could these interviewees simply have been wrong?

This is, in the end, a difficult question to resolve, but several issues raised by these statements deserve to be noted. The first is that all of these comments were noting a decline from an exceptionally high level of popular support for the revolution in 1963–64. Even though the drop-off may have been considerable, it has to be measured in terms of the elevated starting point. Thus the level of support which the revolution still enjoyed prior to the Tet Offensive was considerably stronger than these implicit comparisons with the past suggest.

Measuring Civilian Morale and Levels of Popular Support for the Revolution

In addition, the accounts make it clear that much of the loss of support was situational. The revolution was encountering problems, and the peasants made cost–benefit calculations about the utility of continuing to take risks on behalf of an enterprise that looked like it was stalled. This is the key point. Stalemate worked to the advantage of the revolution ("the guerrilla wins if he doesn't lose") and could therefore survive and even prevail at much lower levels of popular support than it had enjoyed during the high tide of 1963. Nevertheless, as the United States discovered in the Korean War ("die for a tie"), it is far more difficult to keep up home-front morale without the prospect of imminent and decisive victory, and there is no reason why this should not apply to the supporters of the revolution as well.

The subject of individual and collective morale is almost impossibly elusive, as the Rand interview project (titled "Studies of Viet Cong Motivation and Morale") discovered over time. There is, first of all, the problem of drawing conclusions from disparate individual accounts. For every negative assessment, there is a positive one.

Further complicating the assessments of civilian morale at this critical juncture of the revolution is the difficulty of connecting two crucial dimensions of the revolutionary support base, or even fully understanding each one separately. The first is the scale of intensity of commitment by different groups of revolutionary supporters. There is, first of all, the small but totally dedicated "hard core" at the center of the movement, comprised of leading Party members at every level and key cadres from the village level on the civilian side and the platoon level on the military side on up. A surrounding group of full-time revolutionaries, such as the village guerrillas, some ordinary or less committed Party or Labor Youth members, lower-level military cadres and rear services personnel, and a wide range of people engaged in "troop proselytizing," propaganda, liaison, supply, security and clerical tasks comprised a second circle, which we will call the "revolutionary infrastructure." Their loyalty was to the revolution, but their initiative, leadership skills, level of risk acceptance and/or perseverance was lower than that of the hard core. The third circle is the "backbone elements" (*nong cot*). These were extremely committed civilians who were selected by the Party to galvanize the support of other villagers. Although they linked

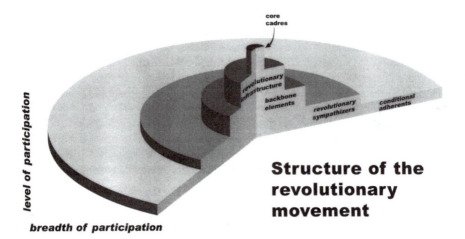

Figure 13.1   **Structure of the Revolutionary Movement** *(Diagram by Lynn Thomas)*

ordinary civilians who were sympathetic to the revolution with the Party's infrastructure, the Party felt it was important that other villagers should perceive these activist sympathizers as "like themselves" and thus different from full time revolutionaries. A fourth circle were people who were sympathetic to the movement but too preoccupied with family or personal interests to make continual sacrifices on its behalf, especially during periods of difficulties. We shall call these "revolutionary sympathizers." Beyond these, at the outer margins of the support structure of the movement, were apolitical or extremely risk-averse peasants who were highly sensitive to cost–benefit calculations. They might be termed "conditional adherents," who could be mobilized when the revolution was strong but not when it was in trouble.

The four circles of support for the revolution are illustrated schematically in Figure 13.1. The vertical dimension in this figure measures the level and intensity of support. The "hard core" would always operate at the upper limit of support for the revolutionary cause, while the level of support given by conditional adherents would fluctuate widely depending on the situation, and the level and intensity of support of the other groups would fluctuate within a narrower range. The horizontal dimension of the revolutionary support base is the size and extent of each of these components. In general, as the size of each group expands, the intensity of its commitment to the revolution becomes more variable (remember Lenin's "better fewer, but better"). At the same time, when the revolution gains momentum, the size of the inner circles with a higher level of commitment increases, bolstered by the greater activism of people moving from the outer circles to a higher level of involvement in the revolution.

Thus both the level of intensity of each segment of the revolutionary movement and its numbers are in constant flux. These two dimensions of the structure of support for the revolutionary movement can be imagined as something resembling a telescope, whose inner and smallest section (the hard core) is always fully extended to the heights of maximum commitment, but whose surrounding sections extend or retract according to the ups and downs of the situation. It is the latter groups to which "rational actor" calculations are more applicable. During the Tet Offensive, as we shall see, the width of the circles of support surrounding the "hard core" expanded, and the level of activism briefly surged to the height of the hard core itself. Over time, as the level of activism of the outer groups fell, the size of these groups also contracted, with the conditional supporters dropping away from the movement altogether, and many in the other groups fell into a lower category of commitment to the revolution.

The width and scope of each section of the "telescope" also varies with the situation. The inner core is generally fairly small and consistent in size. The immediate surrounding segment of lower-level full-time members of the resistance is somewhat more variable, as the "infrastructure" is diminished by casualties and disruption of revolutionary-controlled areas. "Backbone elements" were especially prominent in the early 1960s when the movement was expanding. The "backbone elements" were also essential to the "popular associations" which mobilized civilians support for the revolution. During the subsequent years there was little reference to this group in the interviews, and it appears that this group became smaller and less active. Revolutionary sympathizers, the next surrounding segment, fluctuate even more in both numbers and level of participation, and the outer circle of conditional or opportunistic supporters are generally mobilizable only during periods of revolutionary upswing.

The "telescope" image measures only observable behavior. Assessing attitudes and loyalties—which are themselves different things—can be even more complex. Villagers' attitudes in 1966–67 reflected a sharp drop in their confidence that the war was going well for the revolution. The progression of this changing attitude as reflected in the interviews roughly paralleled the progress of the GVN pacification program, and probably was not the same in villages outside the pacification target area, such as those in northern Cai Be and Cai Lay. Even in the villages that were hit hardest by pacification, the fact that peasant support for the revolution dropped off when survival became the dominant issue in the countryside does not necessarily mean that loyalties had changed. In this sense attitudes (including loyalty) cannot be inferred from behavior (such as refusing to carry out revolutionary tasks or leaving the village against cadre orders).

In addition, no generalization can account for all the villagers. Here again we should note that a decline in support for the revolution did not necessarily mean an expansion of the GVN support base, at least in terms of people who were willing to make substantial sacrifices for the Saigon government. But, as we shall see, the GVN proved surprisingly resilient in facing the challenge of the Tet Offensive, and did in fact expand its base of support, largely from the ranks of those whose interests had always been opposed to the revolution, but who were not galvanized into making a political choice until the shock of Tet.

Despite the fact that much of the revolution's lost support during this period was at least temporarily revived in the period during and immediately after the Tet offensive, the picture of declining support for the revolution in 1966 and 1967 does, in fact, presage a long-term trend. We can see in retrospect that the natural class base for the revolution was beginning to erode with the "middle peasantization" of the countryside, discussed in earlier chapters. In the early 1960s there were sharp cleavages among villagers, based largely on class, although there was no uniform pattern of class structure among the villages of My Tho.

It might be expected that the wealthier peasants would be quicker to jump ship than the poorer peasants. A hamlet Farmers' Association cadre from Binh Duc said, "Before, when the GVN was weak in this area, the families which were angry with the Front as well as the upper middle peasants and rich peasants had to keep quiet and to resign themselves to pretend that they were eager to support the Front. Apart from these families, there are also a certain number of families whose relatives worked for the GVN. These families had to do the same and, therefore, we reported that 90 percent of the population of the area supported the Front. At present, the tide has changed. The GVN has become stronger in this area, while the Front has been getting weaker. This is a good opportunity for the angry families to act against the Front—secretly, of course. They will certainly give information about the Front's activities to the GVN and become supporters of the GVN. That's why I told you that the percentage of supporters of the Front has greatly diminished" [DT174]. Here it is the class status of the peasant which is the controlling factor, and it is the wealthier peasants who can now (discretely) express their opposition to the revolution.

However, the exodus of the wealthier peasants from the villages sometimes inadvertently resolved the class tensions which the revolution had manipulated. In Xuan Son village, "there had been some problems between the social classes in 1964–65 because the Front intentionally stimulated the hatred of poor peasants toward the rich peasants and landlords. Now [1967] there are no more problems because there are no more rich peasants and landlords" [DT293]. Without land to offer and class tensions to exploit, the revolution was left only with appeals to community solidarity and patriotism. Strong revolutionary villages now became weaker because they were the main targets of the bombing and shelling, and therefore, like Xuan Son, increasingly depopulated, and also because there was no longer anything tangible and immediate in terms of benefits that the revolution could offer its dwindling base of supporters.

Obstacles to Mobilizing Villagers in 1967

The obstacles to mobilizing the villagers were as much situational as psychological. The cadres were simply unable to gather groups of villagers together. This meant that as the popular associations collapsed, there were no auxiliary mechanisms for political mobilization, and the leading village cadres had to go laboriously from house to house for every task, from indoctrination to taxes, while also trying to evade the increasingly frequent U.S. and GVN operations. Communications with the district were also made much more difficult, and the village cadres began to feel an increasing sense of isolation. And, of course, they were no longer protected and supported by the local and main force units as before.

Some cadres in the most intensively patrolled villages around the U.S. base still managed to hang on. A Long Hung Party committee member said, "The activities of the Front cadres in my village are now very limited. All the cadres have retreated to Ap Tay hamlet in Kim Son village except for a certain number of cadres having a high fighting spirit, who have been assigned by the village Party committee to stay in the village to harass the Allied fighting forces and assassinate those villagers who show a friendly attitude toward the pacification force. These cadres who are staying in the village exploit families sympathizing with the Front to build secret bunkers to hide themselves all day long, with food supplied by those families, and they carry out their sabotage and terroristic activities at night.

This can be done because of the lack of searches by the pacification forces in the village" [DT185]. The intensive patrols kept the cadres off balance, made it impossible for them to hold meetings among themselves, let alone with the villagers, and disrupted communications between higher and lower levels. The cadres, however, were still able to find ways of hiding and operating in the village.

Increasing difficulties in mobilizing peasant support made life much more difficult for the cadres. To begin with, cadres now had to perform some of the onerous labor tasks that they used to assign to the villagers. In Diem Hy, the cadres were "angry at having to do the labor which they had been previously been exempted from. Many times we reported our dissatisfaction to the village chapter, but it replied that we just had to try to endure it" [DT241]. These additional duties, piled on top of demands that already made the life of a village cadre very hard, created some family conflicts. "Seeing that I had to be out almost every night, my wife got mad and grumbled a lot. Once she simply couldn't restrain herself and shouted at me, 'You and your comrades can go to hell! If you want to follow them, why don't you just leave once and for all?' I felt very depressed whenever she complained about my activities. She was not alone among the cadres' wives in complaining about their husband's zeal; all the other cadre wives did also. It's easy to understand why they were unhappy. Whenever I called on a cadre friend, I never failed to notice angry expressions on his wife's face. My friends would get the same look from my wife" [DT241].

In Thanh Phu village (Cai Lay) the remaining cadres evidently tried to carry on as before, despite the fact that they no longer had a support base to perform routine tasks. "All the popular associations have disintegrated, and yet the village Party committee refuses to disband them. It still tries to maintain the pretense that these associations still exist and thus refuses to accept reality. For this reason, its directives don't conform to reality. For example, it still orders the hamlet Farmers' Association Ban Can Su to motivate the Liberation Youth Association and the Farmers' Association to send volunteers to serve as civilian laborers to carry the dead and wounded from the battlefield. What's more, the bombing, shelling, and military operations have paralyzed all activities in the village. Sometimes the cadres flee from the village for an entire week, without daring to come back to perform their missions. Generally speaking, 90 percent of the Front's infrastructure at the hamlet level has disintegrated. At the village level, there are only a few village Party committee members to provide leadership, and without the people to support them they can't do anything. Only the mobile Front military units are still able to carry out their missions" [DT229].

Despite Difficulties, Revolutionary Military Operations Continue in 1967

The major problems of the revolution in 1967 were caused not by GVN pacification programs, however, but by the ferocity of the war itself. Depopulation of the revolutionary areas had been going on since 1965, and severely crippled the operations of the revolution. U.S. military operations not only intensified the dangers and accelerated the depopulation, they also created even larger and more frequent waves as they passed through the villages. This was not the leisurely cruise ship of the ARVN operations during the early 1960s, which might hit a given area once or twice in a year, but a succession of power boats that would come through a given area many times. Hardly had one set of waves subsided when a new sortie came through.

Concentrating on the pacification centers of Tam Hiep and Binh Duc also diverted the ARVN from challenging the revolution in its base areas. Despite the massive firepower of the U.S. Ninth Division, and the erosion of revolutionary control around the main pacification areas in Chau Thanh district in the eastern part of the province, the main force units were still able to operate in the 20/7 area. During the increasingly frequent encounters with U.S. troops, the concentrated battalions generally held their own. The cases of the 263rd and 261st Battalions illustrate the military stalemate which was achieved. On the one hand, the U.S. and GVN troops were not able to dislodge main force units from a key area of the province. On the other hand, the operational area of these units was substantially reduced due to the increased dangers of movement, and the support that they could offer to cadres, guerrillas, and villages targeted for pacification was accordingly diminished.

Increasing Difficulties in 1967 Cause the Party to Turn its Attention to the Urban Areas

The population hemorrhage from the liberated areas had started in 1964 in a few places, accelerated in 1965, and become widespread in My Tho in 1966. In many places, part of the village population had been able to hang on by living out in the rice fields, away from their houses in the treelines, which were now targets for U.S.–GVN air and artillery because they also served as bases for the guerrillas and concentrated units. Now even this expedient would no longer guarantee survival, and only a few hundred people remained in villages like Cam Son at the eye of the storm in the 20/7 zone, while the rest took refuge in squalid refugee camps. Losing their population base was a major problem for the revolution.

The carefully crafted pacification programs in places such as Binh Duc and Tam Hiep had been generally successful, but the vast security resources required to displace the cadres and guerrillas from these few villages meant that this approach could not be used on a large scale. Perhaps without conscious design, the U.S. forces, led by the Ninth Infantry Division, hit on another solution to the problem: drain the pond to catch the fish. Whether or not depopulation was a deliberate strategy, it became increasingly the consequence of the military operations of American and GVN forces in My Tho.

For their part, the revolutionary strategists also began a shift in approach. Having failed to defend their base areas sufficiently to retain the population, the revolutionaries decided to turn the tables by attacking their enemies not just on the periphery, but in their very "lair." The 1968 Tet Offensive was designed with a very broad strategic objective in mind: to demonstrate to Washington decision makers that the conflict was stalemated, and that the war could not be won militarily. But though the nationwide attacks on urban centers in the Tet Offensive were designed for a larger purpose, some of the local strategy in My Tho had already been headed in this direction. Attacks on district towns were attempted in 1967, but more often a lower-cost tactic of mortar shellings of district towns and the My Tho province capital were favored in order to shake up rear areas of their opponents and take some of the military pressure off the liberated areas by forcing the U.S. and GVN to pay more attention to defending urban areas against small special operations and mortar units.

Attacking the urban areas also served the purpose of causing peasants who moved there for safety to reconsider the benefits of living in a potential target zone. In Thanh Phu (Cai Lay), "The Front also threatened those who lived near towns and cities, telling them that they should return to the village because the situation might change. When the Front liberated these towns and cities, it wouldn't protect their lives and property." Here again, the logic of the Tet Offensive attacks on towns and cities is prefigured. Prior to Tet, however, the warnings did not have much impact, despite the increased shellings of GVN areas. "The cadres said what they pleased," said the head of the Thanh Phu village Farmers' Association, but "none of the villagers paid any attention to their propaganda line" [DT203].

Conclusion

Civilian morale was clearly at a low ebb by 1967. The village Farmers' Association chief from Thanh Phu (Cai Lay), one of the strongest revolutionary villages in the province, said that the people were too dispirited by the prospect of reverting to a drawn-out guerrilla war to cope with the U.S. troops, and that the cadres began to lose their credibility.

> .... in 1965 the Front had to announce that the Americans were deliberately transforming the conflict into a limited war, that they were bringing satellite troops into South Vietnam and increasing their war potential, and for this reason the Front would have to revert to guerrilla warfare and it would fight for ten or twenty more years until it could carry out a general offensive and uprising. At that time the people realized that the Front would never tell the truth about anything—from the length of time it would take it to liberate the south to its tax policy, its draft policy, and so on.
>
> Each year the cadres told the people about the tax policy: "Please make an effort. This is the last year of our struggle, because this year we will carry out a general offensive, bring the war to an end, and achieve the revolution." The draft policy was getting harsher, and putting a heavier demand on the people each year. From having enough to eat, the people came to lack everything. Now they have become exhausted and paralyzed in body and spirit. Gradually, the people lost their determination, then they lost their zealousness, then they stopped responding to the Front's appeals and the participating in the Front's activities, and then they finally abandoned the Front to move into the GVN areas.
>
> This unfavorable and dangerous situation deflated the Front's movement, and weakened it further and further. Since it couldn't motivate the peasants, the Front naturally disintegrated and collapsed. Besides, no matter how much propaganda the Front made, the people remained frightened of the war, so it was unrealistic of the Front to force them to stand the fighting and make sacrifices for ten or twenty more years. This was a bad political move, and the people gradually left the Front for the GVN areas. The Front became isolated. It won't be able to find a way out unless the North helps it with lots of money and manpower [DT203].

This bleak view of the revolution and its prospects on the eve of the Tet Offensive is, of course, the perspective of a cadre who had just undergone a personal crisis of belief, but it is not unrepresentative of the interview accounts, and is certainly consistent with the general picture of My Tho between 1965 and 1967 presented in the interviews. It suggests that the Tet Offensive may in some way have been a response to the problems outlined in this cadre's analysis, and an attempt to shore up the credibility of the revolution in areas like My Tho. It also correctly forecast the importance of support from North Vietnam in the last phase of the war. Still, as the following chapter shows, the revolution in My Tho had resources and residual support that this account would not have predicted. As later chapters will discuss, it was not the losses in the costly Tet Offensive that ultimately made the Northern forces decisive to the outcome in the province and in the country, but the sustained U.S.–GVN counteroffensive that followed Tet, especially in 1969 and 1970. Finally, as the concluding chapters will discuss, it is possible that after the U.S. withdrawal, a revival of the guerrilla movement in My Tho and the Mekong Delta would have enabled the war to be concluded in much the same way as it nearly had been in 1965.

Still, the military and political changes that had taken place in My Tho and the delta during the 1965–67 period would have forced some change of strategy and tactics even if the Tet Offensive had not occurred. Despite the heavy losses and constant pressure it suffered during the spring and summer of 1967, the 514th Battalion, which had received an upgraded set of more demanding offensive missions in 1966, had been told at the time that "in the future the unit would have to attack towns and cities, and use tactics previously reserved for regular forces and, in particular, would have to carry out street fighting" [DT190]. This reorientation of mission was determined well before the Tet Offensive, but it shows that the province and military region were already experimenting with the idea that the best defense was a good offense, and that—rather than try to protect liberated areas with its "umbrella defense"—the concentrated units might do better by forcing the GVN to defend its own rear areas, thus relieving pressure on the countryside.

The year 1967 closed with the revolutionary units battered but intact, the civilian cadres increasingly stymied by loss of access to population, and a demoralized civilian population increasingly unwilling to participate in risky activities. Even with the hindsight of history, knowing the next act of the drama, this does not seem an inaccurate picture of the My Tho situation at year's end. The Tet Offensive showed graphically that this was not the only reality, however, and that underneath this surface view vast and unseen forces were stirring.

14

Tet: The Untold Story of the "General Offensive and General Uprising"

Confident that the war situation was well in hand, South Vietnamese President Nguyen Van Thieu went to celebrate the traditional lunar new year holiday of Tet in his wife's native town of My Tho. The special security precautions that normally accompanied his movements around the country did not indicate any particular problems in My Tho, and Thieu settled in to enjoy his family holiday.[1] The U.S. advisors in the Mekong Delta were equally convinced that the military situation was under control. In December 1967 plans indicating a major attack on the city were captured, but when by late January 1968 it had not taken place, the Government of the Republic of Vietnam (GVN) forces and the U.S. advisors concluded that the assault had been compromised by the loss of the plans and therefore called off. On the eve of Tet 1968, the United States and its Saigon allies were confident. "Three weeks before the Tet Offensive, Brigadier General William R. Desobry held a farewell news conference after eighteen months as U.S. military advisory chief in the delta. Desobry said that the Viet Cong forces were 'poorly motivated, poorly trained' and that the South Vietnamese Army 'has the upper hand completely.'"[2]

When the Tet attack by the revolutionaries hit My Tho on the night of January 30–31, 1968, only the presence of special detachments providing security for President Thieu near the province compound, and some tactical mistakes by the attacking revolutionary forces, saved the city from being overrun. Only on the second day of the offensive, when President Thieu was evacuated to Saigon by helicopter, did the attacking forces become aware of his presence in the town.[3] This was one of many unforseen circumstances which undermined the Party's offensive plan. The two attacking regiments were driven out of the city after three days by a determined defense of the Army of the Republic of Vietnam (ARVN) and by province forces and, ultimately, by devastating U.S. firepower. Of Ben Tre, the province capital south of My Tho across the Mekong River, a U.S. major reportedly remarked, "It became necessary to destroy the town to save it," but the same might have been said of My Tho. The U.S. advisory team reported after the first week of the offensive: "An estimated 25% of the city was burned, 5,000 residences have been destroyed and 25% of the people are homeless. The psychological impact of a calamity of this importance cannot be measured so close to the event, but it is obviously enormous."[4]

In the excitement, shock, and turmoil of the nationwide revolutionary offensive, and the natural focus on the major cities, what was happening in the countryside went largely unreported. By the time the situation had stabilized in late spring of 1968, the extraordinary turnabout that had occurred in the villages of My Tho had subsided. However, perhaps the most remarkable aspect of the Tet Offensive in My Tho was that the demoralized and increasingly passive civilian population participated energetically, and often enthusi-astically, in tasks which they had shunned during the previous year. This view from the villages is the main missing dimension of most accounts of this critical turning point of the war. Another important point raised by the Tet Offensive in My Tho is what it can tell us about how the local situation in the province fit into the "big picture" of the war.

U.S. Military Reports on the Situation Prior to the Tet Offensive

Despite the arrival of U.S. troops and the intensified military and pacification operations, 75 percent of the hamlets in My Tho were still under predominantly revolutionary control in December 1967. Beneath the surface of an apparent drop-off in numbers and effective-ness of revolutionary forces in My Tho and a sharp reduction of military activity in some of its main military units during 1967, the basic structure remained intact. As events would soon show, the appearance of decline was deceiving. Not only were the familiar forces of the 514th and 261st Battalions undergoing refitting for combat, additional battalions were being formed. Despite the casualties and defections of civilian cadres, the number of Party members in the province had risen to 6,000.[5] This compares with the 4,000 Party members at the time of the Geneva Accords in 1954, 1,500 in 1961, and 7,000 in 1973.

Some indications of unusual activity prior were picked up and recorded in the U.S. Advisory Team's monthly report. "The VC had laid extensive plans for an attack on My Tho to have been accomplished prior to TET to bolster their propaganda efforts. However, due to the discovery of these plans through captured documents found on the bodies of four high ranking VC (one the Battalion commander of the 514th), and due to intensified RF-PF (Regional Force-Popular Force local military) operations in Chau Thanh district, these plans did not materialize."

A much more ominous indication of things to come was a document captured by a U.S. Special Forces detachment not far from the Stone Buddha Pagoda on January 28, 1968, with a roster of politically active GVN supporters in My Tho city, complete with home addresses, dated December 30, 1967, and another document dated January 6, 1968, with a full account of the activities of GVN province officials and police.[6] Sometime in Decem-ber 1967 the deputy head of the Region Military Intelligence Section was captured during a sweep operation. It is unclear how much he revealed to the Saigon authorities. A postwar revolutionary history simply states that he "talked" (*khai bao*).[7] However, this interroga-tion apparently provided detailed though incomplete and misleading information on the identities and roles of some of the units which would soon participate in the assault on My Tho city.

It appears that the apparent intelligence windfall for the United States and Saigon of capturing the second ranking revolutionary military intelligence officer in the central Mekong Delta the month before the Tet Offensive was counteracted by the incomplete and prob-ably deliberately misleading information he provided to his adversaries. As summarized by the U.S. advisor's report, this interrogation made no mention at all of an impending large scale attack (let alone the idea that the province capital would be the target) or even a significant change in missions. The units mentioned were portrayed as intent on attack-ing "friendly bivouacs" or on "defensive missions." No mention was made of the clone units such as the 261B Battalion which was part of the Dong Thap Regiment, or the 514B, units, or the fact that the 267th and 269th were probably clone units whose original counterparts were attacking Saigon and its surrounding areas. Nor was mention made of units such as the province battalion of Kien Tuong and a clone unit of the Ben Tre province battalion which were being sent to My Tho for the Tet attack. The questions raised by the document captured on the body of the slain commander of the 514th Battalion with attack plans for My Tho city do not seem to have been reflected in the information provided by the MR2 military intelligence officer, who may have successfully thrown his interrogators off the track by providing some limited information already known to them, and putting it in the context of a "business-as-usual" approach to military operations in the near future.

One reason for the failure to anticipate the Tet attacks in My Tho was the general consensus about the diminished military capabilities of the revolutionary forces. Not only did the information from prisoners and defectors suggest that these forces were considerably understrength, but they had been on the defensive for most of the previous year and inactive for extended periods of time. These units had encountered severe problems in recruitment and resupply, their operational area had been reduced, especially around My Tho city and the eastern part of the province, and the aggressive U.S. operations in their base areas seemed to have thrown them off balance. Increasingly, it was difficult to avoid detection, and the main force units paid a heavy price whenever they were uncovered.

Issues Raised by the Tet Offensive

How, then, did these battered units manage to pull off the totally unexpected feat of penetrating and occupying part of My Tho city? This is an important question, but the even more remarkable fact is one that went completely unnoticed at the time, and even decades later is still largely ignored. Unlike Saigon and other cities, including My Tho itself, where a "General Uprising" was called for but never materialized, nearly the entire rural population of My Tho—for whatever reasons—was immediately and effectively mobilized in support of the offensive. Taxes, which had been increasingly hard to squeeze out of the peasants, were now paid in advance. Civilian laborers who had evaded the cadres before now performed hazardous duties, sometimes for months on end. Young men who had escaped the draft now signed up in large numbers, as did many women. Guerrillas who had resisted being sent out of their villages now willingly left for the heavy fighting around My Tho and the district towns.

In short, a *rural* uprising did take place in My Tho. It did not last long. By the time of the second offensive in May 1968, the surge of support for the revolution had subsided, and was progressively ground down by the high costs of being involved in the heaviest fighting of the war, which lasted through 1969. By 1970 much of the province was "pacified," and by 1971 many people had concluded that the war in the Mekong Delta was nearly over. The deactivation of this massive, if brief, show of popular support for the revolution will be described in subsequent chapters. However, in order to understand both the nature of support for the revolution and how it changed over time, it is vitally important to understand this little-noted "general uprising" in the countryside during early 1968.

As far as My Tho is concerned, the most important issue raised by the Tet Offensive is whether the heavy toll on their own troops and cadres, and the loss of territory and population in the Mekong Delta and elsewhere, forced Hanoi's leadership to attempt a risky gamble that a go-for-broke offensive would speed up the resolution of the war and stem the erosion of the revolutionary movement. This was the theory favored by General Westmoreland and U.S. National Security Advisor Walt Rostow, who felt that Tet was a desperate roll of the dice, forced on Hanoi by the realization that they were losing the war, and time was not on their side. The extent to which the Tet Offensive was influenced by Hanoi's perception that the war was gradually grinding down the revolutionary forces and that it had to be brought to a head because of unacceptable attrition is one of the still-unresolved historiographic problems of the Vietnam war. The evidence cited below of complete confidence in victory at the COSVN level would not indicate that Tet was a desperation move.

Certainly the top revolutionary leadership did recognize the great difficulties the movement was encountering in places like My Tho, but there is no explicit evidence that this was a major factor in the Tet decision. As the previous chapters have shown, the revolutionary movement in My Tho had suffered significant setbacks, and this was no doubt the case in many other areas. However, reality is one thing, and perceptions of reality are quite another. Lower-level cadres who had to struggle with the problems of carrying out policies in increasingly unfavorable circumstances were painfully aware of these difficulties, though their more insulated superiors at higher levels did not seem to acknowledge this, and continued to press for attainment of unrealistic goals. It is also certain that the civilian population and many in the revolutionary movement itself were weary of the war. Yet the fact remains that the revolutionary movement in My Tho, depleted as it was on the eve of the Tet Offensive, still controlled 75 percent of the province and was rebuilding its military forces to a level surpassing previous years.

When and How was the Tet Decision Relayed
to South Vietnam and My Tho?

One of the mysteries of the planning for the Tet Offensive is how much (and when) the lower levels such as those in My Tho knew about the specific nature of the plan, and the extent of changes that may have taken place in the basic plan between June 1967, its formal transmittal to the South in October 1967, and the final Hanoi Politburo resolution of December 1967. Not only is the exact evolution of the Tet decision still unclear nearly four decades after the event, there is also still some confusion about when the Tet plan was actually transmitted to the South, and to provinces such as My Tho.

Stepped up recruiting and intensified mobilization in the villages in the summer of 1967 indicate that My Tho province was already preparing in a general way for the Tet Offensive before COSVN received the Tet directive from Hanoi in October 1967, but the specific objectives discussed in a Region directive in September were not yet connected directly to the Tet plan of coordinated offensive against major towns and cities. "Le Hong Thang"—probably a pseudonym for Sau Duong, the Region 2 Party secretary—sent a letter to My Tho and other provinces on September 2, stating that "the time is ripe to totally defeat the third enemy dry season offensive." Therefore, "in compliance with the Central Committee and COSVN strategic plan," a decision has been made to concentrate on "stepping up a general attack in the Winter–Spring campaign of 1967–68," whose primary objective is to "create favorable conditions which will lead to the seizure of power" in South Vietnam. To achieve this, Region 2 will make special efforts "to conduct concentrated attacks with an ever higher tempo and an ever larger scale to destroy large units of enemy forces and drive them on the defensive." In addition, armed forces in the region were directed to "cut lines of communication, maintain heavy pressure on cities and towns, encircle enemy military bases, step up violent and repeated raids on enemy command posts, logistical installations, and also isolate small enemy elements to facilitate their destruction." The goal was to ensure that "no area would be safe for the enemy." The Winter–Spring campaign, said the region secretary, "is a decisive phase for final victory."[8] Another, earlier summary of this letter by U.S. intelligence noted that the objective of these attacks was to "frustrate the pacification program, to support the people's uprising, and to crush the enemy's forces."[9]

The "Winter–Spring Offensive" and Aims of the Tet Offensive in My Tho

In late September, the My Tho province military affairs committee issued a "top secret" directive outlining the tasks for the 1967–68 Winter–Spring campaign in the province. The objective was to "score the greatest victories," which would lead to an "important turn" of the war situation, "thus contributing greatly to the common effort to defeat the U.S. imperialists in a relatively short period of time." Guerrilla war was to be developed to the "next higher step," and military forces should "achieve coordination for concentrated attacks to completely destroy the enemy unit in each attack." Emphasis would be placed on "attacks on enemy rear base areas, cities and towns, and communication lines."[10]

Chin Hai, who had replaced the ailing Chin Om as My Tho province Party secretary,[11] wrote a draft of this directive on September 25, 1967. It referred to a Resolution from the Party Central Committee, and directives from COSVN and Region 2 which would be further explained in "supplementary reorientation" indoctrination sessions. In addition to the internal Party indoctrination, the troops and cadres were to pass on to the civilian population the idea that something big was about to happen. "If we want to have a mass general offensive and uprising movement we must exert ourselves to the limit in paying attention to the mission of spreading the word and mobilizing [co dong] the people." My Tho province should "go all out in focusing on the buildup of troop strength and maintaining troop strength, and each echelon must take responsibility for this. This mission cannot be taken lightly . . . [hiatus in original] in order to respond to the requirements for attacking the enemy in a timely fashion." Chin Hai's draft message concluded that the political mission outlined "stems from these new requirements imposed by higher levels. The coming period will require very intense and urgent [khan truong] efforts to respond fully to the requirements on time and at the right time. . . . [hiatus in original] In the coming period, the revolution cannot wait for us to organize indoctrination sessions of the type that drag on inconclusively."[12]

In conjunction with attempts to harass and disrupt the GVN presidential election on September 3, 1967, several district towns were mortared. So was My Tho city—for the first time in the war, according to the province U.S. senior advisor's report of September 30, 1967. The main target of this accelerated activity against GVN-controlled areas would be Highway 4. Although the main Tet objective of My Tho province was the attack on the province capital, from the perspective of the region and higher levels, the main strategic contribution My Tho could make in the period before, during, and after Tet was shutting down the critical lifeline of Highway 4 connecting the Mekong Delta with Saigon. U.S. military intelligence captured a draft of the September My Tho Winter–Spring offensive plan, and concluded that the "main objective appears to be disruption of communications along Highway 4." The document itself stated that the "Objective of the province during the forthcoming period is to meet requirements of sabotaging lines of communication during the Winter–Spring offensive in compliance with orders from higher headquarters and from the Military Affairs Committee of My Tho province."[13]

An appraisal of the success of these directives passed on through a general indoctrination on the situation through December 1967 concluded that, with a string of "bitter failures," the "enemy had to give up their plans to search for and destroy VC main forces in the Mekong Delta. Concurrently, their intention to clear lines of communication was foiled. In October 1967 the U.S. and GVN planned a large scale operation in My Tho province," with elements of four divisions to relieve pressure on Highway 4. "However, their plan was smashed by our forces. Violent attacks were launched on cities and towns throughout the Military Region and the enemy was compelled to withdraw their troops in operations to rescue urban areas where they were pinned down."[14] Offensive operations against the towns and cities would undermine rural pacification by pulling troops out of the countryside.

My Tho's Preparations for the Tet Offensive

The shift in focus to the cities and GVN rear bases, the foundation of Saigon's control system, required that the revolution's relatively weak position in the urban areas be urgently strengthened. This effort began prior to the October Tet order to COSVN, and even the June Hanoi Tet decision. Until this time the province capital of My Tho had been a backwater of the conflict. It was a nearly uncontested area of GVN control, and there had been little overt revolutionary action in or against My Tho city. A captured security directive dated July 15, 1967, noted the results of surveillance on the local U.S. Central Intelligence Agency (CIA) office in My Tho, along with GVN security activities, and warned that the influx of refugees from liberated areas to GVN-controlled areas was providing a valuable source of information to the GVN on revolutionary organizations. The list included in this document revealed that the number of urban agents operating in My Tho was not impressive, even allowing for the fact that the list may have been incomplete. My Tho city had a total of fifteen agents divided among four unspecified missions. Go Cong town had a single agent, and the towns of Cai Lay and Cai Be had three and six agents, respectively, for "mission A2."

Evidently these agents were not very effective. "The above cadre especially those in charge of mission A3, failed to collect information on units and agencies and to dominate GVN local administrative personnel. As a result, document states that in July, August, and September 1967 the Security Section of My Tho will implement the provisions of the order from N2 [Military Region 2] under the guidance of SAN2 [security section of Military Region 2] to improve the capability of these cadre."[15] From this document, it is apparent that the intelligence capability of the revolution in the urban areas of My Tho needed considerable expansion and improvement. According to the province Party history, there were four Party chapters in My Tho city, thirty Youth Group members, 200 members of revolutionary popular organizations, and 500 sympathizers in the city, along with an armed urban unit of seventy people. The Party chapters in the villages surrounding the province capital were said to have twenty-five to thirty Party members, the village guerrillas ranged from six to twelve, and the "organized civilians" 200 per village.[16] A slightly different account comes from the province military history. According to this source there were only about twenty Party members in My Tho city attached directly to the city Party committee, along with fifty activist sympathizers, although this study claims that there were three companies of urban armed units with a strength of 120 to 140 each. These units were responsible for the four sectors or wards of the city. Given the fact that the city Party committee was stationed in My Hanh Dong and Nhi Binh villages, some dozen kilometers from the city itself, it is open to question how effective their organizational preparations for the offensive were.[17]

In 1967, the Party raised the status of My Tho city in its territorial organization from a mere province capital to an autonomous city on a par with Can Tho and Hue, and began a major strengthening of the city revolutionary organization in October. A city cadre said proudly that My Tho even "surpassed those two cities because of its revolutionary tradition" [DT313]. This cadre said:

> From the French period to the present, there had always been workers' movements, etc., in My Tho province. Even though these movements had not been strong, they had some repercussions. Besides, the population of My Tho had been swollen by the large influx of refugees. These people understood the policies of both the GVN and the Front. They had, to some extent, enjoyed the favors of the Front, or benefited from the Front's policies. So they still had some sympathy for the Revolution. These were the favorable factors for the Revolution, and the Front was determined to occupy the areas on the edge of the city of My Tho at all costs in order to create an opening to the vast liberated areas outside, and bring the influence of the Revolution surging into the city. Only in this way would the Front be able to build up its infrastructure organizations and rely on these organization to carry out fierce phases of assaults, in line with the balance of forces in the city. Previously, the Front—and in particular, the region Party committee of Region 2—left the city in the hands of the city cadres, and let them do whatever they could, because the region didn't grant the city the strategic importance that it deserved. Beginning in 1967, when the question of taking over the government in My Tho was raised, the region realized that it would have to take over the government right in the city, because if it only seized power in the countryside it wouldn't be able to completely finish off the GVN. Raising My Tho City to the level of a city Party committee was designed to prepare and create a new strategic position. Starting from the middle of 1967, the military forces and the specialized branches got under way to carry out the mission [DT313].

At this time, in mid-1967, the military region's main interest in My Tho province was still in its potential for controlling or disrupting major lines of communication, especially Highway 4. This decision of the region to upgrade the importance of My Tho province capital did, however, result in a major infusion of cadres to work in and around My Tho city in 1967. Muoi Ha, one of the top three cadres in My Tho province, and head of the military affairs section of the province, was transferred to become the head of the My Tho city Party committee [DT308]. The city cadre mentioned above was himself detached to My Tho, and claims (probably with considerable exaggeration) that the number of cadres in the city was raised from twenty to over 1,000. Many of these cadres were, however, unable to actually operate inside the city itself [DT313].

In October, after COSVN received the Tet order, it was passed on to the leaders of the provinces around South Vietnam, who started to make their own detailed plans. The code clerk of the My Tho province Party committee recalled that message traffic in the few months before the Tet Offensive was three to four times heavier than usual. The daily messages were as long as thirty or forty typewritten pages. This heavy flow of messages continued until the offensive began [DT337]. Despite the fact that these extraordinary battle preparations were taking place all over South Vietnam, even the signals and communication people working for the Southern Command at COSVN did not know the exact date and purpose of the attack until two hours before the offensive started.[18]

Some village cadres reported receiving the "hit the streets" *(xuong duong)* directive in October [DT386]. Documentary evidence suggests that this was almost certainly not the Tet order itself, but a general phase of mobilization whose ultimate purpose had not yet been revealed. The terminology used to name this directive was taken from a recently coined slang phrase in the political vocabulary of Vietnam that had originated in the urban struggles of Saigon in the 1964–66 period. "Hit the streets" referred to the mass Buddhist and student demonstrations in the streets of Saigon. In the rural setting, "hit the road" toward My Tho in support of the military attacks at Tet would be a more accurate rendition of what *xuong duong* required of the villagers, but at that time they could not have known this. The word *duong* could mean any road, street, or path, urban or rural, but the origins of the phrase *xuong duong* were definitely urban, and it is probably better translated as "hit the streets" to suggest this implication. The use of a quite recent term coming from the cities shows the fallout effect of the political discourse at the national level in the countryside. The fact that a number of interviews mentioned this term suggests not only that the province Party leaders used this phrase to describe the first wave of Tet indoctrination, but that it resonated with the villagers as well. Although the phrase had come into currency even in the countryside, and the peasants knew it was a term of the cities, its implication of an urban uprising was evidently not clearly understood in the villages at the time.

In Thanh Phu (Cai Lay) village and hamlet cadres studied what was called the "hit the streets reorientation" for two days, sometime in October (according to an interviewee's recollection in 1971). "There were five of us at the meeting in the hamlet. By order of the " 'hit the streets directive,' " Each hamlet unit leader had to recheck to see how many hamlet guerrillas there were in each hamlet, and how many of these could be transferred to higher levels—to be sure we had enough strength to supply the needs of the battlefield in case something unexpected happened. In my hamlet there were eight guerrillas, but I promised that we would be able to recruit twelve more to get a full complement of twenty. This was based on the number of youth still in the hamlet" [DT386]. In the large village of Thanh Phu (Cai Lay) there were still nearly 100 youth who had not joined either side, and several dozen of these were in this cadre's own hamlet.

In addition to an order to conduct a census of military-age youth, which was also mentioned in several other interviews, the October hamlet indoctrination also specifically mentioned the prospect of a major development in the war situation. "The main part of the 'hit the streets' resolution was that the situation was a very good and favorable situation, and that an unexpected coup might occur, and we would await the order of the Front for the overthrow. That's all they said. Because of this we would have to recheck our forces to be certain we had enough strength if this situation occurred. If we sent the young men with enough strength up to the concentrated troops, would there be enough to replace them? That's as far as they went" [DT386]. The October–November preparation at the hamlet level gave the people and cadres an inkling of a major mobilization, but it was still a conditional possibility, ostensibly dependent on some event in the cities such as a coup and, therefore, not a situation whose timing could be controlled by the Front. The precise outline of the Tet Offensive, or even its general timing and urban orientation, were not clearly spelled out. However, the village cadres were confident. "They said the situation was ripe, and all we had to do was wait for it to happen. When it did, we would grasp the opportunity and seize victory and peace" [DT386].

The province itself probably did not get a specific picture of the Tet Offensive until late November. Even then, the full plan and the exact dates may not have been spelled out. The official Party history of My Tho is vague about the order for the Tet Offensive and says only that "Carrying out the [December 1967] Resolution of the Politburo and the Resolution of the Party Central Committee's 14th Plenum [January 1968], which contained the plan to initiate an offensive and uprising in the Spring of 1968, the Region Committee chose My Tho city to be the main focal point of the offensive and uprising."[19] This suggests that political decisions and operational plans prior to January 1968 did not lay out the full scope of the offensive.

Rehearsals for the Tet Offensive

In November, the province succeeded in a daring attack on the district town of Cai Lay, in what was—in retrospect—clearly a preparation for Tet in several ways. First, it was part of the strategy of putting pressure on the "urban areas." Second, it was a test run of techniques of attacking cities and towns. Third, it was a test of the ability to coordinate simultaneous multiple attacks. Finally, it was possibly a deception operation, to keep attention focused on the western part of the province, while three battalions were preparing to move in for the attack on My Tho province capital. A platoon leader from the 263rd Battalion who participated in the attack was told that the main mission of his unit was to destroy the Regional Force camp in Cai Lay district. "On the afternoon of November 3rd, my company held a meeting between the company command staff and the various platoon leaders. We were instructed that the upcoming attack on Cai Lay district headquarters aimed at scoring a military victory at Highway 4 in order to create a more favorable political atmosphere in favor of the Front, by cutting off the traffic between Saigon and the delta" [DT261].

His unit was also told that another big unit would join in the attack with them, but not the identity of the unit (it was the 261st Battalion). "However, we knew from experience that it would be a big attack. Whenever we were told that we had to coordinate with other units, we sensed that the stakes would be important" [DT261]. After a mortar attack on the town, and a daring crossing of the river flowing beside the town, the 263rd launched a devastating attack on Cai Lay and its defenders before withdrawing.

This major assault on Cai Lay was a kind of rehearsal for Tet, especially in coordinating simultaneous attacks on multiple targets, as with the shelling of the city of My Tho in conjunction with the assault on Cai Lay town. In December, a plan for an attack on a post in Cai Be district was captured. This major operation was to involve three battalions (the 261st, 263rd, and 267th) but was called off for some reason, even before the documents were captured.[20]

In addition to being a rehearsal for Tet, these planned multibattalion attacks in western Dinh Tuong may also have been deception operations. In neighboring Ben Tre, "to throw the enemy off the track of our preparations, from October 1967 the armed forces of the province and districts conducted many attacks on the enemy" in various outlying districts.[21] The celebrated siege of Khe Sanh had also been, in part, a deception operation. General Tran Van Tra writes that, "according to plan, prior to 'N' Day, we launched strong attacks on Khe Sanh [January 20, 1968] in order to draw a large number of U.S. and Saigon puppet troops from the inner cities to this remote but important area, to divert the enemy's attention and thus help our urban forces in the secret deployment of their units."[22] Possibly the activity in Cai Be and Cai Lay districts in the period leading up to Tet had the same purpose.

Indoctrinating Revolutionary Forces for the Tet Offensive

By December, the village cadres began to receive more specific indications of the upcoming offensive. In battered Cam Son village, a hamlet guerrilla (who was quite atypical of this level in having attended high school in the district town) was given the "reorientation indoctrination" for the upcoming period. Originally, this indoctrination had been scheduled for October, but the fierce battles in the village forced a postponement. A district cadre came down and read from a prepared document. "Because the trainees received no documents," said the guerrilla, "it was impossible to find out what the most important item in the course" was. There certainly was no explicit discussion of the timing or scope of the upcoming offensive. The village trainees were assured that the United States would not dare to expand the war to the North, "because the Soviet Union is now very powerful," an indication that one of the major Party concerns about the possible U.S. reaction to the offensive was reflected in this indoctrination. The three-zone strategy of coordinating actions in the jungle-forest, the deltas, and the cities was discussed at length [DT286]. A translated summary of the December indoctrination states that the role of the Mekong Delta was to "pin down U.S. and puppet troops." In the cities "we should use brutal force to terrorize the people" [this is certainly not an exact rendition of what was originally said, since the revolution did not view its "revolutionary violence" as "terrorism"]. "Each zone should be self-sufficient as far as resources and manpower are concerned," they were told— an injunction which was somewhat at odds with the strategic concept of using main force battalions from places such as the Mekong Delta in the attack on Saigon.

To the extent that any instruction stood out in the minds of the trainees, it was that "the most important point, which was often emphasized, was that cadres should warn people of future hardships and prepare them for these hardships" [DT286]. Perhaps the Party was already concerned because of reports about raising expectations of an early end of the war too high, although the excited talk by cadres at all levels of a "once-in-a-thousand-years" offensive close to Tet drowned out any cautions and caveats that might have been issued. Though the prospect of bringing about a speedy end to the war served the Party well in the early stages of the Tet Offensive, it cost the revolution heavily later on. It is clear from the interviews that even in the pre-Tet preparation, when the full extent of the plan had not yet been revealed to lower-level cadres and civilians, some overeager cadres exceeded their mandate by giving the villagers the impression that this would be the final major push of the war.

Some defectors who left their units and villages at the end of 1967 reported that the local cadres had begun to issue promises that an imminent end to the war was in sight (for example, by stating that this would be the "final contribution" of the people and that an "overall resolution of the conflict was imminent"). "Indeed, the Front has promised that the war will end in the very near future and that the Revolution will be victorious," said a young man from the 20/7 zone who defected in late December. But he also had heard this before, and dismissed it as empty talk to encourage contributions from a war-weary population. "Yet since 1960," he said, "not only hasn't the war not ended, but it has become fiercer and more terrible every day" [DT281.]

A young man from Phu Phong, who left the revolution in 1971, described how he joined the revolution just before the Tet Offensive. "The Front made intense preparations for the Tet Offensive. The cadres frequently gathered the people in meetings. The young men and the women had to attend indoctrination sessions about their duty as youth in the current situation. The preparations lasted about a month, from November to December. I joined the Front at the beginning of December, when all the youth were forced to serve in the Front forces. I was then married, and couldn't go into hiding to avoid my military service. At that time, a large number or youths joined, some to serve as civilian laborers, others to transport wounded away from the battlefield. Generally speaking, almost all the youths in Phu Phong village joined the Front at that time" [DT308]. Although the respondent retroactively explained this as the result of effective coercion, this would not explain why coercion had not worked for the previous year or two. The cadres "held meetings in the settlements and hamlets, and mentioned the big victories of the Front, [which was] winning everywhere, in order to motivate the people. They incited the hatred of the people by saying that the Americans had dropped bombs to destroy the people's crops, and shelled and killed the people. The cadres talked about incidents that had happened in the village to make the people hate the Americans. When they were motivating the people, they didn't say anything about political matters. It was only on the way [to carry out the Tet Offensive] that the cadres said that this time we were going to take over this or that city in order to end the war, because this was an opportunity that only occurred once in a thousand years" [DT308]. Thus the people were not told explicitly what was going to happen and when, but during the three months prior to Tet, the accelerated pace of mobilization activities made it clear that something very big was imminent.

Receiving the Order to Attack

The My Tho city cadres racing from their base in western Dinh Tuong to get to the city in time to coordinate with attacking troops had little time to think about anything but the mission at hand. The urban cadres were to help guide the region main force units to their targets. For the first time, the revolutionary forces were fighting on terrain that their enemy knew much better than they, and carrying out an attack in a city, even one as small as My Tho, would be a complicated operation.

Just as the Tay Son leader Quang Trung had asked his troops to celebrate Tet in advance in 1789 so that they could attack the Chinese troops intervening in Vietnam's civil war, occupy Hanoi during the lunar holiday and catch them by surprise, some units had their own early Tet celebrations. A newly assigned elderly former village deputy Party secretary was told on the 28th that the My Tho city rear services organization would celebrate on the 30th of the lunar year, which was Monday, January 29, 1968. The section head gathered the cadres together and told them that the urban military unit had given this order, and a member of the unit even planned to have his official engagement ceremony on that occasion. When the time came, however, nothing was said or done about a ceremony. The group went ahead anyway and held the joint ceremony in the late afternoon. At 1830 hours, while the ceremony was going on, a special order came in to move out, so the ceremony was abandoned in mid-course, and the logistics unit fanned out to do its job carrying ammunition and supplies for the units that were already in place, poised for the attack [DT308].

Although the province had been receiving daily instructions from the military region on Tet preparations, the attack order came only ten days before the opening of the offensive. The province Party committee's code clerk said, "The most special thing was that the General Offensive and Uprising order was sent to the province ten days before the offensive, and the directive ordered the province to immediately prepare to educate the people. Ten days prior to the general mobilization directive [the actual attack order on the eve on Tet], the region's directive to the province used the term 'General Offensive and Uprising' in a directive for the first time. I didn't know what a General Offensive would be like. It was necessary to prepare forces in the villages and arm them with rifles as well as ideologically, and with resolve to score accomplishments in the Spring of 1968 to offer as a gift to Uncle Ho and the Party. The mobilization would let the people know that the General Offensive and Uprising stage was at hand, and would be a huge once-in-a-lifetime victory, and would fire up the masses" [DT337]. During the period of preparation for the offensive, political struggles, military proselytizing efforts to demoralize the GVN soldiers, and guerrilla attempts to surround and put pressures on military posts were intensified [DT337].

At the region level, the frantic last-minute preparations for the offensive led to communications difficulties. Tam Phuong, the military commander of Region 2, recalled: "Close to the day of initiating the campaign, COSVN called Sau Duong [the region Party secretary] to report [on the preparations for the offensive] and to receive last-minute instructions. I went down to the port [in Thanh Phu, a coastal district in Ben Tre province which was an offloading point where supplies from the North were received] to supervise and energize the supply of ammunition and its transportation to the battlefield. At the very moment Sau Duong and I were away from the office, Nam Be, who was the standing committee member of the region committee, received the order for 'D-day' [ngay N], but the envelope had a notation, 'only to be opened by the comrade Party Secretary of the Region Committee and the commander of the Military Region.' For this reason the Party secretary and I lost 12 hours in receiving this." Because of the secrecy and extreme compartmentalization in passing on this order, the front-line commander (Nguyen Van Si) was still scrupulously observing the Tet cease-fire order, and was delayed in moving his troops into place for the attack on My Tho city.[23]

According to the province code clerk, the final directive received by the My Tho province Party committee arrived by radio on Monday, January 29, at noon, but was not decoded until 10 o'clock that night. (Neighboring Ben Tre province received its orders on January 27, according to its province military history.)[24] The directive from the region to My Tho province was only two typewritten pages, shorter than many of the written operations orders that had been sent in the fall by the military region concerning the Winter–Spring offensive. The directive ordered the attack to commence at midnight on January 30, and the open fire was scheduled for the early hours of January 31, 1968. The last-minute nature of this order led to some confusion and operational mistakes, and contributed to the 514th Battalion's failure to open fire at the preordained time along with the 261st Battalion [DT337].

When the Region 2 order to get in position to launch the attack arrived, the province Party committee was at the opposite end of the province on the border with Kien Phong. At 2200 on the 29th, the entire province headquarters was loaded into ten sampans with nine persons in each, and set out for Go Luy, the "unofficial revolutionary capital" of the province in Nhi Binh village near Ap Bac, and close to a GVN agricultural extension chicken farm. The trip was accomplished with astonishing speed and ease, and in two hours the province headquarters was in place. Province cadres set out to organize the logistics, the distribution of new recruits, and the many urgent tasks of the offensive. On the night of the 30th, the attack was set in motion [DT337]. Before the attack, the reorganized My Tho city Party committee had its headquarters at Ap Bac, near Go Luy, but a considerable distance from the city. Taking advantage of the relaxation of security on the eve of Tet, the leading cadres contacted their "legal" agents in the city and started to move into the province capital. "Even at the time," said one, "while we were on our way, we still believed that we were going to carry out attacks on the occasion of Tet, like in any other year. Cadres like me didn't understand that a general offensive would be carried out" [DT313].

What If the Offensive Failed?

The cadres in the villages, however, concluded from the intense mobilization in the countryside that a major offensive of some kind was imminent. In the enthusiasm of the buildup for what most cadres thought would be the decisive push of the war, the local consequences of failure had not been clearly thought out, even at the highest levels of the Southern command at COSVN. At the Hanoi level of grand strategy, three scenarios of success, partial success, and military failure but strategic success had been considered. The December Politburo resolution stated that, if the assault was only a limited success, the U.S. and GVN forces would be able to hold on to the major cities, reconsolidate, and continue the war—but not alter the fundamental stalemate. In the worst-case scenario, the war would escalate and spread to North Vietnam, Laos, and Cambodia, but this would not succeed either, because it would stretch U.S. resources beyond the breaking point and possibly trigger a Soviet and/or Chinese response. But that was the "big picture" view. What would happen in places like My Tho if the offensive failed?

In the aftermath of the war, General Tran Do, the deputy political commander of COSVN and the political counterpart of General Tran Van Tra, addressed this issue. A local history of the conflict in Dong Thap Muoi, the Plain of Reeds, and the territorial base of the Military Region 2 headquarters says the following: "The Politburo and the Party Central Committee had predicted three possible outcomes of the Tet Mau Than attack, but according to comrade Tran Do, deputy political commander of the B2 region [e.g., South Vietnam excluding Central Vietnam, that is, COSVN's jurisdiction from the border of the Central Highlands to Ca Mau peninsula] at the time, 'looking back on the documents of the Politburo and the Central Committee I feel that the three possibilities were really only one possibility. That is, they only predicted the possibilities of what would happen after we had achieved victory.'"[25]

The Plain of Reeds history comments, "Looking back on those documents, the guiding idea was that the war would be terminated." This history quotes the Region 2 military commander at the time, Le Quoc San [Tam Phuong], as ascribing this to a "once-and-for-all" *(dut diem)* mentality.[26] One of the problems that the local Party leadership saw at the time was that little attention had been paid to the possibility of preserving revolutionary assets in the towns and the cities if the offensive was repulsed. "The 'General Offensive and Uprising' concept wasn't linked to the phrase 'legal,' and this matter wasn't really discussed." The question was what would happen when the revolutionary agents in the urban areas who had been living under a "legal" cover exposed themselves during the offensive. Exposure would end their usefulness as clandestine urban cadres. "But," continues the Plain of Reeds account, "there was a delicate problem *[co van de]* in Region 2 connected with this question." Eighteen years afterward, this "problem" was "reconsidered" by comrade Tran Do, the deputy political commander of B2 at the time. Tran Do wrote, "I still remember that after phase 1, on the occasion of COSVN sending me down to where Tam Phuong was [MR 2], I met Sau Duong, who at the time was the Party secretary of the region, and got into an argument with him. Now, thinking back on it, I believe I was stupid. Sau Duong raised the question of how we could continue the attack in such a way that we could maintain a legal position for the people. But at the time there was a mind set of a 'once-and-for-all attack' *[danh dut diem]* and bringing power into the hands of the people, so I wasn't pleased to hear this man talk about maintaining a legal position *[thay ong nay noi den van de giu the hop phap, xem ra khong xuoi tai]*, so I argued with him that this was the moment to rise up and seize power, and that anyone who was opposed would be brought before a court and tried with no messing around. Why still talk about maintaining a legal position?"[27]

Despite this angry and ominous threat by the powerful General Tran Do, the region Party secretary argued back. As the Northerner Tran Do recalled, Sau Duong told him, "No way, brother! We have been here a long time, and we see that as a matter of history, an uprising is not that easy. If we fight this battle, we also have to consider the possibility that the situation will not develop favorably, that the enemy will counterattack. Then what do we do? If they come back, how will the people [e.g., revolutionary supporters and activists] live? So there is no way we can't think about the legal status of the people." Tran Do writes that, "listening to him put it that way, I had to admit that he was right."[28] This remarkable exchange gives a vivid picture of the different perceptions of the cadres at the top and the cadres on the spot. Tran Do's candid admission that at COSVN the thinking was dominated by the conviction that Tet would be a "once-and-for-all affair" stands in sharp contrast to the caution of the top region leader in Central Nam Bo, who, in the marshes of the Plain of Reeds, was himself far removed from the realities of the big cities.

In his postwar memoirs, Sau Duong bluntly writes that "With respect to the balance of forces when sending a military spearhead into the cities, Region 8 clearly couldn't guarantee a knockout blow in the towns and cities, to establish a firm foothold there or to cling to the outskirts of the towns and cities to create a strategic opportunity and put pressure on the negotiations for peace in South Vietnam." If the attacks in Saigon and Hue had succeeded, he adds, it might have been a different story. The implication is that the overall plan was flawed, and its failure in the Central Delta was not due to the inadequacies of the local revolutionary leaders. After the first phase of the offensive, the Region proposed a shift of strategy to focus on expanding control in the countryside, arguing that this would be more suitable for their capabilities. For this, the Region was criticized by COSVN for question the Party's wisdom and for a "diminished strategic resolve" (*sut giam quyet tam chien luoc*). "Afterwards a number of comrades in Long An and Region 8 were still aggravated and puzzled about why they had to carry out the option (*kha nang*) of clinging to the outskirts of the cities and towns and suffer heavy casualties and erosion of forces? This was the second scenario [*kha nang hai*] of the plan for attacking the cities, in case it did not deliver a knockout blow [*dut diem*]. Looking back on it and considering it carefully, this scenario was not reasonable in using military forces to attack into the cities. If you couldn't deliver a knockout blow that would mean that the enemy was still strong and you had to retreat. If you couldn't win the first time [first attack] when the enemy was caught off guard, when the enemy had woken up and organized a tight defense, then stopping at the outskirts of the cities would simply mean that the enemy would counterattack and we would be ground down [*tieu hao*]."[29]

Although the main postwar controversy among Vietnamese revolutionaries in the South revolved around the decision to prolong the attacks on the outskirts of the urban areas once the main offensive had failed, it is clear that Sau Duong and other local leaders in the Mekong Delta had deep reservations about the overall offensive plan, and its failure to consider what to do if the main offensive was repulsed. The brief but massive rural uprising that accompanied the first wave of the Tet Offensive suggests that the failure to exploit the power vacuum in the countryside was a missed opportunity, as Sau Duong and others had argued at the time. We shall return to the issue of the political legacy of the perception gap between the top revolutionary leaders in the South, and the regional commanders who had to carry out their orders. It should be noted, however, that even these critics of the Tet Offensive assaults on the cities agreed that the larger strategic purpose of "diminishing the strategic resolve of the Americans" and creating a major turning point in the war was achieved, albeit at great cost.[30]

Launching the Attack

Eight battalions were poised for the attack, a coordinated assault of unprecedented scale for the military region. Even the Kien Tuong province local force battalion had been diverted from the attack on the province capital of Moc Hoa and sent to My Tho, because My Tho city had been designated the main target for the entire region.[31] From Ben Tre came the 516B Battalion, a "clone" of the original province local force unit. In addition, the

261A, 261B, 263rd, 265th, 267th, and 514th Battalions were all thrown into this attack.[32] The 514B Battalion was assigned to attack Go Cong and pin down GVN forces there. Captured documents indicate some shifting of units before and after Tet, and the "clone" organization of twin units with the same basic numerical designation was obviously intended to create uncertainty in the minds of enemy military intelligence about the exact extent of the force they confronted. This still creates difficulties for historians attempting to clarify the details of military operations during that period. Nevertheless, the main outlines of the battle force are clear.

One of the urban cadres involved in the attack on My Tho city described the plan and the attack. "The main attacking force was to occupy the province Administration building and the command headquarters of the Seventh Division. But when they advanced toward Hung Vuong Street [the main street of My Tho, leading past the ARVN Seventh Division Headquarters to the province headquarters], past the bus station [about two blocks from Hung Vuong Street], they were stopped and met with a fierce counterattack. Actually, if the command staff of the revolutionary forces hadn't made any mistakes, they probably would have advanced all the way to the center of town. The command staff of the communist operation didn't study the terrain in advance. They only studied it on maps, and didn't have any actual reconnaissance carried out. So during the attack they hit the wrong places. They attacked one target and thought they were attacking another, and they mistakenly thought that they had occupied their target, while in fact they hadn't entered the town itself" [DT313]. The interviewer asked where the liaison agents were who were supposed to have guided that attack. "It's painful to have to talk about this again. Before the attacks, liaison agents were recruited in sufficient numbers, but about an hour after the attack began, the liaison agents suddenly all fled. It would be funny if it weren't so tragic! The attacking troops had to call on the fighters who used to live in the city to show them the way. But these fighters had left the city ten years before to join the Front, and during this time the city had changed a lot. Again they led the troops in the wrong direction, because they couldn't recognize the old roads, especially at night. The disadvantage right at the start of the attack was of enormous magnitude. I still feel extremely angry when I talk about this, because if careful preparations had been made, if on-the-spot reconnaissance had been carried out, and if a reconnaissance unit had been used to lead the way, the Front would have occupied the city on the second day of Tet" [DT313]. In addition to the confusion and misdirection, President Thieu's decision to celebrate Tet in his wife's native city of My Tho had not been taken into account.

The presence of President Thieu contributed to the problems of the attack, because several units had been kept on alert, both as a standard security precaution and because the United States had been warning him of an impending danger and urging him to keep all forces in South Vietnam at a higher level of readiness during the Tet truce. Nevertheless, by late morning following the attack, two Ranger battalions had been airlifted from My Tho and flown by helicopter to reinforce Saigon. A U.S. helicopter also picked up President Thieu, who returned to Saigon.[33] Thus the additional security that had come with President Thieu left with him as well. As noted earlier, other Ranger units and much of the Seventh Division were withdrawn from the countryside to assist in the city's defense.

A major reason for the lack of military success was that the U.S. and ARVN operations of late 1967 kept the region from transporting enough ammunition to meet the requirements of the military plan of attack on My Tho. The plan called for an initial artillery salvo of 1,000 to 2,000 rounds, but because of an ammunition shortage only 36 rounds were fired. In some ways this was due to the contradiction between maintaining maximum military pressure in late 1967 while at the same time trying to prepare for the offensive. The aggressive guerrilla attempts to cut Highway 4 led to an intensive series of operations by U.S. and Saigon forces which also had the effect of blocking the flow of supplies for revolutionary units. Tam Phuong, the region military commander, states, "After the high points of attacking the Highway in 1967, the puppet Seventh Division and the Third Brigade of the U.S. Ninth Division along with local forces concentrated their efforts to break this up and spread troops out to block Highway 4, so that transporting ammunition from the Nguyen Van Tiep canal down to Highway 4 to ensure sufficient supplies for the main target in My Tho city and in the towns of Go Cong and Ben Tre was very difficult, especially with regard to artillery shells."[34]

From the beginning of the attack, problems of coordination plagued the region command. Both the 261A and the newly formed 261B Battalion mistakenly felt they had reached their objective and stopped to await orders from the command staff. The confusion and disarray is evident in the urban cadre's account of the opening phase of the attack. "In the bus station where the troops could penetrate, they couldn't generate any support, so what could they expect from the underground organizations inside the town? In the bus station, the security cadres only succeeded in capturing a few GVN security agents. The forward propaganda squads started making appeals through megaphones, but their voices were drowned out by the fighting and nobody could hear them. The supply and first aid teams had to work without stopping. Since the troops hadn't advanced into the other sectors of town, how could the undercover organizations and cadres there dare to come out? That was the situation in the First Sector. In the Second Sector, toward the Cho Dui market, the GVN people were still moving about in droves, so how could the undercover cadres there dare to come out?" [DT313]. The Second Sector on the east side of the city had been assigned to the 514th Battalion, "but I don't understand why the 514th Battalion kept hanging around the bus station, and why it couldn't advance toward their assigned area of operation. All five battalions were bunched up in the same area—from the Trung Luong intersection to the bus station" [DT313].

While the main direction of attack came from the west, along the connector road leading from the Trung Luong intersection where Highway 4 coming from Saigon to the north turns west, parallel with the Mekong River across the middle of the province, the province forces of My Tho, the 514th Battalion, and the Kien Phong province battalion had been assigned the eastern sector. Neither of these units encountered much success in penetrating the city, though their mission was to play a supporting role to the main assault by the region forces. The 261A Battalion opened fire as scheduled at 0100 on Wednesday. "It was only at 1400 on the second day of Tet that the region realized that they had occupied the wrong target, but by then the bombings and shellings of the counterattack became fierce and practically razed that area to the ground. In their attack plan, the Front predicted there would be bombings and shellings, but it didn't occur to them that the Americans and the GVN would sacrifice their own forces to such an extent. Unable to withstand the violent counterattack and suffering heavy losses, the night of the second day of Tet, the 261A and

261B Battalions had to withdraw from the town and take up a position on the outskirts. Once there, they received the new plan and tactical guidelines, because by this time, the region was at least aware of the situation and ordered the five battalions who had been delayed for three days to quickly attack the town from four directions" [DT313].

The new plan was to have the 267th Battalion come back down the initial assault route from Trung Luong intersection to the northwest of the city, while the 261A and 261B Battalions moved in from a position directly north. The 514th Battalion was deployed to the east to move in across the bridge separating the "old market" sector of My Tho east of the Bao Dinh river from the residential and administrative section. Because of heavy losses in the first two days of the attack, the 261A and 261B Battalions remained in their positions north of the town. The 267th and 514th Battalions, attacking from the west and east, made partial penetration of the town during the day, but got bogged down and were forced to withdraw at night. By this time most of the Seventh Division and the Ranger units in the province had been pulled in to reinforce, and the fighting raged around the edges of the city for several weeks.

Not all the attacking units performed with distinction. The newly formed 261B Battalion, with its heavy complement of new recruits, was strongly criticized after the operation was over. Its political officer reported to the regiment that although the unit killed 853 enemy and destroyed eleven posts in February 1968, its military successes were "limited by lack of determination and overestimation of the enemy on the part of personnel." In addition, the evacuation of the wounded was not done well, and many killed in action were left on the battlefield or carelessly buried. The unit encountered severe replacement difficulties, and problems with the new recruits—especially those from Ben Tre province, who wanted to go home. "They were afraid of the [intensity] of the war. They requested discharges and refused to fight," said the exasperated political officer.[35] In a report several weeks later, at the end of March, the political officer reported a crisis in troop morale due to "repeated military failures" during the offensive, especially the unsuccessful attacks on My Tho city. Battalion cadres feared that more difficulties would come during the rainy season, which would make operations more difficult, while replacements were hard to get. Squad cadre and ordinary combatants were afraid of the intensity of the war, he said. They "lacked determination and had lost their confidence in final victory." The failure of the offensive resulted in forty desertions by cadre and combatants. The morale crisis had seriously affected both company and platoon cadres. The political officers of Second and Third Companies and the Company Commander of Second company "refused to fight." Platoon cadre were "no better than C[ompany] and D [battalion] cadre, and several of them had either refused to fight or attempted to desert.[36] Clearly this was a special case of a newly formed unit without the experience or leadership of the established units, but this itself was also an indication that hasty recruiting and too rapid expansion of forces created serious problems.

Assessing the Attack on My Tho City

As a result of the heavy fighting, no substantial political agitation took place during the initial Tet attack on My Tho—certainly nothing approaching a "general uprising." Part of this was due to the fact that the attack had stalled, and the city was entered but not taken over. As a city cadre said, "In the end, the four battalions were not able to penetrate the center of town, so the political sections lay in one place, waiting, unable to do anything" [DT313]. Even if the city center had been occupied, as long as heavy fighting continued, any sort of political demonstration by civilians would have been out of the question. As General Tran Van Tra said of the Tet attack on Saigon, "it was completely unrealistic for us to set the goal of the General Offensive–General Uprising in terms of 'taking complete power into the hands of the people,' which our cadres and combatants would interpret as dealing the enemy a 'knock-out' blow. Since the General Offensive could not destroy the bulk of enemy forces—meaning that our attacks could not be decisive—simultaneous uprisings by the masses would be less than successful."[37]

The city cadre later explained that the revolution had erred on the side of leniency, and did not take sufficient advantage of its opportunity to hit hard at the Saigon administration while it had the chance. "To tell you the truth, during the Tet attacks, the Front didn't shoot anyone by mistake, instead they released a lot of people by mistake. The troops captured a lot of cruel GVN officials, but since they didn't know who was who, they let all of them go. This happened because the Front didn't have enough people planted in GVN organizations. Therefore, in order to achieve success, the Front should at least be able to gather information and destroy the hamlet and village governing apparatus, and its failure to do so resulted in many adverse consequences for the Front later on. If the Front couldn't destroy the GVN governing apparatus, then this apparatus would turn around and destroy the infrastructure organizations of the Front" [DT313].

Despite the list of GVN political supporters that had been drawn up (complete with home addresses), not only did the revolution not have enough agents to identify prospective targets, the fact that the military units were unable to gain complete control over the main part of town made it impossible to do the systematic house-to-house arrests (and subsequent executions) that took place in Hue, or even in Cai Lay district, although the region commander later claimed that 120 police and civil servants had been arrested in sector 2. The region's overall verdict on the attack was that "we didn't meet the requirement of a knockout blow *[dut diem]* against the city, and our forces suffered heavy casualties."[38]

By the fifth day of the attack on My Tho city it was clear to Tam Phuong, the Region 2 military commander, that the attack had failed. Tam Phuong wanted to pull out and turn the focus of attack against the vulnerable rural areas. Sau Duong, the region Party secretary, sent a radio message ordering him to continue the attack. At the same time, Tam Phuong also received a separate message direct from COSVN, also ordering a continuation of the assaults on the city. Reluctantly, Tam Phuong followed orders despite his own deep reservations and those of other commanders on the spot, for fear that his superiors would consider him "demoralized about the strategy *[giao dong ve chien luoc]*." Even so, Tran Do, then the deputy political officer for COSVN military forces, did arrive shortly afterward to criticize the entire region Party committee (evidently including Sau Duong) for being "demoralized" and lacking a firm resolve to attack the cities, which he stated was the "highest-level policy *[thuong sach]*," implying that the locals hadn't grasped the "big picture" and had failed in their duty.[39] Tran Do recanted this criticism after the war (and became a harsh critic of the lack of democracy in the Communist Party in the 1990s).

The Tet Attack on Cai Lay District Town

The rehearsal for the attack on Cai Lay the previous November was in part a diversion to draw attention away from the larger attack on My Tho, but it also turned out to be a genuine dress rehearsal for Tet. In the district town of Cai Lay, the Tet Offensive started in the early morning of January 31, around 0200, an hour after the opening assault on My Tho city. At first artillery was fired into the town, and the townspeople thought the noise came from the GVN district troops. Heavy firing continued throughout the night, but the revolutionary troops did not assault the town until the following morning. A young high school student who had not yet joined the revolution recalled seeing unarmed ARVN troops racing to get to the safety of the district compound shortly after the firing began. Around noon the next morning he saw "VC" running down the narrow alleys around his house. GVN troops ran up to counter, and fierce street fighting broke out [DT374].

A document captured in the vicinity of Ba Dua in early March 1968 illustrates the plan for the takeover of Cai Lay. It cites the example of Cai Lay as a model to be followed in the attack on another area identified only as "K1"—possibly Ba Dua or even the larger town of Cai Be, which had not yet been heavily attacked. As summarized by the translator, "Speaking of the uprising, document reveals that the population will be armed in the struggle for power, but should retain their legal status (as they had done in Cai Lay district). The uprising of the populace of K1 will be conducted by streets and blocks. The liberation of the village should be followed by consolidation of power, organization of the resistance force and the people's court for the elimination of reactionaries, establishment of the National United Front for Peace and Democracy Committee [Alliance for Peace and Democratic Forces] for the city, economic blockade, and political isolation and evacuation of the population from K1.[40]

Far from rising up in support of the revolutionary troops, the civilians in Cai Lay town cowered inside their homes, behind locked doors, paralyzed with fear. A row of houses between the bus station and the district compound went up in flames and was burned to the ground. The assault did not, however, succeed in overrunning the district compound. For the next two weeks, the revolutionary troops mounted sporadic assaults against the GVN forces in the town. These assaults pinned the GVN troops down in their compound and allowed political cadres to enter parts of the town to operate along with the troops and, on the fifth day of the offensive, they came to the house of the high school student, as well as all the surrounding houses in the neighborhood. As he discovered later, the urban cadres had lists of the political leanings of the town residents, and guided the soldiers. "Has your family been all right these past few days?" they asked. The student invited the cadre to drink a cup of tea. "There's no time," replied the cadre, "But now let's be happy in welcoming peace. I hope you will make a contribution in bringing about peace" [DT374].

For the noncommitted urban residents in places like Cai Lay, especially those who were identified on secret lists prepared by agents in the town as "passive" or from a non-worker-peasant class background, the revolution did not appeal to class consciousness or even anti-imperialism. They invoked the prospect of peace, evidently in the hope that this would get the fence sitters to support them if only to help bring the war to a quick end. But even for some of these, like the high school student, who already despised the GVN, more was required than merely hoping for peace. The cadre returned later in the day and told the student, "I'm now really going to give you a task. You know which houses belong to members of the police, the security agents or military officers, or to people who have opposed the revolution, so I want you to write down clearly the names of those counter-revolutionaries." The student wrote down the names, but none of them were at home. The cadre returned to tell the student that he was turning him over to another handler. Willingly or not, the student had joined the revolution as a secret agent [DT374].

How did he feel about writing down the names of his neighbors, asked the interviewer? "At the time, I didn't feel anything," replied the former student. "I looked on these people as the enemy and only wanted to kill them in order to have peace. Then I just went ahead and did it to bring about a quick peace, and didn't think about the fact that this was going to harm my friends." Asked by the interviewer how he could consider enemies "friends," he replied, "Friends in the sense that we fooled around together, so I could bribe them into not drafting me. That's the only reason I wrote down their names—I didn't write the names of my real friends." Despite his willing collaboration in this tracking down of "counter-revolutionaries," all of them (according to his account) managed to flee, and none was found by the cadres. A few days later his new handler came back and told him that he didn't need to write down any more names, but needed to indicate more accurately where the houses of those he had already listed were. There were also, he said, a large number of Cai Lay town people serving as agents under the command of his handler. For another four months he continued to provide lists and maps showing the guerrillas which routes were safe [DT374]. Evidently, the revolutionary forces in Cai Lay did not place much confidence in their new-found friends. A directive from the region was captured in early March which said that "Emphasis should also be placed on lessons drawn in recent operations in Cai Lay and Kien Phong where losses of fifth columnists were suffered and the overall success of operations was denied due to lack of confidence [in] the fifth columnists by the military units involved.[41]

Uprising in the Countryside

In the countryside the story was completely different from the urban areas of My Tho. Although no uprising took place in the city of My Tho or the district towns, a mass mobilization in the rural areas was in progress from the outset of the offensive, and even before. The terminology used in the interviews reflects that atmosphere of the time. The almost universal term was *phan khoi,* which is often blandly translated as "enthusiastic." Despite the fact that this term was overused by the cadres and often devalued to describe even a lukewarm response from the people, in this case it is clear that the interviewees meant it in its original sense. It is translated here as "fired up," which is not exact, but is a closer approximation to the emotion described. Another commonly used term, particularly for the young men who had avoided the draft until Tet but who now joined in droves, was *hang*—also usually translated as "enthusiastic." Here it indicates that they were more than merely upbeat, they were "really into it." Other interviewees use the term *hao thang* indicating that the people were caught up in the excitement and thrill of impending victory. *Hao thang,* is a venerable term frequently encountered in the Chinese classics of strategy and deception, such as *The Romance of the Three Kingdoms,* and also implies being carried away by the prospect of victory—to the point of being disastrously careless or over-confident (or, in Stalin's memorable phrase, "dizzy with success"). It is revealing that the descriptions of the people's attitudes while the Tet Offensive was still unfolding use the term *phan khoi,* whereas the term *hao thang* appears in the retrospective analyses.

Because of the preparations prior to Tet, the villages had already begun to mobilize, but it was not until the attack on My Tho city signaled the opening of the offensive that the purpose of this activity became clear. In Thanh Phu (Cai Lay), the village had been prepared for some action since October, but did not get the order to move—or even know the attack had started—until the second day of the offensive. A hamlet unit leader got the order to send eight hamlet guerrillas to the village, and retain twelve others in the hamlet. The eight who went to the village "were really fired up, because by that time the offensive had started and we propagandized that Saigon had already been occupied and we had already entered all the province and district capitals, and were only waiting for forces to come in from the outside to support them and it would be all over. At the time the people were really fired up." The twelve hamlet guerrillas set off to dig up the district road. The sound of gunfire on the second and third days heightened the highly charged atmosphere of uprising *(khi the len va noi day tung bung).* In this atmosphere, "if we wanted to assemble the masses it was easy to get a crowd, and if we wanted to collect money they were ready to contribute." The cadres' credibility and authority were reestablished, and "in that situation, with the uprising atmosphere, the people believed in the cadres, and at that time they immediately did whatever the cadres told them" [DT386].

The suddenness of the event, combined with the evidence of total mobilization in the countryside, created an unprecedented atmosphere. In Nhi Binh village the cadres were initially glued to their radios. "Every five minutes they shouted through a megaphone the news of which areas had been seized, how the fighting was going, and about the capture of the radio station" [DT316]. In Go Cong, like Cho Gao an area of weak revolutionary control because of its distance from the Plain of Reeds and supporting military units and bases, the response was immediate and electric. A district youth cadre described the mood. "Generally speaking, the atmosphere in every village was one of strong uprising, even in those villages near the market villages and the district town, where new recruits and new guerrillas were also inducted. Before Tet there were villages without a single guerrilla, but when Tet came you could say that even the weakest villages were able to recruit ten guerrillas and send up ten new recruits—that was in the villages that had been the very weakest all along. The liberated villages mobilized platoons of village guerrillas and sent nearly all the remaining youth off as new recruits. Apart from new recruits they were also able to mobilize civilian laborers—about thirty per village. They were sent off with expenses paid, they didn't have to support themselves out of pocket" [DT387]. A captured document listing the strength of village Women's Associations in Hoa Dong district of Go Cong as of April 1968 recorded an average of 400 members per village.[42] A hamlet cadre in Ban Long village said that in his neighborhood any youths that he motivated to go off and serve who evaded their duty were, in the ambiance of uprising, criticized and scolded, and he himself was reproached if he didn't get them to go. "They compared us with other hamlets and asked why it was that they were able to get twenty to twenty-five of forty young men to join, but we couldn't get five or six?" In the end, the youth in the hamlet enthusiastically went off to join the troops—at least in the heady atmosphere of initial success of the Tet Offensive. Later, nearly 80 percent of them returned to the village [DT372].

A woman in her thirties who joined up in the enthusiasm of the offensive said, "I didn't understand what revolution was. I followed the Front because at that time the atmosphere was charged with excitement *[phan khoi]*. The cadres were bustling back and forth all around my house. They would constantly invite me to join the revolution to fight the U.S. and puppets. I listened to what they said, but the main reason was that I was eager to have fun, and wanted to follow the older brothers who were cadres going from village to village." She became a liaison agent. But when it stopped being fun, she was still motivated by what others were doing, and when she rallied in 1971 she explained that "I saw a lot of the sisters coming out to rally, and only then did I dare follow them" [DT384].

In Phu Phong village next to Vinh Kim, mobilization for the Tet Offensive was effective in terms of mobilizing both manpower and resources. As in other villages, the young men who had managed to avoid the draft now found it impossible to do so. Although (as in other interviews) this was ascribed to the increased effectiveness of the village guerrillas in flushing out draft dodgers, it is also clear that social pressure, mass psychology, and political mobilization played key roles. An elderly cadre who had been recruited to reinforce the city unit's logistics section just before Tet recalled: "In the attack everyone from cadres to soldiers to the masses of the people believed that the Tet Offensive would succeed. Therefore, rural boys and girls hit the road to serve as civilian laborers. As many as were needed could be gathered for the battlefields" [DT308].

Reasons for Success in Rural Mobilization During the Tet Offensive

Why did pressure and mobilization work at that time, when it had been largely ineffective for the previous two years? The major change in the overall situation, which affected the "rational peasant" calculations of those who joined the revolution, as well as the "moral economy" effectiveness of community pressures, was that now the prospects for the revolution to achieve a breakthrough looked a lot better than they had. Thus, the individual contribution would be more valuable but, more than this, there would be a possibility of bringing the war to an end by jumping on the bandwagon. At the same time, community pressure was once again a mobilizing tool that could be used by the revolution, after a period in which the fragmentation and demoralization of the village communities had made it extremely difficult for the cadres to rely on this social support.

Popular associations in Phu Phong were revitalized, and the Women's Association cadres energetically appealed to all villagers to do their part. "Were the women as zealous in carrying out their tasks as the men?" a young male village cadre was asked. He replied: "Most of them were eager because they heard the Front's propaganda about the big victories. They were enthusiastic and left with great zeal" [DT308]. In the always sensitive area of finance, the Phu Phong villagers were asked to pay half of their next year's taxes in advance to support the offensive. With the exception of families with many children who were granted exemptions, most paid. Those who didn't were "denounced and insulted." In this newly energized political atmosphere, community pressure once again worked for the revolution. Nearly 4 million piasters were collected as an advance on the following year's taxes, more than triple the total amount collected in 1966 for the regular tax period [DT308].

In neighboring Ban Long village, also next to Vinh Kim, Tet celebrations were in full swing when word of the offensive came. The village Party secretary assembled the village and hamlet cadres and assigned them to gather the villagers together. "According to the indoctrination documents that had been passed out, the General Offensive would cover all of South Vietnam. Hearing this, the people were really fired up, and everyone did whatever was within their capability to do. For instance, the old men stayed home to organize funerals for those who sacrificed their lives. The peasant men who had the strength went out to dig up roads and cut the lines of communication. It has always been said that when the day of General Offensive and General Uprising came, the entire people would rise up and seize power, so at that time the people were confident that it would succeed. Everyone was fired up and at the time no one was thinking that the government out there would counterattack and that they would get into trouble for having participated. The people with one accord rose up." The villagers streamed toward Vinh Kim and assembled there with people from other villages, and the cadres led them up to Highway 4. Not an airplane was in sight, and with no bombing and no GVN resistance, the mass movement swept the countryside for between three and ten days (depending on the account), until the planes came, the bombing started, and the insurgents deserted back to their villages [DT372].

One consequence of the Tet Offensive was to eliminate for a short time the external influences that had invaded the traditional quiet of rural life. The most important change was that there were no helicopters and airplanes suddenly intruding into the villagers' world. Along with this, the roads and Highway 4 had been dug up and interdicted, so no vehicles—military or otherwise—were moving in most of the province. The countryside had reclaimed its bucolic pace of life (except for the bustling mobilization and the guerrilla attacks on posts), and the revolution was now able to dictate the conditions of rural life without significant challenge from the machines and technology of its urban-based opponent. This was taken by many people in the countryside as evidence of a decisive shift in the war. A guerrilla from My Long, in the heart of the 20/7 zone, said that there and in neighboring Nhi Qui, the Tet Offensive resulted in the youth joining civilian labor teams for three to four months. "The people were really fired up and said 'this is a once-in-a-thousand-years opportunity—friends and relatives, we are about to have peace! *[sap co hoa binh ba con oi].*' At the time there were no vehicles running because the roads had all been dug up" [DT330]. In Nhi Binh, another big village straddling Highway 4, the guerrillas controlled the strategic route for more than ten days, according to a village cadre [DT312].

Many of the interviewees commented on the absence of airplanes and helicopters, which had become a constant threatening presence in their lives. For the province committee, used to being stationed in "free-fire zones" which were constantly bombed and shelled, this was a welcome respite. "For three days there were no planes," said the code clerk, "and we could move around freely, which made the brothers in the protection unit really happy. We ran out to Highway 4, and felt the Front had won a big victory" [DT337]. For these cadres, reaching Highway 4 and standing there without fear of detection and death after years of hiding in the backwaters of the province must have had an impact like Balboa reaching the Pacific Ocean. A veteran military cadre in charge of training new recruits said, "Before Tet, planes were flying all the time, but at Tet 1968 there was not a plane in the sky for a week, so the people really believed a victory was being won" [DT338].

A hamlet guerrilla from My Duc Tay at the edge of the Plain of Reeds commented, "From the beginning of 1968 to the middle of the year, people were really enthusiastic, because sometimes you would only see one plane in a month. The posts had all withdrawn, leaving only those around Highway 4." During the first few days of the offensive there were "no airplanes in sight. Everything was quiet as a tomb. At that time people got very excited and enthusiastic and told each other, 'in a few days I will go back in there and fix up my orchards.' Only when the GVN counterattack began did we know we had failed. In July and August 1968, when Americans began to land troops in wave after wave, I knew the offensive had failed. At the time a lot of cadres were arrested and a number killed. People moved to New Life Hamlets to live. All buffalo and oxen were killed by airplanes. A number of youth came to tell me, 'The situation has become so violent that I can't stand it any longer. I have to go now'" [DT371]. In this remote village, the counterattack did not come until August 1968, presumably because the U.S. and GVN forces were preoccupied with reclaiming more critical areas. But when the counterattack came, it had the same impact as in villages which were hit earlier. The rural idyll was over for the peasants, and along with it their dream of leading a normal life and "fixing up their orchards." The war returned with a vengeance, and the intensity of the violence after Tet reached unprecedented levels.

Demoralization Following the Collapse of the Tet Offensive

Those who believed, from either conviction or calculation, that peace could be obtained only by revolutionary victory were devastated by the failure of the Tet Offensive to achieve a quick and decisive outcome. In Nhi Binh the guerrilla ranks had swelled from ten before to the offensive to more than forty [DT312]. The counterattack in Nhi Binh began on the fourth day, in the form of intensive bombing and shelling. The villagers "were very discouraged. They saw that the conflict was going to drag on, and that there would be many more ups and downs, that it would not be ended overnight. So they became demoralized. The first few days they believed, and they went all-out. Whatever they were told to do, they did with conviction. Later, when they were told to do something, they did it without conviction and sometimes fled halfway through. When the counterattack came on the fifth day, they were still serving as civilian laborers carrying ammunition and wounded. They still did it, but without much spirit of voluntarism [ho it co tinh than xung phong ra lam]. They were afraid of the bombing and shelling" [DT316].

By March 1968, said a committed village cadre, the movement in Nhi Binh had "died down" because U.S. troops were stationed in the village and artillery blanketed the area, killing a large number of cadres and civilians, and creating an atmosphere of fear and apprehension among both cadres and villagers [DT312]. The villagers asked the cadres how they could win, if they were unable to take advantage of a situation in which their opponent was taken completely by surprise—an opportunity that was not likely to reoccur. The cadres replied that in a conflict there were always ups and downs, but inevitably another Tet-type opportunity would arise. "When it does, we'll let you know," the cadres told the villagers. "Please try to keep the faith and stay alert, and when the time comes you will know." Some villagers believed this, but the majority did not because they saw the cadres, who had been a close and constant presence during Tet, now forced to operate at a greater distance from the villagers, while the local GVN authorities increasingly became the dominant factor in the daily life of the village [DT316]. A cadre from Binh Duc village, next to the U.S. military base, reported that the villagers were disillusioned by the failure of the revolution to take over the cities as they had promised. "Then gradually the response of the ARVN and the American troops forcibly separated the people from the revolution. They caused a lot of difficulties to the people and destroyed their crops with bombing and shelling, and this was why the people had to suffer privations. If they stayed in the liberated areas they wouldn't be able to earn their living, so they had to flee to the strategic hamlet areas" [DT301]. This sense of closeness/distance is a crucial factor in analyzing the nature of support for the revolution, and it will be examined in detail in the following chapters.

A young man from My Hanh Dong village, a traditionally strong revolutionary village astride the supply route to Cambodia, gave a different impression of how long the glow of Tet enthusiasm lasted. Ironically, in some cases it was more persistent and longer lasting among the villagers than among the cadres, who, like the Resistance veteran, tended to be more pessimistic precisely because of their greater experience and knowledge of the situation. "When preparations for the General Offensive of Tet Mau Than were being made, the cadres propagandized that victory was around the corner, and the towns and cities of the South would be liberated, so the people were very confident. Although the General Offensive was defeated, the majority of the people in the village didn't know it, so, except for a small minority, they still continued to believe. The minority saw the GVN soldiers going on sweep operations and the liberation cadres fleeing, so they didn't believe, and asked, 'Why is it that all I see is cadres running and hiding all the time?'" [DT332].

Retrospective Assessments of the Tet Offensive in My Tho

Whether it took days, weeks, or months, the rural uprising in My Tho gradually subsided, village by village. Both the initial magnitude of the revolution's success in sweeping large numbers of youth along in the high tide of revolutionary enthusiasm, and the sad consequences for the villages in the following years, are reflected in the case of Thanh Hung village, where a village guerrilla later reported: "In 1971, pacification came [to his hamlet]. The hamlet had no more young people, because those who were of age all joined up to follow the Front and leave the village in 1968" [DT370]. The great surge of youth enlistment following the Tet Offensive drained the countryside of young men and created great difficulties for the revolution in the subsequent period.

When the counterattack reached Go Luy on the fourth day, the province committee stationed there was forced to flee by motorized sampan to Hoi Cu village in Cai Be, between Highway 4 and the Plain of Reeds. Unlike the lightning move across the province just before Tet, which took only two hours, it took them six days to move half that distance to Hoi Cu. During the chaos of the frantic escape, the province committee lost contact not only with its superiors and subordinates, but with its own sections. When the province committee finally was able to reorganize its temporary headquarters, lassitude infiltrated the ranks of the support personnel, and some members of the security unit deserted. Radio contact with the region was reestablished, and the province organization was bombarded with questions about which roads had been seized. The region also passed along news of great victories in battles in Hue and Saigon [DT337].

In its report to the region, the province committee blamed the failure to accomplish the primary mission of seizing the towns and province capital on lack of coordination in the military operation—for which it had no responsibility. The opening of the attack was not synchronized, and the military lacked tactical coordination in combat. Units lost their way in the province capital. The rear service supply was a mess. The people could not be motivated to rise up. The code clerk noted that the pattern of province reports to the region was that if it was news of victories, the report would be very prompt, but there would be long delays if the news was bad. Moreover, because the province could not get on top of the situation of its subordinate units and districts, it took seven or eight days before the first summary report was sent to the region. The overall assessment of gains and losses was not sent for a month because of the confused situation and the difficulty of contacting the districts [DT337].

About a month after the offensive, indoctrination documents were sent to the villages to explain why the attack had not succeeded in seizing the cities and ending the war. The cadres passed on the explanation in the indoctrination materials that there had been many big successes in hitting at the main bases of the enemy, but a lack of coordination was responsible for the offensive coming up short. This, of course, put the blame on the implementation of the plan rather than on the plan itself. A hamlet cadre from Ban Long said that Tet was explained as a partial success, in that it had resulted in the expansion of liberated territory and pushing back some posts. The people attending these sessions, he added, did not say that since they had gone all-out in support of the revolution and it had not succeeded, they would no longer contribute, but they appeared sad and depressed because it now looked like the war was going to drag on [DT372]. The short-term failure of the Tet Offensive cost the Party heavily by damaging its credibility. As one village cadre ruefully observed, "We lost prestige among the people because of excessive propaganda about victory" [DT386].

After the war, a military history of My Tho province gave the following evaluation of the Tet Offensive in the province. Despite the concentration of forces and the bravery of the soldiers, it said, "in the overall battlefield of the region as well as the My Tho battlefield, in a situation where the balance of forces was that the enemy had far more numbers than we did, we couldn't accomplish the targets set out for the three phases of the campaign, especially seizing and occupying the key targets in My Tho city during phase one of Tet Mau Than (January–February 1968). After phase one we suffered casualties that could not be replaced in time, and lost the element of surprise in the General Offensive and Uprising, and yet still had to carry out phases two and three in order to coordinate with the entire region, so that armed forces suffered even greater casualties. The main force regiments suffered casualties of up to 60 to 70 percent, and the local forces and guerrillas that had just been pulled up encountered fierce fighting and were affected by enemy psychological measures and deserted in rather large numbers. The enemy energetically responded right from the beginning with counterattacks that pushed our forces way out and resumed pacifying the countryside while we still continued to attack the cities in phases two and three and didn't quickly turn to expand the rural liberated zone, counter enemy sweep operations, and disrupt pacification. Thus, after three phases of the General Offensive and Uprising of 1968 we lost our strategic position [mat the] and our effective forces [mat luc] and the movement encountered a lot of difficulties."[43]

Although the Tet Offensive succeeded in its larger strategic purpose of forcing the war into a new phase, and ultimately led to the disengagement of the United States from the conflict, the revolutionaries in the South paid a very high price. The "Viet Cong" or Southern forces, especially in the big units, suffered devastating losses. As the war went on, North Vietnamese regular forces increasingly took over the brunt of the heavy fighting. The upsurge in revolutionary participation in the villages resulting from the uprising of the initial phase of the offensive gradually subsided. Many of those who, in the flush of anticipated victory, had joined up in one capacity or another, fled or quit. In My Tho, the casualties in the concentrated units did not come primarily from the offensive itself, but from the bombing and shelling of the U.S.–GVN counteroffensive, especially after the ineffective "second offensive" of May 1968.

In My Tho city, the buildup of urban cadres before Tet was negated by the heavy losses they suffered. Many were arrested. A young woman from Ben Tre, who was transferred to the My Tho city Party organization as a replacement after Tet, said that the city cadres had felt that the Tet Offensive in the city had been a partial success in that, according to their estimate, 50 to 60 percent of the town people in My Tho had "responded" to the revolutionary call. The evidence was that they participated in "violent actions *[bao dong]*" such as stopping vehicles and going on face-to-face demonstrations. By the time of her arrival in 1969, however, there was little evidence of this responsiveness. In part this was due to what the people had seen and experienced during the offensive. "In those days the people in the neighborhood had witnessed big battles and seen soldiers killed or disappear." What really bothered them, however, was the guerrilla attack on the passenger-carrying three-wheeled lambrettas, when "civilians were killed, so they were repelled and disgusted *[chan ghet]* [DT317].

The Tet Offensive was not only the crucial turning point of the Vietnam conflict, but its political effects continued to be felt in Vietnam long after the war ended. It is thus doubly important for understanding the revolutionary conflict in My Tho because it decisively affected the larger context in which the province revolutionary movement was set, as well as having a profound impact within the province itself. In the long term, it marked the beginning of the U.S. disengagement, which led ultimately to the final confrontation between the contending Vietnamese factions. Despite the massive impact the U.S. post-Tet counterattack had on the movement, the gradual departure of U.S. troops made it inevitable that the Mekong Delta, with its crucial resources of population and food, would once again become a critical theater of the war. In the short term, the massive let down from the Tet euphoria was a major setback to the revolution in My Tho and elsewhere.

For the GVN, it had the opposite effect. The war had been brought to the doorstep of the Saigon government—in the words of one interviewee, "right into the bed of Nguyen Viet Thanh," the ARVN Seventh Division commander whose heavily guarded residence was in My Tho city and who had nearly been taken hostage [DT313]. These close encounters had a contradictory effect in the once impregnably secure urban areas. On the one hand, they brought many of the opponents of the revolution off the fence. Tet galvanized a new source of support for the Saigon government, and elicited a new level of commitment from its existing supporters. With the negotiations in motion, it was only a question of time before the U.S. troops left, and it was clear to both the GVN and the fence sitters that they could no longer rely on the Americans to take care of their interests and bear the brunt of the fighting. Not only had there been highly visible assassinations during the brief occupation of the cities and towns, some troops did not treat the civilian population well. An after-action report from the 261B Battalion said that "inadequate emphasis" was placed on civilian proselytizing activities, and noted that "during the attacks on My Tho city, personnel of D261B treated the civilian population with roughness and confiscated their property."[44]

Probably the most damaging legacy of the Tet Offensive for the revolution was the impact that the decision-making process itself had on the leaders at the front lines, who had to bear the brunt of the miscalculations of their superiors and felt responsible to those who they ordered to their deaths in attacks which they knew were increasingly futile. In early February COSVN had ordered the attacks on My Tho city to continue, when it was evident to local commanders that they could not succeed. Tam Phuong, the commander of military forces in Region 2, notes that it was the top Party leader in the South, Pham Hung himself, who gave the order to continue the attacks on My Tho city in March even while taking away Regiment I and transferring it to Long An. The region commander was stunned. "I was disconcerted because this mission was extremely onerous and hard to carry out, but because it had been ordered from above and I saw that the comrades in command of the other military regions and units received their missions and silently left, so I didn't know how to take this up with my superiors."[45] In August, COSVN ordered a third-wave offensive despite the heavy casualties. Tam Phuong notes that the battalions were down to 70 to 100 troops, the local forces and guerrillas had been seriously depleted, and "the mass movement had collapsed [sa sut]. In particular, the military commanders at each level had a lot of doubts and questions, and were flustered in commanding, building up, and utilizing the troops."[46]

Tam Phuong comments that the misguided orders from above were the result of a lack of two-way communication in the decision process and a failure to observe the time-honored Party practice of self-criticism, learning from mistakes, and adjusting to reality. Beyond the tactical misjudgments, "The even more important shortcoming was a lack of democracy, a lack of criticism and self-criticism in the after-action reviews, and a failure to listen closely to the lower levels." Significantly, it was not until Vietnam embarked on its postwar *doi moi* (renovation) reforms that some of the higher-level Party leaders admitted their errors. General Tran Do, for instance, had angrily rejected as defeatist Sau Duong's (the Region 2 Party secretary) insistence on a "plan B" if the maximum goals of the offensive were not met, and refused to allow Tam Phuong, the region military commander, to withdraw after the fifth day of the assault on My Tho city, when it was clear that it could not succeed. After the war, General Do acknowledged that the leadership had been "subjective" and had commanded the offensive "without a scientific basis." Perhaps it was a belated "lesson learned" from this experience that led General Do to emerge at this very time as the most prominent and highly placed Party leader demanding extensive democratic reforms.[47]

The conclusion that Tam Phuong drew from this experience would resonate with many mid-level Vietnam commanders in the U.S. Armed Forces. "In the face of a coercive [go ep] leadership and command like this, at that time no one really dared to set forth any other ideas [about] not continuing the attacks on the city. But in the case of subordinate cadres and Party members, they shouldn't only rigidly carry out orders from above, they also have a responsibility to the cadres, Party members, soldiers, and compatriots for victory and defeat on the battlefield, for the unit that they themselves command. This failure to show the courage of a Communist Party member, and to fully live up to the responsibility for the blood of the cadres, soldiers, and compatriots by not forcefully reporting the real difficulties of the battlefield and formulating an appropriate combat operational plan is a bitter lesson for me."[48]

Conclusion

New energy on the Saigon side, combined with the losses suffered by the revolution, were key elements in the problems it encountered during the 1968–71 period. An even more important explanation, however, was the escalation in intensity and destructiveness of U.S. operations in My Tho. In some ways the shock of Tet, and the habituation of the U.S. public and officials to the massive destructiveness of the post-Tet counteroffensive and "destroying to save," cleared the way for a new method of operations. From the local perspective, the most significant immediate impact of the Tet Offensive was the virtual abandonment of the already inadequate restraints on the use of massive firepower in populated areas.

These post-Tet reverses suffered by the revolution raised the question of whether the feat of tapping a latent reservoir of support for a second time could be accomplished, or whether the Tet experience was so traumatic that even the younger generation could never again have any illusions about a dramatic turnabout in the fortunes of the revolution. By 1971, even this crucial issue was to some extent besides the point, since the reservoir had dried up or, rather, been displaced into fragmentated tiny wellsprings of potential support in areas securely controlled by the GVN. To use another liquid metaphor, the U.S.–GVN counteroffensive "drained the pond to catch the fish," by carrying the depopulation of the countryside even beyond the already dislocated situation of 1966–67.

15

Tragic Farewell

No period of the war since the rapid expansion of the revolutionary movement in the Concerted Uprising of 1959–60 saw as dramatic a reversal of fortune as the three years following the Tet Offensive. In early 1968, the Government of the Republic of Vietnam (GVN) was reeling from the unexpected scope and intensity of the general offensive, but by the middle of the year the Saigon government had taken the counteroffensive and the outer layers of revolutionary support mobilized at Tet began to fall away. By the end of 1968 and throughout 1969 the war reached its peak intensity, as "accelerated pacification" operations by U.S. and Army of the Republic of Vietnam (ARVN) units hammered the revolutionary forces and reversed the gains they had made at Tet. These operations pushed back the concentrated units, forced them to split up, and made it possible for the GVN to reestablish an increasingly numerous and effective network of small military posts, manned by province and district militia, in areas where they had been forced to withdraw by the Tet Offensive and also in areas where, before Tet, small militia groups were too vulnerable to the big revolutionary units to operate. Despite the eventual withdrawal of the U.S. Ninth Division, whose effective but destructive operations had been largely responsible for the turn of the tide in My Tho, most of My Tho province and the Mekong Delta was under predominant GVN control by 1970, and the revolution reached its lowest ebb in the conflict in 1971.

This post-Tet period posed challenges for both sides, which were met in ways that engender controversy long after the event. For the United States, it indicated that current military tactics were not working. As a result, the U.S. military adopted the method of "draining the pond to catch the fish" and directed an unprecedented level of violence at the villages, which resulted in the depopulation of large parts of the countryside and the further isolation of the revolutionary forces. Not surprisingly, this led to a catastrophically high level of civilian casualties during the year following Tet, and raises questions of moral accountability for U.S. commanders that, in some ways, go beyond the issues raised at My Lai.

Here is another case in which a local study can illuminate some important issues of the Vietnam war. For both the United States and the revolutionaries, there was a vast difference between local realities and the perspective and beliefs of those higher up, who were insulated from the consequences of their policies. The devastating operations of the U.S. Ninth Division, which wreaked havoc on the people of the central Mekong Delta, were designed by the top command of this unit, and were not the product of panicked and vengeful low-level units in the heat of battle. On the Vietnamese side, the top Communist Party authorities clung to their plan of attacking the cities long after most revolutionaries on the front lines had realized the futility of this costly strategy. It is clear from some postwar local histories that this policy was controversial at the time, and continues to cast doubt on the wisdom of some top Party strategists of that era.

"New Optimism" Following the Tet Offensive

It took some time for even normally optimistic U.S. officials to fully appreciate the magnitude of the change that occurred in the year following the 1968 Tet Offensive. When they did, a "new optimism" arose in Vietnam among both the Saigon government officials and their U.S. advisors. The American public by this time was inured to upbeat news from Vietnam because of the steady stream of cheery assurances emanating from U.S. officialdom over the course of the war. The *Washington Post* reported right after President Richard Nixon's inauguration that a comprehensive policy review of Vietnam policy elicited "galloping optimism" among American officials in Vietnam, despite the skeptical tone of the questions posed in Washington. The answers to questions about how the war was going "for the most part reflected the dominant theme of high American officials in South Vietnam that the war, to quote one official, 'is going better than at any time since 1961.' " The optimism reflected a view that "it is not so much a question of allies doing better as the enemy doing much, much worse, and the population becoming increasingly disenchanted with the war." Ironically, the upbeat mood from Americans in Vietnam was not well received in Washington, where there was "a reluctance on the part of NSC [National Security Council] staffers to 'believe the good news.'"[1]

Eventually the "new optimism" gained converts in Washington, and the political imperatives of finding a way out of the war persuaded U.S. decision makers that it was not just a question of heavy "Viet Cong" casualties, but that the root cause of the turnaround was an improved allied effort, including the GVN forces. In October 1970 the *New York Times* reported that "opinion in US has been polarized for so long that it has not kept up with realities of Vietnam and is about [two years] behind current events." U.S. officials maintained that the "allies have never been stronger and [the] enemy never weaker," though there was still uncertainty about how the South Vietnamese would perform on their own. Because of the legacy of previous overconfidence and the resulting credibility gap between official pronouncements and the U.S. public, "officials are reluctant to express their new optimism openly . . ."[2]

In Washington, the Nixon administration increasingly interpreted the problems of the revolution and the improved performance of the GVN as evidence that the Vietnam albatross could be lifted from America by turning the fighting over to Saigon—the policy of "Vietnamization." The fact that this term was originally devised by the French (who also, less felicitously, called it the "yellowing" of the conflict) as a desperate attempt to break the impasse in which they found themselves was not emphasized by the Nixon administration, which tried to sell this as a new policy capable of bringing about an honorable exit to the war. In the Mekong Delta, "Vietnamization" led to the withdrawal of the U.S. Ninth Division—the only major U.S. unit operating there—by mid-1969.

There was a large element of truth in the "new optimism," even though it had minimal impact on a war-weary U.S. public. However, just as General William C. Westmoreland, commander of U.S. forces in Vietnam, had overestimated the revolution's problems and underestimated its resilience and recuperative powers prior to Tet, the Nixon administration did not fully appreciate the factors that might lead to a revolutionary comeback. First, failing to learn the lesson of the previous administrations, they assumed that the revolution was critically dependent on outside aid, and that diplomatic pressures or incentives could induce the Soviet Union and China to lean on Hanoi, to provide an acceptable exit for the United States. Second, they assumed that the reserves of manpower from the North could be interdicted either militarily or diplomatically, and that the depleted revolutionary movement in the South would wither on the vine and be unable to recover. Third, the HES (Hamlet Evaluation Survey) scores for July 1969, the month the U.S. Ninth Division left Dinh Tuong for good, show that military success was not easy to translate into political success or gains in territorial security. Despite the shattering impact that U.S. forces had on revolutionary military units in the year and a half following the Tet Offensive, a comparison of maps based on HES scores for 1967, 1969, and 1971 suggests that the major gains in pacification in Dinh Tuong occurred after the U.S. Ninth Division had left the province. It could be argued that this constitutes evidence of the success of Vietnamization though, as the following chapter contends, "pacification" was more due to bombing and shelling that drove much of the rural population into safer areas (the GVN controlled zones which were the source of the devastation) than improved GVN performance. And, finally, the Nixon Administration assumed that with continued military aid and financial assistance from the United States, the Saigon government could translate its material superiority into a victory or, at least, something less than a clear-cut defeat.

One way this could be done was to induce the North Vietnamese to lie low for a while, to allow a "decent interval" to pass, after which the United States would no longer be held responsible for the outcome.[3] With the passage of time, a communist victory in Vietnam would not be perceived by the world as a major blow to American global credibility. This scenario would offer the United States the prospect of disengaging with a gradual withdrawal of troops while turning the war over to the Saigon government. It might be coupled with a negotiated settlement, but it did not depend on a formal accord. Of course, this "decent interval" scenario was based on one lesson the Nixon administration *did* learn, namely, that Vietnam was not the linchpin holding the "Free World" together, and that loss of South Vietnam would not in practical terms be a crippling blow to the U.S. global position. It was mainly the psychological impact of a defeat that concerned Nixon and his National Security Advisor Henry Kissinger.

Another way to end the costly and divisive U.S. presence in Vietnam was to negotiate a favorable settlement. While Vietnamization might be a prolonged process, and depended in large part on the performance of the Saigon government and army, a negotiated solution might bring a quicker end to the war and an earlier exit for the United States. If a negotiated solution could be achieved that was perceived to give a fighting chance to the United States's ally, it would not necessarily require that Saigon maintain decisive military superiority. Over the next several years, it became clear that the main problems in reaching such a settlement were (1) getting Hanoi to drop its insistence that the Saigon government would have to be dismantled prior to an agreement—which was partly a negotiating ploy and partly based on a genuine fear of repeating the 1954 approach of agreeing to a military cease-fire before reaching a political solution (which had backfired badly on the Party), and (2) having both Saigon and the United States agree to a settlement which left North Vietnamese troops in the South after a U.S. withdrawal.

My Tho and the Larger Context of the War Following the Tet Offensive

Details of the larger diplomatic context of the conflict are beyond the scope of this study, though there are some points at which this big picture intersects with the local dimension of the war in My Tho. The most important of these is what it tells us about the policy of Vietnamization which, along with negotiations, was one of the two main pillars of the Nixon disengagement strategy. Second, the revolutionary political and military policies in the Mekong Delta reflect some of the Communist Party's calculations about the connection between internal political strategy and the Paris negotiations. Elections and the formation of the Provisional Revolutionary Government in mid-1969 were largely pro-forma maneuvers carried out with an eye toward Paris rather than a real broadening of the political base of the revolution, and the way in which this new development was reflected at the village level gives an indication of the Party's political and diplomatic intentions. Third, some of the impact of the U.S. invasion of Cambodia in 1970 may be seen by examining how it affected the conflict in My Tho. Fourth, the Party fought a costly and losing battle to resist the "accelerated pacification" program, until it finally concluded that it would be smarter to lie low until the United States completed its withdrawal. It seems likely that Hanoi was unwilling to exercise greater flexibility in negotiations during this period, at first because it wanted to be in a better military position than its GVN opponent following the U.S. withdrawal, and kept throwing its forces at the opposition despite heavy losses, and then because it implicitly acknowledged the weakness of the revolution in the South (in 1971, as the next chapter will discuss) and simply waited for the United States to leave before resuming intensive military pressure in 1972 just before the signing of the Paris Agreements.

Either of the Washington scenarios for ending the U.S. military involvement in Vietnam could benefit from a major military effort in the final phase of U.S. involvement. Punishing the revolutionary forces and driving them onto the defensive would buy time for Vietnamization and the "decent interval." Military gains and pacification progress would strengthen the U.S. hand at the negotiating table. Finally, it would require more expensive and prolonged assistance from Hanoi's allies, thus putting an added strain on its diplomatic strategy. Although it seems paradoxical that Nixon's Vietnam policy involved escalation of the intensity of the war even as it deescalated its troop presence, the escalation was intended to make withdrawal possible. As this chapter shows, the whirlwind post-Tet Offensive operations of the U.S. Ninth Division pushed most big revolutionary units out of the province by 1969, and when these troops were poised to return in early 1970 the Cambodian invasion diverted them into other areas. Large-scale military operations did not resume in My Tho until the 1972 Easter Offensive.

The Tet Offensive triggered a massive counterattack by U.S. and Saigon forces. Hanoi's strategic calculation that the offensive would move the war to a new stage was correct, and in the long run this led to a negotiated withdrawal of the United States from the conflict. In the short run, however, the consequence of Tet was very different. Just as the 1964–65 escalation prompted the unwanted intervention of the United States, the Tet Offensive did not lead immediately to a deescalation of the conflict, rather, the U.S.–GVN response pushed war to an unparalleled level of intensity. Party leaders had carefully laid out a list of scenarios which they thought exhausted the possible range of U.S. responses. What they did not anticipate was that Washington might escalate the violence and expand the war into Laos and Cambodia (but not North Vietnam) and, at the same time, enter into negotiations while conducting a military withdrawal.

Party leaders had assumed that once the United States realized that "limited war" was not working, they would probably deescalate. If they did not, the only remaining possibility would be a major increase in U.S. military forces, with all the political and economic dislocations that would ensue, and an expansion of the war into the rest of Indochina, including North Vietnam. If that happened, the United States would fail because of a combination of the increased political, economic, diplomatic, and strategic strains of a much larger commitment of forces, and a probable sharp increase in Soviet and Chinese assistance.

Instead, over the course of the next several years, the United States capped and then reduced the level of its troops and made up for this by an even greater reliance on devastating firepower. This had tragic consequences for the civilian population of My Tho, which suffered extremely heavy casualties during the prolonged U.S. exit. The 1970 invasion of Cambodia expanded the war, but not in the way Hanoi had predicted. This invasion was not, in fact, part of a major expansion of the ground war, and the anticipated corollary of a partial U.S. invasion of North Vietnam. It was instead a desperation measure by President Nixon to push the Communist forces off balance long enough for the United States to extricate itself from the conflict (the "decent interval") and do so "with honor," while turning over the fighting to the GVN (the policy of "Vietnamization").

Draining the Water to Catch the Fish: Depopulating the Countryside

Up until the Tet Offensive, the much maligned General Westmoreland had earnestly attempted to minimize civilian "collateral damage" and preferred to fight in remote areas, partly out of concern for the effects on Vietnamese noncombatants of U.S. forces substituting firepower for American lives. In places such as My Tho, the existence of large "free-fire zones," where no clearance was required for bombing and artillery, meant that the restrictions did not apply to these areas and civilians living in these zones were considered to be "VC supporters" and, hence, legitimate targets. Also, the GVN was not bound by any of these restrictions, since it was the authorizing authority for airstrikes and shellings within the province, and it picked up American tactics such as "H and I fire" (harassment and interdiction fire) with gusto. The idea was to randomly shell suspected bases and liaison routes on the off chance that enemy cadres or troops might be passing by. The main purpose of this "H and I fire" was psychological—to keep the revolutionary forces off balance. For the civilians in the province, this was the most serious threat to their daily lives, until the Tet counteroffensive.

Westmoreland had relied on "search and destroy" operations in remote jungles and mountains. His careful and legalistic "rules of engagement" had tried to build in safeguards against the consequences of unrestrained military operations in heavily populated areas. Even General Westmoreland, however, became frustrated with the high costs and slow progress of pacification, and just before the Tet Offensive he considered the relative merits of a depopulation strategy. In a memorandum on "The Refugee Problem" dated January 4, 1968, Westmoreland wrote: "The success of the communist insurgency program is dependent upon control of the people. . . . In order to thwart the communist's [sic] designs, it is necessary to eliminate the 'fish' from the 'water,' or to dry up the 'water' so that the 'fish' cannot survive. Therefore, only two options are available in a practical sense; either the communists and their political control must be driven from the populated areas and security provided to keep them out, or the people must be relocated into areas that will facilitate security and prevent communist control apparatus from re-entering the community." The original draft of his memorandum stated: "The first course of action is very time consuming and expensive in terms of troop[s]," which was then corrected with a handwritten insertion that the first course of action is "preferred but it is" time consuming. "The second course of action," Westmoreland wrote, "can be carried out relatively quickly and is not as expensive in security troops as the first course of action. Although the military situation does not always permit, it is desirable to prepare well in advance for the relocation of the population. However, expediences [sic] may have to be resorted to as a military necessity." He concluded, "In summary, there are two basic ways of eliminating communist influence: one, by tediously catching the 'fish' (the VC) and letting the 'water' (the people) remain in place; two, by draining off the 'water' and recapturing it at another location and allowing the 'fish' to strangle. Discrimination must be exercised in choosing the method to be employed. The relocation of the population should not in all practicability be disallowed, since it can save lives, destruction, and time. However, the refugee care must be anticipated and sympathetically planned."[4]

Westmoreland's successor as Commander of U.S. forces in Vietnam, General Creighton Abrams, was an aggressive tank commander from the General Patton school, and had little patience for these niceties. Abrams abandoned "search and destroy" for "clear and hold" in populated areas. Some historians have argued that this was a strategic innovation by Abrams. In fact, "clear and hold" was part of Westmoreland's 1965 strategy for deploying U.S. troops. After phase I of "search and destroy" operations, Westmoreland envisioned a phase II, in which pacification would be resumed along with "clearing" and "securing," and a phase III which would "extend and expand clearing and security operations throughout the entire populated area of the country."[5] This shift was to have devastating consequences for many civilians in My Tho and other Mekong Delta provinces, but it opened the way for a pulverizing series of assaults on revolutionary troops and cadres that pounded them into quiescence by 1971.

Nearly unnoticed in the clamor of debate about negotiations and troop withdrawals, units such as the U.S. Ninth Division had taken off the kid gloves. During a six-month operation called Speedy Express, U.S. Ninth Division units claimed over 10,000 "VC KIA" (killed in action), but only came up with 900 weapons. An alert stringer for *Newsweek* magazine noticed the discrepancy some time later, and suggested the hypothesis that the vast gap between weapons and bodies may have indicated that a large number of those killed by the U.S. Ninth Division were not "VC" at all, or at least not armed troops. The implications of this possibility are in some ways more disturbing than the My Lai massacre, which happened just after Tet but was only uncovered the following year. In the furor over My Lai, it is curious that Speedy Express did not attract more attention. Unlike My Lai, which could be blamed on a few failed officers, the civilian casualties of Speedy Express were a consequence of official policy. Even the increasingly optimistic John Paul Vann criticized General Julian Ewell, commander of the Ninth Division for inflicting ex-

cessive civilian casualties in his quest for increasing the "body count" and the highly decorated Col. David Hackworth, a battalion commander in this division, stated that "I knew
Vann was right. Americans should never have been deployed in the Delta—especially
under the command of 'the Butcher of the Mekong Delta,' with his insatiable appetite for
body counts."[6] Ewell had clearly caught on to the new "catch the fish" approach. Hackworth
describes him as "a tightly wrapped, thin-lipped, hard charging West Pointer who meant to
drain the Delta before the Delta pulled the plug on him."[7]

Re-focus on the Mekong Delta After the Tet Offensive

The human costs of the post-Tet period to the people of My Tho were largely overshadowed by the reverberations of that epochal event. By the time memories of Tet had
faded, the attention of the outside world had shifted to the dramatic reversal of the fortunes of war, as the revolutionary forces were beaten back and the U.S. and Saigon
forces seized the initiative. After the Tet Offensive had been repulsed in the area around
Saigon, U.S. and GVN officials decided to make the Mekong Delta a top priority. With
the failure of the second May 1968 offensive around Saigon, the military resources that
had been concentrated on the defense of Saigon could now be diverted to the delta and
other places around Saigon.

As planning for a revived pacification program proceeded in mid-1968, William Colby,
the deputy director of the Civil Operations and Revolutionary Development Support
(CORDS) pacification bureaucracy, suggested to his boss Robert Komer (whom he soon
succeeded as director) "that its first priority be placed on the Mekong Delta provinces
south of Saigon. The Tet attack had devastated many of the communities of that area, but it
was clearly the key to a successful national pacification campaign, since it contained a
disproportionate percentage of the people of the nation, especially the rural population—
some six million in all—and was the rice basket for the whole country. Komer agreed to
the logic, even though we both knew we were taking on a large job, as the density of the
Vietnamese army units there was thin compared to some of the more northern areas, and
there was only one American division stationed in that area. But this was the point of the
exercise. Pacification was not a military chore but one of local security and development,
so that it was in the Delta that the need for it was obviously the greatest."[8] Priority for the
Mekong Delta took the form of expedited deliveries of better weapons to the province
forces in the area, and expansion of the Regional Force and Popular Force units there. It
also resulted in the dispatch of John Paul Vann to take over the CORDS operations in the
Mekong Delta.

In Colby's view, the main reason why pacification in the delta was crucial was that it
would support the "Vietnamization" program, by freeing South Vietnamese regular units
from pacification duties so they could take the place of the departing U.S. troops and
confront the main force units of the revolution. "The challenge, therefore, was to accelerate pacification to match the withdrawal of the Americans, which began in July 1969. The
first troops, happily, were taken from the Delta, to remove all American units from its
heavily populated terrain, so inappropriate for the American 'body count' mentality. The
geographic objectives of pacification did not greatly change, but, as I said to John Vann,
our real objective now was to replace the departing American units facing the regular

North Vietnamese Army units in the northern and mountain provinces on the nation's frontier."[9] The idea of turning more of the war over to the ARVN had been under serious discussion since before the Tet Offensive, but now became a major element of the Nixon administration's Vietnam policy. Pacification thus became indispensable to Vietnamization and, in Colby's opinion, the Mekong Delta was the key to the success of pacification.

The delta was also important for Communist Party strategists, first of all for the reverse of the reasons that Colby had stated (it was the key to preventing pacification and frustrating Vietnamization) and also because of the role that the delta played in their own plans. Although the Tet Offensive had achieved its goal of stretching the opponent's resources thin, creating a vacuum in the countryside that facilitated the intense but brief rural General Uprising, in the counteroffensive after Tet, the process subsequently began to work in reverse. Armed forces from adjacent provinces had to be sent to My Tho to assist in coping with the U.S. and GVN attacks. My Tho was the priority area of Military Region 2 because of its geographic centrality, which made it crucial to the control of the most vital communications routes to the Mekong Delta of both sides.

"Accelerated Pacification" and the Phoenix Program

The transition from counteroffensive to pacification began with an improvised "accelerated pacification program," a "three-month blitz starting in November [1968]."[10] The objective was to upgrade 1,000 hamlets from an "insecure" rating (on the Hamlet Evaluation Survey scale this meant category D or E, the two categories which indicated dominant but not complete revolutionary influence in a hamlet, or category V, for complete "Viet Cong" control) to "a relatively 'secure' state," meaning a HES rating of C or higher.[11] This first phase of post-Tet pacification was largely indistinguishable from the intense military counteroffensive, but it did mark the beginning of a shift to a clearer focus on pacification operations, and it regained some of the territorial control that had been lost by the GVN during and after Tet.

"Accelerated pacification" (*binh dinh cap toc*—though, as William Colby noted, even the GVN called it "APC") was not a carefully crafted or ingeniously implemented program. It was based on a simple but devastating tactic, described by the revolution as "draining the pond to catch the fish" (a phrase also used by General Westmoreland), in which the "draining" was essentially a rural depopulation strategy which, whether by accident or design, worked by making life in non-GVN areas unlivable for civilians. This strategy, however, had a potentially fatal flaw. Pacification would not be complete until the displaced civilian population returned to their homes. When they did, they would again be available for mobilization by the revolution *if* the cadres and guerrillas were still there to reactivate them. And, needless to say, bombing civilians out of their homes was not the most direct route to "winning hearts and minds."

The post-Tet pacification program was based on a different strategy than its previous incarnation. The previous strategies had concentrated on expanding control of territory and, thus, over the population in that territory. The "drain the pond" approach focused mainly on the population, and used a variety of means to physically move civilians from insecure areas into GVN controlled territory, rather than relying on expanding the area of GVN control. Whereas the "oilspot" and other theories were agnostic on the question of whether GVN security depended on eliminating the cadres and guerrillas or simply pushing them out of the area, the post-Tet strategy clearly assumed that they must be "neutralized" even though the logic of "draining the pond" would suggest that the cadres could be simply left in a depopulated wasteland to wither on the vine. The most notorious method of doing so was the Phoenix program, soon to become an infamous term in the lexicon of the Vietnam War. William Colby, as director of the CORDS pacification bureaucracy, frequently attempted to explain, with some irritation, that Phoenix was not an assassination program, and that "neutralizing" cadres did not necessarily mean killing them. In a technical sense, this was true. "Neutralizing" could be accomplished by capturing cadres or inducing them to defect, or simply to stop working. The spirit of Colby's objective is captured by the use of "wanted posters." Colby compared these to the "Wanted—Dead or Alive" posters of the American Wild West.[12] There were financial inducements for information. As advertised on the Phoenix "wanted posters," rewards would be given by the police merely for information. Nothing was said about qualifications such as "information leading to arrest and conviction"—it was assumed that arrest *meant* conviction.

The charge that Phoenix was an assassination program was more troubling to Colby, who wrote that "many casual readers of the press and of journals of extreme opinion still believe—and what's more believe that I have admitted—that Phoenix was responsible for the assassination of 20,000 Vietnamese, innocent as well as guilty. And this charge is repeated in some circles whenever my name comes up, bidding fair to become an accepted myth about me."[13] Colby argued that the 20,000 had been killed, not assassinated, and that 85 percent of these had been killed during military operations and only about 12 percent by police or other security forces carrying out their duties—i.e., the result of resisting arrest. Finally, Colby pointed to his own directive on the subject, which stated that Phoenix operations were "specifically not authorized to engage in assassinations or other violations of the rules of land warfare, but they are entitled to use such reasonable military force as is necessary to obtain the goals of rallying, capturing, or eliminating the VCI [Viet Cong infrastructure] in the RVN [Republic of Vietnam].[14]

Leaving aside the debating point about the "loophole" implicit in the statement that necessary force might be used for, among other things, "eliminating the VCI" (did this mean the general goal of eliminating the revolutionary organization, or did it mean doing this by killing the cadres?), there is no doubt that Colby—like most intelligence professionals—preferred live captives who could provide information. It also seems farfetched to draw a distinction between military members of the revolution, whom it was legitimate to kill, and civilian members, who, at least in the view of some of Colby's critics, had a presumptive right to due process. This is one of the many polemical aspects of the Vietnam war where liberal critics missed the point by selectively applying American concepts and values to a reality that was quite different. The civilian cadres regarded themselves as soldiers of the revolution, were quite willing to use "revolutionary violence" when necessary, and certainly did not accept the idea the GVN civil officials were "out of bounds" as targets of the conflict, which would be the logical parallel of this civil–military distinction.

Ironically, the focus on the Phoenix program by the antiwar movement in the United States pushed a much more important concern into the background. It was not the relatively few targeted assassinations, carried out mostly by GVN forces, that should have been the paramount moral and political concern of the United States. In fact, the Phoenix program degenerated into a morass of individual vendettas and settling of accounts, as well as an extortion program—activities which had gone on for time immemorial and were examples of general abuse of power. A study of this program concludes that even if taken at face value, the actual operations of Phoenix personnel accounted for only 7 percent of all those killed or captured by U.S.–GVN forces.[15] The Phoenix program was only one among many institutions and organizations that gave people acting "under the color of authority" the means to victimize others for personal reasons. More troubling than the Phoenix program in terms of actual American moral responsibility for the consequences of war was the widespread and often indiscriminate killing of civilians as a result of U.S. bombing, artillery, and military operations. This is an issue that was debated among Americans in general terms at the time, under the blanket rubric of "war crimes." Some antiwar forces issued blanket denunciations of the entire war as a criminal enterprise. Highly publicized *mea culpas* of American soldiers, such as the "Winter Soldier investigations," spotlighted atrocities of individuals and small units. So did the indelible crime of the My Lai massacre.

While America's attention was directed toward Phoenix and My Lai, the intensified operations of the U.S. Ninth Division in populated rural areas and the more relaxed procedures for protecting civilian life resulted in a significant escalation of civilian casualties— already unacceptably high even before the Tet Offensive. The evidence in the interviews does not shed much light on this period, first because the worst years for civilian deaths (1968–69) were not covered contemporaneously in the interviews, and second because civilian deaths were not new to the My Tho countryside. Only the scale of civilian death was different, and this tended to be indicated, several years after the event, by general phrases such as "the most ferocious period of the war." By this time civilian deaths had become a familiar feature of the war, and did not often merit special mention.

A related moral and political issue is the reliance on a pacification strategy based on a de-facto policy of depopulation. "Draining the pond to catch the fish" was the antithesis of the carefully calibrated policy of which pacification "czar" Colby dreamed, but it much better describes the reality of places like My Tho in 1968–71 than does Colby's account of carefully orchestrated intelligence, and bringing law and order with economic benefits to the countryside. It could be that the U.S. Ninth Division, which was the main architect of this policy in 1968 and 1969, did so as an unplanned by-product of operations conducted for other purposes. But General Westmoreland's "draining the water" memo of January 1968, cited above, suggests that it was either official policy or a reflection of thinking at the highest levels of military command in Vietnam. Professor Samuel Huntington wrote that the United States had unwittingly blundered into the right strategy to win the war— "forced draft urbanization," in which the negative element of refugees fleeing the countryside would be turned into a positive manpower source now denied to the enemy and under Saigon's control.

The Tide Turns Against the Revolutionary Forces After the Tet Offensive

In March 1968, the command of Military Region 2 convened a conference of its subordinate provinces and commands to evaluate the results of the first phase of the Tet Offensive.[16] This first comprehensive post-Tet evaluation by Region 2 also resulted in a redirection of the military efforts within the region, because of the heavy counterattacks. "After phase 1," says one military history of the region, "Region 8 [the old Resistance designation for Region 2, or Central Nam Bo] was regarded as having 'a diminished strategic resolve' *[sut giam quyet tam chien luoc]* for the reason that Region 8 saw that they had to shift their efforts to concentrating forces inside [the liberated areas], and then turning to liberate the rural areas, and sent a part of the region main force in a once-and-for-all attack of the My Phuoc Tay Agroville, as well as attacks on rural bases and posts, in order to support the three points of attack of the masses and liberate the entire countryside to take advantage of the collapse of [GVN] soldiers's morale after phase 1."[17] The fact that the attacks on towns and cities had to be abandoned, and the return to the defense of the countryside, was demoralizing evidence that the Tet Offensive was over, and that it had failed to hold on to the early gains achieved in the region—but is not what led to a "diminished strategic resolve" on the part of the region.

Postwar local histories have clarified the real issues underlying the phrase "diminished strategic resolve." Local military and political leaders in the upper Mekong Delta who were closest to the realities in the countryside were angered by the Party Central Committee's (COSVN's) dogged refusal to admit that the strategy of throwing all forces at the cities had become obsolete and counterproductive by at least mid-1968. The forces that were chewed up in ineffectual attempts to maintain pressure on the urban areas, Saigon in particular, could have been better used in taking advantage of opportunities to expand revolutionary control presented by the U.S.–Saigon retreat from the countryside following the initial shock of the Tet Offensive (described in the previous chapter). When the U.S.–GVN counterattack came, these forces were needed to oppose "accelerated pacification" in the villages.

A 1994 history of the war in Long An, published in Hanoi, was very critical of COSVN for clinging to an outmoded strategy. It concluded that "shifting direction to fight 'pacification' in the countryside took place far too late (after the enemy had regained control over almost all the countryside and left us in an isolated position in the area on the outskirts [of the urban areas], and so we encountered far too many problems."[18] Although the problem was especially acute in Long An because it was the springboard for attacking Saigon—a goal the top Party leaders were reluctant to abandon—other Southern provinces, including My Tho, also stuck with this urban-oriented strategy until the resources for doing so were exhausted, forcing a retreat to the rural areas. Even when the first formal strategic readjustment came in mid-1969 (discussed below), the move came far too late and even then the shift in strategy was not clearcut.

A My Tho city cadre said that this policy shift from the cities to the countryside did not come quickly enough, and the delay cost the revolution heavily in terms of lost opportunities. Describing the period immediately after the Tet Offensive, he said:

> Granted the [National Liberation] Front couldn't take over My Tho, what was most dangerous was the fact that it failed to destroy the GVN governing apparatus and the underground organizations suffered the consequences of this failure. Once this happened, the Front didn't consider the local conditions in My Tho in order to devise a method and a principle of operation appropriate to the situation here. Instead, it thought My Tho was like Hue or Saigon. And so it lost its influence among the cadres, while the population—who didn't understand the situation—thought it was a big Front victory.

The situation being what it was following the Tet attack, once it was confirmed that it was impossible to take over the city, the troops that were concentrated on the edge of the city should have turned around and helped to enlarge the liberated areas on the edge of town. With their strength at the time, they were well equipped and had more troops than they needed, so the Front forces should have turned around and liberated the country- side and created a firm foothold for the Front by wiping out all the GVN village and hamlet governing apparatuses, and they could have turned the situation in the cities around. They were bogged down like that, and yet they forced the troops to stay put on the edge of town in order to hold on to the area, thereby making the troops targets for the enemy bombings and shellings. If you hold the battlefield that way, you'll get cut to pieces [DT313].

The strategy proved to be a very costly departure from the elusive guerrilla tactics that had so often given the revolutionary troops a tactical advantage. More importantly, the Tet- inspired zeal of the remobilized peasantry began to dissipate. In the traditionally strong village of My Loi (Cai Be), by mid-1968 the revolution had to stop using public pressure and "reduction of prestige" sessions to intimidate and humiliate people who refused to carry out assigned tasks, because so many villagers began shirking these duties that it was impossible to invoke social pressure [DT331].

By the middle of 1968 the province Party committee headquarters, which had relocated to Hoi Cu village, was forced to cope with continuous operations which went on for three to four months, as well as intense bombing and shelling [DT337]. A member of the prov- ince committee staff said that by the end of 1968, the numerical strength of units in the province was "way down, and couldn't be replaced" [DT337]. A captured document re- vealed that at a Military Region 2 conference on guerrilla warfare in mid-September 1968, provinces like My Tho had been criticized for failing to properly implement the Three- Year Recruitment plan. Among other measures, this plan called for getting partial invalids who had been allowed to return to their villages to enlist in the village guerrillas. Accord- ing to this document, "no Party members in twenty-six villages of My Tho province volun- teered to join the guerrillas," and in another village in the region only two of seventy Party members served in guerrilla units.[19]

By the end of 1968, the Party acknowledged that in most of My Tho the "guerrilla forces had been sent up as replacements to the main force units during the offensive waves of 1968 and each village only had one or two cells of guerrillas remaining, or even only one or two guerrillas left."[20] The 514th Battalion had a major clash in the heart of the 20/7 zone with the ARVN Seventh Division at the end of the year and sustained heavy casual- ties. A villager from My Long reported that he did not see the 514th after that [DT355]. In Binh Duc village, the conclusion that the war would go on for a long time did not fully register among those mobilized by the Tet Offensive until the beginning of 1969, but "as the situation dragged on, a number of them deserted" [DT301].

Many revolutionary adherents began to take stock of the gains and losses of the year following the Tet Offensive, and realized that the war was not going to end soon. Even during the fierce initial U.S. and GVN counterattacks, the very intensity of the military operations may have given the impression that the war could not last long at that accel- erated pace, and that the high-tempo fighting would force an early resolution of the conflict. However, when the fighting continued month after month, even at this accelerated pace, this prospect seems to have faded away. The Party continued its attempts to bolster morale by holding out the prospects of an early end to the war even well into 1969. A village guerrilla from Tam Hiep reported that in the main political indoctrination session of 1969 he was told that peace was just around the corner *(sap em roi)* [DT304].

The issue of peace posed thorny political and psychological problems for the revolutionaries. On the one hand, they wanted to persuade those making sacrifices on the villages and the battlefields that their contributions were having an impact at the negotiating table, and that they must try even harder if they wanted the war to end quickly. On the other hand, the Party had consistently warned against the dangers of becoming overreliant on the diplomatic process, and tried to discourage any illusions about a quick and painless political end to the war. The messages sent to the cadres and troops were to some extent working at cross purposes. One said that their contributions would support the negotiations and bring peace, while the other told them to forget about negotiations, that the only absolute guarantee of peace was to bring about an end to the war through victory on the battlefield.

However, many who had joined in the enthusiasm of Tet stayed on permanently, or until they were killed. Even among those who ultimately left, some endured the fierce combat until 1969 or even 1970. Others, however, were discouraged by the prolongation and escalation of the war. A young man who had been with the revolution since 1960 finally lost faith after the Tet Offensive, because he thought that if the revolution could not end the war under those circumstances, it wouldn't get a second chance. Even so, he said that 90 percent of the young men in Cai Lay had joined the revolution at Tet, and that they only started to desert in 1969 [DT385]. The official Party history records that by the beginning of 1969 the entire area of My Tho province and city, along with Go Cong, had thirty-three liberated villages and 120 liberated hamlets with a combined population of 300,000 people under revolutionary control.[21] The rural population of the province in 1969 was around 540,000 by the GVN's count. The U.S. province advisor's report for April 1969 (covering the period up to the end of March 1969) stated that "the GVN now controls 61 percent of the population and 41 percent of the hamlets." This was "an all time high since Tet 1968." A comparison of the HES scores of January 1968 and July 1969 show that this claim was based on the assumption that a "C" or contested hamlet was essentially under the control of the GVN. The comparison reveals that much of the province was still under the predominant control of the revolutionary side. The major difference is that many of the "V" (under total "Viet Cong" control) hamlets of 1968 had shifted to the "D" category (predominant "Viet Cong" influence) by July 1969.

One village cadre felt that the turning point was not the counteroffensives of 1968, but the pacification of 1969. "It was not until mid-1969," he said, "when the GVN pacification was going strong and the infrastructure organizations had been destroyed and the cadres had fled, that the people lost confidence in the Front" [DT305]. The province Party history seems to point to the middle and latter parts of 1969 as the period when the difficulties became serious to the point of immobilizing operations. By April 1969, "two-thirds of the villages in Go Cong province [which had been split off from My Tho in 1968 because of communications difficulties] had been seized by the enemy." B52 strikes in Cai Be and Cai Lay, along with defoliation and continuous helicopter reconnaissance, made even the base areas along the Nguyen Van Tiep Canal extremely vulnerable. "The enemy continuously ambushed the communication corridors and brought our liaison and supply activities to a halt." Intense ARVN operations following the departure of the U.S. Ninth Division also had a major impact, and by the latter part of 1969 "the province Party committee headquarters had to move constantly. The concentrated troops of the region and province had to split up into companies and platoons." GVN pacification efforts and general cadre demoralization took a heavy toll on the revolutionary ranks. "They carried out their psychological warfare and Chieu Hoi activities with a lot of poisonous and crafty schemes. These schemes caused us a significant amount of damage."[22] A village guerrilla near the Tam Hiep priority pacification area and the province airfield said that in his view, "in 1968 we were able to continue fighting, and through 1969 people were still confident." It was not until 1970, he argued, that demoralization set in [DT302].

The U.S.-GVN Counter Offensive:
Breaking Up the Big Revolutionary Units

Pacification in the post-Tet period was a three-step process. The first step was pushing back the concentrated units into remote areas and forcing them to break up into smaller units, less able to pose a threat to the GVN, especially the regional and popular force militia in the villages. This, in turn, would free up U.S. and ARVN units to operate in smaller units and cover a wider area with more frequent operations. With this kind of support, the second step could be taken. A network of small posts could be extended into previously untenable areas. After this, as a third step, the civilian population would be regrouped around these posts, using the threat of burning or dismantling their houses as an incentive for villagers who were reluctant to move. With the population relocated in GVN-controlled areas, the village and hamlet cadres would be isolated and would find it difficult to survive—let alone carry out political and military activities. Thus isolated, the cadres would be easier targets for "neutralization."

According to interviews in 1971, by the middle of 1968 even the leading units of Region 2 were having difficulty maintaining their effectiveness. The 261st Battalion was able to operate in the exposed terrain of Cho Gao district—something it had not been able to do in 1967—but it was ineffective, and ultimately had to retreat west of Highway 4. In August and September 1968, however, the 261st returned to Cho Gao near Binh Phuc Nhat village. A village cadre proposed using a platoon of the battalion to shell the nearby post, and a company to attack it "in order to push forward the popular movement in the village." The plan was foiled by the appearance of a GVN unit from Go Cong, which resulted in a battle that lasted for one day and one night. The firepower of the 261st was by this time "so weak that they were routed," leaving behind nearly a company of dead [DT305]. Next, the smaller and more mobile 514th Battalion also seems to have gradually retreated from the eastern part of the province. By 1969, Northerners began to fill the ranks of these traditional "Viet Cong" units [DT390]. Even company-sized units were probably closer to platoons, because following the first wave of Tet attacks, the strength of the 514th and its clone 514B "suffered continuous losses, so they rarely had more than a hundred men. It was impossible to reinforce them" [DT313].

Impact of the U.S. Ninth Division on My Tho

Although the U.S. Ninth Division devised some quite effective infantry tactics, and had a major impact because of its intensive infantry operations, the main contribution to pacification was the bombing and shelling, which forced people into GVN-controlled areas. "Infantry troops were crucial," said the Binh Duc Party secretary, "and posts are dangerous. Even twenty American troops dared penetrate deep into a liberated area to attack, whereas ARVN wouldn't dare do this even with two or three companies." Although this made life difficult for the cadres, the major blow to revolutionary control was not the ground operations. "Gradually the response of the ARVN and the American troops forcibly separated the people from the revolution. They caused a lot of difficulties for the people, destroyed their crops and belongings with bombings and shellings, and this is why the people had to suffer privations. If they stayed in the liberated areas they wouldn't be able to earn their living so they had to flee into the Strategic Hamlet areas" [DT301].

Some of the military setbacks suffered by revolutionary forces were due to the effective operations of the U.S. forces in the delta, which turned the tactics the revolution had devised against it. A circular dated July 9, 1968, instructed various units to take precautions against a new enemy tactic for surprise attacks, that relied on "silence" tactics. "The enemy positions troops in the field at night. When discovered and attacked by our troops they remain silent, pretending they are not in the location, but when our troops are within range they react with grenades and then open fire. They also hide in fortified bunkers to avoid mortar attacks and when our troops approach they call for artillery fire."[23] Thus the elaborate system of fortified bases devised in the early 1960s no longer worked, because the other side had learned to use the same fortifications (when they did not destroy them), and the "umbrella of security" did not deter U.S. forces from entering revolutionary areas in small units.

It was not so much the tactics as the superior mobility and firepower of the U.S. Ninth Division troops that enabled them to operate in more dangerous areas with fewer troops than the ARVN. The "jitterbugging" and "piling on" tactics of using small units to locate revolutionary units and then massively reinforcing them was made possible by the lavish use of air transport, which quickly brought reinforcements in helicopters, and air power, which protected the searching small units and bailed them out of trouble if they encountered a stronger revolutionary unit. The Binh Duc Party secretary said that "When the Americans were still here, their regular troops were very active, so they didn't need to set up posts at night or to have many units operating. They only relied on aerial bombings day and night without letup and sent their ground troops deep into liberated areas" [DT301].

Civilian Casualties from Bombing and Shelling

The U.S. Ninth Division commander later wrote that "all of the efforts put into civic actions could be undone in an area by one destructive operation. Our part of the delta, with a little over three percent of the country's land surface, had ten percent of the country's population. When we broke down into small units covering large areas, the possibilities for damage increased." Nevertheless, he concluded that the policy of adopting "urban rules of engagement as well as our own 1000 meter buffer zone around populated areas to prevent excessive use of artillery" had led to "only moderate civilian casualties" during the period of "very heavy combat over an extended period of time in late 1968 and early 1969."[24]

The overall U.S. strategy, however, was to substitute firepower for manpower wherever possible, and Ninth Division operations in My Tho and Kien Hoa exemplified this approach. The problem was that the firepower accompanied the ground troops on their excursions throughout the province looking for enemy units and, therefore, was not aimed at particular confirmed targets but served primarily to "soften up" the areas the small U.S. units were about to probe. It should not be surprising, therefore, that the "collateral" damage to nonmilitary people and property caused by these bombings and shellings was extensive. Judging from the interviews, the most destructive period of Ninth Division activities, operation "Speedy Express," was not an isolated case. In a lengthy study of the Ninth Division's operations in Vietnam co-authored by the division's commander, the only apparent reference to operation Speedy Express is a statement that when the Ninth Division received a unit citation from the Vietnamese chairman of the Joint General Staff in June 1969, "Here for the first time a major unit was receiving an award for humanitarian interest in the Vietnamese people while at the same time being cited for gallantry in inflicting over 10,000 casualties on the enemy during a four month period."[25]

The cited casualty figure is close to the statistic compiled at the end of the six-month-long operation in My Tho and Kien Hoa. Historian Ronald Spector writes: "In operations in the Mekong Delta from December 1968 to June 1969, the 9th Infantry Division reported a body count of almost eleven thousand enemy dead and only 267 U.S. fatalities, a kill ratio of 40.8 to one. Strangely enough, only about 751 weapons were captured. Pacification advisors in the Delta suspected that many of those killed were not Vietcong fighters, but civilian 'supporters' willing or unwilling and innocent bystanders. Admiral Salzer concluded that one brigade commander of the 9th Infantry Division was 'psychologically . . . unbalanced. He was a super fanatic on body count. He would talk about nothing else during an operation. . . . Maybe he was a good commander but you could almost see the saliva dripping out of the corners of his mouth. An awful lot of the bodies were civilians.' In 1972 Kevin P. Buckley of *Newsweek* charged that close to half of the eleven thousand 'enemy' killed by the 9th Infantry Division had been civilians."[26]

Impact of Deteriorating Security Situation
on Cadres and Revolutionary Organizations

The effect of these civilian deaths on the revolutionary movement cannot be measured solely in terms of the numbers who were actually killed. As the above accounts indicate, the fear of death was sufficient to induce large numbers of villagers to move into GVN areas. It also made mobilizing for civilian labor activities in support of the revolution much more difficult, right from the time of the post-Tet counteroffensive of 1968. A cadre from Binh Duc said that the villagers' spirits "dropped because the war got fierce, and people didn't believe in the Front's victory any longer. Only about five or six people were killed doing civilian labor duty, but it had a big effect on the policy." The cadres tried to counteract this by holding solemn funeral ceremonies for the villagers killed during civilian labor missions, called them "fallen heroes," and had the popular associations give assistance to their families. This was evidently not enough to alleviate the fears of going on these missions. In some cases it did not mollify the families of those who were killed, and some of these turned the lessons they had learned about political agitation on the very cadres who had taught them. The former village Party secretary said, "There were cases where people whose relatives were killed came and cursed the cadres in the style of "face-to-face struggles" [DT301].

How much of this intensive bombing and shelling actually put the village cadres and guerrillas out of action is unclear. A prisoner who had operated in Nhi Binh village said, "the Americans rained down about 100 artillery shells per person, but our people are still there. The trees are still there, so the liberation brothers are still there" [DT312]. Even if most cadres survived the onslaughts, they took a psychological toll. As noted above, the village Party secretary of Binh Duc complained of the psychological oppressiveness of a life of hiding in bomb shelters, hardly daring to come up for a breath of fresh air [DT301].

The province Party committee, which had been staying in Hoi Cu village for several years, was also forced to move. A code clerk who traveled with the province headquarters said that "beginning in 1969 the situation was not quiet and we had to flee the bombing and shelling. Sometimes we didn't have time to eat or breathe, and the GVN expanded their area of control daily." In 1969 the province headquarters "moved to Long Trung village near the Ba Rai River for about a year. Long Trung was then pacified and its terrain cover destroyed, so they moved to Thanh Hoa in Cai Lay, but were subjected to continuous bombing. They then moved to Long Tien in mid-1970" [DT337]. A village guerrilla from Cam Son, near Long Trung and Long Tien in the heart of the 20/7 zone, said that "no big units have come into Cam Son since 1969. Too many posts have been set up" [DT339]. By the end of 1970, 353 posts and watchtowers had been set up in the post-Tet pacification push, bringing the total in Dinh Tuong province to 633 (with another 157 in Go Cong).[27]

Revival of Pacification Following the Tet Offensive

The evidence from the interviews suggests that although many cadres were killed along with guerrillas and civilians in 1968–69, it was not until the concentrated units had been dispersed and pushed back and the GVN consequently was able to extend a thick network of militia posts into formerly contested and liberated villages and hamlets that the core cadres in the villages began to encounter real difficulties. Depopulation was the main cause of these difficulties, since the cadres could no longer mobilize the villagers, and were left without a source of protection and supply, and even without a mission. However, as the next chapter will examine in detail, "draining the pond" did not result in catching all the "fish" in the rural areas of My Tho, and the surviving cadres were able to hold on and wait for conditions to change. Still, the critical phase of the pacification process was the extension of the GVN control structure based on an interlocking network of posts, which blanketed the area with militia. The "accelerated pacification" operations and the associated bombing and shelling had paved the way for this, both by removing the threat of concentrated units to these posts and by forcing a major demographic redistribution in the countryside. Those people who had fled from the liberated or contested areas were regrouped around these posts, farther from the cadres and closer to the GVN authorities.

"The total effect of VCI eliminations on the VC effort in Dinh Tuong province," cautioned the October 1968 report of the American province advisor, "must be termed slight." November's report indicated some progress, but the decrease of the percentage of population under "VC control" from 39.5 percent to 31.3 percent "reflects not only the loss of VC hamlets, but lower estimated population in hamlets still controlled by the VC," an evidence of the role depopulation played in the pacification effort. About half the rise in GVN-controlled population from 590,000 to 640,000 (unlike the HES population figures, this included urban areas) was attributed to a rise in the population of My Tho city, clearly as a result of refugees. As of October 1968, the province chief was reluctant to commit resources to opening the road north from Cai Lay to the My Phuoc Tay Agroville and Kien Tuong province, for fear of becoming overextended. Still, this difficult task had been accomplished by February 1969. Two major items of progress were reported at the end of November 1969. One was that for the first time the number of killed, captured, or defected exceeded the U.S./GVN estimate of the revolution's ability to recruit in the province—the fabled "crossover point" on which General Westmoreland had based his strategy of attrition. Ironically, by this time Westmoreland had been replaced by General Creighton Abrams, who had abandoned this concept.[28]

As pacification continued to gain, the Vietnamization program also moved along. The August 1969 sector report noted that all of the U.S. Ninth Division had left the province except for a battalion which was providing security at the Dong Tam base. From this time on, American ground troops were not a factor in the Mekong Delta—though U.S. air power was still a major prop for Vietnamization.

There were still some concerns about how well pacification would fare during the Vietnamization process. A comprehensive study of pacification done by a U.S. military historian after the war concludes that the departure of the U.S. Ninth Division "ended the innovative riverine operations with the U.S. Navy and made the ARVN 7th Division responsible for securing the southern approaches to Saigon. Thus, the responsibility for military support of pacification fell fully on the 7th Division. Its desertion rate rose rapidly, becoming in September 1969 the highest of any ARVN division. The number of defectors also dropped after the 9th Division left, a sign that the ARVN unit was putting less pressure on the enemy. The 7th made such feeble efforts that Dinh Tuong province advisor Colonel Harry Amos referred to the division as being 'adamant in refusing to act against the infrastructure.' " This study adds that, "The continued activity of the infrastructure and the psychological and military threat of the Viet Cong vitiated popular support for the Saigon government. During the accelerated [pacification] campaign, the government had been unable to convince the citizens of Dinh Tuong that it could protect them."[29]

As the next chapter shows, this judgment about the psychology of the civilian population may have been correct, but the evaluation of the ARVN requires some qualification. The ARVN and other GVN forces did, in fact, "pacify" most of Dinh Tuong by 1971, at least for a time. A comparison of province maps of HES scores in 1967, 1969, and 1971 suggests that more pacification occurred between mid-1969 when the U.S. Ninth Division departed and 1971 than in the 1967–69 period when U.S. troops were present. Of course, the U.S. Ninth Division laid the groundwork for this by breaking up and pushing back the military forces of the revolution. Yet, though the ARVN did not approach pacification with the offensive zeal of the U.S. Ninth Division, it managed to find other ways to extend Saigon's reach in the absence of a major challenge from the revolution's big military units, as the next chapter will discuss, including rural depopulation as a result of heavy bombing and shelling and forced relocation of civilians.

Impact of Pacification on Life in the Villages

Many of the problems for the revolutionary movement that had been building in the period before Tet 1968 reemerged in 1969, but now the magnitude of these difficulties was much greater. Loss of population resulted in the erosion of the popular associations, which were the key foundation of the revolution's entire support structure. Taxes were difficult to collect, and recruiting for military units came to a standstill. Now the village and hamlet cadres were increasingly unprotected, as the military units were pushed out of the province and this, in turn, made their activities among the dwindling population in revolutionary areas difficult and dangerous.

For the cadres and their supporters in former revolutionary strongholds such as Hung Thuan on the border between My Tho and Kien Phong province, or My Loi near the Plain of Reeds, life was increasingly miserable. Even noncadres who wanted to cling to their native hamlets found the situation grim. A young woman who was a marginal supporter of the revolution described how the bombing and shelling had forced the remaining population to move to the middle of the rice fields. "Out there in the rice fields the sun beats down on you and there are no trees and bushes for shade. Every family made a tiny hut to live in to make it through the day. With regard to food, living in the rice fields is harder than living along the riverbank where there are fruit trees and fish, and life is easy and more pleasant." In My Loi, in July 1969 the cadres were still able to mobilize the few remaining villagers to go on civilian labor missions for a few days, only to find that the supply routes had been cut off by ARVN operations and there was nothing to transport [DT334].

In Thanh Hung village, life for the peripheral supporters of the revolution was even more miserable. A seventeen-year-old girl had studied to be a medic for a few months but ended up returning to her original job doing civilian labor missions, because there were no people left to care for in the revolutionary area where she stayed. In 1968 she was drafted during the Tet Offensive to go to My An with a group of twenty porters, mostly male. After a week of indoctrination on the goals of the revolution, they performed regular rice transportation missions from My An to My Loi, about three times a month. Unlike the previous system, under which civilian laborers were drafted periodically, in the post-Tet period all the civilians in heavily bombed areas like My Loi had fled, and the porters now were considered full-time members of the revolution. When they were not on mission, they lived in small scattered cells, in open fortified trenches. "In there, it was very depressing. Our cell had only four people and there was no one nearby. We just cooked meals and passed the time in the trench until we had a mission. Sometimes a jet plane would bomb very close to where I was and I was afraid that the trench would collapse and kill me. Many times the planes strafed around us, and there were times when the soldiers came in on operation. It was very dangerous." Living in the open, with only a sheet of nylon to fend off the rain, she eventually contracted malaria. Evidently, the two boys and two girls in her cell lived chastely together and "only talked about everyday things, never about love." "The most bombing and shelling was in 1969. That was when the pacification soldiers and the ARVN came in on operations daily." Finally, the other girl in the cell, a very close friend, was killed by ARVN soldiers. The survivors could only cover her with a piece of plywood in a crude burial [DT334].

Several Party histories report frankly on the cadre demoralization of the period. Despite the dispatch of COSVN and region cadres to help out the local organizations, the situation continued to deteriorate, and some of these outside cadres were themselves killed. They "shared the hardships of the comrades in Chau Thanh and Cai Lay districts in My Tho, who said dejectedly, 'there isn't a day that goes by when we don't bury a comrade. The enemy is all around us, if we want to retreat, we don't know where to go. We can only rig grenade traps, but they kill more of us than the enemy.'"[30] By the beginning of 1970, bombing (including the dreaded antipersonnel cluster bombs, or CBUs), defoliation, clearing of trees and foliage which concealed cadre hideouts, and forced population regroupment created great difficulties for the revolution. "The headquarters of the province and district Party committees had to move constantly. In our ranks there emerged demoralization [tu tuong dao dong] and confusion. A number left their posts and fled for safety, and some went out and surrendered to the enemy."[31]

Security Situation in Late 1969 and 1970

It may be significant that it was evidently not until mid-1969 that COSVN fully understood the plight of the revolutionary forces in the Mekong Delta, which they had been ordering into the breach from their remote jungle redoubts. The Long An province study notes that the leaders of a key zone bordering Saigon got to meet Pham Hung, the head of COSVN, in mid-1969, for the first time since the Tet Offensive. "Since the receipt of the order to attack Saigon, this was the first time that Subregion 3 of Long An had gotten an opportunity to report directly the difficulties in the outskirts of the urban areas [vung ven] and to present the thoughts and viewpoints of the Subregion about the linkage between the urban outskirts and the rural areas to the rear. This was a matter that COSVN was intensely researching. But the reality-based reports of the Subregion became very important in determining the strategic direction for the next period. It was clear that reports by wireless and by written documents coming from the battlefield had not adequately reflected the realities of combat, and usually suppressed and downplayed the intense difficulties and the painful truth. Comrade Pham Hung was very moved when he heard about the situation in Long An."[32]

The revolutionary military forces were experiencing even greater difficulties at the end of 1969, though there was a flurry of military activity toward the end of the year. Whether from necessity or by design, some of the main force units in My Tho began withdrawing toward the Cambodian border. A postwar history of the Plain of Reeds says that this was part of a plan of drawing U.S./ARVN forces away from the key pacification areas and creating conditions for a subsequent attack on the populated areas. "As for the Region Main Force, during this period, the notable battles were fought by . . . [the 261st Battalion] on the Cai Be district battlefields, which had received orders to concentrate and hit hard at the puppet army, to bring about an American withdrawal, make it impossible for the puppets to become stronger, and at the same time pull the enemy forces which are concentrated on supporting pacification to the distant border regions, creating conditions for the local areas to energize [xuc tich] their forces so that when we move into 1970 there will be larger attack phases. We must do what it takes to make the Mekong Delta surge forward."[33] This explains the intensification of military activity noted by the American advisors in late 1969.

The revolutionary forces themselves had been reinforced, and the 88th Regiment of the North Vietnamese Army (NVA) was brought into the Plain of Reeds. On December 2, 1969, the 88th Regiment and province forces from Kien Tuong attacked the district town of Kien Binh "to widen the corridor along the [Cambodian border]." The attack inflicted heavy casualties on the defending GVN forces but at a very high price for the 88th Regiment which suffered heavy casualties and was forced to withdraw, while the Kien Tuong province 504th Battalion managed to penetrate briefly into the GVN district headquarters. "This was a battle which achieved its basic purpose," said the Plain of Reeds history, "but did not result in victory, so that the price paid in sacrifices [casualties] was even higher." However, in this retrospective view, this high price brought about some returns, and "the small nameless battles that popped up in many places caused the GVN colonel who commanded Kien Tuong sector to admit in his report of December 1969, 'From their bases along the Vietnam–Cambodia border the Viet Cong have continued to threaten the province capital of Kien Tuong as well as the posts along the border, and have attacked our local forces on operations.'"[34] Although the Saigon government was occasionally compelled to reconsider its priorities because of lack of sufficient forces, by 1970, the GVN was clearly gaining the military initiative in Dinh Tuong. As the bases for revolutionary main force units contracted in the face of increased ARVN pressure, the results were soon felt in the pacification program. Despite the arrival of North Vietnamese units in the delta, the sector advisors retained their optimism and the August 1970 report stated that "the GVN now controls 91 percent of the province" and that Cho Gao district for the first time had all of its hamlets in the ABC categories, that is, with no hamlets remaining under dominant revolutionary control. (In the December 1970 HES report, all of the hamlets of Binh Ninh village were rated "D." Apparently Binh Ninh had not yet been reinstated to the HES in August 1969). By September 1970 the province had pushed its pacification activities into the very fringes of the Plain of Reeds, and had begun to clear the area along the canal connecting Hau My village and My Phuoc Tay, as well as continuing to try to consolidate the area around Cai Nua, the key post controlling Route 20, the road between Highway 4 and the strategically critical strongpoint at Hau My on the Western fringe of the Plain of Reeds. The following month, the ARVN Twelfth Regiment of the Seventh Division stepped up operations around the "wagon wheel" at the very center of northern Cai Be in order to consolidate the ambitious plan to interdict concentrated units from the stepping-off point of "base 470."

Both the region and the province leaders tried desperately to stem the tide of pacification by deploying their dwindling forces to challenge the GVN occupiers, but there were not enough troops to go around. A leading cadre of the My Tho province unit described the problems he encountered in northern Cai Be during this period.

> From 1969 to 1970 the GVN launched the pacification program, which had a major impact. I must say that there is no question that the pacification campaign had a powerful negative impact on the morale of the cadres and the rural people. During the Tet Offensive the plan was to seize land and expand out from it like an oilspot. Unexpectedly, the pacification program shrank these areas bit by bit, like a piece of meat drying in the sun. That idea of expanding the liberated areas after the Tet Offensive was gradually defeated, and then land was lost and there were no more people. Both cadres and people lost their confidence gradually, until it finally collapsed altogether. At the time the infra-

structure and the armed units tried continuously but didn't succeed. The cadres and units fled from one place to another, but there were no safe havens. It was the same for me. I was at the time the deputy commander of the province unit in charge of Route 20. I used the 514th Battalion to hit continuously along the road, with the aim of blocking pacification going deep into the liberated areas. Lt. Col. Hap, the Cai Be GVN district chief, and I clashed all the time. Lt. Col. Hap couldn't ever get across Road 20 or pacify that area. I tried hard to hold on to that area but gradually it shrank, though not rapidly as in other places. I was still able to hold on to the operational area and was able to station an entire battalion there. MR2 [Military Region] cadres could come and go in that area. At the time the situation in the areas to the east, like northern Cai Lay, northern and southern Chau Thanh, had deteriorated alarmingly, just like soap bubbles exposed to the sunlight. The cadres took refuge but had no place to hide. The province Party committee had to send me to northern Chau Thanh district to destroy pacification. I restored Front control in Tan Hoi and Tan Phu for a time, but then Route 20 was lost. This time a direct order from MR2 sent me back to Route 20. It was not a routine order from just the province Party committee. This was because Route 20 in northern Cai Be was the key area *[moi truong]* of the region. If we couldn't hold Route 20, the region couldn't come in [to My Tho]. This was the key gateway for the region to send cadres and materiel from up there [the Plain of Reeds] down here. I returned to Route 20 and northern Chau Thanh had all its villages cleared and the cadres all ran like hell and hid. I felt really let down. My life was miserable and my struggle was really worthless. I couldn't hold the territory and I myself had to be exiled like a sacrificial beast. I saw clearly that I couldn't do anything under those circumstances. The province unit at the time only had six people. I returned to Route 20 and sent Ba Kieu, the deputy unit commander, to Tan Phu to block pacification. A few days later he was shot and killed. Tu Luong [the "Chinese King"] replaced Ba Kieu [DT415].

The dilemmas posed by stretching forces too thin, which had always plagued the GVN, now became a major problem for the revolution. Even the redoubtable "Chinese King," a guerilla war specialist who had been sent to the Ap Bac area to replace a deputy province unit commander who had been killed and to arrest the decline of the guerrilla movement in Northern Chau Thanh, eventually had to flee [DT415].

Despite the military gains by the GVN, even the "new optimists" must have found it difficult to believe what the HES statistics for December 1970 told them. These figures indicated that there were only forty-eight contested hamlets and four "VC hamlets" left in Dinh Tuong province, and that the GVN controlled a population of 550,146, with 12,869 in the contested category according to the January 1971 U.S. province advisor's report. According to the HES, there were only 350 people living in "VC-controlled" areas by the end of 1970. Although it is clear that pacification had spread to most of the province, it is not credible that only 350 people out of a population of nearly 600,000 remained in areas of revolutionary control, and it is difficult to credit the 12,869 figure of those living in contested areas. In the next chapter we will examine the meaning of these figures and assess them in the light of other available data. Even assuming that this was an accurate reflection of the territorial security situation in which these categories of population lived, we must investigate whether this also reflects changes in political attitudes and behavior as well as territorial security—in short, how deep-seated and permanent was the remarkable pacification of 1969–70? This question will be addressed in the following chapter.

By 1970, the rapid pacification progress naturally slowed, as the majority of the hamlets were now considered to some degree "secure." In June the province mounted an operation to go after the last major base area in the 20/7 heartland, in Cam Son village. Although the news looked upbeat, for the first time the sector report noted the arrival of an entire North Vietnamese unit in the province. The Eighty-eighth NVA Regiment, with 450 men, was confirmed present in the province. A leading province military cadre said that in October 1970 the province received 180 North Vietnamese, "including both cadres and soldiers to reinforce the units—especially the 514C Battalion, which at the time had only 120 people, including both cadres and soldiers" [DT415]. Vietnamization in the Mekong Delta now had to cope with the arrival of Northern troops to fill the void left by the local concentrated units, which had dwindled in strength, broken up into smaller units, or gone to Cambodia to regroup.

The Invasion of Cambodia

The major change in the strategic context during the period from Tet 1968 to the end of 1970 was the invasion of Cambodia. It came shortly after the U.S. advisors had expressed concern about the arrival of a North Vietnamese unit in My Tho, and an upsurge of revolutionary military activity at the end of 1969. But the predicted local assaults in My Tho in early 1970 did not happen, and in the late spring an unexpected development occurred that caused further problems for the revolutionaries in the Delta. The fall of Prince Norodom Sihanouk and the subsequent U.S.–GVN invasion of Cambodia had the short-term effect of buying some time for Vietnamization to succeed, as President Nixon had hoped. This "incursion" had tragic consequences for Cambodia, however, and did not change the ultimate course of the war. Some evidence exits that the Cambodian invasion did break up a planned offensive. A city cadre in My Tho said that a major offensive had been planned for May 1970, but that it had been disrupted by the Cambodian invasion [DT317].

Cambodia had been a valuable asset for the revolution during the years following Prince Sihanouk's breaking of relations with the United States in 1964. As mentioned above, the Cambodian supply routes became much more important in the Mekong Delta after the partial interdiction of the "port" along the coast of Ben Tre. The Plain of Reeds history explains this background.

> Before 1970 we had very good fraternal relations with the friendly country of Cambodia. Cambodia wanted to maintain a position of neutrality, so it turned a blind eye *[lo di]* and let us use the port of Sihanoukville to transport weapons to the Plain of Reeds for further distribution to various places. The historical hatred that our enemies tried to exploit and revive to divide our peoples had been dissipated, and there was a mutual sympathy based on our mutual view of the U.S. as a common enemy, so that the Vietnamese revolution was helped in many ways that history will never forget to give thanks for. So in a situation where the Americans and the puppets were carrying out pacification and violent attacks a number of cadres were able to go over to friendly territory—it wouldn't be too much to call it "sacred territory." But the Region committee directed that we must try by every means to cling to the battlefield and be on the spot in order to hold the movement steady. And the price paid for holding on at that time was very steep.[35]

Clearly, some tension was created by the region directive to keep as many assets as possible in and near the Mekong Delta villages while they were suffering such heavy casualties, especially in view of the fact that some of the main force units that had been their main protection had withdrawn to the safety of Cambodia. In early 1970, however, Military Region 2 sent a unit called Regiment 3 to My Tho along with the 269th demolition Battalion and a company of the 267th Battalion in order to prepare for a campaign aimed at retaking lost territory in the rural areas of the province.[36]

A former buffalo herder, who claimed to have joined the 269th Battalion during the pre-Tet 1968 mobilization at the age of fourteen, described the battalion's activities in attacking the Tan Son Nhat airport, the "Y" bridge, and other notable Tet battles. The U.S.–GVN counteroffensive drove the unit back to Hau Nghia, and finally to a base area in the Ba Thu region of the "parrot's beak" in Cambodia, where it spent much of 1968 and 1969. According to the Plain of Reeds history, both the 269th and 267th Battalions had been hit so hard during the Tet Offensive that they were forced to retreat to the Cambodian border area to recuperate.[37] At the end of 1969 the 269th Battalion was reinforced. The My Tho province history states that in February 1970, Region 2 ordered the 269th "sapper" or demolition battalion to My Tho, along with the 267th Battalion, which was supposed to move to the outskirts of My Tho city to participate in a campaign to "expand the liberated zone *[chuyen vung]*."[38] Although the bulk of this effort was directed toward the villages, the assignment of a regular company to operate in the vicinity of the province capital showed that even in early 1970 the "urban outskirts" idea was not dead. The Cambodian crisis seems to have interrupted the full implementation of this plan.

There is no mention of the presence of either of these units returning to My Tho during 1969 or 1970 in the U.S. province advisor's reports. A squad leader from the 269th Battalion indicated that his unit continued to stay in Cambodia. At the end of 1969 the unit was reinforced and the entire battalion was assembled and told that there might be a coup against Sihanouk. "Before the coup, there was an order that 'if the Cambodians attack us, we should not fight back.' Sometimes the Cambodians grabbed our weapons, because theirs were nonautomatic Chinese weapons, and they were so taken with our automatic weapons that sometimes they snatched them from us. After the overthrow of Sihanouk, the military medical stations and rear services stations were kicked out by the Cambodians. Our commanders then ordered that if Cambodians came to talk to us, we must keep a distance of 3 meters, and if they tried to snatch our weapons we could shoot to kill. At the time, the cadres were afraid that the Cambodians would follow the nationalists" [DT350]. This was a sharp change from the generally amiable relationship that had prevailed prior to the coup. Cambodian soldiers who had fired all their allotted ammunition during drunken sprees bought replacements from the Vietnamese troops at 5 piasters per round. When Vietnamese troops went to Cambodian houses to buy rice, they were often feted with meals of ducks or chicken—expensive delicacies for a Cambodian peasant. In other cases, however, the Cambodians took advantage of Vietnamese "guest" status by refusing to make change for purchases and walking off with the extra money. On the Vietnamese side, some young Vietnamese civilians residing in Cambodia left their Cambodian girl friends in the lurch when they became pregnant.

As the U.S. and ARVN units invaded Cambodia, the 269th and other units tried to resist, but were not strong enough to do more than harass the ARVN units, which chased the 269th but could not catch it. The offensive was accompanied by heavy U.S. bombing and GVN artillery.

> We retreated to block Highway 4 to Phnom Penh, with our two remaining companies. The other units were the [NVA] 308th and 102nd Divisions. After the coup in Cambodia, we blocked the road to stop transport vehicles from coming through. Two other companies went up there, and our companies stayed back along the border to wait for the approaching ARVN troops. We were hit hard by artillery from Duc Hue and Kien Tuong. The airplanes destroyed every house around. I heard that guerrillas shot down two planes. At the time I was in the trenches and saw two planes collide and go down. According to the people, General Do Huu Xuan was in one of those planes. [General Do Cao Tri's helicopter went down in this area about that time. Mai Huu Xuan was a notoriously corrupt political general who rarely ventured near a battlefield] . . . The Cambodians really hated the Americans. We shot down two planes, and at that time two planes had been coming in to shoot up the houses of the people, because it was a liberated area, with children joining the liberation [DT350].

During the invasion, the fighting was so fierce that the 269th was unable to care for its wounded or take away its dead. After several days, however, the ARVN pulled out and the 269th returned to Ba Thu to refit. Many scattered units caught in the path of the invasion were decimated because they did not have enough strength to resist. During one clash, more than seventy Cambodian civilians—men, women, and children—were killed by ARVN fire because they had taken refuge in the trenches with the 269th troops and were mistaken for combatants.

The Cambodian invasion had both a short-term and a long-term impact on My Tho. Its immediate effect was to deflect the arrival of the additional troops that had been earmarked for the province. It also further isolated the revolutionary movement in My Tho from important base areas and from contact with other provinces. The Cambodian invasion forced the Region 2 command out of its "Tam Thuong" base area near the Cambodian border above the town of Chau Doc, where it had been for thirteen years.[39] The region base then moved deep into Cambodia, even farther from its area of responsibility. After the war, Tam Phuong (the top military commander of the region) wrote, "In the years when things were very fierce on the battlefield, especially from 1969 on, the enemy was stationed all over the place and there was no way that the [region] installations could go down to the battlefields down there." He did, however, criticize his own failure in the 1961–65 period to move closer to the action when it was easier to do so.[40] The following year, however, the region leaders moved into the very heartland of My Tho province to prepare for a stepped-up campaign of military action.

To justify the invasion of Cambodia, the Nixon administration argued that it was necessary to disrupt the communist base structure and supply lines in order to throw them off balance and buy time for Vietnamization to succeed. The fact that the timetable for success was set by the 1972 U.S. presidential elections was evident to all parties concerned. Despite the tragic consequences of the invasion for Cambodia, there is some evidence that the invasion did have some impact on places like My Tho. The note of concern by U.S. province advisors about the success of Vietnamization seems to have evaporated after this event. The fact that the Party apparently gave up on the idea of continuing large-scale military offensives during the period following the Cambodian invasion may also have been influenced by the difficulties caused by the disruption of base areas and supply lines, even though the failure to locate, let alone capture, the vaunted "Pentagon East" COSVN command headquarters discredited the initial rationale for the operation.

Over the longer term, the results were less favorable to Vietnamization. The ARVN proved unable to continue its operations in Cambodia, and though the overthrow of Sihanouk cut the main supply line to the Mekong Delta, it also led to the rise of the Khmer Rouge. Saigon's early enthusiasm about being joined by an anticommunist ally in Cambodia began to diminish as the ineffectiveness of the Lon Nol regime became apparent—as did its hostility to all Vietnamese, regardless of political coloration. Even so, the Vietnamese revolutionary forces continued to use the Cambodian base areas effectively, despite opposition from Lon Nol and, increasingly, the Khmer Rouge. Although the revolutionary forces were able to operate in all theaters of the three countries of Indochina, the ARVN found this beyond its capacity, and its attempt in early 1971 to cut off the Ho Chi Minh trail in central Laos marked the beginning of the end for Vietnamization.

For My Tho, the years 1970 and 1971 were the most difficult of the entire conflict. If the war had been limited to that province alone, a revival of the revolutionary movement would have been extremely difficult. Yet the nucleus of the movement held on, without the support of military forces that they had enjoyed in earlier years, until the tide began to turn with the Easter Offensive of 1972, which led to a resurgence of the guerrilla movement in the Mekong Delta. In the interim, the revolution was stripped down to its hard core. Both the "time of troubles" of 1970–71 and the subsequent revival illustrate the nature of the support for the revolutionary movement, and the conditions under which it could be mobilized. For this reason, the period of its greatest weakness actually reveals some of the most tenacious strengths of the movement.

The Vinh Kim district chief referred to this group of village officials and notables as "a pack of mangy dogs." The banner extols the GVN Land to the Tiller program in this 1971 photo.

Nguyen Van Hoi, a fourth generation landlord and one of the wealthiest people in Vinh Kim, tends his bonsai plants in 1971.

Nguyen Van Hoi's grand villa is pockmarked from bullets and mortar fragments in 1971.

Entrance to an underground bunker in Hoi's house. Hoi gave refuge to revolutionary cadres here throughout the war.

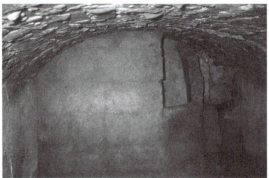

The underground bunker.

Aerial view of the area around Phu Nhuan Dong village, which was a priority pacification zone in Dinh Tuong in 1972.

Pacification plan for the Phu Nhuan Dong area, 1972.

A heavily bombed area in northern Dinh Tuong, 1972.

A "mini-base" where cadres retreated for survival in 1971–72 like Br'er Rabbit in the briar patch.

An ARVN post in northern Dinh Tuong, 1972.

ARVN soldiers suffer casualties during pacification "mini-base" clearing operations.

Refugees often lived in makeshift shelters along the sides of GVN-controlled roads.

GVN military post along canal in northern Dinh Tuong province, 1972.

Le Quoc San (Tam Phuong) was the top military commander in the central Mekong Delta for most of the "Vietnam War" period.

Muoi Tan was the deputy commander of the revolution's province military unit in My Tho at the time of his defection in late 1971, which nearly resulted in the capture of Tam Phuong. Muoi Tan was arrested and executed after the war.

A revolutionary *dac cong* special operations or sapper unit, located in My Duc Tay village only 350 meters from the A Rac GVN militia post, listens to radio reports from its reconnaissance team on GVN military activities in 1971.

The operations officer of the *dac cong* company prepares a tactical plan for an attack on a GVN post on Route 20 in Hau Trinh hamlet, Hau My village, Cai Be district, My Tho province in 1971.

Tran Minh Phu (Sau Phu) was one of the most skilled military commanders in the central Mekong Delta throughout the 1960–75 period.

A photo taken on January 29, 1973, two days after the Paris Agreements were signed, has the following caption: "Cai Lay: A North Vietnamese captain (C) poses with South Vietnamese soldier (L) and Viet Cong soldier (L [*sic*: actually on the right in the photo]) following a secret meeting in a graveyard off Highway Four near here" (UPI, Corbis).

Nguyen Minh Duong (Sau Duong) resting on the Ho Chi Minh trail on his way to Hanoi to attend a series of Politburo meetings following the Paris Agreements.

Civilian porters carry ammunition in Cho Gao district. Despite the ups and downs of the war, the revolution was able to mobilize effective civilian support for its final offensive.

Tran Van Tra returns to the South in late January 1975 after a trip to Hanoi to meet with the top Party leadership.

Students and underground urban cadres seize a cache of weapons stored at the Nguyen Dinh Chieu high school in My Tho town on April 30, 1975.

The vice chairman of My Tho's People's Revolutionary Committee in 1982 had participated in the August 1945 revolution in My Tho town. His son, a student at Nguyen Dinh Chieu High School, was active in the seizure of weapons there and the subsequent takeover of My Tho town. The person on the far right was a member of the C.207 urban operations unit of My Tho town during the conflict.

Revolutionary forces enter the GVN compound in
Cai Lay district town on May 1, 1975.

Mass meeting in My Tho to celebrate revolutionary victory.

The revolution's flag flies over Cai Lay district, May 1, 1975.

Revolutionary cemetery in Tien Giang (My Tho) province, 1999.

Tablets with names of deceased revolutionaries from Long Hung village.

16

Holding On

Between the invasion of Cambodia in April 1970 and the Spring "Easter Offensive" of April 1972 the revolution in My Tho and other provinces in the Mekong Delta faced the most difficult challenges of the entire post-1959 conflict. The serious decline in the revolutionary movement which started in 1969 reached its nadir in 1971. This chapter contends that the success of pacification in 1970–71 was temporary and largely the result of the depopulation of large areas once controlled by the revolution, as a consequence of incessant bombing and shelling. To the extent that the "pacification" of My Tho's rural areas was accompanied by programs such as the much-ballyhooed new land reform of the government of the Republic of Vietnam (GVN), initiated in 1970, these programs were a consequence rather than a cause of the Saigon government's security gains in the countryside. Most peasants who temporarily or permanently deserted the revolution were not influenced primarily by economic incentives or appeals from the GVN, nor did they transfer their allegiance to Saigon even if they ultimately rejected the revolutionary side.

Because the less determined or less committed followers of the revolution left or became temporarily inactive, it is possible to examine more closely what constituted the "hard core" of the revolutionary movement in My Tho, and to discern the lines between different levels of support and commitment for the movement. By doing this, we can get a sense of both the scope and intensity of support for the revolution, how these different levels of support among various sectors of the population changed over time, how numerous each revolutionary circle was—from the fully committed to the conditional supporters —and to what extent these variations were determined by temporary changes in circumstances as opposed to fundamental shifts in political loyalties. How many who had supported the revolution at one time or another were only fair-weather friends, or opportunistic "rational peasants"? Ironically, by putting the extent of commitment among revolutionary supporters to its hardest test, the adversity of 1970–71 makes it possible to see some of the reasons for the movement's strength at a time of apparent weakness.

Both the large and sudden intake of new recruits who had been swept up by the exhilaration of the Tet Offensive in My Tho, and the heavy losses of both civilian and military cadres following the Tet Offensive, led to inevitable changes in both the quality and quantity of local cadres in the province. A leading province military cadre said:

> With regard to the quality and ability of the new group of cadres, you have to divide it into periods. The 1966 period was the fiercest, so that the group that joined from 1966 to 1968 had ability because they had to withstand the rigors of a ferocious battlefield. They were not skilled, but war had taught them and given them experience. The Tet 1968-and-after group were really weak, couldn't accomplish anything. What motivated the Tet

1968 group to join in large numbers was opportunism, not anything more fundamental. The 1960 Concerted Uprising reverberated for a long time among the masses, so the youth that joined then did it out of a fundamental commitment. The new group were opportunists who thought that the Tet Offensive was going to end the war and in a few days the Saigon government would collapse. This was the opportunity for them to atone for their crimes and when the revolution won, even if they weren't covered with glory, at least they could live freely and make a living without being hassled. When the opportunity ended, naturally they faded away and ran. The ones who are still around are there because they are stuck, or have gotten in too deep so they had to keep on. This is different from the Concerted Uprising, like the youth I told you about who followed our armed propaganda team for three days and pleaded to join. He was an ordinary civilian so we couldn't take him. He wept and I was very touched. I feel that the confidence and belief *[niem tin]* of the youth at that time was very powerful, but now it is gone. It has burned away [DT415].

This was the judgment of a deeply discouraged and disillusioned cadre and, as this chapter will show, many highly motivated people joined the revolution in My Tho during the 1968–71 period. Nevertheless, there was a difference between different generations of cadres, from the Resistance cadres, to the Concerted Uprising movement or "movement" cadres who joined in the early 1960s, to the "Ho Chi Minh class" who joined in 1968 and after.

Parallels Between the Revolution's Problems
in 1970–71 and Earlier Periods of the Revolution

It was not the first time the movement had been at a low ebb. During the six years between the Geneva Accords of 1954 and the Concerted Uprising, the military arm of the revolution had been deactivated and the cadres jailed or chased into hiding. A closer parallel to the 1970–71 period, however, was the years just before to the battle of Dien Bien Phu and the signing of the Geneva Accords. In the early 1950s the French made political accommodations with the powerful religious sect forces of the Hoa Hao and Cao Dai in the Mekong Delta and, in conjunction with their own "Vietnamization program," turned much of the fighting over to these local groups. The result was much like what happened later, in 1970–71. Viet Minh military units were forced out of the populated areas of My Tho province. Soon the guerrillas had to take refuge in the Plain of Reeds, and then the political cadres followed in temporary exile from their villages. My Tho became a "white zone," with no secure revolutionary bases in most of the villages.

However, when the military situation began to deteriorate for the French in other parts of Vietnam in late 1953, the results were soon felt in My Tho. The religious sects withdrew into a defensive posture, and the Viet Minh cadres and guerrillas returned to My Tho. Within a few months, the security situation was transformed from near-total "pacification" to clear Viet Minh dominance. Because the war was ended by diplomacy in Geneva, and the military forces of the Southern movement evacuated from the Mekong Delta and the rest of South Vietnam, it is difficult to say how much the turnabout in the delta would have contributed to a complete revolutionary victory—but the very fact that it happened left a strong and lasting impression on its followers.

Many of the older cadres and their supporters recalled this period in interviews done during 1971, and cited this as evidence of their belief that the revolution could come back. The resurgence of the movement in the Mekong Delta after the Easter Offensive of 1972 demonstrated the resilience of the revolutionary movement, and the depth and tenaciousness of its latent sources of support. It also raises the question of why the movement did not simply collapse when it was so near the brink of disaster, and why the peasants did not join a bandwagon to deliver the coup de grace to the cadres and end the war—as they had tried to do to the Saigon government in the 1968 Tet Offensive. Moreover, the Saigon government was beginning a land reform which for many peasant cultivators held out the prospect of permanent title to the land they tilled. If the peasants were, as many have alleged, apolitical or opportunistic, this would have been their chance to contribute to an early end to the war and bring about the peace for which they all yearned, as well as ensure their economic future.

Why Did the GVN Lose the Dominance Attained in 1971?

Although the revolution lost much support during this period, some of this loss was temporary. As the cadres had maintained, a significant latent base of support for the revolution remained, which could be reactivated when circumstances changed. Even the support that was more definitively lost to the Party and the revolution did not necessarily shift to the Saigon government. The bulk of the disaffected peasants who turned away from the burdensome and often brutally enforced demands of the revolution did not become GVN loyalists. The revolution's base of support was shrinking, but its core was very deep, while the potential base of support for Saigon was expanding but very shallow, and the GVN leadership core proved hollow when put to the ultimate test. The asymmetry of each side's base of support was a vital reason why the GVN was never able to translate the superior material incentives it could offer into a committed base of support that was willing to stick with it to the end.

How could the GVN have lost its overwhelming dominance over the revolutionary forces in the Mekong Delta within a year, from 1971 to 1972? Part of this can be explained by the increase in North Vietnamese troops and the decline of U.S. military support, but the crucial factors were political and psychological. Much of the GVN's inability to translate military strength into political superiority was due to the fact that even while the Party alienated supporters and pushed them around, its nationalist credentials dating from the August revolution were still far superior to those of the GVN, whose origins dated back to the colonial period and which was so obviously and directly dependent on foreigners.

It is certainly true that as the war went on, this began to change, as more and more Vietnamese began to see some merit in the GVN claim that it represented the "nationalists" and came to feel that the nationalist credentials of the revolutionaries did not compensate for their ruthlessness and their incessant demands. Nonetheless, peasants who routinely referred to the Saigon forces as the "Nationalists" *(Quoc Gia)* when the situation demanded, also made it clear that in using this term, they did not mean that they regarded the GVN as more patriotic than the revolutionaries. The term simply referred to the Saigon administration —another way of saying the "government" or "the authorities." The alternative was to call them "puppets" or "illegitimate authorities" *(nguy)*, as the revolutionaries demanded, but when the cadres were out of earshot it was safer to use nonprovocative language to avoid being branded a "Viet Cong" by the expanding pacification forces of the GVN. However, the Saigon government was unable to consolidate the substantial forces in Vietnamese society who, either from personal interest or from personal injury by the revolution, might have become firm and committed supporters.

Even the top leadership of the GVN felt that the Saigon government's overwhelming dependence on foreign assistance was a major political handicap. This is clearly reflected in Rand Corporation interviews with a number of leading figures in the GVN not long after the end of the war. One former GVN general said, "Since the dependence and subordination of the Vietnam government was so obviously demonstrated by the predominant presence and power of the Americans, the Vietnamese general public could not refrain from viewing their government as a puppet deprived of all national prestige, lacking in a national mandate and thus being untrustworthy. In [such] a highly ideological struggle as the Vietnam war, this aspect had a strong negative impact and worked much to the detriment of the RVN [Republic of Vietnam] cause. Moreover, reacting to the negative attitude of the Vietnam public, RVN officials were unwilling or afraid to take any initiative and were thus reduced to adopting a defensive attitude."[1] The Rand study noted that the "long list of negative statements made by former South Vietnamese leaders about their own leadership was punctuated only rarely by positive statements about anyone, military or civilian, although some senior commanders were praised."[2] If this was the view at the top, it is not surprising that there is scant evidence of loyal and enthusiastic support for the Thieu government at the bottom, in the villages of My Tho.

Institutionalized corruption stemmed from the top of the GVN system, centered around President Thieu and his main supporters. The Rand Corporation study of the defeat of the GVN, based on interviews with leading generals from the Army of the Republic of Vietnam (ARVN), concluded that in the view of these leaders themselves, corruption was "a central feature of the South Vietnamese regime."[3] At the local level, corruption and high-handedness was the experience of most rural Vietnamese, and this did not endear the GVN to them as a system of government—even though it was objectively less demanding and oppressive than the revolutionary system of control (when it was able to function). The very corruption and inefficiency of the Saigon government should have provided some protection and relief for the hard-pressed peasants, but for those at the bottom of the ladder who could not afford to pay, and who were subject to the periodic harassment of Saigon soldiers, the cash nexus was not an attractive trade-off for the strict but more equitable values of the revolutionary-controlled communities.

The GVN Alienates Potential Supporters in the Villages

Two examples of the local abuse of power and inability to build bridges between the Saigon system and local communities illustrate the problem. Captain Minh, the populist GVN Vinh Kim (Sam Giang) district chief of 1966 (discussed in an earlier chapter) was long gone by 1971, and the current incumbent dealt summarily with the village notables who had enthusiastically supported Minh. A visiting American journalist was regaled with a litany of complaints from villagers about GVN policies and personnel, ranging from being forced from their homes into "secure" locations to being forced by GVN militia to clear mine-infested areas. "The people are usually Vietcong sympathizers," said an American advisor, "and even if they're not they've learned where the booby traps are. If we tried to clear those areas with soldiers, we'd lose a lot of men. So we put the soldiers behind the civilians and have them do it. . . . You'd be surprised how few civilians we lose."[4]

Although village democracy had been promoted with great fanfare as an example of the political progress being made by the GVN, relations between the Saigon district chief and the elected Vinh Kim village council were at a low ebb. The village council accused the GVN district officials of corruption but, wrote Peter Jay of the *Washington Post,* "Perhaps the greatest source of resentment against [the district chief, Major] Dai among the village leaders is the authority that he has over them, as elected officials of their villages and hamlets, and the arrogance with which he exercises it. Residents of Vinh Kim are proud of their village, which according to local historians has a past 'rich in heroes and famous men'—including a number of celebrated guerrilla fighters. [Dai] mentioned this tradition in a tirade he delivered to a council of village elders, which is repeated with anger and without prompting by those who heard it. 'He told us that he didn't see any heros and famous men in Vinh Kim,' a council member recalled. 'He said all he saw were a lot of mangy dogs.'"[5]

The village notables in Vinh Kim were caught between two forces. Reviled by the GVN district chief, they were also targets of revolutionary assassination. Some secretly supported the local cadres, whether out of genuine sympathy for the revolutionary cause, nationalist fervor, community solidarity, or simple prudence as insurance against the eventuality of a revolutionary victory. Don Oberdorfer of the *Washington Post* discovered on a return trip to Vinh Kim in 1980, that Nguyen Van Hoi, a village notable during the pre-1975 period with extensive Saigon contacts was still a notable in revolutionary Vinh Kim. He "was introduced as 'advisor' to the Red Cross in the village and 'an honored person.'" He proudly told Oberdorfer that the "leaders of the 'liberation forces' in the village took refuge against Saigon government sweeps. Since he is among one of the richest men in the village, a fourth-generation landowner here, the hiding place, by his account, was both unsuspected and undetected throughout the war."[6]

For other "village notables," however, life in Vinh Kim had its perils, even in nominally "secure" areas. In February 1969 a U.S. advisor reported that "Some twenty people—men women and children—were clustered around the water pump shop of Le Van An, Chairman of the Administrative Committee of Vinh Kim village and an elected village official. During the confusion a young boy reached around the corner from the adjacent shop and handed Le Van An a grenade wrapped in paper. The grenade exploded in An's stomach and he died in about one hour. . . . This is the second prominent Vinh Kim citizen closely associated with GVN and US to [be] assassinated. . . . last week Pham Ky Ngoi [a well-known journalist who lived in Vinh Kim] was assassinated on [the] night of 22 Feb by VC execution squad who came to his house and knifed him."[7] This and other similar incidents involving children involved in terrorist incidents raise unanswerable questions about the motivations and level of understanding of these pre-teenagers and, therefore, what conclusions can be drawn about the significance of the involvement of children in terrorism.

In Phu My village the local GVN militia leaders only had to worry about the revolutionary side. They were two co-opted warlords of religious sects, Tu Hue and his Cao Dai troops, who played a major role in the GVN recovery after the overthrow of Ngo Dinh

Diem in 1963, and Huynh Hoa, with his Catholic militia. The GVN district and province authorities could not afford to alienate them. Both men had been extremely effective military leaders, but outside their own religious communities they did not win hearts and minds for the GVN [DT179, DT233]. The elected local representatives of the fledgling village democracies of the "Tan family" villages around Phu My wrote an angry open letter to top GVN officials which was published in a Saigon newspaper in September 1971. They accused Huynh Hoa of corruption and abuse of power.

> During the past two months he has made use of his power, has done his best to domineer while not heeding any of the wishes of the people. At any moment he is ready to scold loudly the people and the village officials by heavy, nasty, uneducated words. With any type of work and with people not under his authority (as subordinates) he also uses rough words and threats without caring, as would a person of higher authority than the district or even the Province Chief. Nobody dares to make trouble or act contrary to his wishes because he will abuse power and immedialy [sic] get revenge for anyone who opposes him. With regard to the "land to the tiller" policy of the government he takes back the rice land of the poor because he in [sic] the landlord, for his own interests he stands up and uses his power to force the people to labor for the public good without pay. This does not mean constructing entrenchments around an outpost, but forcing people to bring their buffalo and plow his fields, pull weeds, make dikes, in order to obtain personal benefits. At night, whenever he returns to the village to rest . . . he orders PSDF [People's Self-defense Forces or part time village militia] to guard far from the village while his well trained soldiers guard the market to allow him to open a party, organize card games, drink liquor throughout the night with wealthy shopowners, causing the people in the market to spend sleepless nights every time he returns to the village. These are several examples out of thousands.[8]

The purpose of the petition was to get the GVN regime to "investigate, and demolish the people who harm the intention and policy of the government which favors the people."[9] It is doubtful that the GVN could or would dispense with the critical services of effective military leaders such as Huynh Hoa but, as in the case of Vinh Kim, the building of local democracy and consolidation of the natural anticommunist base in the rural areas ran aground on the abuses of this type by GVN representatives.

Pacification Reduces the Revolutionary Movement to Its Hard Core in My Tho

In the final analysis, the differences between the GVN and the revolution went deeper than politics. As the war became more and more devastating, and Vietnamese society was torn apart by "forced draft urbanization" and wartime social maladies, the shrinking zones of the revolution were the last bastions of peasant conservatism. It may have been this that the Party had in mind in the mid-1969 directive called Resolution Nine, which called for a remobilization of peasants on the basis of traditional Vietnamese values. People who had once lived in revolutionary-controlled areas routinely referred to them as "in there," or "inside" *(o trong),* in contrast to the GVN areas, which were "out here" or "outside" *(o ngoai),* indicating that the GVN areas were somehow alien and external to the peasants' world. To some, especially the poor peasants who were the firmest base of social support for the revolution, the revolution promised, not a "revolution" which would produce an urbanized and industrialized brave new world, with modernistic machines, factories, and labor heroes, but a bedrock defense of their conservative rural social values against the inroads of unwanted and negative social changes in the urban areas—which were so pervasive that they penetrated into even the most remote villages through returning refugees. Though the revolution had begun in the "modernizing" villages such as Vinh Kim during the early years, by 1971 it was strongest in the "backwater" villages farther removed from the communications and commerce of market villages along or near the main roads of My Tho. And this was true even though, as some fragmentary figures on revolutionary strength in Chau Thanh district suggest that some villages right on Highway 4, such as Duong Diem and Nhi Binh, still had a fairly strong revolutionary movement.

By 1971 the revolution had largely lost its ability to control villages and hamlets by direct coercion, and the cadres themselves were preoccupied with a grim struggle for individual survival. Sporadic military activity was still possible in a few areas of the 20/7 zone, but most of the concentrated units operated—with difficulty, and in groups of much smaller size—in northern Cai Be and Cai Lay districts. The district local forces were ineffective, as were most of the village guerrilla units. In most villages of the province, the remaining cadres and guerrillas went into hiding to await more favorable conditions.

Like Br'er Rabbit in the briar patch, the cadres holed up in tangled clumps of vegetation and brambles that had taken over the now nearly totally depopulated former liberated areas, protected by a maze of grenade traps that made it too costly to attempt to penetrate their hideouts. By mid-1971 the GVN had launched a program of clearing the trees and vegetation from these areas to literally flatten these cadre "minibases." The few remaining civilians who had clung to their rice fields were resettled—by force if necessary—into clusters around the small military posts that now blanketed the province. This resulted in nearly total isolation of the cadres, and completed the regrouping of the civilian population under the watchful eyes of GVN local officials and militia.

In this way, the long-standing U.S.–GVN ambition of "draining the pond to catch the fish" had, in essence, been accomplished. Yet the cadres held on, even though their ranks were severely depleted. This was the true "hard core" of the movement, whom no appeal to material interest or psychological blandishment could persuade to abandon their commitment to the revolution. It was, however, a somewhat different group than the "movement cadres" who had been brought in during the 1960–63 period to replace the Resistance cadres purged by Directive 137, or even the "Ho Chi Minh class" of youth who had joined the revolution during and after the Tet Offensive.

For one thing, the attrition of both the "movement cadres" and the Tet generation forced the Party to recall some of these Resistance veterans. A village cadre said that "the current generation of cadres has been nurtured a long time. They are the backbone cadres who went underground during the six years of peace but because they were either dissatisfied or purged they became angry and quit. Now the Party asks them to resume their work according to their capacities. This started to happen at the beginning of 1970. To sum it up, this group of village cadres are all former cadres except for one or two young cadres. These competent cadres are all over forty years old, and they have lots of experience in both the political and the military field and far surpass the young cadres and Concerted Uprising cadres. . . . For example, Bay Thanh, formerly head of the Farmers' Association. During the Concerted Uprising he became disgruntled and quit. But now he is back in charge of a hamlet finance–economy section and the people have great confidence in him" [DT308]. Another older cadre, Tu Tien, who had been the village Party secretary of Ban Long, had been purged in the mid-1960s because he complained that he was too old to be able to operate in the swampy area to which he was assigned. A village cadre said that "from the Destruction of the Oppression period only Tu Tien is left. The group from 1963 and 1964 all have gone up to district and were killed. In 1964, when I joined there, Tu Tien was the village Party secretary." In 1971 Tu Tien's Party membership was restored, no doubt because of the serious shortage of cadres. "He has talent and virtue and prestige among the people. When he talks they listen, and have full confidence in him" [DT308].

Older cadres who had been promoted to district now had to return to the villages to fill the leadership void left by death and defection of the village cadres. A hamlet guerrilla described the situation in his village in 1971. "My Long is now weak. Many cadres have been killed or have rallied [to the GVN]." Tam Canh, a veteran cadre from the Resistance, returned to assume the role of village Party secretary. The village organization was still relatively strong, with several dozen Party members, mostly between thirty and fifty years old. "District cadres continue to drop by from time to time and they try to consolidate the movement, but it doesn't improve because all the youth are gone. There is no one to send up to the big units. The older cadres say, 'If it goes on like this, probably our village will run out of people and only we will be left.' " One reason for the high attrition rate was that the Party members among the cadres had to set the example, and expose themselves to more risks. "It's easier to die as a Party member because you have to be in the vanguard to set the example," said the hamlet guerrilla, "like the hamlet unit leader. He was a Party member and had to go first. So he ran into a grenade trap and was killed." The interviewee preferred the less dangerous role of an ordinary hamlet guerrilla. "The hamlet guerrillas didn't study the Party line. I wasn't keen on advancement and just wanted to stay in the hamlet. But I saw all the guerrillas getting killed, so I rallied" [DT330].

My Long was not alone in having a fairly large number of Party members left in the village in 1971. My Loi village, which had eighty Party members before the Tet Offensive, still had fifty in 1971 [DT331]. The following year, 1972, the Party had still had a substantial 4,000 members in the province,[10] compared with 6,000 in 1968. The 1970 figures for revolutionary strength in fifteen villages of southern Chau Thanh district list 49 village guerrillas or about 3 per village, 360 hamlet guerrillas, and 261 Party members or a little over 17 per village.

"Middle Peasantization": Class Struggle Recedes While the Revolution's Socio-economic Base Shrinks

Despite the depopulation of the countryside and the severe depletion of their ranks, the cadres held on. These cadres represented the true "hard core" of the movement, whose commitment to the revolution was unshakeable. As the Party would have predicted, the cadres who stuck to stick it out were driven by class interests and attitudes. Many peasants from better-off backgrounds had dropped by the wayside, often because their motivation was not strong enough to overcome the fear of death and the grinding frustration of an unending war or, as the poor peasant members of the revolution asserted, the middle and rich peasants who had grown up in more comfortable circumstances were not as adaptable to extreme hardship.

By 1971 the Party leaders in My Tho were beginning to grasp the extent of the transformation of the rural class structure in the province. A Party member from Diem Hy village said that as of 1971 the cadres in the village were all poor peasants. "They didn't take middle peasants, and by now have combined both old and new middle peasants. Old middle peasants were those whose parents and grandparents had been middle peasants and had money and possessions, and new middle peasants were those who had become prosperous during the war since 1960 and had money and possessions." In earlier years, middle peasants were accepted as Party members but "they couldn't become members of the Party chapter committee or district cadres. They could only help out in the popular associations and would only be allowed to transfer [into more important areas] after a long period of testing and enduring hardships." The interviewer commented that the Party appeared to be right in thinking that middle peasants could not stand the hardships, because in Diem Hy as of 1971 the remaining thirteen cadres were all poor peasants. The respondent answered that Diem Hy was a special case, and that some other villages still had middle peasant cadres [DT398]. Class background was not an infallible predictor of ability to withstand hardships. Of 102 people interviewed in 1971, 62 were "ralliers," and among this group there were 8 middle peasants, 39 poor peasants, and 8 very poor peasants. This could, however, be explained by the relatively larger numbers of poor peasants in the larger group from which these interviewees came, and the fact that there were fewer middle peasants remaining in the revolutionary ranks in My Tho. It is also probably true that a large number of those who stuck it out in the villages during this period of extreme difficulty were poor or very poor peasants.

Some respondents asserted that by 1971 the Party no longer made distinctions between those who had become middle peasants because of the Party land reform and those who had inherited their class status. As in Diem Hy, in Phu Phong, "the village government no longer refers to middle peasants. Since it has given land to the poor people, they are now lumped in with the middle peasants and the whole group is called new middle peasants [dong hoa toan the danh tu trung nong moi] and the government only attacks landlords and feudalists." "How does it attack landlords and feudalists?" the interviewer asked. "For example, in the case of someone who shouts loudly and disturbs the peace or drinks a lot, the cadres will immediately push the people to criticize them. Now the attacks are aimed at the imperialists and the feudalists. Naturally, attacking the feudalists means attacking the imperialists. The movement to attack the feudalists is very strong. Anyone who behaves in feudalist fashion receives an immediate visit from the cadres, who come to guide and criticize him. They no longer have to bring these people to village meetings, feudalists are attacked every day in the village" [DT308]. Thus the term "feudalism," which had once described the cluster of political, economic, and social practices that buttressed mandarinal rule and landlord exploitation, now referred to offensive and unacceptable individual behavior patterns rather than class attributes.

One way of viewing this amalgamation of old and new middle peasants is that the infusion of former poor peasants into the ranks of middle peasants had further tied the expanded middle peasant strata to the revolution. Another way of viewing it is that once the former poor peasants became middle peasants, they took on the interests and outlook of that class and diluted the hard-core base of the revolution. Either way, class conflict had been subtly transformed into a conflict of values and lifestyles. The sharp edge of class interests had been dulled by "middle peasantization" and the decline of the landlords. "Feudal" now became a code word for "un-Vietnamese" behavior and values. Although the Party's strongest rural supporters were still the poorest peasants in the rural areas, their numbers had declined both because of "middle peasantization" and because of the refugee exodus from the village. Thus the revolutionary movement's core base of support remained very deep, but also was progressively narrowed by the consequences of the war. Those who remained in the vicinity of the cadres were usually relatives or older people with a strong family "revolutionary tradition." Since the Party could not appeal to them on the basis of conferring material benefits, it played the role of supporting and enforcing their view of how rural society should function, which, despite the Party's attempts at transforming rural social practices in the early 1960s, remained quite traditional.

Probably this happened largely because the cadres and their families now constituted a distinct "society" within the larger society, as is vividly expressed by a cadre from Phu Phong village. "The cadres remaining in the VC areas have all their relatives in the revolution, parents, wives and children, so they have all these entangling relationships. If they come out here [the GVN zones] they will lose all their prestige with regard to their own families who are still in there. The families of the cadres are tightly bound together, so they stayed in the village and clung to their land. They cannot leave. These cadres work with great zeal and devotion because they believe the propaganda of their superiors who tell them that peace will come soon, and that if they don't work for the [National Liberation] Front the war will drag on and peace will come much later. I noticed the cadres are sick of war, but because of the situation they all have to work for the Front" [DT308].

Almost inadvertently, the Party role in My Tho had changed from social engineering to guardian of peasant social conservatism, because the family network now overlapped the political network in the places where the cadres and their families lived. Even in reaching out to the villagers who had moved to the GVN zones, the moral edge that the cadres retained was based both on their courage in "sticking it out" and on the fact that they were now the representatives of the last vestiges of "authentic" rural life. The class agenda and the original factors that gave rise to the revolution in the first place persisted even though they were now overlaid with these concerns about traditional values and life style.

The Party recognized that it took special dedication and temperament to stick it out under these circumstances, and though there was a general feeling that poor peasants had both the motivation and the life-training to bear these hardships, anyone who could take it was welcomed. The middle peasant who served as the Party leader in Binh Duc after the formal dissolution of the Party chapter said, "Before, the revolution emphasized the question of class. At present, if they are sticky about class origin they won't find enough manpower to carry on the war. So the emphasis on class has been diminished" [DT301]. The increased emphasis on solidarity against the GVN, and the reduced importance of the land question, all contributed to the lower urgency attached to class background. The irony was that as class background was officially deemphasized, the class basis of the cadres became more pronounced than ever.

"Rational Peasants" and Political Commitment

To carry on in the conditions of 1970–71 took an exceptional level of commitment. It was mainly the poorest peasants who were able to maintain this commitment, partly because they saw their interests as welded to the revolution, and partly because they were more used to enduring unending hardships than peasants brought up in more comfortable circumstances. Still, given this background of penury and deprivation, why didn't they abandon ship when the revolution had temporarily run aground? Why wasn't the promise of land reform, now being energetically pushed by the Saigon government, or the lure of life in the urban areas, where even a cyclo driver earned many times more than most poor peasant families, enough to make them quit?

Here we run into a question that penetrates to the heart of the nature of the revolutionary movement: Why did people join, and what sustained them through periods that imposed heavy costs and provided few benefits? The Vietnam war has produced a classic confrontation of explanatory models, whose most notable proponents are Samuel Popkin and James Scott, both professors of political science. Scott's classic study (see Bibliography) of the deep causes of revolution emphasized the "moral economy" of peasant communities. When the peasants were pushed over the brink of survival, they were also pushed beyond the limits of toleration and acquiescence, and were literally forced into revolution—sanctioned by the ultimate value of the "moral economy," the primacy of survival of the community and individuals and families within the community. Popkin's "rational peasant" (see Bibliography), by contrast, was an autonomous political actor, who is able to calculate behavior on the basis of self-interest. As in most "rational actor" explanations of political behavior, the context of political action is not the moral universe of a community, but the costs and benefits of action to the individual.

Needless to say, this crude and oversimplified account of Scott and Popkin's views does not catch the subtlety and richness of argument in these contemporary classics, but this thumbnail sketch is a necessary introduction to much of the following discussion about the nature of revolutionary movement. Three issues are especially important. First, is the basis of political action the isolated individual assessing possible gains and losses from acting or abstaining from action, or is the key point the social and community context within which the individual makes these decisions? This leads to a second point, the relative weight of values or beliefs versus self-interest as political motivator. Those who stress values more than interests logically point to the social and community context in which political decisions are made. Finally, there is the question of how to account for different levels of intensity of political commitment within a single social or political movement. The Vietnamese revolution, for example, had an unshakable inner core, described above. It also had a much broader base of marginally committed adherents at the outer edges of the movement, and a variety of different levels of commitment in between. How do we account for these differences? Can they be measured? Do the committed "hard core" operate on a completely different level of behavior (motivated exclusively by values or beliefs) than the outer layers of the movement (who are more self-interested or "rational peasants" in their behavior)? The 1970–71 period raises all of these questions. Why did the cadres hang on? What effect did alternative options provided by life in GVN areas (salary, lifestyle, etc.) have on the cadres and their followers? And, perhaps most important, to what extent did "pacification" merely temporarily suppress active support for the revolution, as opposed to eliminating it? Was there still, even in the revolutionary nadir of 1971, a latent base of support for the revolution? If so, under what conditions could it be revived?

There are no conclusive answers to these questions, but some tentative findings based on the analysis of this and other chapters may be advanced. The cadres hung on for both "rational peasant" and "moral economy" reasons. As "rational peasants," they had invested too much of themselves in the revolution to abandon what they had achieved, and they also had a stronger belief in the ultimate victory of the revolution, which made holding on a more appealing option. Because they tended to come from the poorest strata of rural society, the countervailing benefits they could expect from the Saigon government were not, in their view, attractive. Land reform under the auspices of the GVN was not much of a lure, for reasons we will consider shortly. Moreover, the hard-core cadres had already seen that the results of land reform depend on who holds political power, and the track record of the GVN in defending the interests of poor peasants was not good. These cadres could not expect anything like the power and prestige that they enjoyed by virtue of their positions in the revolutionary movement if Saigon won and they again ended up at the bottom of the social scale.

Rational calculations are not enough, however, to explain the tenaciousness of the hard core. What rational person would continue to risk hardship and probable death on the mere expectation of some distant payoff? The cadres' strong belief in ultimate victory did not mean that they thought that victory would be quick or easy, and most of them were prepared for a prolonged period of privation and danger, without any assurance of being around at the end to reap the rewards. Even ideology is not a complete or satisfactory alternative explanation. Ideology is a sort of halfway house between a purely rational actor whose instrumental calculations are based solely on personal costs and benefits, and a type of political behavior that is shaped by values and beliefs. It is also compatible with self-interested behavior, especially for downtrodden workers or peasants who believe that they will be the primary beneficiaries of the revolution.

Peasant Conservatism

To a surprising degree, peasant conservatism provides a better explanation for the decision of My Tho's revolutionaries to stick it out through hard times than does either ideology or rational calculation. Dramatic changes in the lifestyle of the urban areas had washed back into the rural heartland, as "bar girls" and "cowboys" (prostitutes and young, urbanized, libertine males) occasionally returned to their villages for brief visits, or were encountered by villagers or family members in their decadent urban native habitat. A seventeen-year-old girl from a middle peasant background in My Thanh village, on the border of the Plain of Reeds, explained that she did not want to leave the heavily bombed village for the GVN areas because she was afraid that her land would be confiscated by the revolution. Besides, she added, "I like the peaceful life of the countryside better than the Ba Ton market [near Cai Lay district town]." Clearly it was not peaceful in the conventional sense, but she meant that when the bombs and artillery were not falling, the village still retained its quiet, slow-paced ambience, which she preferred to the frenetic pace of the GVN marketplace. "I was arrested when the ARVN came in on operation and called me out of my trench," she said. "I am happy because I will be released today. I saw television at the Ba Ton market, and don't like the style of provocative dress and the rock music I see on TV. Like every young person I like to be fashionable like everyone else, but in the countryside you can't dress as in the cities." Still, while she was in Ba Ton, "I had a really beautiful *ba ba* made" [DT334]. Although the *ba ba* outfit of a plain white tunic blouse and black pants was the costume of most peasant women, the urban fashion had changed the simple rough cotton to sleek and form-fitting synthetic fabrics, which, depending on how ostentatious or provocative they were, were criticized by the conservative peasants and cadres in the rural areas.

During this complex 1971–72 period, as the war moved toward its final phase, peasant conservatism was evident in the shrinking areas of revolutionary control and influence while throughout much of the rest of the countryside the uprooted refugees and the shattered families of the province lived in an anomic and atomized world. Under these conditions, calculations based on individual interest were clearly more likely to motivate behavior than the collective values and social pressures of small communities which no longer existed as cohesive social units. In general, villages which were more distant from the GVN areas and which had a long history of revolutionary control were hostile to GVN fashions and cultural influences. This was not simply a political position of the cadres, but a deep-seated peasant conservative reaction to urban influences which offended their sense of propriety. At this level, it was these attitudes and values more than political control which sealed off the "liberated" areas from the Saigon zones. By 1971, few areas were under the tight cadre control of earlier years, and the cadres' inability to control the economic activities of the peasants—evidenced by the lack of success in controlling commercial relations with GVN areas—shows the declining direct control of the revolution over the activities of people living in the rural areas.

Control of social comportment and attitudes was maintained not by the cadres but by community consensus—at least in those hamlets where a remnant community still existed. The fact that the communities in the formerly liberated zones were largely older people and mostly poor peasants gave a distinctive cast to their social attitudes. Peasant conservatism was even more pronounced in the remote villages, because the peasants with money and contacts in the urban areas had already fled, leaving behind a nativist hard core of poor peasants, who saw the towns as alien and exploiting entities, which only reinforced their conservatism. Not all poor peasants were immune to the lures of urban fashion, but those who tried to keep up were in the minority. A young man classified as a poor peasant from My Long village, in the heart of the 20/7 zone, said, "Women in the village who dress in urban styles are criticized." "At the time," he added, "I was really a 'cowboy' and was called in for criticism many times. One time they threatened to kill me, and said all my relatives worked for the GVN." To deflect this suspicion and criticism, he joined the hamlet guerrillas in September 1970. "I had a relative who was a GVN soldier, who came back dressed like a cowboy. He got beaten up. I was the only one in the village who dressed like that" [DT330].

Binh Phuc Nhat in Cho Gao is an example of a village near a GVN-controlled area which began to see changes as early as 1966. The war had not hit the village as hard as more remote areas, but there was a strong and functioning revolutionary movement there through the Tet Offensive. One problem area had been in recruiting women. A few young women volunteered to serve as cadres, but their effectiveness was limited. A village cadre observed, "They were young, and had not yet married. In my view they joined only because they thought it would be fun. Not long after they joined, they started having affairs and getting into trouble. They started wearing thin clothes, and wore the newest fashions day in and day out. They wore 'sandals and shoes' and sashayed around *[ong eo]*." The peasants complained that "The minute they step out of the house they start to act like our fathers or grandfathers *[Cha moi buoc ra khoi nha cung lam ong lam cha nguoi ta]*" [DT311].

"Wearing thin clothes" meant abandoning the sturdy and shapeless simple white cotton blouses and black pants that peasant women traditionally wore, in favor of more revealing form-fitting and somewhat transparent synthetic fabrics with bright colors and decorative patterns. "Wearing shoes and sandals" *(di giay di dep)* was a sarcastic peasant reference to young women putting on airs. Shoes and even plastic sandals were considered to be an affectation in an environment where most people went barefoot because it was more appropriate in the muddy rice field environment. From the traditional point of view, acting like "fathers or grandfathers" was clearly inappropriate behavior for young women. These young female cadres were neither the right age nor the right gender to exert authority over their elders.

Although this peasant conservatism had been an enduring feature of the villages, it was not until after the Tet Offensive that it became a major social and political issue. A poor peasant from Than Cuu Nghia village, next to the province airbase, where U.S. soldiers and their camp followers were highly visible, was told by the cadres that "the foreign countries who have come to take over Vietnam have tried to alter behavior out here [in the towns]. [The cadres] said that these foreign countries invading Vietnam have given rise to bad behavior among the Vietnamese. Before people wore loose-fitting pants and now they are skin-tight. This has given rise to prostitution and has made the Vietnamese bad. The peasants found this line of argument appealing because they only wanted to live a simple and honest life, and not give rise to any decadent behavior. There is a lot of bad behavior in the village compared with before, a lot of fooling around even with married people. The communists feel this is not right and the masses also denounce it. They say that this is behaving like the GVN or the U.S." [DT302]. Even in this village near a major GVN base there was a feeling, at least among the older peasants, that the strict communist morality was more in tune with traditional virtues of rural life than the decadent ways of the Saigon areas.

Although the Communist Party had always stressed puritanical virtues, and generally enforced them with rigor, they had not always been seen as the upholders of rural tradition. During the land reform phase of the Resistance, the local village power structure had been turned upside down. The terror of the early years of the Concerted Uprising was also deeply upsetting to the village pattern of finding ways to maintain social harmony even in the face of deep-seated conflict. Once the terror had served its purpose, however, the Party was able to turn social solidarity into a positive, and unite the majority of the villages behind its program, as discussed in earlier chapters.

Cadres still tried to uphold the revolutionary changes in things like marriage and funeral ceremonies. The simple civil "declaration ceremony *[le tuyen bo]*," an exchange of wedding vows before the assembled neighbors presided over by a cadre, was intended to cut down on extravagant banquets and gifts, so that the resources thus saved could be used by the revolution. In the earlier years, the cadres succeeded in enforcing this practice, but by 1971 only the cadres themselves continued to use the simple ceremony. In My Long, "Only those who worked for the Liberation followed the new ceremony, and the ordinary people still followed the old wedding customs. The cadres didn't like the people to follow the customs of the old days, which they regarded as feudal, but the people still went ahead. Wedding and engagement ceremonies were happy occasions—the 'declaration ceremonies' were not" [DT330]. Clearly there were still issues on which peasant traditionalism diverged from Party policy, but not everyone in the revolutionary areas was attracted to the old ways.

To some extent, peasant solidarity and conservatism was a function of age and class. Older and poorer peasants tended to be the most negative about urban influences. For the youth, however, the lure of "modernization" could be appealing, and it was not simply a question of Saigon's decadent blandishments. A village guerrilla from My Long village in the heart of the 20/7 zone was deeply impressed by the stories of the Northern soldiers passing through about life under socialism, where people were "organized into groups and cells" and could "buy things with ration cards." In addition, "people wore proper clothing up there—sandals and shoes—not just any old thing. They took cars to work and got a monthly salary" [DT330]. A young guerrilla from Huu Dao also was captivated by the tales of socialism recounted by Northern soldiers passing through his village. "They said that in the North, life is structured in an orderly routine *[nen nep]*. When you go to work, there is someone to care for the children. They said that in the North, whoever worked received points and those who didn't work got no points. They said life in the North was very pleasant. . . . They said that it was a bit difficult during the bombing, but before that life was easy" [DT365].

A still-committed revolutionary who had been entrusted with recruiting penetration agents in the major GVN base area of Hau My on the fringe of the Plain of Reeds said that "actually, I didn't contact anyone for military proselytizing after I was recruited in December 1969 because I saw that the youth in Hau My were living it up and having a lot of fun. They dressed like cowboys and sang all day. If I had tried to recruit them they would have denounced me right away" [DT333]. It is clear that the attraction of being a "cowboy" was a lifestyle issue, not a political commitment, though it did have political implications. The "cowboy" lifestyle was only possible in the GVN areas, and those who were drawn to it knew all too well what a revolutionary takeover would mean for this playboy existence. Nevertheless, the fact that the GVN condoned and abetted this lifestyle did not necessarily mean that people who enjoyed its tolerance would defend it to the death.

On the face of it, the unplanned and partial assumption by the Party of the role of guardian of peasant conservatism seems to underscore the strength of communitarian traditions in the countryside, and suggest a strengthening of the "moral community." It raises the question of who was leading the "revolution" at this stage. To a considerable extent, the Party had to adapt itself to the requirements of survival, and depended heavily on the meager supplies and tenuous communication link with the outside provided by the thin clusters of poor peasants who clung tenaciously to their land near the minibases. Although the Party continued to devote a great deal of energy to maintaining a regularized system of ideological indoctrination for village cadres, it was not ideology but rather identification of the peasants with those who shared their life and hardships that induced support for the cadres—and, therefore, for the revolution. Political identification was a simple "us" versus "them" distinction between those peasants who still clung to their village ways "in there" and those who had left the community to live "out there." At this juncture, the Party was not trying to remake rural society, but to blend in with it for survival.

The GVN Tries to Win Over the Peasants
with a "Land to the Tiller" Program

However, it is also true that the vast social dislocation of the war which atomized the rural communities also strengthened the "rational peasant" individualism of many people struggling to survive in an environment in which familiar community social mechanisms had broken down. Although individualism cut into the base of voluntary support for the revolution, in part because the revolution had little to offer a "rational peasant" by 1971, this lost support did not shift to the side of the Saigon government—even though the GVN appeared to be able to deliver precisely the type of material benefits that could win the peasants over. Though water pumps and fertilizer revolutionized rural production, and enriched some of those who still were able to farm, they did not translate into committed political support, either in gratitude or out of self-interest.

Even the Saigon land reform, which was a massive attempt at social engineering, failed to have a decisive impact because it was too little, too late. Had the same reforms been carried out earlier the story might have been different, but the point is that reform was simply not possible until this time. It was only the depopulation of the countryside, the insecurity which made farming dangerous, the final withering away of the landlord class and the shift of their family resources into more secure urban ventures such as real estate and small shops, or well-connected children in the GVN civilian and military structure, and the dramatic shrinkage of the rural labor force by military mobilization of most of the able-bodied males that made land reform feasible in 1971. According to a revolutionary postwar study, the percentage of South Vietnam's population still living in the countryside in 1971 had declined from 80 percent a decade earlier to 70 percent, and of this only 35 percent or 4.1 million of 11 million were "primary laborers *[lao dong chinh]*" or male breadwinners of a family. In surveys conducted in several villages of Ben Tre province, between 60 and 77 percent of agricultural workers between the ages of sixteen and sixty were women.[11] As an earlier chapter points out, the escalation of the war in 1965–66 appears to have resulted in the end of land distribution in liberated areas. A cadre who had returned from regroupment in North Vietnam to his village in My Hanh Dong stopped actively working for the revolution because of bad health, but after the 1968 Tet Offensive asked the village cadres to give him some land so that he could bring his family back from where they were living in Cambodia and support them in his native village. "When I came back to village, I didn't get any land, and had to work as a hired hand. The cadres said, 'when we divided the land you weren't here. Now there is none left.' I asked them to give me a little to support my family. They replied that they couldn't reopen the land decisions *[chinh sach ruong dat bay gio khui ra khong duoc]*. Since the land had all been divided, some of it had been sold. There were no orders on how to deal with muddled land tenure issues *[xao canh]*. There were a lot of abandoned rice fields, but to clear them would cost more than 20,000 piasters for 4 or 5 *cong* [a *cong* is 1/10th of a hectare] and I didn't have the money. About half the villagers have fled to GVN areas. Some come back to work their fields, some trade in GVN areas. The only people working fields are women and old men" [DT338]. A hamlet guerrilla from My Duc Tay village also reported that the Party had forbidden any changes which would "muddle" land tenure, and had stopped talking about land reform because the current needs of the revolution were "to increase friends and decrease enemies" [DT371].

In most cases, the liberated areas had more land than people to work it, so land distribution was not a burning issue. Moreover, in some places there was not a great deal of incentive to farm more land than required for bare subsistence, because of heavy revolutionary taxes. In Thoi Son village, by 1971 no GVN land reform had taken place, and 40 or 50 *cong* of uncultivated land had been lying fallow for two or three years but was not considered worth the expense to reclaim [DT341]. In My Long village, in the heart of the 20/7 zone, a lot of abandoned land still nominally belonged to landlords (it had almost certainly been distributed to tenants earlier). All but about 10 percent of this land, however, was in areas that were too insecure to farm because they were near the bushes and trees in which the cadres were hiding—places that were constantly shelled. As for the small amount of land that was out in the open, away from the minibases and the shelling, "people simply grab a piece of land to work. The landlords themselves request that this land be worked so that it will not become overgrown. When the situation is quiet, they will come back and reclaim the land. They don't take any tax or rent, so both sides are happy" [DT342]. In My Duc Dong village, the landlords came back from the towns periodically and tried to collect rent. A village guerrilla from Tam Hiep said that where he lived, "Mr. Ca, a landlord, is still in the hamlet. He has many fields under cultivation. Now tenants only pay about 10 percent to the landlord." Even so, rents were higher than before the Tet Offensive [DT304]. This was probably both because of greater GVN control in the area and because land had become increasingly valuable, since the fields of the village that bordered Highway 4 had been switched over to highly profitable vegetable plots. This intensive cultivation was done mostly by individual owners, however, and did not lend itself to the now nearly obsolete landlord system.

The decline in landlord power is revealed by a report that these landlords "nowadays have to beg tenants to give them a little rent so they can live." If the tenant was "afraid" of the landlord, he might give up to 2 *gia* in rent; if not, he would give 1 to 1.5 *gia* [a *gia* is 40 liters by volume]. One of the factors that undermined the landlords' bargaining position was that a lot of land in the large village of My Duc Tay went uncultivated because field rats would eat much of the crop [DT371]. In My Hanh Dong village there was over 100 hectares of uncultivated land, and the landlords, who still owned a lot of land in the village, found it hard to collect rent, and could do so only by appealing to the "sympathy *[tinh cam]*" of their tenants [DT391]. By contrast, in the neighboring village of My Hanh Trung, where 50 hectares of land still belonged to the landlords, they continued to collect rent from tenants at the rate of 2 *gia* a *cong*, because they continued to pay tax to the revolution and therefore their land had not been confiscated [DT377].

There was, to be sure, a shortage of land in most areas that were secure enough to be farmed. In many areas where some security had been restored, rice fields which had been out of cultivation had become overgrown with weeds and brush and were too expensive to clear and reclaim, so the remaining cultivable land was in even heavier demand. In many areas there was also a labor shortage. The war had left most villages bereft of able-bodied males. Since reclaiming land required exceptionally strenuous physical labor, this also meant that the older men and women still on the land could not expand their cultivation. However, what the relative absence of young and middle-aged males meant most of all was that any land reform settlement which ratified the ownership of whoever was the current tenant would leave many questions when the soldiers and refugees returned to the land.

Saigon's land reform may have had some impact in solidifying political support for the GVN, but in the end it was too little, too late. Data on this subject, however, are hard to come by. Stuart Callison's study, *Land to the Tiller in the Mekong Delta*, based on interviews conducted in 1971 and 1972, updates some of Robert Sansom's earlier data on one village in Dinh Tuong (Long Binh Dien) [see Sansom's *Economics of Insurgency*], but the fact that Long Binh Dien was a relatively secure village and close to a well-traveled and secure province road makes it difficult to extrapolate to other areas of the province. Moreover, the Dinh Tuong data are from only a single village in the province. Perhaps the greatest problem in analyzing the political impact of land reform in this late phase of the war is establishing the extent to which economic benefits actually affected loyalties and/or behavior. In a concluding chapter to his study of the early 1970s "Land to the Tiller" (LTTT) program in the Mekong Delta, written after the collapse of the GVN, Callison observes: "The exact degree of the greater political support creditable to the LTTT Program alone cannot be identified, but it was clear that support for the insurgents in the Delta was waning in the early 1970s as the whole package of the government's rural development program was being favorably received."[12]

Like many observers, Callison concludes that land reform "and other elements of the Republic of Vietnam's [RVN] counter-insurgency effort in the Mekong Delta reduced the insurgent forces to very low levels of potency in the early 1970's." He adds that, "One of the ironies of the tragic conflict in Vietnam is that by 1975 the RVN had apparently won the war of insurgency, considered the more intractable threat by their American ally, and then lost the conflict to a *conventional* invading army due to reduced logistical support and a classic battlefield blunder."[13] We will consider the relationship between guerrilla and regular war and between Southerners and Northerners in the next chapter. Here we focus on the question of whether the "insurgency" had in fact been defeated, and the role that land reform may have played in pacification.

The GVN "Land to the Tiller" law, signed by President Nguyen Van Thieu in March 1970, went far beyond the reforms of the Diem regime and, in some crucial respects, beyond the previous revolutionary reforms—on paper, at least. The law allowed retention of a maximum of fifteen hectares, but only if the owners themselves cultivated the land. Those who received land in the Mekong Delta area could get up to 3 hectares of land free of charge. Priority was given to current tillers, no matter how they had come to occupy the land. In this regard, the LTTT reform was substantially different from the Diem reforms, which did not recognize the Viet Minh land distribution, gave priority only to tenants recognized by the landlord, and then only if they had the cash to purchase the land. It was also different from the revolutionary land distribution of the early 1960s, which treated purchasers of land from the Diem reforms who had displaced tenants as usurpers of the land.

Moreover, the GVN would give permanent legal title to the land, in contrast to the clearly provisional grants of usage and cultivation rights made by the revolution, which wanted to retain the right to reallocate land according to political requirements and did not want to complicate a later move toward cooperativization by encouraging a mentality of private ownership among the peasants. To reimburse those who lost land, U.S. aid and deferred payments allowed the GVN to buy off the remaining landlords without charging the recipients. The landlords were to be compensated at a rate equal to 2.5 times the average annual paddy yield of their land (on a five-year basis). They would be paid 20 percent in cash and the rest in government bonds over an eight-year period.[14]

"In proposing the LTTT Program the GVN had three major goals in mind," writes Callison. They were "(1) social justice, (2) agricultural development, and (3) political pacification. Greater social justice would be achieved simply by abolishing the land-tenant system, thus reducing the exploitative features of the current system and enlarging the class of small, middle-class, owner-cultivator farmers. Land distribution would enhance agricultural development programs by giving the farmers incentives to ownership to care for their land and enabling them to retain the total product of their labor and investment, which was expected to induce greater efforts to raise production and 'provide the basis for a sound agricultural economy.' Of more immediate concern, the program was expected to 'undercut the Viet Cong land program and gain the farmers' political support,' thus shortening the struggle to defeat the communists."[15] Thus, the GVN land reform had the explicit political objective of supporting pacification by neutralizing what was assumed to be the major political appeal of the revolution—the promise of land to the poor peasants.

To some extent, the "Land to the Tiller" program may have had a short-term impact in eroding support for the revolution, but it was only one piece in a much larger picture. First, the LTTT program essentially ratified changes already made by the previous reforms—including the most fundamental of these, the revolutionary reforms of the Viet Minh period and the early 1960s. Second, the LTTT program was politically possible only because of the massive disruptions of the war, which made land both less desirable (in the case of land in insecure areas) and less vital to survival (because of the artificial war economy, which allowed a large number of people to survive without being engaged in agricultural production). Third, because of the military mobilizations of both sides and the refugees, the cultivators tended to be mainly women and older men. Callison's Long Binh Dien survey of farmers reveals an average age of 56.8 years for men (17 of his 45 respondents) and 47.0 for women (28 of 45).[16]

Fourth, the final stages of the war were not similar to the early contest for political loyalties of the rural peasantry. By this time basic decisions about political loyalty and action had been made by most people, and had far deeper roots related to the intersection of individual and family experiences with the civil war than the day-to-day calculations of the "rational peasant." Fifth, the GVN land titles were only as valuable as its prospects for survival, and there was clearly a wide range of opinions on this important point by the Dinh Tuong peasants of the early 1970s. In Tam Hiep village, which bordered prosperous and secure Than Cuu Nghia on one side and some of the remaining minibase areas on the other (and which was rated a "reasonably secure" B by the Hamlet Evaluation Survey in mid-1971), the people were afraid to accept GVN land titles for fear that "those guys [*may cha]*" would come out to confiscate them. "Now, during pacification, people who were given land [by the revolution] are allowed to keep it. They make out a paper and give it to the GVN, which will recognize it. But people are afraid to take land from the GVN reform because they are afraid the Viet Cong will cut their throats" [DT304]. A study by the Control Data Corporation noted that "In Dinh Tuong some dare not apply for title because they fear Viet Cong retribution."[17] This could, of course, work in reverse. The former deputy Party secretary of Binh Trung village said that as pacification eroded revolutionary control in 1969 and 1970, "people who received land from the Front became very worried, because they see the movement is now receding *[thoai trao]*" [DT310]. But since the GVN accepted whoever was actually tilling the land as the legitimate claimant no matter how they had gain access to it, the recipients of land from the revolution had less to fear.

The limited available data on the link between land reform and political views do not support the conclusion that the GVN was able to secure the loyalties of delta peasants with land titles. The titles did not actually result in a shift of tenure, since it simply ratified the right of the existing cultivator to be on the land. To the extent that the LTTT program had a direct and immediate effect on the cultivator, it was in ending the onerous rents to landlords, which resulted in a very significant impact on peasant income, as Callison's data suggest. This does not seem to have redounded to the credit of the GVN. As noted above, Callison concluded that "The exact degree of the greater political support creditable to the LTTT Program alone cannot be identified." The Bush survey found that only 12 percent of their respondents in Dinh Tuong answered affirmatively to the proposition that "Farmers fully support the Government now. The GVN did what it promised. The GVN understands what farmers need and is really helping us." Even fewer (8 percent) agreed with the statement that "LTTT defeats Viet Cong propaganda. It reduces their influence in the village. Because all are owners, Viet Cong can not move freely in the hamlet. There is no Viet Cong terrorism now." Not a single respondent said that "There is no more Viet Cong 'tax' squeeze."[18]

Finally, the classic guerrilla struggle for control of the villages that had characterized the conflict in the early 1960s had been eclipsed (but not entirely supplanted) by the big-unit war and the infusion of North Vietnamese troops, and land reform was fundamentally irrelevant to that aspect of the war. The image of North Vietnamese tanks crashing through the gates of Saigon's Presidential Palace and inducing the final GVN surrender has left the impression that the war was won by massive conventional force from the North. If so, then land reform was clearly not the way to defeat the communists. The next chapter will argue, however, that guerrilla war in the Mekong Delta remained an important, if secondary, aspect of the overall conflict—especially after the Easter Offensive of 1972. As noted earlier, this chapter contends that the success of pacification in 1970–71 was temporary and, to the extent that land reform was related to pacification, it was a consequence rather than a cause of GVN security gains in the countryside.

The Revolution Attempts to Reverse the GVN's Pacification Gains

As the revolution tried to cope with the practical problems resulting from the loss of territorial control, it devised an ambitious plan to reverse the GVN pacification gains, which it called "upgrading the zone *[chuyen vung]*." This plan was aimed at turning Saigon-controlled areas back into revolutionary-controlled zones. In a mirror-image adoption of the

Saigon Hamlet Evaluation (HES) security classification program, the Party devised its own ABC scoring system. This was not a new device. It was used sporadically in some areas undergoing GVN pacification before the Tet Offensive. Now, however, the ABC system was revised and incorporated into the *chuyen vung* strategy as a belated response to the January 1970 Central Committee Resolution Eighteen directive on "defeating Vietnamization," which was translated into a counter-pacification policy by Region 2 in September 1970.

A preview of the general direction of the plan came during the July 20, 1970, campaign, when the head of the region permanent office, Viet Thang ("Victorious Viet," who had been the Party leader in My Tho during the late 1950s) came to My Tho with Tam Phuong, the military commander of Region 2, and Sau Phu, who had commanded the 261st Battalion in the early 1960s. They selected southern Cai Lay district as a pilot area for counter-pacification and took direct command of the effort.[19] The My Tho province committee met in September 1970 to consider COSVN's evaluation of the revolution's reaction to the GVN pacification program of 1969 and early 1970. Some postwar histories suggest that this meeting revived the "urban outskirts *[vung ven]*" concept of the 1968–69 period (see the previous chapter), but this time it seems that the "outskirts" referred to areas around village posts in rural areas.[20]

The province committee distilled the discussion of this September meeting into a simple slogan: "Stand fast on the land, stick close to the people, and stay close to the enemy *[ba bam]*." The main objective was to restore a toehold for military units in and near the populated areas of My Tho. To this end, the province committee devised its own HES scheme with four classifications: A hamlets were "completely liberated, B hamlets had [GVN] posts but the enemy in them was surrounded, and we were in control night and day, C hamlets had posts and a repressive administrative machinery, but it was in exile [not located in the hamlet], the enemy was able to break out on operations and we were only in control part of the day or at night." The fourth category was "weak hamlets where the enemy was in total control."[21]

This policy did not reach the villages until March 1971, and there were slight differences in the criteria used to grade the security level of a hamlet in the village version. Generally the village version was less rhetorically evasive about the loss of revolutionary control and more practical in its specific criteria. In Thanh Phu (Cai Lay) for example, there were (by the cadres' count) three A hamlets, three B hamlets, and seven C hamlets. "An A hamlet was not yet pacified and was controlled by [the] Front. Cadres could operate day and night but people lived in the rice fields and the cadres were still in the jungle. You couldn't stay in a B hamlet." In mid-1971, the GVN HES ratings on the remaining two listed hamlets (reduced from four in 1969) were "D" and "E." The "upgrading the zone" strategy aimed at turning B hamlets into A hamlets. A "B hamlet has a post. C hamlets are completely controlled by the GVN. This ABC classification was sent down at [the] same time as the counter-pacification program [1971]." A leading village cadre said:

It wasn't hard to classify these hamlets, because there were clear criteria which related to the presence of posts and the ability of cadres to operate. The district classified them based on the report of the head of the *mang* [intervillage sector]. The *chuyen vung* or upgrading of hamlets policy was crucial and had priority over all other tasks. The cadres and party members had to study it thoroughly. This policy came down in March 1971. The cadres were told it would be a difficult job but that they had to strive to carry it out because of its importance. We had to get B hamlets up to A to provide a foothold for the troops in the hamlets. Only if they could concentrate in the hamlets could the troops widen the battlefield and make the military the "lever" *[don xeo]* for politics. Only if the military was strong would there be enough strength to cope with the situation, that is, to reclaim land and people. The broad plan was laid out but not the details, and it depended on the locality. The first thing was to isolate the posts so that they couldn't break out *[bung ra]* and operate. When we had to get them to pull back into their posts, then we would call on the people to join the popular associations and participate in revolutionary tasks, and push the movement forward to a high level, along with kicking out the security agents and the village council from the village. Finally the isolated posts would be knocked off *[tieu diet]* [DT386].

The plan was, of course, nothing less than a call to repeat the Destruction of the Oppression and Concerted Uprising of 1960–61. This village cadre was skeptical.

I feel that we didn't have enough forces to succeed in upgrading hamlets. We just studied the policy and listened to it. The policy of isolating posts sounded grand, but there was nothing to it apart from setting grenades along the path to and from the post and sniping. The grenades were easy but sniping was not, because the guerrillas were afraid of being discovered and killed. Now it is not easy to attack a post because they are carefully defended and have solid fortifications. The Vanh Dai *[vanh dai* was the "perimeter" surrounding GVN areas] Company has forty people but lacks weapons like the B40, B41, and DKZ, so it couldn't strongly attack the post, and doing it with infantry alone wouldn't work. Also it was very hard to concentrate the company and it was easily discovered. Basically there were no results. No posts were attacked and there were only a few ambushes around the Tong Doc Loc canal. They still set grenades and sniped at posts but without much result apart from wounding a few soldiers. No hamlets were upgraded [DT386].

During 1971, GVN pacification seemed like an unstoppable juggernaut which could not be resisted with the meager military forces at hand, and without a population base.

Isolation of the Village Cadres

The GVN attempt to clear the land of places to hide made life even more difficult for those cadres who were still in the hamlets that were undergoing pacification. A hamlet guerrilla who had reluctantly rejoined the movement after having rallied to the GVN during the fierce assaults of the U.S. Ninth Division in his village of Hoi Cu said that the situation there in 1971 was "more dangerous than when the Americans were conducting sweep operations at the beginning of 1969. The terrain has been cleared and the guerrillas and cadres have had to flee from the hamlet. They come back at night to collect taxes and bolster the morale of the people. During the day, if they don't have to hide, they will bring the money to the hamlet and get the people or family members to go out to the market to buy them some food. But it is precisely because the cadres are still lurking around the hamlet that the soldiers chase after them and take advantage of the occasion to grab ducks and chickens and threaten the people with all sorts of things" [DT378]. Because of the heavy bombing and shelling in 1969 and 1970, most people in An Thai hamlet had already moved out to live in the Strategic Hamlet or along Highway 4. Only twenty or thirty old people were left in the hamlet. The treelines and orchards were all heavily booby-trapped, and no one dared go near them. "For the last two years, I haven't seen any new recruits or civilian laborers from the hamlet." GVN district officials often came into the hamlet to urge people to move back to the hamlet and resume farming "but no one went back because the hamlet was still contested and every time the [GVN] soldiers went on patrol they fired indiscriminately into the hamlet." The situation in the hamlet, he said, was "half fat and half lean *[nua nac nua mo]*" [DT378].

Clearing out the trees (done by the GVN troops) put an end to some of the onerous work that some peasants had been made to do for the cadres. In the shrinking areas of revolutionary presence it was not really possible to talk of "control" of an area, since the cadres could rarely project their influence among the civilian population, which now consisted of scattered families living in the middle of the rice fields. The cadres themselves stayed concealed in the treelines, and tried to create an impenetrable hedge of vegetation, laced with grenade traps, to discourage GVN soldiers from entering these redoubts. They were still somewhat dependent on the nearby civilians for the extensive labor needed to build these pale shadows of the former "combat hamlets." The techniques of creating a thicket of brambles, bamboo fences, and obstacles were the same as in the old combat hamlets, but there were no "hamlets" to enclose, and there was little in the way of combat since the cadres simply evaded any troops that were bold enough to enter these minibases.

The cadres' isolation and the encroachment of GVN control had subtly transformed the "inside" into an archipelago of secluded minibase islands, largely cut off from the civilian population, as illustrated by a respondent who said that in My Hanh Trung the two strongest revolutionary hamlets in the village "didn't have a single civilian" [DT377]. Inability to circulate among the civilian population also changed the cadres' work style. It was not often possible to gather even small groups of peasants, so the cadres had to find ways of reaching them. In the depopulated hamlets of My Hanh Trung,

> In Xom Choi and Ca Mau hamlets the cadres operated openly. In Nang Trung hamlet they operated furtively and at night. About three or four times a month they would come around and ask the people to do civilian labor duty (four people at most). The guerrillas would come to the house and people were forced to go—they couldn't refuse. Or they would come in to collect taxes and spread the news of victories. The guerrillas and the cadres came into each house to pass on the victory news or collect taxes—it was certainly not possible to assemble the neighborhood. Usually the guerrillas and cadres operated between six and seven o'clock in the evening because the [GVN] soldiers would have finished their patrols. Operating at night was disadvantageous because the people wouldn't open their doors, but at that time [early evening] the people hadn't yet gone to sleep, their doors were still open, so [the cadres could] burst into *[dot nhap]* the homes [DT377].

The changes in the relationship between the cadres and the peasants is implied in the use of the term "burst into" the homes, suggesting that, like unwanted guests or gangs carrying out "home invasions," the cadres had to force themselves on a reluctant peasantry.

Considering that they usually did so only when they came demanding labor or taxes, this picture is probably not far wrong, for there was no time or security for patient explanation and preparatory socializing.

Cut off from the civilian population and unable to farm, the cadres eked out a primitive existence. A hamlet finance cadre from Tan Hoi described this life in 1971. "If you go into the hamlet, you have to have an armed escort and might even be shot or killed. For the last twenty days or so we just ate rice with salt. Even if we had money, we couldn't do anything because there wasn't anyone there to sell us anything. In the orchards in villages on the other side of Highway 4, like Long Tien, Long Trung, Cam Son, Xuan Son, and Hoi Son, you could eat fruit from the orchards but you couldn't stand this diet for long. In the villages on this [north] side of Highway 4, like My Hanh Dong, My Hanh Trung, My Phuoc Tay, Tan Hoi, Tan Phu Dong, and Tan Binh, the orchards are mostly squash and bamboo. There is no fruit to eat, just a few coconuts. In the dry season we could catch fish, but in the rainy season the place was flooded, so how could we scoop up the fish? If we did, there was no rice. Recently [summer 1971], we only hid. The people are all gone, who would we operate with? By day they would come back to the rice fields, but we didn't dare come out. By day there were soldiers all over the place" [DT391].

Life in Recently Pacified Hamlets

By 1971 the security situation had turned sharply in favor of the GVN, but there were still pockets of contested territory. Since most villages in the province (with the exception of some along the fringe of the Plain of Reeds) had been brought under some degree of GVN control, the major strategy of pacification in early 1971 centered around bringing the remaining population living in outlying areas of hamlets under the control of the GVN. This was achieved by a combination of extending the network of militia posts into the newly pacified areas, blanketing a given zone with mutually supporting GVN militia units that restricted the movement of the cadres, and driving them on the defensive. To complete the isolation of the cadres, the GVN embarked on a major program of resettling the peasants still living out in the rice fields. They were ordered to dismantle their houses and move close to the nearest post, where they could be more closely supervised. A second phase of the 1971 pacification, starting about mid-year, switched the focus from gathering the population into GVN areas to extending Saigon's territorial control by eliminating the remaining cadre bases. Given the fact that the GVN claimed that 96 percent of the Dinh Tuong population was under government control as of early 1971, it might be asked what more pacification remained to be accomplished?[22]

One answer was that "GVN control" meant hamlets rated A, B, or C, and some of the C hamlets were actually in contested areas. The logic of the HES rating system was that A and B would reflect complete and nearly complete GVN control, while D and E would be the equivalent for the revolutionary side. V meant total "Viet Cong" control and was considered "off the scale" as far as rating gradations of area security was concerned. C was "in between" and therefore meant "contested" or mixed control, although it usually indicated areas that the revolution considered "weak" from their perspective. In previous years, the U.S. advisor reports had sometimes lumped C hamlets with A and B hamlets in a category indicating GVN control, though sometimes only A and B were used for this purpose. By

1971, the HES ratings were clustered at the top of the ABC scale, and in this context a C hamlet seems to have been considered "relatively insecure." Because nearly the entire province of Dinh Tuong was considered "pacified" in 1971, the question of what these letter ratings indicated once more re-emerged. Richard Hunt, who has written the most comprehensive general study of pacification, observes that

> CORDS [Civil Operations and Revolutionary Development Support, the U.S. organi-
> zation in charge of pacification in Vietnam] revised HES again in 1971 to reflect the
> changing character of the war, giving greater weight to political factors (the infra-
> structure, terrorism, level of development) that affected security. Under the 1971 HES,
> over 84 percent of the population lived in hamlets rated A or B at the end of December
> 1971, roughly the results of the previous year, which were measured by less stringent
> standards. How could CORDS project an image of progress if it continually had to
> make the measurement criteria more rigorous? Each iteration of HES seemed to raise
> questions about the validity of the previous version. Ultimately it was hard to recon-
> cile the changes in HES with the general notion that security was continually improv-
> ing. The problems with HES stemmed from its inception, when U.S. officials yield to
> the temptation to publicize HES data as evidence of progress. HES was designed as an
> internal management technique, which was a valid use. As a public relations tool,
> HES was disastrously misused.[23]

Hunt writes that "A special assessment of HES in 1972 concluded that it generated anomalies, showing improvements, for example, 'in cases where thousands of area residents are forced by tactical activity from their relatively insecure C villages into camps located in AB rated zones. In other words, though population has been uprooted, and territory lost, the HES will nevertheless show at least a temporary pacification advance in terms of AB population.' The reliability of some reports declined after the South Vietnamese took responsibility for preparing them under Vietnamization."[24]

Although delicately phrased, the U.S. study's conclusion that there were cases of peasants being forced from their homes by "tactical activity" was an indirect admission of the depopulation strategy employed during pacification in places like Dinh Tuong. It also notes that increased control over population does not necessarily bring about increased control over territory, in fact, the reverse can sometimes happen. The Dinh Tuong province advisor's report of April 1971 recorded 255 hamlets of the 477 total hamlets as being in the AB category, and 424 in the ABC category. Previous HES figures had focused largely on the hamlet as a unit of security control, and tended to include the entire hamlet population in whatever rating the hamlet received. So, if a hamlet had a HES rating of B, and a population of 500, the entire 500 would be considered to be living under GVN control, even if a portion still lived in parts of the hamlet that were in fact controlled by the cadres. The logical next step was to bring the entire population of these hamlets under Saigon control in fact as well as on paper. The 1967 HES listed Cam Son village in the 20/7 zone as having four hamlets with a combined population of 3,540. By August 1971 it listed only two hamlets with a combined population of 300 and both rated E. A resident of Cam Phong hamlet said that there were only two families there, but this extreme depopulation was not reflected by the HES, which no longer listed Cam Phong hamlet [DT332]. Another hamlet cadre from Cam Phong said that Cam Son village was pacified, but that the GVN operated only around the posts. "If the Seventh Division is not on operation, the Front could continue to operate because the soldiers just hang around the posts" [DT320].

The separation of the cadres and the civilian population created three different groups in the village. The first were the cadres and their families, who stayed in the unpacified parts of the village. Second were the hard-core supporters and sympathizers, the "backbone cadres." These were not actually "cadres," although it is significant that some interviewees like DT308 now used this term to refer to people who had earlier been reformed to as "backbone elements" to distinguish them from full time revolutionaries. They were the indispensable links between the cadres and the third group, the ordinary civilians, who had all taken refuge in GVN areas, mostly along the provincial route running through the village or near the post. The finance clerk reported that "a number of cadres told me that if they hadn't organized at least five or ten underground cadres in a pacified hamlet, they wouldn't be able to operate" [DT308].

In those hamlets in which the GVN established a post, the civilian population was regrouped to the vicinity of the post, where the militia could keep them under surveillance and prevent the cadres from having regular contact with them. This was not a voluntary program, and those who refused to move risked having their houses shelled or burned to the ground. A hamlet guerrilla from My Long said in May 1971 that "before, the GVN gave time for people to disassemble their houses. But now if there are houses that haven't been taken down, the ARVN does it. My own mother's house was burned. She had gone out to a GVN area and wasn't home at the time, so they burned it. If you are at home they didn't burn it but just pulled it down. There were no explanations by the GVN. They just pull down the houses and tell the people to leave. Of the thirty-eight homes in the hamlet, two have been burned and the others have been pulled down." The initial order to move was given in early 1970. "The people asked to stay to finish the harvest and they were afraid that if they moved far away it would be dangerous going back and forth to their fields. Some got the GVN to put it off until this year. Families with possessions still in the hamlet leave a person to take care of them and those who have moved everything out took everyone with them. Now there are less than twenty people in the hamlet" [DT330]. In My Hoa hamlet of My Duc Dong village, by mid-1971 all the residents had been regrouped around the nearest post.

> At present, everyone has returned to the hamlet [post]. No one is still out in the rice fields, so there is no more dismantling or burning houses. At the beginning, the people refused to return to the hamlet, partly because the VC forbade them to, and partly because they were afraid there would be no security if they returned to the hamlet. After that, the Eleventh Regiment was stationed right in the hamlet, and they threatened the people that if they didn't move there, they would have no grounds for complaint if they were shelled, even if people got killed. The regiment mortars shelled the rice fields around where the people were all night. They got scared and all moved to the hamlet, and were reimbursed for the expense of dismantling and moving their houses, and got sheets of corrugated tin for roofing. Afterward, the people were told by the village council to submit applications for indemnification for their property losses during the Tet Offensive. The village council estimated the damage and put it on paper. Many families got damages appraised at 30,000VN or 40,000 piasters [DT357].

This was the right and left hand of the GVN. On the one hand, peasants were brutally forced to move. On the other hand, they got compensation not only for the move, but even for the damages from the Tet Offensive—another round in the bidding war for peasant loyalty. Needless to say, everyone benefited from this largess, which came ultimately from the U.S. taxpayer, because the village officials undoubtedly took their cut as they passed the money along.

For pacification to succeed, it would eventually have to extend its territorial control into the formerly contested and liberated areas, and ensure enough security so that most people could return to their original homes, and most land could be reclaimed and cultivated. Despite impressive gains in security, this goal was never achieved. It had been an article of faith among many of the U.S. specialists on "pacification" that real success in counterinsurgency depended on "nation building" and "community development." However, with the departure of U.S. troops from My Tho, these efforts subsided. In Thanh Phu village (Chau Thanh), next to the Dong Tam base where the U.S. Ninth Division had been stationed, "When the Americans were still here, the village council came in every week to assemble the people to discuss community development and to check family registers, etc. Since the Americans left, they have rarely come in, especially since the beginning of 1971 to present [mid-1971] they have not been in my hamlet at all—I myself don't know the reason" [DDT395]. By this time the development aspect of pacification had given way to a heavy emphasis on the security dimension. Though it is clear that the more secure situation led to a great deal of spontaneous economic development, whether this was translated into stronger community institutions in GVN areas is open to question.

Much of the pacification in 1969–70 had been based on a depopulation strategy, "draining the pond to catch the fish." This continued into 1971, and it was the clear intention of the GVN to regroup the people remaining outside their control around the military posts that constituted the core of GVN security in the hamlets. The interviews show that in most cases GVN village officials constantly warned people living in "pacified areas" not to go to the outlying areas to farm, giving the reason that it was too dangerous. A representative case is the village authorities in Vinh Kim, who assembled the people every month and lectured them on security. "They urged the people not to go to live or work in the deep areas, because it could be dangerous if the two sides started shooting at each other" [DT343]. In some cases, such as An Thai hamlet of Hoi Cu, GVN officials did urge people to resume farming, but the insecurity caused by the random firing of the GVN's own patrols as well as their harassment of the few civilians who had stayed on discouraged people from doing so [DT378]. Even when the GVN began to expand its territorial control in mid-1971 by attempting systematically to level the "minibases," this still was not linked to a resettlement of these areas.

Despite Pacification, the Revolution Is Still Active in My Tho

Although the GVN overwhelmingly dominated My Tho in 1971, the province's rural areas were not totally desolate, and the revolution continued to be active in a number of ways. A young man from My Tho had been trained as a musician in the revolutionary base areas around Ba Thu in Cambodia during the 1967–70 period. While he was in Cambodia he found that "Cambodians liked the Vietnamese. Vietnamese entertainments were also attended by Cambodians, and Vietnamese artists did a program in the Cambodian language for them." He returned to My Tho and traveled around the province with a small entertainment team, giving shows.

> I began to specialize in the study of music in 1970 and studied the accordion about eleven months. I liked the accordion because it was more forceful and lively than the guitar. When you are young, playing the accordion is like a breeze in the jungle. I only heard the Region entertainment group play. They were really good. I studied with an instructor along with another student, an ethnic Chinese from Cambodia. I played better than the Chinese girl—women always play worse than we do. Our method was modeled a bit on the French. I studied until the end of 1970 and was sent back to My Tho in February 1971 to the province entertainment troupe. When I was young it seemed like there were a lot of them, but now because of the fierce war they had split up into small groups. Songs were by composers from "in there"—the ones at the Region were better than at province. I also liked music from the North. The entertainment group had eight people. We had to do everything—dance, act, and sing. I was a poor singer and in plays I only did small roles. Before, the province group did songs of the musicians of that time. Now we do new music which I like better. I don't like *vong co* [traditional Southern music] because it is too sad and it puts me to sleep. The older people like different things, but most like *vong co* more than anything. The young people like me are more progressive. The province entertainment group only traveled when it was quiet. We didn't go to difficult places like Cho Gao. We did go to Chau Thanh, however. We went all the way up to Tan Huong and also to Tam Hiep, but not to Binh Duc or Vinh Kim. Most places were north of Highway 4. Our audiences were 100 to several hundred, up to 400. They only came because they enjoyed listening. Performances were at night. We were not worried about airstrikes. People like *cai luong* [reformed opera] the most, and the group also did *cai luong*. It wasn't only peasants who performed, but also students from out here. I liked Southern folk songs *[dan ca Nam Bo]*. We performed 400–500 meters away from the post, far enough so they couldn't hear. We couldn't go where there were a lot of posts, like Binh Duc or Cho Gao. Sometimes we went into weak [contested] areas only 300 meters from the highway. I was arrested when we arrived for a performance. A plane landed troops. I was the only one captured and they really threatened me [DT401].

The interviewer asked, "Impartially speaking, who do people still support?" The answer was that "Although the war has been terrible, the people still live cheerfully. They like to watch entertainments. When we come in people say, 'Why is it that you nephews have been so long in coming back here?' So we had the impression that the people still loved us and still liked our music. They certainly weren't apathetic *[ue oai]* or unhappy when we came." Asked how he liked the music in the Saigon zone, he replied, "the music out here is too far out *[qua troi]*!" [DT401].

Even in places like Tam Binh and My Long villages, in the heart of the 20/7 zone and a priority area for GVN pacification, the revolution was still able to assemble an occasional crowd despite the collapse of the popular associations. "The Farmers' Association and Labor Youth were still strong in 1969, but starting from 1970 it began to fall apart. Many were killed, many rallied, many went to big units. At the time [1969], the Farmers' Association was still strong. At every meeting more than forty people attended in the hamlet. The Women's Association only had about six or seven people in the hamlet. Now [1971] the popular associations don't exist because ARVN has leveled the terrain *[pha dia hinh]*.

When we could still operate, the popular associations met hamlet-wide and sometimes even on an intervillage level with Long Tien, Ban Long, My Long, Phu Phong. An entertainment group performed. There was recently a performance this year [1971] in Tam Binh. They put on an anti-pacification play and showed scenes of police oppressing the people, making them pay bribes and so on. They had large speakers—you could hear it from the post—but [the GVN soldiers] were afraid and didn't do anything. My Long was still strong because all the cadres were still there, although the guerrillas were demoralized. The singers were really good, they danced a rice-threshing song from Korea. The women had on beautiful makeup. The people, seeing boys and girls dancing and holding hands, roared with laughter." Evidently the mobile movie teams were no longer able to function in 1971, however. "Films about the North were shown, praising the happy life in the North. We saw films in 1969 and 1970" [DT330].

Although the village cadres were largely passive, holed up in their "minibases," they were able to maintain a presence in almost every village, and they were able to come out and appear suddenly in populated areas often enough to remind people that they were still around. Even in villages that had been extensively "pacified," such as Binh Duc and Thanh Phu in the shadow of the U.S. Ninth Division base at Dong Tam, cadres could still operate, and the "province town unit" C207 continued to move around [DT395]. The cadres were able to hang on even in areas that had been cleared of trees and defoliated. One long-time base at the intersection of the villages of Nhi Binh, Huu Dao, and Binh Trung was cleared, but the contiguous area of potential hiding places was nearly a square kilometer, only half of which was cleared. "In the middle of this configuration *[doi hinh]* there is a stream which goes down to Dau Manh Pagoda, and then there is a river which goes up to Duong Diem market and the post. The [guerrilla] unit is in this area. If you clear out this area, then they will go over to the other side of the stream. You can clear all you want, they will still be there. You can shell them or bomb them, but they will go down in their bunkers and wait for it to end, then they'll come out again. They stand guard, and if you come in this way they will simply move. If you destroy the whole terrain configuration they will go somewhere else" [DT398]. These segmented clusters of tree cover, called minibases by the U.S. advisors and "terrain configurations *[doi hinh]*" by the cadres, were too numerous to eliminate without denuding the entire province, along with its orchards, which—though heavily damaged—were still an important potential source of income for the peasants.

In the violent aftermath of the 1968 Tet Offensive, Binh Duc village was in the eye of the storm of the U.S.–GVN counteroffensive. About thirty cadres and a squad of guerrillas were dispersed throughout the village to maintain a foothold. The accelerated pacification took a heavy toll on the cadres. There was also internal dissension and a flagrant case of corruption with tax money that weakened the village organization. In October 1969, after several village secretaries (including Hai Duc, who had become famous for reportedly killing 78 enemy) and most of the other cadres in the village had been killed, the Binh Duc Party chapter was disbanded. With no formal revolutionary organization in the village, an armed propaganda team was set up (as had been done in the 1959–60 uprising), consisting of a few guerrillas from Binh Duc and a few guerrillas borrowed from nearby Thanh Phu village. Their main mission was to collect taxes, though the security situation made this difficult. Only about 30 percent of the taxes could be collected. Part of the problem was that roving gangsters posed as tax collectors to shake down the civilian population. This made life more difficult for the genuine guerrillas, because the high turnover and secrecy had made it difficult for the people to tell who really represented the revolution, so the armed team coming to collect was often greeted with suspicion [DT301].

The village guerrillas in Binh Duc were deprived of the umbrella of protection of larger units, and were therefore very reluctant to attack even small GVN units for fear of giving away their position. They had to do their own liaison with the district, because there were no longer any liaison agents to do so. Because they were not familiar with this work, and because they had to be more cautious than liaison agents, the process took twice as long. Binh Duc was not alone in its problems with liaison. In Long Dinh village, a trip to Nhi Binh village which used to take two hours required two days by 1971 [DT384]. Binh Duc's few guerrillas were not strong enough to do more than collect taxes occasionally, but they were supported by thirty or forty guerrillas from the neighboring villages of Thanh Phu and Long Hung. Together, these guerrillas clung to what was still grandly termed an "anti-American annihilation perimeter [*vanh dai diet My*]" even though the Americans had left and the "perimeter" "only consists of a small orchard" [DT301]. Despite the vastly reduced effectiveness of this small force, it does illustrate the story of 1971, which was the ability of the cadres and guerrillas to hang on, and the failure of the GVN to eliminate them.

Still, the situation in 1971 was bleak for the revolutionaries in My Tho. Their military forces had been reduced in numbers. A postwar military history of the province states that "Cadres and Party members were arrested, killed, and wounded in ever-increasing numbers. The masses in the province base area were down to 40,000 people, the majority being old people, women, and children. The numbers in the province and district armed forces declined day after day." The remnants of the 514A Battalion were absorbed in the 261st Battalion. Despite the claims of several postwar histories that recruiting was still possible in My Tho, both the 261A and 261B Battalions were forced to rely on filler troops from North Vietnam. The 514C Battalion's strength ranged from fifty to seventy men. Saigon's military assets in the province numbered 31,000, and in Go Cong 12,944. There were nearly 700 posts in My Tho and 326 in Go Cong.[25]

GVN Success in 1971 Bore Seeds of Future Problems

In some ways the GVN success in setting up a network of posts was a contributing factor in this failure to take advantage of the military weakness of the revolution. The posts made Saigon complacent and reduced the scope and intensity of GVN ground operations, leaving the cadres and guerrillas with safe havens and some respite. The Binh Duc leader described the change caused by the departure of U.S. troops. "When the Americans were still here, their regular troops were very active so they didn't need to set up posts or to have many units operating. They only relied on aerial bombings day and night without letup, and sent their ground troops deep into liberated areas. After the Americans withdrew, the GVN set up many posts. Each village built something like eight or nine posts, whereas the Americans used to have only two or three posts at most. The increase in the number of posts created a lot of obstacles for the VC. Before, the Americans used shellings and bombings to the maximum and were only concerned about protecting their bases and barracks, so it was easy for the Viet Cong to hide, provided they built fortified bunkers. The increase in posts restricted the VC from carrying out their attacks a lot" [DT301].

This temporary success, however, created further problems for the GVN. "At present, the VC have to disperse their forces very thinly and then at night gather to attack posts. Then they withdraw to their base 2 or 3 kilometers away. Before, the Viet Cong didn't dare attack like this, because if they did the Americans would send ground troops in to search the area under attack and bomb and shell heavily. But if the ARVN are attacked, they only try to cope with the VC within a radius of 1 kilometer or less. So the VC are safe after they withdraw, even though greatly hampered by network of posts. GVN bombing and shelling affects them only a little" [DT301]. The cadres and guerrillas would either try to find a wooded area very close to the base, to cut down on the shelling, or they would find an area beyond the 1-kilometer radius that the post could effectively patrol. The minibases outside this radius were only occasionally invaded by larger infantry operations, and the impenetrability of the maze they had created gave them plenty of time to escape.

Despite Hardships the Revolution Maintains Its Forces in 1971

According the official province Party history, in 1971 the province was able to recruit 739 new Party members, of whom 426 were "not uncovered" by the GVN and presumably operated undercover in Saigon-controlled areas. Elections were held for five district committees and forty-seven of the villages, and 247 "not uncovered" hamlet Party chapters were set up, again probably in areas under GVN control. Nearly 1,500 cadres and Party members were given training, and 859 new Party Youth Group members were recruited (300 of whom were "not uncovered" or clandestine members). Over 2,600 Farmers' Association members and 1,800 Women's Association members were on the rolls, although interviews suggest that these were mostly inactive though still dues-paying members. In an attempt to quantify the outer circles of support for the revolution, the province Party organization listed 1,263 *nong cot* or "backbone elements," indicating supporters who were not part of the formal cadre structure but who could be relied on to take the lead in encouraging others to carry out Party orders. Four thousand "military proselytizing political forces" were listed, presumably people who had agreed to persuade family members to defect from the Saigon armed forces.[26] Although the Party history does not give province totals for Party members and guerrillas for 1971, the 1972 figure for Party members under province leadership was 4,000.

On the military side, the province claimed to have enlisted 482 new recruits for the concentrated units, while "developing 1,374 armed hamlet and village forces, including 275 village guerrillas, 288 hamlet guerrillas, 411 secret guerrillas, while the rest were security and secret Self-defense forces."[27] A captured document listed the 1970 strength of revolutionary forces in Chau Thanh district at 33 village cadres, 49 village guerrillas, 360 hamlet guerrillas, 261 Party members, 265 Youth Group members, 1080 Farmer's Association members and 1,744 Womens' Association members.[28]

Holding On: Preserving Forces and Waiting for the Next Strategic Opportunity

In January or February 1971 COSVN made its first comprehensive strategic reassessment of the situation since Resolution Nine in mid-1969. COSVN Directive 01 of 1971 concluded that "The enemy has achieved some temporary results, but is steadily failing at implementing his basic schemes. . . . They failed to destroy or wipe out the revolutionary infrastructure or our local and guerrilla forces, which continued to remain in their areas of operation."[29] The tone of this document was far more subdued than that of an earlier Party strategic reassessment in a 1969 document called Resolution Nine, and the great changes that had taken place since 1969 were evident more in what Directive 01 did *not* say. There was no mention of aggressive large-scale military operations, and main force units were not mentioned as having "continued to remain in their area of operations." The modest accomplishment of the past several years was that "We managed to maintain, and in some areas even expand, our control over villages and hamlets in spite of the presence of enemy outposts."[30] The main accomplishment in this devastating 1968–71 period lay in "holding on" while waiting for the storm to subside and new strategic opportunities to emerge.

The war had been transformed by three factors: expansion of the battlefields to Cambodia and Laos, the withdrawal of U.S. troops and the "Vietnamization" of the fighting, and pacification. The spread of the war to the rest of Indochina created new strategic and diplomatic issues. Vietnamization posed a new test for the contending sides, who were now left to fight it out among themselves in the absence of the Americans. The apparent success of pacification appeared to give the GVN a strong advantage, but it was based fundamentally on rural depopulation. Thus two questions remained to be answered in My Tho. The first was whether the overwhelming GVN security advantage in the Mekong Delta could be reversed if the larger strategic context changed. The second was how much of the civilian population, now displaced as refugees and numbed by the prolonged war, would respond if the revolutionary movement should stir again.

17

Civil War

From a seriously weakened position in 1971, the revolution in My Tho and elsewhere in the Mekong Delta made a military recovery during and after the Spring "Easter" Offensive of 1972. The offensive revived the guerrilla warfare movement in South Vietnam, blunted the previous momentum of Saigon's pacification program, expanded the revolution's territorial control, widened its sphere of military operations in South Vietnam, and led to the signing of the Paris Agreements in January 1973 and the final withdrawal of U.S. forces. The main engine of this transformation was troops that had infiltrated from North Vietnam, whose impact on the military balance paved the way for the final victory of April 1975. The result was not, however, simply a conquest of the South by the North. After the departure of U.S. troops, the conflict reverted to what it had been before: a civil war.

After the 1973 ceasefire, the focus of the conflict shifted back to the Mekong Delta and the populated areas around Saigon. The heavy fighting of the previous year was temporarily suspended by the constraints of the Paris Agreements, and both sides turned their attention to the struggle for control of the most heavily populated rural areas. By mid-1973, Hanoi finally acknowledged the complaints of angry guerrillas leaders in the Mekong Delta that they had been put on the defensive by the restraints on armed struggle imposed by the strategy of clinging to the formalities of the Agreements in an attempt to keep open the possibility of a political solution. Resolution 21 of the Party's Central Committee in Hanoi authorized the unrestrained resumption of armed struggle. It also recentered attention on the Mekong Delta, and the struggle for control of land and people. "We must resolutely attack and counterattack the enemy," it said, "and firmly maintain and expand our initiative in every aspect, defeating the enemy's encroachment operations into the liberated areas or pacification of the delta zones and adjacent areas. Carrying out this injunction requires linking it with the requirement of securing people *[gianh dan]* and gaining sovereignty *[gianh quyen lam chu]* in order to secure a strong position to defeat the enemy."[1] Translating this decision into specific terms, the southern command issued COSVN Resolution 12 in September 1973, which designated the Mekong Delta as the main battlefield, for it was here that "the enemy had selected their focus of pacification, grabbing land and people and scooping up resources."[2]

This chapter will trace the main events leading to the conclusion of the Vietnam war as they affected My Tho, the Spring Offensive of 1972 (which is hereafter referred to as the Easter Offensive, as it was dubbed by American journalists at the time, in order to distinguish it from the 1975 spring offensive), the Paris Agreements and cease-fire of January 1973, the early post-cease-fire struggle between the two sides in 1973, and Hanoi's conclusion that a political solution was no longer possible.

During the final years of the war the Mekong Delta and provinces such as Dinh Tuong were, in many ways, sideshows in the final stage of the conflict. The heaviest fighting in the Easter Offensive of 1972 and the final offensive of the war in 1975 was in central Vietnam and the area northwest of Saigon. Resolution 21 anticipated a prolonged period of struggle in which the people and resources of the delta would be the key to laying the foundation for final victory. The end of the war came sooner than Hanoi anticipated, however, and the final offensive moved from central to south Vietnam, involving Dinh Tuong only at the very end. However, the delta did play an important role in tying down potential government of the Republic of Vietnam (GVN) reinforcements to these other battlefields, and the guerrilla warfare movement showed signs of revival which would have caused serious problems for the Saigon government if the war had been prolonged further, and considerably strengthened the local revolutionary position for the post-cease-fire struggle. The outgoing head of the U.S. military advisory mission wrote in mid-1974: "Taken from a country-wide perspective, even a total GVN victory in the lower Delta would not be decisive in 'winning' the battle with the Communists; however, GVN failure to secure and control this rich and fertile area would have an extremely serious negative impact on the GVN's ability to survive."[3] President Nguyen Van Thieu is reported to have told the commanding generals in Military Region III (surrounding Saigon) and Military Region IV (the Mekong Delta), "I am placing the struggle for survival of South Vietnam in your hands."[4]

For the purposes of this study, the extent to which the revolutionary movement in Dinh Tuong flourished or declined is of greater concern than the specific course of military events there. Nonetheless, the military activities of the last phase of the war are an important indicator of the state of the revolutionary movement, even though most of the major battles were fought by North Vietnamese units and not the local guerrillas. As has been emphasized throughout, the Northern troops were part of the overall revolutionary movement, and they were as much a part of the local picture as was the U.S. Ninth Division in earlier years. Although these Northern troops had their own command structure and logistics system, they were still heavily reliant on the local population for food and on the guerrillas for their familiarity with the local terrain. Moreover, there is some evidence that a significant revival of the local guerrilla movement took place in the last years of the war.

As a result of the years of conflict in which large areas of countryside were depopulated, however, the revolution had lost much of its support base. After the cease-fire some of the displaced refugees returned to areas controlled by the revolutionary forces, but it was a far cry from the vast population base that had supported them in the early years of the war. A hard core of sympathizers continued to provide vital sustenance to cadres, troops, and guerrillas, but this core social base of the revolution had shrunk to a definite minority status, which had a significant impact on Hanoi's ability to incorporate postwar South Vietnam into a socialist framework.

Still, the revolution was able to extend its influence beyond its area of direct control, as evidenced by the increasing effectiveness of its taxation, and a rebound in its ability to attract new recruits. Whether a prolonged low-level political-guerrilla strategy would have gradually tipped the balance against the Saigon government after the January 1973 cease-fire cannot be known, because the big-unit fighting eventually resumed, and this overshadowed the changes taking place in the hamlets during the post-cease-fire period. Although the "Viet Cong" had been critically weakened, the Saigon government was unable to consolidate its position in Dinh Tuong, despite the advantage of its proximity to Saigon, and the presence of one of the GVN's best units, the Seventh Division of the Army of the Republic of Vietnam (ARVN). This is a reminder that political as well as military strength in a civil conflict is relative, not absolute.

Complexity of Understanding the Final Phases of the Conflict

Since the end of the war in 1975, the sharp contrasts between North and South, and the inability of Hanoi to successfully implant socialist institutions in the South, the "reeducation" camps and refugees, and the general postwar hostility of Southerners to Hanoi's rule have led many to the natural conclusion that the Vietnam war, in the end, was in fact a simple military conquest by the North. The last few years of the war were more complicated than this, however. There was substantial support for the North Vietnamese military presence among revolutionary supporters in the South, and the question therefore is how numerous these supporters were in places such as My Tho. Furthermore, the Northern military forces revived the revolutionary movement in the South from its low ebb of 1971, so another key question is why, how, and how far the movement was revived and with what implications for understanding the dynamics of the revolution in the final phase of conflict. In addition, the revolutionary strategy from the beginning was based on the assumption that victory would come from the interactive strength of all its parts: North and South, city and countryside, military and political. Dinh Tuong did play its role in the final collapse of the Saigon government, though the final takeover of the province was a result of the fall of Saigon rather than a cause.

We must be cautious, therefore, about understanding the Vietnam war through the images of its concluding act. At the same time, what happened *after* April 30, 1975, is an extremely important indicator of the social and political changes that had taken place throughout the war. If the U.S.–Saigon players were so mesmerized by short-term issues that they missed the more fundamental long term changes unfolding before their eyes, this was also true of the revolutionary side. From the high tide of anti-French patriotism in the Resistance, to the revolutionary fervor of the late Diem period, and its revival during the Tet Offensive, the base of support for the revolution contracted until the firmly committed supporters were certainly a minority even of the rural population by the end of the war.

It seems that the patriotic fervor of the revolutionaries overrode their training in Marxist class analysis, and they were unable to see the larger implications of the fact that the class structure of South Vietnamese rural society had undergone a sweeping transformation since 1945. Landlordism on the grand scale of the French period had completely disappeared, even by the early 1960s. Devastating rural conflict drove many off their land, and mass military mobilization by both sides stripped the countryside of able-bodied farmers. More land was abandoned than could be reclaimed and farmed. Although too little and too late, the GVN land reform did have some impact on the once powerful appeal of the revolutionaries to landless peasants. Many rural residents had fled to the cities and became cut off from their ties to the land. Of course, incipient agricultural mechanization also promised to change substantially the demand for rural labor, indicating a possible return to landlessness and rural unemployment, but this had not yet become a factor when the war ended.

Most important, what had once been vivid and wonderful imagined visions of the rewards of revolution conjured up by persuasive propaganda now began to be toned down by the realities of the way the revolution had thus far progressed in both North and South. The peasants had seen how uncertain the benefits of revolutionary land grants were. Even if the land was not reclaimed by returning owners under the protection of the Saigon government, as had happened several times during the thirty-year conflict, taxation by the revolution could be as oppressive as the rents to landlords. Finally, one unanticipated consequence of the arrival of North Vietnamese troops into the Mekong Delta was that through contacts and conversations with them the Southern peasants began to get an intimation of life under socialism, and most did not like what they heard—especially the prospect that their land would be collectivized.

Unfortunately for the Saigon government, the declining enthusiasm for the revolution did not lead to a corresponding increase of support for the GVN. At the national level this was due to a failure to consolidate a potentially strong political base of the growing numbers of people who had lost their enthusiasm for the revolution, were personally or politically opposed to it, or feared a communist victory in the South. At the local level in places like My Tho, the problem lay in the behavior of many of its officials and troops, which alienated the people who were turning away from the revolution on the grounds of self-interest, political persecution, or plain apathy. These significant groups could not be mobilized by Saigon for a last-ditch stand against the revolutionary forces, but they did, along with the traditional opponents of revolution, become the base of a social stratum that defied Hanoi's attempts to extend socialist institutions and practices to the South after 1975. However, in the 1972–75 period, although the *breadth* of support for the revolutionary movement was diminished, the *level* of support among the remaining followers of the revolution increased substantially from 1970–71.

Even before the Easter Offensive, the "new optimism" of 1969 had given way to anxious concerns prompted by the withdrawal of U.S. ground forces, despite the nearly complete pacification of the delta in 1971. "Vietnamization" was now going to face its ultimate test, and many were doubtful that it would succeed. The departing bureau chief of the *Washington Post* wrote a sober assessment of his tour in an article titled "Vietnam: The Optimism Has Faded," and noted that "with the possible exception of [GVN President] Thieu and a few others who in their public utterances still talk of victory, it is hard to find a South Vietnamese who expects that the war will be won. It may not be lost, or at least not for quite some time, and meanwhile life for many of those in the cities and countryside who are not actually engaged in combat has improved significantly. . . . But the central fact about the war in Indochina is that it is still going on. [GVN] Vietnamese casualties are still high—28,000 dead last year [1971], more than any year since 1968—and the only hope of a settlement appears to lie in the hands of the Americans and the Chinese. Mr. Nixon's impending trip to China is discussed here with a touching mixture of wistfulness and war-weary cynicism."[5]

Strategic Context of 1972

Revolutionary strategy had always placed the Mekong Delta in a larger context, linking the guerrilla action there to main force military combat in the mountain–forest zones (such as War Zones C and D northwest of Saigon and the Central Highlands) and political action in the urban areas. Now the global and regional strategic context had become a vital aspect of revolutionary planning as well, affecting both the timing and the priorities of military actions in the delta. Hanoi's thinking is reflected in a June 1971 resolution of the Central Military Commission, which was to evolve into the offensive of 1972. The overall objective was to "concentrate all efforts on military and political attacks in the three zones of South Vietnam, the main battlefield, and throughout the Indochina battlefield." The main focus in South Vietnam would be, "Coordinating strong blows from main force units in the mountain–forest zone with attacks and uprisings in the deltas and political struggle along with strong armed struggle in the urban areas, attacking the three pillars of the 'Vietnamization' policy, and creating a new situation advantageous to us in the event of a cease-fire, creating conditions to push the revolutionary movement steadfastly forward in the new situation."[6] The objectives were both military and political. Defeating Vietnamization would help bring about a negotiated settlement and cease-fire as well as create a better military position for the revolutionary forces in that situation.

A conjunction of factors led to Hanoi's abandonment of the "economy of forces" approach of 1971, in which they scaled back military activities while waiting for the American withdrawal to diminish the U.S. military threat to the revolutionary position. It seems likely that by the time of Resolution Nine in mid-1969, and certainly by 1970, the planners in Hanoi did not want to do anything that would slow down or even reverse this withdrawal. They had also concluded that until a new strategic opportunity presented itself it would be futile to wear down their own forces in inconclusive engagements. Directive 01 of January/February 1971 emphasized the importance of "holding on" and opposing pacification. It was transmitted to My Tho in July 1971 (leaving open the question of whether the directive had been modified in the interim). The province stressed "clinging to the people and the hamlets" and "preparing for phase two of countering the [GVN] pacification plan."[7] The Easter Offensive reflected the Party view that this approach had served its purpose and that, with the U.S. ground forces nearly gone and the offensives of the anticommunist forces in Laos and Cambodia blunted, a changed situation provided new strategic opportunities to be exploited.

Encouraged by the setbacks to the anticommunist military forces of Phnom Penh and Laos in 1971 and early 1972, Hanoi turned its attention to South Vietnam. In February 1972, the Central Military Commission, a committee of the Party's top political and military leaders, declared that "The task of the first order is to concentrate leadership of the war and reinforce our strength on the battlefield in all respects, mainly in the South Vietnam battlefield."[8] The subsidiary missions laid out in this February decision were the following: (1) Destroy a large portion of Saigon's armed forces, shatter their defensive dispositions one by one, and enlarge the liberated areas. Although the GVN forces had now become the main combat objective, U.S. forces should also be attacked and attrited. (2) Push the attack and uprisings in the important rural delta areas, and step up the guerrilla warfare movement. (3) Push the urban political struggle movement and sharpen the enemy's internal contradictions. The directive called for the Southern revolutionaries to "basically defeat" Saigon's pacification program, as well as to "liberate the greater part of the rural delta areas."[9]

A Close Call: The Military Region Commander Is Nearly Captured

Even before the final plan for the offensive had been formulated, preparations for a major military push were underway in Dinh Tuong. At the end of 1971 top commanders from Military Region 2 came to the province to take direct charge of military operations and "prepare for a new phase of activities." Tam Phuong, military commander of Region 2, led this group. He was accompanied by Sau Phu, commander of the 261st Battalion in the early 1960s and now the deputy chief of staff for the military region. The destination of this group was the 20/7 zone in the heartland of My Tho. When they reached the critical juncture of this journey, the dangerous crossing of Highway 4 at Hoi Cu village, the group awoke to find that they had been surrounded by GVN troops. They quickly realized that they had been betrayed from within their own ranks.[10]

Muoi Tan was a native of Hau Thanh village in Cai Be, on the fringe of the Plain of Reeds. He came from a revolutionary family. His brother rose to become the head of the My Tho province committee office before being killed in 1970, and his wife's brother became a member of the Cai Be district Party committee in 1956. Muoi Tan had been a member of the province armed propaganda team in 1959, and had risen through the ranks because of his boldness and leadership ability, eventually becoming the deputy commander and chief of staff of the province unit. However, the long conflict took a heavy psychological toll on him. By 1970, the year of his brother's death, Tan realized that although many of the original eleven members of the province armed propaganda unit had risen to battalion commands or positions of province-level leadership, he was the only one who had survived intact. The others had all been killed, crippled, or had lost their health. The war dragged on and the revolution seemed stymied in My Tho. Seeking some solace in an otherwise bleak situation, Tan started a liaison with a younger woman, and was severely criticized by his superiors. Finally he contacted the GVN province authorities and laid out a plan to capture Tam Phuong's group as they traveled to the 20/7 zone. The plan almost succeeded. Although completely surrounded, Tam Phuong kept his wits about him and avoided the trap set for him by his quick response to the situation. Although the GVN forces came within a stone's throw of Tam Phuong, they missed their target. A providential downpour and the expert guidance of a local guerrilla allowed Tam Phuong to slip through the encirclement.

Muoi Tan's action was a replay of a similar episode during the anti-French Resistance when, during the period of French pacification success in My Tho in the early 1950s, the deputy commander of the province unit cooperated with French intelligence while still with the unit and then defected. A similar incident had occurred in 1957 when the leader of the small province guerrilla unit which later became the 514th battalion surrendered to the GVN and revealed all the unit's hideouts in the province, and again in 1962 when a defecting deputy commander of the 514th battalion led GVN forces to inflict heavy casualties on the revolution's Region military training center in Kien Tuong province. Tan's actions were also devastating to the province military forces, because he knew their operational patterns and hiding places intimately. Because the region forces were also stationed in his area of responsibility, they were also threatened. In fact, Muoi Tan had requested that a leading cadre in a North Vietnamese unit turn over to him a map indicating its operational routes and hiding places. After the war, this officer remarked, "I have a quirk—I'm not sure whether it is good or bad—which is that I am not very trusting. In this case it stood me in good stead." The North Vietnamese officer replied that he only answered to his own region command channels, and would comply only if ordered to by them. Muoi Tan dropped the issue.[11] After the war, Muoi Tan was arrested and executed.

Following this narrow escape, Tam Phuong began to lay the groundwork for a military comeback in the province. Some of the Tet Offensive thinking began to resurface as the top Party leaders began to devise a plan to reverse the setbacks of the previous years. Tam Phuong wrote, "The Mekong Delta and the delta in Region 5 [central Vietnam] were the main targets of the attack on pacification and a big expansion [of territory]. The main target in the Mekong Delta was Military Region 8 [Region 2]. In attacking pacification we would use the approach of a 'comprehensive attack' campaign *[tien cong tong hop]*. This attack and uprising would be the largest strategic offensive since the Tet Offensive. In this offensive we would coordinate three spearheads of attack: a blow from the main forces, attacks on pacification, and the urban movement."[12] The difference between this and the Tet Offensive, of course, was that the main forces would not be attacking the cities, which would be left to the political forces of the "urban movement." The primary task was to use the main forces to disperse the ARVN and begin the process of fighting back against "pacification."

Underlining the importance of My Tho, Sau Duong, the Region 2 Party leader, also came down to My Tho, which had been designated the top-priority province in Region 2. The region approved Tam Phuong's plan to designate the 20/7 zone as the priority area in which to win back control of territory and population.[13] As the highest priority zone in the top priority province in the Mekong Delta, the 20/7 was to be the ground zero of the 1972 revolutionary effort south of Saigon.

Preparing for the Easter Offensive

The forward command post of Region 2, with Sau Duong and Tam Phuong, moved around in the heart of the 20/7 zone and, along with the My Tho province Party committee, which was also located there, began to lay the groundwork for an offensive. Sau Duong observes that the "bases" of the cadres and military units were not like those of the anti-French Resistance period, but simply referred to any place that offered "a place to stay while carrying out a mission during a defined period of time. For this reason, [even] if that place was near an enemy post, it could still serve the purpose . . . if it could serve as a base to live in." From the end of 1971, the command headquarters of Region 2 (still referred to by Sau Duong as Region 8, as during the Resistance period) was transferred in phases from the Cambodian border to the 20/7 zone just south of Highway 4. It would be a mistake, writes Sau Duong, to compare the "bases" in the 20/7 with the large expanses of territory in the Plain of Reeds that served as base areas in the Resistance. These 20/7 "bases" were often located in an area of about a square kilometer bounded by GVN posts on all sides. In such a cramped and fluid situation, Sau Duong recalled that "many times when hearing the brother cadres report that our Region had liberated hundreds of villages and was administering tens of thousands of people, I just laughed."[14]

Following the attempted capture of Tam Phuong, Sau Duong and his Region command group arrived at the base of the My Tho province committee in Long Tien village in the 20/7 zone at the beginning of October 1971. By this time, Chin Hai had replaced the ailing Chin Om as the My Tho province Party Secretary. Unlike the austere areas where the Region headquarters had stayed along the Cambodian border, the 20/7 zone was "a rich area with many people, with abundant orchards, fresh water, a lot of rice, and tasty fish and shrimp. It was also right next to the lifeline of the enemy, Highway 4, and an international waterway—the upper branch of the Mekong River. It would be very painful for the enemy to lose this area." When Sau Duong arrived in late 1971, "every hamlet" in the 20/7 zone was covered with posts. Everywhere you looked there was the [GVN] yellow three striped flag flapping from high observation towers—you could even see the soldiers standing guard on them."

When Sau Duong later described this situation at an expanded meeting of the Politburo in Hanoi in 1973, his listeners were stunned and skeptical. How was it possible to operate under such circumstances? This perception gap between the northern and southern leaders of the revolution may have contributed to the disagreements over strategy following the cease fire, described later in this chapter. When he arrived at the My Tho province committee base in the 20/7, Chin Hai explained that it was located in a one square kilometer area in Long Tien village surrounded by seven or eight posts "so that the outer defensive perimeter of the province committee was itself the defensive perimeter of the [GVN] posts, and the province committee was less than 500 meters from them." The province committee survived much as the village cadres described in the previous chapter, with a protective tangle of obstacles and grenades making movement into their area very costly and slow.

The My Tho province committee did not rely only on physical defensive measures. Chin Hai laughingly told Sau Duong that "over half the posts in the zone had secret contact with us, and the remainder, except for a few cruel tyrants, were passive and watched over the bricks [of their post] while drawing a salary *[giu gach an tien]*. To say nothing of the fact that enemy soldiers agreed to supply us with information, and protect us within the fences of the posts when the enemy mounted big military sweeps or B-52s rained bombs on the base." These local accommodations did not extend to higher levels, however. During the two months Sau Duong and Tam Phuong were in the 20/7 zone in the late 1971, the GVN received reports that two "Viet Cong generals" were in the area. A flurry of operations was launched, guided by Muoi Tan's intimate knowledge of the province committee's bases. Sau Duong describes a cat-and-mouse game of staying one step ahead of the attacking forces while circulating through the villages surrounding Long Tien. This routine began to wear on Sau Duong. "I had the impression that the enemy was constantly following at the heels of our group."

This constant pursuit also affected the province committee, who often had to worry about protecting themselves instead of carrying out their broader responsibilities. Sometimes Chin Hai himself would serve as a guard and lookout for the Region command as it moved around. On one occasion, the members of the Region protection unit were so exhausted that Chin Hai had to pick up an AK and stand guard along the Ba Dua road to Cai Lay district town while the Region group crossed to the other side. Sau Binh, the deputy province Secretary of My Tho had to serve as a liaison guide to take Sau Duong's group to Thanh Hoa village, near Cai Lay. Returning to the Long Tien base, the Region group was attacked by GVN province forces of Dinh Tuong, which were not strong enough to accomplish their mission. When the GVN forces pulled out, Sau Duong found a note inside the house he had been staying; "With fond greetings to brother Quyet! This is Nai. I came here but didn't meet you. Best wishes and good health." Nai had been a member of the Region protection unit when it was stationed along the Cambodian border. He had since defected to the GVN after being sent to a combat unit and denied permission to marry a women who was regarded by the revolution as a "swan" (*thien nga,* traditionally a beautiful woman of dubious character, but in this context it could also mean a female Mata Hari recruited by the GVN from the urban areas to use her charms to gain intelligence on the revolutionary side) and was now accompanying the attacking GVN forces. Knowing that Quyet and Nai had served together in his protection unit, Sau Duong wondered if this was not a subtle message of warning from Nai that the GVN now knew exactly where the Region command was. "I still think constantly about this," writes Sau Duong. "The episode with Nai's letter left behind is a serious lesson about looking at and evaluating a person. Even in the case that they have joined the enemy." Unlike the confrontations with the faceless Americans, the conflict had once again truly become a civil war.

With their 20/7 zone location revealed, the Region command moved north of Highway 4 to Hung Thanh along the Nguyen Van Tiep canal and finally settled in a base 500 meters from the Stone Buddha Pagoda, fomerly a revolution base but now a GVN post. Tam Phuong, the Region military commander and the My Tho province committee stayed behind in the 20/7 zone, but both were now relieved of the responsibility of the protecting the Region headquarters, and the attention that its presence in the exposed 20/7 zone had drawn from the GVN. While in Hung Thanh, Sau Duong was called to COSVN, still based along the Cambodian border. COSVN military commander General Hoang Van Thai gave Sau Duong the Easter Offensive plan to read. Sau Duong's reaction was that the plan would stretch revolutionary forces too thin. "I felt that the campaign was somewhat heavily weighted toward military attacks to liberate provinces, districts, and villages in Region 8. The campaign would be spread over four provinces north of the upper branch of the Mekong River and there was even the intention to expand the campaign to Ben Tre. The COSVN main forces had assembled two divisions for the campaign along with three regiments of Region 8, the province battalions and district local forces and village guerrillas. In all, the forces added up to an army group *[quan doan].* As for supplies, ammunition, and explosives, the list looked quite sufficient. I knew that by this time the 559 [Ho Chi Minh trail] and the 759 [sea supply routes] had been linked up for a long time, with enough capacity to provide supplies for big battles for big battles in the South."

It was Sau Duong who represented the Region in putting his signature on the Easter Offensive attack plan, but he did so with misgivings. In addition to the problem of trying to do too much with too few forces, he was concerned that the COSVN forces (mostly North Vietnamese units) did not know the guerrilla war environment of the Mekong Delta well enough, and worried that not enough attention was being given to the political aspects of the campaign. In retrospect, Sau Duong felt that "The opportune moment for the campaign was lost because Region 8 opened fire in April 1972 in accordance with the coordinated plan agreed on by COSVN and Region 8. But it was only in June 1972 that COSVN sent its main force troops down [to the upper delta], so the enemy was ready to counter this."[15] Two of the regiments the Region had at its disposal in early 1972 were Regiment I (E1) and North Vietnamese Regiment 88, along with six specialized battalions (demolition, artillery, etc.).[16] One additional battalion and five companies were earmarked for Dinh Tuong as reinforcements, but only one-third of these additional forces had arrived in the province by the end of March 1972.[17] The improved situation of for the revolutionary forces in Cambodia allowed the dispatch of elements of some units stationed there to the Mekong Delta. A native Southerner who belonged to the Dong Nai regiment, formerly from Military Region 1 (eastern Nam Bo), said that one of three platoons in his company was sent to My Tho because the "liberated area [in Cambodia] had expanded and they didn't need as many soldiers" [DT409]. Two regiments of the North Vietnamese Army (NVA) Fifth Division also moved from Cambodia to the Plain of Reeds and eventually to Dinh Tuong.

The 1972 Easter Offensive

On March 11, 1972, the Politburo and the Central Military Commission met jointly in Hanoi to lay out specific objectives for what became known as the Easter Offensive. The main thrust was directed at the area just below the Demilitarized Zone (DMZ), and the aim was to expand a large liberated area, change the balance of military forces, and the complexion of the entire war. Although the primary focus of the offensive was in the northern provinces of South Vietnam, the overall plan called for the Mekong Delta to undermine pacification so that the delta could play its role in the "three-zone" strategic division of labor. Liberated areas should be enlarged "wherever and whenever possible," a language which suggests that this was a secondary objective, and a difficult task given the weakness of local guerrilla forces in the delta. Revolutionary forces in the delta were directed to tie down Saigon military forces to prevent them from reinforcing other areas. The directive stated that the paramount objective was to eliminate as much of the ARVN main forces as possible and to inflict demoralizing losses on them, in order to "quickly change the balance of forces so we can advance to final victory." On March 23, 1972, the Politburo gave its final approval to the plan, and the attacks unfolded on March 30 with massive assaults on ARVN positions along the DMZ.[18]

COSVN ordered the military region command back to the Plain of Reeds above Hau My, to Kien Tuong's Zone 4, "in order to create a springboard [to the populated areas of My Tho] and prepare for COSVN to send forces down to launch a coordinated campaign on a large scale."[19] Tam Phuong hastily moved from the 20/7 zone to the Plain of Reeds. As before the Tet Offensive, last-minute orders from above required frantic last-minute preparations. "Time was of the essence," recalled Tam Phuong, "and we had to 'scramble' [vat chan len co ma chay] to organize cadres to prepare the battlefield, transport weapons and ammunition, and lay out a combat plan."[20]

The first attacks in this area started on April 7, and were aimed at creating a stronger foothold in Dinh Tuong and expanding a secure base area in the Plain of Reeds and Dinh Tuong north of Highway 4 to protect the supply lines running south through that province to Ben Tre, and to serve as a staging area to push east into Cho Gao and Go Cong.[21] This initial attack was led by the North Vietnamese 88th Regiment, which pushed down to the Nguyen Van Tiep Canal and retook important areas of the Plain of Reeds bordering Dinh Tuong.

There is some evidence that the higher levels of the revolutionary movement once again held out to their subordinates the prospect that the war could be ended quickly by a maximum effort. A cadre from Military Region 2 said that the region "prepared morale for the

Concerted Uprising in accordance with the resolve of COSVN to gain final victory" [DT404]. Tam Phuong, the region military commander, concluded that "with regard to leadership and command, I feel that there was a large shortcoming, which includes both our estimate of the enemy—we were still subjective and simplistic and not scientific and objective. We laid down a resolve [quyet tam] and set out objectives that were too high in view of our actual capabilities, so the effectiveness of the campaign was reduced."[22]

At the time, however, there was a feeling of expansive confidence at the top leadership levels. To underline the importance of this campaign, General Hoang Van Thai, COSVN's deputy Party secretary and Hanoi's leading military commander in the area, took direct charge. The key objective was to "use a portion of COSVN's main forces to utilize surprise and punch through the [Vietnam–Cambodian] border defense line and shatter the line of defense blocking the heart of the Plain of Reeds, in order to create a transportation corridor from rear to front, and quickly penetrate down to Highway 4 and, along with the forces of Military Region 2 [which included three North Vietnamese regiments, including E1, E88, and E320], cut the Highway and finish off [dut diem] the districts and subsectors as a means of motivating the masses to rise up as one, and liberate the majority of the people during June and July. After that we will expand the zone to Go Cong and Ben Tre."[23]

Sau Duong, the Region 2 Party Secretary, felt that the results of the Easter Offensive were significant, but short of the objectives set out in the offensive plan. The offensive had inflicted heavy casualties on the GVN forces "flattened 436 posts, annihilated Vinh Kim sub-sector, heavily damaged Long Khot, Thien Ho, and Ba Dua sub-sectors, the command base of the Seventh Division and command base of the 16th Regiment. [It] liberated 79 villages, 1,044, hamlets, and won back 900,000."[24] Perhaps Sau Duong was smiling to himself as he wrote these lines in his memoir, just as he had earlier laughed at such claims made by subordinate cadres in his presence during the conflict. On the next page of his memoirs he indirectly criticizes that Easter Offensive plan for being over ambitious by noting that the results were far less than called for in the plan. The initial objectives of the Easter Offensive, as far as Region 2 was concerned, were to launch "a general coordinated offensive to destroy the new pacification of the enemy." COSVN's orders were to "annihilate each enemy battalion and regiment, bring the Seventh Division to its knees, along with the commando brigades [ARVN Ranger, Paratroop, and Marine units], ... Liberate a number of district towns and sectors and, circumstances permitting, liberate a province town. Finish off the posts and forces repressing the people, and liberate the greater part of My Tho and Kien Tuong provinces, and part of Kien Phong, Go Cong, and Ben Tre provinces. Cut off Highway 4 and the Cho Gao canal, surround the cities and cut off Saigon from the lower Mekong Delta." Sau Duong concludes that "Thus the campaign fell short of achieving its objectives. The COSVN leadership did not see the full extent of difficulties of Region 8 in coping with the enemy. Even though the U.S. Ninth Division had withdrawn from My Tho, the enemy pacification and encroachment plan in the strategy of Vietnamization of the conflict had been effectively implemented. The forces and strategic posture of Region 8 had just been rebuilt so that sending COSVN main force units down to crush the enemy could not be easy."[25] Despite his reservations about the Easter Offensive, Sau Duong concluded that it was a strategic success in preparing the ground for the Paris Agreements and the final withdrawal of U.S. military forces.[26]

Impact of the Easter Offensive in the Mekong Delta

The Easter Offensive did succeed in three important respects. First, the Easter Offensive attacks in Dinh Tuong and the Plain of Reeds helped regain access to the base areas vital to the concentrated big units. Second, it did shatter the GVN defense line, which had sealed off the upper delta from the revolution's base areas in Cambodia. Finally, it revived the guerrilla warfare movement in the delta to the point where GVN units withdrawn to reinforce ARVN units in other regions had to return to the delta. An initial assessment by the U.S. Central Intelligence Agency at the end of April 1972 concluded that "In a short time, the Mekong Delta has changed from the most secure and prosperous part of the country to a source of considerable apprehension to South Vietnamese commanders. The main threat to pacification in the delta is not resurgent Viet Cong forces, although they have sharply stepped up harassing attacks, but rather North Vietnamese main-force reinforcements which have recently moved into the delta region in strength. The balance of opposing forces in the delta has shifted significantly in recent weeks as a result of the infiltration of two North Vietnamese regiments into the upper delta, the movement of two more North Vietnamese regiments in Cambodia to positions just west of Chau Doc province, and the departure of the South Vietnamese 21st Division to fight north of Saigon. Formerly there were only six main-force enemy regiments fighting in the delta. Now there are ten which pose an immediate threat to the region."[27]

As in the early years of the conflict, the revolutionary forces were still far weaker than Saigon's military assets in Dinh Tuong, but they were once again finding room to operate and securing base areas and supply routes throughout the province. This was not, however, a replay of the revolutionary expansion of the early period. The major difference was that the population had been redistributed into areas more easily controlled by Saigon, which the ill-fated Strategic Hamlet program had failed to do, and most were now numbed by the unrelenting and seemingly unending conflict. There were few eager volunteers to fill the ranks and move from guerrilla to main force operations. It was the North Vietnamese troops who filled this void.

The promised reinforcements from Military Region finally began arriving at the beginning of May, including Battalion 2009B and five infantry companies from the military region. The province history notes that "this was the first time My Tho had received troops from the rear area of the North (Nam Ha was the sister province) as reinforcements for the province and district forces."[28]

COSVN saw an opportunity to draw ARVN forces away from the Mekong Delta. The second phase (July 1972) had the objective of "sucking the enemy up to the [Cambodian] border line, and speedily sending the COSVN main forces down to the battlefield to attack in coordination with the local forces to open up [intervillage] *mang,* and the areas south and north of Highway 4 to create a firm foothold to develop the offensive posture."[29] Although it had been pulled out of the delta, the ARVN Seventh Division was forced to return to Dinh Tuong to defend against a series of attacks lasting from May to September 1972. The top U.S. military advisor in the Mekong Delta, Major General Thomas Tarpley, reported, "The battle for Dinh Tuong province began with enemy attacks on district towns, attempting to take advantage of the movement of the 7th ARVN Division to the Cambodian border. The enemy, consisting primarily of the Dong Thap I and Z15 Regiments, launched a series of attacks against Sam Giang [Vinh Kim], Cai Be, and Cai Lay district towns during the period 17 May–11 July. All of these attacks failed, with heavy enemy losses. The enemy suffered over 800 killed during these battles, forcing him to withdraw to sanctuaries to refit. Friendly losses in the actions were relatively light." General Tarpley noted, "The continued enemy threat in Dinh Tuong, however, necessitated the bolstering of friendly forces in that province." Moreover, the optimistic tone was a bit premature. Vinh Kim was about to receive one of the most devastating blows of the war.

GVN Pacification Undermined by the Easter Offensive

The purpose of these military operations in the Mekong Delta was to undermine pacification and revive the guerrilla warfare movement. The Easter Offensive in central Vietnam and northwest of Saigon served to distract the GVN from this vital area. In the Mekong Delta, the strongest blow was not struck until the main part of the Easter Offensive in Central Vietnam and northwest of Saigon was well underway. Another consequence of the resumption of large-scale fighting was a diversion of Saigon's military resources from the pacification program. As Saigon's forces were refocused on the main force battles, and as the North Vietnamese units expanded their area of operation, the province security situation deteriorated. Dinh Tuong's HES scores, measured largely by the number of people in "secure" hamlets, had dropped 23.3 percent by August.[30] Another State Department analysis of the overall situation in the Mekong Delta reported, "a decline in government population control every month since the first of the year. 742,000 rural people have shifted out of the reportedly secure category. . . . The lower delta provinces of Chuong Thien and An Xuyen and the upper delta province of Dinh Tuong report the most substantial reverses."[31]

The second phase of the province offensive in July 1972 was aimed at eliminating the Vinh Kim subsector command, and a series of attacks was launched on July 2. The Party later claimed that fourteen posts had been eliminated and the villages of Ban Long, Huu Dao, and Binh Trung were liberated, and Kim Son village "basically liberated."[32]

Although the revolutionary Region 2 military commander's retrospective judgment of the Easter Offensive in My Tho and Region 2 was critical,[33] his adversaries at the time had a different assessment. By August 1972, the U.S. advisors in My Tho were alarmed. "Acknowledging that Communist troops strength in Dinh Tuong province has now reached its highest level since the 1968 Tet Offensive, Lt. Col. John Ramsey, deputy senior advisor of the province said simply, 'We've got North Vietnamese soldiers up to our ears.'"[34] U.S. advisors estimated that "in Dinh Tuong alone there are 5,000 well-equipped North Vietnamese and Vietcong troops," and that "the size of this force has grown in recent weeks as more enemy soldiers have slipped in from sanctuaries in Cambodia."[35] Jacques Leslie of the *Los Angeles Times* was told by U.S. advisors that "Communist soldiers control the northern half of one of Dinh Tuong's seven districts, Sam Giang [Vinh Kim], and hold large pockets in other districts. And they have brought anti-aircraft artillery and SA-7 Strella heat-seeking missiles, forcing South Vietnamese to declare some areas 'off limits' to helicopters. Said Capt. David Dressler, top advisor in Cai Lay district: 'This is the first time I've known of any area in this province to be declared off limits to choppers. And it's the first time the North Vietnamese have moved Strellas this far south.'"[36]

At the same time, elements of the NVA Fifth and Seventh Divisions, which had previously fought in An Loc north of Saigon and then moved into Cambodia, were now moving into Dinh Tuong. "Several times North Vietnamese forces have laid siege to district towns [in Dinh Tuong], then suddenly faded away. A four day battle at Vinh Kim, capital of the Sam Giang district, caused 250 North Vietnamese and Vietcong deaths against 95 South Vietnamese killed and more than 200 wounded. Most important, however, was the impact on Vinh Kim's residents. Though it ended a few weeks ago, about half the villagers still spend the night in My Tho, Dinh Tuong's capital, and stay in Vinh Kim only during the day. 'they do not feel secure at this time,' said Maj. Thomas J. Davis, top advisor in Sam Giang. 'This was probably one of the major goals of the attack.' Davis said that after the battle, the Vietcong frightened the people by setting up loudspeakers on the bank of the Mekong River near Vinh Kim and announcing they would return. This sort of tactic has not been used here since before the 1968 Tet Offensive."[37] The *New York Times* reported that hundreds of homes had been destroyed in this assault and that every building had been damaged before the attacking troops were driven off. Three thousand residents fled during the fighting.[38]

Showing a bravado that had been missing from revolutionary operations for several years, the revolutionaries even warned the villagers in advance of the attack. A *Newsweek* dispatch from its Saigon bureau in August said, "The attack last month on Vinh Kim provides an excellent example of the VC delta tactics. The American advisors in Vinh Kim didn't know it, but the villagers knew the attack was coming as early as June. 'One month before the attack the other men ["those gentlemen"] (the VC) told us they would attack the district,' says . . . the head of the local electrical cooperative. 'They said they were bringing in more soldiers and for us to leave when the attack began. They said they didn't want the people to get hurt.' [He] and other villagers said that in the months before the attack, Vietcong cadre would come into the village in broad daylight to talk to the people less than a hundred yards from the US advisory compound and the government's district headquarters. Not even the forewarned villagers, however, expected the size of attack which came. Five hundred communist soldiers approached Vinh Kim from five different directions." The attackers overran half of the U.S. advisors' compound and left an adjacent post a charred ruins. Two relieving Regional Force companies were ambushed in classic style as they rushed to relieve the beleaguered district. "The size and ferocity of the attack amazes Maj. Davis. 'They're standing and fighting. We call in B-52s and they're still there. Those people are not backing down. This is really a different ball game from what we're used to in these parts.' " This new wave of military action caused the GVN to withdraw from 12 posts while "consolidating" others, which "left the entire northern half of the [Sam Giang] district, including populated areas, under Vietcong control." Remarkably, only six civilians were killed in the attack. Although they had been forewarned, when they tried to leave, "the GVN district chief would not open the barbed wire gate across the road leading out of town."[39] Another report stated that in Sam Giang district, "The government has been forced to abandon 30 outposts out of nearly 60."[40] Ba Dua, a strong point south of Cai Lay, was also hit by revolutionary forces. The Cai Lay U.S. advisor reported that "they're using the same old tactics . . . and they're just as good as they were in the early 1960s." He added that "from what I understand, they've collected two million piasters in taxes already this year. We're on four major infiltration corridors here you know and we've had to pull out of the areas near the Plain of Reeds. Here in Dinh Tuong province we're right in the middle of their plans."[41]

ARVN Seventh Division troops along with Ranger units fought a series of battles in Dinh Tuong and the Plain of Reeds during the summer of 1972, including a major engagement to relieve the beleaguered base in Hau My, which was the main GVN control point between Dinh Tuong and the Plain of Reeds. While the Saigon forces held their own, they did so largely with the aid of over 100 B-52 air strikes. B-52s had broken the back of the North Vietnamese offensive in central Vietnam, and were assuming an unprecedented role in the Mekong Delta. Between July 8 and early August 1972, fifty B-52 strikes hit Dinh Tuong province. A U.S. advisor in Cai Lay district dryly observed, "I didn't think that we could ever have B-52s in here because the population is spread out . . . but a lot of the people have been moving away from the immediate areas of bombing."[42] The question remained, however, how the Saigon forces would do if they had to operate without this powerful support. The U.S. State Department analysis concluded that the "shift of ARVN main forces left the burden of defending pacification to the territorial forces. Their performance in rising to this task has been mixed. In many cases, they share the ARVN's reluctance to risk casualties in offensive operations and its predilection to rely on air strikes to dislodge enemy forces."[43]

The Party Attempts to Rebuild its Forces in My Tho

Although the main battles in the late spring and summer of 1972 were fought by North Vietnamese troops, there was also a resurgence of local guerrilla activity. Prior to the Easter Offensive, the village guerrilla and local forces were understrength and ineffective. District local force units in Cai Be and Chau Thanh had been reduced to less that a platoon in strength. Cai Be had attempted to increase its forces starting in mid-1971, and managed to assemble a platoon "comprised mainly of guerrillas taken up from the villages and about six or seven youth grabbed from secure areas" [DT413]. Despite that fact that this raised the numbers of the Cai Be unit from twenty-seven to forty-seven by April 1972, the fighting spirit of the new and reluctant recruits left something to be desired. The expansion was the direct result of a reinforced North Vietnamese military presence starting from the beginning of 1972, which provided more security for cadres and guerrillas in northern Cai Be, and favorably impressed the civilian sympathizers of the revolution. "From January to May 1972," said one interviewee, "the Cai Be local forces were able to expand to forty-seven and the cadres were able to expand their activities in the villages and hamlets, since it was easier thanks to the sympathy of the people toward the North Vietnamese *bo doi* [troops]. The level of tax collection and the contributions of rice, fish sauce, salt, etc., also rose considerably over the 1971 level. In general, the people's morale rose very high thanks to the presence of the North Vietnamese troops" [DT413].

While the fighting subsided in the late summer of 1972, the revolution stepped up its recruiting and preparations for a negotiated settlement. This time the results, even as presented in the official Party history, were marginal exploitations of gains made in the earlier phases of the offensive. Summing up the entire period of the Easter Offensive, the Party history asserts that in Dinh Tuong nineteen villages and 126 hamlets were liberated with a total of 164,000 people, and that 30,000 of these had returned to their former residences from Saigon-controlled areas. The offensive had put revolutionary forces in a position to threaten the roads and canals, and had gained a toehold in weak areas such as southern Cai

Lay, Go Cong, and Cho Gao. During this period 670 Party members were recruited along with 2,650 members of the Farmers' Association and 2,400 members of the Women's Association.[44]

By the beginning of 1973, the total number of Party members in the Dinh Tuong and Go Cong provinces (mainly in Dinh Tuong) combined were 7,000 party members and 30,000 people "in various revolutionary organizations."[45] (It is not clear how much of an increase this was over the previous year. As noted in the previous chapter, the 1972 total was 4,000, which may have included only those Party members under the command of the province, and not all those in other "revolutionary organizations" such as the military units and organizations under the control of Region 2.) Thus the new recruitment for the Party during 1972 was a little less than 10 percent of the total number of Party members in the province—somewhat higher if only Party members under direct province control are considered. These figures on recruitment are roughly comparable to the totals for 1971 and, even if they are accurate, do not suggest a major rebuilding of the revolutionary organization as an immediate result of the offensive. Thus the claim that nearly one-third of the province population was under revolutionary control is implausible—though the HES reported 742,000 in the Mekong Delta as a whole shifting out of the "GVN control" category, and this total was due largely to changes in only three of the delta provinces, including Dinh Tuong.[46]

North Vietnamese Troops in the Central Mekong Delta

It was not local recruitment which was driving the resurgence of the revolutionary movement in Dinh Tuong. North Vietnamese troops had been operating in the central Mekong Delta since 1969, when the 88th Regiment moved into the area, and at about the same time Southern main force units began to receive North Vietnamese replacements for their heavy losses. During 1971 Region 2 received 2,376 North Vietnamese troops, and it got another 7,808 in 1972.[47] As the top-priority province in the region, My Tho presumably was allocated the largest portion of these troops. By 1972, the Southern concentrated units, even with these replacements, had become too weak to operate effectively. Reaction to the North Vietnamese presence in the delta was mixed. Some civilians feared that their presence would be a magnet for fighting, and hoped they would simply go away. Others were enthusiastically supportive. Many cadres appreciated the additional security these forces provided. Others detected a superiority complex among the Northerners, and felt resentful.

When North Vietnamese units came in for the first phase of the Easter Offensive, some people in areas which had not seen fighting for some time were angry. Villagers in Duong Diem "didn't supply the North Vietnamese *bo doi,* and even cursed them because as a result of their presence in the village people's houses, property, and orchards were extensively burned. The people felt the North Vietnamese didn't have enough strength to defend the people's lives and property, so they not only didn't supply them but cursed them as well" [DT410]. Duong Diem was a category B village at the time, and the resumption of fighting clearly frightened these villagers who had grown used to the temporary respite brought on by pacification. By contrast, in the still strong (but sparsely populated) revolutionary areas in large villages such as Hau My and My Thanh on the fringe of the Plain of Reeds, "the people really received the *bo doi* warmly when we passed by," and said "try hard boys, peace is nearly here" [DT408]. A guerrilla from Cai Lay said that civilians had to put up with the North Vietnamese coming to stay in their houses whether they liked it or not, but that attitudes depended on their family situation. "Some families with children in ARVN seemed not to be pleased but had to accept it. There were no problems between the *bo doi* and the people. First of all, they didn't hassle or tease the women in the house, and during the day they swept the house. They really ingratiated themselves to the people *[mua chuoc long dan],* so the people liked them." At first the villagers had been frightened by their presence, but after they got to know the *bo doi,* "now when they come in, they are delighted" [DT414].

All accounts confirm that the North Vietnamese troops were extremely well disciplined in their dealings with the local population, and that this was a sharp contrast to the behavior of GVN troops. In Cai Lay a village guerrilla used to observe GVN troops on operation who "burned sixteen of the people's houses, crushed their rice plants with APCs, and grabbed three or four pigs, about 100 bushels of rice and four or five "shrimp-tail" sampan motors. When they left, the people wailed and shouted and said they were cruel and so forth." By contrast, when the *bo doi* came through, "I saw that each time they clashed with the GVN people brought food out for them—they would never do things like [the ARVN]. During all time I was in there I never saw them plunder anything" [DT414].

A member of the province protection unit who operated alongside North Vietnamese filler troops admired their discipline and said that because they had lived in the North, "they had a high level of education, so that on theoretical matters they could talk well. But when it came to getting the job done, they were just like us [Southerners]. They weren't any better in their virtue or behavior." In his view, these northerners "were contemptuous of the people down here, because they felt they had followed the GVN so they didn't have confidence in them, and didn't have respect for them or their customs." Among themselves, the North Vietnamese said, "the people here almost all have family members serving as soldiers for the Nationalists, so they can't be trusted," and also contemptuously added that "these people down here are completely uncultivated *[khong co hoc thuc gi ca].*" Nevertheless, they were polite in face-to-face encounters with Southerners. "Some did civilian proselytizing well, some not, but whether good or bad, wherever they went bombs and shells followed, people were killed and houses burned. People didn't want them to come, but it was their zone so the people couldn't say anything" [DT409].

Some North Vietnamese believed that the people could be trusted but not the local cadres. At the beginning of 1972, "the *bo doi* came to station troops [in northern Cai Be district] but lived separately and didn't maintain liaison with anyone. They organized their own security and had no liaison with the local infrastructure. The North Vietnamese announced straight out that they didn't need the support of the local infrastructure because they operated and moved according to a military map that they brought with them and didn't need the guerrillas to lead the way. They boastfully said, 'We believe in the South Vietnamese people, but cannot have any confidence in the local cadres.'" Not surprisingly, there was considerable tension among the local cadres, who wanted to be notified when the *bo doi* entered people's houses. "The North Vietnamese *bo doi* simply barged into civilian houses regardless of whether they were good citizens or bad citizens, to ask them to buy things or give them food and drink." When the locals cautioned them about the security risks involved in these indiscriminate contacts, the *bo doi* replied, "We don't need you m . . . f . . . ers to educate us—all we need is the sympathy of the people." These troops did a very effective job of winning hearts and minds among the people, even while they were alienating their fellow revolutionaries, and the Southerner who observed this situation conceded that, "In general the people were very pleased and really had confidence in the North Vietnamese troops." The confidence faded after the momentum of the Easter Offensive slowed down, and villagers attitudes toward the *bo doi* began to change. "A few days before I rallied," said a member of the Cai Be local force unit who came out at the beginning of September 1972, "the people had begun to ridicule *[che nhao]* the North Vietnamese. Every time one came into a civilian house they would ask, 'So how long will it be until victory? How is the war going to end when there are so many deaths?' The North Vietnamese smiled and didn't reply" [DT413].

After several months of intense fighting in mid-1972, it became clear to the North Vietnamese that military maps would not be enough, and they would need some support from the local guerrillas to navigate around the hazardous booby traps seeded throughout the liberated areas. The Cai Be district local forces used the *bo doi* for their own purposes and, on their own, attacked GVN troops coming to reinforce units fighting with the North Vietnamese. This was done without any coordination with the *bo doi*. The local force commander said, "Screw the North Vietnamese *[ke ba noi tui Bac Viet]*. We'll operate on our own." The North Vietnamese, in turn, "charged the local forces with being arrogant. 'You Southerners have just a handful of guys. What can you accomplish? *[Tui Nam Bo chung may, con may thang thi lam duoc cai gi?]*'" [DT413].

The local forces and guerrillas were so enraged that they secretly exulted when wandering *bo doi* triggered grenade traps. "They just got what they deserved," said the Cai Be unit leader. The North Vietnamese angrily called the village guerrilla leader of My Thien and threatened, "If my guys continue to step on grenades, I'll exterminate the lot of you!" The local force and guerrillas even shot and killed several drunken North Vietnamese wandering around shooting off their weapons, taking advantage of the noise and confusion to avoid blame. The Cai Be local force leader told his troops, "Don't let anyone push you around like that. If we don't undermine North–South solidarity and are still able to uphold the honor of Nam Bo, let's do it! If someone gets killed in the dark of night, no one will know who did it" [DT413].

Both local cadres and civilians began to get a picture of life in the socialist North from conversations with the *bo doi,* and they generally did not like what they heard. A guerrilla from Cai Lay overheard people in his village complaining that "If the North Vietnamese side wins, we probably won't be able to live. Communal eating, all mixed together—how can you live like that?" Even members of his guerrilla unit said, when no Northerners were around, that they did not want to live in agricultural cooperatives. "They just wanted to live on their own, and eat their own food like we Southerners have always done." The picture the *bo doi* had painted of collective life was not appealing to the guerrillas. "Go to work at eight in the morning and come back in the afternoon to rest," was the way the *bo doi* described it. "If you worked a lot, you would earn a lot." What bothered the Southerners was the restrictions on individual choice and the bureaucratic obligations to the collective. "If you raise a pig and it dies, you are in trouble, and have to make reports and the like. If you raise two chickens or two pigs and want to eat one of them, you have to sell the other to the State. Every one of the Northerners who came in said the same thing, and this scared the majority of the people in the South" [DT414].

Thus the presence of North Vietnamese troops in Dinh Tuong was a mixed blessing for the revolution. Their military contribution was the key to the revival of the local movement, but at the same time there was friction. How representative the extreme situation in Cai Be was is open to question, since other interviews show that local cadres were grateful for the support. Evaluating the political impact of the North Vietnamese troops on the Dinh Tuong civilian population is even more difficult. From the limited interview data, it appears that regional animosities were limited to relations between the *bo doi* and the local cadres, and that the civilian population either found the North Vietnamese sympathetic or, if they "cursed" them, did so not because of any personal or political reasons, or out of regional animosity, but because their presence was an immediate danger to the villagers.

Impact of the Easter Offensive on the People of My Tho

Popular reaction to the Easter Offensive itself is equally difficult to gauge. Many of the accounts cited above describe initial enthusiasm, when the revolutionary forces looked strong, tailing off as the momentum of the offensive subsided. Even at the beginning of the offensive, many people were cautious, and harked back to the parallel of the Tet Offensive. Asked whether the people in his contested village of Tan Hoi had contributed a lot to the revolution during the Easter Offensive, a rallier replied, "Not a lot, only a little, because through the many phases of this long war they had accumulated a certain amount of experience. For example, at the time of the Tet Offensive the Front attacked all over the place, but in the end didn't achieve any results and weren't able to hold on to any place for a prolonged period, so that in the Concerted Uprising phase of the April 1972 offensive, the people's confidence in the Front was diminished. For this reason, they contributed only a little in manpower and materiel because they thought that the Front was not yet able to win final victory, and not yet able to bring peace and independence to the people" [DT412]. The "not yet" formulation, and the continued adherence to the ultimate ideal goal of the revolution (to bring peace and independence to the people) suggest that in this person's view, it was not a rejection of the aims of the revolution, but only a pragmatic calculation that contributions at this time would not have the desired effect.

The increasing shrewdness of peasant political calculations is captured by a former Region 2 cadre, who describes the growth of a capacity for independent judgment among ordinary people, even on great matters of war and peace which they had once considered way above them.

In my view, evaluating [the attitudes of] some of the people and [GVN] soldiers is very hard. Moreover, the masses and soldiers now know a lot about the patterns *[qui luat]* of this war. The pattern of victory today and defeat tomorrow repeats itself over and over again, and has become a fact of life. Today you open up this area into a liberated zone and tomorrow it is again encroached on and seized [by the GVN]—this story has become routine and widespread by now, so the masses are very cautious. The reality is that now they really take pains to calculate things *(chiu suy xet lam)*. At the time of the Concerted Uprising in 1960, the masses totally believed that the Front would win, but victory did not arrive. Then came the Tet Offensive and the people thought that would be a sure thing, but in the end the Front was unable to bring victory. When it came to the

Concerted Uprising of April 1972, even though the Front resolutely carried out a strategy designed to gain victory, the masses and the soldiers were hesitant, and didn't dare to respond to the uprising because their experience showed them that the pattern of victory and defeat went on and on. Even though for a while the revolution was able to open up the liberated area in the 20/7 zone, the people saw clearly that victory and defeat in a campaign was temporary. For this reason, stirring up the mass movement to an uprising was very difficult and the soldiers couldn't be induced to revolt spontaneously [khoi nghia] [DT404].

A disillusioned province military cadre who had fought for the revolution throughout the war, and who had been one of the original members of the tiny pre-uprising province armed force, said sadly, "After the Tet Offensive, as far as the people were concerned the Just Cause had not completely disappeared, but their belief [in the revolution] had declined a lot. Many people asked themselves, now where does the Just Cause lie? A feeling of skepticism [nghi ngo] had appeared among the people" [DT415]. This conclusion, reached by a discouraged but experienced long-time member of the revolution, may well have reflected the basic political reality of My Tho toward the end of the war, though there is no way to verify these scattered observations other than to note that almost all of the handful of interviews in 1972 and 1973 lend some support to this observation.

From Offensive to Cease Fire

Officially, the Party had no such apprehensions. The overall assessment of the Easter Offensive was that it changed the balance of forces "in a direction favorable to us," both locally and nationwide.[48] This formulation did not assert that the revolutionary forces were now stronger than the GVN, but only that the balance was shifting in a favorable direction. Clearly the Easter Offensive was designed with the Paris talks in mind, and aimed at improving Hanoi's negotiating position. The offensive was also meant to put the revolutionary forces in a better position after a settlement was reached, either for a prolonged period of political-guerrilla struggle or, if that failed, a return to large-scale military action. Despite the introduction of North Vietnamese troops in the province, the absolute air superiority of the U.S.–GVN and the awesome power of the B-52s seem to have discouraged a concentration of forces that could have delivered a knockout blow to key ARVN military positions along the Plain of Reeds.

By the summer of 1972, rumors of a cease-fire were prevalent in the countryside and in the Mekong Delta. A reporter was told by U.S. officials that "since the beginning of July, Viet Cong have told villagers to raise Communist flags and perform certain administrative tasks if a cease-fire comes about. The practice has been most widespread in the Mekong Delta, where North Vietnamese and Viet Cong troops have been gradually building up since the beginning of the offensive more than four months ago."[49] From July to October the number of combat incidents in Dinh Tuong dropped from 274 to around 100. In mid-November the relative lull and the "change in Communist tactics over the past three months has been so dramatic that one American officer called it 'a new phase in the war.'"[50]

The famous "peace is at hand" abortive cease-fire of October 31, 1972, had mixed effects on the province. A Tan Phu village guerrilla reported that his unit had been continuously active prior to this, urging the people to sew flags, and preparing for land-grabbing operations to exploit the cease-fire. The indoctrination of villagers about the cease-fire began on October 15, and the twenty families in the revolutionary-controlled corner of the village were fired up. "They were happy and awaited the cease-fire in order to return and annihilate the tyrants," he said. On the eve of the abortive cease-fire, the guerrillas were each issued a fistful of rice, and linked up with the North Vietnamese troops so that the next day, after the cease-fire was signed, within the space of twenty-four hours we would attack and grab land and people *[gianh dat gianh dan]*." But nothing happened, and the disillusioned guerrilla eventually rallied—ironically, only three days before the real cease-fire [DT406].

Rumors of a cease-fire also preoccupied the North Vietnamese troops who had come to Dinh Tuong. In regular indoctrination sessions the cease-fire was discussed only in general terms, and the cadres took pains to avoid indicating a specific date, "because they were afraid we would slack off on our missions waiting for the cease-fire to come. . . . Nobody wanted to die in the last days of the war" [DT407]. In the Thanh Phu (Cai Lay) village unit, some guerrillas said among themselves, "The hell with it! If there's going to be peace, just let it happen; whoever takes over, just do it and get on with it *[Em thi em me no cho roi, ai nam thi nam me no cho roi]!* If we go on like this we could be killed at any time" [DT414].

When the real cease-fire came on January 27, 1973, there was no time for speculation and reflection. The revolution had set out a formidable set of tasks for the cadres, and the Saigon government was equally determined to take advantage of the situation. Responsibility for the unraveling of the cease-fire lies with both sides, but the fundamental reason is the nature of the agreement itself. Like the Geneva Accords of 1954, the Paris Agreements set up a framework for a political resolution of the conflict that would work only if all parties saw it as being in their interest. Since the Saigon government could only lose by sharing power with the Provisional Revolutionary Government (PRG) there was not much of an incentive for it to push for a political resolution of the conflict. As at Geneva, the main consequence of the agreement was to remove the external party, in this case the United States, from the fighting, with the hope that the Vietnamese parties could sort it out themselves.

An Uneasy Truce

Truce violations were routinely committed by both sides, though the few available interviews seem to point to the GVN side as the more frequent and serious transgressor. Retrospective Party accounts view their approach during this period as too complacent, which is an indirect admission of a more passive stance in the early post-cease-fire phase. The probable explanation is that the Party wanted to deprive the GVN of any pretext to avoid fulfilling the political clauses of the Paris Agreements, since the benefits in any political concessions would go to the PRG. Some diplomatic pressure may also have been exerted by Hanoi's allies to give at least the appearance of respecting the accords. Eventually it became clear that this strategy was not working to the revolution's advantage. Saigon was retaking some areas that it had lost during the Easter Offensive and, like the government of Ngo Dinh Diem in the 1950s, the Thieu administration showed no signs of wanting to engage in political competition with the revolutionary side. By mid-1973, Hanoi changed its strategy and resumed the all-out military struggle which ended with the defeat of Saigon's forces on April 30, 1975.

From the few interview sources, the general picture of the immediate aftermath of the cease-fire was of GVN encroachment putting the revolutionaries on the defensive, although there are significant exceptions to this pattern. A member of the Province Protection Unit, who left the revolution in mid-February 1973, said, "For the past week the Front hasn't attacked any posts but has just penetrated deep into the weak areas where people are, to hold on to the people. The Front hasn't attacked areas with [GVN] soldiers, but if the soldiers barge into the liberated zones they will be attacked—if not, they will be left alone" [DT409]. A member of the People's Committee of My Tho province, who left in October 1973, told an interviewer, "I have to say impartially that it was the GVN that conducted many operations in the liberated areas after the cease-fire. They do it not to seize land or to pursue the liberation forces. These operations are mainly to set up the posts that were lost in the Uprising [Easter Offensive]. They didn't set them up right on the same place as before, but several hundred meters away." The clashes that did occur, he said, were largely related to these post-building operations or GVN operations to resupply isolated posts. In contrast to the all-out military attack of the uprising, "now that peace has come, the attack has shifted to politics with the slogan, 'Struggle, repel, attack *[dau, duoi, danh],*' with 'struggle' as the main priority" [DT411].

The Paris Agreements took effect at 0800 hours on January 28, 1973, and its provisions began to be implemented—but not without some friction. In My Tho the Region 2 PRG delegation to the four-party military commission called for in the accords was reportedly given quarters in a chicken house on the former U.S. base—which still reeked of its former occupants. Among the early charges of cease-fire violations throughout the country made by the PRG delegation were a series of attacks on hamlets along Highway 4 that were alleged to be under revolutionary control.[51] Although many people were wary, others were exuberant. "In Tan Hoi village," said one, "the people were really fired up. Everything had quieted down at that time. Then I heard the sound of firecrackers going off mixed in with the muffled firing of guns, signifying the happiness and enthusiasm of the people." When after a few days the sound of real gunfire continued, the people became bitter and pessimistic [DT412]. A province cadre who operated in the heart of the 20/7 zone said, "At the beginning of the cease-fire, people were all fired up and believed in the revolution. How could they not believe after the Concerted Uprising [Easter Offensive], which liberated all the posts in the deep areas, and the meetings and boisterous demonstrations? Then the GVN fought back and the movement subsided. Then, when the cease-fire came, the people were again fired up and confident, but this time their enthusiasm was subdued, and not boiling up like during the Concerted Uprising" [DT411].

Jacques Leslie of the *Los Angeles Times* and a French colleague were the first foreign correspondents to enter a revolutionary zone after the cease-fire. On the third day of the cease-fire Leslie parked his car along Highway 4 and, guided by the directions of a farmer, entered the revolutionary-controlled area. "We were in Binh Phu," he reported, "a 100 percent Viet Cong-controlled village of seven square miles and 6,800 people. We were amazed that the Viet Cong occupied territory so close to the main road through the Delta—from where we stood at one point, we could see cars plying it. I'd driven that stretch many times without suspecting the Viet Cong were so close." Leslie could see "battle smoke twisting upwards in the distance," but was skeptical of the local evidence of GVN cease-fire violations, which appeared to reflect earlier fighting. During a walk of over four miles and several hours, artillery shells landed within 200 meters of the group. They were guests of honor at an entertainment and political rally of several thousand people. Leslie's scoop encouraged another half-dozen journalists to come to Binh Phu, until the overwhelmed village revolutionary leader begged them to stop so he could get on with his work.[52]

Both sides tried to stake out as much territory as they could, by blanketing the countryside with their flags. The "battle of the flags" actually made it easier for the GVN to draw the line between two zones of control, and it was clearly Saigon's policy to try to eliminate the contested areas between them, not because Saigon acknowledged the sanctity of the remaining areas of revolutionary control or expected the revolutionaries to accede to whatever line the GVN was able to establish, but because they wanted to reclaim territory lost during the Easter Offensive and continue their pacification operations. "Who did the people blame for violations of the cease-fire?" one interviewee from a contested village was asked. "In my view they don't blame anyone. They see that the Front still is firing its weapons and the GVN is firing its weapons, so that both sides are violating the cease-fire. I heard some people say, 'The GVN can plant its flags, but the Front can't.' Several hours before the ceasefire, the Liberation planted flags but they were all immediately torn down by the GVN. When the GVN tells people to put up its flags they dare to do it, but if the Liberation orders it, no one would dare. If you put up a Liberation flag you had to do it yourself. But, in the end, when the GVN came in the people took down all the Liberation flags and put up GVN flags." Having won the battle of the flags, the GVN ordered people in the contested parts of the village to move into the Saigon zones. Those who refused had their houses bulldozed. The Party tried hard to widen its zone of control. "Their sole aim now is to expand their area of operation so that the North Vietnamese *bo doi* can come in, but they haven't been able to do this. In fact, their zone has contracted and GVN posts are getting more numerous" [DT412].

In mid-February 1973 the My Tho province Party committee met in Long Tien village to assess the initial results of the cease-fire. It focused on the question of how to respond to GVN cease-fire violations, but seemed to stress encroachments into the "deep liberated areas" more than the contested zones, and proposed countering these primarily with political struggle.[53]

According to General Tran Van Tra, the My Tho province leadership had to hide their more aggressive actions from their superiors. Like Tra, these leaders vividly remembered the failure of the "politics first" strategy of the 1954–59 period. Tra wrote, "my heart still ached with grief for those comrades who fell during that period, holding weapons which they did not dare shoot, and grief for the many local movements that were drowned in blood." Because of Hanoi's desire to exploit the political and diplomatic possibilities of the Paris Agreements, and the injunction to maintain the cease-fire, Southern revolutionaries felt that they were the victims of an unrealistic policy imposed on them by a distant leadership. "Because they were afraid of being criticized for violating the policy [military proselytizing]," wrote Tra, "in My Tho the guerrillas had to hide the fact that they were organizing attacks (hide them from their superiors) on posts that had been illegally established in our bases. In Mo Cay, Ben Tre, in the face of a situation of enemy encroachment attacks which the armed forces couldn't respond to and which pushed them into constant retreat, the brothers could only gripe that 'the only thing left is to crawl under the porch to live.' In the end they had to attack on their own to reestablish the district base area."[54]

Assessing the Political-Military Balance of Forces
in My Tho in Mid and Late 1973

The difficulties of assessing the relative strengths of the contending sides in the renewed civil war are acute. Comparisons of the political and security situation often led to sharply different conclusions. This was noted even before the cease-fire by American journalists such as Sydney Schanberg of the *New York Times* who reported in mid-1972 that control of the Mekong Delta was "a matter of perspective." An American advisor in Dinh Tuong assured him that the province was 80 percent controlled by the GVN, and that "Every North Vietnamese thrust has been blunted and thwarted." On a trip to the district town of Cai Be, however, a local pharmacist told him that he wouldn't venture a mile out of town because it was too dangerous. After a pause for thought, he made a clarification. "I should correct that. I am a timid man. The brave ones go maybe a mile and a quarter." Schanberg found that despite the "surface sense of security," yet "while vehicles speed freely along the American built two lane highway most of the time, the Communists and the war are never more than 500 yards away."[55] Jacques Leslie's trip to Binh Phu right after the cease-fire is another confirmation of this.

In the summer and fall of 1973 more American reporters visited villages in Dinh Tuong and produced a mixed picture of the state of the revolutionary movement. The June 1973 attempt in Paris to restore the cease-fire, known as "Cease-fire 2," was unsuccessful, though a *New York Times* reporter in My Phuoc Tay found that "the upsurge of fighting that many military analysts had predicted failed to materialize" and that the forest of red-and-blue revolutionary flags which had blossomed in January at the time of the original cease fire were now reduced to two flags in the village.[56] Another *New York Times* journalist visited Long Tien in the heart of the 20/7 zone in July 1973 and reported that "The South Vietnamese Army sent an additional regiment into the area two or three months ago, and since then, government control of the region—at least along the major roads—appears to have increased. The dirt road that runs through Long Tien still bears gaping holes where land mines exploded, but the road is now busy with traffic, testifying to its relative safety. Army officers say that Vietcong snipers no longer shoot at buses. A farmer, watching the army's rather casual artillery bombardment of the Vietcong flags, observed that when such flags were put up a year ago "there would be planes dropping bombs, artillery fire all the night, and the gunfire was like the winter rain."[57] Again there was a rebuilding of roads and the appearance of normal traffic into formerly forbidden zones. Although the ferocity of the war had diminished, and places like Long Tien enjoyed a temporary respite, the fighting dragged on in other areas of the province. Even where there were military setbacks and revolutionary units were pushed out of some areas, the underlying political strength of the revolution seemed to grow precisely because of the restoration of some normality in civilian life.

Perhaps the best illustration of the difficulties of assessing the situation in this "civil war" period are the contrasting pictures of Hau Thanh village painted by an American reporter and a former member of the revolutionary movement familiar with the area. In 1971 Hau Thanh had been considered a very weak area of revolutionary control, with a mere eight village guerrillas and a handful of village civilian cadres, though larger military units could still operate in the area [DT403]. After the cease-fire, the military activities of the revolutionary side had declined even further, but the political base of support seems to have become stronger. "At first glance," reported Thomas Lippman of the *Washington Post* on a November 1973 trip to Hau Thanh, "the evolution of peace in this Mekong Delta village looks like a tidy little success story for the government of South Vietnam. A month before the cease-fire, Hau Thanh was an unhappy and embattled place where the government was barely hanging on. The chief road was insecure, it was risky to walk to the main village pagoda. Vietcong troops mined trails and canal banks. B-52s were bombing nearby paddies, and only periodic sweeps of South Vietnam's 9th Division kept the Communists from penetrating the marketplace at the center of the village. Now the road is unthreatened, and a team of army engineers sent in to repave it. The soldiers play volleyball in the village square at dusk, their weapons stacked in the compound. A construction crew is extending the market. Village officials move from home to office unescorted. There is no problem getting to the pagoda next to which a new government militia outpost has been set up where the Vietcong used to roam."[58]

"But what has happened in Hau Thanh over the past month is actually little short of a disaster for the Saigon government. Not only does the Vietcong control most of Hau Thanh's territory, it has the political allegiance of most of the people. Worse still, from the point of view of a government that regards accommodation with the Communists as treason, the two sides are living and mingling with one another in a condition approximating peace, with the NLF tolerating Saigon's control of the administrative machinery and the government officials acquiescing in the NLF's political dominance." Lippman was given guidance by local Buddhist monks into the revolutionary-controlled part of the village, where he was given a rousing reception in "a festive, glad handing four-hour romp through huts and paddies and canals." "I don't understand it," an anti-Communist Vietnamese who also visited Hau Thanh told Lippman, "The people look so happy." As he returned to Saigon territory, Lippman was handed off from one set of guides to another. "At each transfer, the new escort knew where the guests had been and what their own task was, and seemed to take it on willingly, smiling in a conspiratorial denial of the rules laid down by Saigon. They were all in it together and made no effort to hide it."[59]

A seasoned revolutionary veteran, however, painted a picture of revolutionary weakness in Hau Thanh. A province military cadre who was a native of the village said in a May 1973 interview that the village Party secretary had only been in the movement for a few years. "He's still a kid and can't do anything at all. Village cadres can now do immediate tasks but can't perform longer-term missions. At most they can carry out 20 percent of what the province orders" [DT415]. The probable reasons for this more negative assessment illustrate the caution with which all the interviews need to be evaluated. First, by 1973 this cadre was disillusioned with the revolution, and his impression of revolutionary weakness in Hau Thanh and other places was both a reflection of his despair and a justification for his defection. A more important reason is that precisely because of his long experience in the revolutionary movement, a level of organization and support which appeared impressive to an outside observer appeared inadequate to this former revolutionary, who had seen the movement at much greater heights, and was used to demanding a very high level of performance from cadres. Even if the village cadres of Hau Thanh could carry out only 20 percent of what the province ordered, it appears to have been, by any objective standard, a relatively effective 20 percent.

Resolution 21: Hanoi Authorizes a More Aggressive Posture

The Party leadership, however, was not looking for mere coexistence or accommodation with the Saigon government, especially in view of the inroads that the GVN had been making into revolutionary and contested zones. By mid-1973 Hanoi was finally persuaded by reports from the South that the cease-fire had broken down irreparably, and attempts to resolve the conflict politically would be futile. Resolution 21 of the Party's Central Committee made it clear that once again, "the revolutionary path in the South is the path of revolutionary violence *[bao luc cach mang]*. Whatever the situation, we have to seize the opportunity and hold fast to the strategic line of being on the attack" *[duong loi chien luoc tien cong]* and be flexible in leadership to push the Southern revolution forward."[60] The implication is that it was lack of flexibility and rigid adherence to an unrealistic policy that was now being corrected. Still, in the specific area that guerrilla leaders in the South like Tran Van Tra criticized most forcefully, lack of aggressiveness in contested areas, Resolution 21 said only that in these contested areas the revolution must "firmly maintain our strategic position *[the]* and forces *[luc]* and move ahead step by step."[61] Evidently this cautious formulation was enough to give the green light to commanders in the South to take more aggressive measures as they saw fit.

General Tran Van Tra's account of the final phase of the war describes a debate about strategy between advocates of concentrating heavily equipped main force units in a given area and his own somewhat qualified advocacy of force dispersal. Resolution 21 had designated the Mekong Delta as the main battlefield and therefore a priority area for a force buildup, but "At that time the issue arose among both military and civilian cadres of how to build up the forces in the delta." Some advocated concentrating on eastern Nam Bo and lining up forces "to lock horns like buffaloes fighting," while others favored "choosing another area to attack by surprise, meaning the Mekong Delta, in order to concentrate forces and fight there." Tra and other COSVN leaders ultimately rejected this proposal, along with the Maoist idea that "the rural areas would have to be liberated first and only then could you liberate the urban areas."[62] This, Tra said, ran counter to the Party's strategy of "attack, attack" in all three zones (delta, mountain–forest, urban) with mixes of political and military struggle appropriate to each zone. "In the strategy of attack," he argued, "the blows struck by main force units are very decisive, but the main forces with their constantly improving equipment and technique cannot possibly be concentrated for big battles in the open terrain of the deltas with their networks of streams and swamp." Given the enemy strength and the nature of the terrain, concentrating forces would "amount to paralyzing ourselves, falling into a weak and passive position," and would multiply the strength of the enemy by playing into his hands. Experience showed, said Tra, that in the Mekong Delta the optimum-sized unit was a regiment with light weapons (in the Resistance and in the 1960s, the battalion was viewed as the largest feasible concentrated force). If a division was to be used, it would have to be armed and organized differently than a division equipped for the mountain–forest areas. These main force units would have to be able to integrate their operations with those of local force and guerrilla units."[63]

Hanoi's official July decision to endorse the resumption of large-scale military operations did not reach My Tho until mid-October 1973, when the province Party committee met to discuss its implications for the local revolutionary movement. A major objective of the new plan was to create a large and contiguous liberated zone on both sides of Highway 4 in order to facilitate cutting the lifeline of Saigon in the Mekong Delta. Two North Vietnamese regiments, the 320th and 2nd were called in to support the expansion of the liberated zone along the Nguyen Van Tiep Canal. According to the official provincial revolutionary history, the military offensive during the October–December 1973 period forced 100 posts to withdraw, liberated 10 villages and 50 hamlets with a population of over 50,000, and induced nearly 5,000 families to return to their former place of residence in the revolutionary-controlled zones.[64] Allowing for the usual hyperbole and statistical inflation, this account does reflect the breakdown of the cease-fire, and the reescalation of the war.

The Party Considers 1973 As a Year of Regaining Lost Momentum

Following Resolution 21 in mid-1973, the revolutionary forces in Dinh Tuong put increasing military pressure on the GVN, with the consequence that by late spring of 1974, at the end of the dry season, Saigon had been forced to relinquish many of its gains during the previous year. General Tra wrote that "As for us, at the end of the dry season we had retaken all the liberated areas that the enemy had seized before January 28, 1973, including even the area north of Highway 4 in My Tho, where the enemy had massively encroached after the cease-fire. Not only that, but we even expanded the liberated area in twenty villages with about 300,000 people in the Mekong Delta."[65] Tra's account implies that the year 1973 was largely a holding action, when the revolutionary forces recovered from early setbacks, and reversed them by the first quarter of 1974, when the scales of territorial control began to tilt the other way. In all three zones of control, "the organized masses, the guerrilla forces, and our local forces expanded. The contested zone had spread into the zone controlled by the enemy in all the military regions of B2 [Nam Bo]."[66]

Tra's admission that 1973 was a year of limited military progress for the revolutionaries in the upper Mekong Delta is echoed by the My Tho revolutionary history as well as the assessment of Tam Phuong and Hanoi's top military leaders. A resolution of the Central Military Commission in Hanoi dated April 1974 stated that the GVN had been "pushed back in Region 9" [the lower delta or western Nam Bo] but merely "halted" in Region 8 [central Nam Bo or Region 2 of the Mekong Delta].[67] In January 1974 the My Tho province Party committee met to assess the year following the cease-fire and concluded that while there were some accomplishments, "compared with the goals set out for 1973, there were many shortcomings. The main reason is that the various levels didn't completely grasp the mission of comprehensively building the liberated areas in a way that could change the balance of forces between us and the enemy." Among the measures the Party leadership decided on to strengthen the liberated areas was a target of returning 10,000 families to their former homes and enlisting 2,000 youth into the armed forces.[68]

Conclusion

If the story in Dinh Tuong for 1973 was the resumption of full-scale armed struggle, the story of 1974 was a gradually accelerating shift in the balance of military forces which seriously threatened Saigon's hold over the countryside even before the 1975 final offensive. During this year there was a complex interplay between continually escalating conventional warfare and the concurrent rebuilding of the local revolutionary organizations. In large part this rebuilding was made possible by a combination of expanding zones of revolutionary control and the return of civilian population to these zones. Unfortunately, the range of sources to describe and analyze this process is very limited. A single interview was conducted in 1974. Thus the final two years of the struggle in Dinh Tuong must be pieced together by comparing accounts from official sources. On the U.S. side these are mainly the military advisory reports and periodic assessments from the State Department's representative in the delta. On the revolutionary side, a variety of memoirs and official histories from central to provincial level shed some light on this period. Given the inevitable problems of limited perspective and information inherent in such sources, much of the analysis of the last phase of the war must rely on an assessment of the strengths and weaknesses of these sources, a careful comparison of them, and logical inference from the limited available data. It is just one more irony of the Vietnam war that after the almost microscopic documentation on which much of this study is based, the most dramatic chapter of the conflict unfolded largely beyond the reach of the historian's craft, but it is to this final task of recall and reconstruction that we now turn.

18
The Final Chapter

After a year of inconclusive political and military struggle in Vietnam, a subtle but decisive shift in the balance of forces occurred during 1974. Because it was not clearly perceived by contemporary observers, it is hard to define the exact point at which the balance tipped irreversibly toward the revolutionary side. It is also difficult to distinguish the effect of the decline of the government of the Republic of Vietnam (GVN) throughout the entire country from the deterioration of its control in My Tho. But some analyses made by various revolutionary leaders at the time, as well as contemporaneous comments made in U.S. reports, offer some clues. At the beginning of 1974, American advisors were concerned that "the dominant fact is the enemy's strength." At about the same time, the Communist Party concluded that the GVN was now critically overextended, and that once again revolutionary strategy had the opportunity to exploit this weakness by stretching the Saigon defenders out into isolated defensive positions, which could then be attacked at the initiative of the revolutionary side. This also meant that the revolutionary forces would not be able to concentrate in places like the upper Mekong Delta to clear out large and secure base areas, and would have to disperse into smaller units over a wide range of terrain in order to prevent the GVN from concentrating its own forces. It was a price the revolution was more than willing to pay. In the end, the surrender of Saigon was the catalyst that led to the collapse of a critically weakened GVN position in Dinh Tuong. Following the military blitzkrieg by North Vietnamese troops in central Vietnam, there was a General Offensive which ultimately swept into Saigon, crashing through the gates of the Presidential Palace. However, there was no General Insurrection in the cities, which had been the standard Party vision of how the conflict would end. In the Mekong Delta, Saigon's implosion simply made further resistance pointless, and the tattered but still coherent GVN security structure in Dinh Tuong unraveled within hours of General Duong Van Minh's capitulation.

By the end of 1974, two developments convinced Hanoi and the Party Central Committee Office of South Vietnam (COSVN) that the time was ripe for a sharp acceleration of their plans to conclude the "national democratic revolution" in the South, and defeat the Saigon forces. First, the growing hostility to the GVN leadership of Nguyen Van Thieu and the widespread corruption of his regime rekindled urban political agitation on a scale that had not been seen in South Vietnam since the Buddhist crisis of 1966. The fact that the leadership of this political opposition came from former supporters of Ngo Dinh Diem, who were appalled by the social breakdown of a war-torn society, and from hard-line anticommunist Catholic priests protesting the corruption of the Thieu regime, reveals an important shift in South Vietnamese society. Although there were no doubt many revolutionary sympathizers among Thieu's urban opponents, the prime movers came from the right rather than the left.[1] Nevertheless, Party leaders saw in this urban movement a chance to return to their "three zone" strategy, which relied on political struggle in the cities to support guerrilla war in the Mekong Delta and big unit attacks in the remote mountain–forest areas.

Even in the placid backwater of My Tho city, some anti-Thieu protests were heard in 1974, revealing the extent to which the Thieu government's grip on power was slackening. It is important to note, however, that there is little evidence that the urban political crisis was an indicator of a revival of Party strength or of revolutionary appeal in the towns and cities. More likely, it was a response to the twin squeeze of economic decline (unemployment and inflation) and corruption—which had been tolerable when U.S. dollars sloshed into every corner of Vietnam, but became insupportable as the post-American intervention economy contracted. It should also be noted that in Dinh Tuong and surrounding provinces, there was a major turnover in district and province leaders in 1974, ostensibly related to corruption, which reflected political instability within the GVN's own ranks.[2]

The other major GVN vulnerability of which the Party took note in late 1974 was also related to the economic contraction and reduction in aid that followed the withdrawal of American troops. GVN forces were now being forced to fight a "poor man's war." In past years an outpost under attack could call on nearly unlimited artillery support, and often airstrikes as well. Since the Tet Offensive, the GVN had relied heavily on U.S. airpower to beat back the revolution's big units. Now, in the aftermath of the Watergate scandal, the planes were gone, the aid and material assistance was threatened, and Saigon's forces were increasingly on their own. As many accounts by former Saigon officials and Army of the Republic of Vietnam (ARVN) officers reveal, the GVN had great difficulty adjusting to this fact.

On the revolutionary side, troops from North Vietnam continued to pour into the South, and aid from Hanoi's socialist friends continued to flow—although Hanoi later accused China of scaling down its assistance starting in 1974. Men and supplies were not abundant in all of the revolutionary zones, however, and the upper Mekong Delta was one of the weaker areas in terms of manpower and logistics. No doubt this would have changed had the war gone on longer, but in the end the forces in the upper Delta were racing to keep pace with events in other areas, which had accelerated beyond their ability to respond. It is symptomatic that the main force units sent up from the Delta to attack Saigon from the south heard the final surrender announcement over the radio as they gazed at Saigon from well outside the city. The collapse of the GVN in My Tho coincided with the surrender in Saigon. It is important to note, however, that a substantial revival of revolutionary territorial control had taken place in the upper Delta, including Dinh Tuong, even before the final offensive unraveled the GVN positions elsewhere in the country. This resurgence was even stronger in the lower Delta, which indicates that any plan the GVN may have had for withdrawing into an enclave of Saigon and the Mekong Delta would have run into major problems even if GVN forces had managed to hold a defensive perimeter north of Saigon. The revolutionary comeback in the Delta began as a result of the 1972 Easter Offensive, stalled during the immediate cease-fire period in early 1973, resumed in mid-1973, but did not really gather critical momentum until 1974.

Momentum Shifts Toward the Revolution in Spring 1974

Even though expansion of My Tho's revolutionary zones in 1973 had been less successful than the provincial and Southern Party leadership desired, they concluded that the situation in late spring of 1974 was favorable enough to present a new strategic opportunity. COSVN now began to perceive that Saigon's forces were stretched thin, to the point where they could be forced to abandon some areas in order to hold others. From the perspective of revolutionary strategy, this was the perfect opportunity to exploit the opponent's weaknesses and "contradictions." "Throughout the [1974] dry season, especially in its final several months," wrote COSVN's General Tran Van Tra, "their forces in IV Corps, the Mekong Delta, were sucked back, mostly to My Tho and the Kien Tuong–Cambodian border, while in Hau Giang [lower Delta around Can Tho] the 21st Division had to break up into individual battalions but still couldn't maintain the morale of the Civil Guard [Regional Force] and Self–defense Force [Popular Force]."[3] Tra asserted that this led the IV Corps commander to abandon some smaller posts and use the militia taken from them to beef up larger and more important posts and replace manpower losses. In his view, this process, which began in the spring of 1974, set in motion a gradual GVN retreat that led ultimately to its disastrous withdrawal from the Central Highlands in the following year.[4] American military observers acknowledged that in the first quarter of 1974, "throughout the Delta outposts were shelled and attacked as enemy forces attempted to open rice supply routes. During the month of February 1974 49 outposts were temporarily abandoned due to enemy pressure or overrun and subsequently retaken."[5] By the end of June 1974 the Defense Attache's Office (DAO) acknowledged the net loss of 144 posts in the Mekong Delta since the cease-fire.[6]

Both the guerrilla forces and the North Vietnamese main force units in My Tho had developed substantially by the beginning of 1974. The My Tho province Party history claims that every village now had two to three squads of guerrillas, while some had platoons, and the village of My Hanh Dong had expanded to sixty guerrillas. Each district was said to have one or two companies. The long-lost balance between guerrilla, district, province, and region forces was now said to be restored, and the local guerrillas were capable of coordinated operations with local and main force units. This was evidenced in a series of operations in northern Cai Lay spearheaded by the 88th Regiment of the North Vietnamese Army (NVA) and the NVA 320th Regiment, which the province Party historians claimed ripped large holes in the GVN position along the critical zone bordering the Plain of Reeds and forced forty-seven posts in Cai Be to withdraw. Equally important, the revolutionary forces were now able to secure a foothold east of Highway 4 in Cho Gao province and begin to lay the groundwork for interdicting the Cho Gao Canal, the only route besides Highway 4 capable of large-scale supply of rice from the Delta to Saigon.[7]

By 1974, North Vietnamese forces had become even more vital to the struggle in the Mekong Delta. The newly formed North Vietnamese Eighth Division, consisting of the 88th, 24th, and 320th regiments was put under the direct command of Military Region 2.[8] However, although the balance may have been gradually shifting, there were no major military breakthroughs for the revolutionary side until the end of 1974. The ARVN continued to hold important bases in the Plain of Reeds, preventing the large revolutionary units from operating freely there and consolidating a completely secure base. Despite this, the

North Vietnamese and local force units were able to hold on to their positions in the 20/7 zone, and expand their control in the exposed areas of Cho Gao and Go Cong east of Highway 4. At the beginning of 1975, even before the start of the final Great Spring Offensive, the GVN military position in Dinh Tuong had deteriorated significantly.

Although much reduced in size, the United States retained a small military support staff known as the Defense Attache's Office (DAO), which issued periodic country-wide situation reports, including the Mekong Delta and Dinh Tuong. On the revolutionary side, a variety of Hanoi histories of the conflict, provincial histories (of My Tho [Dinh Tuong] as well as the neighboring provinces of Kien Tuong and Ben Tre), provide a basis for understanding this perspective on the war. Both sides present a fairly optimistic picture of their progress throughout 1974, but both express concern that they were not doing better. More important, both sides cite very different evidence of their success. On the GVN side, it was their ability to hold positions in the Plain of Reeds and stand up to the North Vietnamese units. On the revolutionary side, it was the ability to harass the GVN and expand their sphere of operations into new areas, especially the once-"pacified" exposed areas east of Highway 4.

Battle for Control of the Plain of Reeds

"One year after the cease-fire," reported the DAO in February 1974, "there is an uneasy equilibrium. The dominant fact is the enemy's strength. Positioned better. Structured better. Unharrassed by US air."[9] Despite this perceived improvement of opposition forces, the DAO was cautiously optimistic about the ARVN's performance. At the beginning of 1974, the DAO listed three primary threat areas in the Mekong Delta: the Seven Mountain region of Chau Doc province along the Cambodian border, Chuong Thien province in the lower Delta, and Dinh Tuong, which alone accounted for about 30 percent of the incidents in all of Military Region 4 for that reporting period. "The areas South of QL [National Highway] 4 and adjacent to TL-20 [provincial route 20] /LTL-29 [interprovincial route 29] in Cai Lay and Cai Be districts were especially active, and short-term interdictions occurred during the quarter. Activity in the Tri Phap area continued at past levels as ARVN probed the perimeter of the Communist controlled sector."[10]

The DAO's May 1974 Quarterly Assessment report was considerably more upbeat, largely because of the ARVN Seventh Division's success in the Plain of Reeds. "The high point of the quarter and the entire ceasefire period, was the penetration of the Tri Phap village area in Kien Tuong province, commencing 13 February." In fact, the DAO was so impressed with this performance that they billed it as the long-delayed avenging of the 1963 ARVN defeat at Ap Bac. This rhetorical excess is perhaps an indication of how scarce good news from the ARVN front was during this period. Nonetheless, the ARVN did maintain a fairly strong hold on the key areas of the Plain of Reeds throughout 1974, and into 1975. This did not stop the revolutionary forces from operating in the area, but did inflict heavy casualties on some of the North Vietnamese units, and prevented them from achieving a completely secure base and logistics area in their traditional sanctuary. Moreover, while the ARVN was occupied in holding a position deep in its enemy's territory, the North Vietnamese and local guerrilla forces were expanding the scope of their operations closer to the vital GVN lifeline of Highway 4.

Tri Phap was a village about 10 kilometers north of Hau My, which Saigon considered the "gateway to the Plain of Reeds" and which was, from the revolutionary perspective, a "gateway to the gateway." Right after the January 1973 ceasefire, the DAO province reporter for Kien Tuong wrote that "Infiltration of NVA men and materiel continues down the long established corridors along the sparsely populated border with Kien Phong and through eastern Kien Tuong to the tri-border with Kien Tuong-Kien Phong-Dinh Tuong. Tri Phap village itself was lost by the GVN during the 1972 Offensive and remains under hostile control, its defense becoming ever more formidable as Base Area 7170 becomes ever more important to the VC/NVA effort in the Delta."[11]

The revolutionary side called this area Zone 4 of Kien Tuong province. At the time of the Easter Offensive in 1972, COSVN had designated Huynh Cong Than to take charge of this area. Than had led the guerrilla movement in Long An before being called up to the region level and was now assigned to hold on to this key link in the supply lines from the Cambodian border to My Tho and Ben Tre. In his postwar memoir he writes, "After the Paris Accord, Region 8 had two important liberated areas, the 20/7 zone in My Tho and Zone 4 in Kien Tuong."[12]

Just before the Easter Offensive, the province chief of Kien Tuong had designated the Tri Phap area as the key target of pacification for 1972, and ordered GVN forces to "clear out the terrain cover and the minibase clusters [can cu lom] along the canals and streams of Tri Phap." At this point, the main force presence had been reduced to the point that the GVN could plan for this to be done largely by local militia. The idea was to strip all vegetation from along the network of canals in this area, to deprive the revolutionary forces of cover and concealment, as had been done in parts of Dinh Tuong in 1971.[13] The Easter Offensive deflected this plan, and the arrival of larger North Vietnamese units in the area required a major commitment from the ARVN to the area of Tri Phap. By the end of June 1974, according to the Kien Tuong province history, the GVN had moved twenty-four battalions, sixty-eight artillery pieces, and two M113 armored personnel carrier squadrons to the Plain of Reeds and had attempted to seal off the Tri Phap area by establishing four company- or battalion-sized bases and several smaller posts in the area. "In the sweeps and destruction attacks from these keypoints," said the Kien Tuong account, "the enemy caused a certain amount of property damage. The life of the people was thrown into turmoil, and the people had to temporarily take refuge elsewhere, and production of food encountered difficulties."[14]

Both sides had two sets of plans for the Plain of Reeds. One approach was purely military, and each side aimed at controlling this terrain which offered the revolution's forces essential networks of liaison and supply routes and, in good times, secure base areas. An alternative plan was broader in scope and longer-term in concept. Saigon had long harbored the dream of turning the Plain of Reeds into a populated and prosperous area, with the underlying intention of creating a solid pro-government base that would deny this traditional refuge of rebels and dissidents to its opposition. According to the Kien Tuong province history, the pre-Easter Offensive GVN plan was to pacify 85 percent of the territory and control 95 percent of the population. In addition, Saigon was said to be planning to move 400,000 people, including a large number of anticommunist Hoa Hao sect members—in a move reminiscent of the French alliance with the sects in the early 1950s—and even overseas Vietnamese. From their ranks, 10,000 soldiers would be recruited.

A pro-GVN base would be created which would squeeze out the revolutionary forces, block their transportation routes, deny them a population to tax, and facilitate an economic blockade of whatever revolutionary areas remained.[15] This was, of course, a revival of an older idea from the Ngo Dinh Diem period, which had been implemented on a small scale in the form of the Agrovilles at Hau My and My Phuoc Tay in Dinh Tuong. As before, however, a deteriorating military situation made this vision impossible to implement. And, as the political and military situation deteriorated, the militantly anticommunist Hoa Hao also turned against the Saigon government, as they had turned against the French in 1954.[16] For its part, the Kien Tuong Party organization also wanted to expand and repopulate its areas, especially province Zone 4 (which included Tri Phap), and to pressure the few district towns in the province, assure unbroken supply lines, and "succeed in controlling 60,000 people" and creating a "production breakout from the population" who were presently cut off from their land or unable to put it into production.[17]

U.S. Assessment of Revolutionary Intentions and Capabilities in 1974

Despite the fact that by the late spring of 1974 the DAO was generally optimistic, and had presented the ARVN operations in the Tri Phap area as the long-awaited proof of its ability to deal with the military challenge of the communists without extensive U.S. support, in the same report there was also a more somber assessment of the overall balance in the Delta and the potential capacity of the revolutionary forces. DAO's May 1, 1974, report observed that "Of particular interest this year is the NVA's unprecedented emphasis on infiltration to COSVN" and that an increasing portion of North Vietnamese infiltration was being directed not toward Central Vietnam and the Central Highlands, but to COSVN's area of command in Nam Bo, including both the area northwest of Saigon and the Mekong Delta.

In their report at the beginning of November 1974, the DAO noted improvements in communist military logistics due to the rainy season and the increased ease of sampan transport, and some relative gains caused by a decline in territorial forces (militia) strength of the GVN in the upper Delta. The DAO perceived "little change in either the level or intensity of activity in the northern Delta (VC MR-2) during the quarter," though there was some military activity in the western two-thirds of Dinh Tuong province as well as Kien Phong province. "In mid-September [1974] communist units began a minor campaign to weaken RVNAF control in central and northeastern areas of Dinh Tuong province with the objective of facilitating logistical input into central VC MR-2." Both sides suffered casualties in these operations, and the DAO judged it a "costly stand-off period for both contestants."[18]

Despite the fact that the DAO characterized the middle of 1974 as a continuation of a "stand-off," which implied that not much had changed since the beginning of the year, or even since the cease-fire, there were some points in its November 1974 report that seem (especially in retrospect) to indicate that important challenges for the GVN were in store. Perhaps the most significant of these is the observation that the ARVN was now forced to fight a war with far fewer resources. "The enemy appears to have accurately assessed ARVN's recent reluctance to expend large quantities of artillery to support small isolated outposts under attack, and has exploited this situation by sharply increasing attacks on such positions. Lack of reactive fire support combined with sharply reduced air support has had a noticeable effect on the morale of RF/PF [Regional Forces / Popular Force] defenders. RVNAF intentionally abandoned many smaller outposts of marginal value. Each loss of an outpost, whether by intention or force, expands the enemy's area of influence."[19]

The growing weakness of Saigon's territorial forces concerned the American advisors, and somewhat dimmed the luster of the ARVN's performance in maintaining a hold on the Plain of Reeds, since there was some evidence that the revolutionary forces had simply avoided the larger units to concentrate on the more vulnerable militia. "The burden of security with the Region [IV Corps] fell increasingly on territorial forces," the DAO reported, "as the enemy found success in avoiding major unit confrontations and concentrated instead on vulnerable targets of opportunity." At the same time, the revolutionary forces had beefed up their firepower, while the GVN's air and artillery support was declining. "SA-7 missile activity continued at a high level in the southern Kien Phong/western Dinh Tuong missile belt. Fifteen missiles were fired during the period. Three aircraft, including a China Airlines C-123 chartered by Air America were destroyed." Attempts to interdict the roads increased sharply, and there was evidence of effective sapper operations in the four bridges destroyed in Dinh Tuong during the quarter.[20]

If things looked bleak for the GVN in Dinh Tuong province over the third quarter of 1974, the situation was about to get much worse. Already in November, the province report noted "a more intense phase of activity" with "the number of VC incidents sharply increasing." Highway 4 was now often blocked until nine or ten o'clock in the morning. "Détente" in Chau Thanh, Ben Tranh and Cho Gao districts, which had enjoyed relative security "is now apparently over as heavy fighting has erupted in these districts against outposts, village offices, and police stations."[21] The DAO province report for December stated that in the "period ending 14 Dec. 1974, the intensity of VC aggressive operations during this reporting period created the most depressing and demoralizing situation since the ceasefire. No area escaped attention; in fact relatively secure villages were subjected to enemy pressure." Sappers destroyed the electric transformer station on the outskirts of the province capital and province roads were being cut off. Unlike DAO province reports from the upper Delta earlier in 1974 which reported that the GVN was holding its own under pressure, now "GVN forces are generally reacting defensively to the enemy's initiatives."[22]

Hanoi and COSVN Plan Strategy for 1975

From September 30 to October 8, 1974, the Politburo met in Hanoi to analyze the situation and devise strategy for the coming year. It concluded that the situation was favorable enough that a ripening strategic opportunity could be exploited and pushed along. In this spirit, the Party leadership put forth a goal of winning the war in the South in two years, and selected the Central Highlands as the focus of large-scale continuous attacks during 1975. The Central Military Commission was directed to follow closely the U.S. reaction to the offensive of the 1974–75 dry season. Party Secretary General Le Duan concluded the meetings by saying that it was now time to lay down a resolve to finish the "national democratic revolution" in the South (although that had also been mentioned in Resolution 21 the previous year).[23] At the same time, in early October 1974, COSVN met and determined that 1975 would be a "hinge year" (a phrase also used to describe 1965 prior to the U.S.

intervention) and 1976 would see the victorious conclusion of the war."[24] The tone of these declarations and the contrast with the cautious assessments of early 1974 indicate how much and how quickly the situation had changed, at least in the eyes of the top Party leadership.

At the highest levels of the Party there were some who were not entirely sure about this optimistic assessment, perhaps recalling the overblown expectations for the Tet Offensive. General Tra acknowledged that "It was not easy to come to a consensus on this. There were all sorts of considerations to be weighed and analyses to be tossed back and forth."[25] Everyone agreed that the Saigon regime of Nguyen Van Thieu had been politically weakened by corruption scandals and general ineffectiveness, and that it had affected GVN troop morale. However, people like Tra felt that the guerrilla movement was still insufficiently developed, and that the main forces did not yet have a capacity to strike big knockout blows.

Some also cautioned that revolutionary actions would have to be cleverly devised so as not to provoke a U.S. intervention—perhaps thinking back the 1963–64 strategy of "go for broke." "All these concerns were very correct," wrote Tra. Nonetheless, Pham Hung, the top Politburo member in the South, was optimistic. Hung asserted that "The enemy is in a total crisis, even including the central puppet government, so it is not only in one dimension or one geographical area. The puppets will collapse with every increasing speed like a vehicle plunging down a slope, which can't cope with a sudden emergency." Whatever weakness the revolutionary side had would be overcome in the impending rainy season, leading to a successful dry-season offensive in 1975, which would, in turn, set the stage for ending the war in 1976.[26] The exact process by which the Party reached the conclusion in late 1974 that Saigon was weakening much faster than they had hitherto anticipated is not entirely clear, but it was in part due to a perception of political instability at the center, and perhaps reassurance that U.S. reintervention was very unlikely following the resignation of President Nixon in August, rather than any dramatic changes on the battlefield. "Even if you offer them candy," said Hanoi's Premier Pham Van Dong sarcastically, "they wouldn't come back."[27]

Even in Dinh Tuong, the political situation in the towns began to simmer, according to the province history. "In the towns and cities and the suburban areas the masses continually participated in struggles demanding democracy and a better standard of living. The anticorruption movement unfolded in an atmosphere of tension and pulled in many participants. On September 13, 1974, on the occasion of thirteen Catholic priests from Saigon coming down to My Tho, a big meeting was organized in the My Tho market to expose and denounce the corruption of the puppet president and demand his resignation. We mobilized 200 people to participate in order that they understand better the basic nature of the enemy administration."[28] It is telling that the initiative came from the strongly anticommunist Catholic priests, who at the time were in the forefront of opposition to President Thieu, and that this Saigon-based movement was spreading to places such as My Tho. Despite the fact that the Party took credit for assembling a fairly modest crowd, it is revealing that they had to be further educated about the "basic nature" of the GVN, suggesting that they were not even revolutionary sympathizers, and an indicator of how far the population in the urban areas had drifted away from the revolution. Still, even these small signs of urban unrest in the usually politically quiescent town of My Tho was an indication of the growing discontent with the Thieu government among the base of GVN supporters, which must have encouraged the Party planners to believe that the balance was shifting against their opponent even in the "urban areas."

Tra reveals that in the October 1974 meeting of COSVN, "we also discussed the possibility of a fast change in the situation, the puppet troops and puppet government might collapse earlier than we anticipated, particularly if a sudden political military event [coup] happened right in Saigon. In that event, possibly the B2 battlefield could, on its own, advance to the final assault on the enemy lair and nerve center and bring the war to an end, not wasting the opportunity." The problem was that COSVN lacked the main force troops for such an adventurous move. Tra asked for and was granted more regular troops, which were to be transferred to the South Vietnam battlefield by "unrolling the mat," that is, a sequential shuttling of forces to the nearest zone south of them, rather than waiting for troops to come all the way from the North.[29]

Since the 1975 dry-season campaign was designed to lay the groundwork for a final win-the-war offensive in 1976, Tra was directed to lay out a plan for attacking Saigon. He was especially concerned about the prospect of the GVN pulling back to a defensible position linking Saigon and the Mekong Delta, and frequently referred to General James Gavin's "enclave strategy" of pulling back into a defensible position in highly populated lowland areas such as the Mekong Delta. Tra recalled that the Diem government was once saved from a coup by reinforcements from the Delta and that the French had focused on securing Saigon and the Delta in laying the groundwork for their reconquest of Vietnam in 1946. At the time (late 1974), he admits, Thieu denounced this as a surrender, but Tra was sure that when push came to shove, Thieu would be forced to consider shrinking back to a truncated South Vietnam consisting of Saigon and the Mekong Delta.

Thus COSVN's planning for an assault on Saigon was not designed simply as a conventional military attack on an objective (Tra implied that this had been the problem in the 1972 offensive, planned by unimaginative Northern generals in central Vietnam), but would have to be conducted in a way that would cut off this last strategic option of the GVN, and accelerate demoralization and confusion in Saigon. Although Hanoi had targeted the Central Highlands as the main priority for 1975, a concern about keeping the GVN from retreating to the Delta and undermining its existing forces there and preventing them from reinforcing Saigon was an integral element of COSVN's thinking about the final stage of the war; in Tra's words, "If you want to liberate Saigon, first of all you have to isolate it from its surrounding areas, don't give it a route to escape or regroup, don't let it get reinforcements, surround it so there is no escape—only disintegration and panicked confusion."[30] COSVN plans for My Tho were heavily influenced by this concern about isolating Saigon from the Mekong Delta. My Tho was to concentrate on expanding the liberated areas in the Plain of Reeds to bring them closer the Highway 4, and facilitate cutting off this lifeline, as well as conducting attacks which would tie down the ARVN Seventh and Ninth Divisions and prevent them from reinforcing Saigon. It also discussed contingency plans to send two regiments from the lower Delta to strengthen an attack on Saigon from the south. The other priority was to strengthen the revolutionary position east of Highway 4 in the traditionally weak and exposed area of Cho Gao district and Go Cong. "To assure the attack from the south of Saigon," writes Tra, "the COSVN command headquarters planned to create two routes of troop advance: one from Long

Dinh [in the 20/7 zone] and My Tho through Cho Gao, Tan Tru, Tan An and Can Duoc, Can Giuoc and Nha Be, and the other from Ben Tre through Go Cong, and up through Can Duoc, Can Giuoc, and Nha Be to attack Districts 7 and 8 [in Saigon]. Both routes had to go through our weak zones and had a lot of enemy posts, the terrain was difficult as well as being far from our liberated base areas," so considerable advanced planning to prepare these eastern routes would be needed.[31]

Before finalizing these ambitious plans, Tra and Pham Hung were recalled to Hanoi in mid-November 1974 to meet with the Politburo. Tra's deputy Le Duc Anh reminded him, "Please try to present the case to Party Central to ask for more troops for our battlefield. Fourth Army Group is still lame—too weak—the weakest of all the corps, but it is also the main force of the key battlefield. It's hard to figure."[32] Upon arriving in Hanoi, Tra was told that he would get his reinforcements, but that COSVN had to earmark 40 percent of them for the Mekong Delta to strengthen province and district forces. This was because the NVA general staff had now decided that the Mekong Delta would be the main battlefield in 1975, and efforts should be concentrated on opposing pacification and gaining a greater population base to change the balance of forces another step in a favorable direction.

The task of the big units in eastern Nam Bo and the Central Highlands would be to expand the supply corridors to places like the Mekong Delta, and save themselves for 1976 when the big offensive would take place. Tra was not at all pleased to hear this plan of the NVA high command, which envisaged a much smaller scale of military operations, since it contradicted COSVN's own plan, which had already been presented to the Politburo and the Party Central Military Commission. He complained to Le Duc Tho, who responded with a compromise position: conserve forces in 1975 and save up for a massive effort in 1976 to end the war. "We cannot and must not let the war drag on," said Tho.[33] Eventually, Tra persuaded Tho to support a more ambitious attack plan for the spring of 1975, which started with an assault on the Central Highlands town of Ban Me Thuot—whose fall in March 1975 started the cascade of dominoes that led to the collapse of the Saigon government.

Intensification of Revolutionary Military Operations and Guerrilla Activities in Late 1974

While Tra was in Hanoi, the more modest plan based on pushing guerrilla warfare and opposing pacification in the Mekong Delta began to unfold. On December 12, 1974, a series of attacks in all areas of Nam Bo commenced, including attacks on the Tri Phap area and the 20/7 zone in southern Cai Lay.[34] By this time, the region forward command had moved to the Ba Dua area on the western edge of the 20/7 zone.

Chin Om, the My Tho province Party secretary from 1962–68, had just returned after a four-year odyssey. In late 1969, while he was working at the region in charge of the Farmers' Association and Liberation Front activities, his always-fragile health again deteriorated. COSVN sent him to Hanoi via Phnom Penh (while Prince Norodom Sihanouk was still in power) and China. While in transit in Quangzhou, his group reacted with cold disdain to a welcoming Chinese group which thrust copies of Chairman Mao's "little red book" at the Vietnamese delegation. The once warm revolutionary comradeship between the two countries had now soured because of "complicated political developments in China which we didn't much welcome." After a checkup in Hanoi, Chin Om was sent to the Soviet Union with suspected cancer. Although the diagnosis was wrong, he spent a year in Russia convalescing from a variety of debilitating illnesses and was impressed by the solicitude of the Russian doctors. He returned to Hanoi but suffered another heath setback and was in the Viet-Xo [Soviet] hospital when the Christmas bombing of 1972 forced all patients to evacuate the city. In 1973 Chin Om was sufficiently recovered to return to the South in a jeep driven down the Ho Chi Minh Trail to Loc Ninh. Stopping off at COSVN, he was offered the job of running the COSVN Farmers' Association Office, but his old comrades at Region 2 asked that he return to the central Delta. After a tense motor bike ride through hostile territory in Cambodia controlled by Pol Pot, who was "openly provoking" Vietnam, he reached the region forward command. In his travels, Chin Om had experienced the full range of the larger context of My Tho's own war in all its complexity: China, the Soviet Union, the Nixon-ordered bombings, neutral Cambodia under Sihanouk, and post-Sihanouk Cambodia and the Khmer Rouge. Clearly the revolutionary world was not what it had been, but now the revolutionary struggle in Vietnam was reaching its climactic stage.

Chin Om finally reached the Region 2 forward headquarters in the 20/7 zone in October 1974. It was the first time he had been in the province in six years The change was striking. "In 1968, the region only had forces concentrated at the regimental level and the enemy's military forces were intact and operating alongside an American army with all kinds of firepower and a wealth of material supplies. Now the region had divisions with the latest weapons and equipment. The Americans had pulled out. The puppet forces had suffered defeats and were demoralized. The new situation was full of promise. The cadres, soldiers, and masses were fired up and confident."[35]

Military operations in the traditionally weaker eastern part of Dinh Tuong intensified with a surge of military activity in Cho Gao starting in November 1974 which began to seriously undermine the GVN position in this formerly secure district. The 514C Battalion suddenly sprang to life in a series of attacks on posts. As a gesture of psychological warfare, the corpses of Saigon militia killed in these attacks were dragged to the market town of Cho Ong Van and the district capital of Cho Gao to demoralize the GVN supporters there. The NVA 2009B Battalion also joined the battle. The combined operations of these units, says the My Tho province history, opened up the vital liaison route across Highway 4, and gained control of much of the northwestern part of the district, "turning Cho Gao from a weak movement to one where the liberation uprisings and expansion were developing very strongly."[36]

"To support the main battlefield in Cho Gao and Go Cong," writes the My Tho province history, "the region Party committee brought in its own Eighth Division and COSVN's Fifth Division to operate in Zone 4 of Kien Tuong [the Tri Phap area] and in northern Cai Be."[37] In Kien Tuong, the Saigon forces were still strong, with elements of the ARVN Seventh and Ninth Divisions active in the province, confronting the two NVA divisions. The Party history of Kien Tuong makes the extravagant claim that during this December offensive, revolutionary forces in Military Region 2 conquered 320 posts, and "basically" or completely liberated thirty-one villages. "After this phase, the situation in the Mekong Delta took an important turn. We gained control of two and a half million of seven million people, among which 1.44 million were [newly] liberated." Even by this account, however, the operations that had the greatest impact on the overall situation in the South took place in eastern and western Nam Bo, not in the central Delta.[38] For its part, the My Tho history claims that the 1974–75 dry-season offensive resulted in "the liberation of 88 villages, 309 hamlets, basic liberation of 26 villages, liberation of 80,000 people and mobilization of 5,000 families to return to their old homes."[39] Another revolutionary account claims a total of 45,000 "political and military proselytizing forces" at the beginning of 1975.[40]

These impressionistic statistics are belied by the fact that the serious collapse of the GVN position in Dinh Tuong, even as depicted in official revolutionary accounts, does not appear to have happened until the Ho Chi Minh "Great Spring Offensive" of 1975 was well advanced. Still, the deep fissures in Saigon's hold over the upper Delta were clearly in evidence by the beginning of 1975. A U.S. State Department reporter in the Delta covering Dinh Tuong province confirms in his January 1975 report the deteriorating situation in the northwestern part of Cho Gao and the occupation of two villages in the area. Within the town of My Tho itself, a demolition unit blew up the headquarters of a city ward. The routes to Hau My and Moc Hoa in the Plain of Reeds were open only periodically, when military conveys were sent through. Militia units in Dinh Tuong were chronically understrength, and Regional Force battalions averaged 30 to 50 percent of their authorized number.[41]

U.S. Assessment of GVN Ability to Cope with the Growing Threat

DAO reports on Dinh Tuong and surrounding provinces offer fragmentary but suggestive evidence of a perceived decline in administrative capacity as well as military effectiveness during 1974. Major programs such as the Land to the Tiller land reform appear to have bogged down in corruption or were deflected to marginal areas. Because of the decline in U.S. assistance, the GVN once again became dependent on rice from the Mekong Delta, whose provinces were assigned quotas for delivery to a central General Supply Administration in Saigon. (an interesting prefiguring of the fixed price-compulsory quota rice collection system of the post-1975 communist state).These quotas proved increasingly difficult to meet as the GVN gradually lost control over this key commodity in a "battle for rice" as its control over territory slipped and numerous small unauthorized rice mills sprang up, challenging the control that the GVN had previously attained by restricting mills to a relatively few large ventures which could be closely monitored. Province level tax collection was adequate but clearly encountering problems in 1974. DAO province reports noted the increasing unreliability of the HES reporting and the growing tendency of province officials to cover up bad news. As the security situation deteriorated the province and district officials became increasingly passive in performance of their duties. The high turnover of province and district leaders in 1974 was probably both a cause and effect of the slippage of GVN administrative capacity.

The DAO's reaction to the upsurge in revolutionary activity in the Delta in late 1974 and early 1975 was cautious concern. Its February 1975 report noted, "In December, the NVA opened up with great intensity in the Delta, surpassing by far previously recorded activity since the so-called cease fire." In contrast to the gloomy December 1974 conclusion of Warren Parker, the DAO reporter for Dinh Tuong province, that local "GVN forces are generally reacting defensively to the enemy's initiatives," the composite DAO report at higher levels asserted that in January 1975 "RVNAF reacted magnificently. While RVNAF is not yet facing a countrywide offensive, the NVA is clearly determined to make substantial gains in all areas within SVN." In the Mekong Delta, according to the DAO, the purpose of these escalating operations was to "extend control of land and people, and drive wedges into cracks which the VC/NVA perceive in the GVN/RVNAF defense structure." In a more cautious tone, the report concluded that "In line with these objectives to accelerate an already disturbing erosion of RVNAF strength and control in outlying areas, the Communists increased their force structure both quantitatively and qualitatively by forming the 8th and 4th Divisions from already existing units, and by committing the 5th Division to combat missions in the upper Delta."

The DAO noted a strong threat against the Plain of Reeds district town in Tuyen Nhon, and other less intense attacks in Dinh Tuong and Kien Tuong, but did not see any "major loss of terrain control for RVNAF" although "remaining areas of the upper Delta also were hit hard by harassment attacks and numerous shellings." ARVN forces were "kept on the defensive, but did not suffer major losses," although "routes 4, 20, and 29 in Dinh Tuong were frequently mined, as was Route 7A in Vinh Long." The DAO cautioned that "Future pressure could be more severe if the 8th and 5th Divisions are able to conduct coordinated attacks, which could represent the stiffest challenge the RVNAF has faced since the ceasefire." In the lower Delta, the situation was considerably worse, however, and "throughout the southern Delta provinces, VC/NVA units were able to drive RVNAF out of considerable expanses of countryside."

In contrast to DAO's cautious optimism about the military situation in the upper Delta, and the conclusion that the GVN, though threatened, had not yet lost territory in key Plain of Reeds locations like Tuyen Nhon, General Tra wrote that by the time the Politburo and the Central Military Commission met on December 18, 1974 to make the fateful decisions that launched the final military campaign of the war, Tuyen Nhon had already been lost to the GVN. "By that day, all of B2 [South Vietnam] had entered the first phase of the dry season campaign and had scored victories. In the Mekong Delta, huge chunks of the pacification program of the enemy had been destroyed . . . We had liberated the sector [district] of Hung Long in the lower Delta and the district seat and administrative capital of Tuyen Nhon in the upper Delta. This was the first time in the Delta that we had wiped out a district seat and seized control of it."[42]

By this time, the "poor man's war" had considerably limited Saigon's ability to rely on its traditional tactics of countering attacks with massive air and artillery. The DAO reported in February 1975 that "artillery support for outposts under attack was limited to two rounds, after which permission for additional support had to be requested from higher headquarters." Even so, the war of the main force units and major outposts had not yet turned decisively against the ARVN. The war in the villages, however, was another matter. Warren Parker, the U.S. official who reported on Dinh Tuong, gives the following account of the situation in February 1975. "Although the number of VC initiated incidents have decreased during this reporting period, the overall security condition of this province continues to breed pessimism. The enemy continues to have the initiative and to successfully overrun village offices and outposts at will. Except for the district town, enemy forces appear to "own" all of Ben Tranh district and much of Cho Gao. During 1974 in VC Cho Gao district, which includes portions of GVN Ben Tranh and Chau Thanh districts, the VC collected 135.8 *million* piasters in riceland taxes alone. The VC tax goal for Dinh Tuong province for 1975 is 2.4 *billion* piasters, or about five times that of the GVN goal of 0.5 billion piasters."[43] GVN Regional Force companies in the province averaged thirty to forty men and in some, according to the province chief, the officers and NCOs outnumbered the soldiers. "For the last few months, losses average over 300 more than recruitments; and of these losses there are three desertions to one loss due to enemy action." In this situation, Parker noted, "it is no mystery why RF/PF forces avoid contact with the enemy and resort to huddling behind barricades during hours of darkness; nor is it difficult to understand how easily VC forces can dominate the villages and hamlets. It isn't mere military aid which is needed; it is discipline, motivation, incentive, and individual commitment, which is sadly lacking."[44]

Morale in the Regional and Popular Forces was probably not bolstered by an order from the IV Corps commander to the Dinh Tuong province chief to transfer 700 Regional Force soldiers to the ARVN Seventh Division in a desperate attempt to bring that unit up to strength, despite the fact that Dinh Tuong was short 4,806 Regional and Popular Force soldiers at the time.[45] The ARVN also began to evacuate troops from the Plain of Reeds so that they could regroup and protect Highway 4. By these expedients they managed to assemble a force of about 26,000 troops.[46] As the Saigon forces retreated into a shell, the revolutionary side continued to expand its control of population and territory. If it is accurate, the projected 1975 figure for the revolution's province tax of 2.4 billion piasters is a staggering increase from the actual collections of 312,805,539 piasters in taxes for the year 1974. Even if the actual revenues of 1975 were only a portion of the target figure, this is still an impressive leap in the revolution's perceived capacity to collect revenue—and not an implausible one given the fact that the GVN estimated that by February 1975 the revolution controlled about 40 percent of the riceland in the province.[47]

A Rapid Shift in Momentum: Late 1974 and Early 1975

It is not clear exactly when the rapid turnabout in territorial control took place, but the likelihood is that most of the major revolutionary gains came in a relatively short period during late 1974 and the first two months of 1975. General Tra's report to the Politburo conference in Hanoi on December 18, 1974, mentioned the "things which have just recently come up, our strength and forward progress and the enemy's weakness and decline."[48] In early 1974 there was already evidence of the disintegration of the GVN's "Land to the Tiller program."[49] No doubt the erosion of this program was much more serious by early 1975, though this is not mentioned explicitly in U.S. reports of that period—probably because the GVN land reform was by then irrelevant. Clearly, whatever impact the Saigon land reform program had on the local population, its efforts at increasing tax revenues and pushing local development had been eclipsed by the rapid turnabout in territorial control.

General Tran Van Don, at the time a vice premier of the GVN, came to Dinh Tuong in November 1974 to evaluate the situation and, in particular, the security situation along Highway 4, the lifeline to Saigon from the Mekong Delta. According to a DAO report the briefings he received from province officials were "optimistic to the point of fabrication." After a round of on the spot inspections, Don quickly realized that the reality was "entirely different" from his official briefings. He returned to the province to let these officials know that he was now "aware of the true security situation in Dinh Tuong province," and that "the security situation had deteriorated." By hiding the real situation, he told the province officials, they made it difficult for the national leadership to "take proper remedial action or provide adequate support . . ."[50] Even before the start of the final offensive in Central Vietnam, the GVN was in serious, if not terminal, decline in Dinh Tuong.

When Tran Van Tra returned from Hanoi, he plunged into series of meetings with COSVN's military command beginning on March 3. During his absence, COSVN had discussed the problem of how to put pressure on Saigon from the south, and had concluded that it was necessary to step up pressure on Cho Gao district in Dinh Tuong immediately, as well as on Go Cong and southern Long An, "because our movement there was not yet strong and could not guarantee that our armed forces could move in close to [Saigon's] districts 4, 7, and 8." COSVN commanders were also worried about the lack of strength in main force units in this crucial area and called them "still far too weak." To provide some reinforcement, COSVN decided to try to mobilize the old guerrilla warfare support system, especially in central and western Nam Bo, and rely on political and guerrilla forces to back up the regular units. At this point, COSVN's capacity to coordinate all these elements was still limited by its determination to keep the Hanoi decision to launch a major offensive secret, and its high-level cadres were strictly forbidden to talk about (1) completing the national democratic revolution, (2) the aim of ending the war in 1975–76, and (3) the General Offensive and Uprising. As far as the lower levels were concerned, the plan was still as laid out in Resolution 21 of 1973, which, as noted in the previous chapter anticipated a prolonged period of struggle in which the people and resources of the Delta would be the key to laying the foundation for final victory sometime in the future.[51]

In March 1975, the My Tho province Party committee convened a meeting of village Party secretaries in My Hanh Dong village in Cai Lay. This was the first time in years that such an assembly was possible, and is another indicator of how much the security situation had changed. The assembly resolved to "push forward the timetable for the liberation" of the province in accordance with a directive from Military Region 2, and specifically to "basically liberate" the district of Cho Gao, as well as to open up many liaison corridors along Highway 4. By April or May they hoped to have gained control of the main ARVN strongpoints and the districts. To accomplish these ambitious goals, the province formed a new Ap Bac battalion, expanded the district local forces from two to five companies, and made sure every village had from two to four platoons. Military Region 2 sent two regiments from the Eighth Division to operate along with the 514C and 2009B Battalions, with the result that the key road crossing of Highway 4 to the east was now secured by the conquest of most of northern Ben Tranh, and the heavily Cao Dai and Catholic strongpoint of Phu My was totally isolated.[52]

While the province effort was concentrated in the eastern part of Dinh Tuong, the Military Region 2 forces were active in the west. In January 1975, Tam Phuong returned from an eight-month convalescence in Hanoi, with a message from Tran Van Tra that the Politburo had decided to end the war in two years. Stopping over at COSVN, he delivered the message and was reassigned to his old post as head of Military Region 2. Assessing the results of the past months' campaigning, Tam Phuong concluded that the military operations in the Plain of Reeds had failed to secure a strong rear base in this vital area. He proposed a shift of focus to General Le Duc Anh at COSVN. Instead of continuing to battle with the ARVN in the Tri Phap (Zone 4) area, whose open terrain left the region's troops vulnerable to artillery, Tam Phuong now wanted to concentrate on the strategic "wagon wheel" area of northern Cai Be, where six canals come together southwest of Tri Phap. With the ARVN cleared out of this area, Zone 4 would be easier to control. In mid-March, the 24th Regiment finally overcame ARVN forces in the "wagon wheel" area after a fierce series of battles and counterattacks. "In two weeks, we had laid the gut area of the Plain of Reeds wide open, including northern Cai Be and northern Cai Lay districts, Zone 4 of Kien Tuong province, My An district (Kien Phong), and Kien Van district (Sa Dec)," wrote Tam Phuong.[53] The main northern line of defense in Dinh Tuong province was thus undermined. At the same time, other region forces opened up a corridor from Tay Ninh into the Plain of Reeds. Tran Van Tra asserts that by the end of March, "we had completed the expansion and connection of important bases, which were now completed and secured from the Plain of Reeds west of Saigon, running to the east and north of Tay Ninh to Phuoc Long, War Zone A in northern Bien Hoa, and over to Binh Tuy and Ba Ria on the seacoast. Saigon was thus completely surrounded by us from the west to the north and northeast."[54] The obvious missing link was the south, the upper Mekong Delta, and the area southeast of Saigon.

The following month, emboldened by the collapse of the GVN in Central Vietnam, Military Region 2 ordered My Tho to prepare for an uprising, and to gain full control of the Cho Gao Canal and cut Highway 4 in as many places as possible, thus isolating Saigon from the Delta and allowing the region to bring three regiments into position to advance on Saigon from the south. Le Duan, the secretary general of the Party and the former leader of the revolution in the South, sent a letter to Le Duc Tho at COSVN dated March 29, 1975, stating that "In reality, the battle for Saigon has begun." He instructed that "a crucial matter is that we boldly send troop reinforcements right away to carry out the missions of cutting [lines of communication] and strategic encirclement of Saigon from the direction of My Tho and Tan An."[55]

At the beginning of April, COSVN passed on three daunting orders to Military Region 2. The first was to cut the lifelines from the Delta to Saigon: Highway 4 and the Cho Gao Canal. Second, the region was ordered to send an assault force to enter Saigon from the south, and to seize and occupy the General Police Directorate. Third, along with accomplishing these other missions, the region was to liberate its entire territory using its own resources. Realizing that it would be difficult to move large units from My Tho to Saigon, since the intervening territory was considered a "weak area" for the revolution, Chin Hai, the former My Tho province Party secretary, (1968–73) was put in charge of arranging security and providing logistical support for this effort.[56]

The My Tho Province Committee Issues the Order for an Uprising

On April 9, 1975, the My Tho province Party committee issued orders for the uprising, with the intention of overrunning Cho Gao and then advancing on to My Tho city. With three battalions seizing the villages of Quon Long and Binh Phuc Nhat, the revolutionary forces were able to block the critical Cho Gao Canal. "This victory made the enemy in the remaining string of posts hole up inside to defend themselves and created conditions for the masses to rise up and participate in digging up roads, destroying posts, and setting up roadblocks, as well as calling on the soldiers to go home and earn a living." By the middle of April the big units from the region were able to safely cross Highway 4 near the Trung Luong intersection and position themselves for the final advance on Saigon.[57]

Now the pace of events was outrunning the strategic planners. Military Region 2 had intended to use two divisions to seize Moc Hoa, the capital of Kien Tuong, and slice straight down to Cai Lay district town, then on to Tan Hiep near the former province airfield and "annihilate" the ARVN Seventh and Ninth Divisions. When they saw how quickly things were moving, the region decided not to take the chance of getting bogged down in fighting in a remote location like Moc Hoa, and sent the NVA Fifth Division due east across the Plain of Reeds to cut Highway 4 near Ben Luc, the main bridge in Long An province. However, the unit was not strong enough to overcome well-fortified ARVN positions. The region then shifted these units south to Dinh Tuong, to attempt to cut Highway 4 through that province, but they were soon diverted to the advance on Saigon.[58]

The March on Saigon

Both COSVN and Military Region 2 forces were mobilized to drive up from Dinh Tuong and enter Saigon from the south. Chin Hai (Le Van Pham), the former Party leader of Dinh Tuong who replaced Chin Om in 1968 and who was now a leading Military Region 2 cadre, was made the political officer of this makeshift corps.[59] General Tra waited for these forces to get into position. He was worried because the southern route of advance was "the most difficult because the terrain was complicated, it was far from our bases, and the troops would have to pass through areas that had been occupied by the enemy for a long time. The route was long and had to pass through heavily populated areas, and it wasn't true in every case that our infrastructure was more numerous than the families of the puppet soldiers, who had not yet seen the light."[60]

Tra was so impressed by the diary of a cadre who made this difficult march that he quoted it at length in his book. This was a small but important part of the final offensive, writes Tra, small because the southern wing of the assault consisted only of three regiments and two light infantry battalions, with no tanks, anti-aircraft, or heavy artillery like the other much larger wings coming from the north and west of Saigon. Tran Ham Ninh received the order to move from the Highway 4 interdiction mission on to Saigon. The drive from the south on Saigon was important because it emphasized that the city was surrounded and prevented reinforcements from the Delta. Ninh's diary reads:

> April 9, 1975: We say farewell to the beloved 20/7 zone (the area belonging to Cai Be and Cai Lay of My Tho province lying between Highway 4 and the Mekong River). Why is it that this time I feel a lingering nostalgia? Only last week we had to leave for a time, but came back after a few days. Today we depart, will we ever return? No way of knowing. . . . Seated on the sampan going past the My Long base. An enemy battalion ran past here two days ago. The [National Liberation Front] blue and red flag fluttering looks so beautiful. The current slowly moves along, and seems indifferent to whether or not there is still a mercenary's corpse lying in a corner of this base. Coming to Nhi Qui, the sun has not yet set. Guerrillas surround the Bo Keo post, so the enemy artillery fires wildly. The enemy infantry along Highway 4 has not yet retreated. By midnight we are far from the 20/7 zone, but our food and camp are passable.[61]

The next entry reads:

> April 10, 1975: Tan Hoi, a piece of brave and stubborn land. The indomitable base of the My Tho province unit. Today in the command headquarters of the unit there is only Tam Cong [Deputy commander of the province unit. Tam Cong was a poor peasant from Cai Lay who had been launched into a command position in the 514th Battalion and named a "Hero of the Army" during the radical "motivation of the peasants" campaign in 1965, according to DT110]. . . . 1500 on the road over to Tam Hiep to meet the 88th Regiment. The brothers are all ready. Through Bao Dinh [a small river bordering the My Tho province capital], I meet someone I know. Can't say anything, because the army is moving on. As for my friend, he has the task of staying behind and holding on to this land. We skirt around many houses. Inside the houses is complete silence, but certainly the mothers and sisters and kids in those houses can't sleep because the shuffle of feet, even though our step is light, resounds to the bottom of their hearts. They all lie there, tossing, and their hearts go out to us. Because the coordination was not good, we got to Luong Hoa Lac but no one was there to meet us.[62]

The formation continued to trudge silently past Cho Ong Van and Quon Long, where they were supposed to link up with the E24 Regiment, but again coordination was lacking and not all of the other units showed up. On April 15, the two groups were all assembled and departed Quon Long. "So muddy! Who would believe mud up to your stomach!" Finally they reached the Vam Co Dong River. Because they had no transportation across the river, it took until April 30 to reach the outskirts of Saigon, where they heard the surrender announcement over the radio.[63] Other units of the Region 2 assault force did make it into Saigon, and seized the General Police Directorate on schedule.[64]

Revolutionary Takeover in My Tho

In My Tho the revolutionary forces grew as the end drew near. The Region pulled the E1 Regiment out of Ben Tre and sent it along with another battalion to My Tho to reinforce the anticipated final attack on the province town and the ARVN Seventh Division base in Dong Tam. According to the province military history, after the Province Party Committee's April 9 uprising order, the province unit pulled up 1,000 village guerrillas and somehow found 797 new recruits to form a new "Ap Bac" Battalion. The province history asserts that at this juncture there were 28 local force companies: 5 in Cai Be, 7 in Southern Cai Lay, 4 in Northern Cai Lay, 3 in Southern Chau Thanh, 2 in Northern Chau Thanh, and 7 in Cho Gao.[65] It is difficult to assess these claims and evaluate the military effectiveness of these units, but the numbers of people under arms had undoubtedly grown substantially since the 1973 cease-fire. A postwar history of the Party Youth Group in My Tho indicates that its ranks swelled as the triumph of the revolution drew near. "Tested by reality, the number of youth admitted to the Group increased rapidly. Prior to liberation, My Tho province had 3,700 members. After April 30, the total membership rose to 5,200. The membership of the Youth Group in My Tho city rose from 170 to 420 during this period.[66] It is not clear how many of these new revolutionaries were what many Vietnamese contemptuously referred to as "April 30 cadres," who jumped on the bandwagon at a late hour, but it did show which way the wind was blowing.

As the momentum was clearly shifting in favor of the revolution, "military proselytizing" began to have an effect. One revolutionary account describes the surrender of a number of posts, including Quon Long, an important control point along the Cho Gao Canal where "twenty soldiers' families who had been educated by us poured into the post. The mother and the wife of the post commander hugged him tight, which allowed the soldiers to take their weapons and surrender to the revolution."[67] Once again, the situational change was the key to prompting political action. Whether or not they supported the revolution, this family saw the handwriting on the wall and acted to protect their interests by keeping the son/husband alive.

As a result of the revolution's rapid success in Cho Gao, the GVN elements were "cut off from each other, holing up, stretched thin," and this "created conditions for the people of Go Cong and My Tho to serve well the big units of Military Region 2 in mid-April 1975, which crossed Highway 4, crossed the Bao Dinh River [on the edge of the city of My Tho], went over to Cho Gao and assembled at the designated time and place to participate in the assault from the southwest [against Saigon] of the Ho Chi Minh campaign."[68] On April 24, the district town of Cho Gao was surrounded. The big units then went on toward Saigon, leaving three local battalions to finish the conquest of Cho Gao. The district headquarters surrendered at 1130 on April 30, 1975.[69] The long-time nemesis of the revolution, Phu My, was also overrun in the morning. Then came Vinh Kim district, which surrendered at noon.

According to the official revolutionary history of the final days in My Tho, Cai Be district fell next. "At about noon on April 30 about 1,000 masses came in and seized the Cau Sat iron bridge, and about 4,000 people on the spot supported them, with the district forces surrounding the place, and using loudspeakers to call on the enemy to surrender. About 300 [soldiers] remaining in the subsector waited for our forces to arrive to turn over power. At 1830 hours on April 30, the local armed forces and masses came to force the district chief to surrender, and Cai Be town was completely liberated."[70] Cai Lay district held out longer, although parts of the town were taken over starting from 0800 on April 30. A nearby battalion of the ARVN Seventh Division was persuaded to disperse, and an M113 taken over from ARVN was brought into the district town. The district chief, with only two platoons, held out until 0300 on May 1, when he was forced to surrender.[71]

In My Tho itself, both clandestine agents and "legal" supporters of the revolution were active during the morning of April 30, spreading rumors and attempting to demoralize the GVN. At around 1500 hours a group of students at the prestigious Nguyen Dinh Chieu High School forced the school principal to open up a small arsenal of weapons under his control, and distribute them to teachers and students to set up a "protection unit" for the school. One of the student leaders who was active in the revolutionary takeover of My Tho city was the son of a high-level province cadre, who himself had been a leader in the student revolutionary movement in My Tho in 1945 during the August Revolution, and after 1975 became the vice chairman of the province party committee. Despite the close police surveillance of the city's population, this young revolutionary had lived and studied undisturbed in My Tho while his father led the guerrilla struggle from villages.[72]

At 1630 hours, revolutionary troops filtered into the heart of the city, where about 2,000 confused ARVN soldiers were milling around on the main thoroughfare of Hung Vuong, and by 1700 the My Tho Party committee told them to turn in their weapons and go home.

A high school teacher in My Tho said that there was no fighting. The troops suddenly appeared, and from then on were in control of the situation.[73] At about the same time, a group of demonstrators led by the armed security police of Military Region 2 took over the jail and released all the political prisoners, and the armed city unit along with some activists in the city took over the province headquarters. By 2300 on April 30, most of My Tho was in revolutionary hands. On the eastern side of the city an ARVN armored squadron continued to hold out. At midnight, the E1 Regiment entered the city and commenced an attack on this unit. By 0500 the following morning My Tho was completely under revolutionary control.[74]

Outside the city at the Dong Tam base, headquarters of the Seventh Division, commanding General Tran Van Hai gave orders to resist to the end. Some units that had been operating in Cho Gao tried to retreat to Dong Tam, but were stopped east of My Tho city by a mob of demonstrators, and the force abandoned their vehicles and melted away. The soldiers in Dong Tam, seeing that no reinforcements were coming, also shed their uniforms and left. General Hai committed suicide at 0300 on May 1. In all, the revolutionary side counted nearly 30,000 GVN soldiers involved in the final defense of Dinh Tuong.[75] At noon on May 2, the last resisting ARVN unit surrendered the Hau My base.[76]

Many of the main actors in this revolutionary drama survived to witness the end. However, the exceptional hardships of many years of demanding struggle had taken their toll on the health of many top Party leaders in the central Mekong Delta. Chin Om had been sent to the Soviet Union in 1970 for treatment, and did not return to My Tho until 1974—and then only with the intercession of Sau Duong, the Region 2 Party secretary who was in Hanoi in April and May 1973 attending a series of expanded Politburo meetings. Sau Duong persuaded the Unification Commission of the Communist Party Central Committee to allow Chin Om to return to the South.[77] Chin Om's account leaves it unclear whether special intervention was needed to allow him to return to the South because of the Party's solicitude for his health, or because the Party may have felt it needed a younger and healthier leadership in the South for the closing act of the "national-democratic" revolution and its next phase of "building socialism." Sau Duong himself was soon removed from the front line of leadership in the central Mekong Delta. After his meetings with the Politburo in May 1973, he was sent to East Germany for convalescence and medical treatment. He briefly returned to Region 2 in March 1974 to be present at a Party election to determine his successor as Party secretary of Region 2. After several close ballots, a younger leader (Huynh Chau So, also known as Nam Be) defeated Viet Thang—a veteran former Party leader in My Tho, and Sau Duong was transferred to COSVN.[78] In 1976 he was asked to step down from his position in the Party Central Committee in order to "reduce the number of comrades who are old and in bad health and select comrades to put into the Central Committee who are of an age where they can rejuvenate the new Central Committee.[79]

Viet Thang ("Victorious Viet") had been a leading region cadre since the early 1960s, and it was he who headed the transitional military government of My Tho City *(uy ban quan quan)* after the revolutionary takeover.[80] Chin Hai (Le Van Pham) was in charge of the political and logistics support for the move of region forces through the eastern districts and later became the province Party committee secretary of My Tho once again. Ba Chim (the "Birdman") had been in charge of the region Party committee office since 1967, and was likely in My Tho at that time. It is possible that the last five province Party leaders were all in My Tho in April 1975. Chin Om, Sau Danh, the main military leader of the province for most of the post-1960 period, and the recently appointed province Party secretary, Sau Binh (Nguyen Cong Binh), who had been in charge of the revolutionary movement in Cai Be district for much of this time, awoke near Ap Bac on April 30, 1975, to observe an ARVN helicopter being shot down by local guerrillas. They turned on the radio just in time to hear the last GVN leader, General Duong Van Minh, read the surrender proclamation over Radio Saigon.

Because My Tho city had been elevated to a separate status equivalent to a province at the start of the offensive and because the surrounding troops were mostly controlled by Region 2, the region was in charge of things there and Cai Lay became the central focus of the province's efforts. The revolutionaries had planned to make Cai Lay their provisional province capital. Chin Om was dispatched together with Sau Binh to participate in the takeover. At 2100 they entered the district town. The Cai Lay district chief held out until his troops got word that a captured ARVN artillery base at My Phuoc Tay was about to shell his headquarters.[81] The troops melted away, and by the middle of the night the GVN district chief had surrendered and was put in the town jail. Chin Om writes:

> On May 1, 1975, Cai Lay town was decked out with flags. The civil servants were all present in their offices. All aspects of life returned to normal. The markets still were held, electricity and communications were uninterrupted, the sanitation workers cleaned up the huge piles of garbage that littered the streets. Every corner of the town was crowded with people. The masses from the rural areas flocked in to see the liberated town. The atmosphere was upbeat. It truly was a big festival celebrating the historic victory. I heaved a sigh of relief. Suddenly, I felt as though a heavy weight had been lifted from my shoulders.[82]

The Revolutionary Victory in My Tho in Historical Perspective

Whether the finale of the long struggle for My Tho involved a "general insurrection and uprising" is hard to say. Even if it did, it would be harder still to assess the inner meaning of a mass movement in this last act of the war, and whether these were true revolutionary supporters, opportunists, or simply ordinary people who wanted to put an end to the long struggle. Some official revolutionary accounts stress the importance of mass demonstrations. Other descriptions echo Chin Om's emphasis on how quickly things returned to "normal" and how little disruption accompanied this stunning transfer of power. The real key was the hopeless military situation, even though there were many more GVN armed troops than revolutionary soldiers in Dinh Tuong, especially after most of the main force units were called to Saigon. Had the contest been confined to this single province, the outcome would no doubt have been different. But it was, and always had been, a conflict set in a much larger context.

The fact that the remaining ardent revolutionary supporters in Dinh Tuong (and probably most of South Vietnam) were certainly in a minority by the end of the war did not save the Saigon government from collapse. Even if the official claim that the revolution's provincial support base rested on 45,000 "political and military proselytizing forces" by the beginning of 1975 is correct, this accounts for less than 10 percent of the province population of over half a million. The number of Party members in the province was about 7,000 in the final years. The revolution was decisively aided by the North Vietnamese troops, who compensated for the lack of Southern troops after the Tet Offensive. Yet the critical factor was the Saigon government's inability to coalesce those who might have supported it into a movement that could muster the necessary cohesion to withstand the revolutionary challenge.

Saigon collapsed from within as much as from external assault, and fell apart from the top down rather than the bottom up. This is a complex and contentious issue and, unfortunately, the strong and weak points of the Saigon regime which are so central to analyzing the revolutionary victory lie outside the main line of inquiry of this study. But even the limited insight into this question offered by the experience of My Tho indicates that the struggle was lost by the GVN as much as it was won by the revolutionary side, despite the remarkable resilience of the revolutionary movement in the provinces, and the surprising rebound of its local strength toward the end of the war.

For the Party the triumph was marred by the fact that, just as the war was won, the revolution itself was slipping away. The causes of this erosion were changes in the world situation, the vast social changes that had taken place within Vietnam itself during the long conflict, and, ironically, the revolution's success in politically educating the peasant masses to understand and promote their own interests. None of these changes was fully apparent at the time, and can only be understood in historical retrospect. Colonialism had ended, though the American attempt to hang on to a sphere of influence by imposing a proxy government looked close enough to the old imperialist style to convince many Vietnamese that their patriotic duty lay in fighting for real independence. After the U.S. withdrawal, and as the Nixon Doctrine signaled a cutting loose from these neo-colonial entanglements, the nationalist argument lost some of its force. In addition, the ideological struggle of the Cold War, which had convinced many Vietnamese that they were on the side of progressive mankind, and backed by loyal and powerful allies, was already beginning to fade, especially after President Nixon's visit to China. Despite the Soviet Union's eagerness to fill the void left by the U.S. retrenchment, we now know that the deep ideological passions of the Cold War had just about run their course by the time the Vietnam war ended, and its geostrategic foundations had been greatly eroded.

More important, Vietnam itself had changed in fundamental ways during the conflict. The landlordism that had fueled peasant resentment and attracted a mass rural following to the revolution had nearly disappeared even by the middle of the conflict, and the land question itself had been pushed into the background by the war. An urban middle class of consumers, artificially created though it was, pulled many active, educated, and articulate people away from the revolution. The Communists' own brutality was brought home by such episodes as the Hue massacre by the revolutionaries of GVN officials and civilians following the Tet Offensive in 1968. This alienated many who might otherwise have supported the revolution on patriotic grounds. The war itself devastated the countryside and sent large numbers of refugees to the towns and cities where, cut off from their roots, they became a kind of *lumpenproletariat*, thinking mainly of survival day to day. Large-scale military mobilization created a linkage to the GVN which, if not based on enthusiastic loyalty, did draw many soldiers away from the revolution and toward the GVN, if only because they were fighting for their own survival. Tran Van Tra's revealing concern about the peril of the final march from My Tho on Saigon—that it had to go through populated areas where the families of soldiers outnumbered the revolutionary supporters—is an indication of how far these Saigon connections had permeated even rural South Vietnamese society.

The fervent, if belated, nostalgia for the old South Vietnamese flag among millions of overseas Vietnamese is an indication that societies and polities do change over time. The overwhelming political advantage of the revolution in seizing the nationalist laurels was gradually eroded over time, even though to the end many, if not most, high Saigon officials would in more introspective moments confess their feelings of inadequacy on the issue of nationalism compared to their communist brethren. Despite the intelligence and competence of many of its adherents, as a system, the GVN was crippled by institutionalized corruption, and as a political movement it generally failed to produce widely respected and effective leaders—with some notable exceptions. Its dependency on foreign support undermined its nationalist appeal for many Vietnamese.

In exile, the tone of these former GVN officials and soldiers has become much more confident and articulate, and the old inferiority complexes have faded into the past, especially as their once-formidable revolutionary foes floundered in guiding Vietnam into the twenty-first century. Among many overseas South Vietnamese formerly bitterly critical of GVN leaders, the past has been reformulated and the GVN reconstituted as a remembered golden age of democracy and prosperity. This was definitely not the view of most Vietnamese in the 1960s and 1970s, including many of those who later became revisionists while in exile, but in historical retrospect, a long-term trend toward some alternative to the communist version of nationalism and social organization can be discerned even though there is no consensus on what it is. Nevertheless, the remarkable achievements of the revolutionaries during three decades of opposition to foreign intervention have left a powerful legacy which still endures.

Even during the war, as some interviews suggest, Vietnamese peasants were apprehensive about their future after a communist victory. As later events made clear, individualism is deeply ingrained in the rural South Vietnamese. The revolution had a major transformative impact on these peasants, by educating them to understand and struggle for their own interests. When, after the war, these interests diverged from those of the Communist Party, it is hardly surprising that these shrewd and well-informed peasants stood up for themselves. For their political education, they have the Party to thank. The "moral economy" gave way to the "rational peasant" in no small part because of the unintended consequences of the revolution's own very successful efforts to raise the political consciousness of the masses.

Tragically, it was often the most idealistic of the revolutionaries who were the victims of the war. Many of the seasoned Viet Minh cadres, who were the bulwark of the revolution in the struggle against the French, were cast aside when the new phase of the conflict started in 1960. They were replaced by a remarkable generation of daring and energetic young people, whose motivations were also generally quite idealistic, who were moved by patriotism, and who believed strongly in the visions of a just society. Many of these people, who were mostly in their early twenties when the conflict reignited, were later killed, ground up in an unrelenting and unending war. Some of them tired of the struggle and opted out. Others had the idealism squeezed out of them by hard reality and painful personal choices. Their eloquent voices are heard in the interview citations. Those who survived and held on to the end were often the toughest, most doctrinaire, and unrelenting revolutionary true believers. In their position there was, in fact, no other way to survive.

These were not always, however, the people most qualified to lead Vietnam on to the next stage of its development. They had performed prodigious feats of bravery and even heroism. Their grit, dedication to a cause, and determination must inspire awe and admiration. But they also had learned habits of survival that stifled the development of a more open system in the postwar period and, with some very notable exceptions, their belief in austerity and sacrifice, though admirable in war, did not translate well into economic development and prosperity. Most of all, the idea that the revolutionary movement was more important than any individual interests often led to a callous disregard for the rights and welfare of the very people who were its ostensible beneficiaries, and was too often a license for abuse of power by cadres who disdained the idea of a bourgeois rule of law and argued that revolutionary ends could justify almost any means. Nevertheless, one legacy of the conflict was that the enormous costs incurred in carrying out orders from the top that had been devised in secrecy and isolation and with no debate about the consequences for those most directly affected, led many Southern guerrilla leaders to advocate greater openness and democracy in Vietnam's political life after the war. Vietnam's post Cold War economic reforms have led it in directions inconceivable to its wartime revolutionary leadership.

The final irony is that it was the United States, or perhaps the war itself, that produced the greatest revolution in Vietnam, building on a process started by the revolutionaries but taking it in a different direction. This happened as a result of the cruel and painful dislocation of an entire society and the devastation of war. To some extent, it was the massive disruption of rural life and the resulting atomization of Vietnamese society that finally and definitively erased landlordism and the feudal structure of rural society. It made a more egalitarian society possible by reshuffling the deck on land tenure, and by opening up avenues of economic, social, and even political advancement that were impossible in the old society. This shaking loose the bonds of tradition had its painful costs, to be sure, eroding family structure, proliferating social vices, and reckless profiteering and corruption. It is telling that toward the end of the war, the great appeal of the communists in their shrunken enclaves in Dinh Tuong was as peasant conservatives who stood for the old rural virtues in opposition to the deracinating wave of influences from the urban areas that washed over the countryside.

For better or for worse, the painful but impersonal dislocations of war were, in the end, a stronger revolutionary force than the rational but harshly authoritarian social engineering of the communist revolutionaries. Perhaps this is the social equivalent of Schumpeter's "creative destruction" inherent in capitalism, and by clearing away the detritus of the old society the war laid the groundwork for a more participatory and egalitarian society sometime in the future. Considering the immense and tragic costs for the people of My Tho on all sides of the struggle, however, the price exacted for these changes by the long revolutionary struggle has cast a long shadow over the future.

Notes

Notes to Chapter 1

1. George C. Herring, "The Big Muddy," book review of *A Time for War: The United States and Vietnam, 1941–1975,* by Robert D. Schulzinger (New York: Oxford University Press, 1997), *Los Angeles Times Book Review,* p. 7, May 11, 1997.

2. Ronald Spector, "Cooking Up a Quagmire," book review of *Dereliction of Duty,* by H.R. McMaster (New York: HarperCollins, 1997), *New York Times,* section 7, p. 31, July 20, 1997.

3. Examples include Michael Lind, *Vietnam: The Necessary War: A Reinterpretation of America's Most Disastrous Military Conflict* (New York: Free Press, 1999); Lewis Sorley, *A Better War: The Unexamined Victories and Final Tragedy of America's Last Years in Vietnam* (New York: Harcourt Brace, 1999); Mark Moyar, *Phoenix and the Birds of Prey* (Annapolis, MD: Naval Institute Press, 1997).

4. David D. Gilmore, "Everything Went Wrong," book review of *Father, Soldier, Son: Memoir of a Platoon Leader in Vietnam,* by Nathaniel Tripp (South Royalton, VT: Steerforth Press, 1996), *New York Times,* section 7, p. 29, February 2, 1997.

5. Thomas Lippman, "Albright's View of Hanoi Predates Tet Offensive," *Washington Post,* June 27, 1997.

6. Samuel L. Popkin, *The Rational Peasant: The Political Economy of Rural Society in Vietnam* (Berkeley: University of California Press, 1979); James C. Scott, *The Moral Economy of the Peasant: Rebellion and Subsistence in Southeast Asia* (New Haven: Yale University Press, 1976).

7. The "Scott-Popkin debate" is, of course, far more complex than this brief summary suggests and, in the eyes of many scholars, the early discussions of these two important books were based on misleading dichotomies. The present study does not employ or challenge either approach directly, but uses the oversimplified distinction in this paragraph to alert the reader to an analytic framework which is more implicit than explicit in this work.

8. "'By God, we've kicked the Vietnam syndrome once and for all!' So said President George Bush in a euphoric victory statement at the end of the Gulf War, suggesting the extent to which Vietnam continued to prey on the American psyche more than fifteen years after the fall of Saigon." George C. Herring, America and Vietnam: The Unending War," *Foreign Affairs,* Winter 1991, p.104.

9. Matt Steinglass, "Vietnam and Victory," *Boston Globe,* December 18, 2005. "Supporters of the American invasion and occupation of Iraq have often argued that it has little in common with the Vietnam War. But judging by President Bush's new 'National Strategy for Victory in Iraq,' unveiled November 30 and promoted in a series of recent speeches, the administration itself may have started to see some parallels. The document envisions a three-pronged security strategy for fighting the Iraqi insurgency: 'Clear, Hold, and Build.' It is no accident that this phrase evokes the 'clear and hold' counterinsurgency strategy pursued by the American military in the final years of the Vietnam War. For months, as the *Washington Post*'s David Ignatius and *The New Republic's* Lawrence Kaplan have reported, influential military strategists inside and outside the Pentagon have been pushing to resurrect 'clear and hold' in Iraq, claiming that the U.S. effort to suppress the Viet Cong was actually a success."

Notes to Chapter 2

1. This account of Nguyen Thi Thap's return visit to the South is taken from her memoir, *Tu Dat Tien Giang* [From the Land of the Upper Delta] (Ho Chi Minh City: NXB Van Nghe Thanh Pho Ho Chi Minh, 1986), pp. 11–22.

2. Tran Van Giau, "May Dac Tinh Cua Nong Dan Dong Bang Cuu Long-Dong Nai" [Some Special Characteristics of Peasants in the Mekong Delta and Dong Nai], in *Mot So Van De Khoa Hoc Xa Hoi Ve Dong Bang Song Cuu Long* [Some Social Science Questions Concerning the Mekong Delta] (Hanoi: NXB Khoa Hoc Xa Hoi, 1982), p. 2.

Notes to Chapter 3

1. This account of Nguyen Thi Thap's role in the August 1945 revolution is taken from her memoir, *Tu Dat Tien Giang* [From the Land of the Upper Delta] (Ho Chi Minh City: NXB Van Nghe Thanh Pho Ho Chi Minh, 1986), pp. 258–80.

2. Dan Ton Tu [Sau Vi], "The Year I Turned 21," in *Dong Chi: Hoi Ky Cach Mang* [Comrades: Revolutionary Memoirs] (Tien Giang: NXB Tong Hop Tien Giang, 1987), pp. 17–29.

3. Ibid., p. 19.

4. Nguyen Thi Thap, *Tu Dat Tien Giang,* p. 24.

5. Ibid., p. 24.

6. Ibid., p. 39.

7. Dan Ton Tu, "The Year I Turned 21," pp. 26–28.

8. Ibid., p. 29.

9. Nguyen Thi Thap, *Tu Dat Tien Giang,* pp. 31–32.

10. The unification of rival communist groups, of which Ngo Gia Tu's was one, did not take place until 1930.

11. Nguyen Van Nhan (Ba Chim), *Lon Len Cung Cach Mang* [Growing up with the Revolution] (Tien Giang: Ban Tuyen Giao Tinh Uy Tien Giang, 1995), p. 46.

12. Nguyen Thi Thap, *Tu Dat Tien Giang,* p. 267.

13. Ban Nghien Cuu Lich Su Dang, *Tia Lua* [A Shaft of Fire] (Tien Giang: NXB Hoi Van Nghe, 1986), p. 85.

14. Pham Cao Duong, *Vietnamese Peasants Under French Domination: 1861–1945*, Center for South and Southeast Asian Studies, University of California, Monograph Series, no. 24 (New York: University Press of America, 1985), p. 119.

15. An official biography describes Bay Phong (Nguyen Thin) as coming from a middle peasant background, but shows a photograph of Phong dressed in an imposing *ao dai* (traditional scholar's gown) with turban, the formal dress of the upper gentry at that time. This biography decorously omits the incident of Phong taking money from his mother. *Nhung Nguoi Con Uu Tu Cua Tinh Tien Giang* [The Outstanding People of Tien Giang], vol. 2 (Tien Giang: NXB Ban Tuyen Giao Tinh Uy Tien Giang, 1993), p. 5.

16. The story of the theft by Bay Phong is told in *Dong Chi: Hoi Ky Cach Mang* [Comrades: Revolutionary Memoirs] (Tien Giang: NXB Tong Hop Tien Giang, 1987), pp. 9–16.

17. Huynh Kim Khanh, *Vietnamese Communism: 1925–1945* (Ithaca, NY: Cornell University Press, 1982), p. 85.

18. Nguyen Ngoc Luu, *Peasants, Party and Revolution: The Politics of Agrarian Transformation in Northern Vietnam, 1930–1975*) (Ph.D. dissertation, University of Amsterdam, 1987) p. 153.

19. Doan Thanh Nien Cong San Ho Chi Minh Tinh Tien Giang [The Ho Chi Minh Communist Youth Group of Tien Giang Province], *Lich Su Doan Va Phong Trao Thanh Nien Tinh Tien Giang* [History of the Party Youth Group and the Youth Movement of Tien Giang Province] (Tien Giang: Xi Nghiep In Tien Giang, 1996), p. 23.

20. Ban Nghien Cuu Lich Su Dang, *Lich Su Dang Bo Tinh Tien Giang 1927–1954 (so thao)*, vol. 1, p. 30.

21. Doan Thanh Nien Cong San Ho Chi Minh Tinh Tien Giang, *Lich Su Doan Va Phong Trao Thanh Nien Tinh Tien Giang*, p. 24.

22. Huynh Kim Khanh, *Vietnamese Communism: 1925–1945*, p. 64.

23. Ban Nghien Cuu Lich Su Dang, *Lich Su Dang Bo Tinh Tien Giang 1927–1954 (so thao)*, vol. 1. The discussion of this early history of the Party is on pp. 34–38.

24. Nguyen Van Nhan, *Lon Len Cung Cach Mang*, p. 46.

25. Ban Nghien Cuu Lich Su Dang, *Lich Su Dang Bo Tinh Tien Giang 1927–1954 (so thao)*, vol. 1, p. 106.

26. Alexander Woodside, *Community and Revolution in Modern Vietnam* (Boston: Houghton Mifflin, 1976), p. 121.

27. Pham Cao Duong, *Vietnamese Peasants Under French Domination: 1861–1945*, p. 66.

28. Ibid.

29. Nguyen Ngoc Luu, *Peasants, Party and Revolution*, p. 139.

30. Ban Nghien Cuu Lich Su Dang, *Lich Su Dang Bo Tinh Tien Giang 1927–1954 (so thao)*, vol. 1, p. 51.

31. Ibid., p. 54.

32. Ban Nghien Cuu Lich Su Dang, *Tia Lua*, p. 45.

33. Lady Borton, *After Sorrow: An American among the Vietnamese* (Tokyo: Kodansha International, 1996), p. 46.

34. Ban Nghien Cuu Lich Su Dang, *Lich Su Dang Bo Tinh Tien Giang 1927–1954 (so thao)*, vol. 1, p. 44.

35. Nguyen Thi Thap, *Tu Dat Tien Giang*, p. 36.

36. Ibid., pp. 42–43.

37. Ibid., p. 49.

38. Ibid., pp. 67–73.

39. Ban Nghien Cuu Lich Su Dang, *Tia Lua*, p. 47.

40. See David Marr's discussion of *Phu Nu Tan Van* in *Vietnamese Tradition on Trial, 1920–45* (Berkeley: University of California Press, 1981), pp. 220–28.

41. Ban Nghien Cuu Lich Su Dang, *Tia Lua*, p. 44. The women mentioned were Nguyen Thi Luu, Nguyen Thi Thu, Mai Quynh Hoa, and Nguyen Thi Kiem.

42. Nguyen Thi Thap, *Tu Dat Tien Giang*, pp. 101–6.

43. Ban Nghien Cuu Lich Su Dang, *Lich Su Dang Bo Tinh Tien Giang 1927–1954 (so thao)*, vol. 1, pp. 77–78.

44. Ibid., vol. 1, p. 89.

45. Nguyen Thi Thap, *Tu Dat Tien Giang*, p. 123.

46. Ibid., p. 130.

47. Ibid., p. 129.

48. Ibid., p. 131.

49. Ibid., p. 135.

50. Ban Nghien Cuu Lich Su Dang, *Lich Su Dang Bo Tinh Tien Giang 1927–1954 (so thao)*, vol. 1, p. 90.

51. Nguyen Thi Thap, *Tu Dat Tien Giang*, p. 146.

52. Cited in Ban Nghien Cuu Lich Su Dang, *Lich Su Dang Bo Tinh Tien Giang 1927–1954 (so thao)* vol. 1, p. 94.

53. Nguyen Thi (Nguyen Ngoc Tan), *Nam Thang Chua Xa* [Months and Years Not Long Past] (Ho Chi Minh City: NXB Van Nghe TP Ho Chi Minh, 1986), p. 131.

54. In Duong Diem village, the constable became a member of the ICP in 1930. Ban Nghien Cuu Lich Su Dang, *Tia Lua*, p. 13.

55. Nguyen Thi, *Nam Thang Chua Xa*, p. 132.

56. Ban Nghien Cuu Lich Su Dang, *Lich Su Dang Bo Tinh Tien Giang 1927–1954 (so thao)*, vol. 1, pp. 105–6.

57. Huynh Kim Khanh, *Vietnamese Communism: 1925–1945*, pp. 255–56.

58. Ban Nghien Cuu Lich Su Dang, *Lich Su Dang Bo Tinh Tien Giang 1927–1954 (so thao)*, vol. 1, p. 99.

59. Duong Quang Dong, "Phuc Hoi Co So Dang" [Reestablishing the Party Infrastructure], in *Mua Thu Roi: Ngay Ham Ba* [The 23rd of That Autumn], vol. 1 (Hanoi: NXB Chinh Tri Quoc Gia, 1995), p. 59. The My Tho province Party history says that Duong Khuy was appointed Party secretary at the beginning of 1943. Ban Nghien Cuu Lich Su Dang, *Lich Su Dang Bo Tinh Tien Giang 1927–1954 (so thao)*, vol. 1, p. 107. Christoph Giebel cautions against relying on the historical reminiscences of Duong Quang Dong, and calls him "a historian's nightmare." Christoph Giebel, *Imagined Ancestries of Vietnamese Communism: Ton Duc Thang and the Politics of History and Memory* (Seattle: University of Washington Press, 2004), p. 27.

60. Duong Quang Dong, "Phuc Hoi Co So Dang," pp. 62–64.

61. Le Van Thang (Tran Van Tra), "Ngon Lua Cach Mang Kong Bao Gio Tat Trong Nhan Dan Nam Bo" [The Revolutionary Flame of the Nam Bo People Will Never Be Extinguished], in *Mua Thu Roi: Ngay Ham Ba,* vol. 1, p. 44.

62. Nguyen Thi Thap, *Tu Dat Tien Giang,* pp. 259–60.

63. Le Van Thang, "Ngon Lua Cach Mang Kong Bao Gio Tat Trong Nhan Dan Nam Bo," pp. 43–44.

64. Nguyen Thi Thap, *Tu Dat Tien Giang,* pp. 260–61.

65. David G. Marr, *Vietnam 1945: The Quest for Power* (Berkeley: University of California Press, 1995), p. 192. For Marr's analysis of the Eighth Plenum, see pp. 169–72.

66. *Nhung Nguoi Con Uu Tu Cua Tien Giang,* p. 45.

67. Nguyen Thi Thap, *Tu Dat Tien Giang,* p. 260.

68. Nguyen Van Nhan, *Lon Len Cung Cach Mang,* p. 47.

69. Ban Nghien Cuu Lich Su Dang, *Lich Su Dang Bo Tinh Tien Giang 1927–1954 (so thao)*, vol. 1, pp. 114–16.

70. Marr, *Vietnam 1945: The Quest for Power*, pp. 134–36.

71. Phillipe Devillers, *Histoire du Viet-Nam de 1940 à 1952* (History of Viet Nam from 1940 to 1952) (Paris: Editions du Seuil, 1952), p. 85.

72. Ngoc Hien, "Comrade Duong Khuy," *Nhung Nguoi Con Uu Tu Cua Tien Giang,* p.48.

73. *Nhung Nguoi Con Uu Tu Cua Tien Giang,* p. 29.

Notes to Chapter 4

1. Tran Huu Nghiep, "Nhung Ngay Toi Lam Uy Vien Mat Tran Viet Minh Tinh My Tho Nam 1945" [The Days in 1945 When I Was a Committee Member of the Viet Minh Front in My Tho], in *Thoi Viet-Minh* [The Viet Minh Period] (My Tho: Ban Tuyen Giao Tinh Uy, 1991), p. 42. Nghiep says he was given this figure by Duong Quang Dong, who was a member of the *Xu Uy.*

2. Ban Nghien Cuu Lich Su Dang [Party Historical Research Section], *Lich Su Dang Bo Tinh Tien Giang 1927–1954 (so thao)* [History of the Tien Giang Province Party Headquarters 1927–1954 (draft)], vol. 1 (Tien Giang: Xi Nghiep In Tien Giang 1985), p. 192.

3. Ban Nghien Cuu Lich Su Dang [Party Historical Research Section], *Lich Su Dang Bo Tinh Tien Giang 1927–1954 (so thao)* [History of the Tien Giang Province Party Headquarters 1927–1954 (draft)], vol. 1 (Tien Giang: Xi Nghiep In Tien Giang 1985), p. 192.

4. David G. Marr, *Vietnam 1945: The Quest for Power* (Berkeley: University of California Press, 1995), p. 464.

5. *Nhung Nguoi Con Uu Tu Cua Tien Giang* [The Outstanding People of Tien Giang] (Tien Giang: NXB Ban Tuyen Giao Tinh Uy Tien Giang, 1992), p. 58.

6. Ibid.

7. "Dong Chi Duong Khuy" [Comrade Duong Khuy], in *Nhung Nguoi Con Uu Tu Cua Tien Giang*, pp. 45–46.

8. Ban Nghien Cuu Lich Su Dang, *Tia Lua*, p. 54.

9. *Cach Mang Thang Tam: Tong Khoi Nghia o Hanoi va Cac Dia Phuong* [The August Revolution: The General Uprising in Hanoi and the Regions] (Hanoi: NXB Su Hoc, 1960), p. 331.

10. The life of North Vietnam's peasants during the famine is eloquently illustrated by interviews with survivors in Gerard Chaliand, *The Peasants of North Vietnam* (Baltimore: Penguin Books, 1969).

11. Ban Nghien Cuu Lich Su Dang, *Lich Su Dang Bo Tinh Tien Giang 1927–1954 (so thao)*, vol. 1, pp. 116–17.

12. Dan Ton Tu (Sau Vi), "Cach Mang Thang Tam tai My Tho" [The August Revolution in My Tho], *Saigon Giai Phong*, August 20, 1973, p. 3.

13. Ban Nghien Cuu Lich Su Dang, *Lich Su Dang Bo Tinh Tien Giang 1927–1954 (so thao)*, vol. 1 (Tien Giang: 1985), pp. 121–22.

14. *Cach Mang Thang Tam: Tong Khoi Nghia o Hanoi va Cac Dia Phuong*, pp. 333–34.

15. Ban Nghien Cuu Lich Su Dang, *Lich Su Dang Bo Tinh Tien Giang 1927–1954 (so thao)*, vol. 1, pp. 120–21.

16. Vo Tran Nha, ed., *Lich Su Dong Thap Muoi* [History of the Plain of Reeds] (Ho Chi Minh City: NXB Thanh Pho Ho Chi Minh, 1993), p. 69.

17. Hien was the son of the village chief of Tan Thuan Binh village in Cho Gao district, who had hosted Tran Van Giau's *Xu Uy* meeting in 1943 "Dong Chi Duong Ky," p. 42. The former Viet Minh police chief of My Tho says that Tran Van Hien was from Cho Gao and the son of "Mr. Hoai, a village official" [DT136].

18. Tran Huu Nghiep, "Nhung Ngay toi Lam Uy Vien Mat Tran Viet Minh Tinh My Tho Nam 1945," pp. 43–44. Nghiep claims Tran Van Hien came to his house to recruit him to serve in the Viet Minh Front Committee of My Tho. At Hien's side was a "light complected, rather short and not very talkative person named Duong Khuy." Only later did Nghiep discover that the man was the province Party secretary at that time (p. 44).

19. Nguyen Thi Thap, *Tu Dat Tien Giang*, p. 286.

20. Nguyen Van Nhan, *Lon Len Cung Cach Mang*, pp. 53–54.

21. Ban Nghien Cuu Lich Su Dang, *Lich Su Dang Bo Tinh Tien Giang 1927–1954 (so thao)*, vol. 1, p. 158.

22. Ibid., p. 146.

23. Nguyen Thi Thap, *Tu Dat Tien Giang*, pp. 293–94.

24. The My Phong decisions are listed in Ban Nghien Cuu Lich Su Dang, *Lich Su Dang Bo Tinh Tien Giang 1927–1954 (so thao)*, vol. 1, p. 147.

25. Tran Huu Nghiep, "Nhung Ngay toi Lam Uy Vien Mat Tran Viet Minh Tinh My Tho Nam 1945," p. 46.

26. Ibid., pp. 47–49.

27. Nguyen Van Nhan, *Lon Len Cung Cach Mang*, p. 59.

28. Ibid.

29. Nguyen Thi Thap, *Tu Dat Tien Giang*, pp. 298–99.

30. Nguyen Chi Cong, *Song Mai Voi Nhan Dan*, pp. 34–35.

31. Nguyen Thi Thap, *Tu Dat Tien Giang*, p. 297.

32. Ibid., p. 303.

33. Ibid., p. 42.

34. *Tran Danh Ba Muoi Nam*, vol. 1, p. 59.

35. Nguyen Van Nhan, *Lon Len Cung Cach Mang*, pp. 61–63.

36. Ban Nghien Cuu Lich Su Dang, *Lich Su Dang Bo Tinh Tien Giang 1927–1954 (so thao)*, vol. 1, p. 160.

37. Nguyen Thi Thap, *Tu Dat Tien Giang*, p. 371.

38. Ibid., p. 372.

39. Ibid., p. 379.

40. Nguyen Van Nhan, *Lon Len Cung Cach Mang,* pp. 63–64.

41. Ban Nghien Cuu Lich Su Dang, *Lich Su Dang Bo Tinh Tien Giang 1927–1954 (so thao),* vol. 1, p. 163. The reference to three companies can be found in Vo Tran Nha ed., *Lich Su Dong Thap Muoi,* p. 67.

42. Vo Tran Nha, ed., *Lich Su Dong Thap Muoi,* p. 67.

43. Ibid., p.73.

44. "Overview," in *Mua Thu Roi Ngay Ham Ba: Hao Khi Dong Nai—Ben Nghe—Cuu Long,* vol. 3, p. 46.

45. Tran Van Tra, "Chien Tranh Nhan Dan Khoi Dau Tu Nam Bo Nhu The" in Ibid., p. 107.

Notes to Chapter 5

1. Vo Tran Nha, ed., *Lich Su Dong Thap Muoi* [History of the Plain of Reeds] (Ho Chi Minh City: NXB Thanh Pho Ho Chi Minh, 1993), p. 74.

2. So Giao Duc Tien Giang [Tien Giang Province Education Service], *Lich Su Tien Giang* [History of Tien Giang] (Ho Chi Minh City: Nha May In Quan Doi, 1986), p. 33.

3. Vo Tran Nha, ed., *Lich Su Dong Thap Muoi,* pp. 73–74.

4. *Nhung Nguoi Con Uu Tu Cua Tien Giang* [The Outstanding People of Tien Giang] (Tien Giang: NXB Ban Tuyen Giao Tinh Uy Tien Giang, 1992), p. 65.

5. Vo Tran Nha, ed., *Lich Su Dong Thap Muoi,* p. 75.

6. *Nhung Nguoi Con Uu Tu Cua Tien Giang,* p. 72.

7. Nguyen Chi Cong, *Song Mai Voi Nhan Dan* [With the People Forever] (My Tho: NXB Tong Hoi Tien Giang, 1986), p. 43. Reference to the complete liberation of Hau My is in Vo Tran Nha, ed., *Lich Su Dong Thap Muoi,* p. 77.

8. Nguyen Van Nhan (Ba Chim), *Lon Len Cung Cach Mang* [Growing up with the Revolution] (Tien Giang: Ban Tuyen Giao Tinh Uy Tien Giang, 1995), p. 64.

9. Ibid., pp. 65–67.

10. Vo Tran Nha ed., *Lich Su Dong Thap Muoi,* pp. 80–81.

11. Nguyen Van Nhan, *Lon Len Voi Cach Mang,* p. 68.

12. Ibid. p.73.

13. Ibid. pp. 68-69.

14. Ban Nghien Cuu Lich Su Dang [Party Historical Research Section], *Lich Su Dang Bo Tinh Tien Giang 1927–1954 (so thao),* vol. 1 (Tien Giang: 1985), pp. 181–82.

15. Nguyen Van Nhan, *Lon Len Voi Cach Mang,* pp. 94–95.

16. Vo Tran Nha, ed., *Lich Su Dong Thap Muoi,* p. 99.

17. Ibid., p. 84.

18. Bo Quoc Phong, *Lich Su Cuoc Khang Chien Chong Thuc Dan Phap 1945–1954,* vol. 3, p. 66.

19. Huynh Minh Hien, "Nho Dong Thap Muoi, 'Thu Phu' Cua Nam Bo Trong Nhung Nam Dau Khang Chien" [A Remembrance of the Plain of Reeds, the 'Capital' of Nam Bo During the First Years of the Resistance], in *Mua Thu Roi, Ngay Ham Ba: Doc Lap Hay la Chet* [The 23rd of That Autumn: Independence or Death], vol. 2 (Hanoi: NXB Chinh Tri Quoc Gia, 1996), p. 374.

20. Vo Tran Nha, ed., *Lich Su Dong Thap Muoi,* p. 105.

21. Bo Chi Huy Quan Su Tien Giang, *Tieu Doan 309,* p. 83.

22. Ibid., p. 80.

23. *Tran Danh Ba Muoi Nam,* vol. 2, p. 198.

24. Nguyen Van Nhan, *Lon Len Cung Cach Manh,* p. 74.

25. A. M. Savani, *Visages et images du Sud Viet-Nam* (Saigon: 1955). This book was written as a troop information guide for French troops in the South, but it appeared a bit late to serve the purpose. The preface indicates that the writing was completed in late 1953.

26. Ibid., p. 118.

27. For a discussion of Leroy, see the introduction by Mai V. Elliott (translator), to *No Other Road to Take: Memoir of Mrs. Nguyen Thi Dinh*, Cornell Southeast Asia Program Data Paper 102 (Ithaca, NY: Cornell SEA Program, 1976).

28. Ban Nghien Cuu Lich Su Dang, *Lich Su Dang Bo Tinh Tien Giang 1927–1954 (so thao)*, vol. 1, p. 222.

29. Ibid.

30. See the discussion of this issue in Edwin E. Moise, *Land Reform in China and North Vietnam* (Chapel Hill, NC: University of North Carolina Press, 1983), chaps. 8 and 9. Moise's characterization of the Fourth Plenum of January 1953 is on p. 173.

31. Nguyen Van Nhan, *Lon Len Cung Cach Manh*, p. 74.

32. Bo Chi Huy Quan Su Tien Giang, *Tieu Doan 309*, p. 109.

33. Nguyen Van Nhan, *Lon Len Cung Cach Manh*, p. 76.

34. Vo Tran Nha, ed., *Lich Su Dong Thap Muoi*, pp. 131–34.

35. Bo Chi Huy Quan Su Tien Giang, *Tieu Doan 309*, p. 120.

36. A. M. Savani, *Visages et images du Sud Viet-Nam*, pp. 120–21.

37. Vo Tran Nha, ed., *Lich Su Dong Thap Muoi*, p. 141.

38. Le Viet Thang, "Vo Trang la Con Duong Song" [Armed Struggle Is the Path to Survival], in *Lon Len Cung Cach Manh*, pp. 133–34.

39. Nguyen Van Nhan, *Lon Len Cung Cach Manh*, p. 76.

40. Vo Tran Nha, ed., *Lich Su Dong Thap Muoi*, p. 146.

41. So Giao Duc Tien Giang, *Lich Su Tien Giang*, p. 37.

42. Vo Tran Nha, ed., *Lich Su Dong Thap Muoi*, pp. 147–50.

43. Bo Chi Huy Quan Su Tien Giang, *Tieu Doan 309*, pp. 128–29.

44. A. M. Savani, *Visages et images du Sud Viet-Nam*, p. 121.

45. Bo Chi Huy Quan Su Tien Giang, *Tieu Doan 309*, pp. 129–43.

46. So Giao Duc Tien Giang, *Lich Su Tien Giang*, p. 38.

47. Rand Corporation memorandum, "A Translation from the French: Lessons of the War in Indochina," May 1967, vol. 2, trans. Victor J. Croizat, p. 114.

48. Nguyen Thi Thap, *Tu Dat Tien Giang*, pp. 452–55.

Notes to Chapter 6

1. George McT. Kahin, *Intervention: How America Became Involved in Vietnam* (New York: Alfred A. Knopf, 1986), pp. 61–64.

2. Gareth Porter, "Imperialism and Social Structure in Twentieth Century Vietnam" (Ph.D. diss., Cornell University, Ithaca, NY, 1976), p. 294.

3. Ban Nghien Cuu Lich Su Dang [Party Historical Research Section], *Lich Su Dang Bo Tinh Tien Giang 1954–1975* [History of the Tien Giang Party Headquarters, 1954–1975], vol. 2 (Tien Giang: Xi Nghiep In Tien Giang, 1986), p. 6. Province Party leader Viet Thang states that there were 2,000 Party members in My Tho at the time of the Geneva Accords. Le Viet Thang, "Vo Trang la Con Duong Song" [Armed Struggle Is the Path to Survival], in *Lon Len Cung Cach Mang* [Growing up with the Revolution] (Tien Giang: Ban Tuyen Giao Tinh Uy Tien Giang, 1995), p. 193.

4. Le Quoc San, *Cuoc Do Suc Than Ky* [The Incredible Trial of Strength] (Hanoi: NXB Quan Doi Nhan Dan, 1991), p. 32.

5. Ban Nghien Cuu Lich Su Dang, *Lich Su Dang Bo Tinh Tien Giang 1954–1975*, vol. 2, p. 6.

6. Ibid., p. 21.

7. Tran Van Tra, "Nhung Chang Duong Lich Su Cua B2 Thanh Dong" [Historical Stages in the B2 Brass Fortress], vol. 1, *Hoa Binh Hay Chien Tranh* [War or Peace] (Hanoi: NXB Quan Doi Nhan Dan, 1992), p. 184.

8. Nguyen Thi Thap, *Tu Dat Tien Giang* [From the Land of the Upper Delta] (Ho Chi Minh City: NXB Van Nghe Thanh Pho Ho Chi Minh, 1986), pp. 448–51.

9. Ibid., p. 451.

10. Ibid., p. 453.

11. Ibid., p. 455.

12. Tran Van Tra, "Nhung Chang Duong Lich Su Cua B2 Thanh Dong," vol. 1, pp. 32–33.

13. Ibid., p. 173.

14. Bo Chi Huy Quan Su Tien Giang [Tien Giang Military Command Headquarters], *Tieu Doan 309* [The 309th Battalion] (Tien Giang: Xi Nghiep In Tien Giang, 1990), p. 166.

15. Nguyen Van Nhan, *Lon Len Cung Cach Mang*, p. 80.

16. Le Viet Thang, "Vo Trang la Con Duong Song," p. 139.

17. Ban Nghien Cuu Lich Su Dang, *Lich Su Dang Bo Tinh Tien Giang 1954–1975*, vol. 2, p. 12 Another source claims that "We put people into 60 to 70 percent of the enemy's basic level administration." Nguyen Thanh Son, ed., *Cuoc Khang Chien 30 Nam Quan Dan Tien Giang* p. 120.

18. Ban Nghien Cuu Lich Su Dang, *Lich Su Dang Bo Tinh Tien Giang 1954–1975*, vol. 2, p. 12.

19. Nguyen Tran, *Cong va Toi* [Accomplishments and Misdeeds] (Xuan Thu: 1992), p. 233.

20. Le Viet Thang, "Vo Trang la Con Duong Song," pp. 152–54.

21. Ban Nghien Cuu Lich Su Dang, *Lich Su Dang Bo Tinh Tien Giang 1954–1975*, vol. 2, pp. 11–12.

22. Ban Nghien Cuu Lich Su Dang, *Lich Su Dang Bo Tinh Tien Giang 1954–1975*, vol. 2, p. 8.

23. The decree ordering these changes was dated October 22, 1956. Huynh Minh, *Dinh Tuong Xua va Nay* [Dinh Tuong Yesterday and Today], privately printed, nd., p. 41.

24. Ban Nghien Cuu Lich Su Dang, *Lich Su Dang Bo Tinh Tien Giang 1954–1975*, vol. 2, p. 16.

25. Nguyen Tran, *Cong va Toi*, p. 297.

26. Nguyen Chi Cong, *Song Mai Voi Nhan Dan*, p. 56.

27. Ban Nghien Cuu Lich Su Dang, *Lich Su Dang Bo Tinh Tien Giang 1954–1975*, vol. 2, p. 16.

28. Nguyen Thanh Son, ed., *Cuoc Khang Chien 30 Nam Quan Dan Tien Giang*, p. 125.

29. Nguyen Tran, *Cong va Toi*, p. 231.

30. Ibid., p. 302.

31. Ibid., p. 229.

32. Nguyen Thai, *Is South Vietnam Viable?* (Manila, privately printed, 1962), p. 133.

33. Nguyen Thanh Son, ed., *Cuoc Khang Chien 30 Nam Quan Dan Tien Giang*, p. 131.

34. *Tim Hieu Phong Trao Dong Khoi o Mien Nam Viet Nam* [Understanding the Concerted Uprising Movement in South Vietnam] (Hanoi: NXB Khoa Hoc Xa Hoi, 1981), p. 61.

35. Ibid., p. 63.

36. Ban Nghien Cuu Lich Su Dang, *Lich Su Dang Bo Tinh Tien Giang 1954–1975*, vol. 2, p. 13.

37. Nguyen Tran, *Cong va Toi*, p. 256.

38. Ibid., p. 260.

Notes to Chapter 7

1. Nguyen Thanh Son, ed., *Cuoc Khang Chien 30 Nam Quan Dan Tien Giang* [The Thirty-Year Resistance of the Army and People of Tien Giang] (Tien Giang: Xi Nghiep In Tien Giang, 1986), p. 137. For some reason, this reckoning explicitly excludes the clandestine chapters made up of Party members whose identities were known to the GVN.

2. One well-informed source said that there were twenty-two draft revisions of the version of Resolution 15 before it took its final form. It was apparently initially drafted sometime in 1957 by the Reunification Commission in Hanoi under the supervision of Le Duan and Pham Hung. The twentieth revision evidently met the requirements of Le Duan, who submitted it to the Fifteenth Plenum of the Central Committee, which met from December 1958 to January 1959 to discuss the situation in South Vietnam. Despite some reservations by members of the Central Committee, who were hesitant to confront the United States at that time, the decision was made to approve a mix of armed and political struggle in the South. But the written version of this draft resolution at the Fifteenth Plenum had to be revised three more times before it was resubmitted to the Central Committee in a supplementary meeting of the Fifteenth Plenum in May 1959. Interviews in Hanoi 1999 and 2000.

3. Le Quoc San, *Cuoc Do Suc Than Ky* [The Incredible Trial of Strength] (Hanoi: NXB Quan Doi Nhan Dan, 1991), p. 52.

4. *Tim Hieu Phong Trao Dong Khoi o Mien Nam Viet Nam* [Understanding the Concerted Uprising Movement in South Vietnam] (Hanoi: NXB Khoa Hoc Xa Hoi, 1981), p. 40.

5. Nguyen Van Nhan (Ba Chim), *Lon Len Voi Cach Mang* [Growing up with the Revolution] (Tien Giang: Ban Tuyen Giao Tinh Uy Tien Giang, 1995), pp. 114–15.

6. Nguyen Thanh Son, ed., *Cuoc Khang Chien 30 Nam Quan Dan Tien Giang,* p. 118.

7. Le Quoc San, *Cuoc Do Suc Than Ky,* p. 35.

8. *Tran Danh Ba Muoi Nam* [The Thirty-Year War], vol. 3 (Hanoi: NXB Quan Doi Nhan Dan, 1988), p. 68.

9. Thayer, *War by Other Means: National Liberation and Revolution in Viet-Nam 1954–60* (Sydney: Allen and Unwin, 1989), p. 105.

10. *Kien Tuong: Lich Su Khang Chien Chong My, Cuu Nuoc (1954–1975),* pp. 61–62.

11. Vo Tran Nha, ed., *Lich Su Dong Thap Muoi,* p. 190.

12. *Kien Tuong: Lich Su Khang Chien Chong My, Cuu Nuoc (1954–1975),* p. 69.

13. Ibid., p. 70.

14. *Tran Danh Ba Muoi Nam,* vol. 3, p. 69.

15. Le Viet Thang, "Vo Trang la Con Duong Song," p. 157.

16. Nguyen Chi Cong, *Song Mai Voi Nhan Dan* [With the People Forever] (My Tho: NXB Tong Hoi Tien Giang, 1986), p. 67.

17. Ibid., p. 164.

18. Ibid., p. 172.

19. Le Quoc San, *Cuoc Do Suc Than Ky,* p. 34.

20. *Luoc Su Dang Bo Cong San Viet Nam Tinh Ben Tre* [Summary History of the Party Headquarters of the Communist Party of Vietnam in Ben Tre Province] (Ben Tre: Chien Thang Printing House, 1985), pp. 141–42.

21. Le Viet Thang, "Vo Trang la Con Duong Song," p. 194.

22. Vo Tran Nha, ed., *Lich Su Dong Thap Muoi,* p. 199. Tran Van Tra said that, unlike other battles which the GVN did not report to the United States, this battle "was certainly known to the U.S. Embassy" because of its scale and significance. Tran Van Tra, *Nhung Chang Duong Lich Su Cua B2 Thanh Dong,* p. 131.

23. Le Quoc San, *Cuoc Do Suc Than Ky,* pp. 39–46.

24. *Tran Danh Ba Muoi Nam,* vol. 3, p. 87.

25. Tran Van Tra, *Nhung Chang Duong Lich Su Cua B2 Thanh Dong,* p. 162.

26. Vo Tran Nha, ed., *Lich Su Dong Thap Muoi,* p. 199.

27. Le Quoc San, *Cuoc Do Suc Than Ky,* p. 40.

28. Cuoc Khang Chien Chong My Cuu Nuoc 1954–1975, p. 69.

29. Nguyen Chi Cong, *Song Mai Voi Nhan Dan,* p. 76.

30. Le Viet Thang, "Vo Trang la Con Duong Song," p. 195.

31. Ibid., pp. 194–96.

32. Ibid.

33. *Ban Nghien Cuu Lich Su Dang, Lich Su Dang Bo Tinh Tien Giang, 1954–1975*, vol. 2, p. 21.
34. Le Viet Thang, "Vo Trang la Con Duong Song," pp. 196–97.
35. Nguyen Tran, *Cong va Toi* [Accomplishments and Misdeeds] (Xuan Thu, 1992), p. 199.
36. Ibid. p. 256.
37. Ban Nghien Cuu Lich Su Dang, Lich Su Dang Bo Tinh Tien Giang, 1954–1975, vol. 2, p. 22.
38. Le Viet Thang, "Vo Trang la Con Duong Song," pp. 198–200.
39. Ban Nghien Cuu Lich Su Dang, *Lich Su Dang Bo Tinh Tien Giang, 1954–1975*, vol. 2, p. 21.
40. Le Quoc San, *Cuoc Do Suc Than Ky*, p. 62.
41. Ban Nghien Cuu Lich Su Dang, *Lich Su Dang Bo Tinh Tien Giang, 1954–1975*, vol. 2, p. 22.
42. Le Viet Thang, "Vo Trang la Con Duong Song," p. 201.
43. Ibid., pp. 201–2.
44. Nguyen Chi Cong, *Song Mai Voi Nhan Dan*, p. 80.
45. *Tran Danh Ba Muoi Nam*, vol. 3, p. 110.
46. Ibid., p. 209.
47. Nguyen Thanh Son, ed., *Cuoc Khang Chien 30 Nam Quan Dan Tien Giang*, p. 144.
48. Ban Nghien Cuu Lich Su Dang, *Lich Su Dang Bo Tinh Tien Giang, 1954–1975*, vol. 2, p. 22.
49. Le Viet Thang, "Vo Trang la Con Duong Song," p. 209.
50. Le Quoc San, *Cuoc Do Suc Than Ky,* p. 65.
51. Le Viet Thang, "Vo Trang la Con Duong Song," p. 212.
52. Ibid., p. 213.
53. Ban Nghien Cuu Lich Su Dang, *Lich Su Dang Bo Tinh Tien Giang, 1954–1975*, vol. 2, p. 23.
54. Nguyen Thanh Son, ed., *Cuoc Khang Chien 30 Nam Quan Dan Tien Giang*, p. 147.
55. Ban Nghien Cuu Lich Su Dang, *Lich Su Dang Bo Tinh Tien Giang, 1954–1975*, vol. 2, p. 24.
56. Ibid., p. 25.
57. *Tran Danh Ba Muoi Nam*, vol. 3, pp. 147–48.
58. Ibid., p. 152.

Notes to Chapter 8

1. Nguyen Chi Cong, *Song Mai Voi Nhan Dan* [With the People Forever] (My Tho: NXB Tong Hoi Tien Giang, 1986), pp. 83–84.
2. Ibid., p. 84.
3. Le Viet Thang, "Vo Trang la Con Duong Song" [Armed Struggle Is the Path to Survival] in *Lon Len Cung Cach Mang* [Growing up with the Revolution] (Tien Giang: Ban Tuyen Giao Tinh Uy Tien Giang, 1995), pp. 235–36.
4. The following account of Party history in Long Trung village is taken from Nguyen Thi (Nguyen Ngoc Tan), *Nam Thang Chua Xa* [Months and Years Not Long Past] (Ho Chi Minh City: NXB Van Nghe TP Ho Chi Minh, 1986), especially pp. 128–52.
5. Ibid., p. 129.
6. Nguyen Van Tao, *Tan Dai Tu Dien Viet-Anh* [Modern Vietnamese-English Dictionary] (Tokyo: NXB Tan Van, 1969), p. 1864.
7. Nguyen Thi, *Nam Thang Chua Xa*, p. 152.
8. CDEC (Combined Document Exploitation Center) document no. 01-0519-70. A postwar Party history states that "half" the Party members at the end of 1961, a total of 20,000,

were in the armed forces. If this figure is correct, then the total number of Party members was 40,000. *Tran Danh Ba Muoi Nam* [The Thirty-year War], vol. 3 (Hanoi: NXB Quan Doi Nhan Dan, 1988), p. 160.

9. Doan Thanh Nien Cong San Ho Chi Minh Tinh Tien Giang [The Ho Chi Minh Communist Youth Group of Tien Giang Province], *Lich Su Doan Van Phong Trao Thanh Nien Tinh Tien Giang* [History of the Party Youth Group and the Youth Movement of Tien Giang Province] (Tien Giang: Xi Nghiep In Tien Giang, 1996), p. 123.

10. Giai Thich Dieu Le Dang [Explaining the Party Rules], Kien Tuong Indoctrination Training, January 10–11, 1964, p. 5.

11. "Chuong Trinh Cong Tac To Chuc Cho Gao Nam 1965" [Program for the Organization Task in Cho Gao for 1965].

12. Doan Thanh Nien Cong San Ho Chi Minh Tinh Tien Giang, *Lich Su Doan Van Phong Trao Thanh Nien Tinh Tien Giang*, p. 149.

13. Tran Danh Ba Muoi Nam, vol. 3, p. 156.

14. Bon Bai Hoc ve Cong Tac Dang cua Huyen Uy [Four Lessons About the Party Work of the District Committee] (Tien Phong Publishing House, October 15, 1965, Pike Archive), p. 37.

15. Max Clos, "The Situation in Vietnam," in Vietnam: History, Documents, and Opinion on a Major World Crisis, ed. Marvin E. Gettleman (Greenwich, CT: Fawcett, 1965), p. 436.

16. An American advisor's positive appraisal of Phuc, as well as Le Minh Dao, can be found in Edward P. Metzner, *More Than a Soldier's War* (College Station: Texas A&M University Press, 1995). Tran Van Phuc's account of his own lengthy and harsh incarceration after the war is in Edward P. Metzner et.al., *Reeducation in Postwar Vietnam* (College Station: Texas A&M University, 2001).

Notes to Chapter 9

1. Ban Nghien Cuu Lich Su Dang [Party Historical Research Section], *Lich Su Dang Bo Tinh Tien Giang, 1954–1975* [History of the Tien Giang Party Headquarters, 1954–1975], vol. 2 (Tien Giang: 1986), p. 29.

2. *Cuoc Khang Chien Chong My Cuu Nuoc 1954–1975* [The Anti-American National Salvation Resistance 1954–1975] (Hanoi: Bo Quoc Phong, 1988), p. 81.

3. *Tran Danh Ba Muoi Nam* [The Thirty-Year War], vol. 3 (Hanoi: NXB Quan Doi Nhan Dan, 1988), p. 157.

4. Le Quoc San, *Cuoc Do Suc Than Ky* [The Incredible Trial of Strength] (Hanoi: NXB Quan Doi Nhan Dan, 1991), p. 98.

5. Ban Nghien Cuu Lich Su Dang Lich Su Dang Bo Tinh Tien Giang, 1954–1975, vol. 2, p. 27.

6. Ibid., p.28.

7. Vo Tran Nha, ed., *Lich Su Dong Thap Muoi* [History of the Plain of Reeds] (Ho Chi Minh City: NXB Thanh Pho Ho Chi Minh, 1993), p. 225. This account says the demonstration took place in 1960. The official My Tho Party history says it happened after the formation of the National Liberation Front in My Tho, that is, in early 1961. Ban Nghien Cuu Lich Su Dang, *Lich Su Dang Bo Tinh Tien Giang, 1954–1975*, vol. 2, p. 24.

8. Nguyen Minh Duong, "Ap Bac—Thanh Qua Cua Su Ket Hop Hai Chan Ba Mui" [Ap Bac—The Result of the Combination of the Two Legs and Three Spearheads], in Ban Tuyen Van Giao Tien Giang [Tien Giang Propaganda, Culture and Education Section], *Chien Thang Ap Bac: Ky Yeu Hoi Thao Khoa Hoc* [The Ap Bac Victory: Summary of a Scientific Conference] (Tien Giang: Nha In Tien Giang, 1993), p. 60.

9. A district cadre commented that Chinese weapons were first seen in the delta in 1962 [DT135]. A soldier in the province rear base protection unit reported a single shipment of arms from the North in 1963 [DT22]. A detailed discussion of the subject in a Hanoi book on the logistics of the war says that the first shipments came in 1962 as a result of Ca Mau province

taking the initiative to send four boats to the North to pick up weapons. Perhaps taking the cue from this, the North started to send weapons in March 1963. The first such shipment went to Ca Mau. By the end of 1964, sixty-seven shipments of arms had been sent to the South, totaling 3,864 tons. General Rear Services Directorate, *Tong Ket Cong Tac Hau Can Chien Truong Nam Bo-cuc Trung Bo.*

10. Cadre notebook of member of the province Military Affairs Section, ca. 1965.

11. Later in the war, the Southern military command concluded that experience showed that a regiment-sized unit with light arms was the optimum-sized unit. See the discussion on this point in Chapter 22. Tran Van Tra, *Ket Thuc Cuoc Chien Tranh 30 Nam* [Terminating the Thirty-Year War], vol. 5 (Ho Chi Minh City: NXB Van Nghe, 1982), p. 90.

12. Le Duan, "Gui Anh Muoi Cuc va Cac Dong Chi Nam Bo," p. 37.

13. *Tran Danh Ba Muoi Nam,* vol. 3, p. 158.

14. Vo Tran Nha, ed., *Lich Su Dong Thap Muoi,* p. 230. The province Party history says the transfer of the Seventh Division occurred in April 1961. Ban Nghien Cuu Lich Su Dang, *Lich Su Dang Bo Tinh Tien Giang,* 1954–1975, vol. 2, p. 27. It seems likely that this was the date of the decision to move, but that the division did not become operational until the summer.

15. Ban Nghien Cuu Lich Su Dang, *Lich Su Dang Bo Tinh Tien Giang, 1954–1975,* vol. 2, p. 24.

16. Vo Tran Nha, ed., *Lich Su Dong Thap Muoi,* p. 217.

17. Nguyen Thanh Son, ed., *Cuoc Khang Chien 30 Nam Quan Dan Tien Giang,* p. 143.

18. Ibid., p. 215.

19. Vo Tran Nha ed., *Lich Su Dong Thap Muoi,* p. 243.

20. Nguyen Cong Binh et al., Le Xuan Diem, and Mac Duong, *Van Hoa Va Cu Dan Dong Bang Song Cuu Long* [Culture and People of the Mekong Delta] (Hanoi: NXB Khoa Hoc, 1990), p. 427.

21. Jeffrey Race, *War Comes to Long An* (Berkeley: University of California Press, 1972), p. 1.

22. Huynh Minh, *Dinh Tuong Xua Va Nay* [Dinh Tuong Yesterday and Today] (Huynh Minh, n.d.), p. 255.

23. Nguyen Thanh Son, ed., *Cuoc Khang Chien 30 Nam Quan Dan Tien Giang,* pp. 141–51.

24. Ban Nghien Cuu Lich Su Dang, *Lich Su Dang Bo Tinh Tien Giang, 1954–1975,* vol. 2, pp. 20–24.

25. Ibid., p. 34.

26. Ban Nghien Cuu Lich Su Dang, *Lich Su Dang Bo Tinh Tien Giang, 1954–1975,* vol. 2, p. 29.

27. Ibid.

28. Nguyen Minh Duong, *Cuoi Doi Nhin Lai (hoi ky)* [Looking Back Over a Lifetime (memoir)] (Tien Giang: Xi Nghiep In Tien Giang, 2000), pp. 353–54.

29. Nguyen Minh Duong, "Ap Bac—Thanh Qua Cua Su Ket Hop Hai Chan Ba Mui," p. 60.

30. Neil Sheehan, *A Bright and Shining Lie* (New York: Random House, 1988), pp. 42–68.

31. Nguyen Thanh Son, ed., *Cuoc Khang Chien 30 Nam Quan Dan Tien Giang,* pp. 159–64. This source says that there were 182 American advisors in the seminary at the beginning of 1962. Neil Sheehan says that the U.S. advisory detachment based at the seminary was over 200 by the end of 1962.

32. *Tran Danh Ba Muoi Nam,* p. 177.

33. *Cuoc Khang Chien Chong My Cuu Nuoc cua Nhan Dan Ben Tre,* p. 101.

34. *Luoc Su Dang Bo Dang Cong San Viet Nam Tinh Ben Tre* [Summary History of the Party Headquarters of the Communist Party of Vietnam in Ben Tre Province] (Ben Tre: Chien Thang Printing House, 1985), p. 164.

35. "Report on the SVN Situation from the End of 1961 to the Beginning of 1964."

36. Ban Nghien Cuu Lich Su Dang, *Lich Su Dang Bo Tinh Tien Giang, 1954–1975,* vol. 2, p. 35.

37. Neil Sheehan, *A Bright and Shining Lie,* p. 50.

38. Le Viet Thang, "Vo Trang la Con Duong Song," p. 241.

39. Ibid., p. 244.

40. Ibid., p. 249.

41. Vo Tran Nha, ed., *Lich Su Dong Thap Muoi*, p. 255.

42. Le Viet Thang, "Vo Trang la Con Duong Song," p. 250.

43. Ibid.

44. Nguyen Minh Duong, *Cuoi Doi Nhin Lai*, p. 352.

45. Le Viet Thang, "Vo Trang la Con Duong Song" p. 252.

46. Ban Nghien Cuu Lich Su Dang, *Lich Su Dang Bo Tinh Tien Giang, 1954–1975*, vol. 2, p. 37.

47. Ibid., pp. 88–89.

48. Neil Sheehan, *A Bright and Shining Lie*, p. 119.

49. *Cuoc Khang Chien Chong My Cuu Nuoc 1954–1975*, p. 96. There is a slightly different version in Le Duan's "letters to the South," in which he writes to General Nguyen Chi Thanh that, after the Ap Bac battle, "The Americans saw that they *could not* defeat us [emphasis added]." Le Duan, *Thu Vao Nam*, p. 69.

50. "Throughout his next Vietnam visit, in early 1966, Joe saw signs of American success. He reported that the famous 514th Vietcong Battalion, known as the 'ever-victorious,' was 'really in dreadful shape,' beset by defeat, defection, and unpopularity in the villages." Robert W. Merry, *Taking on the World: Joseph and Stewart Alsop—Guardians of the American Century*" (New York: Penguin, 1996), p. 429.

51. *Tran Danh Ba Muoi Nam*, vol. 3, p. 189.

52. Tran Van Tra, "Luan Ve Tran Ap Bac Lich Su" [Commentary on the Historical Battle of Ap Bac], in Ban Tuyen Van Giao Tien Giang, *Chien Thang Ap Bac: Ky Yeu Hoi Thao Khoa Hoc*, p. 25.

53. Nguyen Thanh Ha (Muoi Ha), "Chien Thang Ap Bac Nhin Lai 30 Nam," p. 126.

54. Ibid., pp. 127–28.

55. Nguyen Minh Duong, "Ap Bac—Thanh Qua Cua Su Ket Hop Hai Chan Ba Mui," p. 64.

56. Tran Minh Phu [Sau Phu], "Ap Bac—Buoc Chuyen Bien Moi Cua Quan Dan Mien Nam" [Ap Bac—A Step in the New Transformation of the Army and People of the South]," in Ban Tuyen Van Giao Tien Giang, *Chien Thang Ap Bac: Ky Yeu Hoi Thao Khoa Hoc*, p. 75.

57. Tran Van Tra, "Luan Ve Tran Ap Bac Lich Su," p. 29.

58. Neil Sheehan, *A Bright and Shining Lie*, p. 207.

59. Ban Nghien Cuu Lich Su Dang, *Lich Su Dang Bo Tinh Tien Giang, 1954–1975*, vol. 2, p. 40.

60. Nguyen Chi Cong, *Song Mai Voi Nhan Dan*, p. 95.

61. Le Quoc San, *Cuoc Do Suc Than Ky*, p. 131.

62. Nguyen Thanh Son, ed., *Cuoc Khang Chien 30 Nam Quan Dan Tien Giang*, p. 180.

63. Nguyen Chi Cong, *Song Mai Voi Nhan Dan*, pp. 97–99.

64. Vo Tran Nha, ed., *Lich Su Dong Thap Muoi*, p. 279, refers to a COSVN directive on destroying Strategic Hamlets dated August 28, 1963.

65. Nguyen Chi Cong, *Song Mai Voi Nhan Dan*, p. 100.

66. Le Quoc San, *Cuoc Do Suc Than Ky*, p. 131.

67. Nguyen Chi Cong, *Song Mai Voi Nhan Dan*, pp. 97–100.

68. Ibid., p. 99.

69. Ban Nghien Cuu Lich Su Dang, *Lich Su Dang Bo Tinh Tien Giang, 1954–1975*, vol. 2, p. 42.

70. Nguyen Thanh Son, ed., *Cuoc Khang Chien 30 Nam Quan Dan Tien Giang*, pp. 180–81.

71. Nguyen Minh Duong, *Cuoi Doi Nhin Lai (hoi ky)* [Looking Back Over a Lifetime (memoir)] (Tien Giang: Xi Nghiep In Tien Giang, 2000), pp. 369.

72. Le Quoc San, *Cuoc Do Suc Than Ky*, p. 135.

73. Vo Tran Nha ed., *Lich Su Dong Thap Muoi*, p. 272.

454   NOTES TO CHAPTERS 9 AND 10

74. Le Quoc San, *Cuoc Do Suc Than Ky,* pp. 132.

75. Ban Nghien Cuu Lich Su Dang, *Lich Su Dang Bo Tinh Tien Giang, 1954–1975,* vol. 2, p. 42.

76. Nguyen Chi Cong, *Song Mai Voi Nhan Dan,* p. 97.

77. Neil Sheehan, *A Bright and Shining Lie,* p. 345.

78. Memorandum From the Joint Chiefs of Staff's Special Assistant for Counterinsurgency and Special Activities (Krulak) to the Secretary of Defense (McNamara), Foreign Relations of the United States (FRUS) 1961–1963, Volume III, Vietnam, January–August 1963, SACSA 468-963 Washington, August 16, 1963.

79. *Nghi Quyet Hoi Nghi TUC lan thu II* [Resolution of the Second COSVN Plenum], pp. 2–4. Vietnamese original identified as CDEC 6 028 0155 70. Document captured by U.S. forces in 1969. Deals with the period 1960–64. Pike Archives.

80. "Report on the SVN Situation from the End of 1961 to the Beginning of 1964."

81. Ibid.

82. Ibid.

83. "Report: General Political Situation at the End of 1963 (Consolidation of Situation During the 4th Quarter)," January 25, 1964. J2-MACV Log.10–96, October 16, 1964. Document captured October 1, 1964.

84. Ibid.

85. "Report on the SVN Situation from the End of 1961 to the Beginning of 1964."

Notes to Chapter 10

1. Resolution of the Ninth Plenum, December 1963, marked "Top Secret." Vietnamese original in Pike Archives. Cited hereafter as "Resolution Nine 1963."

2. Ibid., p. 6.

3. Ibid.

4. Ibid., p. 7; emphasis in the original.

5. Ibid., p. 12.

6. *The Pentagon Papers,* Senator Mike Gravel Edition (Boston: Beacon, 1971), vol. II, p. 17.

7. Ibid., p. 18.

8. "Report: General Political Situation at the End of 1963 (Consolidation of Situation during the 4th Quarter)," January 25, 1964, J2-MACV Log. 10-96, October 16, 1964. Document captured October 1, 1964.

9. Le Quoc San, *Cuoc Do Suc Than Ky* [The Incredible Trial of Strength] (Hanoi: NXB Quan Doi Nhan Dan, 1991), p. 137.

10. Ibid., p. 138.

11. Nguyen Minh Duong, *Cuoi Doi Nhin Lai (hoi ky)* [Looking Back Over a Lifetime (memoir)] (Tien Giang: Xi Nghiep In Tien Giang, 2000), pp. 370–75.

12. Ibid., pp. 377–78.

13. Ban Nghien Cuu Lich Su Dang, *Lich Su Dang Bo Tinh Tien Giang, 1954–1975,* vol. 2, p. 44.

14. *Tran Danh Ba Muoi Nam,* vol. 3, p. 234.

15. Ban Nghien Cuu Lich Su Dang, *Lich Su Dang Bo Tinh Tien Giang, 1954–1975,* vol. 2, p. 44.

16. "Report: General Political Situation at the End of 1963 (Consolidation of Situation during the 4th Quarter)."

17. *The Pentagon Papers,* Senator Mike Gravel Edition, vol. II, p. 28.

18. *Qua Trinh Cuoc Chien Tranh Xam Luoc cua De Quoc My va Quy Luat Hoat Dong cua My Nguy Tren Chien Truong B2 (Du Thao)* [The Development of the American Imperialist's War of Aggression, and the Patterns of Operation of the U.S. and Puppets on the B2 Battlefield (Draft)] (Hanoi: Quan Doi Nhan Dan Viet Nam, 1984), p. 127.

19. *The Pentagon Papers*, Senator Mike Gravel Edition, vol. II, p. 31.

20. Ibid., p. 43.

21. Ibid.

22. Ibid.

23. "List of Liberated Villages in My Tho Province," J2-MACV Log 10-286, October 18, 1964. Document captured August 1, 1964.

24. "Tong Ket Tran Tan Cong Chi Khu Quan Su Cai Be (Dinh Tuong) Dem 19 Rang 20 Thang 7 Nam 1964," [After Action Report on the Battle of Cai Be Sub-sector (Dinh Tuong), the Night of July 19, 1964], original in Vietnamese of document captured October 1, 1964. Item 21 of J2-MACV document listing 11/64.

25. Ibid.

26. Ibid.

27. Ibid.

28. Le Quoc San, *Cuoc Do Suc Than Ky*, p. 173.

29. "Tong Ket Tran Tan Cong Chi Khu Quan Su Cai Be (Dinh Tuong) Dem 19 Rang 20 Thang 7 Nam 1964."

30. The list of attendees is from Vo Tran Nha, ed., *Lich Su Dong Thap Muoi*, p. 295. Details on their connection with My Tho are from the interviews as well as this source.

31. Vo Tran Nha, ed., *Lich Su Dong Thap Muoi*, pp. 297–98.

Notes to Chapter 11

1. "LBJ Goes to War," in *Vietnam War: A History*, PBS television documentary series.

2. Le Duan, "Gui Anh Xuan" [To Brother Xuan], dated February 1965, in Le Duan. *La Thu Vao Nam* [Letters to the South] (Hanoi: Su That, 1985), p. 68. "Brother Xuan" is identified in a footnote as General Nguyen Chi Thanh, ibid., p. 398.

3. Ibid., p. 71.

4. Ibid., p. 72.

5. Ibid., p. 76.

6. Le Quoc San, *Cuoc Do Suc Than Ky* [The Incredible Trial of Strength] (Hanoi: NXB Quan Doi Nhan Dan, 1991), p. 183.

7. Ibid., p. 184.

8. Nguyen Minh Duong, *Cuoi Doi Nhin Lai (hoi ky)* [Looking Back Over a Lifetime (memoir)] (Tien Giang: Xi Nghiep In Tien Giang, 2000), pp. 379–81.

9. Le Duan, "Gui Anh Xuan," [To Brother Xuan], dated February 1965, in Le Duan. *La Thu Vao Nam* [Letters to the South] (Hanoi: Su That, 1985), pp. 86–93.

10. Ibid., pp. 95–97.

11. Ibid., p. 110.

12. Ibid., pp. 111–12.

13. Ibid., p. 113.

14. Ibid., p. 142.

15. Ibid., p. 124.

16. Ibid., p. 129.

17. DT Documents Reel I, "Chi Thi: Day Manh Cao Trao Thi Dua . . . vuot muc chi tieu 6 thang cuoi nam 1965" [Directive: Push Forward the High Tide of Emulation . . . surpass the target for the last six months of 1965], signed BQS KY [My Tho Province Party Committee Military Affairs Section], dated October 9, 1965. The David W.P. Elliott collection of Vietnamese communist documents [microform], Cornell University Library.

18. Tran Huu Dinh, *Qua Trinh Bien Doi Ve Che Do So Huu Ruong Dat Va Co Cau Giai Cap o Nong Thon Dong Bang Song Cuu Long (1969–1975)*, pp. 28–29.

19. Ibid., p. 29.

20. Lam Quang Huyen, *Cach Mang Ruong Dat o Mien Nam Viet Nam*, p. 41.

21. Ban Nghien Cuu Lich Su Dang, *Lich Su Dang Bo Tinh Tien Giang 1954–1975,* vol. 2, p. 32.

22. Tran Huu Dinh, *Qua Trinh Bien Doi Ve Che Do So Huu Ruong Dat Va Co Cau Giai Cap o Nong Thon Dong Bang Song Cuu Long (1969–1975),* p. 41.

23. Ibid., pp. 38–39.

24. Ibid., p. 41.

25. Ibid., p. 42.

26. Le Duan, "Gui Trung Uong Cuc Mien Nam" [Letter to Central Office, South Vietnam, i.e., COSVN], dated November 1965, in Le Duan, *La Thu Vao Nam,* p Le Duan, "Gui Trung Uong Cuc Mien Nam" [Letter to Central Office, South Vietnam], p. 156.

27. Nguyen Van Cong, *Song Mai Voi Nhan Dan* (With the People Forever) (My Tho: NXB Tong Hoi Tien Giang, 1986), pp. 107–08.

28. Ban Nghien Cuu Lich Su Dang [Party Historical Research Section], *Lich Su Dang Bo Tinh Tien Giang 1954–1975* [History of the Tien Giang Party Headquarters 1954–1975] (Tien Giang: 1986), vol. II, p. 48.

29. Nguyen Van Cong, *Song Mai Voi Nhan Dan,* p. 108.

30. Ban Nghien Cuu Lich Su Dang, *Lich Su Dang Bo Tinh Tien Giang 1954–1975,* vol. II, p. 49.

31. Nguyen Van Cong, *Song Mai Voi Nhan Dan,* p. 108.

32. Tran Bach Dang, "Ky Niem Sau Sac Voi Anh Sau Di [Profound Impressions of Brother Sau Di]," in Bo Quoc Phong, Vien Lich Su Quan Doi Vietnam [Ministry of National Defense, Vietnam Institute of Military History], *Dai Tuong Nguyen Chi Thanh: Nha Chinh Tri Quan Su Loi Lac* [General Nguyen Chi Thanh: Outstanding Political and Military Leader] (Hanoi: NXB Quan Doi, 1997), pp. 112–13.

33. CDEC document 10-116-65. The document was captured by the Dinh Tuong police on October 3, 1965. The translation is dated December 7, 1965, and titled "Report Concerning the Enemy [RVNAF] Situation During the First Half of CY [Calendar Year] 1965." The citation is from p. 21 of the translation.

34. *Nhung Nguoi Con Uu Tu Cua Tien Giang* [The Outstanding People of Tien Giang] (Tien Giang: NXB Ban Tuyen Giao Tinh Uy Tien Giang, 1992), p. 186.

35. Ibid., p. 190.

36. Nguyen Minh Duong, *Cuoi Doi Nhin Lai (hoi ky),* p. 381.

37. Ibid., pp. 385–86.

38. Ibid., pp. 387–88.

Notes to Chapter 12

1. Nguyen Cao Ky, *How We Lost the Vietnam War* (New York: Stein and Day, 1978), p. 83.

2. *The Pentagon Papers: The Senator Gravel Edition* (Boston: Beacon, n.d.), vol. II, p. 516.

3. Ibid., vol. II, p. 533.

4. Ibid., vol. II, p. 544.

5. Thomas C. Thayer, *War without Fronts: The American Experience in Vietnam* (Boulder, CO: Westview, 1985), p. 141.

6. Ibid., p. 143.

7. Stanley Karnow, *Vietnam: A History* (New York: Penguin, 1984), p. 502.

8. David Halberstam, *The Best and the Brightest* (New York: Random House, 1972), p. 186.

9. William Colby, *Lost Victory* (Chicago: Contemporary Books, 1989), p. 192.

10. The Pentagon Papers: The Senator Gravel Edition, vol. II, p. 598.

11. Ibid., p. 576.

12. Ibid., vol. II, p. 578.

13. Ibid., vol. II, pp. 576–77.

14. Dinh Tuong Province U.S. Senior Advisor's Report, December 1, 1966. U.S. Army Center of Military History, Washington, D.C.

15. Untitled and undated section on Dinh Tuong province of a U.S. government post-Tet estimate of the consequences of the attack, p. 2. Notation in handwriting indicates that this was "received from McIlvaine of VSSG/State." U.S. Army Center of Military History.

16. Marguerite Higgins, "Vietnam Town Regains Prosperity," *Washington Star,* August 10, 1965.

17. Thayer, *War without Fronts: The American Experience in Vietnam,* p. 225.

18. Ibid., p. 221.

19. Jerry M. Tinker, "The Refugee Situation in Dinh Tuong Province," Field Research Memorandum 6 (McLean, VA: Human Sciences Research, Inc., August 1967), p. 2.

20. Ibid., pp. 36–37.

21. Ibid., p. 10.

22. Ibid., p. 12.

23. Of the 272 interviewed, 69 answered the question about returning home and, of these, about a third said they made frequent visits home to harvest crops. A note appended to the table titled "Return Visits to Native Village" says "No. of refugees *not* returning: 203, or 74.6%."

24. Philip Taylor, Fragments of the Present: Searching for Modernity in Vietnam's South (Honolulu: University of Hawai'i Press, 2001), p. 162.

25. A prominent US official wrote "This brings me to the question of the so-called National Liberation Front, which is the political facade, made in Hanoi, for the Viet Cong movement. I doubt if any of you can name a single leader of the National Liberation Front. But these are faceless men installed by Hanoi to give the appearance of bourgeois and truly South Vietnamese support for the operation. . . . So there should be no doubt of the true nature of the Viet Cong and its Liberation Front, or that they are a completely different movement from the political opposition to Diem. As to the latter, and its present emergence into a truly nationalistic amalgam of forces—regional, religious, military, and civilian—I can perhaps best refer you to the excellent lead article by Mr. George Carver, an American with long experience in Saigon, in the April [1965] issue of *Foreign Affairs.* Mr. Carver tells a fascinating story of the emergence of these new nationalistic forces in South Viet-Nam, with all their difficulties and weaknesses, but with the fundamental and overriding fact that they are the true new voice of South Viet Nam and that they have never had anything to do with the Viet Cong."

Address by William P. Bundy Before Dallas Council on World Affairs on May 13, 1965, "Reality and Myth Concerning South Vietnam," Department of State Bulletin, June 7, 1965, p. 893. Ironically, in this article for *Foreign Affairs* on truth in political packaging George Carver did not disclose his identity as the CIA's top official in charge of Vietnam affairs.

26. Dinh Tuong Province U.S. Senior Adviser's Report, November 1, 1966. U.S. Army Center of Military History, Washington, D.C.

27. Peter A. Jay, "The Unpopular Maj. Dai: Thieu's Man in the Village," *Washington Post,* July 3, 1971.

28. Nguyen Minh Duong, *Cuoi Doi Nhin Lai (hoi ky)* [Looking Back Over a Lifetime (memoir)] (Tien Giang: Xi Nghiep In Tien Giang, 2000), pp. 402–3.

Notes to Chapter 13

1. Nguyen Thanh Son, ed., *Cuoc Khang Chien 30 Nam Quan Dan Tien Giang* [The Thirty Year Resistance of the Army and People of Tien Giang] (Tien Giang: Xi Nghiep In Tien Giang, 1986), p. 131.

2. Le Quoc San, *Cuoc Do Suc Than Ky,* pp. 234–35.

Notes to Chapter 14

1. President Thieu had received an intelligence briefing just before his departure for My Tho. "In any event, at 1800 29 January the allied cease-fire went into effect in all of South Vietnam except I CTZ (Corps Tactical Zone). President Thieu, unmoved by an intelligence briefing concerning indications of impending attack against urban areas, left Saigon soon after the declaration of the cease-fire to spend the Tet holidays at the coastal *[sic]* city of My Tho (IV CTZ). James J. Wirtz, *The Tet Offensive: Intelligence Failure in War* (Ithaca, NY: Cornell University Press, 1991), p. 218.

2. Don Oberdorfer, *Tet* (New York: Avon, 1971), p. 169.

3. Nguyen Thanh Son, ed., *Cuoc Khang Chien 30 Nam Quan Dan Tien Giang* [The Thirty Year Resistance of the Army and People of Tien Giang] (Tien Giang: Xi Nghiep In Tien Giang, 1986), p. 230.

4. U.S. My Tho Province Advisory Team, Monthly Report, February 7, 1968.

5. Ban Nghien Cuu Lich Su Dang [Party Historical Research Section], *Lich Su Dang Bo Tien Giang 1954–1975* [History of the Tien Giang Party Headquarters 1954–1975] (Tien Giang: 1986), vol. II, p. 57.

6. CDEC Bulletin 10,502, March 20, 1968. Documents captured on January 28, 1968.

7. Nguyen Thanh Son, ed., *Cuoc Khang Chien 30 Nam Quan Dan Tien Giang,* p. 227.

8. CDEC Bulletin 8416, December 5, 1967.

9. CDEC Bulletin 8429, November 3, 1967.

10. CDEC Bulletin 8733, January 1, 1968.

11. Nguyen Thanh Son, ed., *Cuoc Khang Chien 30 Nam Quan Dan Tien Giang,* p. 223.

12. Le Van Hai [Chin Hai] for the My Tho Province Military Affairs Section, "Chi Thi Cong Tac Chinh Tri Dot Dong Xuan 1967–1968 (du thao) [Directive on the Political Mission for the 1967–1968 Winter–Spring Campaign (draft)]," The David W. P. Elliott Collection of Communist Documents, NLF Documents, microfilm reel deposited at Cornell University Library, Reel I, Directives.

13. CDEC Bulletin 7952, November 11, 1967.

14. CDEC Bulletin, 13,546, June 21, 1968.

15. CDEC Bulletin, 6849, August 17, 1967.

16. Ban Nghien Cuu Lich Su Dang, *Lich Su Dang Bo Tien Giang 1954–1975,* vol. II, p. 59.

17. Ibid.

18. Quan Doi Nhan Dan Viet Nam, *Lich Su Bo Doi Thong Tin Lien Lac, tap II, 1954–1974 so thao* [Draft History of the Communications and Liaison Troops, vol. II, 1954–1975] (Hanoi: Nha In Quan Doi Nhan Dan, 1985), p. 186.

19. Ban Nghien Cuu Lich Su Dang, *Lich Su Dang Bo Tien Giang 1954–1975,* vol. II, p. 59.

20. CDEC Bulletin 8739, January 1, 1968.

21. Ban Nghien Cuu Lich Su Dang, Luoc Su Dang Bo Dang Cong San Viet Nam Tinh Ben Tre, p. 181.

22. Tran Van Tra, "Tet: The 1968 General Offensive and General Uprising," p. 44.

23. Le Quoc San, *Cuoc Do Suc Than Ky,* p. 251.

24. Bo Chi Huy Quan Su Tinh Ben Tre, Cuoc Khang Chien Chong My Cuu Nuoc Cua Nhan Dan Ben Tre (luoc su), p. 174.

25. Vo Tran Nha, *Lich Su Dong Thap Muoi,* p. 334.

26. Ibid.

27. Ibid.

28. Ibid., p. 335.

29. Nguyen Minh Duong [Sau Duong], *Cuoi Doi Nhin Lai (ho ky)* [Looking Back Over a Lifetime (memoirs)] (Tien Giang; Xi Nghiep In Tien Giang, 2000), pp. 414–15.

30. Ibid., p. 12.

31. Vo Tran Nha, *Lich Su Dong Thap Muoi,* p. 330.

32. CDEC Bulletin 13,868, July 1, 1968, contains a summary of an incomplete draft of the attack plan (possibly for the second wave of the attack) which lists 261A, 261B, 265, and 267. A citation for combat achievements contained in CDEC Bulletin 13,803, June 29, 1968, further identifies battalions 263 (P60) and 516 (516B) as having participated in the initial assault on My Tho city on January 31, 1968. The history of the revolution in Dong Thap locates the 504th Kien Tuong province unit in this assault.

33. Oberdorfer, *Tet,* p. 167.

34. Le Quoc San, *Cuoc Do Suc Than Ky,* pp. 250–52.

35. CDEC Bulletin 13,827, June 29, 1968. Report dated March 4, 1968, signed by Vu Trong, the political officer of the 261B Battalion, and sent to Battle Group I (Regiment I).

36. CDEC Bulletin 13,861, July 1, 1968.

37. Tran Van Tra, "Tet: The 1968 General Offensive and General Uprising," p. 53.

38. Le Quoc San, *Cuoc Do Suc Than Ky,* pp. 254–56.

39. Ibid., pp. 276–77.

40. CDEC Bulletin 10,430, March 17, 1968. Document captured in the vicinity of Ba Dua, March 10, 1968.

41. CDEC Bulletin 10,466, March 19, 1968, captured March 10, 1968.

42. CDEC Bulletin 16,355, September 9, 1968.

43. Nguyen Thanh Son, ed., *Cuoc Khang Chien 30 Nam Quan Dan Tien Giang,* p. 238.

44. CDEC Bulletin 13,827, June 29, 1968.

45. Le Quoc San, *Cuoc Do Suc Than Ky,* pp. 268–69.

46. Ibid., p. 273.

47. Ibid.p.277.

48. Ibid. pp.277–78.

Notes to Chapter 15

1. Ward Just, "Observers Assert War Is Turning Around," *Washington Post,* reprinted in the *Ithaca (NY) Journal,* February 27, 1969.

2. *New York Times,* October 9, 1970.

3. It appears that one of the proponents of a proto-"decent interval" concept in the aftermath of the Tet Offensive was an unlikely source—the normally hawkish former Secretary of State Dean Acheson. "I took it that the purpose of [American] efforts was to enable the GVN to survive and to be able to stand alone *at least for a period of time* [emphasis in original], with only a fraction of the foreign support it had now. If this could be accomplished at all or only after a very protracted period with the best that present numbers could do, it seemed to me that the situation was hopeless and that a method of disengagement should be considered." Lloyd C. Gardner, *Pay Any Price: Lyndon Johnson and the Wars for Vietnam* (Chicago: Ivan R. Dee, 1995), p. 446. The focus on a "decent interval" had not hitherto been a prominent element of U.S. policy, and it is instructive that Acheson focused on it in the post-Tet atmosphere. Henry Kissinger's refinement of this was to focus on finding ways to achieve a decent interval at a much lower level of commitment and to disguise the likely consequences of disengagement.

4. General William C. Westmoreland, memorandum titled "The Refugee Problem," dated January 4, 1968. The Westmoreland Papers, Box 15, Folder 28 History File I, document 23. LBJ Library.

5. *The Pentagon Papers,* Senator Mike Gravel Edition (Boston: Beacon, 1971), vol. III, p. 483.

6. David H. Hackworth, *Steel My Soldiers' Hearts* (New York: Touchstone, 2002), p.370. "'Ewell's crowing about killing twenty-two thousand VC in the last year was pure bullshit,' Vann went on. 'A lot of the dead were civilians. I told him to look at the weapons-to-body ratio. Flat ridiculous. Two hundred to one.' He paused, a sardonic smile flickering across his lips, but his eyes stayed serious." Ibid.

7. Ibid., p.2.

8. William Colby, *Lost Victory* (Chicago: Contemporary Books, 1989), p. 256.

9. Ibid., p. 272.

10. Ibid., p. 254.

11. Ibid.

12. Colby, *Honorable Men: My Life in the CIA* (New York: Simon and Schuster, 1978), p. 273.

13. Ibid.

14. Ibid., p. 271.

15. Dale Andrade, *Ashes to Ashes: The Phoenix Program and the Vietnam War* (Lexington, MA: D. C. Heath, 1990), p. 186.

16. Bo Chi Huy Quan Su Tinh Ben Tre [Military Command Headquarters of Ben Tre Province], *Cuoc Khang Chien Chong My Cuu Nuoc Cua Nhan Dan Ben Tre (luoc su)* [The Anti-American Resistance of the Ben Tre People (draft)] (Ben Tre: Xi Nghiep In, 1985), p. 183.

17. Vo Tran Nha, *Lich Su Dong Thap Muoi*, p. 335.

18. Thuong Vu Tinh Uy Long An [Standing Committee of the Long An Province Party Committee], *Long An: Lich Su Khang Chien Chong My Cuu Nuoc (1954–1975)* [Long An: History of the Anti-American National Salvation Resistance (1954–1975)] (Hanoi: NXB Quan Doi Nhan Dan, 1994), p. 306. Interestingly, this book, written by a Northerner under the direction of the Long An Party committee, appears to put the responsibility for being out of touch with the situation not on Hanoi, but on COSVN.

19. CDEC Bulletin 17,604, November 1, 1968.

20. Ban Nghien Cuu Lich Su Dang, *Lich Su Dang Bo Tien Giang 1954–1975*, vol. II, p. 65.

21. Ibid.

22. Ibid.

23. CDEC Bulletin 19,637, January 14, 1969.

24. Lieutenant General Julian J. Ewell and Major General Ira A. Hunt, Jr., *Sharpening the Combat Edge: The Use of Analysis to Reinforce Military Judgment* (Washington, DC: U.S. Department of the Army, 1974), p. 181.

25. Ibid., p. 183.

26. Ronald H. Spector, *After Tet: The Bloodiest Year in Vietnam* (New York: The Free Press, 1993), p. 221.

27. Ban Nghien Cuu Lich Su Dang, *Lich Su Dang Bo Tien Giang 1954–1975,* vol. II, p. 69.

28. Lewis Sorley, *A Better War* (New York: Harcourt Brace, 1999), p. 22.

29. Richard A. Hunt, *Pacification: The American Struggle for Vietnam's Hearts and Minds* (Boulder, CO: Westview, 1995), p. 191.

30. Vo Tran Nha, *Lich Su Dong Thap Muoi*, p. 347.

31. Nguyen Thanh Son, ed., *Cuoc Khang Chien 30 Nam Quan Dan Tien Giang*, p. 251.

32. Thuong Vu Tinh Uy Long An, *Long An: Lich Su Khang Chien Chong My Cuu Nuoc (1954–1975),* pp. 280–81.

33. Vo Tran Nha, *Lich Su Dong Thap Muoi*, pp. 371–72.

34. Ibid. p. 371.

35. *Lich Su Dong Thap Muoi*, pp. 344–45.

36. Nguyen Thanh Son, ed., *Cuoc Khang Chien 30 Nam Quan Dan Tien Giang*, p. 251.

37. *Lich Su Dong Thap Muoi*, p. 346.

38. Ban Nghien Cuu Lich Su Dang, *Lich Su Dang Bo Tien Giang 1954–1975,* vol. II, p. 69.

39. *Lich Su Dong Thap Muoi*, p. 341. This source claims that the region base moved to My Tho, but the memoir of Tam Phuong indicates that it went to Cambodia.

40. Le Quoc San, *Cuoc Do Suc Than Ky,* p. 408.

Notes to Chapter 16

1. Stephen T. Hosmer, Brian M. Jenkins, and Konrad Kellen, *The Fall of South Vietnam* (New York: Crane, Russak, 1980), p. 71.

2. Ibid.

3. Hosmer et. al., *The Fall of South Vietnam*, p. 74. See also the discussion of corruption in Gabriel Kolko, *Anatomy of a War* (New York: The New Press, 1985), pp. 208–213.

4. Peter A. Jay, "The Unpopular Maj. Dai: Thieu's Man in the Village," *Washington Post*, July 3, 1971.

5. Ibid.

6. Don Oberdorfer, "Return to the 'Rice Roots' of Vietnam," *The Washington Post*, July 17, 1980.

7. Dinh Tuong Province Senior Advisor report to USAAG IV Corps, February 1969.

8. Translation of an open letter to the GVN Prime Minister, Interior Minister, and Dinh Tuong Province Chief, published under the heading, "People Complain," by the *Tieng Noi Dan Toc* newspaper (Saigon) on September 20, 1971. Allan Goodman Collection, Hoover Institution, Palo Alto, California.

9. Ibid.

10. Ban Nghien Cuu Lich Su Dang [Party Historical Research Section], *Lich Su Dang Bo Tien Giang 1954–1975* [History of the Tien Giang Party Headquarters 1954–1975] (Tien Giang: 1986), vol. II, p. 74.

11. Lam Quang Huyen, *Cach Mang Ruong Dat o Mien Nam Viet Nam* [The Land Revolution in South Vietnam] (Ho Chi Minh City: NXB Khoa Hoc Xa Hoi, 1985), pp. 117–18.

12. Charles Stuart Callison, *Land to the Tiller in the Mekong Delta: Economic, Social and Political Effects of Land Reform in Four Villages of South Vietnam*, Monograph Series No. 23, Center for South and Southeast Asian Studies, University of California Berkeley (Lanham MD: University Press of America, 1983), p. 337.

13. Ibid., p. 336.

14. Callison, *Land to the Tiller*, pp. 81–82.

15. Ibid., p. 86.

16. Ibid., p. 126.

17. Henry C. Bush, Gordon H. Messegee [and] Roger V. Russell. With the assistance of Vu Van Binh, *The Impact of the Land to the Tiller Program in the Mekong Delta*, monograph "Sponsored by ADLR, USAID, Vietnam under Contract No. AID-730-3449," and published by Control Data Corporation, 1972. Available in Honnold/Mudd Library, the Claremont Colleges, Claremont, California.

18. Ibid., p. 46.

19. Nguyen Thanh Son, ed., *Cuoc Khang Chien 30 Nam Quan Dan Tien Giang* [The Thirty-Year Resistance of the Army and People of Tien Giang] (Tien Giang: Xi Nghiep In Tien Giang, 1986), p. 257.

20. Ibid.

21. Ban Nghien Cuu Lich Su Dang, *Lich Su Dang Bo Tien Giang 1954–1975*, vol. II, p. 71.

22. Dinh Tuong Province Senior Advisor's Report, March 1971.

23. Richard A. Hunt, *Pacification: The American Struggle for Vietnam's Hearts and Minds* (Boulder, CO: Westview Press, 1995), p. 260.

24. Ibid., p. 261.

25. Nguyen Thanh Son, ed., *Cuoc Khang Chien 30 Nam Quan Dan Tien Giang*, p. 261.

26. Ban Nghien Cuu Lich Su Dang, *Lich Su Dang Bo Tien Giang 1954–1975*, vol. II, p. 72.

27. Ibid.

28. CDEC Log No. 03-1076-72.

29. Gareth Porter, *Vietnam: The Defnitive Documentation of Human Decisions* (Stanfordville, New York: Earl A. Coleman Enterprises, 1979), vol. II, p. 551.

30. Ibid., vol. II, p. 554.

Notes to Chapter 17

1. *Cuoc Khang Chien Chong My Cuu Nuoc 1954–1975* [The Anti-American National Salvation Resistance 1954–1975] (Hanoi: Bo Quoc Phong, 1988), pp. 291–92.

2. Tran Van Tra, *Ket Thuc Cuoc Chien Tranh 30 Nam* [Terminating the Thirty-Year War] (Ho Chi Minh City: NXB Van Nghe, 1982), vol. 5, p. 89.

3. Defense Attache Saigon RVNAF Quarterly Assessment 4th Quarter FY 74, August 1, 1974. These reports are cited hereafter as DAO.

4. Tran Van Tra, *Ket Thuc Cuoc Chien Tranh 30 Nam* vol. 5, p. 86.

5. Peter A. Jay, "Vietnam: The Optimism Has Faded," *Washington Post,* January 16, 1972.

6. *Cuoc Khang Chien Chong My Cuu Nuoc 1954–1975*, p. 247.

7. Ban Nghien Cuu Lich Su Dang [Party Historical Research Section], *Lich Su Dang Bo Tinh Tien Giang, 1954–1975* [History of the Tien Giang Party Headquarters, 1954–1975] (Tien Giang: 1986), vol. II, p. 71.

8. *Cuoc Khang Chien Chong My Cuu Nuoc 1954–1975*, p. 253.

9. Bo Chi Huy Quan Su Tinh Binh Dinh [Binh Dinh Province Military Command Headquarters], *Binh Dinh: Lich Su Chien Tranh Nhan Dan 30 Nam (1945–1975)* [Binh Dinh: History of the People's War (1945–1975)] (Binh Dinh: 1992) pp. 380–81.

10. Le Quoc San, *Cuoc Do Suc Than Ky* [The Incredible Trial of Strength] (Hanoi: NXB Quan Doi Nhan Dan, 1991), pp. 341–47.

11. Discussion in Ho Chi Minh City, July 1999.

12. Le Quoc San, *Cuoc Do Suc Than Ky,* p. 367.

13. Ibid., p. 368.

14. Nguyen Minh Duong [Sau Duong], *Cuoi Doi Lai (hoi ky)* [Looking Back Over a *Lifetime (memoirs)*] (Tien Giang: Xi Nghiep In Tien Gang, 2000), pp. 429–31.

15. Ibid., pp. 443–72.

16. Ibid., pp. 366–67.

17. Ban Nghien Cuu Lich Su Dang, *Lich Su Dang Bo Tinh Tien Giang, 1954–1975,* vol. II, pp. 75.

18. *Cuoc Khang Chien Chong My Cuu Nuoc 1954–75,* p. 255.

19. Le Quoc San, *Cuoc Do Suc Than Ky,* p. 368.

20. Ibid.

21. *Qua Trinh Cuoc Chien Tranh Xam Luoc Cua De Quoc My Va Quy Luat Hoat Dong Cua My-Nguy Tren Chien Truong B-2* [Evolution of the U.S. Imperialist's War of Aggression and Standard Operating Methods of the U.S. and Puppets in the B-2 Battlefield] (Thuan Hai: 1984), pp. 214–15.

22. Le Quoc San, *Cuoc Do Suc Than Ky,* pp. 388–89.

23. *Kien Tuong; Lich Su Khang Chien Chong My, Cuu Nuoc (1954–1975)* [Kien Tuong; History of the Anti-American National Salvation Resistance (1954–1975)] (Hanoi: NXB QDND, 1993), pp. 194–95.

24. Nguyen Minh Duong, *Cuoi Doi Nhin Lai* (hoi ky), p. 470.

25. Ibid., pp. 471–72.

26. Ibid., p. 471.

27. "Pacification in South Vietnam: A Preliminary Damage Assessment," Central Intelligence Agency, Directorate of Intelligence Memorandum, April 25, 1972, pp. 5–6.

28. Ban Nghien Cuu Lich Su Dang, *Lich Su Dang Bo Tinh Tien Giang, 1954–1975,* vol. II, p. 76.

29. Le Quoc San, *Cuoc Do Suc Than Ky,* p. 380.

30. CORDS, Pacification Studies Group, "Evaluation: Impact of the Enemy Offensive on Pacification," October 5, 1972.

31. "South Vietnam: The Communists Strengthen the Base for Political or for Protracted War," U.S. State Department Bureau of Intelligence and Research, October 6, 1972, p. 3.

32. Ibid., vol. II, p. 78.

33. Le Quoc San, *Cuoc Do Suc Than Ky,* pp. 388–89.

34. Jacques Leslie, "Strategic Delta Province Again Alive with Reds," *Los Angeles Times,* August 3, 1972.

35. Sydney H. Schanberg, "Control of Mekong Delta a Matter of Perspective," *New York Times,* August 25, 1972.

36. Leslie, "Strategic Delta Province Again Alive with Reds."

37. Ibid.

38. *New York Times,* July 20, 1972.

39. File report from the Saigon bureau of *Newsweek,* by Nick Proffitt and Ron Moreau, dated August 10, 1972. The "cable-ese" orthography has been changed in this citation.

40. Daniel Southerland, "North Viets Gaining in Mekong Delta," *Christian Science Monitor,* August 2, 1972.

41. File report from the Saigon bureau of *Newsweek,* by Nick Proffitt and Ron Moreau dated August 10, 1972.

42. Leslie, "Strategic Delta Province Again Alive with Reds."

43. "Vietnam: The July Balance Sheet on Hanoi's Offensive," July 17, 1972 p. 5.

44. Ban Nghien Cuu Lich Su Dang, *Lich Su Dang Bo Tinh Tien Giang, 1954–1975,* vol. II, p. 80.

45. Ibid., vol. II, p. 84.

46. "South Vietnam: The Communists Strengthen the Base for Political or for Protracted War," p. 3.

47. Le Quoc San, *Cuoc Do Suc Than Ky,* p. 366.

48. Ban Nghien Cuu Lich Su Dang, *Lich Su Dang Bo Tinh Tien Giang, 1954–1975,* vol. II, pp. 81–82.

49. Jacques Leslie, "Some Viet Cong Units Reported Preparing for Possible Truce," *Los Angeles Times,* August 9, 1972.

50. Jacques Leslie, "Vietnam Delta War Called State of Limbo,"*Los Angeles Times,* November 16, 1972.

51. Tran Van Tra, *Ket Thuc Cuoc Chien Tranh 30 Nam,* Vol. 5, pp. 28–30.

52. Jacques Leslie, *The Mark: A War Correspondent's Memoir of Vietnam and Cambodia* (New York: Four Walls Eight Windows, 1995), pp. 136–59.

53. Ban Nghien Cuu Lich Su Dang, *Lich Su Dang Bo Tinh Tien Giang, 1954–1975,* vol. II, p. 84.

54. Tran Van Tra, *Ket Thuc Cuoc Chien Tranh 30 Nam,* vol. 5, p. 83. Parentheses in original.

55. Sydney H. Schanberg, "Control of Mekong Delta a Matter of Perspective," *New York Times,* August 25, 1972.

56. Joseph B. Treaster, "A Delta Town Is Hopeful but Watchful," *New York Times,* June 16, 1973.

57. David K. Shipler, "Rice Harvested as Delta Fighting Goes on," *New York Times,* July 20, 1973.

58. Thomas A. Lippman, "Two Sides Mingle in S. Viet Village," *Washington Post,* November 3, 1973.

59. Ibid.

60. Tran Van Tra, *Ket Thuc Cuoc Chien Tranh 30 Nam,* vol. 5, p. 72.

61. Ibid.

62. Tran Van Tra, *Ket Thuc Cuoc Chien Tranh 30 Nam,* vol. 5, pp. 89–91.

63. Ibid.

64. Ban Nghien Cuu Lich Su Dang, *Lich Su Dang Bo Tinh Tien Giang, 1954–1975,* vol. II, p. 91.

65. Tran Van Tra, *Ket Thuc Cuoc Chien Tranh 30 Nam,* vol. 5, pp. 112–13.

66. Ibid., vol. 5, p. 113.

67. Ibid., vol. 5, p. 134.
68. Ban Nghien Cuu Lich Su Dang, *Lich Su Dang Bo Tinh Tien Giang, 1954–1975,* vol. II, p. 92.

Notes to Chapter 18

1. "Thieu had begun to lose support from Catholic elements in 1972. The following year the Vatican endorsed a policy of accommodation with the PRG, stimulating a minority of Catholic 'progressives' to become more active on behalf of peace. Far more important was a right-wing resurgence under Father Tran Huu Thanh, one of Diem's close intellectual collaborators and organizer for Nhu, who in June 1974 issued a proclamation against corruption and social decadence signed by 301 priests. Father Thanh was convinced that only a purified state could defeat Communism, and many considered him even more hawkish than Thieu." Gabriel Kolko, *Anatomy of a War* (New York: The New Press, 1985), p. 488.

2. According to DAO (U.S. Defense Attache's Office) province reports, in Kien Phong province the province chief was transferred in November 1973 for "failing to meet rice shipment goals" to Saigon. DAO Kien Phong report November 5, 1973. In the same province four of six district chiefs were replaced in January 1974. (DAO Kien Phong report January 5, 1974). "For no given reason [Go Cong] province chief replaced and the Hoa Dong district chief removed for cause." (DAO Go Cong report February 28, 1974). The Cho Gao district chief in Dinh Tuong "summarily relieved" which "may be related to removal of Hoa Dong district chief (DAO Dinh Tuong report March 31, 1974). The Dinh Tuong province chief was "relieved" in June 1974 (DAO report June 17, 1974. In November 1974 the dismissal of three (of four) Corps commanders, including General Nghi, commander of the Mekong Delta's IV Corps was met with a "ho hum attitude" in My Tho, and the consensus was that "this is typical of the 'punishment' by the President [Thieu] to clean up military corruption." DAO Dinh Tuong report November 4, 1974.

3. Tran Van Tra, *Ket Thuc Cuoc Chien Tranh 30 Nam* [Terminating the Thirty-Year War] (Ho Chi Minh City: NXB Van Nghe, 1982), vol. 5, p. 111.

4. Ibid.

5. Defense Attache Saigon RVNAF Quarterly Assessment 3rd Quarter FY 74, May 1, 1974. These reports are cited hereafter as "DAO Quarterly Assessement."

6. DAO Quarterly Assessment, August 1, 1974.

7. Ban Nghien Cuu Lich Su Dang [Party Historical Research Section], *Lich Su Dang Bo Tinh Tien Giang, 1954–1975* [History of the Tien Giang Party Headquarters, 1954–1975] (Tien Giang: 1986), vol. II, p. 93.

8. Tran Van Tra, *Ket Thuc Cuoc Chien Tranh 30 Nam* vol. 5, p. 131. Tam Phuong identifies the units in Le Quoc San, *Cuoc Do Suc Than Ky* [The Incredible Trial of Strength] (Hanoi: NXB Quan Doi Nhan Dan, 1991), p. 407.

9. DAO Quarterly Assessment, February 1974.

10. Ibid.

11. DAO report Kien Tuong January 31, 1973.

12. Major General Huynh Cong Than, *O Chien Truong Long An* [On the Battlefield in Long An] (Hanoi: NXB QDND, 1994), p. 167.

13. *Kien Tuong; Lich Su Khang Chien Chong My, Cuu Nuoc (1954–1975)* [Kien Tuong; History of the Anti-American National Salvation Resistance (1954–1975)] (Hanoi: NXB QDND, 1993), p. 190.

14. Ibid., p. 213.

15. Ibid., pp. 203, 212–213.

16. "Members of the anti-Communist Hoa Hao Buddhist sect's private army staged a revolt in the Mekong Delta Feb. 1 to protest the government's Jan. 31 order disbanding the 50,000-man force and the arrest earlier in the week of two of its leaders. The rebels set up roadblocks

along a five-mile stretch of highway near Phong Phu, a district capital 90 miles southwest of Saigon, forcing military convoys and civilian traffic to stop. The action precipitated clashes with government troops and at least three persons were reported killed. . . . Following the fighting, the government was reported to have arrested more sect leaders. About 10,000 Hoa Hao followers entrenched themselves around a pagoda at Long Xuyen in defiance of the government. . . . The Hoa Hao had long been at odds with the Saigon regime, demanding special privileges and opposing government efforts to draft its members into the army. The government held the sect's private force was illegal. Feb. 1." 1975 *Facts on File*, February 8, 1975. "S[outh] Vietnamese Govt troops, moving with surprising swiftness, roll into small Mekong Delta village of Thoi Long and round up 60 people. Targets of operation are not Vietcong but members of civil guard of Hoa Hao, Buddhist sect that is 1 of S Vietnam's unique pol[itical] phenomena. Saigon Govt charges that Hoa Hao had taken advantage of confusion created by recent Communist offensive to lure Govt soldiers in Hoa Hao's own guard and had given shelter to draft dodgers. . . ." *New York Times Abstracts*, February 15, 1975.

17. *Kien Tuong; Lich Su Khang Chien Chong My, Cuu Nuoc (1954–1975)* p. 222.

18. DAO Quarterly Assessment, November 1, 1974.

19. Ibid.

20. Ibid.

21. DAO Dinh Tuong bi-weekly province report November 18, 1974.

22. DAO Dinh Tuong bi-weekly province report December 14, 1974.

23. *Cuoc Khang Chien Chong My Cuu Nuoc 1954–1975* [The Anti-American National Salvation Resistance 1954–1975] (Hanoi: Bo Quoc Phong), 1988), p. 298.

24. Tran Van Tra, *Ket Thuc Cuoc Chien Tranh 30 Nam*, vol. 5, p. 141.

25. Ibid.

26. Ibid.

27. Ibid. p.189.

28. Ban Nghien Cuu Lich Su Dang, *Lich Su Dang Bo Tinh Tien Giang, 1954–1975*, vol. II, p. 94.

29. Tran Van Tra, *Ket Thuc Cuoc Chien Tranh 30 Nam*, vol. 5, p. 143.

30. Ibid., p. 149.

31. Ibid., p. 154.

32. Ibid., p. 157.

33. Ibid., pp. 159–60.

34. *Qua Trinh Cuoc Chien Tranh Xam Luoc Cua De Quoc My va Quy Luat Hoat Dong Cua My-Nguy Tren Chien Truong B-2* [Evolution of the U.S. Imperialists' War of Aggression and Standard Operating Methods of the U.S. and Puppets in the B-2 Battlefield] (Thuan Hai: 1984), p. 247.

35. Nguyen Chi Cong, *Song Mai Voi Nhan Dan* [With the People Forever] (My Tho: NXB Tong Hoi Tien Giang, 1986), pp. 113–25.

36. Ban Nghien Cuu Lich Su Dang, *Lich Su Dang Bo Tinh Tien Giang, 1954–1975*, vol. II, p. 94.

37. Ibid., p. 96.

38. *Kien Tuong; Lich Su Khang Chien Chong My, Cuu Nuoc (1954–1975)*, p. 226.

39. Ban Nghien Cuu Lich Su Dang, *Lich Su Dang Bo Tinh Tien Giang, 1954–1975*, vol. II, p. 96.

40. Ban Tuyen Giao Tinh Uy Tien Giang [Tien Giang Province Propaganda and Education Section], *Tien Giang 30–4* [Tien Giang April 30] (Tien Giang[?]: 1995), p. 7.

41. DAO Dinh Tuong bi-weekly province report, January 25, 1975.

42. Tran Van Tra, *Ket Thuc Cuoc Chien Tranh 30 Nam*, p. 183.

43. DAO Dinh Tuong bi-weekly province report, February 22, 1975.

44. Ibid.

45. DAO Dinh Tuong bi-weekly province report, March 22, 1975.

46. Ban Tuyen Giao Tinh Uy Tien Giang, *Tien Giang 30–4*, p. 6.

47. DAO Dinh Tuong bi-weekly province report, March 8, 1975.

48. Tran Van Tra, *Ket Thuc Cuoc Chien Tranh 30 Nam*, vol. 5, p. 185.

49. "D K Shipler survey of land reform in S Vietnam finds program reversing in some areas after reaching near success in dissolving large land holdings and distributing them to poor tenant farmers, thus eliminating one of the Vietcong's strongest pol issues. Plantation owners in secure areas around S Vietnam are coming back to reclaim land they abandoned because of the war. Local officials demand that peasants relinquish land titles they were given a few yrs ago. Moves erode what was one of the most ambitious land-reform programs in Asia, financed largely by US aid and undertaken in '70 as a pol effort to woo peasants. . . . Mekong Delta was area where tenance [sic] had been virtually eliminated. Some legislators and Govt officials are concerned that current backsliding, affecting provs adjacent to Saigon and parts of Central Highlands, will revive land issue for the Communists. . . ." *New York Times Abstracts*, January 14, 1974.

50. DAO Dinh Tuong bi-weekly province report, November 30, 1974.

51. Tran Van Tra, *Ket Thuc Cuoc Chien Tranh 30 Nam*, vol. 5, pp. 207–08.

52. Ban Nghien Cuu Lich Su Dang, *Lich Su Dang Bo Tinh Tien Giang, 1954–1975*, vol. II, p. 98.

53. Le Quoc San, *Cuoc Do Suc Than Ky*, p. 415.

54. Tran Van Tra, *Ket Thuc Cuoc Chien Tranh 30 Nam*, vol. 5, pp. 219–21.

55. Ban Tuyen Giao Tinh Uy Tien Giang, *Tien Giang 30–4*, p. 9.

56. Le Quoc San, *Cuoc Do Suc Than Ky*, pp. 417–20.

57. Ban Nghien Cuu Lich Su Dang, *Lich Su Dang Bo Tinh Tien Giang, 1954–1975*, vol. II, p. 99.

58. Tran Van Tra, *Ket Thuc Cuoc Chien Tranh 30 Nam*, vol. 5, p. 251, 259.

59. Ibid., p. 259.

60. Ibid., pp. 263–64.

61. Ibid., p. 265.

62. Ibid., p. 266.

63. Ibid., pp. 271–73.

64. Le Quoc San, *Cuoc Do Suc Than Ky*, p. 429.

65. Nguyen Thanh Son, ed., *Cuoc Khang Chien 30 Nam Quan Dan Tien Giang* [The Thirty-Year Resistance of the Army and People of Tien Giang] (Tien Giang: Xi Nghiep In Tien Giang, 1986), pp. 322–23.

66. Doan Thanh Nien Cong San Ho Chi Minh Tinh Tien Giang [The Ho Chi Minh Communist Youth Group of Tien Giang Province], *Lich Su Doan Van Phong Trao Thanh Nien Tinh Tien Giang* [History of the Party Youth Group and the Youth Movement of Tien Giang Province] (Tien Giang: Xi Nghiep In Tien Giang, 1996), p. 209.

67. Ban Tuyen Giao Tinh Uy Tien Giang, *Tien Giang 30–4*, p. 12.

68. Ibid., p. 13.

69. Ibid., p. 17.

70. Ibid., p. 23.

71. Ibid., pp. 15–16.

72. Interview in My Tho, August 1982.

73. Telephone conversation, December 1999.

74. Le Quoc San, *Cuoc Do Suc Than Ky*, p. 434.

75. Ban Nghien Cuu Lich Su Dang, *Lich Su Dang Bo Tinh Tien Giang, 1954–1975*, vol. II, p. 102. See http://doanket.orgfree.com/quansu/tuhai1/html for an account of General Hai's suicide.

76. Le Quoc San, *Cuoc Do Suc Than Ky*, p. 434.

77. Nguyen Chi Cong, *Song Mai Voi Nhan Dan* [With the People Forever] (My Tho: NXB Tong Hoi Tien Giang, 1986), p. 121.

78. Nguyen Minh Duong [Sau Duong], Cuoi Doi Nhin Lai (hoi ky), p. 485.

79. Ibid., p. 481. General Nguyen Chi Thanh told Sau Duong in 1965 that the Politburo had already approved his elevation to membership in the Party Central Committee, but formal ratification would have to await the next Party Congress. Because of the war situation, the next Party Congress was not held until 1976, after the end of the conflict.

80. Le Viet Thang, "Vo Trang la Con Duong Song" [Armed Struggle is the Path to Survival], in *Lon Len Voi Cach Mang* [Growing up with the Revolution] (Tien Giang: Ban Tuyen Giao Tinh Uy Tien Giang, 1995), p. 133.

81. Vo Tran Nha, *Lich Su Dong Thap Muoi* [History of the Plain of Reeds] (Ho Chi Minh: NXB Thanh Pho Ho Chi Minh, 1993), p. 441.

82. Nguyen Chi Cong, *Song Mai Voi Nhan Dan* [With the People Forever] (My Tho: NXB Tong Hoi Tien Giang, 1986), pp. 126–28.

Appendix A

The Human Cost

Table A1

Revolutionaries Killed

During the resistance against the French	3,610
During the anti-American conflict	22,142
Unclassified	1,682
Total	27,434

Source: Nguyen Thanh Son, ed., *Cuoc Khang Chien 30 Nam Quan Dan Tien Giang* [The Thirty Year Resistance of the Army and People of Tien Giang] (Tien Giang: Xi Nghiep In Tien Giang, 1986), p. 358.

Table A2

Revolutionary Claims of Saigon Soldiers "Put Out of Action" and Captured in My Tho Province, 1960–1975

"Put out of action"	300,000
Captured	40,000

Source: Saigon Giai Phong, August 8, 1976. This article also claimed that 15,000 American soldiers were "put out of action."

Table A3

U.S. Soldiers Killed in the Provinces of the Upper Mekong Delta, 1959–1975

Dinh Tuong	834
Go Cong	71
Kien Tuong	159
Long An	1,018
Total	2,159

Source: Combat Area Casualties Current File (CACCF), the list of U.S. casualties of the Vietnam War. The search engine used here to locate casualty figures by province can be found at www.noquarter.org, which notes that "The CACCF is a public document updated by the Directorate for Information Operations and Reports at the Department of Defense. Anyone can purchase it from the Center for Electronic Records at the National Archives and Records Administration."

Civilian Casualties: Unknown

Appendix B

Reflections

The saga of revolution in My Tho from 1930 to 1975 was complex and tortuous. Yet, there are some generalizations that may contribute to a better understanding of the Vietnam War (1959–75). Perhaps the most important point is that, contrary to the impression of many Americans who thought that the conflict began when they arrived in the country, there was a long prior history of struggle. The trajectory of past events, and the legacy of the attitudes shaped by these events, imposed constraints on the behavior of all Vietnamese in later stages of the conflict, and, therefore (often unwittingly) on the Americans as well. However important the U.S. role in the Vietnam War, the outcome was fundamentally determined by the actions of the Vietnamese. These actions, in turn, were based on perceptions and beliefs whose historical roots were deep. Hence this project of examining the "Vietnamese War" and the period prior to large scale U.S. involvement in detail is viewed by the author as a precondition for understanding what is more conventionally referred to as the "Vietnam War," which focuses heavily on what the Americans did in Vietnam, and what was done to them.

Although the "Vietnam War" was largely a product of the Cold War and external intervention, the factors which ultimately frustrated the objectives and plans of the United States were home grown. Anti-colonialism and landlordism were the elements that provided the ingredients of a revolutionary movement. The August revolution of 1945 was the crucial historical movement when these ingredients bonded and produced a mass movement. The different tendencies within the revolutionary movement in My Tho, the Vanguard and Liberation groups, each had a distinctive social base. In the immediate aftermath of the August Revolution the two were fused into the larger revolutionary enterprise. Over the longer term, however, many of the urban and rural elites that had been attracted to the Vanguard leadership left the revolution, whose social base increasingly rested on the poorer rural peasantry.

A unique set of historical factors led to a revolutionary triumph in North Vietnam. This study shows why the revolutionary movement in southern Vietnam was initially less successful because of its great diversity of social and political forces and less fortunate historical circumstances (after the Japanese surrender, the south was occupied by the British, who turned a blind eye to the colonial reconquest of the French). Even during the Resistance, the complex mosaic of south Vietnamese society led to temporary French success in "pacifying" the Mekong Delta. An important lesson of this period is that temporary success in one area of Vietnam during a given time period was never enough to thwart the revolutionaries. When the situation deteriorated in other parts of Vietnam, French pacification fell apart. Had the Resistance war continued, the Viet Minh almost certainly would have been victorious in the South as well as the North.

The Geneva Accords resulted in the regroupment of revolutionary armed forces to the North and the demobilization of the guerrillas. Stripped of protection, the remaining revolutionary political cadres were systematically hunted down by the government of Ngo Dinh Diem, which was as little constrained by the internationally mandated protections of political expression in the South as were the forces of Ho Chi Minh in the North. This study does not address the legalities of this period, or even the relative moral standing of the contending sides. The interview data make clear, however, that the short-term gains of the Diem government through rigorous repression of a broad segment of the rural population in places like My Tho had fatal long-term consequences for his rule. Although there was never any question that the revolutionary movement had one power center—in Hanoi—the extent to which the insurgency which ultimately led to the Vietnam War derived from revolutionaries in the South pressuring a reluctant North is evident from the documentation presented here.

One problem with many studies of the revolutionary movement in Vietnam is a tendency to invoke false dichotomies, liberators or terrorists, aggrieved peasants or hardened Leninist apparatchiks. The role of revolutionary violence in the uprisings of 1959–60 and the importance of a few hundred political organizers in My Tho province are amply documented here. Campaigns of sustained terror were relatively rare, however, and usually brief. Their purpose was not only to intimidate or eliminate supporters and officials of the Saigon government, but also to counteract the fear of the Diem regime inculcated in peasants otherwise sympathetic to the revolution, and thus to neutralize Diem's advantage at a time when the revolutionaries were far inferior to the Saigon side in weapons and manpower. It is hard to explain the dramatic surge of revolutionary success in My Tho in terms of the relative handful of full-time revolutionaries, still active in 1959 and 1960, who were up against an adversary whose numbers and weapons were overwhelmingly superior.

A close examination of how the reactivated revolution unfolded after 1960 leads to two conclusions. The first is that there was genuinely widespread support for the revolution in places like My Tho, especially in the 1961–64 period. The tendency of many Western postwar histories to look back at the entire span of the Vietnam War through post-1975 lenses has led to the conclusion that the revolution never had a strong base in South Vietnam. The interview accounts of this period make it absolutely clear that there was a revolutionary high tide during these early years of the Vietnam War. As in 1945 and 1954, the revolutionaries almost certainly would have triumphed had the United States not intervened in 1965. Indeed, almost all contemporaneous accounts by top U.S. decision makers from this period forcefully make this point. This is not to say that the revolutionaries had the political field to themselves. They had many enemies but, in places like My Tho, no real political alternative. Opponents of the revolution, while numerous, were divided and too dependent on outside support.

A second conclusion reached from studying the post-1960 Vietnam War (and, indeed, the Resistance war that preceded it) is that while the revolution was often down, it was never out. Somehow the revolutionaries always found an answer to whatever policies or technologies had given them problems at given junctures. This extraordinary resiliency cannot be explained by a single factor. But whatever the combination of elements that sustained the revolution through hard times, a succession of adversaries with overwhelming material advantages could not duplicate this feat of perseverance over adversity. Many postwar studies of the Vietnam War contend that "if only" certain tactics, programs, or weaponry had been applied in timely fashion, the outcome of the war would have been different. However, the conflict unfolded in historical "real time." There was always a reason why these panaceas were never employed when they might have made a difference. Take two examples: land reform and smart weapons. Saigon's "Land to the Tiller" program might have had an impact on the peasantry had it been done in the 1950s in the place of the Diem reforms (which backfired). But, of course, it would have been unthinkable and politically impossible for Diem to do this-and far more outlandish to think of the French acting along these lines in the late 1940s when the first Viet Minh land reforms were consolidating a base of support for the revolution. It is true that smart bombs and other advanced weapons technology might have been more effective than the less sophisticated weaponry used earlier on by the United States and the Government of Vietnam, but there would have been few targets for them in this phase of dispersed guerrilla war. The revolutionaries did not stand still either. Starting in 1945 with sharpened stakes and machetes, which were adequate for the job at the time, they graduated to SAMS in the 1970s. Of course, these were supplied by China and the Soviet Union, but the point is that the conflict was a dialectic unfolding of action and reaction, in which every new innovation in counter-revolution produced a corresponding racheting up of revolutionary capabilities. The "what if" scenarios are ahistorical and fruitless. What mattered was what happened at the time it was happening and the relative strengths of each side at that precise moment.

Over time, the central issues of the conflict shifted. This study shows not only how important the land question was in the earlier stages of the revolution, but also how the ferocity of the war and the displacement of the peasant population from their hamlets made survival, not land, the main issue for My Tho's rural population. At the same time, the combination of land reform and wartime dislocation fundamentally changed the class structure in the Mekong Delta, and therefore the social base of the revolution. Landlordism was eliminated and along with it the large landless tenant class that had been an important element of the revolutionary constituency. In their place a rural middle class emerged. This study shows how sensitive the revolutionaries were to the "problem" of the middle peasant who, having gained land and a livelihood, might become more attached to it than to the goals of the revolution—and especially the ultimate goal of collectivization. The shrinkage of the social base of the revolution did not, however, prevent the revolutionaries from triumphing even after they became a probable minority in South Vietnamese society. To the extent that the evidence in this study points to any explanation for this, it lies in an asymmetry of motivation and dedication to a cause between the contending sides.

That the North Vietnamese factor was decisive in the end is important, but it also shows that the conflict was from the start set on a national stage. The U.S. assertion that the relevant boundary of the conflict was the Seventeenth Parallel dividing South from North was the key issue at stake in the Vietnam War. The revolutionaries rejected this view as incompatible with their definition of Vietnamese nationalism, and their view prevailed. Despite the many incidents of Southern regionalist antagonism to northerners cited in the interviews, they also make it clear that the southern revolutionaries in My Tho fully shared a commitment to a united Vietnam even though they wanted a much greater say in how it was to be led and were often frustrated by the dominance of a leadership based in the North.

What happened in My Tho sheds light on some historical controversies. The implications of this study for understanding the southern origins of the revived insurgency have already been noted. The essentially stalemated military situation just prior to the Tet Offensive of 1968, despite a year of intensive operations by a U.S. division in My Tho and surrounding provinces, suggests that the offensive was not, as it is sometimes portrayed, a desperation gamble, and that, even in the unfavorable terrain of the Mekong Delta, the revolutionaries had found a way to cope with U.S. combat troops under the rules of engagement that existed prior to Tet. Unnoticed at the time, a massive though brief peasant uprising did take place in the province in February 1968. Studies of the Tet Offensive sometimes point to the fact that no uprisings took place in the cities as evidence of the lack of popular support for the revolution, and it is probably true that in urban areas like Saigon and My Tho city there were few committed supporters ready to hit the streets while the bullets were still flying. Of course, there were many conditional supporters and fair-weather friends of the revolution involved in this uprising. Their purpose was more to end the war than to achieve victory for the revolution. But there was no parallel bandwagoning in favor of the Government of the Republic of Vietnam (GVN) in 1971 when it looked like the revolution was on the ropes. And in addition to the opportunists, many of those who were reactivated in support of the revolution during this short mass movement were latent supporters who were responding to a new situation in which the costs of open support were reduced and the potential benefits increased.

The rural uprisings in My Tho were probably not isolated events. One of the purposes of the assault on the cities, in fact, was to relieve pressure on the revolutionary bases in the countryside. A bitter refrain in postwar revolutionary memoirs of leaders in the Mekong Delta is that they failed to take advantage of the near collapse of the Saigon security structure in the countryside because higher ups in Hanoi and the Party Central Committee Office for South Vietnam ordered them to continue suicidal attacks on the fringes of the urban areas for well over a year following the offensive and long after these ill-considered operations had reached the point of no return. This is the obverse side of the advantage of being supported by Northern forces in the last years of the war. True, these outside forces were crucial to the final victory, but they were also necessary because decisions made in Hanoi had resulted in the decimation of the southern military forces. This happened not only because of the initial losses in the first wave of the offensive, but also over a protracted period of more than a year following Tet Mau Than.

Some studies done long after the war have concluded that the United States might have pressed its military advantage after Tet and won the war. Other books have argued that only after Tet did the United States find a commander (General Creighton Abrams), tactics (the Phoenix program and "pacification"), and policies (the "Land to the Tiller" program) that might have prevailed. What happened in My Tho after the Tet Offensive does not offer much support for these contentions. The military operations of the U.S. Ninth Division in 1968 and the first half of 1969 were militarily effective, but, because they were less inhibited about using massive firepower in populated areas than before Tet Mau Than, they also inflicted devastating casualties on the civilian population, which did not win many "hearts and minds." Pacification was temporarily successful, but largely based on the depopulation of the countryside that resulted from unchecked bombing and shelling of large areas of the province. The Phoenix program in My Tho was ineffective and corrupt (it was too often merely a shakedown opportunity for GVN security forces). The deaths of revolutionaries primarily occurred as a result of military operations, bombing, and shelling. The "Land for the Tiller" program never really got untracked because even in 1971, when most of the province had been "pacified," the former lands of many peasants were either still in places that were insecure, uninhabited (often as a result of a deliberate GVN population removal policy that placed more people in areas controlled by Saigon), or overgrown and uncultivatable. Even for those who got land, there was a question as to whether they would be grateful enough to the Saigon government to support it in adversity. This study presents some vivid, if anecdotal, evidence of the extent to which the Saigon government had alienated the rural notables in towns and villages in My Tho, thus undermining the basis for a noncommunist community of political forces.

Even at the nadir of the revolutionary movement in 1971, a small but determined group of revolutionary cadres held on in the face of overwhelming odds, waiting for the completion of the U.S. withdrawal. In 1972 the "Easter Offensive" was launched. Although the heaviest fighting was in central Vietnam and areas northwest of My

Tho, one of the effects of this offensive was to draw off Saigon forces from the Mekong Delta and relieve the pressure of the beleaguered revolutionary holdouts in places like My Tho. As official U.S. reports and interviews with local observers show, this provided a major setback for "pacification" and brought to a halt programs like "Land to the Tiller." It also cast into question the viability of "Vietnamization" as a means of achieving U.S. objectives after the withdrawal of American combat forces. This study suggests that the apparent near-total domination of the province by the GVN in 1971 was an illusion. The revival of the revolutionary movement was led largely, but not exclusively, by North Vietnamese military forces. It is also clear that a resurgence of the local revolutionary movement was set in motion by the 1972 offensive, but the scope or ultimate significance of this cannot be established by contemporaneous evidence, because only a few interviews were done during this period. These interviews along with independent reports by U.S. journalists do suggest a significant rebound of the local revolutionary movement, however.

What does the way the war ended tell us about the revolutionary movement in My Tho? The image of North Vietnamese tanks crashing through the gates of the Independence Palace suggests a military conquest of the South by the North. In My Tho, North Vietnamese units bore the brunt of the fighting after the 1973 "cease-fire," but these were not the only units on the scene and the revolution showed a surprising revival of its ability to recruit locally in My Tho during this period. The GVN unraveled from the top down in 1975. When Saigon fell, there was still a coherent security structure in Dinh Tuong province, which capitulated after learning of the collapse in the capital. Still, the GVN was clearly on the defensive in the central Mekong Delta from at least mid-1974 on, despite being able to hold onto important bases in places in outlying areas (like the Plain of Reeds) that had once been uncontested revolutionary zones. Reports from My Tho detail the moral and political crisis in the province capital (the Catholic anti-Thieu demonstrations), and the desertions of the demoralized and often unpaid Army of the Republic of Vietnam and regional force soldiers, frustrated by lack of support. The extent to which this was a consequence of overall decline in U.S. support as opposed to corruption and siphoning off resources cannot be answered by this study. The U.S. embassy reporter covering Dinh Tuong at the end of the war reported that

> it is no mystery why RF/PF forces avoid contact with the enemy and resort to huddling behind barricades during hours of darkness; nor is it difficult to understand how easily VC forces can dominate the villages and hamlets. It isn't mere military aid which is needed; it is discipline, motivation, incentive, and individual commitment, which is sadly lacking.

This study helps to explain why the revolutionaries won their thirty-year struggle against externally supported foes. It also suggests why the next phase of the revolution was so difficult. As noted above, the social base on which the revolution had been founded was fundamentally transformed by the end of the war. Southern society was not willing to accept the brand of socialism imposed on them after 1975, as subsequent events made clear. But to view what happened prior to 1965 from the perspective of what happened after 1975 is profoundly antihistorical. The revolution stemmed from real grievances. It built an impressive base of popular support. Most important, it left a deep imprint on the minds of Vietnamese in places like My Tho.

Although this study concludes at a historical point where the "moral peasant" village communities had been largely transformed into atomized "rational peasants," it also contains overwhelming documentation of the deficiencies of a purely "rational choice" approach to the study of the revolutionary movement in My Tho from 1930 to 1975. It is no accident that the rational-choice school of political science flourishes mainly in the United States, where discrete electoral choices can be measured, along with consumer choice in the marketplace. In Vietnam, the choices were about who had the power to establish the basic rules of the game, rather than about the contestants within a mutually agreed on framework. And the economic issues were about the fundamental nature of the socioeconomic system rather than individual economic behavior—although eventually the Party came to grief in trying to override the material interest of the Vietnamese in whose name it was acting. Vietnamese nationalism further complicated the issue because both democracy and capitalism had become identified with the opponents of Vietnamese independence, and this constituted a considerable obstacle to enlisting popular support for political and economic systems that seemed to outsiders to better serve the interests of the majority of Vietnamese.

Some rational-choice approaches have attempted to explain away the obvious problem of accounting for altruistic behavior, self-sacrificing dedication to ideals, or persistence in pursuing goals with uncertain or long-term payoffs at the expense of short-term benefits (including staying alive) by defining it away. "Rational" becomes any choice or behavior that "maximizes values." Beyond this problem of circularity, the rational-choice approach has the additional defect of assuming an individual-centered universe of political choice. In this approach, individuals often appear to focus on self-interested choices, oblivious to surrounding influences. This study shows that the rural village community was the decisive context in shaping values and political behavior up until the mid-1960s, when it was destroyed by the dislocations of the war. Even the revolutionary attempts to remake traditional village society by "pressing it into the mold" of Party-led organizations and "forging" emerging village cadres "by the hammer of the Party" were only partially successful.

And yet, the revolution did provide the peasants with the self-awareness, the information, and the confidence to take control of their own destinies—even when this ultimately led them in different directions from Party desires. Toward the end of the war, the atomization of society by wartime dislocation undercut community pressures, the protracted conflict exposed empty promises and often dissipated the idealism of an earlier period, and the perils of living in a war zone led to an increasing focus on survival and the adoption of a day-to-day time horizon (*sống qua ngày*). This was the rural parallel to the urban intellectual's wartime preoccupation with existentialism, which was denounced by the revolution as an alien mode of thought, fostered by the United States to distract Vietnamese students and intellectuals from the harsh choices presented to them, and a "living for the moment" philosophy that would make them forget their past and avoid thinking about their future. Along with the "middle peasantization" of rural society, these factors ultimately did produce "rational peasants." But the contrasts between two worlds of behavioral choice—individual and collective, value based or driven by "what's in it for me" concerns—were never absolute.

Another conclusion derived from this study is the danger of drawing generalizations from a period as long and complex as that covered by this study, even when the study is narrowed to a single province of a relatively small country. No generalization about political behavior is true at all times for all people. Few generalizations are valid even for a given time period or a specified group of people. The structure of the revolutionary movement was itself complicated. The values, attitudes, and behavior of the core cadres in My Tho were different from their supporting cast: the revolutionary infrastructure and the revolutionary sympathizers. Each group, and individuals within each group, were driven by a different mix of values and incentives. The periodic revitalization of both cadres and especially their peripheral supporters in My Tho (following the setbacks in 1950–52, in 1955–59, 1966–67, and in 1970–71) show that the revolutionary movement did not progress in an upward linear manner and did not recede in a terminal reverse direction. Large groups of people remained latent supporters even when they could not or would not act on their sympathies. This group was clearly much smaller at the end of the war than in its earlier stages, but still remained significant throughout the entire period.

A related point is that nothing lasts forever. The legitimacy gained during the August Revolution and the anti-French Resistance carried the Party through difficult times. But legitimacy is like money in the bank. If the account is drawn down, it must be replenished. The revolutionaries did do this, and received credit for their sacrifice and patriotism. As these interviews show, however, the incessant and uncompromising demands of the Party alienated increasing numbers of former adherents, and gave pause to potential new supporters. The number of middle peasants increased, and, as the Party had feared, they increasingly neglected their benefactors and concentrated on their own interests. Paradoxically, land became less of an issue while a bloated wartime economy offered alternative ways of earning a living, the potent incentive of land distribution began to fade as a powerful motivating force. The gradual withdrawal of the U.S. forces somewhat diminished the once nearly total monopoly on nationalism the revolution had previously enjoyed. In the final analysis, however, the GVN was unable to attract enough active support from those who were turning away from the revolution. The reasons for this would require an extensive study of the GVN and its supporters and potential adherents, but the data presented in this study suggest that while many were no longer willing to actively support the revolution solely on the moral basis of its claims to legitimacy, the Party still had the capacity to deny this legitimacy to the GVN, whose lack of a solid political core was dramatically exposed in the final phase of the conflict.

Vietnamese in the Mekong Delta reacted in different ways to challenges to the revolution's demand for commitment. An important inference from much of the interview data is that the most relevant political distinction in rural My Tho was between the "political class," defined here as those people willing to accept the higher profile and greater risks of being politically involved, and the nonpolitical class, whose constant refrain was "do whatever you like, I remain a simple citizen." Viewing political engagement in this way makes it easier to understand the attitudes and actions of people like the patriotic landlord in Vinh Kim whose friends were important GVN officials and whose son was a GVN local official, but who hid revolutionary cadres in his villa at considerable risk to himself. As a "political" figure, he spanned the complex divide separating local activists. Engagement, networking, and influence were more important than ideology.

An even more intriguing example is someone who does not figure prominently in this book (there is a photograph of him at the end of chapter 3). He is the father of a revolutionary heroine and martyr named Le Thi Hong Gam, who supposedly killed several dozen American soldiers before being killed by U.S. troops. After the war, the father described his life over the span of the conflict. He was a strong revolutionary sympathizer, but evidently not inclined to be a political activist. His sympathies were certainly known to all sides, but he seems to have avoided provoking the GVN local authorities. Amazingly, this convinced partisan of revolution was never arrested by the GVN, though he lived in areas controlled by them for most of the conflict. Part of his success in finding a level of political activism that allowed him to cling to his values while avoiding the risks of overt political action was due to his adopting the protective guise of a devout Buddhist layman, whose concerns for his community were essentially humanitarian. Although many suspected revolutionary sympathizers who were much more marginal to the movement were jailed or persecuted by the GVN authorities, Le Thi Hong Gam's father was untouched. The reason for this is unclear, though he seems to have found just the right combination of local prestige and influence and cautious discretion to enable him to fly under the GVN radar. In the end, cases like this show us how little we know about the local cultural and social complexities of My Tho's villages. Despite the many stories told in the interviews and memoirs cited in this study, and the massive amount of documentation, it is unexplainable anomalies like this that show us we not only do not know many of the answers, but probably also do not know enough to ask the right questions. Whatever insights are offered in the analysis contained in this study are, therefore, ventured with a sense of caution and deep humility.

These cases remind us that the "rational choice" approach also encounters the problem of explaining why some individuals are willing to accept the higher risks of becoming political activists when the risks are disproportionate to the rewards and there are many "free riders" who benefit from their efforts. A simple explanation is that political power protects individual interest. There is plentiful support for this in the litany of complaints about self-serving cadres in this study, yet there are even more contrary examples of self-sacrifice and idealism. Another explanation is that these people are natural "political entrepreneurs" who presumably get some psychic reward from being at the center of things. The Vietnamese phrase "to engage in great affairs of state" (làm đại sự) implies that being politically engaged is both elevating in terms of status and power and dangerous. It must be admitted that this study does not cast much light on this important question, other than documenting that there does seem to be an observable divide between those who are "in the arena" (ở trong cuộc) and those who are "simple citizens." For a political scientist, this failure to account for one of the most fundamental aspects of political behavior—the decision to engage in or avoid political action—is both humbling and challenging. Perhaps others who have addressed this subject in other contexts and circumstances will be able to provide the explanation that is missing in this study.

Of course, there is a broad spectrum between the extremes of self-generated total immersion in political action and complete disassociation from it (which was unwise and usually impossible in a revolutionary-controlled zone). It is important to keep this in mind when confronting perhaps the central issue of most studies of the Vietnamese War—whether the peasants were a neutral force, indifferent to all sides (as some writers allege), or whether they were strongly committed to one side or another (as others maintain). It is my conviction that the data in this study will not support the concept of a neutral peasantry. At the same time, it should caution against inferring too complete a convergence between peasant interests and Party policies. The many instances in which peasants selectively responded to revolutionary orders and appeals, or used the "weapons of the weak" to evade impositions on their self-interest is convincing evidence that this linkage was sometimes tenuous. At the same time, there are many instances of the revolutionaries successfully employing community pressures and coopting village society to the aims of the revolution. The perhaps unintended appeal to peasant conservatism in the last years of the war is also testimony to the deep rural roots of the revolution. It also, however, raises the issue of whether the revolutionaries were the best prepared for a postwar phase of political and economic development, which required different skills and attitudes, rested on a transformed social base, and unfolded in a dramatically transformed world in which colonialism was dead and the Cold War was winding down.

Those who castigate the revolutionaries for their obvious defects—ruthlessness, paranoia, and authoritarian proclivities—should also note that social movements are largely defined and shaped by the forces that produce them. Nationalist movements in more tolerant British colonies tended toward a reasonably open Fabian socialist style of politics. Nationalists in places like Vietnam were forced to be ruthless and secretive because that was the only way an opposition group could survive in the repressive environment of French colonialism, and the repression of the Diem era. Brutality and repression is repugnant in all circumstances, but there was more than a little irony involved in labeling the revolutionaries "terrorists." The tragedy of Vietnam is that the relatively open politics of mass mobilization of the August Revolution was replaced by the closed politics of revolutionary war triggered by the return of the French and the equally authoritarian style of Ngo Dinh Diem—to say nothing of the need to survive American attempts to eliminate the revolutionaries.

Between 1930 and 1975 the Mekong Delta underwent a sweeping set of transformations, many set in motion by the revolutionary movement. Perhaps the most significant of these was the evolution of the mental world of the peasants in the Mekong Delta from subjects to citizens. The massive displacement of the rural population during the war led to an increasingly urbanized society in southern Vietnam, and forever changed the face of Mekong Delta provinces like My Tho, which the French had characterized in the late nineteenth century as "nothing but an agglomeration of villages" with no real towns. In shattering the colonial regime and the structures of oppression in the villages the revolutionary movement also set in motion a protracted conflict, in which immense destructiveness and sweeping dislocations eventually became decisive forces in the emergence of the "rational peasant." The social structure of the countryside was dramatically altered by the growing dominance of the "middle peasants," who gradually displaced the poor and landless peasants as the key social force in the rural areas. It is not surprising that on her return to My Tho in 1975, after a two decade sojourn in North Vietnam, Nguyen Thi Thap ("Sister 10") could hardly recognize the people and the landscape—and that those revolutionaries who survived the entire 1930–75 period as she did were so few.

As a personal observation, the most striking impression from years of interviewing both past and continuing participants in the revolution was the extraordinary powers of observation and analysis that most of these people, formed in the rural backwater of a peasant society, demonstrated. Part of this is probably due to general cultural factors—the Vietnamese respect for education, and the quick intelligence so often remarked on by foreigners. But much of it is also due to the rigorous training they received in the revolutionary movement. It was, to be sure, limited in its perspectives, assumptions, and permitted boundaries. Nevertheless, the constant political indoctrination sessions and the "on-the-job training" of being a revolutionary in a life or death situation constituted a world class university of political science. In the end, the value of the exceptionally rich historical materials based on discussions with people raised in modest circumstances and relative isolation is a testament to them and to the human potential realized by this remarkable group of individuals, no matter what hand fate ultimately dealt them.

Bibliography

Newspaper, Journal, and Periodical Articles

Herring, George C. "America and Vietnam: The Unending War." *Foreign Affairs,* Winter 1991.

Higgins, Marguerite. "Vietnam Town Regains Prosperity." *Washington Star*, August 10, 1965.

Jay, Peter A. "The Unpopular Maj. Dai: Thieu's Man in the Village." *Washington Post*, July 3, 1971.

———. "Vietnam: The Optimism Has Faded." *Washington Post*, January 16, 1972.

Just, Ward. "Observers Assert War Is Turning Around." *Washington Post*, reprinted in *Ithaca Journal*. February 27, 1969.

Keyes, Charles F. "Ethnicity and the Nation-State: Asian Perspective." Paper presented Friday January 17, 2003. Center for International Ethnicity Studies at North Carolina State University's College of Humanities and Social Sciences. http://www2.chass.ncsu .edu/CIES/KeyesPaper.htm

Lescaze, Lee. "No Real Winners in Vinhkim." *Washington Post*, July 19, 1972.

Leslie, Jacques. "Some Viet Cong Units Reported Preparing for Possible Truce." *Los Angeles Times*, August 9, 1972.

———. "Strategic Delta Province Again Alive with Reds." *Los Angeles Times*, August 3, 1972.

———. "Vietnam Delta War Called State of Limbo." *Los Angeles Times*, November 16, 1972.

———. "War Returns to '100% Pacified' Province 30 Miles South of Saigon." *Los Angeles Times*, August 2, 1972.

Lippman, Thomas A. "Two Sides Mingle in S. Viet Village." *Washington Post*, November 3, 1973.

Mirsky, Jonathan. "Wartime Lies." *The New York Review of Books,* October 9, 2003

Oberdorfer, Don. "Now It's the Viet Cong Who Fear the Dark." *Miami Herald*, October 9, 1966.

———. "Tired of Fight, a Viet Cong Chief Switches." *Miami Herald*, October 10, 1966.

———. "Why the Viet Cong Propagandist Quit His Job." *Miami Herald*, October 11, 1966.

———. "Return to the Rice Roots of Vietnam." *Washington Post*, July 17, 1980.

Open letter to the GVN Prime Minister, Interior Minister, and Dinh Tuong Province Chief, published under the heading "A People Complain" by the *Tieng Noi Dan Toc* newspaper (Saigon) on September 20, 1971. Alan Goodman Collection, the Hoover Institution.

Schanberg, Sydney H. "Control of Mekong Delta a Matter of Perspective." *New York Times*, August 25, 1972.

Shipler, David K. "Rice Harvested as Delta Fighting Goes On." *New York Times*, July 20, 1973.

Southerland, Daniel. "North Viets Gaining in Mekong Delta." *Christian Science Monitor*, August 2, 1972.

Steinglass, Matt. "Vietnam and Victory." *Boston Globe,* December 18, 2005.

Taylor, Keith , "Surface Orientations in Vietnam: Beyond Histories of Nation and Region." *The Journal of Asian Studies* 57, no.4 (November 1998)

Treaster, Joseph B. "A Delta Town Is Hopeful but Watchful." *New York Times*, June 16, 1973.

U.S. Government and Government Funded Reports and Translations

American Embassy Saigon cable A-478 to Department of State titled "Post-Tet Situation in Dinh Tuong Province," dated March 27, 1968. This cable was signed by several members of the Embassy political section as well as Ambassador Bunker.

CORDS [Civil Operations and Revolutionary Development Support], Province Briefing Folder; Dinh Tuong (1969?). Available in Hoover Institution Library.

CORDS, Pacification Studies Group. Evaluation: Impact of the Enemy Offensive on Pacification. October 5, 1972.

Defense Attache Saigon RVNAF Quarterly Assessment 4 (series 1973–75).

Dinh Tuong Province Advisor Report (Series 1964–72).

Donnell, John C., Guy J. Pauker, and Joseph J. Zasloff, *Viet Cong Motivation and Morale in 1964: A Preliminary Report.* Santa Monica: Rand, 1965. RM-4507/3-ISA

Memorandum from the Joint Chiefs of Staff's Special Assistant for Counterinsurgency and Special Activities (Krulak) to the Secretary of Defense (McNamara), Foreign Relations of the United States (FRUS) 1961–1963, Volume III, Vietnam, January-August 1963, SACSA 468–963 Washington, August 16, 1963.

"Pacification in South Vietnam: A Preliminary Damage Assessment." Central Intelligence Agency, Directorate of Intelligence Memorandum, April 25, 1972.

Parker, Warren E. Consul General representative. Dinh Tuong and My Tho City. Bi-Weekly Reports. 1975.

"Report on the SVN Situation from the End of 1961 to the Beginning of 1964." CDEC Document Log No. 01–0519–70.

"Report: General Political Situation at the End of 1963 (Consolidation of Situation During the 4th Quarter)." January 25, 1964. J2-MACV Log.10–96, October 16, 1964. Document captured October 1, 1964.

"South Vietnam: The Communists Strengthen the Base for Political or for Protracted War." U.S. State Department Bureau of Intelligence and Research. October 6, 1972.

Tinker, Jerry M. *The Refugee Situation in Dinh Tuong Province.* Field Research Memorandum No. 6. McLean, VA: Human Sciences Research, August 1967.

"Vietnam: The July Balance Sheet on Hanoi's Offensive." U.S. State Department Bureau of Intelligence and Research, July 17, 1972.

Tarpley, Major General Thomas M., Commander Delta Regional Assistance Command. Debriefing Report, January 13, 1973.

Westmoreland, W. C. Memorandum titled "The Refugee Problem," dated January 4, 1968. The Westmoreland Papers, Box 15, Folder 28 History File I, document 23. LBJ Library.

Westmoreland Papers, Box 16, Folder 29, Document 55 Westmoreland to Wheeler, History File February 1–24, 1968, at the LBJ Library.

Untitled and undated section on Dinh Tuong province of a U.S. government post-Tet estimate of the consequences of the attack. Notation in handwriting indicates that this was "received from McIlvaine of VSSG/State."

Zasloff, J[oseph] J. *Political Motivation of the Viet Cong: The Vietminh Regroupees.* RM-4703/2-ISA/ARPA. Santa Monica: Rand, May 1968 (original edition August 1966).

Vietnamese Language Sources

Ban Nghiên Cứu Lịch Sử Đảng. *Lịch Sử Đảng Bộ Tỉnh Tiền Giang 1927–1954 (Sở Thảo)* [History of the Tien Giang Province Party Headquarters 1927–1954 (draft)]. Vol. 1. Tiền Giang: Xí Nghiệp In Tiền Giang, 1985.

———. *Lịch Sử Đảng Bộ Tỉnh Tiền Giang 1954–1975 (Sở Thảo)* [History of the Tien Giang Province Party Headquarters 1927–1954 (draft)]. Vol. 2. Tiền Giang: Xí Nghiệp In Tiền Giang, 1986.

———. *Lược Sử Đảng Bộ Cộng Sản Việt Nam Tỉnh Bến Tre* [Summary History of the Vietnamese Communist Party in Ben Tre]. Bến Tre: Nhà In Chiến Thắng, 1985.

———. *Tỉa Lửa* [A Shaft of Fire]. Tiền Giang: Nhà Xuất Bản Hội Văn Nghệ, 1986.

"Ban Tổng Kết Thành Tích 5 Năm Của Quân Dân Mỹ Tho: 1960–65" [Cumulative Report on Five Years of Accomplishments of the Army and People of My Tho: 1960–65]. David W. P. Elliott Collection of Communist Documents. NLF Documents. Microfilm reel deposited at Cornell University Library. Reel I. Directives.

Ban Tuyên Giáo Tỉnh Uỷ Tiền Giang. *Tiền Giang 30–4* [Tien Giang April 30]. 1995.

Bộ Chỉ Huy Quân Sự Tỉnh Bình Định. *Bình Định: Lịch Sử Chiến Tranh Nhân Dân 30 Năm (1945–1975)* [Binh Dinh: History of the People's War (1954–1975)]. Binh Dinh: 1992.

Bộ Chỉ Huy Quân Sự Tỉnh Kiên Giang [The Command Headquarters of Kien Giang Province] *Kiên Giang 30 Năm Chiến Tranh Giải Phóng* [Kien Giang: 30 Years of Liberation War]. Kien Giang, 1987.

Bộ Quốc Phòng [Ministry of Defense]. *Lịch Sử Cuộc Kháng Chiến Chống Thực Dân Pháp 1945–1954* [History of the Resistance Against the French Colonialists 1945–1954]. Vol. 3. Hà Nội: Nhà Xuất Bản Quân Đội Nhân Dân, 1989.

———. *Lịch Sử Cuộc Kháng Chiến Chống Thực Dân Pháp 1945–1954* [History of the Resistance Against the French Colonialists 1945–1954]. Vol. 4. Hà Nội: Nhà Xuất Bản Quân Đội Nhân Dân, 1990.

Bộ Quốc Phòng và Viện Lịch Sử Quân Sử Việt Nam [Ministry of National Defense and Viet Nam Institute of Military History]. *Đại Tướng Nguyễn Chí Thanh: Nhà Chính Trị Quân Sự Lỗi Lạc* [Senior General Nguyen Chi Thanh: Outstanding Political and Military Leader]. Hà Nội: Nhà Xuất Bản Quân Đội Nhân Dân, 1997.

Bốn Bài Học về Công Tác Đảng của Huyện Uỷ [Four Lessons About the Party Work of the District Committee]. Nhà Xuất Bản Tiền Phong, October 15, 1965. Pike Archives.

Cách Mạng Tháng Tám: Tổng Khởi Nghĩa ở Hà Nội và các Địa Phương [The August Revolution: The General Uprising in Hanoi and the Regions]. Hà Nội: Nhà Xuất Bản Sử Học. 1960.

"Chỉ Thị Về Việc Học Tập và Tổ Chức Lễ Ngày Thành Lập Đảng Nhân Dân Cách Mạng Việt Nam" [Directive to Study and Organize Ceremonies to Commemorate the Establishment of the People's Revolutionary Party]. January 6, 1962. Pike Archives.

"Chỉ Thị: Đẩy Mạnh Cao Trào Thi Đua: vượt mức chỉ tiêu 6 tháng cuối năm 1965." Document titled "Directive: Push Forward the High Tide of Emulation: Surpass the Target for the Last Six Months of 1965," signed BQS KY [My Tho Province Party Committee Military Affairs Section]. Dated October 9, 1965. David W. P. Elliott Collection of Communist Documents. NLF Documents. Microfilm reel deposited at Cornell University Library. Reel I. Directives.

Chiến Thắng Ấp Bắc: Kỷ Yếu Hội Thảo Khoa Học [The Ap Bac Victory: Summary of a Scientific Conference]. Tiền Giang: Nhà In Tiền Giang, 1993.

"Chương Trình Công Tác Tổ Chức Chợ Gạo Năm 196p5." [Program for the Organization Task in Cho Gao for 1965].

"Chương Trình Liên Kết Trong Xã Phát Động Chánh Trị Toàn Dân Của HĐCC" [Integrated Program for Political Motivation of the Entire People by the Forward Supply Councils in the Villages]. Directive dated April 17, 1966. David W. P. Elliott Collection of Communist Documents. NLF Documents. Microfilm reel deposited at Cornell University Library. Reel I. Directives.

Cuộc Kháng Chiến Chống Mỹ 1954-1975 [The Anti-American National Salvation Resistance 1954–1975]. Hà Nội: Nhà In Quân Đội, 1988.

Cuộc Kháng Chiến Chống Mỹ Cứu Nước của Nhân Dân Bến Tre [The Anti-American National Salvation Resistance of the People of Ben Tre]. Bến Tre: Chiến Thắng Publishing House, 1985.

Cuộc Tổng Tiến Công và Nổi Dậy Mậu Thân-1968 [The Mau Than General Offensive and Uprising of 1968]. Hà Nội: Nhà Xuất Bản Quân Đội Nhân Dân, 1998.

Dân Tôn Tử (Trần Văn Vi aka Sáu Vi). "Cách Mạng Tháng Tám tại Mỹ Tho." [The August Revolution in My Tho]. *SàiGòn Giải Phóng*, August 20, 1973.

———. "Năm Tôi 21 Tuổi" [The Year I Turned 21]. In *Đồng Chí:Hồi Ký Cách Mạng* [Comrades: Revolutionary Memoirs]. Tiền Giang: Nhà Xuất Bản Tổng Hợp Tiền Giang, 1987.

Đảng Nhân Dân Cách Mạng Việt Nam Điều Lệ [Party Rules of the People's Revolutionary Party]. Bến Tre: Nhà Xuất Bản Chiến Thắng, June 1964.

"Đề Án Công Tác Tài Chành Năm 1967" [Plan for the 1967 Finance Mission]. David W. P. Elliott Collection of Communist Documents. NLF Documents. Microfilm reel deposited at Cornell University Library. Reel I. Directives.

Đỗ Thúc Vịnh. *Mùa Ảo Ảnh* [The Season of Mirages]. Sài Gòn: Tự Do, 1962.

Đoàn Thanh Niên Cộng Sản Hồ Chí Minh Tỉnh Tiền Giang [Ho Chi Minh Communist Youth Group of Tien Giang Province]. *Lịch Sử Đoàn Và Phong Trào Thanh Niên Tỉnh Tiền Giang* [History of the Party Youth Group and the Youth Movement of Tien Giang Province]. Tiền Giang: Xí Nghiệp In Tiền Giang, 1966. In *Đồng Chí: Hồi Ký Cách Mạng*.

Đồng Nai: 30 Năm Chiến Tranh Giải Phóng [Dong Nai: 30 Years of Liberation War. Đồng Nai: Nhà Xuất Bản Đồng Nai, 1986.

Dự Thảo về Điều Lệ Đảng Cho Miền Nam [Draft Party Rules for the South]. N.d.

"Giải Thích Điều Lệ Đảng" [Explaining the Party Rules]. Tuyên Huấn Kiến Tường, January 10–11, 1964.

"Gởi Các LO-Về Việc Mở Một Đợt Qui Mô Rút ĐPQ, DK, để gấp rút xây dựng lực lượng chủ lực đánh địch nhiều thắng lợi to lớn sắp tới" [To: All Districts—On the Matter of Launching a Major Campaign of Pulling Up Local Forces and Guerrillas to Higher Levels in Order to Attack the Enemy and Win Many Big Victories in the

Near Future]. David W. P. Elliott Collection of Communist Documents. NLF Documents. Microfilm reel deposited at Cornell University Library. Reel I. Directives.

Hậu Giang 21 Năm Kháng Chiến Chống Mỹ [Hau Giang 21 Years of Resistance Against the Americans]. Hậu Giang: Nhà Xuất Bản Tổng Hợp Hậu Giang, 1987.

Hoàng Ước; Lê Đức Bình; and Trần Phương. *Cách Mạng Ruộng Đất ở Việt Nam* [Land Reform in Vietnam]. Hà Nội: Nhà Xuất Bản Khoa Học Xã Hội, 1968.

Hoàng Văn Hoan. *Giọt Nước Trong Biển Ca: Hồi Ký Cách Mạng* [A Drop in the Ocean: A Revolutionary Memoir]. Beijing?: Tin Việt Nam, 1986.

Huỳnh Công Thân. *Ở Chiến Trường Long An* [On the Battlefield in Long An]. Hà Nội: Nhà Xuất Bản Quân Đội Nhân Dân, 1994.

Huỳnh Minh. *Định Tường Xưa và Nay* [Dinh Tuong Yesterday and Today]. Published by author, n.d.

Kiến Tường: Lịch Sử Kháng Chiến Chống Mỹ Cứu Nước (1954–1975) [Kien Tuong: The History of the Anti-American National Salvation Struggle (1954–1975)]. Hà Nội: Nhà Xuất Bản Quân Đội Nhân Dân, 1993.

Lâm Quang Huyên. *Cách Mạng Ruộng Đất ở Miền Nam Việt Nam* [The Land Revolution in South Vietnam]. Thành Phố Hồ Chí Minh: Nhà Xuất Bản Khoa Học Xã Hội, 1985.

Lê Duẩn. *Lá Thư Vào Nam* [Letters to the South]. Hà Nôi: Sự Thật, 1985.

Lê Minh Ngọc. "Về Tầng Lớp Trung Nông ở Đồng Bằng Sông Cửu Long [Concerning the Middle Peasants in the Mekong River Delta]. In *Một Số Vấn Đề Khoa Học Xã Hội Về Đồng Bàng Sông Cửu Long* [Some Social Science Questions Concerning the Mekong Delta]. Hà Nội: Nhà Xuất Bản Khoa Học Xã Hội, 1982.

Lê Quốc Sản [Tám Phương]. *Cuộc Đọ Sức Thần Kỳ* [The Incredible Trial of Strength]. Hà Nội: Nhà Xuất Bản Quân Đội Nhân Dân, 1991.

Lê Văn Hải [Lê Văn Phẩm, Chín Hải], Ban Quân Sự Tỉnh Mỹ Tho [For the My Tho Province Military Affairs Section]. "Chỉ Thị Công Tác Chính Trị Đợt Đông Xuân 1967–1968 (dự thảo)" [Directive on the Political Mission for the 1967–1968 Winter–Spring Campaign (draft)]. David W. P. Elliott Collection of Communist Documents. NLF Documents. Microfilm reel deposited at Cornell University Library. Reel I. Directives.

Lê Việt Thắng. "Võ Trang Là Con Đường Sống [Armed Struggle Is the Path to Survival]. *Lớn Lên Cùng Cách Mạng* [Growing Up with the Revolution], Ban Tuyên Giáo Tỉnh Uỷ Tiền Giang, 1995.

Lịch Sử Cuộc Kháng Chiến [History of the Resistance]. Vol. 1. Hà Nội: Nhà Xuất Bản Quân Đội, 1984.

Lịch Sử Cuộc Kháng Chiến [History of the Resistance]. Vol. 3. Hà Nội: Nhà Xuất Bản Quân Đội, 1989.

Lớn Lên Cùng Cách Mạng [Growing Up With the Revoution]. Tiền Giang: Ban Tuyên Giáo Tỉnh Uỷ Tiền Giang, 1995.

Lược Sử Đảng Bộ Cộng Sản Việt Nam Tỉnh Bến Tre [Summary History of the Party Headquarters of the Communist Party of Vietnam in Ben Tre Province]. Bến Tre: Nhà In Chiên Thắng, 1985.

Một Số Vấn Đề Khoa Học Xã Hội Về Đồng Bàng Sông Cửu Long [Some Social Science Questions Concerning the Mekong Delta]. Hà Nội: Nhà Xuất Bản Khoa Học Xã Hội, 1982.

Mùa Thu Rồi: Ngày Hăm Ba [The 23rd of That Autumn]. Vol. 1. Hà Nội Nhà Xuất Bản Chính Trị Quốc Gia, 1995.

Mùa Thu Rồi: Ngày Hăm Ba [The 23rd of That Autumn]. Vol. 2. Hà Nội Nhà Xuaát Bản Chính Trị Quốc Gia, 1996.

Mùa Thu Rồi: Ngày Hăm Ba: Hào Khí Đồng Nai-Bến Nghé -Cửu Long [The 23rd of That Month: The Heroism of Dong Nai-Ben Nghe-Cuu Long]. Vol. 3. Hà Nội Nhà Xuất Bản Chính Trị Quốc Gia, 1996.

Mùa Thu Rồi: Ngày Hăm Ba: Hào Khí Đồng Nai-Bến Nghé -Cửu Long [The 23rd of That Month: The Heroism of Dong Nai-Ben Nghe-Cuu Long]. Vol. 4. Hà Nội Nhà Xuất Bản Chính Trị Quốc Gia, 1996.

Nghị Quyết Hội Nghị Thường Vụ TƯC đầu tháng 8 Năm 1965 [Resolution of the COSVN Current Affairs Conference of August 1965]. Dated August 28, 1965. This Vietnamese original is also translated as CDEC Document No. 01–0517–70.

Nghị Quyết Hội Nghị TƯC lần thứ II [Resolution of the Second COSVN Plenum], Vietnamese original identified as CDEC 6 028 0155 70. Document captured by U.S. forces in 1969. Deals with the 1960–64 period. Pike Archives.

Nguyễn Chí Công [Chín Công aka Chín ốm]. *Sống Mãi Với Nhân Dân* [With the People Forever]. Mỹ Tho: Nhà Xuất Bản Tổng Hội Tiền Giang, 1986.

Nguyễn Công Bình et.al., *Văn Hoá Và Cư Dân Đồng Bàng Sông Cửu Long* [Culture and People of the Mekong Delta]. Hà Nội Nhà Xuất Bản Khoa Học, 1990.

Nguyễn Minh Đường [Sáu Đường]. *Cuối Đời Nhìn Lại (hồi ký)* [Looking Back Over a Lifetime (memoirs)]. Tiền Giang: Xí Nghiệp In Tiền Giang, 2000.

Nguyễn Thanh Sơn, et. al. *Cuộc Kháng Chiến 30 Năm Quân Dân Tiền Giang* [The Thirty-Year Resistance of the Army and People of Tien Giang]. Tiền Giang: Xí Nghiệp In Tiền Giang, 1986.

Nguyễn Thi. *Năm Tháng Chưa Xa* [Months and Years Not Long Past]. Thành Phố Hồ Chí Minh: Nhà Xuất Bản Văn Nghệ TP Hồ Chí Minh, 1986.

Nguyễn Thị Thập. *Từ Đất Tiền Giang* [From the Land of the Upper Delta]. Thành Phố Hồ Chí Minh: Nhà Xuất Bản Văn Nghệ TP Hồ Chí Minh, 1986.

Nguyễn Trân. *Công và Tội* [Accomplishments and Misdeeds]. Xuân Thu: 1992.

Nguyễn Văn Nhân [Ba Chim]. "Lớn Lên Cùng Cách Mạng [Growing Up with the Revolution]. In *Lớn Lên Cùng Cách Mạng.*

Nguyễn Văn Tạo. *Tân Đại Tự Điển Việt-Anh* [Modern Vietnamese-English Dictionary]. Tokyo: Nhà Xuất Bản Tân Văn, 1969.

Nguyễn Văn Vũ [aka Ba Vũ, real name Nguyễn Văn Dư]. "Về Đất Liền" (Returning to the Mainland). In *Lớn Lên Cùng Cách Mạng.*

Những Người Con Ưu Tú Của Tiền Giang [The Outstanding People of Tien Giang] (Tiền Giang: Nhà Xuất Bản Tuyên Giáo Tỉnh Uỷ Tiền Giang, 1992).

Những Người Con Ưu Tú Của Tiền Giang [The Outstanding People of Tien Giang], Vol. II, (Tiền Giang: Nhà Xuất Bản Tuyên Giáo Tỉnh Uỷ Tiền Giang, 1993).

Notebook of a Cadre of the My Tho Province Military Affairs Section, ca. 1965.

Quá Trình Cuộc Chiến Tranh Xâm Lược của Đế Quốc Mỹ và Quy Luật Hoạt Động của Mỹ-Nguy Trên Chiến Trường B-2 [Evolution of the U.S. Imperialists' War of Aggression and Standard Operating Methods of the United States and Puppets in the B-2 Battlefield]. Thuận Hải: 1984.

Quân Đội Nhân Dân Việt Nam. *Lịch Sử Bộ Đội Thông Tin Liên Lạc, tập II 1954–1975 sở thảo* [Draft History of the Communications and Liaison Troops. Vol. 2. 1954–1975]. Hà Nội: Nhà In Quân Đội Nhân Dân, 1985.

Sở Giáo Dục Tiền Giang. *Lịch Sử Tiền Giang* [History of Tien Giang]. Thành Phố Hồ Chí Minh: Nhà In Quân Đội, 1986.

Thạch Phương và Lưu Quang Tuyên, eds. *Địa Chí Long An* [A Monograph on Long An Province]. Long An: Nhà Xuất Bản Long An, 1989.

Thế Đạt. *Nền Nông Nghiệp Việt Nam Từ Sau Cách Mạng Tháng Tám Năm 1945* [Vietnamese Agriculture Since the August 1945 Revolution]. Hà Nội: Nhà Xuất Bản Nông Nghiệp. 1981.

Thời Việt Minh [The Viet Minh Period]. Mỹ Tho: Ban Tuyên Giáo Tỉnh Uỷ, 1991.

Thường Vụ Tỉnh Uỷ Long An [Standing Committee of the Long An Province Party Committee]. *Long An: Lịch Sử Kháng Chiến Chống Mỹ Cứu Nước (1954–1975)* [Long An: History of the Anti-American National Salvation Resistance (1954–1975)]. Hà Nội: Nhà Xuất Bản Quân Đội Nhân Dân, 1994.

Tìm Hiểu Phong Trào Đồng Khởi ở Miền Nam Việt Nam [Understanding the Concerted Uprising Movement in South Vietnam]. Hà Nội: Nhà Xuất Bản Khoa Học Xã Hội, 1981.

"Tình Hình Phong Trào Đấu Tranh Chính Trị ở Nam Bộ Từ Hoà Bình Lập Lại Đến Nay" [The Situation of the Political Struggle Movement in Nam Bo from the Restoration of Peace to the Present]. Cited in Carlyle A.Thayer, *War By Other Means: National Liberation and Revolution in Viet-Nam 1954–60*. Sydney: Allen and Unwin, 1989, p. 86.

Tổng Cục Hậu Cần, *Tổng Kết Công Tác Hậu Cần Chiến Trường Nam Bộ-cực Trung Bộ (B.2) Trong Kháng Chiến Chống Mỹ* [Summary Review of the Rear Services Mission: Nam Bo and Southern Trung Bo (B.2) Battlefields in the Anti-American Resistance]. Quân Đội Nhân Dân, Tổng Cục Hậu Cần, 1986.

"Tổng Kết Trận Tấn Công Chi Khu Quân Sự Cái Bè (Định Tường) Đêm 19 Rạng 20 Tháng 7 Năm 1964" [After Action Report on the Battle of Cai Be Sub-Sector (Dinh Tuong), the Night of July 19, 1964]. Original in Vietnamese of document captured October 1, 1964. Item 21 of J2-MACV document listing 11/64.

Trận Đánh Ba Mươi Năm [The Thirty Year Battle]. Vol. 1. Hà Nội: Nhà Xuất Bản Quân Đội Nhân Dân, 1983.

Trận Đánh Ba Mươi Năm [The Thirty Year Battle]. Vol. 3. Hà Nội: Nhà Xuất Bản Quân Đội Nhân Dân, 1988.

Trần Giang. *Nam Kỳ Khởi Nghĩa; 23 tháng Mười Một năm 1940* [The Nam Ky Uprising: November 23, 1940]. Hà Nội: Nhà Xuất Bản Chính Trị Quốc Gia, 1996.

Trần Hữu Dĩnh. Quá Trình Biến Đổi Về Chế Độ Sở Hữu Ruộng Đất Và Cơ Cấu Giai Cấp ở Nông Thôn Đồng Bàng Sông Cửu Long (1969–1975) [The Process of Change in Land Tenure and Class Structure in the Rural Areas of the Mekong Delta (1969–1975)]. Hà Nội: Nhà Xuất Bản Khoa Học Xã Hội, 1994.

Trần Thúc Linh. "Làm Đĩ" [Being a Prostitute]. *Tin Sáng* (SàiGòn), August 16, 1971.

Trần Văn Giàu. "Máy Đặc Tính Của Nông Dân Đồng Bàng Cửu Long-Dồng Nai" [Some Special Characteristics of Peasants in the Mekong Delta and Dong Nai]. In *Một Số Vấn Đề Khoa Học Xã Hội Về Đồng Bàng Sông Cửu Long* [Some Social Science Questions Concerning the Mekong Delta]. Hà Nội: Nhà Xuất Bản Khoa Học Xã Hội , 1982.

———. "Từ Tà Lài về Sài Gòn" [From Ta Lai to Saigon]. In *Mùa Thu Rồi: Ngày Hăm Ba*. Vol. I.

Trần Văn Trà. *Kết Thúc Cuộc Chiến Tranh 30 Năm* [Terminating the Thirty-Year War]. Vol. 5. Thành Phố Hồ Chí Minh: Nhà Xuất Bản Văn Nghệ, 1982.

———. *Những Chặng Đường Lịch Sử Của B2 Thành Đồng* [Historical Stages in the B2 Brass Fortress]. Vol. 1. Hà Nội: Nhà Xuất Bản Quân Đội Nhân Dân, 1992.

Võ Trần Nhã, ed. *Lịch Sử Đồng Tháp Mười* [History of the Plain of Reeds]. Thành Phố Hồ Chí Minh: Nhà Xuất Bản TP Hồ Chí Minh, 1993.

Western Language Books and Monographs

Anderson, Benedict O'G. *Java in a Time of Revolution: Occupation and Resistance 1944–1946*. Ithaca: Cornell University Press, 1972.

Andrade, Dale. *Ashes to Ashes: The Phoenix Program and the Vietnam War*. Lexington: D.C. Heath, 1990.

Andrews, William R. *The Village War: Vietnamese Communist Revolutionary Activities in Dinh Tuong Province, 1960–1964*. Columbia: University of Missouri Press, 1973.

Ap Bac: Major Battles in South Vietnam 1963–1964. Hanoi: Foreign Languages Publishing House, 1965.

Bauchar, Rene [Jean Charboneau]. *Rafales sur l'Indochine*. Paris: 1946, p. 71. Cited in Huynh Kim Khanh, *Vietnamese Communism: 1925–1945*. Ithaca: Cornell University Press, 1982.

Borton, Lady. *After Sorrow: An American Among the Vietnamese*. Tokyo: Kodansha International, 1996.

Bush, Henry C., et al. *Impact of the Land to the Tiller Program in the Mekong Delta*. Control Data Corporation, December 1972.

Callison, Charles Stuart. *Land to the Tiller in the Mekong Delta: Economic, Social and Political Effects of Land Reform in Four Villages of South Vietnam*. Monograph Series No. 23, Center for South and Southeast Asian Studies, University of California Berkeley. Lanham, MD: University Press of America, 1983.

Chaliand, Gerard. *The Peasants of North Vietnam*. Middlesex: Penguin Books, 1969.

Clos, Max. "The Situation in Vietnam." In *Vietnam: History, Documents, and Opinion on a Major World Crisis*, ed. Marvin E. Gettleman. Greenwich: Fawcett, 1965.

Colby, William. *Honorable Men: My Life in the CIA*. New York: Simon and Schuster, 1978.

———. *Lost Victory*. Chicago: Contemporary Books, 1989.

Croizat, Lt. Col. Victor. *Vietnam River Warfare, 1945–1975*. Poole: Blandford Press, 1986.

Devillers, Phillipe. *Histoire du Viet-Nam de 1940 a 1952* [History of Vietnam from 1940 to 1952]. Paris: Editions du Seuil, 1952.

Doyle, Edward, and Samuel Lipsman. *The Vietnam Experience: America Takes Over*. Boston: Boston Publishing House, 1982.

Duiker, William. *The Communist Road to Power in Vietnam*. Boulder: Westview Press, 1981.

Elliott, David W. P. "Hanoi's Strategy in the Second Indochina War." In *The Vietnam War: Vietnamese and American Perspectives*, ed. Jayne S. Werner and Luu Doan Huynh. Armonk, NY: M.E. Sharpe, 1993.

———. "Waiting for the East Wind: Revolution and Social Change in Vietnam." *Vietnam Forum*, No. 9. Yale Center for International and Area Studies, Winter–Spring 1987.

Elliott, David W. P., and Mai Elliott. *Documents of an Elite Viet Cong Delta Unit: The Demolition Unit of the 514th Battalion, Part Five: Personal Letters*. Memorandum RM-5852-ISA ARPA. Santa Monica: Rand Corporation, May 1969.

Elliott, David W. P., and W. A. Stewart. *Pacification and the Viet Cong System in Dinh Tuong: 1966–1967*. RM-5788 ISA/ARPA. Santa Monica: Rand Corporation, January 1969.

Ewell, Lt. General Julian J., and Maj. General Ira A. Hunt, Jr. *Sharpening the Combat Edge: The Use of Analysis to Reinforce Military Judgment*. Washington, DC: Department of the Army, 1974.

Fung Yu-lan (Dirk Bodde, trans.). *A Short History of Chinese Philosophy*. New York: Macmillan, 1948.

Gaiduk, Ilya V. *The Soviet Union and the Vietnam War*. Chicago: Ivan R. Dee, 1996.

Gardner, Lloyd C. Pay Any Price: Lyndon Johnson and the Wars for Vietnam. Chicago: Ivan R. Dee, 1995.

Giebel, Christoph. *Imagined Ancestries of Vietnamese Communism: Ton Duc Thang and the Politics of History and Memory.* Seattle: University of Washington Press, 2004.

Hackworth, David H. *Steel My Soldiers' Hearts*. New York: Touchstone, 2002.

Halberstam, David. *The Best and the Brightest*. New York: Random House, 1972.

Hosmer, Stephen T., et al. *The Fall of South Vietnam*. New York: Crane, Russak and Co., 1980.

Kahin, George McT. *Intervention: How America Became Involved in Vietnam*. New York: Alfred A. Knopf, 1986.

Karnow, Stanley. *Vietnam: A History*. New York: Penguin, 1984.

Huynh Kim Khanh. *Vietnamese Communism: 1925–1945*. Ithaca: Cornell University Press, 1982.

Kimball, Jeffrey. *Nixon's Vietnam War*. Lawrence: University Press of Kansas, 1998.

Kolko, Gabriel. *Anatomy of a War*. New York: New Press, 1985.

Leslie, Jacques. *The Mark: A War Correspondent's Memoir of Vietnam and Cambodia*. New York: Four Walls Eight Windows, 1995.

Lieberman, Victor. *Strange Parallels: Southeast Asia in Global Context, c.800–1830, Volume I: Integration on the Mainland.* Cambridge: Cambridge University Press, 2003, pp. 343–43.

Marr, David G. *Vietnam 1945: The Quest for Power*. Berkeley: University of California Press, 1995.

———. *Vietnamese Tradition on Trial 1920–45*. Berkeley: University of California Press, 1981.

———. *Vietnamese Anticolonialism 1885–1925*. Berkeley: University of California Press, 1971.

McGarvey, Patrick. *Visions of Victory*. Stanford: Hoover Institution, 1969.

Merry, Robert W. *Taking on the World: Joseph and Stewart Alsop—Guardians of the American Century*. New York: Penguin, 1996.

Metzner, Edward P. *More Than a Soldier's War.* College Station: Texas A&M University Press, 1995.

Metzner, Edward P., et.al. *Reeducation in Postwar Vietnam.* College Station: Texas A&M University, 2001.

Moise, Edwin E. *Land Reform in China and North Vietnam*. Chapel Hill: University of North Carolina Press, 1983.

Newman, John M. *JFK and Vietnam*. New York: Warner Books, 1992.

Nguyen Anh Tuan. *South Vietnam: Trial and Experience*. Ohio University Monographs in International Studies, Southeast Asia Series, no. 80, 1987.

Nguyen Cao Ky. *How We Lost the Vietnam War*. New York: Stein and Day, 1978.

Nguyen Ngoc Luu. Peasants, Party and Revolution: The Politics of Agrarian Transformation in Northern Vietnam, 1930–1975. N.p., n.d.

Nguyen Thai. *Is South Vietnam Viable?* Manila: 1962.

Nguyen Thi Dinh. *No Other Road to Take: Memoir of Mrs. Nguyen Thi Dinh,* translated by Mai Elliott. Data Paper no. 102, Southeast Asia Program, Department of Asian Studies, Cornell University, Ithaca NY, June 1976.

Oberdorfer, Don. *Tet*. New York: Avon, 1971.

Pham Cao Duong. *Vietnamese Peasants Under French Domination: 1861–1945*. Center for South and Southeast Asian Studies University of California, Monograph Series, no. 24. New York: University Press of America, 1985.

Popkin, Samuel L. The Rational Peasant: The Political Economy of Rural Society in Vietnam. Berkeley: University of California Press, 1979.

Porter, Gareth. *Vietnam: The Politics of Bureaucratic Socialism*. Ithaca: Cornell University Press, 1993.

———. *Vietnam: The Definitive Documentation of Human Decisions*. Vol. 2. Stanfordville: Earl A. Coleman Enterprises, 1979.

———. "Imperialism and Social Structure in Twentieth Century Vietnam." Ph.D. diss., Cornell University, 1976.

Race, Jeffrey. *War Comes to Long An*. Berkeley: University of California Press, 1972.

Sansom, Robert. *The Economics of Insurgency*. Cambridge: MIT Press, 1970.

Savani, A. M. *Visages et Images du Sud Viet-Nam* [Faces and Images of South Vietnam]. Saigon: 1955.

Scott, James C. *Weapons of the Weak*. New Haven: Yale University Press, 1987.

———. The Moral Economy of the Peasant: Rebellion and Subsistence in Southeast Asia. New Haven: Yale University Press, 1976.

Sheehan, Neil. *A Bright and Shining Lie*. New York: Random House, 1988.

Sollom, A. H. "Nowhere, Yet Everywhere." In *Modern Guerrilla Warfare*, ed. Franklin Mark Osanka. New York: Free Press, 1962.

Sorley, Lewis. *A Better War*. New York: Harcourt Brace, 1999.

Spector, Ronald H. *After Tet: The Bloodiest Year in Vietnam*. New York: Free Press, 1993, p. 22.

Stanford Research Institute. Land Reform in Vietnam Working Papers. Vol. 4, Part 1 of 2. Menlo Park: Stanford Research Institute, November 1968.

Taylor, Philip. *Fragments of the Present: Searching for Modernity in Vietnam's South*. Honolulu: University of Hawai'i Press, 2001.

Thayer, Carlyle A. *War by Other Means: National Liberation and Revolution in Viet-Nam 1954–60*. Sydney: Allen and Unwin, 1989.

Thayer, Thomas C. *War Without Fronts: The American Experience in Vietnam*. Boulder: Westview, 1985.

The Pentagon Papers. Senator Mike Gravel Edition. Vol. 2. Boston: Beacon, 1971.

Tran Van Tra. "Tet: The 1968 General Offensive and General Uprising." In Werner and Huynh, *The Vietnam War: Vietnamese and American Perspective*.

A Translation from the French: Lessons of the War in Indochina. Vol. 2. Translated by V[ictor] J. Croizat. Rand Corporation Memorandum RM-5271-PR, May 1967.

Turley, William S. *The Second Indochina War*. New York: Mentor, 1987.

Werner, Jayne S., and Luu Doan Huynh, eds. *The Vietnam War: Vietnamese and American Perspectives*. Armonk: M.E. Sharpe, 1993.

Wirtz, James J. *The Tet Offensive: Intelligence Failure in War*. Ithaca: Cornell University Press, 1991, p. 218.

Woodside, Alexander. *Community and Revolution in Modern Vietnam*. Boston: Houghton Mifflin, 1976.

Index

David Elliott is H. Russell Smith Professor of Government and International Relations at Pomona College. After graduating from Yale University, he served in the U.S. Army from 1962 to 1965. Upon completion of a year of Vietnamese language training at the Defense Language Institute, Elliott served in Vietnam from 1963 to 1965. In 1965, he joined the Rand Corporation, and supervised a study of the revolutionary ("Viet Cong") movement in Dinh Tuong province in the Mekong Delta until the end of 1967. During the course of graduate study at Cornell University, he returned to Vietnam to do research including a follow-up of the earlier Rand Dinh Tuong study in 1971–1972. Upon completion of a Ph.D degree at Cornell, Elliott taught at Cornell for a year, and then took an appointment at Pomona College, where he has taught since 1977.

Villages of Dinh Tuong Province 1954-1975

Cái Bè District

Cai Lậy District

Giao Đức District

Thạnh Phú

Hậu Mỹ

Mỹ Phước Tây

Mỹ Hạnh Đông

Mỹ Thành

Mỹ Hạnh Trung

Tân Phú Đông

Phú Nhuận Đông

Bình Phú

Tân Bình

Tân Hội

Mỹ Thiện

Hậu Thành

Hội Cư

Thanh Hoà

Nhị Mỹ

Nhị Quí

Mỹ Đức Tây

Mỹ Lợi

Phú An

Cẩm Sơn

Long Khánh

Phú Quí

Mỹ Đức Đông

Hoà Khánh

Đồng Hoà Hiệp

Hiệp Đức

Xuân Sơn

Long Trung

Mỹ Long

Long Tiên

Thanh Hưng

An Thái Trung

An Thái Đông

Mỹ Lương

Hội Sơn

Tam Bình

An Hữu

Hoà Lộc

Ngũ Hiệp

Hưng Thuận